S0-BMG-890

Guide to Solaris®

Guide to Solaris®

John A. Pew

Ziff-Davis Press
Emeryville, California

Development Editor	Jeff Green
Copy Editor	Barbara Milligan
Technical Reviewer	Valerie Haecky
Project Coordinator	A. Knox
Proofreader	Kayla Sussell
Cover Illustration	Kenneth Roberts
Cover Design	Kenneth Roberts
Book Design	Laura Lamar/MAX; San Francisco
Screen Graphics Editor	Dan Brodnitz
Technical Illustration	Cherie Plumlee Computer Graphics & Illustration
Word Processing	Howard Blechman, Cat Haglund, and Allison Levin
Page Layout	Tony Jonick
Indexer	Valerie Robbins

Ziff-Davis Press books are produced on a Macintosh computer system with the following applications: FrameMaker®, Microsoft® Word, QuarkXPress®, Adobe Illustrator®, Adobe Photoshop®, Adobe Streamline™, MacLink® *Plus*, Aldus® FreeHand™, Collage Plus™.

Ziff-Davis Press
5903 Christie Avenue
Emeryville, CA 94608

ISBN 1-56276-087-4

Manufactured in the United States of America

10 9 8 7 6 5 4 3 2 1

To Renée

CONTENTS AT A GLANCE

TABLE OF CONTENTS

FOREWORD

THE EVOLUTION OF THE COMPUTING INDUSTRY OVER THE PAST TWO decades has created a new paradigm—a continuum of processing power from hardware toward more sophisticated software. In the early seventies, the computer industry was all about hardware: MIPS and MegaFLOPS. Processing and speed were the big issues of the time and companies strived to put more power at the desktop. Later, the first 1-MIP workstation was announced. People said no one would ever need that much power on the desktop. Today, Sun is building 100-MIP machines for the desktop and the users need for power will probably still not be satisfied.

As hardware became more powerful in the 1980s, software functionality lagged behind creating a gap between hardware performance and the utility that application developers and users could derive from it. Most of the major global computing companies are now investing in resources and technology to develop system software that will take full advantage of this new hardware and close the performance gap. As a result, there seems to be a shift in the computing paradigm toward more advanced software.

Sun Microsystems, Inc. was one of the first companies to recognize this trend by focusing on the UNIX® system software environment and by forming SunSoft, a separate and wholly owned subsidiary, chartered with developing and marketing the Solaris operating system environment. This move to bring the power of Sun's implementation of UNIX to the enterprise computing market was a big step toward closing the performance gap.

SunSoft has established a reputation for outstanding software engineering expertise and has invested thousands of person years into the development of Solaris, probably the most ambitious undertaking in the history of UNIX software. Solaris combines high performance, multiplatform support and enterprise networking with the ease of use of personal computers to give users an advanced 32-bit software solution.

Solaris is a fully distributed computing environment, allowing users anywhere in the world to access and share information transparently. For the end user, it is packed with features such as multimedia mail, networked calendar manager, audio, and graphics support. Most of all, it offers significant performance with its multitasking and multiprocessing support that lets end users truly exploit the power of the hardware on their desktop.

SunSoft will continue to innovate on Solaris. Future releases will include objects, nomadic features, and new interactive technologies, all of which build on the Solaris base.

Though Solaris offers sophisticated features for the software developer and system administrator, at heart, I, too, am the proverbial end user. I want to come into my office, click on my mouse and have everything work simply and intuitively. I found *Guide to Solaris* to be a truly informative book on how to get started with Solaris. The easy text, computer tips, and descriptive examples are enlightening to Solaris users.

End users should seriously consider starting off with this book to gain a base understanding of Solaris and its vast functionality. As we add more features into Solaris and it evolves into the future, this book will become invaluable to users everywhere.

—Edward J. Zander
President, SunSoft
Corporate Executive Officer, Sun Microsystems, Inc.

ACKNOWLEDGMENTS

MY SINCERE THANKS TO SEVERAL PEOPLE WHO WERE INSTRUMENTAL in the design, writing, and review of this book. A very sincere thanks to Jeff Green and Barbara Milligan, the development and copy editors from Ziff-Davis Press, with whom it was a pleasure to work. Their professionalism and commitment contributed greatly to the quality and organization of the book. Thanks also to Ami Knox, the project coordinator at Ziff-Davis Press, for dealing with all the little details of the final copy.

Valerie Haecky did an excellent technical editing job on the entire book. Dale Silva also contributed technical reviews, which were much appreciated and insightful with respect to the Solaris user.

Thanks also to Warren Hogg and Ed Pattermann of SunSoft Product Marketing for their review of and suggestions for the book.

A very special thanks to Karin Ellison of SunSoft Press for giving me the opportunity to write this book and for her encouragement and prodding. And many thanks to the countless engineers and writers of Sun Microsystems for creating and documenting Solaris!

Lastly, my deepest gratitude to my wife and children for their support while writing this book. They have quietly sustained and encouraged me throughout this project. I could not have completed this book without them.

INTRODUCTION

GUIDE TO SOLARIS DESCRIBES THE SOLARIS ENVIRONMENT AND IS written for Solaris users. Programmers and system administrators may also benefit from the material in this book but the intended audience is the new and experienced Solaris user. This book consolidates the information about the most commonly used applications and concepts of Solaris into one volume.

If you are new to the Solaris environment you will appreciate the many explanations and screen shots of fundamental Solaris concepts. Features are described in easy-to-understand language, and you'll also find step-by-step guidelines that will help you get the hands-on experience you need as quickly as possible.

If you are an experienced Solaris user you will find valuable examples that demonstrate common as well as uncommon and advanced features. Many of the programs described in this book have so many features that even experienced users are unaware of them. You may find that there is much to learn about applications that you already use every day.

How to Use This Book

This book is written specifically for Solaris 2.1, which includes the SunOS 5.1 operating system and the OpenWindows 3.1 windowing environment. If possible, you should install this software before using this book. All descriptions and screen shots in the book are from Solaris 2.1 and OpenWindows 3.1.

If you are running an older version of SunOS, such as SunOS 4.1.*x* (which includes OpenWindows version 3), you will find some discrepancies between the descriptions in this book and the way the software actually looks and behaves. However, most of the material on the DeskSet applications (Chapters 3 through 10) is identical for OpenWindows version 3. The material in Chapters 11 through 16 is also largely unchanged from earlier versions, so you should still find this book helpful and instructive.

What's Inside

This book is divided into four parts comprised of 17 chapters.

Part I, "Solaris Fundamentals," contains Chapters 1 and 2, which describe the basics about Solaris and how to get started.

Part II, "The DeskSet," includes Chapters 3 through 10, which describe each of the graphical user interface DeskSet applications.

Part III, "Working from the SunOS Command Line," contains Chapters 11 through 14. These chapters describe some fundamental SunOS commands and concepts as well as how to use the shell, the vi editor, and the network.

Part IV, "System Administration," contains Chapters 16 and 17, which describe some basic system administration tasks that a user may need to perform.

Here is an overview of the contents of each of the 17 chapters in the book:

Chapter 1, "An Overview of the Solaris Environment," describes the basic components of the Solaris environment, including the operating system, the networking environment, and the OpenWindows environment.

Chapter 2, "Getting Started," explains how to log in, set and use your password, and start and exit the OpenWindows environment. It also shows you how to use the shell, use environment variables, and set your search path.

Chapter 3, "OpenWindows Fundamentals," covers the OpenWindows environment. Common OPEN LOOK components are described, as is the Workspace menu, environment customization, and the Help system.

Chapter 4, "The File Manager," is a guide to the File Manager DeskSet application. You learn how to view, create, open, move, copy, and delete files and directories.

Chapter 5, "The Shell Tool, Command Tool, and Text Editor," describes how to use the Shell and Command Tool, and the Text Editor. These tools are combined in this chapter because they share many common features of text manipulation.

Chapter 6, "The Mail Tool," explains the ins and outs of the Mail Tool DeskSet application. You learn how to send and receive mail and organize your mail into folders for easy access.

Chapter 7, "The Calendar Manager," shows you how to schedule appointments using the Calendar Manager DeskSet application. You also learn about the Multi-Browser, which enables you to browse other users' calendars.

Chapter 8, "The Daily-Use DeskSet Applications," describes five DeskSet applications: the Clock, the Print Tool, Snapshot, the Audio Tool, and the Performance Meter.

Chapter 9, "More DeskSet Applications," covers the remainder of the DeskSet applications: the Tape Tool, the Calculator, the Icon Editor, and the Binder.

Chapter 10, "Customizing the OpenWindows Environment," explains some general customization techniques such as scales and fonts, mouseless mode, and customizing menus.

Chapter 11, "SunOS Fundamentals," introduces the SunOS command line. It also describes how to list, display, copy, and move files and directories.

Chapter 12, "More SunOS Fundamentals," picks up where Chapter 11 leaves off by discussing other file operations, how to use the printing system, and how to send and receive mail from the command line.

Chapter 13, "Using the vi Editor," describes how to create and modify ASCII documents using the vi editor.

Chapter 14, "The Shell," shows you how to use the C shell and the Korn shell. Topics discussed include job control, I/O redirection, history, and aliases.

Chapter 15, "Using the Network," shows you how to use the network to log into a remote system, copy files to and from a remote system, and execute commands on a remote system.

Chapter 16, "System Administration for Users," covers some basic system administration concepts and procedures that regular users often need, including: becoming the superuser, monitoring processes, booting and shutting down the system, file system administration, using tapes and floppy diskettes, and network administration.

Chapter 17, "System Administration with the Administration Tool," explains how to use the Administration Tool to manage databases, printer, hosts, and user accounts.

Some Conventions

This book uses the following conventions:

- Text that you type is in **`bold Courier`** font.
- Text that appears on the screen such as the prompt or the output of commands, appears in regular `Courier` font.
- The buttons on the mouse are usually referred to by name. From left to right, these are: SELECT, ADJUST, and MENU.
- The command line prompt shown throughout much of this book is `dugout%`.

  By default, the prompt for the C shell (the default shell for this book) displays the name of the system followed by a percent sign. *Dugout* is the name of the author's system; your prompt will display your own system name.
- A brief description of how to invoke a DeskSet application is included in each of the chapters in Part II of the book. For example, to invoke the Mail Tool you would type

```
dugout% mailtool &
```

You'll see that each example includes an ampersand (&) at the end of the command line. The ampersand indicates to the shell that the application should be started in the background. Background processing is not discussed until Chapter 14, but is included in examples earlier in the book so as not to tie up the window in which the application was started.

An Overview of the Solaris Environment

Getting Started

PART 1

Solaris Fundamentals

CHAPTER

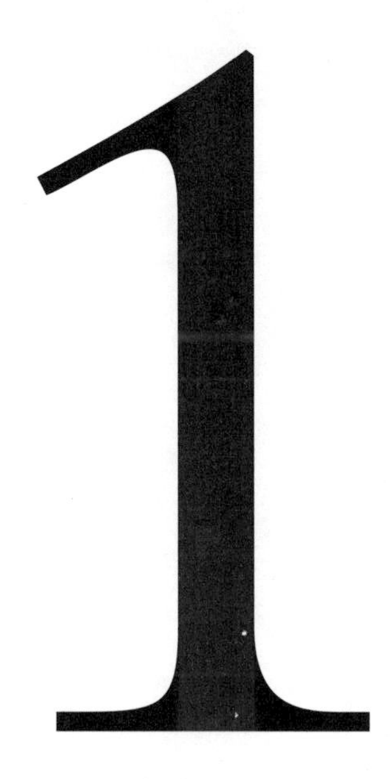

An Overview of the Solaris Environment

What Is the Solaris Environment?

The SunOS 5.1 Operating System

The ONC Networking Environment

The OpenWindows Windowing Environment

The DeskSet Utilities

The Command Line versus the DeskSet Utilities

THE SOLARIS OPERATING ENVIRONMENT RUNS ON SPARC® AND INTEL® microcomputers. It is simple and intuitive enough for beginning users, yet powerful enough for sophisticated processing of all types. Before beginning to work with the Solaris environment, you need to understand what it is and what its components are. This chapter describes all the components of the Solaris environment. Though some of the components are of interest mainly to programmers, end users also should read along to get an appreciation of the breadth and power of the Solaris system.

What Is the Solaris Environment?

The Solaris environment includes an operating system (SunOS), dozens of user programs, a windowing system, numerous libraries, a networking system, and much more. For this introductory discussion we can divide the environment into three major components:

- foundation technologies
- developer environment
- user environment

Let's look at each of these in more detail.

Foundation Technologies

The foundation technologies include the SunOS™ operating system and the ONC™ (Open Network Computing) networking environment. The operating system is a very large and complicated software program that controls the computer hardware (the processor, the disk drives, and the monitor) and that schedules processes to run in the central processing unit (CPU). Included with the operating system are numerous utility programs that you can use for a variety of tasks, such as storing data, searching databases, editing files, and sending mail.

The ONC environment is a family of networking protocols and services that allows you to share files across networks of PCs, workstations, servers, and mainframes, independent of the underlying operating system. Configuring and maintaining the operating system and the network is usually the job of a system administrator. (Part 4 of this book discusses some of the duties of the system administrator.) End users mostly work with the programs and utilities provided with the operating system. Part 3 of this book discusses many of the programs provided with the operating system.

Developer Environment

The developer environment includes tools such as compilers, linkers, and debuggers to help developers write programs. There are also tools to manage source code and measure performance. In addition to tools, there are numerous libraries that make writing programs easier. These libraries include the functionality to do such things as complicated mathematics, text manipulation, and network communication.

The OpenWindows™ windowing environment includes a set of libraries that developers use to write window-based applications. There are libraries for creating OPEN LOOK® user interfaces and for allowing applications to communicate with each other.

User Environment

The user environment is the main focus of this book. The user environment includes the OpenWindows windowing environment and the DeskSet™ programs and utilities. With the OpenWindows environment you can have multiple command-line interfaces on your screen, each in its own window, and you can run DeskSet applications, such as Mail Tool and File Manager, that each have their own graphical user interface.

As a user you will probably run the OpenWindows environment 99 percent of the time. Chapter 2 will introduce you to the environment and provide some basics about how to start it and use it. In the beginning you will probably use the DeskSet programs for most of your work. Part 2 of this book is dedicated to the DeskSet programs. As your sophistication increases, you can begin taking advantage of the additional power available in the many programs included with the Solaris environment. The remainder of this chapter looks at each of these components in a little more detail.

The SunOS 5.1 Operating System

The SunOS 5.1 operating system is based on UNIX® System V Release 4, which was jointly developed by AT&T and Sun Microsystems. The UNIX operating system dates back to the early 1970s, when it was introduced by AT&T. It has since become one of the most popular operating systems for several reasons, including the ease with which the UNIX operating system and UNIX applications can be ported to different hardware platforms, and the ease with which UNIX systems interoperate even when provided by different manufacturers. An organization buying computers for its workforce has the flexibility to acquire machines from different vendors and still be assured that those systems will work together by sharing common UNIX features such as networking and file-system architecture.

The UNIX operating system has many inherent benefits that make it the operating system of choice for thousands of users and developers. It has matured significantly in the last twenty or so years. UNIX System V Release 4 (SVR4) integrates many of the best features of a variety of leading versions of UNIX: BSD, SunOS, System V, and Xenix. The SunOS version of SVR4 offers even more features, including symmetric multiprocessing with multithreads, real-time enhancements, increased security, simplified system administration, and improved internationalization capabilities.

As an end user of the SunOS operating system, you do not need to understand all the intricacies of how the system works. Programmers need to know more of the details of the workings of the operating system so that they can take advantage of its power and features. Some understanding of the features available from the operating system will be helpful to end users, however. Understanding the bigger picture of what is available helps you to make better use of the intelligence of the computer. If you are tabulating marketing statistics or doing word processing, you can do your work faster and more efficiently when you know what tools are available and how to use them. For example, what will you do if you run out of disk space while you are editing an important document? You have been typing for an hour, and now when you try to save your document, you are notified that there is no more disk space available. You needn't lose all your work if you understand that you can save the document onto another file system—one that has available disk space. It is basic concepts like these, and knowledge of available utilities and tools, that help you work faster and smarter.

Let's look briefly at a few of the SunOS operating system's main features.

Multitasking

The SunOS 5.1 operating system is a true multitasking operating system. This means that it can handle multiple tasks simultaneously. Most PC operating systems, like MS-DOS for example, are not multitasking systems. They really can operate on only a single process at a time. In a multitasking operating system, multiple users can work on the same system, each taking advantage of the processing power of the machine. Even with only one user, the system can simultaneously execute multiple operations such as printing a file, receiving electronic mail, recomputing and displaying a spreadsheet layout, and providing notification of a scheduled appointment.

Multiprocessing and Multithreading

The SunOS 5.1 operating system is a multithreaded (MT) operating system. Multithreading provides an environment in which multiple processors can execute the operating system at the same time. Individual applications can also take advantage of multithreading by performing multiple operations simultaneously. This reduces execution-time bottlenecks, thereby improving performance.

Real-time Functionality

The SunOS 5.1 operating system contains the real-time extensions of UNIX SVR4, with important enhancements from SunSoft. These capabilities make the Solaris environment ideal for applications that depend on split-second response, such as on-line transaction processing, telecommunications switching, and military command and control.

Security

New features that improve security have been added to Solaris. New tools enable system administrators to easily increase a system's security level by checking system files' permissions, ownership, and contents, and warning users about potential security problems. Additional security is also provided by means of an encryption and aging technique on user passwords.

Internationalization Capabilities

Internationalization makes it easier to customize applications for different languages and cultures. The SunOS operating system's international support helps software developers localize their applications in different languages so that users can interact with a desktop in their own language. Historically, the UNIX operating system supported the ASCII character set. ASCII, however, does not satisfy the requirements of many languages, so the SunOS 5.1 operating system provides support for multibyte and wide-character code sets. This internationalization allows support for languages such as Japanese and other Asian languages, which cannot be supported with ASCII only.

The ONC Networking Environment

The ONC networking environment is a family of published networking protocols and distributed services that makes it simple to distribute applications and data transparently, no matter where they reside on the network. The Solaris system features new enhancements to the ONC environment, enabling system administrators, end users, and developers to more effectively access, share, and control information across worldwide, multivendor networks.

The ONC environment includes several components:

- NFS® (Network File System) allows users to share files across the network transparently.

- The Remote Procedure Call (RPC) is used by programmers to develop and implement distributed applications across networks.
- The Network Information Service (NIS) is used by system administrators to simplify the management of small and large networks.

Chapters 15 and 16 discuss networking in more detail.

The OpenWindows Windowing Environment

The OpenWindows environment is a set of programs and libraries that together make up a complete windowing system. The OpenWindows environment is based on the X Window System (often referred to simply as X) from the Massachusetts Institute of Technology (MIT). At the heart of the OpenWindows environment is the X11/NeWS™ server, which controls everything being displayed on your screen. There are also numerous DeskSet applications that make it easier for you to use many of the most important user functions such as mail and file management. Additionally, several components of the OpenWindows environment are provided especially for programmers, so that programming is simple and consistent.

The X11/NeWS Server

The X11/NeWS server (often referred to as simply "the server") is responsible for all input and output devices. The server creates and manipulates windows on the screen, produces text and graphics, and handles input devices such as the keyboard and mouse. Applications that use the facilities provided by the server are known as *clients*. The architecture of X allows the server and clients to run on different machines connected by the network. This means that an application can execute on one system while displaying on another.

The X11/NeWS server is a merger of version 11 of the X Window System and NeWS®, the PostScript system-based imaging language. The X11 portion of the server is based on the industry-standard X Window System, mentioned previously. Conforming to the X Window System standard means that applications from different vendors can run under the OpenWindows environment because they share this common standard. The NeWS portion of the server provides extensions that allow PostScript text and images to be easily displayed.

The OPEN LOOK Graphical User Interface

OPEN LOOK is a graphical user interface (GUI). It specifies the way objects appear and behave on the screen. For example, OPEN LOOK defines the behavior of rectangular buttons as having one particular function and oblong buttons as having another. By conforming to a consistent GUI, applications that utilize OPEN LOOK are easy to learn and to use. All OPEN LOOK applications use a set of OPEN LOOK objects that are well-defined: scrollbars, buttons, menus, and so on. Once you understand these basic objects, using any OPEN LOOK application is simple and intuitive. Chapter 3 introduces the OPEN LOOK objects.

Toolkits

The OpenWindows environment includes two *toolkits*, or libraries, that each implement the OPEN LOOK GUI. Programmers may use any one of these toolkits to create OPEN LOOK applications.

OLIT

OLIT is an acronym for the OPEN LOOK Intrinsics Toolkit. OLIT was originally developed by AT&T. Sun Microsystems has expanded and enhanced AT&T's original OLIT to provide new functionality, including drag and drop and support for 24-bit color.

OLIT is especially important as an OPEN LOOK toolkit because it is built on the industry-standard X Toolkit Intrinsics (Xt). The Intrinsics have become a de facto industry standard, especially on UNIX workstations. Another popular toolkit, Motif, is also based on the Xt Intrinsics. Porting between OLIT and Motif is relatively simple because of their common Intrinsics foundation. This simplicity makes OLIT especially attractive to developers who have current Motif applications.

XView

Before the X Window System was adopted by Sun Microsystems, the SunView™ toolkit was the popular toolkit used to create graphical user interfaces. When X became the windowing system of choice, the SunView toolkit was adapted to support the X Window System and was renamed XView™. The XView toolkit was the first X-based toolkit to implement the OPEN LOOK GUI.

XView is a mature, second-generation toolkit. As the successor of the SunView toolkit, XView meets the needs of programmers currently using the SunView toolkit. By using XView and some simple tools, developers can easily migrate SunView applications to the OpenWindows environment.

Drag and Drop

Drag and drop allows you to transfer data between independent applications by using the mouse. Objects such as files, text, or graphics can be moved or copied between applications with a consistent user interface that is supported by all both toolkits. Most of the DeskSet applications support drag and drop. For example, you can drag a file from the File Manager and drop it onto the Print Tool to print the file.

ToolTalk

The ToolTalk® service allows programmers to write applications that can communicate with other applications without having specific knowledge of the other. For example, a desktop publishing program can use the ToolTalk service to automatically load a file or start the program. A file created by the desktop publishing program can be opened by the File Manager, which sends a message by means of the ToolTalk service to either load the file into the already running desktop publishing program, or start the desktop publishing program if it is not already running, and load this file into the program.

The OpenWindows Developer's Guide

The OpenWindows Developer's Guide (DevGuide) is a program that helps developers build programs. It is called a *graphical user interface application builder.* DevGuide allows programmers to quickly create a graphical user interface by providing the ability to design, test, and interactively modify the user interface. After designing the user interface components, DevGuide translates the objects into program code, which can be compiled into an independent running program.

The DeskSet Utilities

The DeskSet utilities are the main interface that most users have to the Solaris environment. The DeskSet applications provide communication and organization facilities that are used daily. DeskSet applications exchange information by means of the drag and drop mechanism. The DeskSet applications follow the OPEN LOOK GUI, which means that their user interface is consistent and easy to use. Figure 1.1 shows the icon for each of the DeskSet applications.

Here is a brief introduction to each of the DeskSet applications:

- **File Manager** The File Manager helps you navigate through your files. It gives you a visual display of files and directories, and permits easy management of these objects. Files can be moved, copied, executed, or removed with simple mouse movements. The File Manager fully supports the drag and drop capability, making many operations extremely simple and intuitive. Chapter 4 discusses the File Manager in detail.

Figure 1.1
DeskSet Icons

- **Mail Tool** The Mail Tool provides an easy-to-use, user-friendly interface for sending and receiving electronic mail (*e-mail*). Mail can be sent, received, and organized into folders. A facility for attaching files to mail messages gives the Mail Tool multimedia capability. For example, an audio message can be attached to a mail message that the receiver can "play." Chapter 6 discusses the Mail Tool.
- **Calendar Manager** The Calendar Manager makes scheduling appointments easy. Not only can Calendar Manager be used to keep track of your own calendar, but its multibrowse facility enables you to check the schedules of co-workers so that meetings can be scheduled at convenient times. Calendar Manager also supports drag and drop so that appointment notices, sent by way of Mail Tool, can be easily scheduled by dragging the mail message with the appointment information from the Mail Tool and dropping it onto Calendar Manager. The Calendar Manager is covered in Chapter 7.
- **Text Editor** The Text Editor is a mouse-based editor that allows you to create and modify ASCII files. The Text Editor makes it easy to copy or move text from one file to another file, or to another application such as the Mail Tool. It also supports drag and drop. Chapter 5 discusses the Text Editor in detail.
- **Shell Tool and Command Tool** The Shell Tool and Command Tool are used to interface to the SunOS operating system. SunOS commands are entered in the Shell or Command Tool. Chapter 5 discusses these two popular DeskSet utilities.

- **Clock** The Clock displays the time for any time zone in the world, in either analog or digital form. The Clock can also be used as an alarm or stopwatch. The features of the Clock program are discussed in Chapter 8.
- **Calculator** The Calculator performs the functions of a hand-held calculator. Functions include algebraic, scientific, financial, and logic operations. Chapter 9 covers the Calculator and describes how to take advantage of its powerful features.
- **Print Tool** The Print Tool provides a convenient interface to the printer. Mail messages, files, and images can be printed directly or by way of drag and drop. Chapter 8 discusses the Print Tool.
- **Audio Tool** The Audio Tool lets you record, play, and edit sound files. Audio messages created by Audio Tool can be sent to other users through the Mail Tool. Chapter 8 discusses the Audio Tool.
- **Tape Tool** The Tape Tool allows you to store information to a tape or other peripheral and easily retrieve it. Chapter 9 includes a discussion of the Tape Tool.
- **Binder** Binder enables you to customize applications on your desktop. Each file type has an associated open and print method. Binder allows you to customize these bindings and also to attach an icon to an application or file so that the File Manager can easily identify it. Binder is discussed in Chapter 9.
- **Snapshot** Snapshot lets you capture and display images on the screen. Captured images can then be stored in files or sent to other users as mail attachments. Existing images can be displayed with Snapshot. A discussion of Snapshot is included in Chapter 8.
- **Icon Editor** Icon Editor lets you create your own icons or change existing ones. Chapter 9 includes a discussion of the Icon Editor.
- **Performance Meter** The Performance Meter visually displays system statistics on local or remote machines with graphical views of CPU usage, load average, disk access, network loading, and more. Chapter 8 includes a discussion of the Performance Meter.
- **Help** A built-in help mechanism is provided for each DeskSet application. Just position the cursor on an application and press the Help key. A Help pop-up window provides basic information about the application and the objects in the application. Additional help is available through the Help Viewer discussed in Chapter 3.

The Command Line versus the DeskSet Utilities

Much of the functionality provided by the DeskSet applications is also available directly by means of the SunOS command line. You might ask, "If the same functionality is available in the DeskSet utilities, why would I ever want to use the command line?" Or your question might be reversed: "If I can do it with the command line, why use the DeskSet utilities?" These are good questions that we will answer in this section.

Let's first consider the advantages to using the DeskSet applications over the command-line interface. The first advantage is a very compelling one: Many of the functions are not available by means of the command-line interface. For example, the Icon Editor does not have an equivalent program available from the command line. The same is true for the Audio Tool, Binder, and Calendar Manager. The Calendar Manager lets you schedule appointments and reminds you of an appointment by a variety of methods: electronic mail, a pop-up notice displayed on your screen, and so on. Although some similar programs are available from the command line, none are as convenient to use and none offer the same notification mechanisms.

Some of the DeskSet applications do have very strong counterparts available from the command line. Two good examples are the File Manager and Mail Tool. Both of these applications give you a graphical user interface for some of the most commonly used SunOS commands.

The mailx program provides almost identical functionality to the Mail Tool. Mailx is the command-line program for reading and sending mail. The features and customization available in mailx and the Mail Tool are very similar. So why use the Mail Tool? If you are new to the Solaris environment and have not used the mail system before, you will find the Mail Tool easy to learn and very intuitive. Mail can be sent, retrieved, and stored with the use of a friendly user interface. All this can be done with mailx, but the odds are that you could learn the Mail Tool in half the time it would take to learn mailx. Also, some features of the Mail Tool, such as the drag and drop facility, are not available in mailx. With the Mail Tool you can use the drag and drop facility to transfer mail messages to other DeskSet applications. For example, you can drag a mail message containing an appointment to the Calendar Manager to schedule the appointment. This is a very handy feature that can become second nature to you after a while.

The File Manager program facilitates some of the most basic SunOS commands. Moving files, copying files, deleting files, and listing files are all functions of the File Manager. Some of the most basic SunOS commands provide the same functionality: **mv** (move), **cp** (copy), **rm** (remove), and **ls** (list). Experienced SunOS or UNIX users sometimes prefer to use the familiar command-line programs rather than the File Manager, because they feel more at home with the SunOS commands.

Personally, I must admit that I use the command-line programs more than 50 percent of the time, because I have been using them for years and can often get the job done faster that way. However, I have also learned that the File Manager provides some valuable shortcuts. For example, I find the File Manager extremely useful when I have a directory with many files in it and I want to move or copy most, but not all, of the files in the directory. Moving or copying all of the files in a directory is a snap when using the command line, but moving all but one or two can be troublesome. I may have to do a lot of typing or write a shell program to do the job. With the File Manager, however, I can select all the files in a directory and then deselect the ones I don't want to copy or move—all with a few simple mouse clicks. Then I can use drag and drop to easily do the operation. (The drag and drop interface cannot be reproduced on the command line.)

Now let's consider the arguments for using the command-line interface rather than the DeskSet applications. As mentioned previously, the command-line interface is often quicker if you know the proper commands. Also, there are times when the graphical interface is not available. For example, if you have a personal computer and modem at home and want to access your Solaris system at work, you will not be able to use the DeskSet programs. Checking your mail, copying files, or checking your appointments are all possible through remote access but not through the DeskSet applications.

When you log into a system remotely, you usually cannot use any of the graphical programs, which include all the DeskSet applications. If you don't know how to use mailx, you won't be able to send or receive mail. If you don't know how to use cp or rm, you won't be able to copy or delete files. These may not be immediate needs, but the time will probably come when you will need remote access.

The moral of this discussion is this: It pays to know both the DeskSet programs and the command-line programs. In this book we will discuss both the DeskSet programs and the command-line interface. We will start with the DeskSet, since it is the quickest way for you to get started if you are a new user of the Solaris operating environment.

Summary

Whether you are an end user, a developer, or a system administrator, the Solaris environment has much to offer. It is a powerful system based on industry standards that offers advanced features and an intuitive interface. The greater your understanding, the greater will be your efficiency and productivity in using the tools and programs provided by the Solaris environment.

In Chapter 2 we'll discuss how to get started by logging in, selecting a password, and starting the OpenWindows environment.

CHAPTER

Getting Started

Logging In

Entering SunOS Commands

The Shell

Preview of the OpenWindows Environment

Logging Out

CHAPTER 1 INTRODUCED YOU TO THE SOLARIS OPERATING ENVIRONment and gave you an idea of its components and power. In this chapter you will learn some basics about how to log in, set your password, and start the OpenWindows environment. You will also learn how to set essential environment variables for things such as the OpenWindows environment and your execution path. Understanding your user environment will make using the Solaris environment easy.

If you are already familiar with the basics of logging in to the SunOS operating system and starting the OpenWindows environment, you may want to skip ahead to Chapter 3. If you are using a Solaris system on which you do not yet have an account, you will need to either check with your system administrator or refer to Chapter 17 for instructions on how to create a user account.

In this chapter you will learn how to

- Log in
- Choose your password
- Change your password
- Enter SunOS commands
- Use the shell
- Set environment variables
- Set your path
- Start the OpenWindows environment
- Create a start-up file
- Enter SunOS commands in a window
- Exit the OpenWindows environment
- Log out

Logging In

Before you can use the Solaris environment you have to log in to the SunOS operating system. If you are more familiar with DOS computers you might wonder why logging in is necessary. With DOS you just turn on the computer and begin working; with the SunOS operating system, however, you have to log in before you can do anything. This is a requirement because the SunOS operating system is a multi-user system, which means it can accommodate multiple users on the system at the same time. Since the early days of the UNIX operating system there have been user accounts associated with every system. This makes it possible for you to keep your data private by "owning" your own files. Other users can use the system but do not necessarily have access to your files.

To log in, you need a user I.D. and a password. These should be given to you by your system administrator. If you do not have a user I.D. and password and are expected to do your own system administration, refer to Chapter 17 to learn how to create a user account.

Your user I.D. is usually your first or last name or perhaps your initials. You will share your I.D. with your co-workers so that they can send you e-mail, browse your calendar, or share your files. Sharing your password, however, is usually considered unwise. Keeping your password private ensures that your files will remain in your control. You can permit other users to read or write to your files on a file-by-file basis, so keeping your password private should not be considered unsociable. It does make it possible to keep private data private.

Let's assume that your user I.D. is *sally*, that your password is *wh1msical*, that your system's name is *dugout,* and that you have not yet logged in to your system. The log-in prompt automatically appears on your screen, as shown here:

```
dugout console login:
```

Your first step is to type your user I.D., *sally*, at the log-in prompt. You will then be prompted for your password. When you type your password the characters you type are not echoed on the screen. This is a security feature to help ensure that your password is kept private. If your password was entered correctly a message appears on the screen and you are granted access to the system. Here is how a successful log-in sequence appears on the screen:

```
dugout console login: sally
Password: [Password is not displayed on the screen]
Last login: Thu Jun 11 23:03:42 on console
Sun Microsystems Inc. SunOS 5.1
dugout%
```

If you make a mistake in typing your password or user I.D., the message

```
Login incorrect
```

will appear, and you will not be given access to the system. You are again presented with the log-in prompt, and you will have to try the entire sequence again.

Choosing Your Password

If this is your first time logging in to the SunOS operating system, you have probably been given your user I.D. and password by your system administrator. If, however, your system administrator has given you a user I.D. and has indicated that your account does not have a password, you will have to provide a new password yourself the first time you log in. If you attempt to log in and you do not yet have a password, the system informs you that you do not have a password and instructs you to choose one.

The prompt

```
New password:
```

indicates that you should type a password. After you have typed it you are prompted to enter it a second time. You must enter the same password exactly as you did the first time, or your password will be rejected and you will have to repeat the process. Here is how the sequence appears on the screen:

```
dugout console login: sally
You don't have a password. Choose one.
passwd sally
New password: [Enter the new password]
Re-enter new password: [Enter the new password again]
Sun Microsystems Inc. SunOS 5.1
dugout%
```

When selecting a password, you must choose a combination of characters that includes at least two alphabetic characters and at least one numeric or special character. Special characters are characters that are neither numbers nor part of the alphabet, such as &, #, -, }, and @. The password must be at least six characters in length. This requirement makes it more difficult for hackers or anyone else to guess your password, thus adding to system security.

Select a password that you can remember without having to write it down. If you make your password so obscure that you can't remember it yourself, you will likely end up having to ask your system administrator to create a new password for you. It's embarrassing to forget your own password!

One technique I like to use for choosing a password is to pick a word that is easy for me to remember and then replace one or more vowels in the word with a numeric or special character. I pick a number or special character that reminds me of the letter I am replacing. For example, if the word I chose was *computer* I might replace *o* with *0* and *e* with *{*. My password would thus be *c0mput{r*. Another good technique is to make up an acronym from a phrase that you can easily remember. For example, you could use *aaadktda* for "an apple a day keeps the doctor away." Of course, you will need at least one numeric or special character in there somewhere. Use your imagination! When choosing your password, remember to use a technique that will help make it easy for you to remember your password but hard for someone else to guess.

Entering SunOS Commands

Now that you are logged in to the SunOS operating system, you are presented with the *prompt*. The default prompt is either a dollar sign ($) or the host name of your system followed by a percent sign (*hostname*%), depending on the shell you are running. (Shells are discussed later in the chapter.) Throughout this book we will use a system whose host name is dugout, so you will see the prompt displayed as dugout%. Following the prompt is a cursor that indicates where the next characters typed at the keyboard will appear on the screen. The cursor indicates that the system is ready to accept commands.

Entering the ls Command

Let's begin by entering a simple command: ls. The ls command lists the files in the current directory. To execute any command, you type the command and press the Return key. For example, enter the ls command now and press Return. The files in the current directory are displayed, and then the prompt is displayed again, indicating that you can enter another command, as shown here:

```
dugout% ls
chapter2   outline
dugout%
```

Some commands include *options* and *arguments*. Both options and arguments provide additional information on the command line that the command uses to alter or specify its behavior. Options usually begin with a dash and specify a behavior for the command. For example, you can run the ls command with the -l option to display a long listing, as shown here:

```
dugout% ls -l
-rw-r--r--  1 pew    staff    20043 Jun 16 22:31 chapter2
-rw-r--r--  1 pew    staff      299 Jun 11 22:01 outline
dugout%
```

The ls command can also take an argument (also called a command-line argument). A command-line argument specifies the object or objects on which the command should operate. For example, you can supply the name of a file or files as arguments to the ls command. When the ls command includes a command-line argument, it lists only the files specified by the argument. For example, to list just the chapter2 program, provide chapter2 as a command-line argument to ls, as shown here:

```
dugout% ls chapter2
chapter2
dugout%
```

You can combine options and arguments. For example, if you wanted a long listing of the chapter2 file, you would specify both an option and an argument, as shown here:

```
dugout% ls -1 chapter2
-rw-r--r--  1 pew    staff    20043 Jun 16 22:31 chapter2
dugout%
```

Changing Your Password

One of the first commands you may need to use is the passwd command. The passwd command is used to change your existing password. It's a good idea to change your password occasionally. As a matter of fact, some companies require users to frequently change their passwords for security reasons. Your system administrator can even force users to change their passwords by setting up *aging* on passwords. When your password "comes of age," you must change it before gaining access to the SunOS operating system. When you execute the passwd command you will first be prompted to supply your old password. This ensures that only you can access and change your password. After you have typed your existing password, you are prompted for the new password. You must then supply the new password a second time, and it must be identical to the first entry. The password is not displayed on the screen when you type it, as shown here:

```
dugout% passwd
Old password:
New password:
Re-enter new password:
dugout%
```

If you make a mistake in typing your old password, or if you do not reenter the new password exactly as you did the first time, you will receive an error message and your password will not change.

The Shell

Now that you have logged in to the SunOS operating system, you are in the *shell.* The shell is a program that provides the interface between the user and the system. You type commands into the shell, and it sees to it that these commands are executed by the system. This is exactly what you were doing in the previous section, when you entered the ls and passwd commands. There are actually three shells available to you: the Bourne Shell, the Korn Shell, and the C Shell. If you are new to UNIX, this may seem confusing. Why the need for multiple shells?

You really need only one shell. The three shells share many common features. The main job of any shell is to execute the commands presented by the user at the command line. Each shell has a few unique features and some slightly different syntax. If you are an advanced programmer, you might even write your own shell, customized to your particular desires, though this is not really very practical. Most people choose either the C shell or the Korn shell as their default shell for day-to-day usage.

The shell provides an environment that makes doing your job easier. Every shell makes it possible for you to type and execute system commands. In addition, most shells provide several other useful features. For example, wouldn't it be nice to be able to repeat a previously entered command without having to type the whole thing again? Both the C shell and the Korn shell have many features like this that provide shortcuts and other time-saving functions that can make you a more efficient user of the SunOS operating system.

You may or may not have to decide which shell to use. If you are using the Solaris system in your work environment, ask a co-worker or your system administrator which shell he or she recommends. You may be told by your system administrator that all users in your company use one particular shell. In that case, you probably will want to go along with the crowd. Using the shell common to your work environment means that you are more likely to get support when you have questions—and that makes a big difference. Throughout this book, most examples that require a shell will be shown using the C shell since it is the default shell for the Solaris environment.

To determine which shell you are currently using, enter the following command:

```
dugout% echo $SHELL
```

The system will respond with one of these three values:

```
/bin/sh [the Bourne shell]
/bin/csh [the C shell]
/bin/ksh [the Korn shell]
```

If you decide that you want to change the shell you are using, notify your system administrator.

There are some essential features of both the C shell and the Korn shell that you need to learn so that you can at least get started with the Open-Windows environment. We will discuss setting environment variables and setting an execution path. Both of these are essential processes and are handled in a slightly different way in each shell.

Setting Environment Variables

The SunOS operating system uses a variety of environment variables to identify such things as your home directory, your default printer, and your time zone. To see your existing environment variables, enter the env command:

```
dugout% env
```

In response to the env command, the system displays the names and values of all your environment variables. For example, your output may look something like this:

```
HZ=100
PATH=/usr/bin
LOGNAME=sally
MAIL=/var/mail/sally
SHELL=/bin/csh
HOME=/home/sally
TERM=sun
PWD=/home/sally
TZ=US/Pacific
```

These are all the variables currently set in your environment. You can probably guess what some of these variables mean. For now, we want to concentrate on two variables: PATH and OPENWINHOME. If you are logging in for the first time, you may not have the OPENWINHOME environment variable set, and your PATH may be limited to a single directory. You will need to set OPEN-WINHOME and expand your PATH before you go any further.

Before you set these environment variables, let's talk about what each of them means. The OPENWINHOME variable identifies the directory location of OpenWindows. OPENWINHOME is a very important environment variable because many things depend on the location of OpenWindows, including run-time libraries, executable files, icons, fonts, and example programs.

The PATH variable sets the *search path*. The search path is the list of directories that are used to determine where to find executable files. When you type a command at the prompt, the shell looks for the command in all the directories specified in the search PATH. If the shell finds the command, it executes that command. If not, it reports back to you that the command was not found. For example, if you try to execute a nonexistent command, the command will fail, as shown here:

```
dugout% dir
dir: Command not found.
dugout%
```

Let's go through the steps required to set these two environment variables. You should first check to see if OPENWINHOME and PATH are currently set in your environment. Use the env command as shown previously. The discussion that follows assumes that OPENWINHOME is not set and that PATH has a limited or incomplete set of directories in its specification. We will demonstrate how to do this for both the Korn and C shells.

First, set the OPENWINHOME environment variable. You must know where OpenWindows is installed. If you are unsure, check with your system administrator. If OpenWindows is installed in /usr/openwin, set the OPENWINHOME environment variable this way:

C Shell:

```
dugout% setenv OPENWINHOME /usr/openwin
dugout%
```

Korn Shell:

```
$ OPENWINHOME=/usr/openwin
$ export OPENWINHOME
$
```

To verify that you set OPENWINHOME correctly, execute the echo command with $OPENWINHOME as an argument. When you precede an argument with a dollar sign ($), the echo command will display the argument's value, as shown here:

```
dugout% echo $OPENWINHOME
/usr/openwin
dugout%
```

Note that if you don't include the dollar sign, then the echo command will just echo the argument itself rather than its value, as shown here:

```
dugout% echo OPENWINHOME
OPENWINHOME
dugout%
```

Now you can set your search path. You should include all the directories that you want searched when executing commands. For starters, use the following directories in your path:

- . (the current directory)
- /bin (one of the standard locations for many SunOS commands)
- /usr/sbin (one of the standard locations for many SunOS commands)
- $OPENWINHOME/bin (the location of the OpenWindows commands)

To set your PATH, enter the following command:

C Shell:

```
dugout% set path=(. /bin /usr/sbin $OPENWINHOME/bin)
```

Korn Shell:

```
$ PATH=.:/bin:/usr/sbin:$OPENWINHOME/bin
```

Now you can check your path by echoing the PATH environment variable:

```
dugout% echo $PATH
.:/bin:/usr/sbin:/usr/openwin/bin
dugout%
```

Notice that OPENWINHOME does not show up in PATH. That is because OPENWINHOME was included with the dollar sign and was therefore expanded to its value: /usr/openwin.

As you become more familiar with your system you may want to expand your search path. Your system administrator may provide you with other directories that you will want to include in your search path.

Creating a Start-up File

The OPENWINHOME and PATH environment variables need to be set each time you log in. Rather than typing these commands each time you log in, you can put them in a *start-up file*. Commands in the start-up file get executed automatically each time you log in. The Korn shell uses .profile as its start-up file. The C shell has two start-up files: .login and .cshrc. The OPENWINHOME and PATH variables should go into the .cshrc file.

Check to see if you already have an existing start-up file by using the ls command you learned about earlier in the chapter.

C Shell:

```
dugout% ls .cshrc
```

Korn Shell:

```
$ ls .profile
```

If the start-up file exists, use the more command to display the contents of the file:

C Shell:

```
dugout% more .cshrc
```

Korn Shell:

```
$ more .profile
```

If you do have a start-up file, but OPENWINHOME and PATH are not set in the file, you will need to add them. If you do not have a start-up file, you must create one and set the OPENWINHOME and PATH environment variables in the start-up file. If you are unfamiliar with how to use an editor to create or modify a file, refer to Chapter 5. If you use the C shell, add these lines to your .cshrc:

```
setenv OPENWINHOME /usr/openwin
set path=(. /bin /usr/sbin $OPENWINHOME/bin)
```

If you use the Korn shell, add these lines to your .profile:

```
OPENWINHOME=/usr/openwin
export OPENWINHOME
PATH=.:/bin:/usr/sbin:$OPENWINHOME/bin
```

Now, each time you log in, these environment variables will automatically be set. Note that if you edit your start-up file, your changes will not take effect until you either log out and log back in, or execute the start-up file.

To execute the start-up file, enter the following:

C Shell:

```
dugout% source .cshrc
```

Korn Shell:

```
$ . .profile
```

Now that your OPENWINHOME and PATH environment variables are set, you are ready to start the OpenWindows environment.

Preview of the OpenWindows Environment

You will learn the details of the OpenWindows environment in Chapter 3, but to get you started, we introduce the basics here. You will learn how to start the OpenWindows environment, how to enter commands in a window, and how to exit the OpenWindows environment.

Starting the OpenWindows Environment

To start the OpenWindows environment, all you need to do is execute the openwin command:

```
dugout% openwin
```

If this doesn't work, you may not have set up your path correctly. You can also try starting the OpenWindows environment with a more complete path specification:

```
dugout% $OPENWINHOME/bin/openwin
```

It takes a minute or two for the OpenWindows environment to start, so be patient. If you have never run the OpenWindows environment before, your system will automatically start some of the DeskSet programs. Your screen will look like the one shown in Figure 2.1.

Entering SunOS Commands in a Window

Now that you have the OpenWindows environment running, you will probably need a window in which to enter SunOS commands. Many of the commands you will use can be executed just by using the mouse. (We'll talk more about this in Chapter 3.) Other SunOS commands are available only when you execute them directly at the command prompt. To enter SunOS commands directly, you will need to use a Command Tool (or a Shell Tool), which is a program that lets you enter commands just as you did before starting the OpenWindows environment. A Command Tool is started by default as part of the default OpenWindows environment, as shown in Figure 2.1. This Command Tool acts as the *system console*. When SunOS or DeskSet applications have warning or error messages to display, they will be sent to the system console. Since this window is conventionally reserved for system messages, you will probably want to open another Command Tool to enter your own SunOS commands.

To start a Command Tool, follow these steps:

1. Position the pointer over the workspace (where no windows appear).

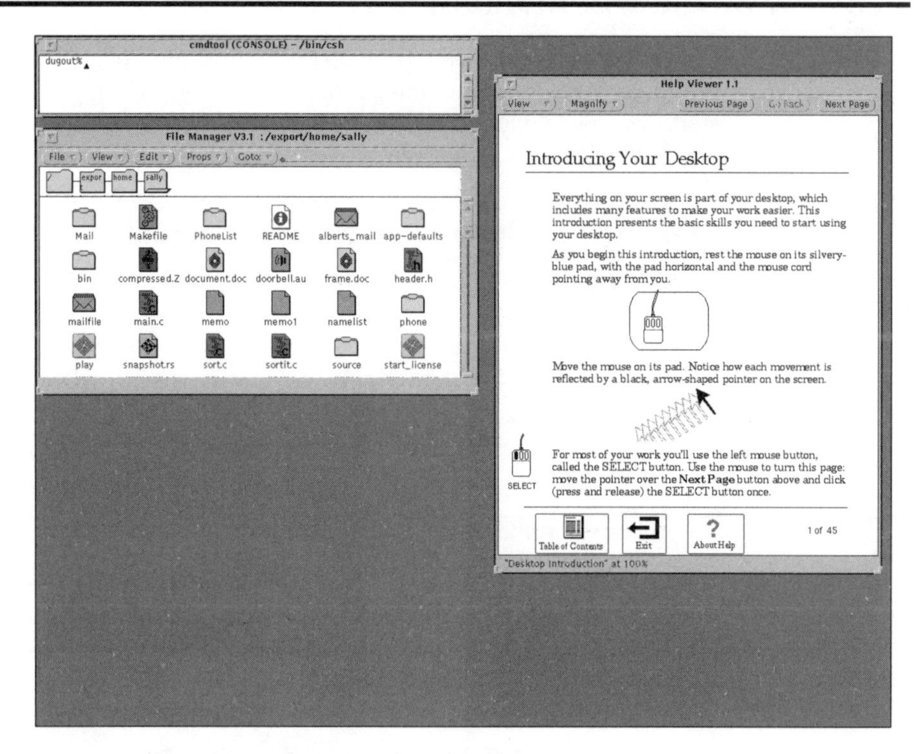

Figure 2.1 OpenWindows default applications and layout

2. Press the right mouse button (called the MENU button). The Workspace menu appears.
3. Drag the pointer across the Programs item in the direction of the arrow (to the right). The Programs menu appears, as shown in Figure 2.2.
4. Position the pointer over the item labeled Command Tool.
5. Release the mouse button. After a few seconds a new Command Tool will appear, as shown in Figure 2.3.

You enter SunOS commands in the Command Tool the same way you entered commands at the shell prompt before you started the OpenWindows environment. One difference is that the window must be *active*. You activate a window by moving the pointer into it and clicking the left mouse button. Depending on the way you set up your environment, it may be necessary only to move the pointer into the window to make it active. We'll discuss this further in Chapter 3.

Figure 2.2
Starting a Command Tool

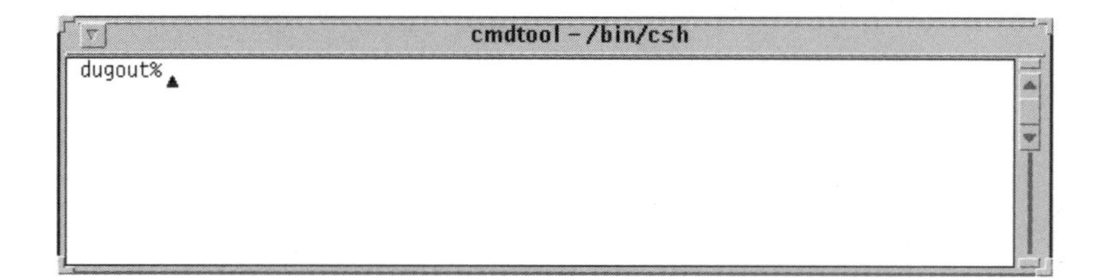

Figure 2.3
A new Command Tool

Each Command Tool has a prompt just as we saw before we started the OpenWindows environment. The default prompt for the Korn shell is the dollar sign ($) and for the C shell is the host name of your system followed by a percent sign (*hostname*%), but prompts can be customized to display just about anything, such as the system host name or the current directory. The Command Tool prompt is followed by the cursor, which is a solid caret if the Command Tool is active, or a dimmed diamond if the Command Tool is inactive. When you move the pointer into the Command Tool and click the left mouse button, the Command Tool becomes active. When you click the left mouse button outside the Command Tool, the caret becomes inactive. This is also called *accepting and losing focus*. When the Command Tool has focus, it is active. When the Command Tool loses focus, it is inactive. Figure 2.4 shows a Command Tool with the ls command entered.

Figure 2.4
Entering commands in a Command Tool

```
cmdtool - /bin/csh
dugout% ls -l .profile
-rw-r--r--   1 sally    staff        491 Sep 29 19:53 .profile
dugout%
```

Exiting the OpenWindows Environment

In later chapters we will discuss in detail how to use the OpenWindows environment. For now, you need to know how to exit the OpenWindows environment. To exit OpenWindows, follow these steps:

1. Position the pointer over the workspace.
2. Press the right mouse button. The Workspace Menu appears, as shown here:

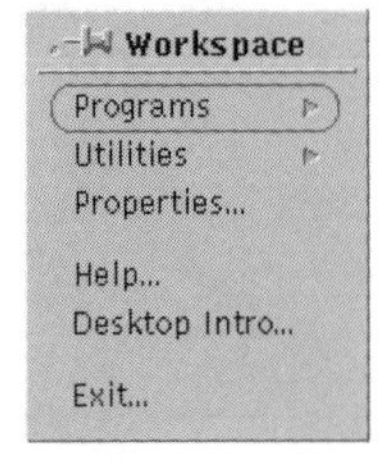

3. Drag the pointer down to the last item, Exit.
4. Release the mouse button. A pop-up window appears, asking for confirmation, as shown here:

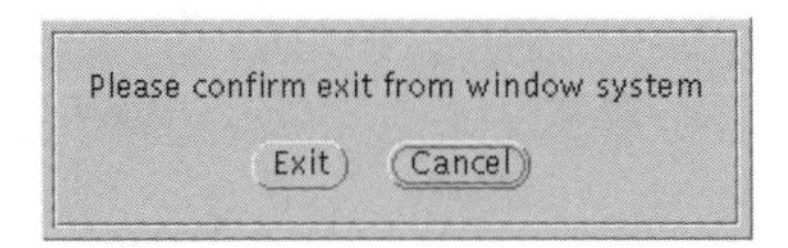

5. Position the pointer over the Exit button, and click the left mouse button. The OpenWindows environment terminates.

Logging Out

When you have finished working in the SunOS operating system, you should log out. If you do not log out, your files can be accessed by anyone who uses your system. By logging out, your account is protected against unwanted use.

To log out of the SunOS operating system, you can either press Control-D or type **exit** at the shell prompt. After you have logged out, you will see the log-in prompt on the screen.

Summary

In this chapter you learned some basics about logging in, setting a password, starting the OpenWindows environment, and entering commands. We have just begun to scratch the surface of the Solaris environment, and we will cover much more in the chapters that follow. The material covered in this chapter is just enough to get you started in running the SunOS operating system and the OpenWindows environment. Part 2 of this book, beginning with Chapter 3, discusses the OpenWindows environment and the DeskSet applications, which will be key components to your success with the Solaris environment.

PART

2

The DeskSet

CHAPTER

3

OpenWindows Fundamentals

Getting Started with the OpenWindows Environment

Basic OPEN LOOK Components

The Workspace Menu

The Window Manager

More OPEN LOOK Components

Customizing Your Environment

The Help System

IN CHAPTERS 1 AND 2 YOU WERE INTRODUCED TO SOME BASIC CONCEPTS about the Solaris operating environment, and you learned how to log in, enter commands, and start the OpenWindows environment. Now you are ready to begin learning more of the details about using the OpenWindows environment that will prepare you for using the DeskSet utilities. In this chapter you will learn about:

- The workspace
- Windows
- The mouse and the pointer
- Base windows
- Pop-up windows
- Icons
- The Workspace menu
- The Window Manager
- OPEN LOOK components
- Customizing your environment
- The Help system

Getting Started with the OpenWindows Environment

In Chapter 2 you learned how to start the OpenWindows environment. Simply enter the openwin command:

```
dugout% openwin
```

This will probably be your first step each time you log in. Now we will discuss some of the details of the OpenWindows system.

The Workspace

The workspace, also called the root window, is the background of the entire screen. All windows, icons, and menus are displayed on the workspace. The workspace cannot be moved or resized. It has its own menu that you can display by pressing the right-most mouse button with the pointer positioned anywhere on the workspace. A typical workspace is shown in Figure 3.1. There are several windows displayed, including the Workspace menu, a pop-up window, several icons, and two running applications.

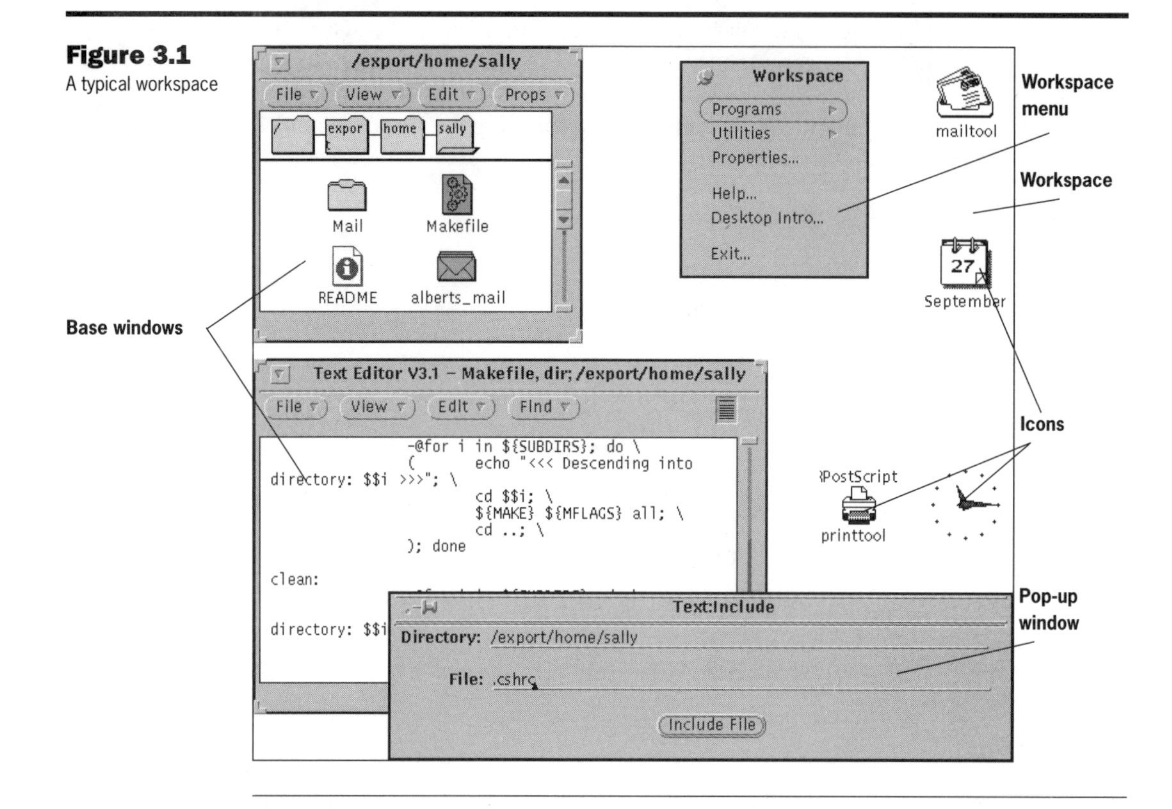

Figure 3.1
A typical workspace

Windows

Every application has its own window or windows. Multiple applications can (and usually do) run simultaneously in the workspace, each having its own window. Windows can overlap and even be obscured completely by other windows. Windows can be moved and resized and can extend beyond the edge of the workspace. There are two different kinds of windows, base and pop-up windows, as we will see in a moment.

The Mouse and the Pointer

You will probably find it necessary to use the mouse when you are using the OpenWindows environment. When you move the mouse on the mouse pad, the pointer on the screen moves. You use the pointer to select items from menus, to move and resize objects, and to perform other tasks.

The mouse has three buttons, and each button has a name. From left to right the buttons are named SELECT, ADJUST, and MENU, known as the

"SAM" mouse, as shown in Figure 3.2. We will use these names throughout this book.

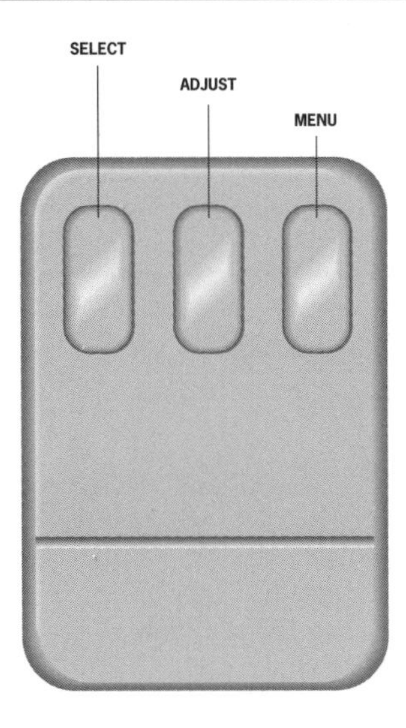

Figure 3.2
The mouse

Each button has a particular function, which is described by its name:

- The SELECT button performs the most fundamental mouse operations, such as selecting an object, activating a button, or manipulating an object.
- The ADJUST button extends or reduces the number of selected objects.
- The MENU button displays a pop-up menu that is associated with the pointer location or the selected object.

You can use mouse buttons in several ways:

Press	Press the mouse button and hold it down.
Release	Release the mouse button. This assumes that you have been pressing the button.
Click	Press and release the mouse button before moving the pointer. This implies that the click and release occur in rapid succession.
Double-click	Click the mouse button twice in rapid succession.

Move	Slide the mouse without pressing any buttons.
Drag	Press the mouse button and hold it down while moving the mouse.

The pointer changes shape to reflect its position and activity. There are many possibilities for cursor shape. Table 3.1 shows several common pointers and their functions.

Table 3.1 Mouse Pointers

Shape	Pointer Type	Description
↖	Basic pointer	The default appearance of the pointer.
	Busy pointer	Indicates that the application is busy and cannot take input.
?	Question pointer	Indicates an invalid selection.
	Text-move pointer	Indicates that text is being moved.
	Text-drop pointer	Same as text-move pointer except that the target indicates it is over a valid drop site.

Everything that appears on the screen, including the pointer, is comprised of a series of dots called *pixels*. Every pointer has exactly one pixel designated as the *hotspot*. The hotspot is the pixel that defines the location of the pointer. For example, when you are moving the pointer into a window, how do you determine when the pointer is "in" the window? The pointer might look like it is halfway in and halfway out. The hotspot is the determining factor. When the hotspot has entered the window, the pointer is said to be "in the window."

Basic OPEN LOOK Components

OPEN LOOK is the name of the graphical user interface (GUI) employed by the OpenWindows environment. The workspace and windows just described are both examples of OPEN LOOK objects. The OpenWindows environment is comprised of many applications that contain OPEN LOOK components. We will describe some basic OPEN LOOK components in this section and talk in more detail about others later in this chapter.

Base Windows

The main window in which an application is displayed is called the *base window*, as shown in Figure 3.3. The base window always has a header that includes a title and a Window menu button. The other objects shown in the figure are optional, though a base window usually has at least one control area or pane.

Figure 3.3
The base window

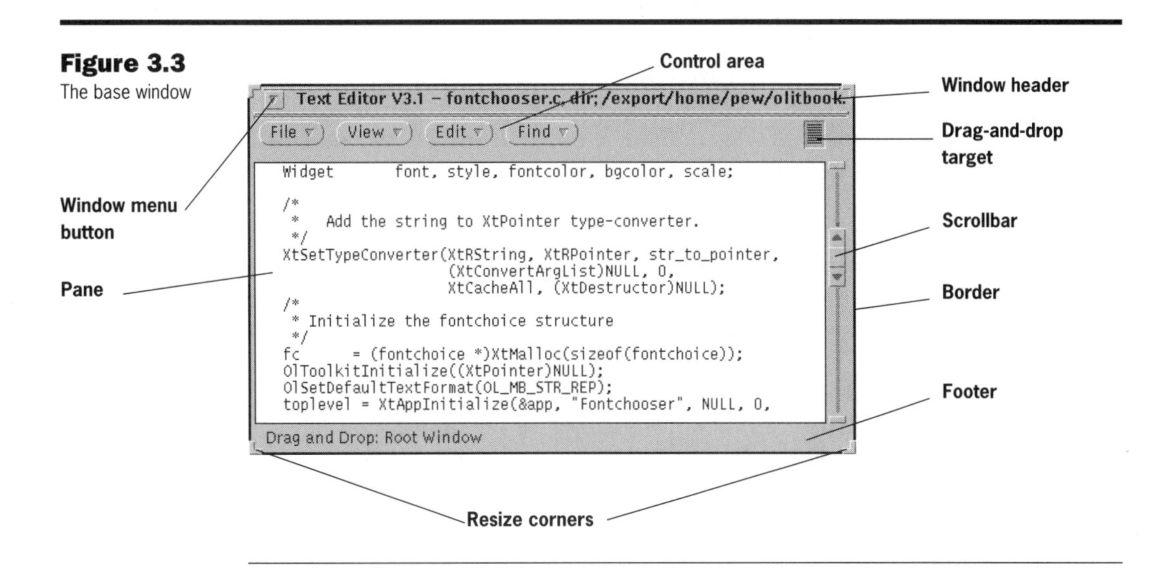

Resize Corners

You use the resize corners to resize a window. If a window does not have resize corners, it cannot be resized. To resize a window:

1. Position the pointer on one of the resize corners.
2. Press the SELECT mouse button.
3. Drag the pointer in any direction. An outline rectangle shows the size as you move the pointer.
4. Release the SELECT mouse button. The window redraws itself with its new size.

You can also constrain the resizing of a window to horizontal only or to vertical only by holding down the Control key on the keyboard while pressing SELECT. After you press SELECT, the direction in which you move first—horizontally or vertically—determines in which direction the resizing will be constrained.

Window Header

Every base window has a header with a Window menu button. With the pointer positioned on the window header, press the MENU mouse button to display the Window menu. We will discuss the Window menu in more detail later in this chapter.

Window Menu Button

The Window menu button is located in the upper-left corner of the window header. Pressing MENU with the pointer positioned on the Window menu button displays the Window menu. Clicking SELECT with the pointer positioned on the Window menu button initiates the default selection on the Window menu. The default selection is usually Close, which closes the window to an icon.

Border

Every window has a narrow border that surrounds it. You can display the Window menu by pressing MENU when the pointer is positioned on the border. This may be especially important if the header is obscured or off the workspace.

Control Area

The control area contains controls for the application. These controls may be buttons, check boxes, menu buttons, and other items.

Pane

The pane is the area where the data is presented. In the example shown in Figure 3.3, the pane contains text. A text pane usually has a pop-up menu associated with it. The Text Pane pop-up menu is displayed when you position the pointer on the text pane and press MENU; the menu contains items for finding, editing, and manipulating text on the text pane. If you hold down the Alt key and press MENU over the pane, the Window menu is displayed.

Footer

The footer region of the base window displays status, error, and state or mode messages.

Scrollbar

The scrollbar permits you to scroll through the contents of the pane. Scrollbars are usually associated with a pane of text or graphics. There are both horizontal and vertical scrollbars. Figure 3.4 shows a horizontal scrollbar.

Figure 3.4
A horizontal scrollbar

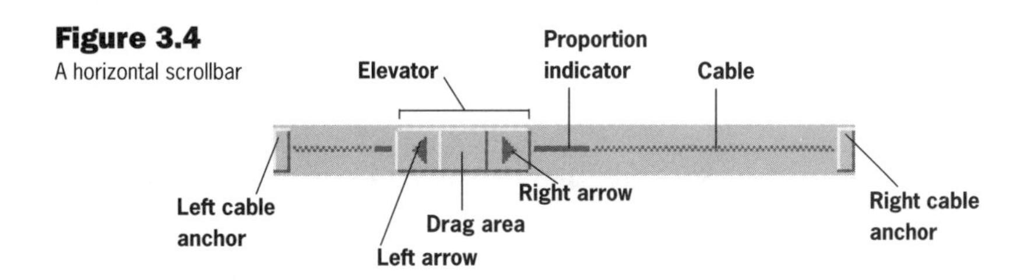

You can manipulate the scrollbar in one of several ways:

- Click SELECT with the pointer on one of the direction arrows to scroll one unit or one line in the direction of the arrow.
- Press SELECT with the pointer on one of the direction arrows to scroll continuously in the direction of the arrow.
- Click SELECT with the pointer on the cable to move the contents of the pane a full page or pane.
- Click SELECT with the pointer on one of the cable anchors to jump to the beginning or end of the contents of the pane.
- Press SELECT with the pointer on the drag area, and drag the elevator to a new position.
- Press MENU with the pointer anywhere along the scrollbar cable, elevator, or cable anchors to display the Scrollbar pop-up menu. Select an item on the menu to control movement of the scrollbar.

The proportion indicator shows the relative size of the visible portion of the pane. The size of the proportion indicator relative to the size of the cable is the same ratio as the size of the viewable area of the pane to the size of the entire pane.

Pop-up Windows

In addition to base windows, pop-up windows are available in many applications. Pop-up windows appear as separate windows that can be repositioned on the workspace independent of the base window. Each pop-up window is associated with a particular base window. When the base window is iconified (see the Icons section a bit later in the chapter), the associated pop-up window or windows also become iconified.

There are four types of pop-up windows:

Command windows are used for setting parameters or for executing commands.

Property windows are used for setting properties of the application or of objects associated with the application.

Help windows provide helpful information about the application or about components of the application.

Notices provide essential information to the user of the application.

Command and property windows are usually displayed when you press a button in the application. Buttons with three dots following the label indicate that a pop-up window will appear as a result of pressing the button. Figure 3.5 shows a base window with a command pop-up window.

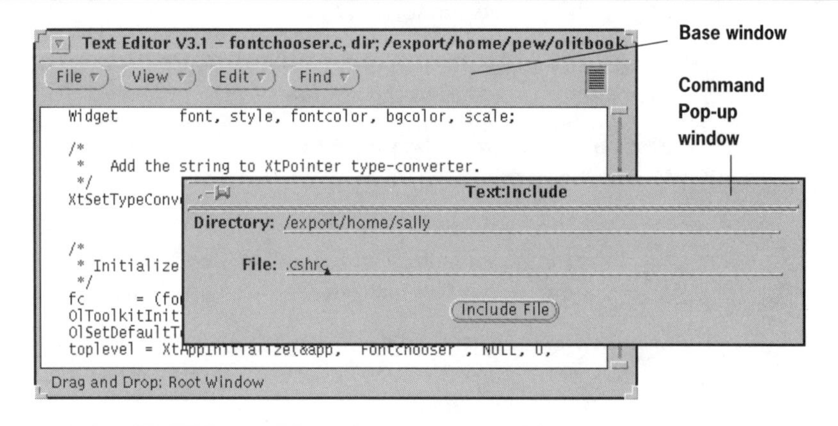

Figure 3.5 A base window with a command pop-up window

Help windows are displayed when you press the Help button on the keyboard. Help is displayed for the object under the pointer when the Help button has been pressed. Figure 3.6 shows a help pop-up window.

Notices are used when important information must be given to the user. The application expects an immediate response; it cannot proceed with any other action until you have responded to the notice. You respond by pressing one of the buttons on the notice (see Figure 3.7).

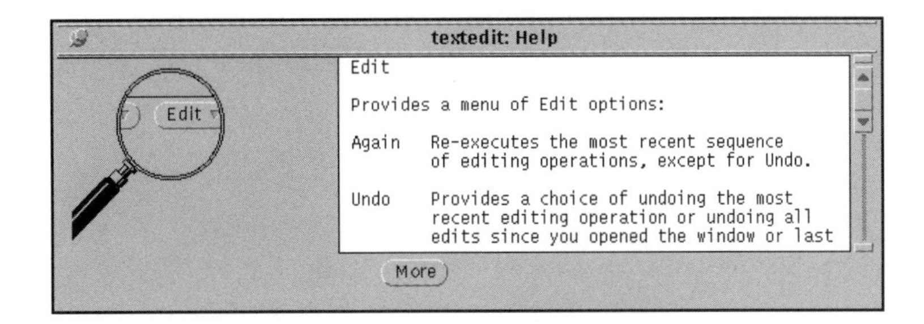

Figure 3.6
A help pop-up window

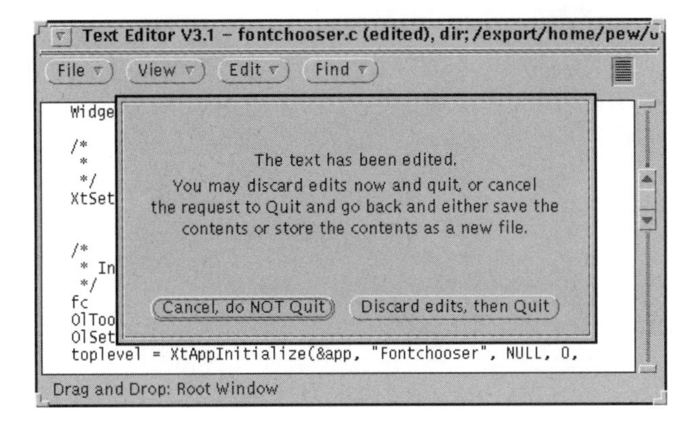

Figure 3.7
A notice pop-up window

Pushpins

Command windows, property windows, and help pop-up windows usually have a pushpin in the left portion of the pop-up header. The pushpin has two states: pinned and unpinned. When the pushpin is pinned, the pop-up window stays on the workspace after the action associated with the pop-up window has taken place. When the pushpin is unpinned, the pop-up window automatically pops down (disappears) when an action is taken.

For example, Figure 3.5 shows a command window with an unpinned pushpin. If you were to push the Include File button, the pop-up window would automatically pop down. An exception to this rule would occur if you specified a file that did not exist, in which case an error message would appear in the pop-up footer and the pop-up window would remain on the workspace. If, however, the command window was pinned, pressing the Include File button would include the file, but the pop-up window would remain on the workspace.

To change the state of the pushpin, move the pointer over the pushpin and click SELECT. This toggles the state of the pushpin. If you are unpinning a pinned pop-up, the pop-up will disappear. (This is one method of dismissing a pop-up.)

Menus and Submenus

A menu displays a list of items you can choose from to initiate some kind of action. You display a menu by pressing the MENU mouse button. For example, you display the Workspace menu by pressing the MENU button when the pointer is positioned on the workspace. You display the Window menu by positioning the pointer on the Window header of an application and pressing MENU. You can also display the Window menu by positioning the pointer on an icon and pressing MENU.

A menu contains one or more items. When an item on a menu has a triangle to the right of the name, this indicates that there is another menu, or a submenu, that can be displayed. Selecting an item on a menu initiates an action or displays another menu.

You can activate menus in one of two ways:

- Press-drag-release
- Click-move-click

To demonstrate the press-drag-release method, let's use the Workspace menu to bring up the Properties window.

1. Position the pointer on the workspace.
2. Press the MENU mouse button to display the Workspace menu, and drag the pointer down to the Properties item.
3. Release the button. The Properties pop-up window appears.

To accomplish the same thing with the click-move-click method, follow these steps:

1. Position the pointer over the workspace.
2. Click the MENU mouse button to display the Workspace menu.
3. Position the pointer on the Properties item.
4. Click the MENU or SELECT button. The Properties pop-up window appears.

Now let's go one step further and use these two methods to pop up a submenu. From the Workspace menu, we will pop up the Utilities menu and select Refresh. The Refresh command redraws all the windows on the screen. First, let's use the press-drag-release method:

1. Position the pointer on the workspace.
2. Press the MENU mouse button to display the Workspace menu, and drag the pointer down to the Utilities item.
3. Drag the pointer in the direction that the triangle is pointing (to the right). The Utilities menu appears, as shown in Figure 3.8.
4. Drag the pointer to the Refresh item.
5. Release the button. The workspace is refreshed.

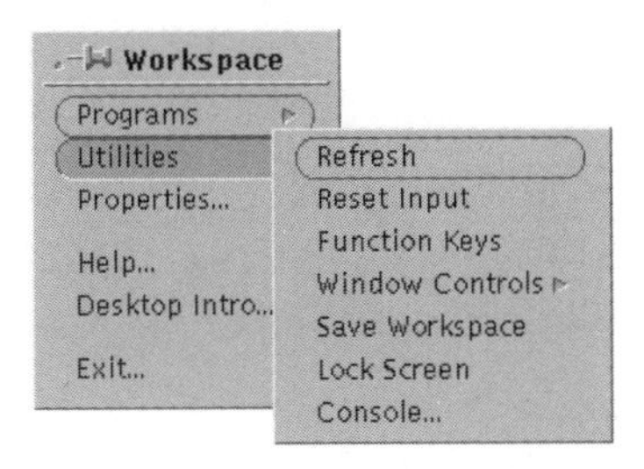

Figure 3.8
The Workspace and Utilities menus

Now try the same thing by using the click-move-click method:

1. Position the pointer on the workspace.
2. Click the MENU mouse button to display the Workspace menu.
3. Move the pointer to the Utilities item.
4. Click the MENU button. The Utilities menu appears.
5. Move the pointer to the Refresh item.
6. Click the MENU or SELECT button. The workspace is refreshed.

You can see in Figure 3.8 that the first item on the Utilities menu, Refresh, has a border around it. This indicates that Refresh is the default selection. Each menu has one item with a border around it. You can activate the default selection of a menu without displaying the menu that it is on by clicking SELECT on the menu button that displays the menu. The MENU button displays the menu, while the SELECT button activates the default selection on the menu without displaying the menu itself. So, because the Refresh item is the default on the Utilities menu, you can activate it by clicking SELECT on Utilities from the Workspace menu.

You can change the default selection of a menu by pressing the Control key, with the pointer over the item that you want to be the default selection. For example, if you want to make Reset Input the default selection on the Utilities menu, you can do so by following these steps:

1. Position the pointer on the workspace.
2. Press the MENU mouse button to display the Workspace menu, and drag the pointer to the Utilities item.
3. Drag the pointer in the direction of the arrow (to the right). The Utilities menu appears.
4. Drag the pointer to the Reset Input item.
5. Press the Control key. Reset Input is now the default item.

The next time you bring up the Utilities menu, you will see that the Reset Input item has the default selection border around it.

Icons

An application can be displayed as either a base window (perhaps with accompanying pop-up windows) or an icon. An icon represents a running application but takes up less space on the workspace than a window. When you do not currently need an application, you can *iconify* it, or change it into an icon. This is often preferred over quitting an application, especially if you are likely to use the application again later. For example, you may use the Mail Tool numerous times throughout the day. When you are not using the Mail Tool, you may want to free up the space it occupies on the workspace. You could quit the Mail Tool, but this means you would have to restart it when you wanted to read mail again. It would be preferable to iconify the Mail Tool and then simply *deiconify* it (redisplay the base window) when you are ready to use it again. This method saves workspace "real estate" and time.

The Workspace Menu

You use the Workspace menu to start applications, set properties, get help, and exit the OpenWindows environment. As you have already seen, you activate the Workspace menu by pressing MENU on any portion of the workspace. (You can also pin the Workspace menu to keep it open on the workspace.) Figure 3.9 shows the Workspace menu. By default, you have six items to choose from in the Workspace menu. The following sections discuss each of these items.

Programs

When you select Programs from the Workspace menu, you bring up the Programs menu. The Programs menu displays a list of the DeskSet applications (see Figure 3.10). Selecting any one of these items starts the corresponding utility. Selecting the last item, Demos, displays another submenu with a list of demo programs. The demo programs range from games, such as solitaire (Xsol), to a program that lets you view fonts (Fontview).

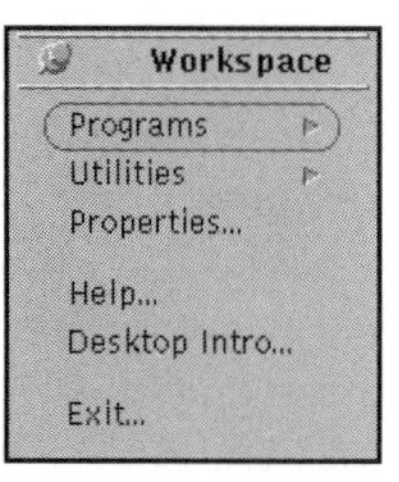

Figure 3.9
The Workspace menu

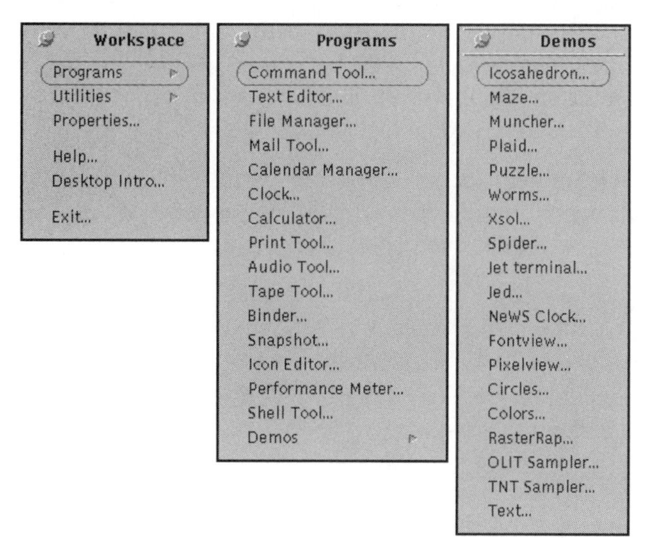

Figure 3.10
The Workspace, Programs, and Demos menus

Utilities

Selecting Utilities from the Workspace menu brings up the Utilities menu. The Utilities menu (shown previously in Figure 3.8) gives you seven items to choose from:

Refresh redraws all windows on the workspace. This is useful when a window or the workspace has become corrupted.

Reset Input runs the SunOS command kbd_mode -u. This can be useful for fixing problems with keyboard input.

Function Keys runs the SunOS command vkbd. A pop-up menu containing buttons for each function key on the keyboard is displayed. This menu can be used to change the keyboard layout for keyboards from different countries.

Window Controls pops up a pinable menu containing four items: Open/Close, Full/Restore Size, Back, and Quit. These functions are identical to the functions provided on the Window menu (see "The Window Manager" later). You can manipulate windows or icons that are selected (shown by the heavy black border) from the Window Controls menu.

Save Workspace saves information about the currently running workspace—including the size and position of windows, the position of icons, and which applications are iconified—so that the next time you invoke OpenWindows, the layout of the workspace, including the applications running and their size and location, will be identical to the layout you had when you saved your workspace.

Lock Screen locks the screen. A pattern is displayed on the workspace, completely obscuring all windows. You must enter your password to unlock the screen.

Console starts a command tool that acts as the console for the system. Error and warning messages come to the Console window. Every running system should have a Console window (and one is provided for you by default when you first start OpenWindows).

Properties

Selecting the Properties item on the Workspace menu brings up the OpenWindows Workspace Properties window. With this window you can select attributes of the OpenWindows environment, such as colors, mouse settings, and languages. We will discuss the Workspace Properties pop-up window in more detail later in this chapter in the section "Customizing Your Environment."

Help and Desktop Intro

Both Help and Desktop Intro invoke the Help Viewer application, which provides on-line information about the OpenWindows environment and various DeskSet utilities. The Help Viewer is discussed in greater detail later in this chapter.

Exit

The Exit item allows you to quit the OpenWindows environment. Before the OpenWindows environment is closed, a notice window asks you to confirm or cancel this operation.

The Window Manager

One of the components of a base window is the header. When the pointer is positioned on the application base-window header, you press MENU to bring up the Window menu. When the pointer is positioned on one of the application's pop-up window headers, you press MENU to bring up the Pop-up menu. These menus are not provided by the application but by the Window Manager. The Window Manager is a special application that manages other applications. It controls window size, position, and stacking order, among other things.

The Window Menu

The Window menu provides seven items, as shown in Figure 3.11: Open/Close, Full Size/Restore Size, Move, Resize, Properties, Back, Refresh, and Quit. Not all of the items are always available for selection. Sometimes one or more of the items is *grayed out* or *insensitive*. This means that the item is unavailable and any attempt to select that item will not work. (Note that the Properties item is always grayed out.)

Figure 3.11
The Window menu

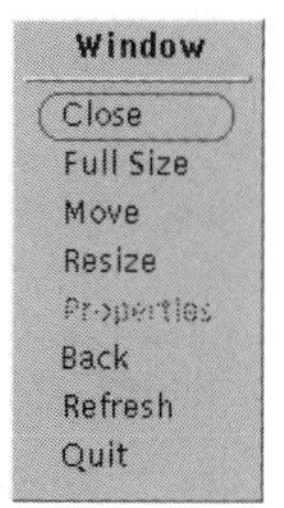

Iconifying Windows

The first item on the Window menu is Close. When you select this item, the application's window disappears from the workspace and is replaced by an icon. The application itself is not terminated. All associated pop-up windows are also iconified with the base window.

You can also use the Window menu button to iconify a window. Pressing SELECT on the Window menu button selects the default choice on the Window menu, which will be Close unless you have explicitly changed the default item.

When an application is iconified, you can display the Window menu by pressing MENU over the icon. In this case, the first item, Close, is replaced by Open. Selecting Open opens, or deiconifies, the application. You can also open an icon by double-clicking SELECT on the icon.

The Open key on your keyboard has the same effect as the Close and Open items on the Window menu. When the pointer is positioned on a base window, you press the Open key to close the application. To open the application, position the pointer on an icon and press the Open key.

Full Size/Restore Size

The second item on the Window menu is Full Size or Restore Size. Selecting Full Size changes the height of an application to the full height of the workspace. When the application is at full size, the second item on the Window menu becomes Restore Size. Selecting Restore Size returns the window to its previous size.

You can invoke the same action by double-clicking SELECT with the pointer positioned anywhere on the header or on the border of any application on the workspace. Double-clicking SELECT when the window is full size returns the window to it previous size.

Moving Windows

The most straightforward way to move a window is to use the press-drag-release method with the pointer positioned on the header or border.

1. Position the pointer on the header or border.
2. Press SELECT.
3. Drag the mouse. An outline of the window is displayed, moving with the pointer.
4. Release SELECT. The window is redrawn at its new position.

Another method of moving a window is to press SELECT while holding down the Alt key, and then dragging the window to the desired location. With this method, you do not have to have the pointer on the header or border—it can be anywhere in the window. This method is particularly useful when the header is obscured or off the workspace.

You can also use the Move item on the Window menu to move windows. Select Move, and then use the arrow keys to move the window. When the window is positioned where you want it, press Return.

Several windows can be moved simultaneously by first highlighting each window you want to move. To highlight a window, click SELECT on the window's header or border. This highlights that window and unhighlights any other windows. (A highlighted window has a thickened border.) To highlight another window at the same time, click ADJUST on the desired window. Now when you perform the move operation, all highlighted windows move together. You can also highlight icons by clicking SELECT or ADJUST on the icon.

Some additional features allow you to modify the behavior of the move operation. If you hold down the Shift key on the keyboard while performing a move (the press-drag-release version), the entire window and its contents move, rather than just an outline of the window. If you hold down the Control key while performing a move, the window is constrained to a horizontal or vertical move only. The Control key has a different function when used in conjunction with the Move command on the Window menu. If you hold down the Control key while using this command and the arrow keys to move a window, the movement of the window is accelerated.

Resizing Windows

The resize corners, provided on most base windows, make it easy to resize a window. With the pointer positioned on a resize corner, press SELECT, drag the resize corner to the new location, and release the mouse button. If you hold down the Control key while resizing a window, the window will be constrained to a vertical or horizontal resizing. If you hold down the Shift key when you press SELECT on the resize corner, the window will move but will not be resized.

You can also use the Resize item from the Window menu to resize a window. Choose Resize from the Window menu, and then use the arrow keys on the keyboard to increase or decrease the height or width of the window. When the window is the desired size, press the Return key.

Window Stacking

The Back item on the Window menu moves the window to the back of the stack. The *stack* refers to the windows that may be stacked on top of each other. Of course, if no other windows are occupying the same space as the window in question, the Back item has no effect.

You can bring a window forward, or to the top of the stack, by clicking SELECT on the header or border of the window. Be careful to single-click. If you double-click, the window will come forward but will also become full size.

Another way to move a window forward or backward is to use the Front key on the keyboard. Pressing Front brings a window to the top of the stack unless it is already at the top of the stack, in which case it is moved to the bottom of the stack (the same as the Back operation from the Window menu).

Refreshing Windows

The Refresh item from the Window menu redisplays the contents of a window. Occasionally, the contents of a window become corrupted and it is necessary to have it redrawn.

Quitting Windows

The last button on the Window menu is Quit. Use this option to terminate an application.

The Pop-up Menu

The Pop-up menu is similar to the Window menu but is provided only when you press MENU with the pointer positioned over a pop-up window. The items on the Pop-up menu (see Figure 3.12) are Dismiss, Move, Resize, Back, Refresh, and Owner?.

Figure 3.12
The Pop-up menu

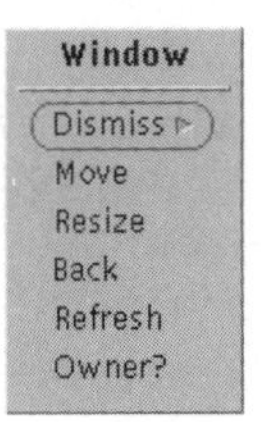

Dismissing Pop-up Windows

The first item on the Pop-up menu is Dismiss, which you use to dismiss, or pop down, a pop-up window. The Dismiss button has a submenu with two choices: This Window, the default, dismisses only the current pop-up window, and All Pop-ups dismisses all pop-up windows associated with the current application.

You can also dismiss a pop-up window by pressing the Open key on the keyboard.

Moving Pop-up Windows

You move pop-up windows in the same way that you move base windows. Position the pointer on the Pop-up header, press SELECT, drag the pointer, and release the mouse button. You can also use the Move item from the Pop-up menu in exactly the same way that you used it on the Window menu.

Resizing Pop-up Windows

You can resize a pop-up window only if it has resize corners. Most pop-up windows, however, do not have them. If a pop-up window does not have resize corners, the Resize item on the Pop-up menu is grayed out.

Pop-up Window Stacking

Pop-up window stacking is identical to window stacking. If you select Back from the Pop-up menu, the pop-up window is moved to the back of the stacking order. If you press the Front key with the pointer positioned on a pop-up window, the pop-up window is moved to the top of the window stack.

Refreshing Pop-up Windows

Refreshing pop-up windows is identical to window refreshing.

Pop-up Window Ownership

The Owner? item on the Pop-up menu allows you to determine which window is the owner of that pop-up window. When you select Owner? on the Pop-up menu, the header of the window that owns the pop-up window flashes quickly five times.

More OPEN LOOK Components

Once you know how to use the standard OPEN LOOK components, you should be able to learn how to use a new OPEN LOOK application in a matter of minutes. Here are some of the basic OPEN LOOK components.

Buttons

Buttons are used for single commands and are typically used in control areas. The label of the button usually describes the command the button initiates. For example, a button labeled Clear probably clears a pane or an associated region. Some buttons have a *window mark* (three dots following the label), which indicates that a pop-up window will be displayed when the button is pressed. You activate a button by clicking SELECT when the pointer is positioned on the button. Here are two buttons, including one with a window mark:

Menu Buttons

Menu buttons are used for displaying menus that contain additional controls. Menu buttons always have a *menu mark*, an outlined triangle following the label. The triangle points to where the menu will be displayed. You activate a menu button by pressing MENU while the pointer is positioned on the menu button. You can activate the menu's default selection without popping up the menu by clicking SELECT while the pointer is on the menu button. Below are two menu buttons. The one on the right has its associated menu popped up.

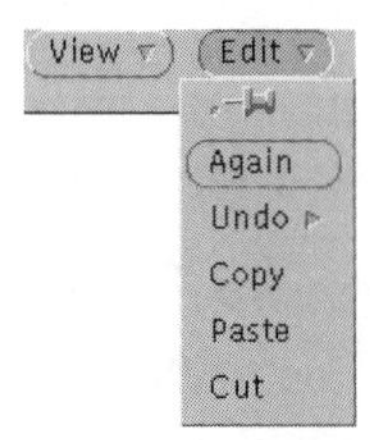

Abbreviated Menu Buttons

Abbreviated menu buttons are very similar to menu buttons. They are also used for displaying menus that contain additional controls. An abbreviated menu button, however, requires less space than a menu button (hence the name "abbreviated"), and the current choice is displayed without the menu. In the illustration below, the current choice is PostScript. You activate an abbreviated menu button by pressing MENU while the pointer is positioned on the button. You can also activate the menu's default selection without popping up the menu by clicking SELECT while the pointer is on the button. Here is an abbreviated menu button:

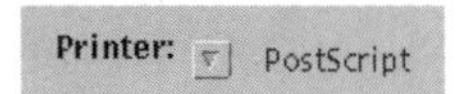

Text Fields

Text fields allow user input from the keyboard. For example, a text field allows you to type the name of a document you want to save. When you position the pointer on a text field and click SELECT, the cursor appears in the text field. Each character you type on the keyboard is displayed in the text field. When a text field cannot display the entire text string, scrolling buttons are displayed to allow you to scroll the text string horizontally. Here is a text field:

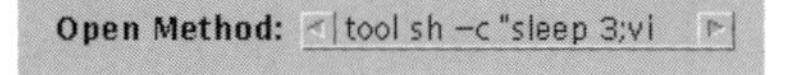

Text Regions

Text regions allow you to input more than one line. Scrollbars are included to scroll the text in the text region.

Numeric Text Fields

Numeric text fields can contain only numbers and have increment/decrement scrolling buttons. You can click on the appropriate scrolling button to increase or decrease the number displayed in the number text field. Here is a numeric text field:

Exclusive Settings

Exclusive settings are used for selecting a state or choice for an attribute. For example, the Snapshot application (see Chapter 8) lets you choose how to capture a screen image—by window, region, or screen. Exclusive settings allow only one choice. They are displayed as contiguous rectangular buttons. The exclusive setting here shows Region as the current choice:

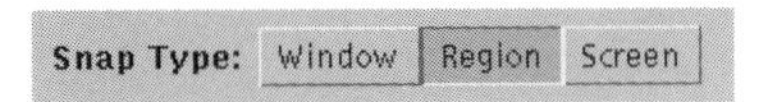

Nonexclusive Settings

Nonexclusive settings are used for selecting multiple values for an attribute. For example, you can set an alarm to give different kinds of signals. The four choices shown below represent different ways the alarm can be registered. One or more of these settings can be used at one time. Nonexclusive settings are displayed as separated rectangular buttons.

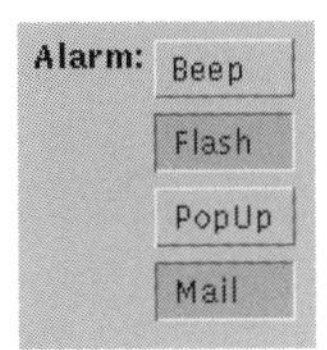

Check Boxes

Check boxes are used for setting a Yes/No or On/Off choice. You toggle a check box by pressing the SELECT button while the pointer is on the check box. In the check box shown here, Owner and Group are chosen, but World is not.

Sliders

Sliders allow you to set a numeric value and to give a visual indication of the setting. You move a slider by pressing SELECT while the pointer is on the drag box, then dragging the pointer left or right, and then releasing SELECT. Another way to move a slider is to click SELECT on the slider bar to either the left or the right of the drag box. The slider moves one unit in the direction of the pointer. The slider shown here is being used as a volume control:

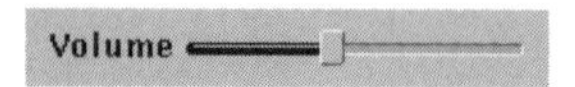

Gauges

Gauges give a visual indication of a numeric value. For example, the gauge shown below indicates the amount of disk space currently in use. Gauges are for display only; they do not take user input.

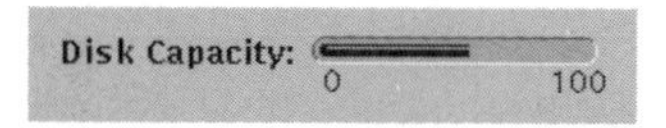

Read-only Messages

Read-only messages provide text that cannot be edited. Here is a read-only message:

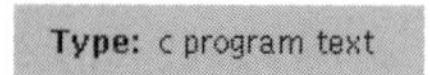

Scrolling Lists

A *scrolling list* is a list of items that can scroll. The size of the list is not bound by the size of the scrolling list. For example, a list of appointments could include dozens of entries, but only a few appear at one time, as shown below. The scrollbar allows you to scroll through the entire list. This saves space, especially for large lists.

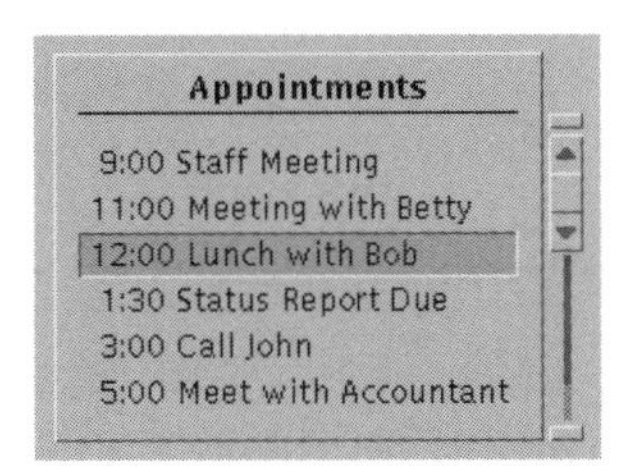

Customizing Your Environment

The OpenWindows environment provides a common set of defaults, including colors, placement of scrollbars, mouse operations, and so forth. In this section we will discuss the customization features available from the Workspace Properties window.

Workspace Properties

Pressing the Properties button on the Workspace menu brings up the Workspace Properties pop-up window. This window allows you to customize six properties in the workspace:

Color lets you change workspace, window, and menu colors. This category is not available on monochrome (black-and-white) systems.

Icons lets you select the default location on the screen for icons.

Menus includes settings for the drag-right distance of the pointer and for the behavior of SELECT on menu buttons.

Miscellaneous includes settings for beep frequency, window manager input focus model, and scrollbar placement.

Mouse Settings includes settings for pointer jumping and multiclick time-out.

Localization includes settings for different languages.

When the Workspace Properties window first comes up, the color category is displayed. (If you are running the OpenWindows environment on a monochrome system, the Icons category will be displayed first.) To change categories:

1. Position the pointer on the abbreviated menu button in the upper-left corner, labeled Category.

2. Press the MENU mouse button. A menu pops up.
3. Drag the pointer to the desired category.
4. Release the MENU mouse button. The new category is displayed.

Figure 3.13 shows the Workspace Properties window with the Category pop-up menu.

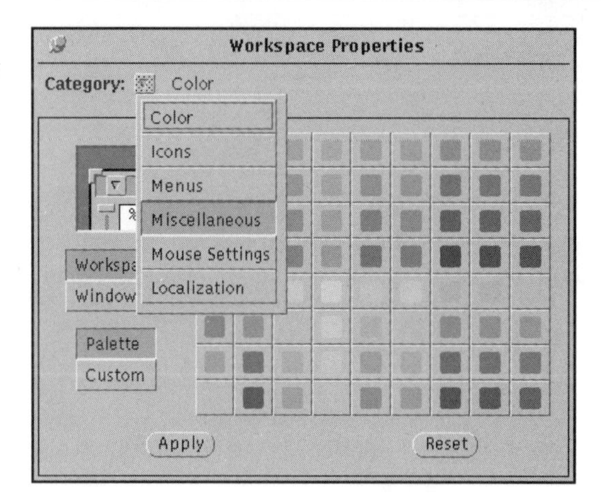

Figure 3.13 Choosing a category from the Workspace Properties menu

When you have set the desired workspace properties, dismiss the Workspace Properties pop-up window by unpinning it or by selecting Dismiss from the Pop-up menu. The Workspace Properties window cannot be iconified.

Color

You use the Color category to select two colors: the workspace color and the windows color (see Figure 3.14). The workspace color is the background color for the workspace. The windows color is the color for the window manager border; it is also the default color used by the DeskSet applications.

To select a color:

1. Click SELECT on Workspace or on Windows.
2. Click SELECT on a color from the color palette. The color is displayed in the inset.
3. Click SELECT on the Apply button. A notice pops up, requesting confirmation, as shown in Figure 3.15.

Figure 3.14
Choosing colors from the Workspace Properties window

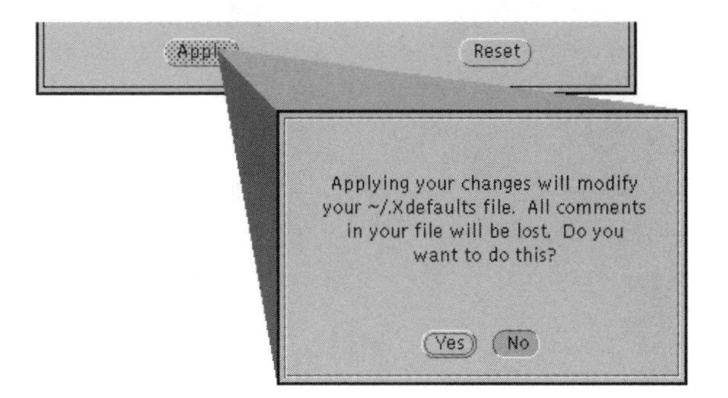

Figure 3.15
Confirming the changes to the Workspace

4. Click SELECT on the Yes button. The color changes take effect.

Clicking the Apply button saves the changes you have made for both the workspace and windows colors. In fact, the Apply button will apply changes made to any of the categories. For example, you can select a new workspace color, then move to a new category such as Icons, make a change there, and then click on Apply. Both the color and icon changes would be applied at that time.

When you click on Apply, a notice pops up, indicating that the ~/.Xdefaults file will be modified and all comments lost. The ~/.Xdefaults file contains (among other things) the information regarding the workspace properties in a format understood by the X Window System. You will probably always want to answer yes to this notice. The only time that you would answer no would be if you had edited the ~/.Xdefaults file yourself, had added comments, and did not want to lose those comments. Only the comments will be lost from the ~/.Xdefaults file. If you have put some custom resource specifications in your ~/.Xdefaults file, you do not need to fear that they will be lost or corrupted.

At any time during the selection, you can also press the Reset button. The Reset button will reset the color selection, or any other selections, made since the last time Apply was selected. This is particularly convenient if you decide against making some changes but aren't sure what all the previous settings were.

If none of the colors provided in the color palette are to your liking, you can customize your own color. Press the Custom button, and the palette is replaced by three sliders representing hue, saturation, and brightness, as shown in Figure 3.16. Adjust the sliders until you have the color you want.

Figure 3.16
Creating a custom color

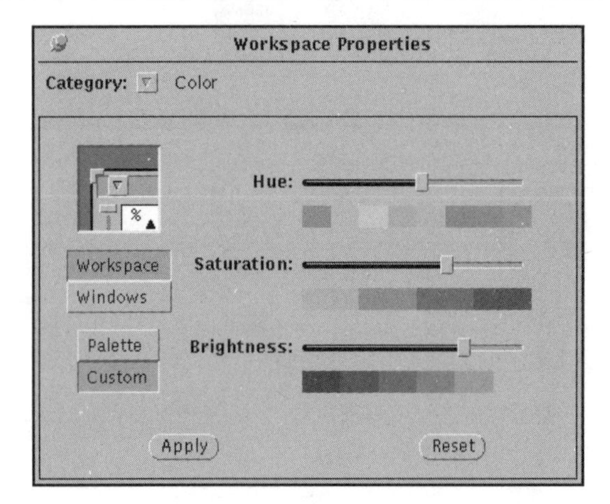

Icons

The Icons category lets you choose where icons will be located. By default, icons appear at the bottom of the screen. If, for example, you want them to appear on the right-hand side of the screen, you select Right from the Location exclusive settings, as shown in Figure 3.17. Changing the location of icons does not affect the icons of any running applications. New programs locate their icons in the newly chosen location. The next time you start the OpenWindows environment, the icons will respond to this new setting.

Menus

The Menus category lets you set two features related to the operation of menus: the drag-right distance and the SELECT button behavior. Figure 3.18 shows the Menus category.

Figure 3.17
Choosing icon location

Figure 3.18
Setting menu properties

The drag-right distance is set to a value representing the number of pixels that you must drag the pointer to pop up a menu. The default value is 100 pixels. As the name implies, the direction of the drag is to the right. The drag-right distance affects only menu buttons whose direction arrows point to the right.

As an example, bring up the Workspace menu, and move the pointer to either the Programs or Utilities button. While holding down the MENU button, drag the pointer to the right, and notice when the next menu pops up. Then go to the Workspace Properties Menus category, change the drag-right distance to a small number such as 10, and apply the change. Now follow the same steps again: Bring up the Workspace menu, move the pointer to either Programs or Utilities, and drag the pointer to the right. Notice how much earlier the menu pops up.

The SELECT Mouse Press feature controls the way a menu button will behave when you press the SELECT mouse button while the pointer is on it. The Selects Default option means that when you click on SELECT, the default item on the pop-up menu is selected without popping up the menu. In addition, the label of the default selection from the menu is previewed in the menu button. The Displays menu option means that when you press the SELECT button over the menu button, it works the same as if you pressed the MENU button.

The File Manager DeskSet application has several menu buttons that demonstrate this behavior. With the Selects Default option set, you can preview the default selection in the menu button. Press the SELECT button while the pointer is on the View menu button. While you are pressing SELECT, the default selection from the menu is displayed in the menu button. If you release the button while the pointer is still on the menu button, the default selection from the menu will be activated. If you do not want to activate the default selection, move the pointer away from the menu button and then release SELECT. Neither of these features affect running applications.

Miscellaneous

The Miscellaneous category sets three features: beep frequency, input focus policy, and scrollbar placement. Figure 3.19 shows the Miscellaneous category.

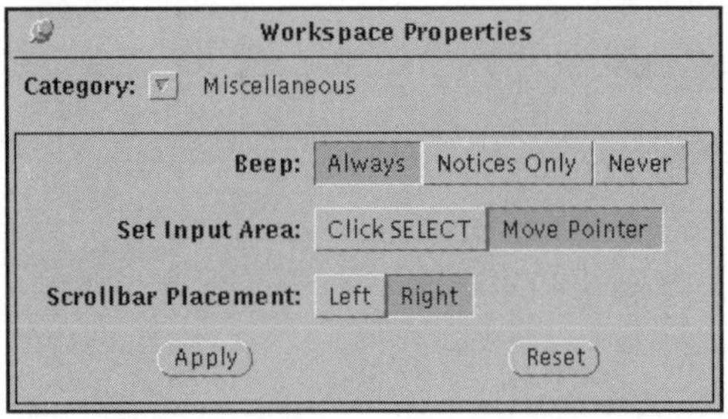

Figure 3.19 Miscellaneous settings

Workspace Properties
Category: Miscellaneous
Beep: Always | Notices Only | Never
Set Input Area: Click SELECT | Move Pointer
Scrollbar Placement: Left | Right
Apply   Reset

The Beep setting has three options: Always, Notices Only, and Never. These options are fairly self-explanatory. The default value is Always; this means that no limitations are made for when the windowing system will provide a beep. Notices Only indicates that a beep will occur only when a notice appears. Never indicates that beeps are turned off.

The Set Input Area setting has two options: Click SELECT and Move Pointer. The Click SELECT option means that if you want to set the input focus to a particular window, you must click the SELECT mouse button in that window. One advantage of this option is that you can set the focus to a window and then move the pointer completely out of the window. The focus will stay in the chosen window until you click SELECT in another window. The Move Pointer option means that the focus is set to whichever window the pointer is currently on. An advantage of this method is that you can simply move the mouse (without an accompanying button click) to move the focus to another window. Try each method for a while to determine which you prefer. Changing and applying the Set Input Area feature takes effect immediately.

The Scrollbar Placement choice determines on which side the scrollbars will be placed. This affects only the applications that are started after the change has been made.

Mouse Settings

The Mouse Settings category lets you set three features: scrollbar pointer jumping, pop-up pointer jumping, and multiclick time-out. Figure 3.20 shows the Mouse Settings category.

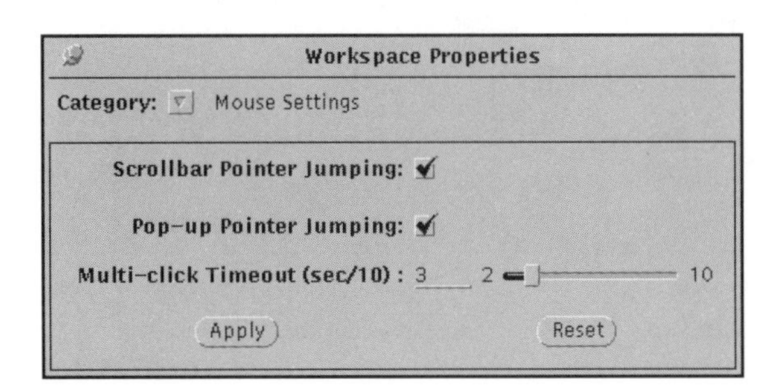

Figure 3.20 Choosing mouse properties

The default setting for Scrollbar Pointer Jumping is True (i.e., checkmarked). This means that when you press and hold SELECT on the scrollbar direction arrow or cable, the pointer jumps in the direction of the movement of the scrollbar.

The Pop-up Pointer Jumping option also defaults to True. With this option set to true, the pointer automatically jumps to the default selection on a pop-up window such as a notice. You may have observed this when pressing the Apply button. A notice appears and the pointer automatically jumps to the Yes button on the notice (if Pop-up Pointer Jumping is set to True). When you make the notice pop down, the pointer jumps back to its previous location. Setting this feature to False turns off this type of pointer jumping.

The Multi-click Timeout feature controls the speed with which the SELECT button must be clicked twice to register as a multiclick or as a double click. Many applications (including most of the DeskSet applications) have certain functionality built around double clicks. Moving the slider to the left or the right adjusts the allowed time between clicks to still register as a double click. There are two ways to adjust the multiclick time-out value. You can use the mouse and pointer to adjust the slider, or you can use the keyboard to type the numeric value in the adjacent text field.

Localization

The Localization category is used for setting the native language that the OpenWindows environment runs in. If you are running the basic OpenWindows environment (in English), this category will not give you any options to choose from. If, however, you are running a localized version of the OpenWindows environment, you will be able to select several locale-dependent options. Figure 3.21 show the Localization category with multiple language choices for the basic setting.

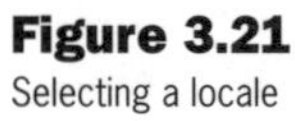

Figure 3.21
Selecting a locale

The Basic Setting option lets you set the native language or country in which the user interface will operate. The Specific Setting choices vary, depending on the Basic Setting choice. For example, Time Format has two choices when the basic setting is Japanese. With the basic setting set to U.S.A., only one time format is available.

The Display Language option lets you determine what language is used for displaying labels of buttons, messages, captions, and so on. The Input Language option lets you determine what language is used for input. You may choose to use one language for display and another language for input.

The Time Format option lets you specify the format used in displaying the time and date. Different locales use different formats; some locales provide multiple time formats to choose from. Figure 3.22 shows the options you are given for setting the time format in the Chinese locale.

The Numeric Format option lets you determine the format for displaying numbers—specifically monetary quantities. The American system uses a period between dollars and cents. Some other systems use a comma.

None of the localization settings affect a running application. Only new applications that you start after applying the changes will inherit the new settings.

Saving Your Workspace

The Save Workspace item on the Utilities menu allows you to save the information about the currently running programs and their locations. The next time you start the OpenWindows environment, all the programs, their sizes, and their locations will be displayed on the workspace exactly as they appeared when you saved the workspace. You can use the Save Workspace feature to customize your workspace and ensure that every time you start the OpenWindows environment all your favorite programs (or icons) will be displayed in the locations and sizes you specified.

Figure 3.22
Selecting a time format

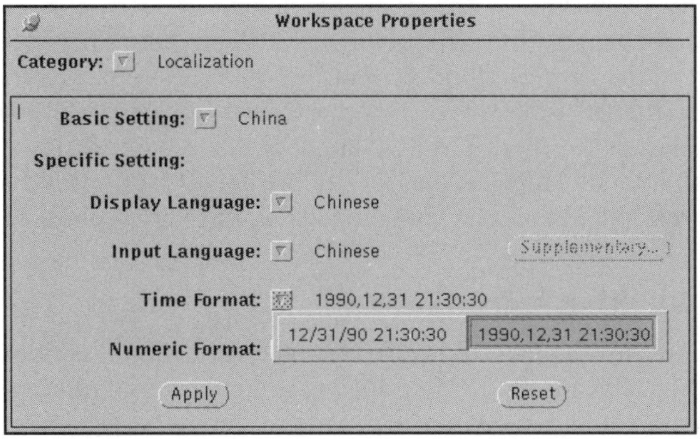

To save your workspace, follow these steps:

1. Organize your workspace the way you want it. Bring up the most frequently used programs and position them on the workspace where you would like them. Also position the icons where you want them.
2. With the pointer positioned on the workspace, press the MENU button. The Workspace menu appears.
3. Bring up the Utilities menu.
4. Select Save Workspace. The pointer becomes busy for a few seconds. Then a notice appears, indicating that the operation is complete (see Figure 3.23).
5. Click SELECT on the OK button.

Figure 3.23
Saving your workspace

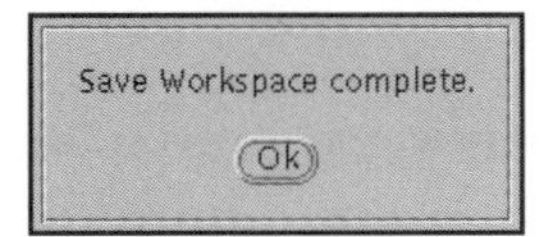

The Help System

Frequently you may need some help in understanding or remembering how a particular DeskSet application or feature works. To find an answer, you can always pull out a book (like this one) or the documentation that is provided with the OpenWindows environment. However, many answers to your questions are available through on-line help. Two types of help are available: spot help and the help handbooks. Spot help provides some written text in a help pop-up that is displayed when you press the Help key while the pointer is on the object in question. The help handbooks are part of a separate DeskSet application called Help Viewer. One of the handbooks is titled *Introducing Your Sun Desktop*. The next section introduces this very useful handbook.

The Desktop Introduction

You can start the Desktop Introduction by selecting Desktop Intro from the Workspace menu. If the Help Viewer is not currently running, it will automatically start. Once the Help Viewer is running, the Desktop Introduction will be loaded and displayed. You can also load the Desktop Introduction by selecting *Introducing Your Sun Desktop* from the Help Handbooks page (see Figure 3.24).

The Desktop Introduction provides a wealth of information about basic OpenWindows concepts (many of which we have discussed in this chapter). Take a few minutes to go through the 45-page introduction, especially if you are new to the OpenWindows environment. Press the Next Page button in the upper-right corner to advance each page. The page titled "Sound and Your Workstation" is especially fun.

Spot Help and Help Handbooks

Spot help is provided for most objects in every DeskSet application. Spot help information is displayed in a help pop-up window when you press the Help key while the pointer is on the object that you need help with. For example, if you are running Mail Tool, position the pointer on the Move menu button and press the Help key. Figure 3.25 shows the spot help for the Move menu button.

Now position the pointer on another object in the same application. Press Help, and the contents of the Help pop-up window are replaced with the new information.

You may also notice the More button on the bottom of the Help pop-up window. (This button is on many Help pop-up windows, but not on all.) When you press the More button, the Help Viewer is invoked with the corresponding help handbook. Figure 3.26 shows the help handbook for Mail Tool.

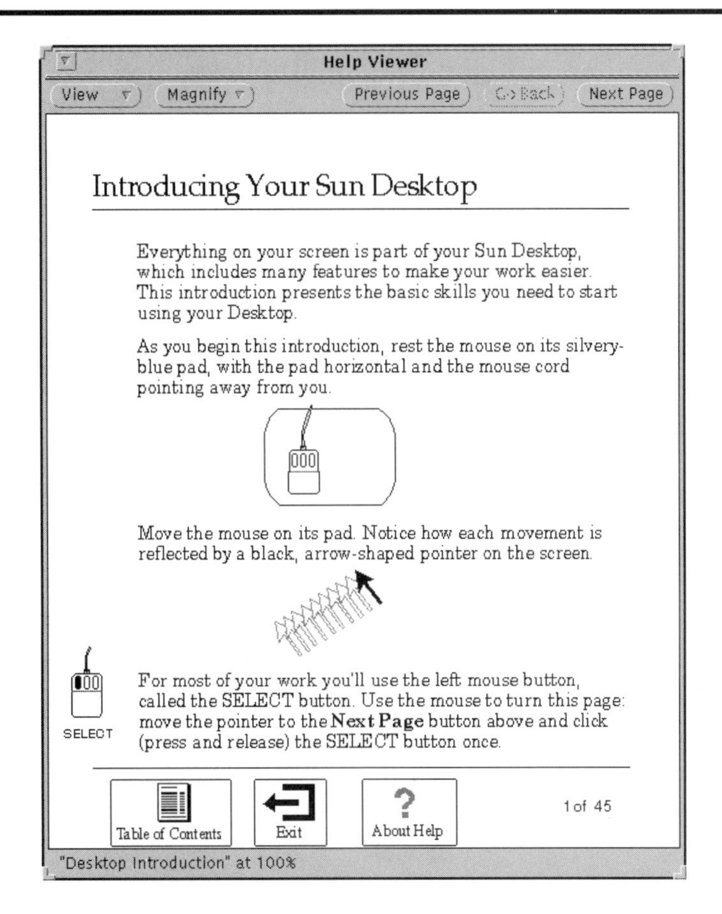

Figure 3.24
The Desktop Introduction

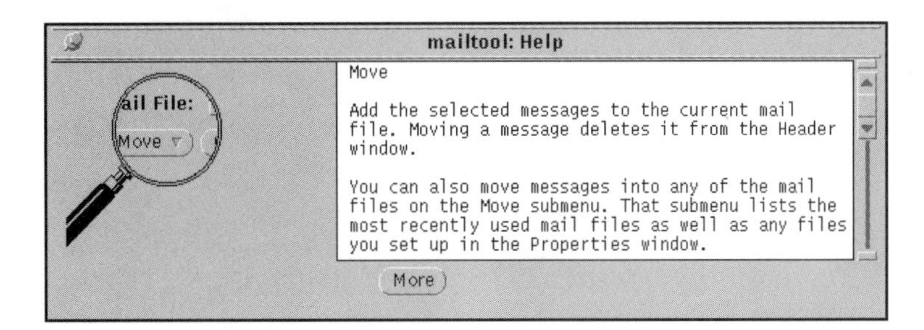

Figure 3.25
Spot help

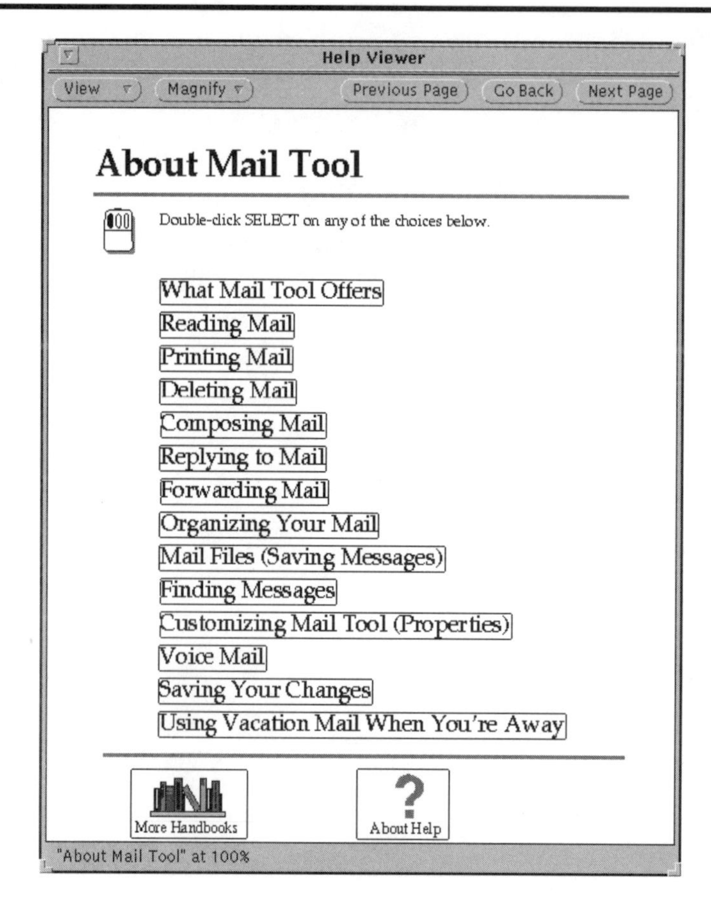

Figure 3.26
The help handbook for Mail Tool

You can read a help handbook without going through the spot help and pressing the More button. The help handbooks are available when you select Help from the Workspace menu. The table of contents for the help handbooks is displayed, as shown in Figure 3.27.

Navigating in Help Viewer

You can get around within Help Viewer in a couple of different ways. The most straightforward way is to use the buttons in the upper-right corner of the application:

Previous Page displays the previous page in the document.

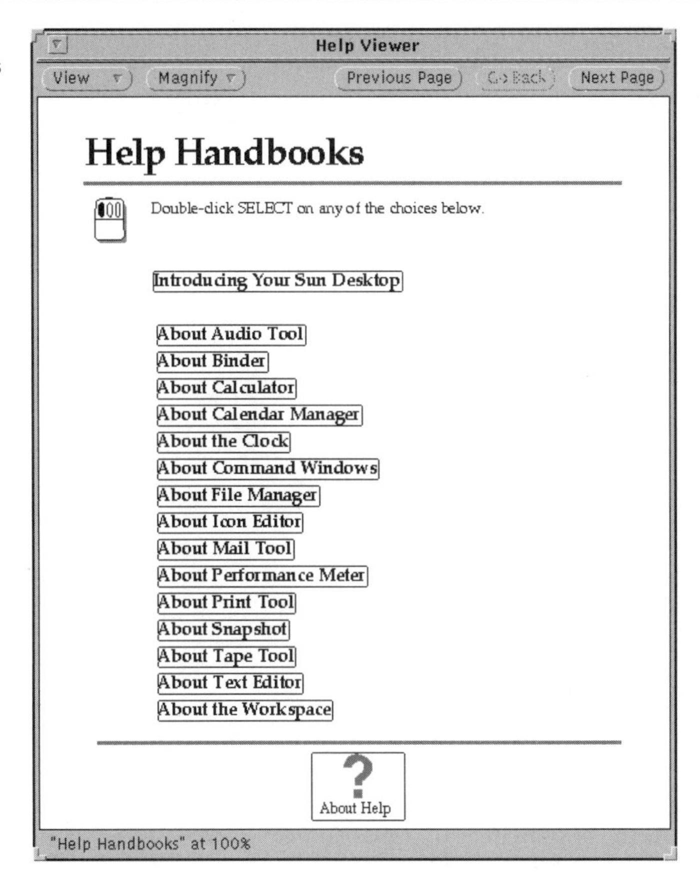

Figure 3.27
The Help Handbooks table of contents

Go Back returns to the previously displayed page. The last 42 pages displayed are remembered. Go Back retraces your steps through hypertext jumps as well as through page turns.

Next Page displays the next page in the document.

You can also use the Viewer pop-up menu to turn pages. Press MENU anywhere on the page to display the Viewer pop-up menu (see Figure 3.28). This menu has the same commands for moving around in the Help Viewer with the addition of a Redisplay item for redisplaying the Help Viewer pane.

You can also use the following keys to navigate through Help Viewer:

PgUp [R9] displays the previous page. Same as the Previous Page button.

Figure 3.28
The Viewer menu

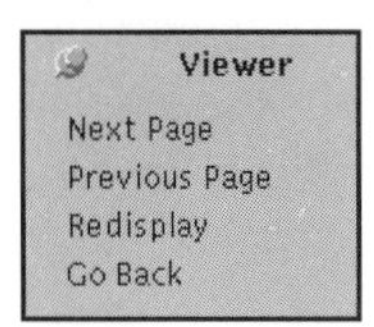

PgDn [R15] displays the next page. Same as the Next Page button.

Undo [L4] goes back to the last page displayed. Same as the Go Back button.

In addition to turning pages, you can follow hypertext cross-reference links within or between documents. Hypertext cross-reference links are identified throughout the handbooks by a rectangular box that surrounds a word or phrase. To follow a hypertext cross-reference, position the pointer on the link (the rectangular region) and double-click the SELECT button. The new page is then displayed in the Help Viewer. You can also follow a hypertext link by selecting the link with the SELECT button (a single click) and then choosing the Follow Link item on the View pop-up menu. The Go Back button (or Undo key) will take you back to the previously displayed page.

Each help handbook begins with a table of contents. Figure 3.26 shows the Mail Tool table of contents. You can use the Next Page button to read each page from the beginning of the handbook. Or you can go directly to the section you are interested in by using a hypertext link. For example, you can double-click on Organizing Your Mail to go directly to that section of the handbook.

At the bottom of each page of a help handbook is a special Table of Contents hypertext link. This link returns you directly to the table of contents. Each page also has an About Help link, which takes you to a handbook that describes how to use both spot help and the Help Viewer.

Customizing the Help Viewer

You can customize the Help Viewer by changing its size and shape, the amount of the page displayed, and the magnification of the page displayed. These techniques are described in the following sections.

Full Page/Partial Page

By default, you will always get a full-page view in Help Viewer. This is the full-page mode. When you resize Help Viewer by using the resize corner, the width and height are constrained to remain proportional so that you always have a full view. The page displayed becomes scaled to the size you set with the resize corner.

The partial-page mode can be selected from the View pop-up menu. This mode lets you choose to display only part of the page while maintaining a constant magnification. A vertical scrollbar is automatically provided so that you can view obscured parts of the page.

Magnification

The Magnify menu lets you change the magnification of the Help Viewer window. Press the Magnify button to pop up a menu that contains four items:

Smaller decreases the size of the window by 10 percent.

Standard Size sets the Help Viewer to 100 percent magnification.

Larger increases the size of the window by 10 percent.

Custom Magnification displays the Custom Magnification pop-up menu (see Figure 3.29).

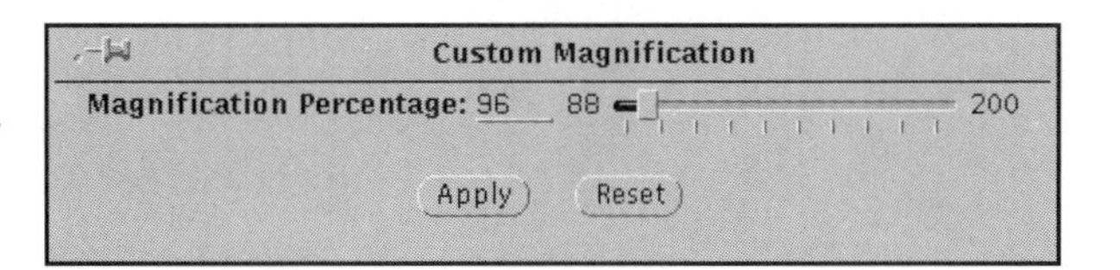

Figure 3.29 The Custom Magnification window

You can select a magnification by moving the slider to the desired size and clicking SELECT on Apply. Pressing the Reset button reverts to the previous setting.

Summary

In this chapter you have learned many important concepts that will help you whenever you use the OpenWindows environment. Understanding these basic concepts will help you learn and use OPEN LOOK applications quickly. You have learned how to use the mouse and how to manipulate objects on the screen with the mouse and the keyboard. You have also been introduced to customizing your environment, and you know where to get help.

Your next step is to become familiar with the DeskSet programs. In the next chapter you will learn how to use the File Manager.

CHAPTER

The File Manager

ORGANIZING AND MANAGING YOUR FILES AND DIRECTORIES IS ONE OF the most fundamental tasks you will perform in the Solaris environment. Knowing how to organize your files into folders and how to manipulate those files will increase your productivity. In this chapter you will learn how to use the File Manager to organize and manage your files.

The File Manager provides a graphical display of the Solaris file system. Files and folders (also called *directories*) are displayed as icons. The File Manager allows you to move, copy, print, and open files. It also shows you the files within the current directory and the path to the current directory. Navigating throughout the file system is as easy as clicking a mouse button.

In this chapter you will learn how to use the features of the File Manager, which allow you to do the following:

- Navigate through the file system
- View files and folders
- Open files
- Start applications
- Create new files and folders
- Rename files and folders
- Move, copy, and link files and folders
- Delete files and folders
- Copy files to and from other systems
- Print files
- Find files and folders
- Create custom commands

File Manager Basics

Before we get into the details of the File Manager, it is important for you to understand some basics about the Solaris file system. Files are organized into directories in the same way that you might put some important papers into a folder. This organization makes storing information convenient and finding information easy.

Directories can contain files as well as other directories (sometimes called *subdirectories*). The Solaris file system is filled with directories and subdirectories, creating a hierarchical directory structure commonly referred to as the *directory tree.* At the top of the tree is the *root directory.* All files and directories originate from the root directory. Figure 4.1 shows a sample directory tree.

Figure 4.1
A sample directory tree

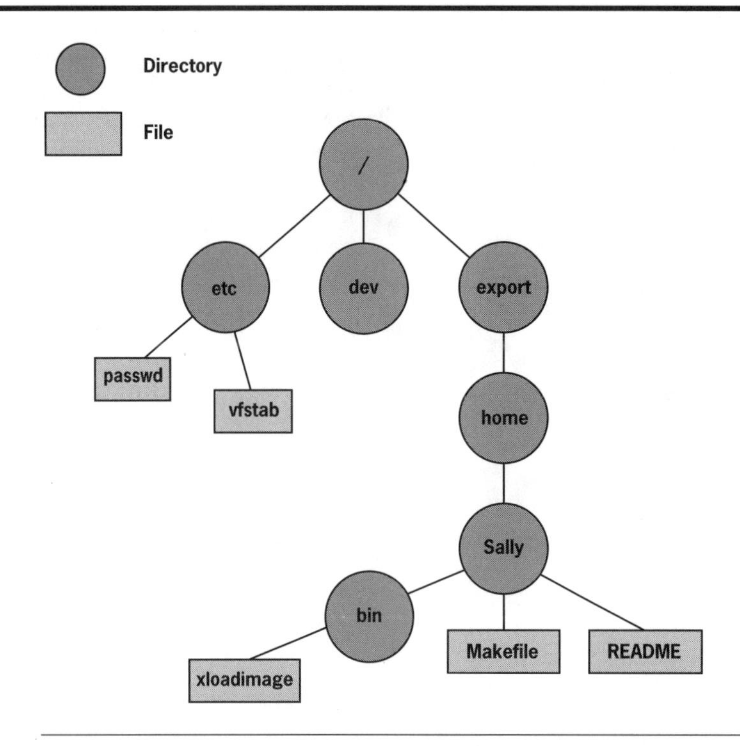

A *complete* or *absolute pathname* refers to a list of directories followed by a file name. The pathname begins with a *slash* (that's a forward slash, not a backslash), and each directory is separated by a slash with the file name as the last component of the path. For example, the pathname

```
/usr/bin/df
```

refers to a file named df that exists in the /usr/bin directory.

A *relative pathname* specifies a file relative to the current location. The pathname may contain one or more directories, or it may contain only the file name. A relative pathname does not begin with a slash. For example, bin/df would be the relative pathname for the df file if the current directory was /usr. If the current directory was /usr/bin, then the relative pathname would be simply df.

The File Manager always maintains a *current directory,* which identifies the File Manager's present location in the directory hierarchy. The files and directories of the current directory are displayed by File Manager. You can use the File Manager to move to different directories and to view and manipulate the files in those directories.

Starting the File Manager

You can invoke the File Manager application either from the Workspace menu or directly at the SunOS prompt in a Command or Shell Tool. To start the File Manager from the Workspace menu, position the pointer over the workspace and press MENU. Select Programs from the Workspace menu to display the Programs menu, and then select File Manager, as shown in Figure 4.2.

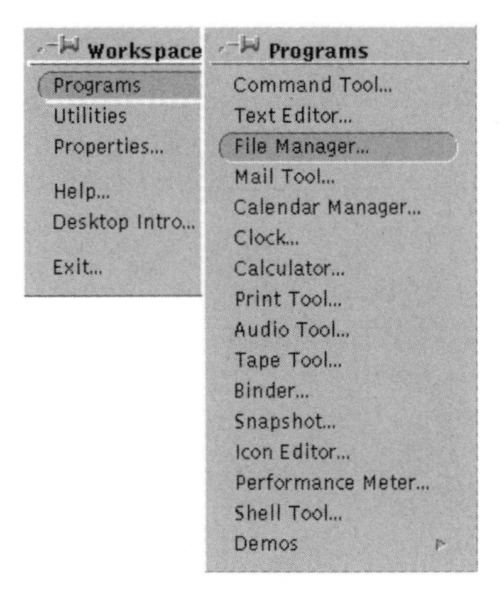

Figure 4.2 Starting the File Manager

To start the File Manager from the SunOS prompt, enter the following command in any Command Tool or Shell Tool:

```
dugout% filemgr &
```

When the File Manager begins, the current directory is the same as the current directory of the Command Tool or Shell Tool from which you invoked the File Manager. If you start the File Manager from the Workspace menu, the current directory will be the same directory from which you started the OpenWindows environment.

The File Manager Base Window

The File Manager base window is divided into three parts: the control panel, the path pane, and the file pane. Figure 4.3 shows the File Manager base window.

The *control panel* contains five menu buttons and a text field. These controls let you change views, open files, set properties, and more.

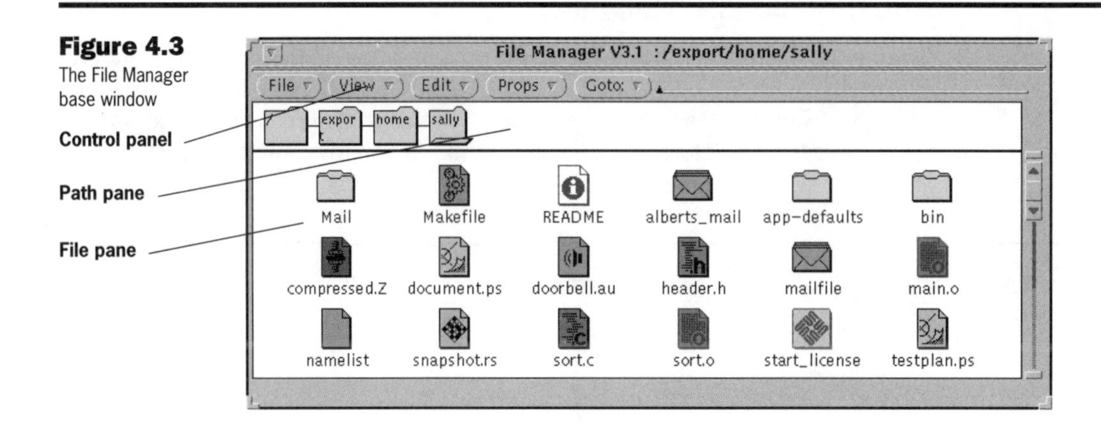

Figure 4.3 The File Manager base window

The *path pane* displays the directory path to the current directory. Two views are available for the path pane: path view and tree view. We'll discuss these different views in more detail later in this chapter.

The *file pane* displays the files and directories in the current directory. Files can be displayed as icons (which is the default display option), or listed with information about size, ownership, permissions, and so on.

The files and folders displayed in Figure 4.3 are shown as icons. There are many different file types, and each type is represented by a separate, unique icon. For example, files containing mail messages are represented by an envelope icon, while folders are represented by an icon that looks like a folder you would file in a filing cabinet.

The File Manager icon looks like the drawer of a file cabinet. The name of the current directory is displayed beneath the drawer, as shown here:

The File Manager also includes a secondary base window called the *Wastebasket.* The Wastebasket allows you to remove files. When files are deleted they are moved into the Wastebasket for later, permanent removal. Or they can be retrieved and moved back into a regular directory. The Wastebasket icon looks like this:

Selecting Files and Folders

One of the fundamental File Manager concepts is *selecting* a file or folder. When a file or folder is selected, it is displayed with reversed colors (monochrome systems display the black and white reversed). You can perform various operations on selected files, such as deletion, print, copy, and so on.

There are several ways to select a file. The simplest way is to position the pointer over an icon and click SELECT. The icon becomes highlighted, and any other icons that were highlighted become deselected. You can select an additional file by positioning the pointer over another icon and clicking ADJUST. (Clicking ADJUST toggles the selection state of a file. If the icon is already selected, ADJUST will deselect it.) Figure 4.4 shows the File Manager file pane with two files selected: Makefile and start_license.

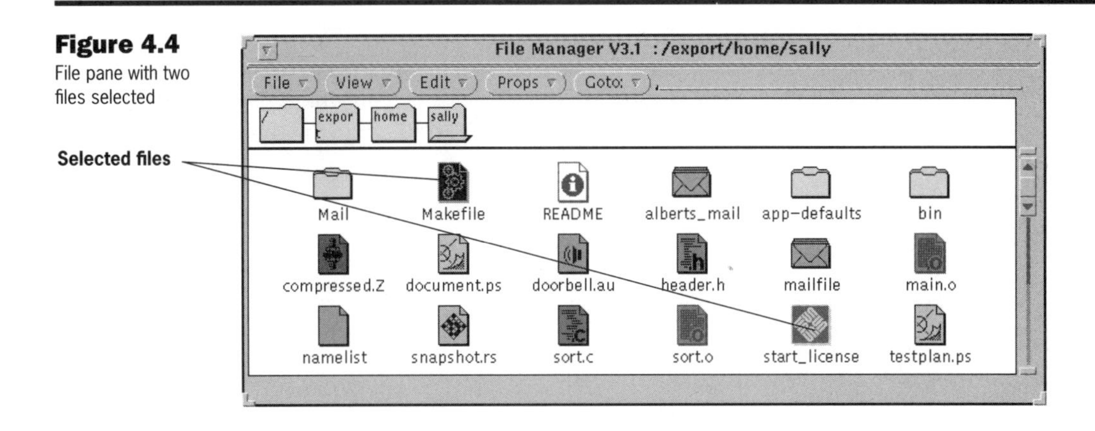

Figure 4.4
File pane with two files selected

Another way to select one or more files is to use the pointer to define a rectangular region. All the icons in the region become selected (and anything else becomes deselected). You do this by following these steps:

1. Position the pointer on the file pane.
2. Press SELECT.
3. Drag the pointer to form a rectangular region enclosing the desired icons.
4. Release SELECT.

All the icons within the rectangular region become highlighted, as shown in Figure 4.5. You can do the same operation with the ADJUST button. The difference is that the selected files will be highlighted without affecting the state of any other icons that are currently highlighted.

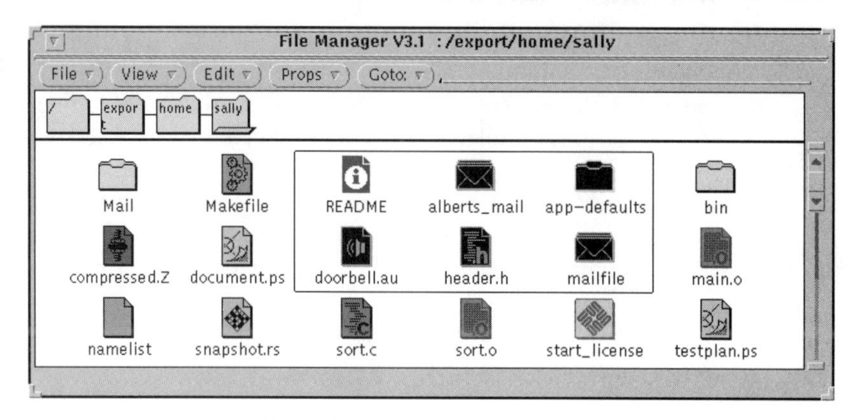

Figure 4.5 Highlighting adjacent groups of icons

If you want to select all the files and folders in the current directory, bring up the File Pane menu by positioning the pointer anywhere over the file pane. Press MENU and then choose Select All. The File Pane menu is shown here:

You can deselect all selected icons at any time by clicking SELECT in the file pane while the pointer is not positioned over any icon.

Navigating through the File System

Now that you know some basics about the File Manager, you can begin to navigate your way through the SunOS file system.

Moving to a New Folder

The files and folders of the current directory are displayed in the file pane. You will often need to change the current directory to look at the contents of another folder. There are several ways to do this.

The Double-click Method

The most straightforward way to move to a new folder is to position the pointer over a folder icon and double-click SELECT. The folder can be in the path pane or the file pane. In either case, the folder represented by the icon becomes the current directory, and all the files and folders it contains are displayed in the file pane.

The Goto Text Field

Another way to change the current directory is to specify the new directory by name in the Goto text field in the control panel. To change folders by using this method, you type the name of the new directory in the text field and press Return, as shown in Figure 4.6.

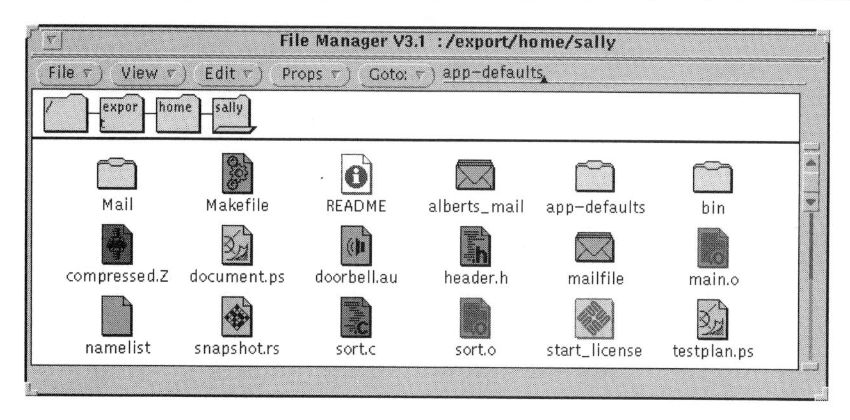

Figure 4.6
Specifying the folder to go to

The Goto Menu Button

When you display the menu associated with the Goto menu button, you will see a list of directories like those shown in Figure 4.7. The items on the Goto menu are the nine most recent directories that the File Manager has used as the current directory. Each time you change directories, the Goto menu is updated.

This is particularly convenient when you are doing some work that requires you to move between two or more directories frequently, especially if those directories are relatively distant. For example, if your work requires you to move between

```
/export/home/sally/bin
```

and

```
/usr/openwin/include/images
```

you could use the Goto menu to easily hop back and forth between the two directories. You could use one of the other methods you have learned for changing directories, but you would have to either type the name of the directory in the text field each time or do a lot of double-clicking.

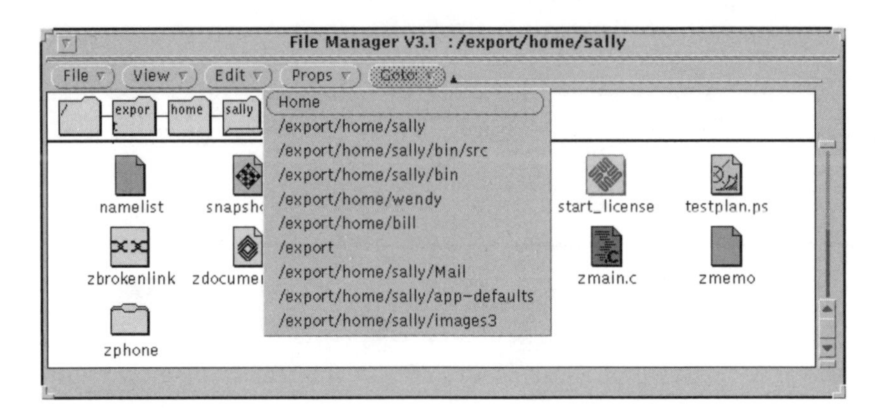

Figure 4.7 The Goto menu

Another thing to notice about the Goto menu is that if the Goto text field is empty, the first item on the Goto menu is labeled "Home." If the text field is not empty, then the first item on the Goto menu is the string of characters in the text field.

The Home item on the Goto menu represents your home directory. Your home directory is your initial directory location when you log in. It contains your start-up files, and it is where you will probably be doing much of your work. Unless you explicitly change it, Home is the default item on the Goto menu. This means that you can click SELECT on the Goto menu button and your home directory will become the File Manager's current directory.

Moving Up the Directory Structure

You can move up one level in the directory hierarchy by selecting Up from the File Pane menu. Moving up the directory hierarchy means changing directories to the immediate parent of the current directory. For example, if the current directory is /usr/openwin/include and you select Up from the File Pane menu, your new current directory would be /usr/openwin.

Manipulating the File Pane

The number of files and folders you can view in a given directory depends on how many files and folders exist in the current directory. If there are only a few files, then you may be able to view all the files and folders in the file pane.

If there are more files than can be displayed in the file pane, you can choose from two methods of adjusting the file pane.

First, you can use the file pane's vertical scrollbar to scroll down to see more files and folders. If all the files and folders in the current directory are visible, the scrollbar becomes insensitive, which means it cannot be used.

Another method of moving about the file pane is to *pan.* Panning is accomplished in the following manner:

1. Press the Meta key (the key with the diamond-shaped symbol on it).
2. Position the pointer over the file pane.
3. Press SELECT. The pointer changes to the panning pointer. (The panning pointer looks like the standard pointer with the arrow pointing down and to the left.)
4. Drag the pointer up or down. The file pane follows the motion of the pointer.
5. Release SELECT and the Meta key.

Finding Files in the Current Folder

Sometimes you may have a directory containing many files. Rather than searching for the file you are looking for by scrolling or panning, you can enter the file name into the Goto text field and press Return. The File Manager highlights the file and automatically scrolls the file pane to bring the selected file into view.

You can also use *wildcard* characters to match multiple files in the directory. Wildcards are special characters that you use to match one or more characters. Here are the three most common wildcard characters:

*	The asterisk matches any number of characters (including no characters at all).
?	The question mark matches exactly one character.
[]	The square brackets identify a set of characters to match.

Let's look at a few examples. Suppose you have these files in your directory:

file1.c	file2.c	file3.c	file4.c
memo1	memo2	memo3	memo4

If you specify ***.c**, it will match all the files that end with .c, because the asterisk matches all the characters that precede the .c. When you enter this into the Goto text field and press Return, all the files that are matched become highlighted (the first row of four files above).

If you specify **memo?**, the question mark will match any single character. In this case, memo1, memo2, memo3, and memo4 would all be selected.

If you specify **memo[24]**, then memo2 and memo4 will be highlighted.

You can also combine wildcards. For example, ***[124]*** matches all the files except file3.c and memo3.

Another way to match a file is to type the name directly into the file pane. (Note that you should first make sure that the input focus is not in the text field. To do this, click SELECT with the pointer in the File pane.) You will see the characters you type appear in the File Manager footer. With this method, a trailing asterisk is assumed as you type, which means that when you type the first character—let's say it's an **e**—the matching is done on e*. Consequently, all the files and folders that begin with an e will be immediately highlighted. Each character you enter subsequently is appended to the string displayed in the footer (except that the asterisk remains at the end of the string). Each character changes the search pattern, and the files that match the pattern are updated with each key entered.

You can use the same wildcards in the file pane that you used in the Goto text field. If you enter a string of characters that do not match any file or folder in the current directory, the File Manager will beep at you and the footer will display a message indicating that it can't find anything that matches the pattern you have input. The next character you type will begin a new search string. If you want to clear the message in the File Manager footer, press Escape.

Displaying Multiple File Panes

You learned earlier how to quickly move between commonly used directories. What is often even more convenient is to have multiple file panes displayed simultaneously. There are two ways to do this:

- Drag a folder from the path pane or file pane, and drop it on the root window.
- Select one or more folders on the file pane, and select Open from the File menu.

In either case, the folder you choose is displayed as an independent file pane in a Folder pop-up window. Figure 4.8 shows the File Manager's box window and the Folder pop-up window.

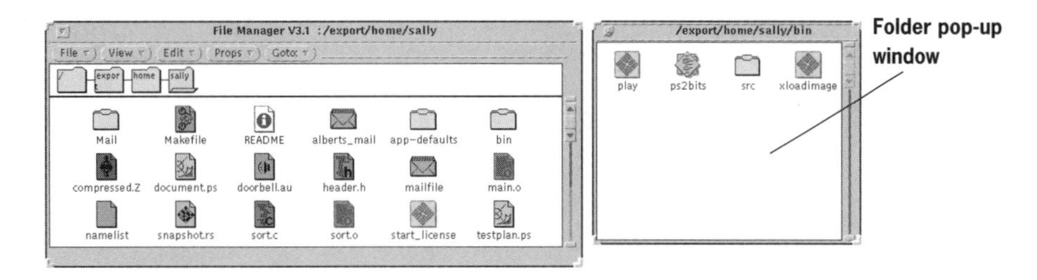

Figure 4.8
The File Manager's base window and the Folder pop-up window

There is no path pane associated with the Folder pop-up window. A File Pane menu, however, is displayed when you press MENU with the pointer positioned anywhere over the pop-up. You can change directories within the pop-up by double-clicking on a folder or by selecting Up from the File Pane menu.

You can display up to six Folder pop-up windows simultaneously. This is extremely useful when you need to copy or move files between directories. Files can be easily dragged from one directory and dropped into another. We'll talk more about drag and drop later in this chapter.

Viewing Files and Folders

The File Manager allows you to display files and folders in a variety of ways. You can display the path to the current directory as a direct path or with the entire directory hierarchy. You can display files and folders with various amounts of information, and you can sort them alphabetically or by date, size, or type.

Switching between Path View and Tree View

The File Manager's upper pane has two display views: *path* and *tree.* When set to path view, it shows the direct path from the root (/) to the current folder. This view takes the least amount of vertical space, leaving more room for the file pane below it. Only the folders that are direct ancestors of the current folder are displayed.

When set to tree view, many folders in the hierarchy are displayed, including sibling directories, child directories, and parent directories. Because these directories can take up considerable horizontal and vertical space, depending on the complexity of your directory hierarchy, horizontal and vertical scrollbars are provided on the upper pane when you use this view. Tree view is especially convenient if you are moving between, or need access to, many different directories.

There are two ways of switching between the tree view and the path view.

The View Pop-up Menu

One way to switch between the two views is to click the menu button on the File Manager control area. This brings up the View pop-up menu, shown here:

The first item on the menu lets you switch the path pane between path view and tree view. When the path view is displayed, the View pop-up's first item is Show Tree. When the tree view is displayed, the first item is Show Path. The Show Tree or Show Path item is the default selection on the pop-up, which means that you can activate that item by pressing SELECT on the View menu button without actually popping up the menu. Try this by clicking SELECT with the pointer over the View menu button. You will see that the path pane toggles between path view and tree view.

The Path Pane Pop-up Menu

Another way to change between tree view and path view is to bring up the Path Pane pop-up menu, which is available when the upper pane is displaying the path view. To display the Path Pane pop-up menu, follow these steps:

1. Position the pointer anywhere within the path pane.
2. Press the MENU mouse button.

The Path Pane pop-up menu is then displayed, as shown here.

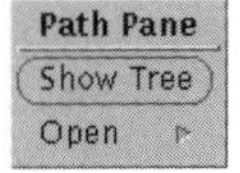

The two items on the Path Pane menu let you change the mode of the path pane and open a selected folder.

Show Tree changes the view of the path pane to tree view.

Open opens the selected folder and makes it the current folder. This item is sensitive only when a folder in the path pane is selected. The files of the chosen folder are displayed in the file pane.

The Tree Pane Pop-up Menu

The Tree Pane pop-up menu is displayed when the path pane is displaying the tree view. To display the Tree Pane pop-up menu:

1. Position the pointer anywhere on the path pane.
2. Press the MENU mouse button. The Tree Pane pop-up menu is then displayed, as shown here:

The six items on the Tree Pane pop-up menu allow you to change views and open a selected folder. In addition, the directory hierarchy of the tree structure can be customized by showing or hiding folders.

Show Path changes the display of the path pane to path view.

Open opens the selected folder and makes it current. This item is sensitive only when a folder is selected. The files of the current folder are displayed in the file pane.

Hide Subfolders eliminates all the subfolders of the selected folder from the tree view. The folders are not deleted from the system, but just removed from the display. This item is sensitive only if a folder is selected and the selected folder has subfolders displayed.

Show All Subfolders displays all subfolders of the selected folder. This item is sensitive only when a folder is selected.

Begin Tree Here changes the top of the displayed hierarchy to the selected folder. This item is sensitive only when a folder is selected.

Add Tree's Parent changes the displayed hierarchy to include the top folder's parent folder. This item is always sensitive unless the top of the displayed hierarchy is root (/).

Viewing Files in the File Pane

You can view files in the file pane in many different ways. Each icon on the file pane represents a file or folder in the current folder. Many kinds of icons can be displayed, with each type of icon representing a different type of file. Figure 4.9 shows a file pane displaying several file types.

Figure 4.9
File pane with several file types

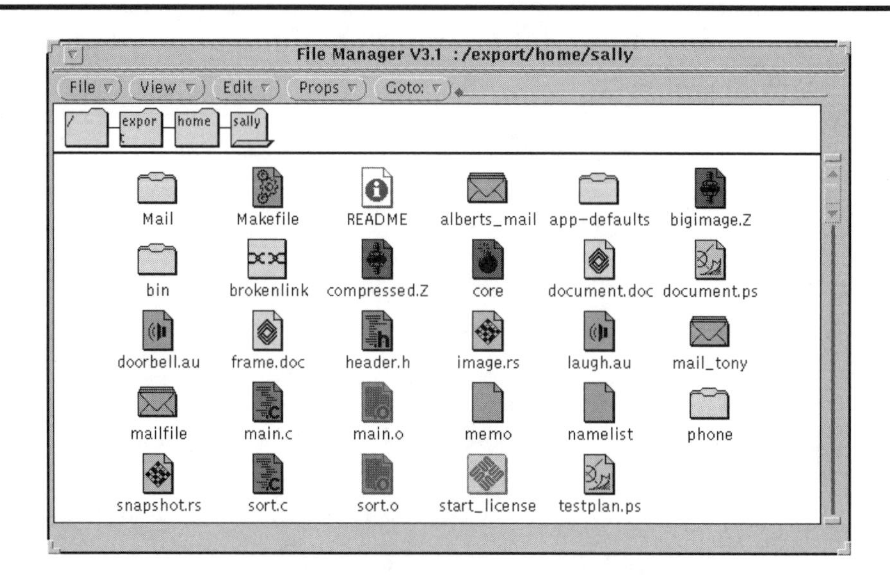

You can change the icons in the File pane to a smaller size so that more files and folders can be displayed. The drawback is that there are only three icon types, indicating whether the file is a folder, a data file, or an executable program. The three small icon types are shown here:

You use the View pop-up menu to choose how to view and organize files in the file pane. The options are as follows:

Icon by Name displays full-sized icons in alphabetical order.

Icon by Type displays full-sized icons grouped by type, as shown in Figure 4.10.

List by Name displays small icons grouped alphabetically. Figure 4.11 shows the file pane with the List by Name option set.

List by Type displays small icons grouped by type.

List by Size displays small icons grouped by size. The largest files are listed first.

List by Date displays small icons grouped by date. The most recent files are listed first.

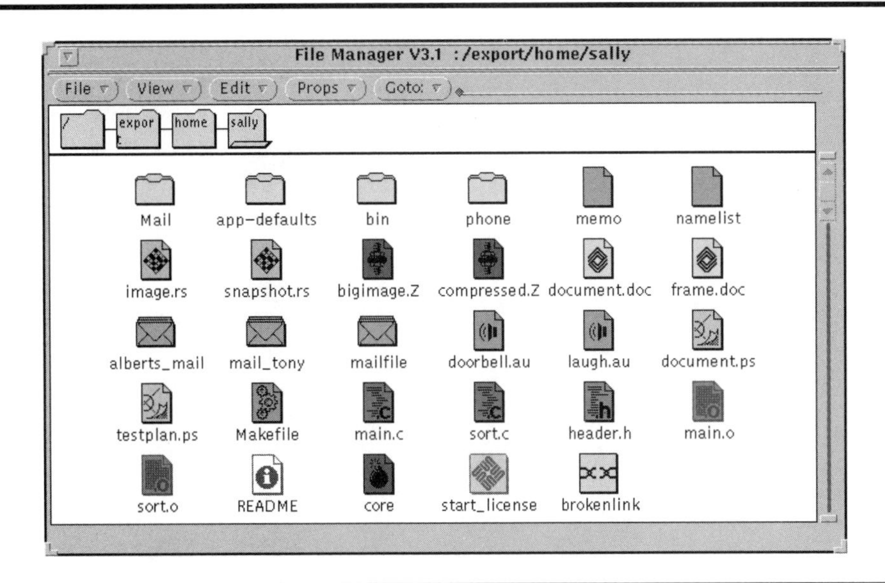

Figure 4.10
Full-sized icons organized by type

Customizing the File Pane

In addition to the predetermined formats available for viewing your files on the View pop-up, customized formats are available from the Customize View pop-up window. To display the Customize View window, select the Customize item from the View pop-up menu. Figure 4.12 shows the Customize View window.

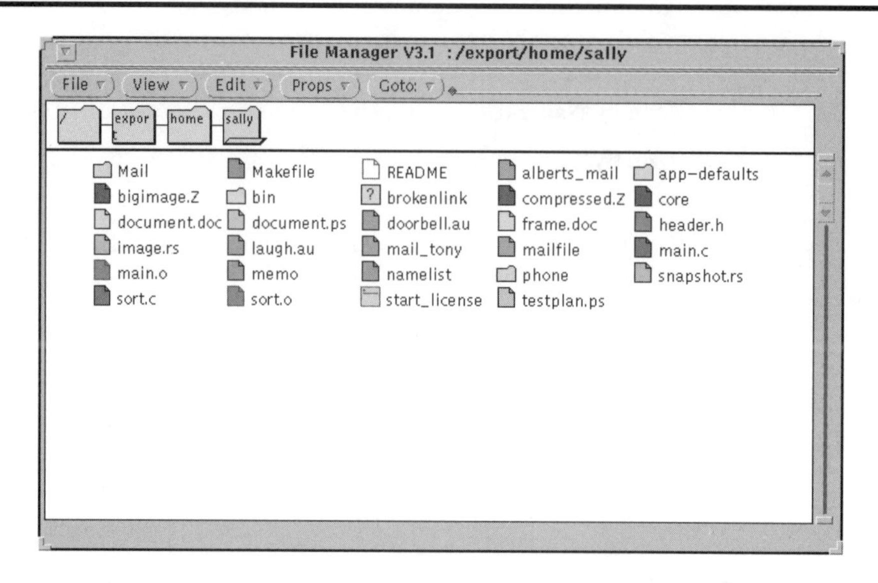

Figure 4.11 Small icons organized by name

Figure 4.12 The File Manager's Customize View window

The Display Mode item provides three choices: Icon, List, and Content. Only one of the three can be selected at one time. The Icon setting displays the full-sized icons in the file pane. The List setting displays the small icons. The Content setting displays the contents of the file if it is an icon or an image file. If it is any other type of file, the full-sized icon is displayed.

At the bottom of the Customize View window are two buttons, labeled Apply and Reset. When you choose attributes on the Customize View window, they do not take effect until you have pressed the Apply button. If you have made one or more selections and then decide you do not want to apply the changes, press the Reset button. All the options will resort to the previously set values.

Displaying Files by Icon

When the Display Mode is set to Icon, the files and folders on the file pane are displayed with full-sized icons. The other fields now available on the Customize View pop-up are Sort By, Hidden Files, and Icon Layout. The Files to View and List Options fields are not available.

Let's consider the other options available when you display files by icon:

Sort By determines how the files and folders are organized on the file pane.

> **Name** lists files and folders alphabetically.
>
> **Type** groups files and folders of the same type.
>
> **Size** lists files and folders by size. The largest files are listed first.
>
> **Date** lists files and folders by date. The most recently modified or created files are listed first.

Hidden Files determines if dot files are displayed on the file pane. Dot files are files or folders that begin with a period.

Icon Layout determines the layout order of files and folders displayed on the file pane. They can be ordered by row, which means that the sorting order goes across a row and then proceeds to the next row, or they can be ordered by column, which means that the icons go from one option column to the next. In Figure 4.12 you can see that the row-by-row option is selected.

Displaying Files by List

With the Display mode set to List, the files and folders are displayed on the file pane with small icons. The options available on the Customize View window are identical to the Icon options, with the addition of the List Options item.

This option allows you to select additional information to be displayed about the files in the file pane. You can select any combination of the choices. If you select none of the choices, the files in the file pane are listed in multiple columns. If you do select one or more of the list options, the files are listed in a single column and the Icon Layout item is unavailable. Figure 4.13 shows the file pane with all options selected.

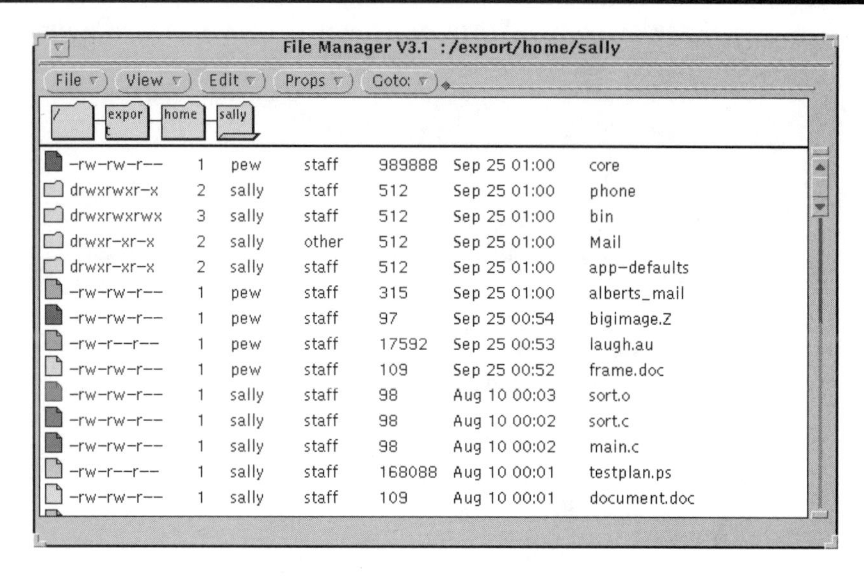

Figure 4.13
Display mode set to List with all list options

You will learn more about these options in Chapter 11. Here is a brief description of each option:

Permissions specifies the read, write, and execute permissions for the owner, group, and world. Specifies also whether the file is a directory, special, link, or regular file.

Owner specifies the owner of the file. Every file has an owner.

Group displays the group ownership of the file.

Date displays the date the file was last modified. This may be the creation time if the file has not been modified since it was created.

Links displays the number of links to the file.

Size displays the size of the file in bytes.

Displaying Files by Content

When the Display mode is set to Content, the contents of a file are displayed as an icon in the file pane. Of course, this works only if the file contains icon or image data. If the file does not contain an icon or image, the regular full-sized icon is displayed. Figure 4.14 shows some of the icons in the /usr/aopenwin/-share/include/images directory.

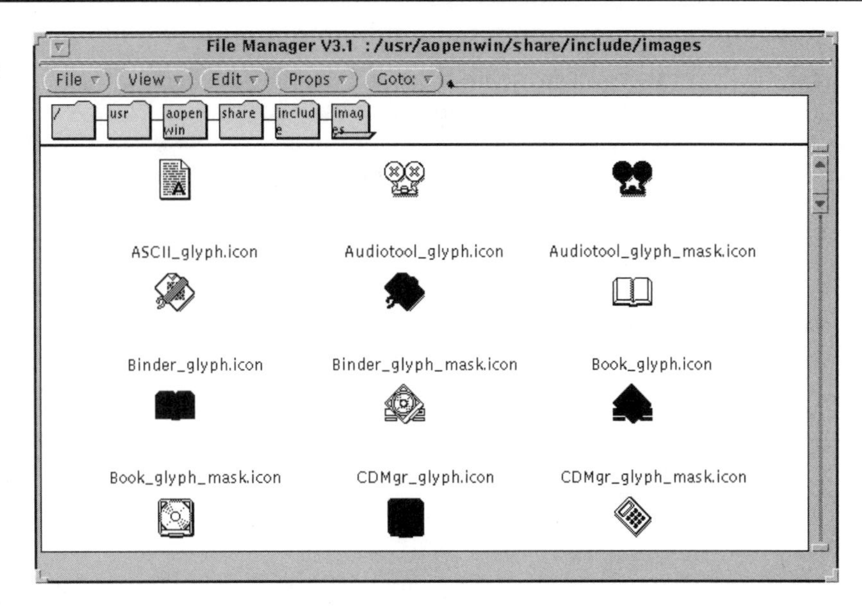

Figure 4.14
Display mode set to Content

When the Display mode is set to Content, the Files to View option becomes active. This option lets you select the types of images to be displayed.

Opening Files and Starting Applications

By now you've certainly noticed that there are many file types displayed by the File Manager. Every time the File Manager displays a new directory in the file pane it has to identify a file type for each file in the directory. It does this in several ways.

The File Manager identifies all the directories and displays each directory as a folder. The File Manager also looks at the file name. Some file names identify the type of the file. For example, all file names that end with .c are assumed to be C programming language files. All file names that end with .ps are assumed to be PostScript files. The File Manager also looks at the permissions of the file (we'll talk in more detail about permissions later in this chapter, in the section titled "File Properties"). If the file has execute permissions, it is assumed to be an executable file. If necessary, the File Manager also examines the contents of the file to determine its type.

Opening a file means something different for each file type. For example, when you open a text file, the file is loaded into a text editor. When you open an executable file, the file is executed. When you open a directory, your current directory changes to that directory. In the following sections you will learn three methods of opening files.

Double-clicking on an Icon

The simplest way to open a file is to double-click on the icon. The File Manager then opens the file. Remember that this means different things for different file types. If you double-click on a PostScript file, the PageView program is started. (PageView displays the image that the PostScript file describes.) If you double-click on an image file, the SnapShot program is started.

Dropping a File onto the Root Window

Another way to open a file is to drag and drop it onto the root window. Here's how you do it:

1. Select a file in the file pane.
2. Press SELECT with the pointer positioned over the selected file.
3. Drag the pointer to the root window.
4. Release SELECT. The file is opened.

One advantage of this method is that you can open multiple files simultaneously. To do this, select the desired files in the file pane, position the pointer over any one of the selected files, and drag it to the root window. All the files selected will be opened. The files needn't be of the same type, either. For example, you could select one PostScript file, one ASCII file, and one executable file. When you drag and drop these to the root window, each one is opened according to its own particular file type.

Selecting Open from the File Menu

You can also open files through the Open item on the File menu. When you click on Open, a menu is displayed with three choices, as shown in here:

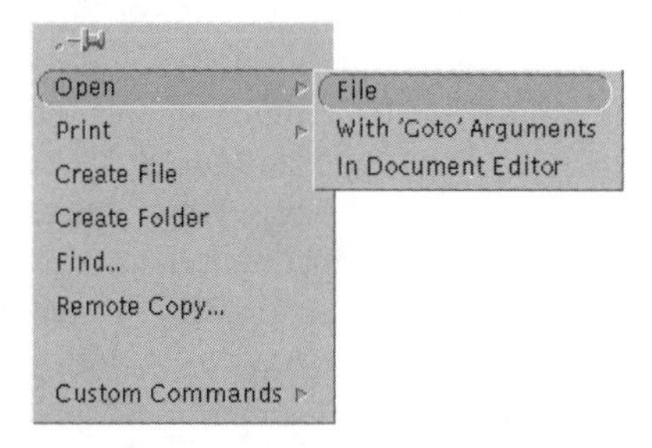

To use this method, you must select one or more files in the file pane and then select one of the items on the Open menu.

The first item on the Open menu is File. Clicking on File is exactly the same as double-clicking on an icon or dropping an icon onto the root window.

The second item, With "Goto" Arguments, opens the file but uses the contents of the Goto text field as arguments to the program that is executed when the file is opened. For example, normally when you open an ASCII file the Text Editor application starts. You can use a command-line argument to position the Text Editor on the screen at the exact coordinates that you specify. If you are invoking the Text Editor from the command line and you want to position it in the upper-left corner of the screen, you issue the following command:

```
dugout% textedit -geometry +0+0 <file>
```

To open a file from the File Manager with the Text Editor positioned in the upper-left corner, you provide the command-line argument by entering it in the Goto text field, as shown in Figure 4.15, and then select With "Goto" Arguments from the Open menu.

Figure 4.15
Specifying command-line arguments in the Goto text field

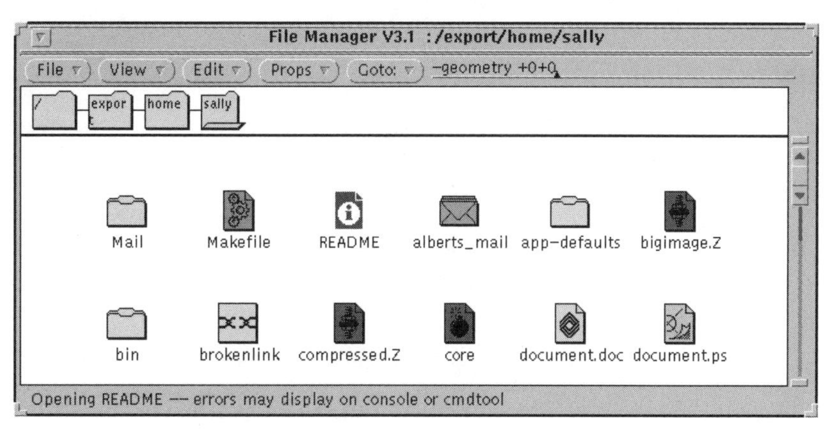

The third item on the Open menu is In Document Editor. This option is useful when you want to edit a file that usually opens in something other than a text editor. For example, a PostScript file usually opens in the PageView program. If you want to edit a PostScript file, you cannot simply open it with a double-click, because that would invoke the PageView program. PostScript files are human-readable ASCII, so there is no reason why they cannot be edited with a text editor. Choosing In Document Editor from the Open menu forces the selected file to be loaded into the document editor, which is the Text Editor by default.

Creating New Files and Folders

The File Manager makes creating new files and folders a simple task. The File menu includes two items for this purpose: Create File and Create Folder.

When you select the Create File item from the File menu, an empty file is created. A new icon appears in the file pane, representing the newly created file. The icon is highlighted, as is the name of the file listed underneath the icon (assuming that you are displaying by icon). The name of the new file is NewDocument. At this point you can press Return and the file will still be called NewDocument, but this probably is not desirable. Instead, you will probably want to choose a name for the file. While the name of the new file is highlighted, type a new name. You can use the Delete or Backspace keys to crasc thc cxisting namc. Whcn you arc satisficd with thc namc, prcss Rcturn. If you do not like the name, you can always change it later, as described in the next section.

To create a new folder, select Create Folder from the File menu. A new folder, called NewFolder, is created. You use the same technique to select a name for the new folder as you did to select a name for a new file.

Renaming Files and Folders

Renaming a file or a folder is a simple task. You select the file or folder and enter the new name. Here are the steps:

1. Position the pointer over the file or folder name. If you are displaying by icon, the name is underneath the icon. If you are displaying by list, the name is to the right of the small icon.
2. Click SELECT with the pointer over the name (not over the icon). The icon and the name are highlighted, as shown in Figure 4.16.
3. Use the keyboard and mouse to enter a new name for the file or folder, and then press Return.

If you choose a name that is already being used in the current directory, the File Manager disallows the name change and reverts to the previous name for the file. Note that you may want to create file names with no spaces so that you can switch between DeskSet and shell programming more easily.

Moving, Copying, and Linking Files and Folders

As you manage your data you will often find it necessary to move or copy files and folders. The concept of moving and copying files and folders is simple.

Moving a file means that it is removed from its current folder and moved into a new folder. The name of the file remains the same. *Copying a file* means that a copy of the original file is created. This copy can have the same name as the original if it resides in another folder, or it can remain in the same folder and be given a new name.

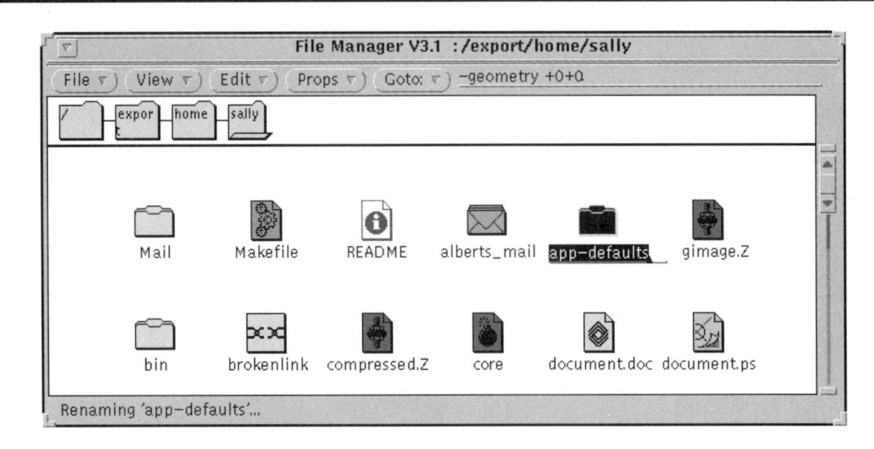

Figure 4.16 Highlighting a file before renaming it

Linking may be a new concept to you. When you link a file, you create a new, special type of file, called a *link,* that "points" to the existing file. The link is not a copy of the original file. All changes made in the original file are reflected in the link file. If you need a second copy of a file so that you can alter the copy while maintaining the original, you should copy the file. If you just need the convenience of accessing an existing file's data from some other directory, you can link the file.

For example, Figure 4.17 shows a file named info in the directory named sally. If you create a link to the info file in a directory named john, you can access the file as if it exists in john. You don't have to worry about keeping the info file in your directory up-to-date, because it is not a separate copy of the info file, but simply a pointer to the original info file in the sally directory. Linking a file is particularly convenient when you need access to the file but don't want to copy it because it may be changing. A linked file also takes up less disk space than a copy of the file.

Using Cut and Paste

If you want to move one or more files or folders, you perform a cut and paste operation. Cutting a file does not permanently remove it. Rather, the file is put on the *clipboard.* The clipboard is a temporary holding place. When you perform a paste, the contents of the clipboard are moved from the clipboard into the pasted directory. Here's how you move a file:

1. Select one or more files.
2. Display the Edit or File Pane menu, and select Cut. (Note that if you press the Cut key on the keyboard, the file is moved to the Wastebasket, not to the clipboard.)
3. Go to the folder that you want to receive the file or files.
4. Select Paste from the Edit or File Pane menu, or press the Paste key on the keyboard.

Figure 4.17
File linked between two directories

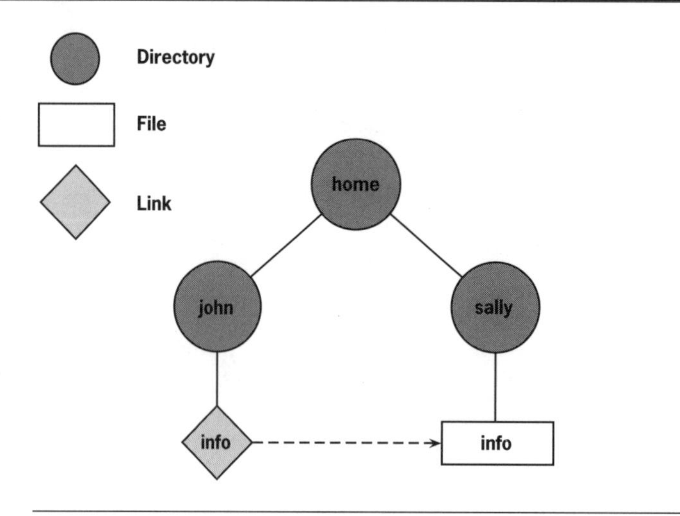

You can go to a folder (step 3) in one of two ways: (1) change the current directory displayed in the file pane, or (2) pop up another file pane by dropping a folder onto the root window.

To copy one or more files or folders, you perform a copy and paste operation:

1. Select one or more files.
2. Display the Edit or File Pane menu and select Copy, or press the Copy key on the keyboard.
3. Go to the folder that you want to receive the file or files.
4. Select Paste from the Edit or File Pane menu, or press the Paste key on the keyboard.

When you copy a file, you can paste it into the same directory. This makes a copy of the file in the same directory. The new file is given the same name as the original, with a suffix such as .1. For example, if you have a file named info that you copied and pasted into the same directory, the new file will be named info.1. If you copy and paste info into the same directory again, the new file will be named info.2.

You'll notice that the Copy item on the Edit and File Pane menus has a triangle on the right side, indicating that it is a menu button. Drag the pointer to the right, and another menu appears, as shown here:

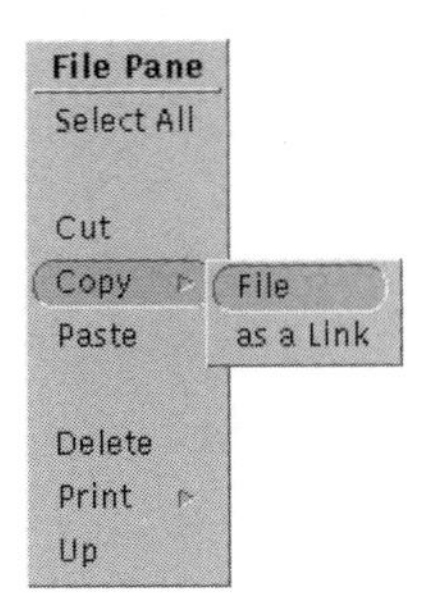

The first item on the menu, File, is the default choice and copies the file as we just discussed. The second item, as a Link, lets you create a link to an existing file. The steps are about the same:

1. Select one or more files.
2. Display the Edit or File Pane menu.
3. Drag the pointer to Copy, and drag right to display the submenu.
4. Select as a Link.
5. Go to the folder in which you want the link created.
6. Select Paste from the Edit or File Pane menu, or press the Paste key.

Remember that a link file does not itself contain any data besides the file to which it is linked. If a link points to a nonexistent file, the link file is represented by a broken chain icon, as shown here:

Using Drag and Drop

Another way to move and copy files and folders is to use drag and drop. When you use drag and drop, you can either move or copy files or folders, but the destination folder must be viewable somewhere within File Manager. The destination folder can be a folder icon in the path pane, a folder icon in the file pane, a Folder pop-up window, or another File Manager application. With cut and paste, you can cut or copy a file and then navigate throughout the directory hierarchy to locate the destination directory. With drag and drop, the destination directory must be viewable at the time the drag begins. You cannot drop a file onto the same folder you dragged it from.

To demonstrate how to use drag and drop, let's drag a file from the file pane and drop it onto a File Pane pop-up window, as shown in Figure 4.18.

Figure 4.18 Moving a file with drag and drop

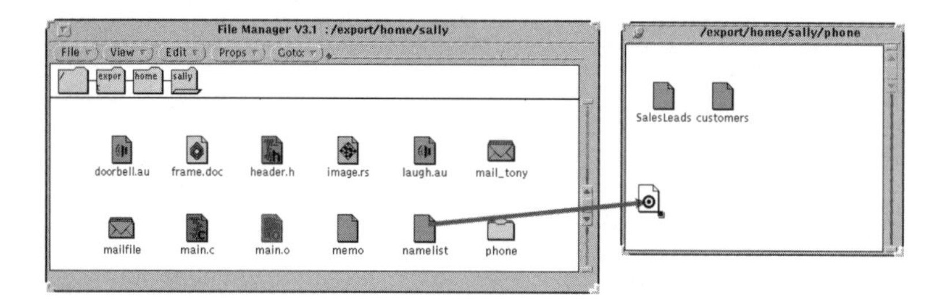

To move a file or files with drag and drop, do the following:

1. Select one or more files or folders.
2. Position the pointer over one of the selected icons.
3. Press SELECT.
4. Drag the cursor to the destination folder.
5. Release SELECT.

The steps to copy rather than move are almost identical. The only difference is that you press and hold the Control key before pressing SELECT in step 3.

If you change your mind while you are dragging, you can interrupt the drag and drop operation by pressing the Stop key on the keyboard. Be sure, however, to press the Stop key before releasing the mouse button.

As you begin a drag operation, you'll notice that the pointer changes shape to match the icon that you are dragging. The pointer makes additional changes in shape when it passes over certain windows. This is called *pointer* or *cursor animation.* When the drag pointer is over a valid drop site, the pointer displays a drag and drop target, which resembles a bull's-eye in the center, as shown here:

The bull's-eye lets you know when you are over a window that will accept a drop.

Another feature of drag and drop is that when you pass the drag pointer over a folder, the folder icon changes. This feature is called *drop-site previewing*. For example, drag a file from the file pane to the path pane, and move the pointer across each of the folders there. As you pass over each folder, the folder icon changes to the shape of an open folder. The open-folder icon indicates that this folder can accept the drop. The File Manager displays in its footer the name of the folder that you are passing over, as shown in Figure 4.19.

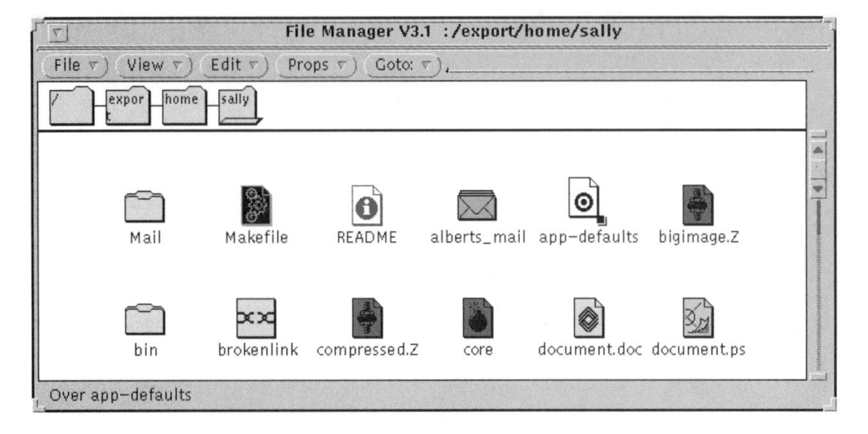

Figure 4.19 The footer displaying the name of the folder

Copying Files to and from Other Systems

You may work in an environment where your computer is connected to a network of other computers running the Solaris environment or some other UNIX derivative. This allows you to transfer information to and from other systems across the network.

If you are using the NFS (Network File System), you may be able to use the File Manager to access directories on remote systems the same way that you access local directories (see Chapter 15 for a complete discussion of networking). With NFS, you treat a remote directory as if it were a local directory. You can use the File Manager to navigate to the remote directory just as you would a regular directory, and use the techniques you have learned thus far in this chapter to move and copy files and folders between systems. This is definitely the easiest way to copy files to and from remote systems. If you are not running NFS but are connected to a network, you can still copy files between systems by using the Remote Copy feature of the File Manager, which we will discuss next.

Using the Remote Copy Pop-up Window

The Remote Copy feature of the File Manager allows you to copy files to and from other systems. Copying files is the only feature available through the Remote Copy window. When you select Remote Copy from the File menu, the Remote Copy pop-up appears, as shown in Figure 4.20.

Figure 4.20 The Remote Copy pop-up

File Manager: Remote Copy
Source Machine:
Source Path:
Destination Machine:
Destination Path:
Copy

Whenever you perform a remote copy, you must provide information about the source and destination. Each remote copy operation requires a machine name and a path for both the source and destination. The source path must include a specific file or files; you cannot specify a directory. The destination path can be either a directory or a file. If a directory is specified, the source file is copied to the remote directory and the file name stays the same. The destination path must include an existing directory on the destination machine but can include a new file name in that directory. This allows you to copy the file to the remote system and give the file a new name.

Let's consider an example. Your system name is *dugout* and you want to copy a file named *memo,* located in /tmp, to a system named *bullpen.* The directory on bullpen that you want to copy the file to is /export/home/sally. You simply enter the information in the Remote Copy pop-up, as shown in Figure 4.21. The new file is named *memo* and resides in the /export/home/sally directory.

One time-saving step you can take is to select the files you want to copy before popping up the Remote Copy window. If you do this, the source machine and source path are automatically filled in for you. Then all you have to do is provide the destination machine and path. Another shortcut, if you want to avoid typing the names of the files you want to copy, is to use drag and drop. If you drag a file from the file pane, you can drop it onto the Source Path field, and the name of the file will be entered there. If you want to copy multiple files at once, you can position the input cursor at the end of the existing Source Path field and repeat the drag and drop operation.

Figure 4.21
Copying a file remotely

File Manager: Remote Copy
Source Machine: dugout
Source Path: /tmp/memo
Destination Machine: bullpen
Destination Path: /export/home/sally
Copy

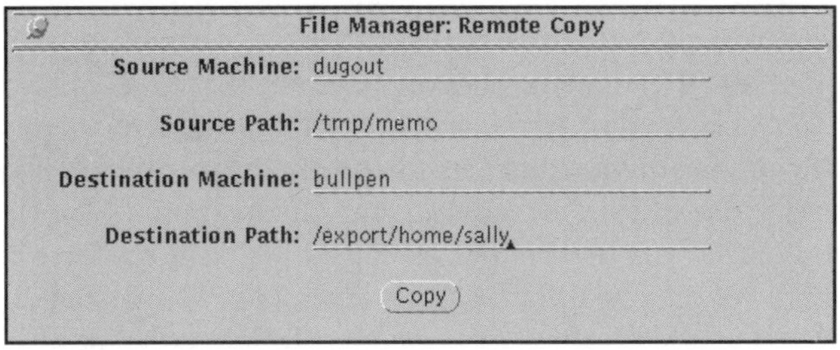

You can copy a remote file to your system by specifying the name of the remote system in the source field, and the name of your system in the destination field. The source path must specify a file or files, and the destination path must include an existing directory.

Once you have provided the appropriate information to the Remote Copy window, press the Copy button to initiate the copy. If the copy does not succeed, a message is displayed in the File Manager footer. Copying a file remotely can fail for a variety of reasons:

- You may not have remote-access permission to the system you are copying from or copying to.
- You may have specified a remote file or directory that does not exist.
- You may not have permission to read the file on the source machine or write the file on the destination machine.

Whatever the problem, a brief message describing the problem will be displayed in the footer.

Deleting Files and Folders

You have learned how to create, copy, move, and link files and folders. Another basic operation is deletion. From time to time, you will want to clean up your directories or free up some disk space, and so you will need to delete files.

You can delete files in one of two ways. One method is to select one or more files or folders and then select Delete from the Edit or File Pane menus. The other method is to use drag and drop, as follows:

1. Select one or more files or folders.

2. Position the pointer over one of the selected files, and press SELECT.
3. Drag the pointer to the Wastebasket.
4. Release SELECT.

When you delete a file, it is not immediately removed from the system. Instead, it is moved to the Wastebasket. Files moved to the Wastebasket are stored in the .wastebasket directory, located in your home directory, until they are permanently removed. Moving files to the Wastebasket is like disposing of a piece of paper in your office wastebasket: you can dig it out of the wastebasket if you decide later that you need it, or you can empty your wastebasket to permanently remove the paper. The same is true of the File Manager Wastebasket: you can retrieve files from it or permanently delete the files.

Using the Wastebasket

The Wastebasket is a part of the File Manager application, but it has its own base window and icon. The Wastebasket icon has two states: empty and full, as shown here:

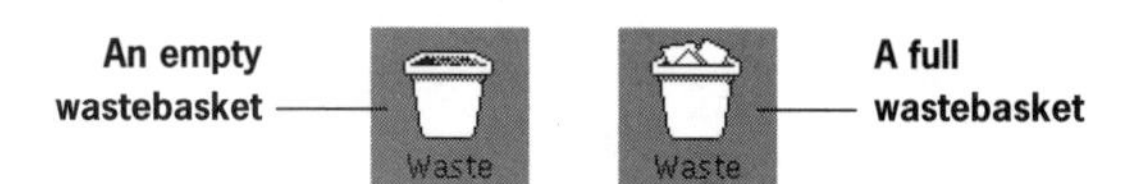

When the Wastebasket is empty, the "empty" icon is displayed. When the Wastebasket contains files, the "full" icon is displayed. You will probably leave the Wastebasket displayed as an icon most of the time. If, however, you need to retrieve a file from the Wastebasket, you will need to deiconify it. The Wastebasket base window is very similar to a Folder pop-up window except that it does not have a pushpin and it has its own menu, as shown in Figure 4.22.

The Wastebasket menu lets you "take out the trash" or retrieve deleted files. Some of the items on the Wastebasket menu are identical to the items available on the Edit or File Pane menu. You can choose Select All, Delete, Cut, Copy, and Paste exactly as described previously. In addition, the Wastebasket menu provides two unique features.

- Empty Wastebasket
- Undelete

When you choose Empty Wastebasket, all the files and folders in the Wastebasket are permanently removed. Once these files are removed, you can't get them back, so be sure before you remove them that you don't need them. If you want to permanently remove some but not all of the files in the wastebasket, first select the files you want to delete and then choose Delete from the Wastebasket menu.

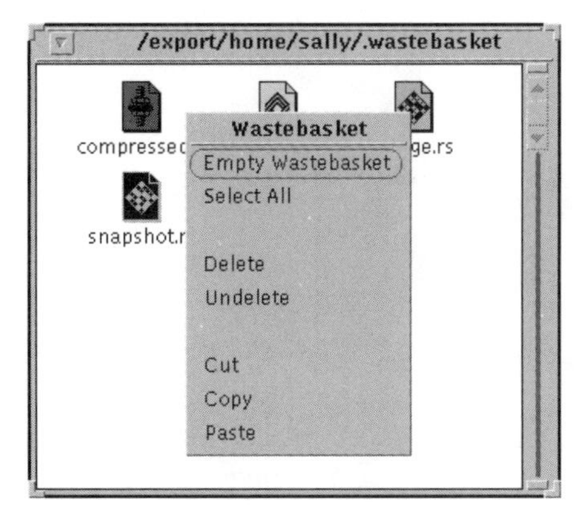

Figure 4.22 The Wastebasket base window and menu

If you want to retrieve any files that you've moved to the Wastebasket, select the file or files and choose Undelete from the Wastebasket menu. The selected files are moved back to the folder from which they were deleted.

Printing Files

You can choose from three ways to print files from the File Manager:

- Use the default print method.
- Use a custom print method.
- Drag and drop a file to the Print Tool.

For basic printing you can just select one or more files from the file pane and then choose Print from the File or File Pane menu. This will send the selected file or files to the default printer. Each file type has its own method of printing, just as it has its own method of opening. If a particular file type does not have its own method of printing, then a default printing method is used. (You can modify the File Manager print method from the File Manager Tool Properties, as we will discuss later in this chapter.)

To use a customized print method for just this particular printing (without changing the default print method), use the Custom Print Properties pop-up window. To display this window, follow these steps:

1. Select one or more files from the file pane.

2. Display the File menu or the File Pane pop-up menu.
3. Position the pointer over the Print item, and drag right to display the Print submenu.
4. Select Custom Print. The Custom Print Properties window is displayed, as shown here:

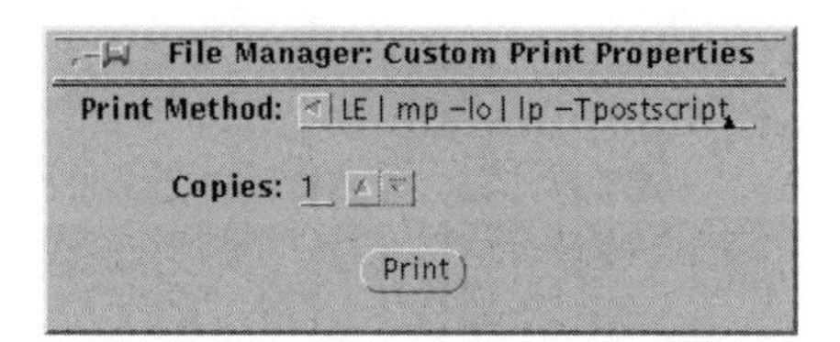

To specify your own print method, replace the Print Method text-field entry with your own customized entry. You may want to do this to execute a special print command or to print to an alternate printer. The $FILE variable is replaced by the name of the file or files you selected in the file pane. You can also specify the number of copies you want printed. When you have entered the appropriate information, press Print to print the files.

The last method of printing takes advantage of the drag and drop feature. You can drag one or more files from the File Manager and drop them onto the Print Tool. You'll learn more about the Print Tool in Chapter 8. For now, all you need to know is that the Print Tool uses the print method associated with each file type when printing files. You can drop the files from the File Manager either onto the Print Tool drag and drop target or onto the Print Tool icon, as shown in Figure 4.23.

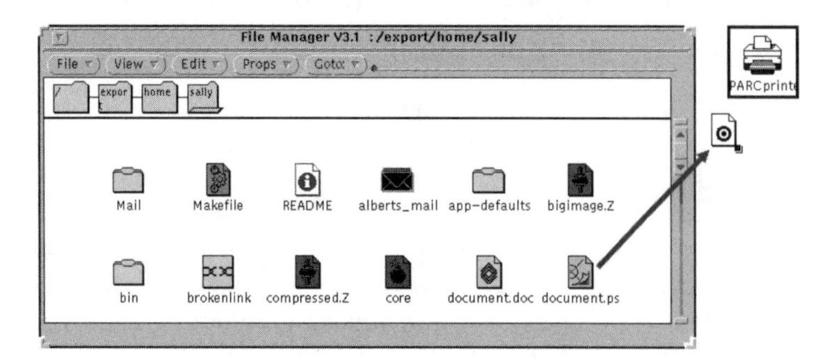

Figure 4.23
Dragging a file from the File Manager to the Print Tool

Finding Files and Folders

You learned a little about locating files in the section "Finding Files in the Current Folder," earlier in this chapter. You were able to select files in the current folder by specifying a name, optionally with a wildcard in the Goto text field or directly in the file pane. Now we will look at a more sophisticated approach to locating files through the use of the Find pop-up window, shown in Figure 4.24. To display the Find pop-up window, choose Find from the File menu.

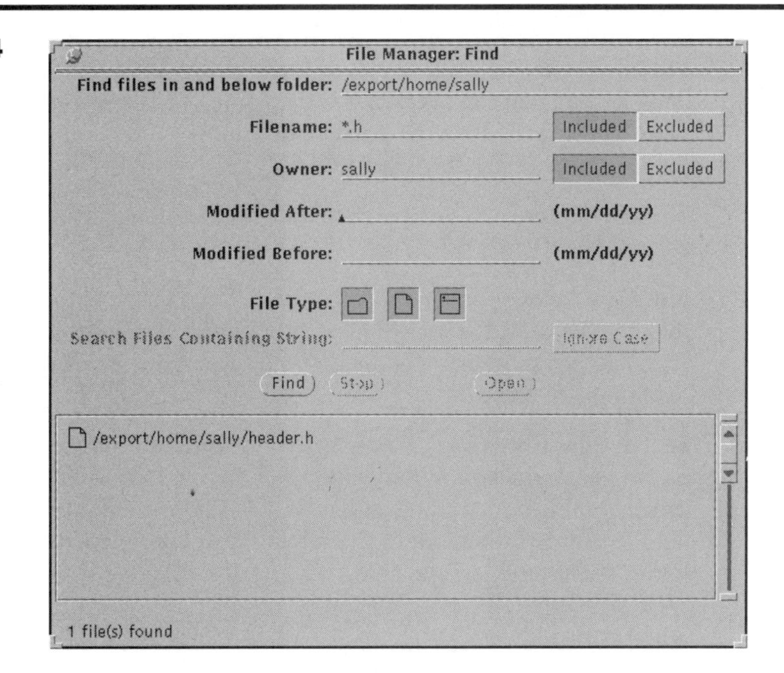

Figure 4.24 The Find pop-up window

The Find feature is useful if you don't know or can't remember the specific location of a file or folder you are looking for. You specify different attributes that describe the characteristics of the file. The search is initiated in the directory that you specify in the Find window. All files and directories that are descendants of the specified directory are examined as part of the find process, and all files that match the attributes specified are listed in the scrolling list at the bottom of the window. Let's look at each of the fields provided by the Find window.

Find files in and below folder identifies the starting point for the search. By default, the current folder is listed in this text field. You can change this to any folder.

Filename specifies the name of the file to look for. You can use wildcards in this field. For example, if you want to find all files ending with .h, you specify *.h in this field. You use the Included and Excluded buttons to the right of the text field to indicate whether you want to find all files that match the pattern specified or all files that do not match the file specified. For example, *.h is in the text field, but if you select Excluded, all files *except* those ending in .h will be matched.

Owner specifies the owner of the file. You can also include or exclude files owned by a specific user.

Modified After tells the search to look for files modified after a certain date. Maybe you can't remember the name of a file you created, but you know you did it last week. You can use this field to eliminate all files from the search created before last week.

Modified Before tells the search to look for files modified before a certain date.

File Type bases your search on file type. You can choose one or more of the three broad categories of files: directories, regular files, or executables. If you do not choose any of the three file types, the search will be independent of the file type.

Search Files Containing String lets you search the contents of the file for a string of characters. When you search for a misplaced file, sometimes the only thing you are sure of has to do with the contents of the file. This field is disabled when either the directory or executable file type is selected from the File Type field.

All of the attributes specified must match before the file can be found. For example, if you specify the Filename as *.h and the Modified Before date as 12/02/93, then only the files that have names ending in .h *and* that were modified before 12/02/93 will be included in the list at the bottom of the window.

Three buttons are displayed above the scrolling list: Find, Stop, and Open. Press the Find button when you are ready to begin a search. The Stop button is active only when a find is in progress. You can press it to interrupt a find operation. Because the files that match your criteria are added to the scrolling list as they are found, there is no need to continue the find operation once the file you are looking for appears in the scrolling list. You can press Stop at any time, and the files in the scrolling list will remain.

You use the Open button to open a file in the scrolling list. To do so, select one of the files in the list and then select Open. If the file you selected is a directory, it becomes the File Manager's current directory.

File Properties

Every file and folder has a certain set of properties such as name, owner, size, and permissions. You can view the details of a file's properties by displaying the File Properties pop-up window. To display the File Properties window, follow these steps:

1. Select a file in the file pane.
2. Press MENU on the Props menu button.
3. Drag the pointer to File, and release MENU.

You can also display the File Properties window by pressing the Props key on the keyboard when one or more files or folders are selected.

The File Properties window is displayed in Figure 4.25.

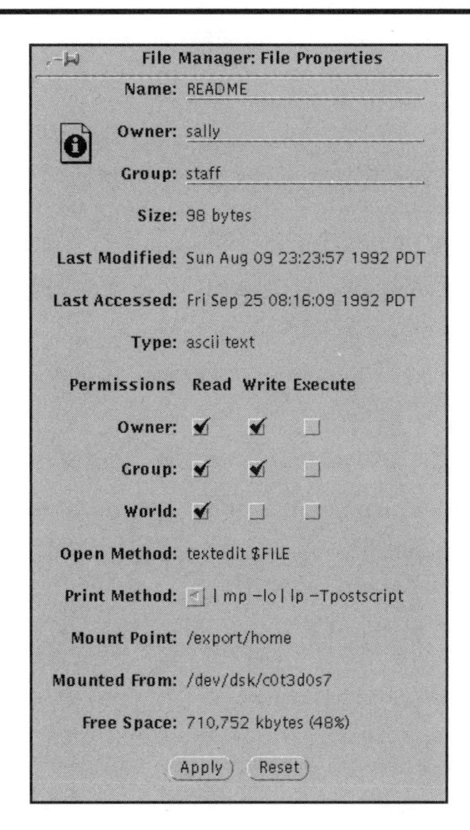

Figure 4.25 The File Properties pop-up window

Most of the information provided in the File Properties window is for reference only and cannot be changed. The only fields that can be modified are Name, Owner, Group, and Permissions. You can change the owner and group only if you have special privileges. Let's take a look at each field:

Name is the name of the file. You can change the name of the file by editing this text field and pressing the Apply button at the bottom of the window.

Owner is the owner of the file.

Group is the group owner of the file.

Size is the size of the file in bytes. If a folder is selected, a rectangular button labeled Contents appears to the right. If you press the Contents button, the size displayed changes to indicate the size of the contents of the folder.

Last Modified is the date and time that the file was last modified.

Last Accessed is the date and time that the file was last accessed. A file is accessed when its contents are examined.

Type is the type of the file.

Permissions specifies the three types of permission: read, write, and execute. These types apply to three categories: owner, group, and world. (See the next section for more on permissions.)

Open Method is the program executed when you open a file. The $FILE variable is replaced by the selected file or files.

Print Method is the program executed when you print a file. The $FILE variable is replaced by the selected file or files.

Mount Point is the directory where the current file system is mounted.

Mounted From is the device that the mount point is mounted from. If it is a remote mount, it includes the server and directory that the file system is mounted from.

Free Space is the number of kilobytes of free space available on the current file system.

Setting Permissions

Only the owner of a file, or a privileged user, can change a file's permissions. The checkboxes on the File Properties window identify the permissions of the file for the three permission categories: owner, group, and world. A check mark indicates that the permission is present. The absence of a check mark indicates that the permission for that category and type is not granted. To change permissions of a file, select the appropriate checkboxes and press the Apply button at the bottom of the window.

You may have some files with sensitive data in them that you do not want anyone else to have access to. In this case, you would turn off all world permissions. You may have other files that you want to share with members of your group. Any user who belongs to the group can access the file according to the group permissions. This provides a convenient way for multiple users to share access to files. Depending on the circumstances, you might want to turn on one or more of the group permissions.

Most of the fields in the File Properties pop-up window can accommodate only a single entry. For example, there is room for only one file name. So, if more than one file in the file pane is selected, some of the fields in the File Properties pop-up window will be insensitive, as shown in Figure 4.26.

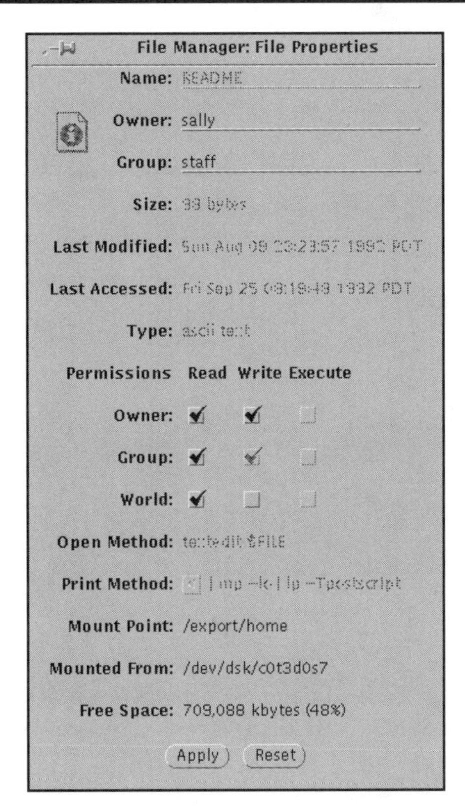

Figure 4.26 The File Properties pop-up window displaying properties for multiple files

When multiple files are selected and the permissions do not match, the checkboxes representing the fields that don't match are dimmed. These checkboxes can still be selected, however. This allows you to set common permissions on multiple files. As soon as you select a dimmed checkbox, it returns to its normal appearance. When you press Apply, the permission takes effect for all the selected files. This is a useful feature when you want to change permissions on many files at once.

File Manager Properties

The File Manager maintains a set of properties that control some of its features. These properties can be set from the File Manager Tool Properties pop-up window. To display the Tool Properties window, follow these steps:

1. Press MENU on the Props menu button.
2. Drag the pointer to File Manager, and release MENU.

You can also display the Tool Properties window by pressing the Props key on the keyboard when no file or folder is selected. The Tool Properties pop-up window is shown in Figure 4.27.

Figure 4.27 The File Manager Tool Properties pop-up window

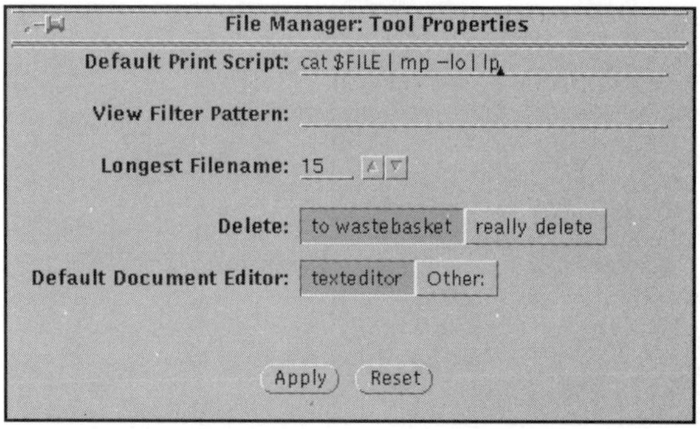

You can set five features from Tool Properties:

Default Print Script is the command executed when a file type does not specify a print method. The $FILE variable is replaced with the name of the file or files being printed.

View Filter Pattern controls the files viewed in the file pane. By default, this field is empty, which means that all files are displayed. You might want to use this feature if you have a folder with many files in it but want to see only the files that end in .c. To display only those files, you simply enter *.c in the View Filter Pattern field.

Longest Filename specifies the maximum number of characters that the File Manager will display as a file name. All others are truncated. You can set this number to anything between 0 and 255.

Delete controls whether a delete operation will move a file to the Wastebasket or will really delete the file from the system. If you set it to Really Delete, then the next time you bring up the File Manager, the Wastebasket will not be displayed.

Default Document Editor is used to set the document editor. When a regular file is opened, a document editor is invoked. By default, this is the DeskSet Text Editor program, but you can choose another editor if you want to. When you press the Other button, a text field appears below the button. The default entry for Other is displayed on the text field:

```
shelltool sh -c "sleep 3;vi $FILE"
```

This starts the vi editor running in a Shell Tool. You can edit the text field to use any text editor you want.

Creating Custom Commands

In addition to the built-in features that we have examined throughout this chapter, the File Manager allows you to create custom commands. To create a command, you must display the Create Command pop-up window:

1. Position the pointer over the File menu button.
2. Press MENU to display the File menu.
3. Drag the pointer to the Custom Commands item, and drag right to display the Custom Commands submenu.
4. Drag the pointer to Create Command, and release MENU. The Create Command window is displayed, as shown in Figure 4.28.

The existing commands are displayed in the Custom Commands scrolling list at the top of the window. To create a new command, begin by pressing the New Command button. When you have entered all the information for your new command, press the Apply button at the bottom of the window. Your new command appears in the Custom Commands scrolling list.

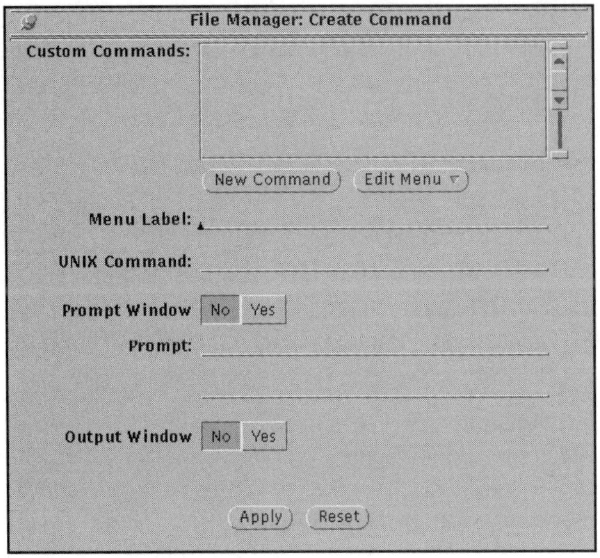

Figure 4.28
The Create Command pop-up window

Let's look at each of the fields on the Create Command window.

Menu Label is where you specify a name for your new command. New commands appear on the Custom Commands submenu.

UNIX Command is the actual command to execute. You can include two variables: $FILE and $ARG. The $FILE variable is replaced by the name or names of the files selected in the file pane. These are the files you want the command executed on. The $ARG variable is replaced by the characters provided by the user in the prompt window.

Prompt Window lets you specify whether to create a window that will prompt the user for information when the user selects the new command. Some UNIX commands require more information than just a file. For example, if you want a custom command that sends a file in a mail message, you need a way to specify the user that the files are to be mailed to. You can use a prompt window for this.

Prompt is where you specify the prompt window. If you choose to include a prompt window, then you need a prompt. For example, if you are sending a mail message as we just described, you need to include a prompt asking for the name of the user to send the mail to.

Output Window specifies whether an output window, showing the output of the command, should be displayed.

Now let's create a custom command. A useful UNIX command that saves disk space is *compress.* The compress command reduces the size of a file by using a special compression algorithm. This is particularly useful when you are dealing with big files. If you are running out of disk space, you can compress some seldomly used files to free up some space. The argument you pass to the compress command is the name of the file or files that you want compressed. Compress changes the name of the compressed file to include a .Z suffix, which helps you easily identify compressed files. To create the compress command, fill in the fields of the Create Command window, as shown in Figure 4.29.

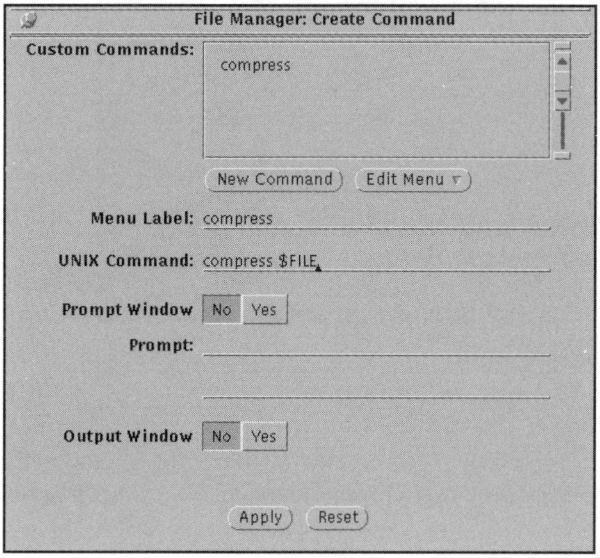

Figure 4.29
Creating a custom command

In this case, we do not need a prompt window or an output window. After filling in the fields, press the Apply button. The compress command is added to the scrolling list at the top of the window.

To execute the compress command, begin by selecting one or more files in the file pane. Then display the Custom Commands submenu and select compress. You will notice that the icon for the file changes to the compress icon. This is because compressed files are a unique file type. The open method for a compressed file uncompresses the file. Therefore, all you have to do to uncompress a compressed file is to open it by double-clicking or by using one of the other methods for opening a file.

Let's consider one more example of a custom command. This time we will create a custom command that sends mail to a specified user. We will need a prompt window in order to get the name of the user or users to send the mail to. Figure 4.30 shows the Create Command window with the appropriate fields for the mail command.

Figure 4.30
Creating a custom mail command

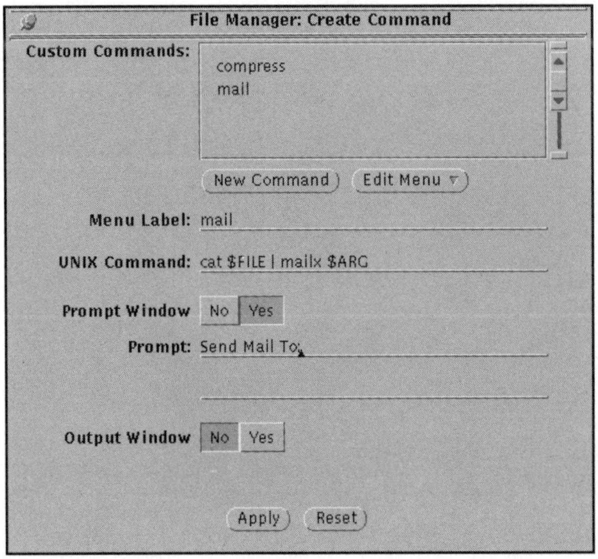

When you execute this command, a prompt window is displayed, asking for the names of the users to send the mail to, as shown here:

Summary

The File Manager is a powerful tool for managing files and directories, with many options for customizing its use. Basic file-management functions such as copying and moving files are available in the File Manager through an intuitive, interactive interface. The drag and drop capabilities are particularly important. As you learn about other DeskSet tools, you may often use the File Manager as the source of a drag and drop operation. Your ability to organize and manage your files and directories will enhance your efficiency when using the Solaris environment.

CHAPTER

The Shell Tool, Command Tool, and Text Editor

THE SHELL TOOL AND COMMAND TOOL ARE TERMINAL EMULATORS THAT you use to enter UNIX commands. The Text Editor is an ASCII text editor that you use to create and modify ASCII files. It provides functions for manipulating and formatting text. These applications are discussed together in this chapter because they have many common features. In particular, the Text Editor and the Command Tool have some editing features that are identical and are also shared by other DeskSet applications such as the View and Compose windows of the Mail Tool.

In this chapter you will learn how to do the following:

- Enter commands
- Create files
- Edit existing files
- Use the Text Editor menus
- Copy and move text
- Load files
- Maneuver throughout the text pane
- Find text
- Format text
- Split the text pane
- Use drag and drop
- Customize the text pane

This chapter begins with a discussion of the Shell Tool and Command Tool and then goes on to the Text Editor.

Both the Shell Tool and the Command Tool give you an interface to the SunOS operating system; they also share many common features. One of the most distinctive differences between the two tools is that the Command Tool provides a scrollbar by default and the Shell Tool does not. The scrollbar allows you to scroll back to text that already has been scrolled off the pane. There are also other differences that you will see throughout this chapter.

The Shell Tool

To start a Shell Tool, you select the Shell Tool item from the Workspace Programs menu, shown in Figure 5.1.

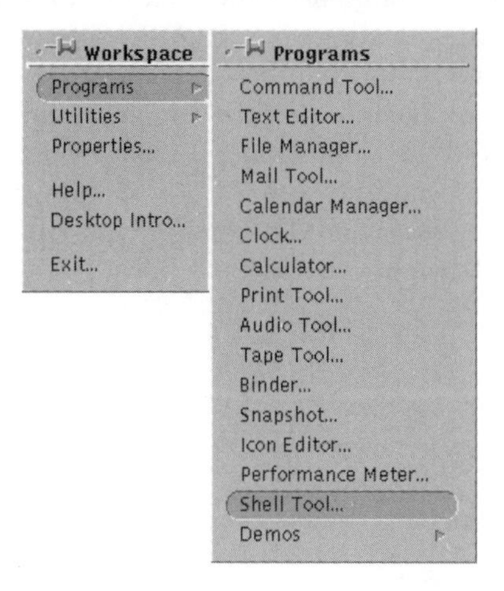

Figure 5.1
Starting a Shell Tool

You can also start a Shell Tool by entering the **shelltool** command at the prompt, as follows, in a running Shell Tool or Command Tool:

```
dugout% shelltool &
```

Starting a Shell Tool on the command line gives you the flexibility of customizing the features of the Shell Tool by setting command-line options that control such things as position, background color, and font. You'll learn more about customizing DeskSet applications in Chapter 10.

The Shell Tool has a simple base window. The base window has no controls and no control area; instead, it has just a pane and the standard window manager border, as shown in Figure 5.2.

The name of the shell being used is shown in the window header. In this case (/bin/csh) it is the C Shell. The Shell Tool icon is a screen and keyboard, as shown here:

Note that the icon also displays the name of the shell.

When the Shell Tool has focus, the cursor is a solid black rectangle, as you can see in Figure 5.2. When the Shell Tool does not have focus, the cursor displays a rectangular outline. How the Shell Tool receives focus depends on the way that your Set Input Area property is set (see the section on setting workspace properties in Chapter 3). You may have to either click SELECT with the pointer in the Shell Tool or just move the pointer into the Shell Tool for it to receive focus.

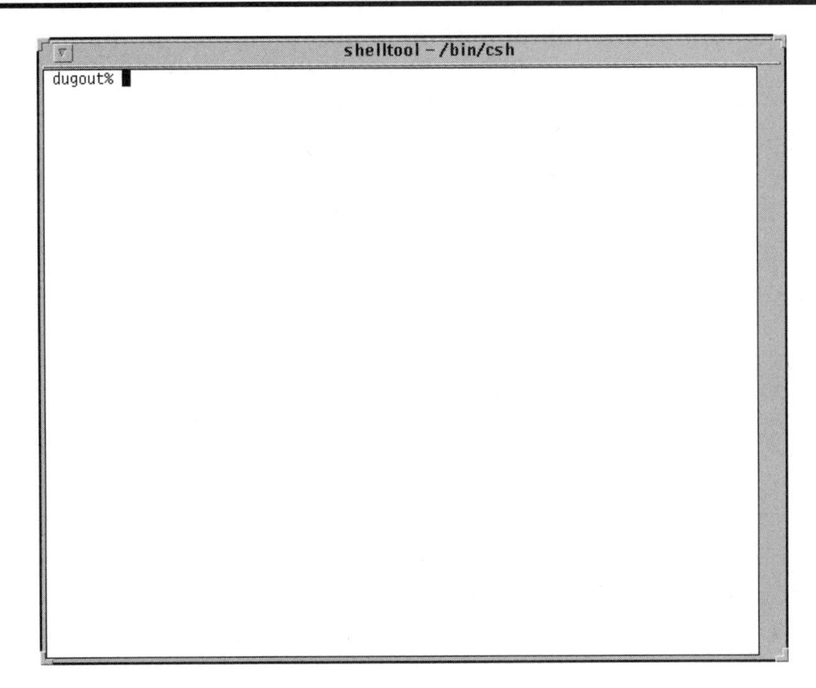

Figure 5.2 The Shell Tool base window

The Term Pane Pop-Up Menu

You manipulate the Shell Tool by using the controls available on the Term Pane pop-up menu. You display the Term Pane pop-up menu by pressing the MENU mouse button while the pointer is positioned anywhere on the pane. The menu looks like this:

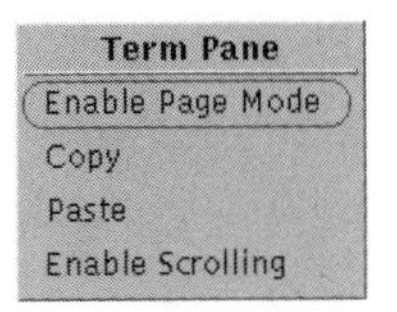

Let's look at each of the items available on this menu.

Enable Page Mode

The primary purpose of a Shell Tool is to let you type commands and then receive output from those commands. It doesn't take long before all of the vertical space of the Shell Tool is filled. When there is no more room for commands or output, the Shell Tool begins scrolling the top edge off the pane. Once the data has been scrolled off the top on the Shell Tool term pane, there is no way to get it back. This can be particularly annoying when you enter a command whose output is greater in length than the vertical size of the Shell Tool. The Enable Page Mode item on the Term Pane menu solves this problem.

When you select Enable Page Mode from the Term Pane menu, the command output stops before scrolling off the pane. One page of text (a page in this context is defined by the size of the Shell Tool pane) is displayed before the output is temporarily halted. The pointer changes to thc shape of a stop sign, indicating that the output has stopped and that there is more data pending. When you have finished examining the output, you can continue to the next page simply by pressing any key. The next page is then displayed, and the output stops again if it has not been exhausted. This pattern repeats until the entire output of the command has been displayed.

When page mode is enabled, the first item on the Term Pane menu is labeled Disable Page Mode. Select this item to turn off the page mode.

Copy and Paste

The Shell Tool provides a standard way to copy and paste text to and from other applications. The process is similar to that of copying and pasting files from within the File Manager (see Chapter 4). Rather than requiring that you copy entire files, though, the Shell Tool provides a way for you to select text and then copy that text and paste it into another Shell Tool or into other applications, such as the Text Editor, or Mail Tool, that support copy and paste. You can also copy text from a Shell Tool and paste it into the same Shell Tool. First, let's talk about how you select text.

There are several ways to select text. Right now we'll look at two ways to do it, and then talk about it in more detail later in this chapter when we discuss the Text Editor. The first method, called *wipe-through text selection,* involves dragging the pointer while holding down the SELECT button:

1. Position the pointer at the beginning or end of the text you want to select.
2. Press the SELECT button.
3. Drag the pointer to the other end of the text you want to select. The text may include only a few characters or several lines.
4. Release the SELECT button.

You will see the selected text highlighted in reverse video.

A better way to select text, especially for larger selections, is to use the SELECT and ADJUST buttons:

1. Position the pointer at the beginning or end of the text you want to select.
2. Click SELECT.
3. Move the pointer to the other end of the text you want to select.
4. Click ADJUST.

The text between the two button clicks will be highlighted.

Once the text is highlighted, display the Term Pane pop-up menu and select Copy. Then move the pointer to the application where you want to paste the highlighted text (which might be a new location in the same Shell Tool) and select Paste from that application's Term Pane menu or from a similar menu.

You can also use the Copy and Paste keys on the keyboard to perform the copy and paste operations. These two keys operate exactly as the Copy and Paste items on the Term Pane menu.

When you copy highlighted text, it is stored by the application in a temporary location called the *clipboard*. When you select Paste, the contents of the clipboard are copied into the pasting application.

Let's look at an example of the way you might use this feature. Suppose you typed a command incorrectly. You intended to type

```
ls -l /etc
```

but instead you accidentally typed

```
ks -l /etc
```

You could just type the entire command again, or you could use the copy and paste feature of the Shell Tool. Follow these steps to take advantage of copy and paste:

1. Type **l**. This is the character that you missed the first time.
2. Select the portion of the previous command that was correct: **s – l /etc**
3. Display the Term Pane menu and select the Copy item, as shown in the upper window in Figure 5.3, or press the Copy key. The highlighted text is then copied to the clipboard.
4. Display the Term Pane menu and select the Paste item, or press the Paste key. The text from the clipboard is copied into the Shell Tool where the cursor is displayed, as shown in the lower window in Figure 5.3.

In practice, you may find it easier to retype such a short command than to use the copy and paste feature. However, if your command is a long one, the benefits of copying and pasting are greater, especially if you don't like to type or if you are a slow typist.

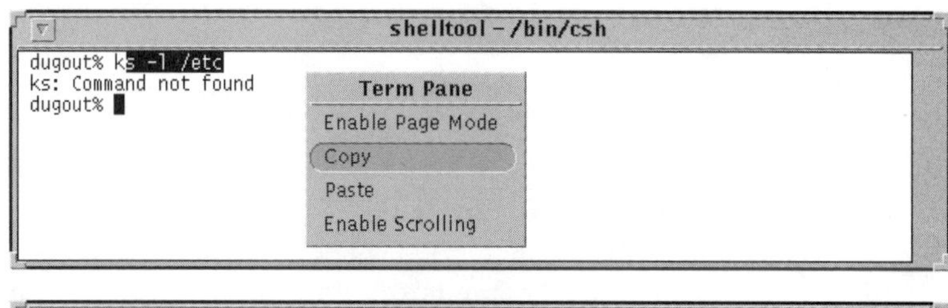

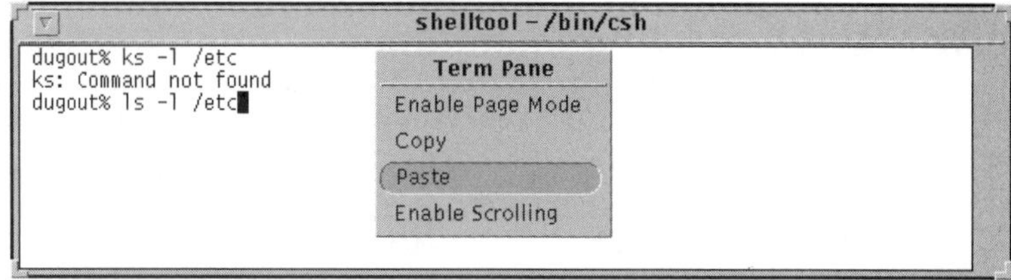

Figure 5.3
Copying and pasting text in the Shell Tool

I use the copy and paste feature frequently to copy a path name from a Command Tool to another application. For example, remember the Goto text field in the File Manager? (See Figure 4.9.) You use this field to change the File Manager's current directory to the one you specify. If you wanted to change the current directory of the File Manager to that of the Command Tool, you could use copy and paste to save yourself some typing. To do this, you first determine the current directory of the Shell Tool by using the pwd command, and then use the output of the pwd command to copy and paste into the Goto text field of the File Manager. You can do this by following these steps:

1. Enter the pwd command in the Shell Tool. The output of the pwd command is a single line that specifies the current directory.
2. Position the pointer over the pwd output.
3. Select the pwd output line.
4. Press the Copy key.
5. Position the pointer over the File Manager's Goto text field.
6. Click SELECT to ensure that the focus is in the Goto text field.

7. Press the Paste key.

Figure 5.4 displays this copy and paste operation between a Shell Tool and the File Manager.

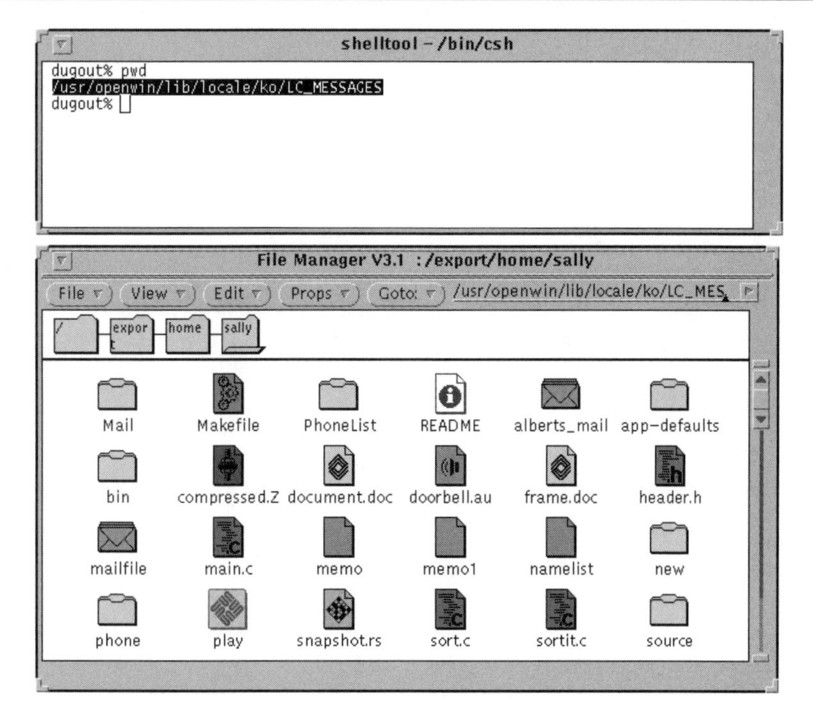

Figure 5.4 Copying a directory name from a Shell Tool to the File Manager

This process is very convenient when you want the current directory of a Command Tool to become the current directory of the File Manager. You don't have to remember the exact path, you don't have to type in that long path name, and you avoid typos.

Enable Scrolling

The last item on the Term Pane menu allows you to enable scrolling. When scrolling is enabled, the Shell Tool essentially gains the added functionality of a Command Tool. A scrollbar is now displayed on the side of the term pane, indicating that the Command Tool mode is in effect. You can toggle the mode back to Shell Tool if you want. When you press MENU on the term pane, you will notice that the menu has changed considerably. We'll discuss the details of the Command Tool in the next section.

The Command Tool

To start a Command Tool, you select the Command Tool item from the Workspace Programs menu. You can also start a Command Tool by entering the following command in a running Shell Tool or Command Tool:

```
dugout% cmdtool &
```

The Command Tool and the Shell Tool have several similarities: they are terminal emulators, they provide a shell interface, and they accept UNIX commands. The Command Tool, however, has some additional features not available in the Shell Tool. As mentioned earlier, the most obvious difference between the two applications is the scrollbar provided by the Command Tool, as shown in Figure 5.5.

Figure 5.5
The Command Tool

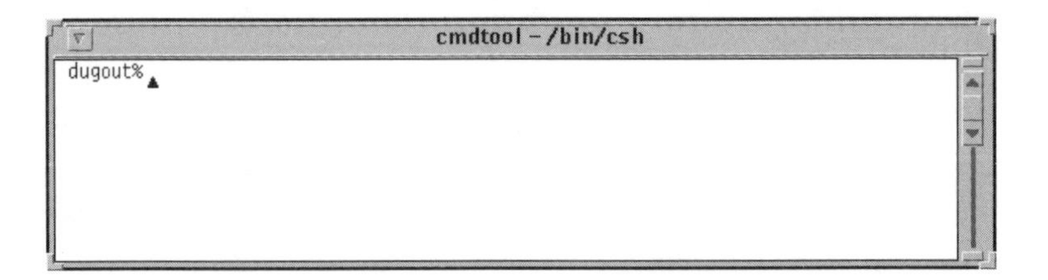

Using the scrollbar, you can scroll the pane up to a position past the top of the visible screen. This means that when text in the term pane scrolls off the top of the Command Tool pane, it is not "lost." This function is extremely useful when you have a command whose output is greater in size than the height of the Command Tool, or when you need to refer to text displayed in the Command Tool earlier in your work session that has since scrolled off the pane.

Another distinguishing feature of the Command Tool is the shape of the cursor. The cursor appears as a solid triangle when the Command Tool has focus, as you can see in Figure 5.5. The cursor appears as a dimmed diamond when the Command Tool does not have focus.

As in the Shell Tool, the only controls available for the Command Tool are on the Term Pane pop-up menu.

The Term Pane Pop-Up Menu

The Command Tool's Term Pane pop-up menu is displayed when you press the MENU mouse button while the pointer is positioned anywhere on the pane.

The menu looks like this:

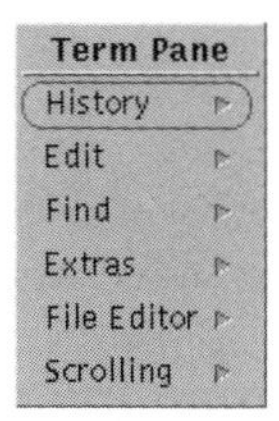

The Command Tool's Term Pane menu has many more features than the Shell Tool's Term Pane menu. The Command Tool allows you to store its contents in a file, edit the contents of the pane, search for strings in the pane, format text, and much more. Some of the features available through the Command Tool's Term Pane pop-up menu are shared by the Text Editor. In this section you'll learn how to use the features of the Term Pane menu that are unique to the Command Tool. The other features that are shared with the Text Editor will be discussed later in this chapter.

History

All the text associated with a Command Tool—both the text that is viewable and the text that already has been scrolled off the pane—is considered the Command Tool's *history* or *history log*. By default, the history is read-only, but you can change it to be editable. The Mode item on the History submenu provides another submenu, the Mode submenu, that lets you choose whether the history will be editable or not. The History and Mode submenus are shown here:

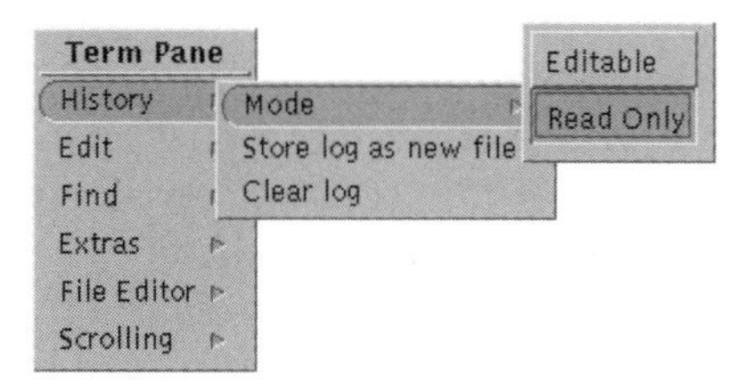

When the history is editable, you can treat it as if it were a file you were editing. You can scroll back through the history and insert, delete, or modify the text of the history as you like. You can also use the arrow keys on the keyboard to move the cursor on the pane when the history is editable.

The second item on the History submenu, Store log as new file, allows you to store the contents of the history as a file. You may, on occasion, execute a command in a Command Tool whose output you will want to store in a file. For example, if you are a programmer, you might compile a large program or a series of programs. The output of the compilation might be several hundred lines long. Compilations are often littered with warning and error messages. If you want a permanent record, or if you find it easier to examine the output in an editor like vi, you may want to store the Command Tool log as a file. When you select Store Log as new file, the Text Store pop-up window is displayed. Figure 5.6 shows the Command Tool with the Text Store pop-up window displayed.

Figure 5.6
The Text Store pop-up window

```
cmdtool - /bin/csh
dugout% cd ../ch5
dugout% make
cc -O  -I../lib -I/usr/openwin/include -c  select.c
"select.c", line 99: warning: argument is incompatible with prototype: arg #2
cc -O  -I../lib -I/usr/openwin/include select.o ../lib/libXs.a
-L/usr/openwin/lib -lXol -lXt -lX11 -o select
cc -O  -I../lib -I/usr/openwin/include -c  xclock.c
cc -O  -I../lib -I/usr/openwin/include xclock.o ../lib/libXs.a
-L/usr/openwin/lib -lXol -lXt -lX11 -o xclock
cc -O  -I../lib -I/usr
cc -O  -I../lib -I/usr
-lXol -lXt -lX11 -o xb
cc -O  -I../lib -I/usr
cc -O  -I../lib -I/usr
-L/usr/openwin/lib -lX
cc -O  -I../lib -I/usr
cc -O  -I../lib -I/usr
cc -O  -I../lib -I/usr
-L/usr/openwin/lib -lX
cc -O  -I../lib -I/usr
cc -O  -I../lib -I/usr/openwin/include tracker2.o mousetracks.o ../lib/libXs.a
-L/usr/openwin/lib -lXol -lXt -lX11 -o tracker2
cc -O  -I../lib -I/usr/openwin/include -c  tracker3.c
cc -O  -I../lib -I/usr/openwin/include tracker3.o mousetracks.o ../lib/libXs.a
-L/usr/openwin/lib -lXol -lXt -lX11 -o tracker3
cc -O  -I../lib -I/usr/openwin/include -c  tracker4.c
cc -O  -I../lib -I/usr/openwin/include tracker4.o mousetracks.o ../lib/libXs.a
-L/usr/openwin/lib -lXol -lXt -lX11 -o tracker4
dugout%
```

```
Text:Store
Directory: /export/home/sally
File: make.out
(Store as New File)
```

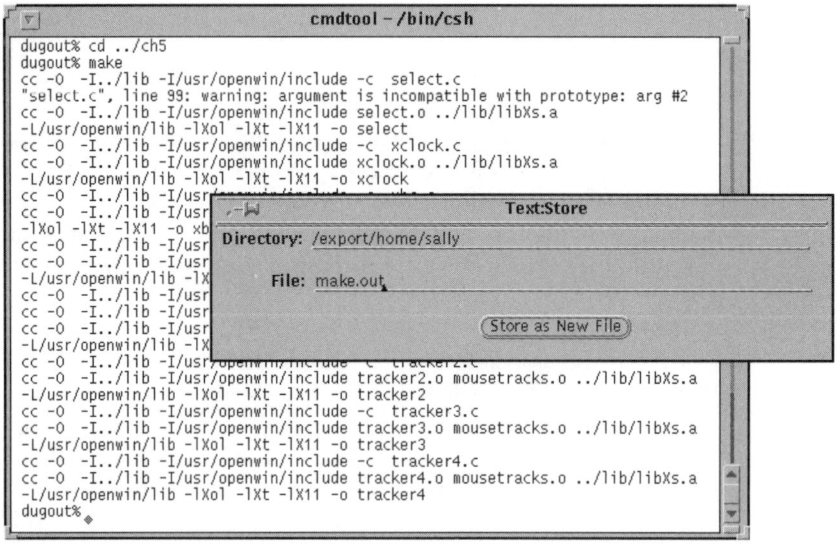

To store the history as a file, enter the name of the directory and the file into the two text fields, and then press the Store as New File button.

The last item on the History submenu, Clear log, allows you to clear the contents of the Command Tool history. Once the history log has been cleared, it cannot be recovered. The history is kept in a file in /tmp. If you run a Command Tool for an extended period of time, the history log file can grow to a considerable size and may become so big that you run out of disk space. Clearing the history log will free this disk space.

Edit

The Edit submenu provides five editing functions: Again, Undo, Copy, Paste, and Cut. Here is the Edit submenu:

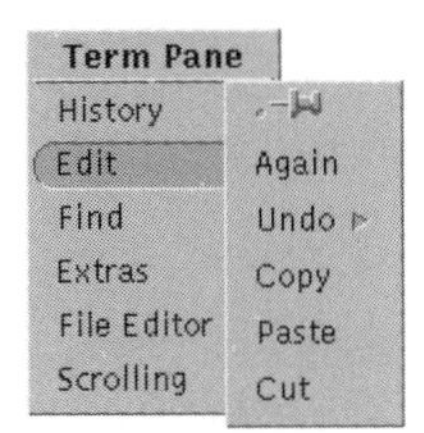

The functions of the Copy and Paste items are identical to those of the corresponding items on the Shell Tool's Term Pane menu. (We will discuss these functions in greater detail in the Text Editor section of this chapter.) Here is a brief description of each of these editing functions:

Again repeats the last command. For example, you can enter a string of characters into the Command Tool and press Again, and the same string of characters will be entered again into the Command Tool.

Undo undoes the last edit. You can undo just the last edit or all edits since the Command Tool was started.

Copy copies the current selection to the clipboard.

Paste pastes the contents of the clipboard into the Command Tool at the position of the cursor.

Cut cuts the current selection and moves it to the clipboard. You can cut only when the history is editable.

Another way that you can activate these five edit functions is to use the keyboard keys with the same labels (Again, Undo, Copy, Paste, and Cut).

Find

The Find submenu lets you search the history log. The submenu looks like this:

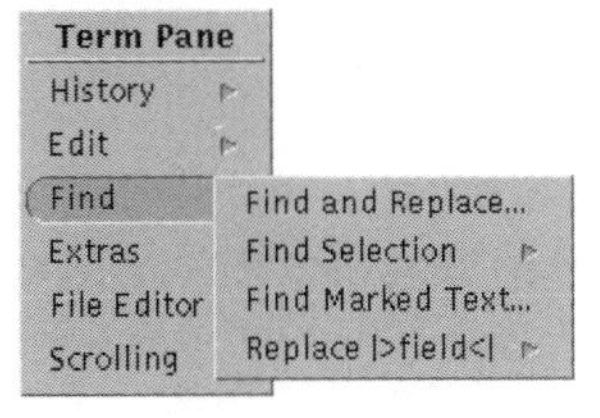

You can specify the text you want to find by selecting it or entering it in a pop-up window. Once the text is found, you can replace that instance of it, or replace it throughout the entire history log. The Text Editor contains the identical submenu and find capabilities. A detailed discussion of the find features is included in the Text Editor section of this chapter.

Extras

The Extras submenu provides some special editing features. You select text and then perform certain operations on that text such as capitalization, formatting, line shifting, and bracket insertion. We will also discuss the Extras submenu in great detail when we discuss the Text Editor. Here is the Extras submenu:

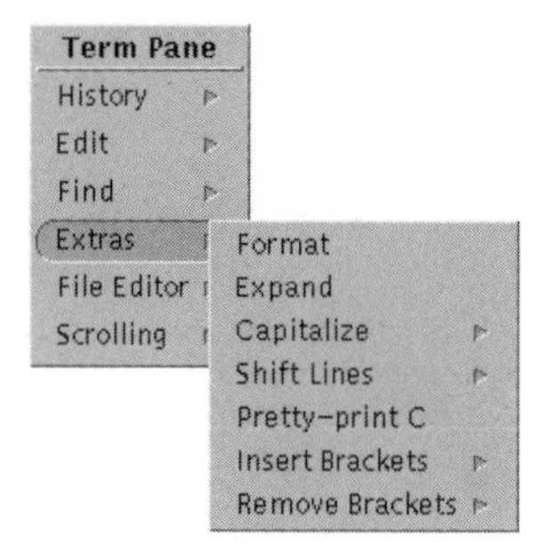

File Editor

The File Editor submenu displays two choices, Enable and Disable, as shown here:

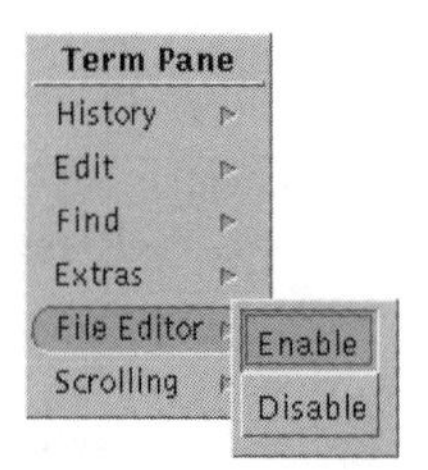

By default, the File Editor is disabled. When you enable the File Editor option, the Command Tool is split into two panes. The top pane displays the Command Tool, and the lower pane displays a text editor. Figure 5.7 shows a Command Tool with file editing enabled.

The File Editor has exactly the same functionality as the Text Editor application discussed later in this chapter. You can use the Text Edit pane of a Command Tool as a normal text editor. I find it useful to do this when I want to do some quick file editing. Rather than start up a new Text Editor, I can enable file editing in a Command Tool, load a file, make the changes, and save the file. This is often faster than starting a new Text Editor application.

Figure 5.7
A Command Tool with the File Editor enabled

```
cmdtool - /bin/csh
dugout% make
cc -O  -I../lib -I/usr/openwin/include -c  tracker1.c
"tracker1.c", line 56: syntax error before or at: staticTextWidgetClass
cc: acomp failed for tracker1.c
*** Error code 1
make: Fatal error: Command failed for target `tracker1.o'
dugout%

File   View   Edit   Find

  Widget   parent, target;
{
  extern void  clear_tracker();
  extern void  track_mouse_position();
  Widget       tracker;

  /*
   * Create the tracker widget and register event
   * handlers for the target widget.
   */
  tracker = XtCreateManagedWidget("mousetracker"
                                  staticTextWidgetClass,
                                  parent, NULL, 0);
  XtAddEventHandler(target, LeaveWindowMask, FALSE,
                    clear_tracker, tracker);
  XtAddEventHandler(target, PointerMotionMask, FALSE,
                    track_mouse_position, tracker);
```

Scrolling

The Scrolling submenu lets you disable the scrolling feature from a Command Tool. With scrolling disabled, the Command Tool acts like a Shell Tool. Fortunately, if you enable scrolling after you have disabled it, the history log is restored. Here is the Scrolling submenu:

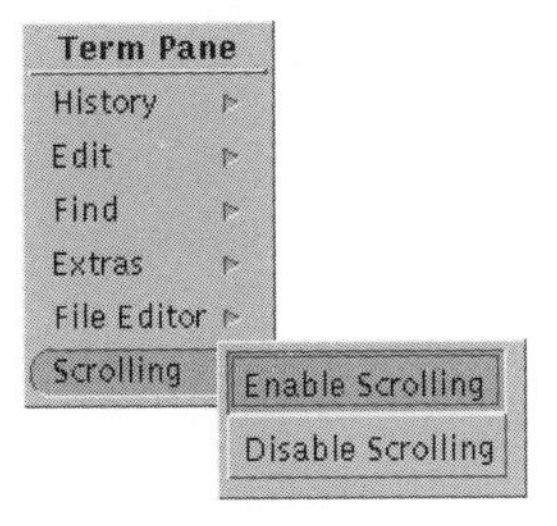

The Console

The Console is a special type of Command Tool. It is used for displaying warning or error messages from the operating system or from applications running under the OpenWindows environment such as the DeskSet programs. You can use the Console for entering commands just as you would any other Command Tool, but it is probably a good idea to reserve the Console for system messages. That way you can avoid confusion about what is a system message and what is the output of a command. You should always have a Console running. If you don't, system messages will be displayed in large type at the bottom of your screen. The messages will corrupt the look of the OpenWindows environment, and you will have to refresh the entire windowing system to correct it. (To do this, select Refresh from the Workspace Utilities menu.)

If you need to start a Console, you simply select the Console item from the Workspace Utilities menu. You can also start a Console by entering the cmdtool command with a -C option, as follows:

```
dugout% cmdtool -C &
```

Text Editor Basics

The basic features of the Text Editor are intuitive and are easy to learn. You enter text by typing characters at the keyboard. You can position the cursor by clicking the SELECT button or by using the arrow keys. You delete characters by using the Delete or Backspace key.

You invoke the Text Editor by choosing Text Editor from the Workspace Programs menu. When you start the Text Editor this way, no initial file is opened. You can begin entering text and then store the text as a new file, or you can load an existing file.

Another way to begin the Text Editor application is to use the textedit command from a Shell Tool or Command Tool. You can also use this command to provide a command-line argument that specifies the name of the file you want to edit, as shown here:

```
dugout% textedit trip_report &
```

If you specify a file that already exists, the Text Editor will be loaded with that file when it starts. If you specify a file that does not exist, a notice appears, requesting confirmation for creating the new file, as shown here:

If you select Confirm, the Text Editor creates the new file and loads it for editing. If you select Cancel, the Text Editor is not started at all.

The Text Editor Base Window

The Text Editor consists of a control area and a text pane, as shown in Figure 5.8.

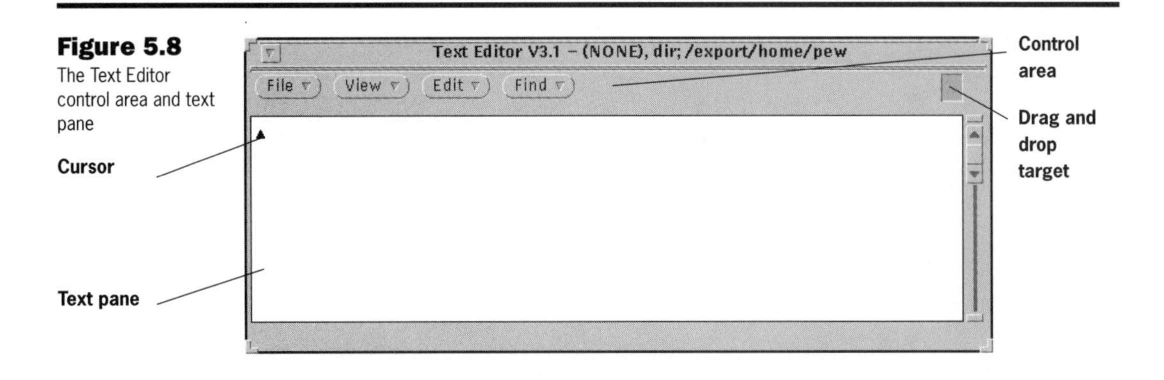

Figure 5.8 The Text Editor control area and text pane

The control area contains four menu buttons and a drag and drop target. The menu buttons provide basic text editor functions such as saving the current file, loading a file, finding a string of characters, and formatting text. The drag and drop target is used to load a file into the Text Editor or to transfer the contents of the Text Editor to another DeskSet application. We will discuss these functions in detail later in this chapter.

The text pane displays the contents of the file being edited. You can use the scrollbar on the right to scroll the contents of the text pane. The text pane also contains a cursor that identifies the current insertion point in the file. When you type characters at the keyboard, they are inserted into the text pane at the cursor location. The cursor is displayed in two ways. When the Text Editor has focus, the cursor appears as a solid triangle. When the Text Editor does not have focus, the cursor appears as a dimmed diamond.

The Text Editor Icon

The Text Editor icon includes the name of the file being edited. If the entire name of the file does not fit into the space provided by the icon, the right portion of the file name is truncated. If the file being edited has changes that have not been saved, the name of the file displayed in the icon is preceded by a right-angle bracket (>). If the Text Editor is editing a file that has not been named, the icon displays NO FILE for the file name. The three variations possible for the Text Editor icon (file has not been named, file has been named, file has been named but changes have not been saved) are shown here:

Creating Text

You create new text in the Text Editor by positioning the cursor at the desired insertion point and typing at the keyboard. You erase text a character at a time by using the Delete key or Backspace key. (You can also use the keyboard Cut, Copy, and Paste keys to add or delete text. This method will be discussed later in this chapter.) You move the insertion point by moving the pointer and clicking SELECT. Start the Text Editor and enter some text by following these steps:

1. Select Text Editor from the Workspace Programs menu.
2. Position the pointer on the Text Editor and click SELECT at the insertion point.
3. Enter some text.

Do this now so that you can experiment with the concepts presented in the next few sections. Enter any text you like.

Note that you cannot position the cursor past the end of the file. The Text Editor does not allow the cursor position to move beyond the last character of the file. When you begin creating a new file, there are no characters in the file, so the cursor can be positioned only in the upper-left corner of the text pane. If you want to have a blank space in the file, you must enter spaces, tabs, or carriage returns to create the blank space.

Maneuvering through Text

You can choose from several ways to position the cursor in the text pane. The simplest way to move the cursor position is to use the mouse and the pointer. Move the pointer to the location on the text pane where you want to insert text, and press the SELECT button. The cursor moves to the position of the pointer.

Another way to move the cursor is to use the keyboard. The arrow keys move the cursor up or down one line at a time, or left or right one character at a time. You can also use the key combinations listed in Table 5.1 to move the cursor. You may often prefer this method when you are doing a lot of typing and you don't want to remove your hands from the keyboard to position the cursor.

Table 5.1 Key Combinations for Maneuvering in Text Editor

Key Combination	Resulting Position of Cursor
Control-F or Right Arrow	One character to the right
Control-B or Left Arrow	One character to the left
Control-.	One word to the right
Control-,	One word to the left
Control-A	Beginning of current line
Control-E	End of current line
Control-P or Up Arrow	Up one line
Control-N or Down Arrow	Down one line
Control-Shift-Return	Beginning of file
Control-Return	End of file

Selecting Text

Many of the features available in the Text Editor require that you first select or highlight some text. For example, to format text, you must first select the text that you want formatted. If you want to cut text from one portion of the text pane and paste it to another, you must first select the text that you want to cut.

When text is selected, it appears in reverse video and is pending delete. *Pending delete* means that the selected text will be deleted and replaced with the new character that you type or paste. Figure 5.9 shows a Text Editor with several lines of text selected.

We've already discussed some basic selection methods, including wipe-through text selection and using the SELECT and ADJUST buttons. You can also select text in the following ways:

- To expand or reduce the size of a current selection, position the pointer at the new beginning or ending location of the text you want to select, and click ADJUST. This method can expand or reduce the size of the selection in either direction.

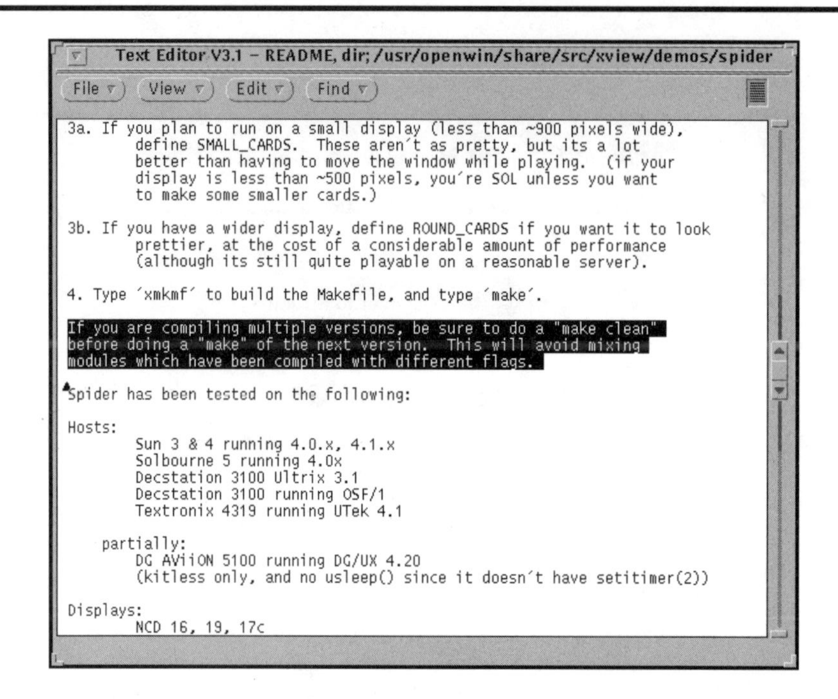

Figure 5.9 Lines selected in Text Editor

- To select a word, position the pointer on the word and double-click SELECT. A word is delimited by a space or punctuation character. If you double-click and keep the SELECT button pressed on the second click, you can drag the pointer to increase or decrease the size of the selection one word at a time.
- To select a line, position the pointer on the line and triple-click SELECT. A *line* is defined as all the characters from the beginning of the line to the carriage return. This may actually span more than one line if text has been wrapped. If you triple-click and keep the SELECT button pressed on the third click, you can drag the pointer to increase or decrease the size of the selection one line at a time.
- To select the entire document, click SELECT four times rapidly.

You may find it necessary to select text that spans more than one visible page but does not include the entire document. You can do this by using the techniques described previously in combination with the scrollbar. When you use the scrollbar to move through the document, the cursor position and the selected text do not change.

Here's an example of how you would select a large section of text:

1. Click SELECT at the beginning of the text you want to select.
2. Use the scrollbar to advance to the end of the text you want to select. The cursor may be out of view, but the insertion point has not changed.
3. Position the pointer at the end of the text you want to select, and click ADJUST.

You have now selected a large portion of text. Some of the selected text may not be visible.

Copying and Moving Text

Earlier in this chapter you learned some basics about cutting and copying text to the clipboard and pasting text from the clipboard. These techniques apply in the Text Editor. You select text by using the methods described in the previous section. Then you perform a cut or copy operation on the selected text, which puts the selected text onto the clipboard. You can paste the contents of the clipboard by moving the cursor to the desired insertion point and then pressing the Paste key on the keyboard or choosing Paste from the Edit menu. (The Edit menu is discussed in more detail later in this chapter.)

Let's demonstrate how to copy text:

1. Select the text to be copied.
2. Press the Copy key on the keyboard, or choose Copy from the Edit menu.
3. Position the pointer at the location where you want the selected text to appear.
4. Press the Paste key, or choose Paste from the Edit menu.

Let's look at an example of moving text by using the cut and paste feature. Suppose you have a document with several paragraphs and you want to swap the order of two of the paragraphs. You would do the following:

1. Select the entire first paragraph.
2. Press the Cut key on the keyboard, or choose Cut from the Edit menu.
3. Position the cursor after the end of the other paragraph.
4. Press the Paste key, or choose Paste from the Edit menu.

This is a convenient way to reposition text without having to reenter it.

Deleting Text

The simplest way to delete text character by character is to position the cursor at the deletion point and press the Delete key. This is often all that is necessary. However, there are other ways to delete text that you may find helpful and time-saving.

One method is to select the text and cut it. The cutting operation moves the deleted text to the clipboard, but you are not required to paste the deleted text. Cutting selected text is a perfectly good method for permanently deleting text.

You can also use the key combinations listed in Table 5.2 to delete characters. These are some of my favorites because I can delete multiple characters—either a word or a line—without removing my hands from the standard hand position.

Table 5.2 Key Combinations for Deleting Text

Key Combination	What It Does
Backspace	Deletes character to the left of cursor
Shift-Backspace	Deletes character to the right of cursor
Control-W	Deletes word to the left of cursor, including trailing spaces
Control-Shift-W	Deletes word to the right of cursor, including leading spaces
Control-U	Deletes from cursor to beginning of line
Control-Shift-U	Deletes from cursor to end of line

Saving Text to a File

The text that you enter or change in the Text Editor is not stored in a file until you save your changes. The File menu contains two items for saving files: Save Current File and Store as New File. If you are editing a file that already exists, all you need to do to save your changes is to press the Save Current File button on the File menu. If you are creating a new file, select Store as New File from the File menu. This selection displays the Text:Store pop-up window, which you use to specify the name and directory of the file you want created. You'll learn the details of how to save files in the File Menu section of this chapter.

The basic Text Editor commands you have learned in this section have provided you with enough information to create and edit files. With this understanding, you can accomplish most of your basic text editing operations. In the next sections we will discuss additional features of the Text Editor.

Text Editor Menus

The Text Editor contains four menu buttons in the control area: File, View, Edit, and Find. A menu is associated with each of these menu buttons. There is also a Text Pane pop-up menu, shown here, that is displayed when you press the MENU button with the pointer on the text pane:

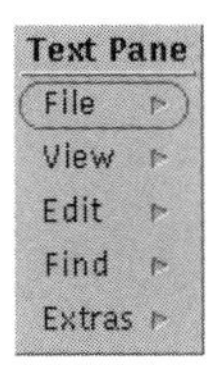

The Text Pane pop-up menu contains five menu buttons: File, View, Edit, Find, and Extras. Notice that the first four items on the menu are identical to the menu buttons on the control area. These four menu buttons are identical in function as well. When you press MENU on the menu button, the associated menu pops up. For example, you can display the File menu either by pressing MENU on the File menu button in the control area or by displaying the Text Pane pop-up menu and pressing MENU on the File menu button. The two menus are identical.

The File Menu

The File menu lets you save a file, load a file, include a file, and clear a file of its contents. The File menu looks like this:

Load File

When you select Load File on the File menu, the Load pop-up window is displayed, as shown here:

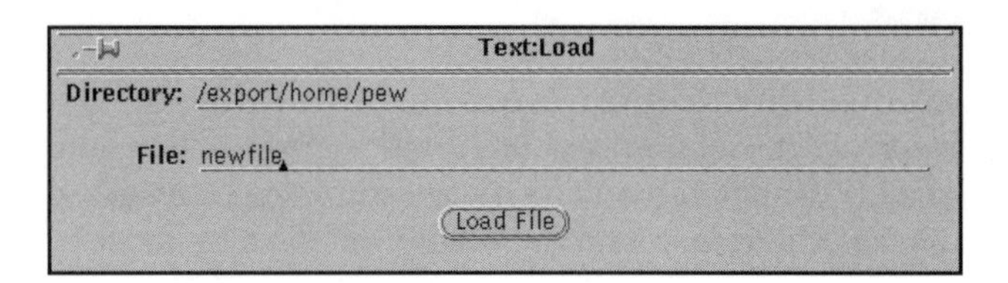

You enter the name of the directory and file that you want to edit in the Load window, and press the Load File button or the Return key. The file is then loaded into the Text Editor.

If you invoke the Text Editor without specifying an initial file, you can use this feature to load a file. You can also use this feature when you have finished editing one file and want to edit another file. Rather than exiting Text Editor or starting another Text Editor, you can load a new file into the existing Text Editor.

If you have been editing a new or existing file, and then you try to load a new file before saving your edits, the following notice will appear:

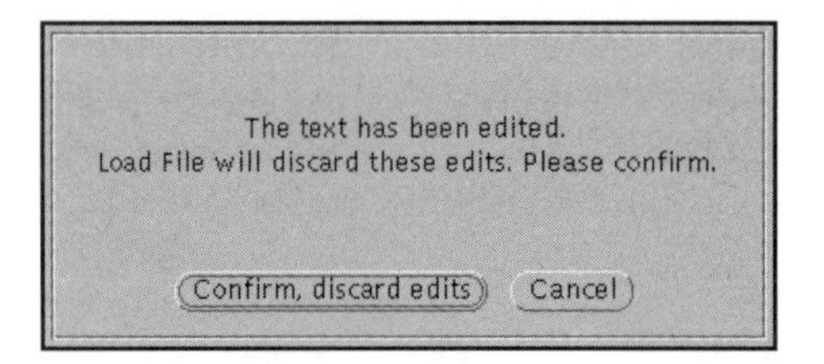

The Text Editor will not throw away your editing without your confirmation. You can either cancel the load-file operation or proceed with loading the new file, in which case your previous edits (since the last time you saved the file) will be lost. There may be times when you want to throw away your edits. If you begin editing a file and then change your mind about your edits, you can reload the same file (as it exists on the disk, without the edits) by displaying the Load pop-up window and entering the name of the file currently being edited. When the notice appears, choose “Confirm, discard edits.” The editing you have done will be discarded, and the file as it exists on the disk will be loaded into the Text Editor.

If you attempt to load a file that does not exist or that you do not have permission to read, a notice appears, informing you that the load was unsuccessful.

Save Current File

The second item on the File menu is Save Current File. When you select this item, the current file is saved to a disk. All the editing that you have done is now stored in the file. To save the current file, you must have a file name associated with the file you are editing. If you have loaded a file or invoked the Text Editor with a file-name command-line option, then you automatically have an associated file name. If, however, you invoke the Text Editor without a file name and just begin entering text, no file name is associated with the text, so you cannot yet save the file. You must first choose Store as New File from the File menu.

If you try to save the current file, and no file name is associated with the text or the file is not writable by you, the following message appears:

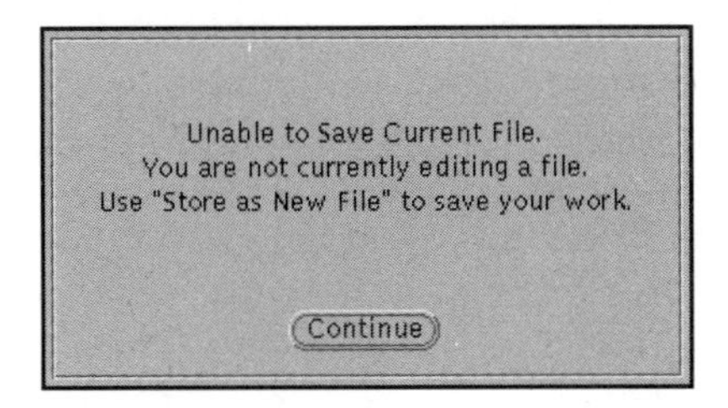

Store As New File

You select Store as New File from the File menu when you want to store the contents of the Text Editor as a new file. This may be a new file that you have created by entering new text, or it may be an existing file that you have made a few changes to and now want to save as a new file, leaving the original file unaltered. In either case, you use the Store pop-up window, as shown here:

Text:Store
Directory: /export/home/pew
File: chapter 5.txt
Store as New File

To store text as a new file, enter the name of the directory and file, and press the Store as New File button.

If you attempt to store the contents of the Text Editor in a file that already exists, and it is not the currently loaded file, the following notice is displayed, warning you that the file you have specified already exists:

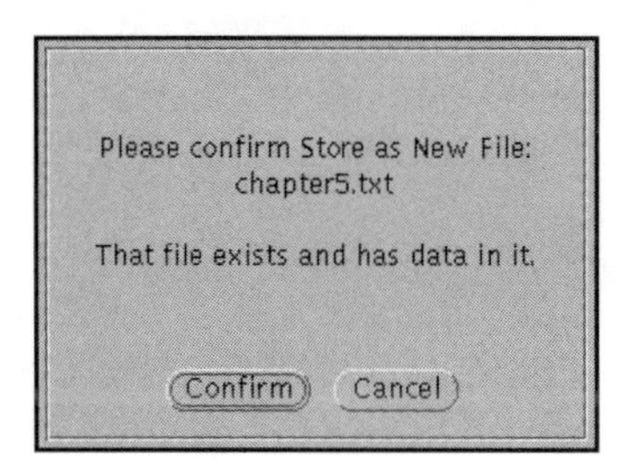

You can cancel the store operation, or you can confirm it. If you confirm it, the existing file will be overwritten with the new file.

Include File

The Include File item on the File menu opens a pop-up window that lets you include or merge a file with the existing text in the Text Editor. This process does not change the name of the currently loaded file, but simply merges the new file with the existing text at the cursor position. If text is currently selected, the included file replaces the selected text. You can use this feature to replace a word, a line, or a paragraph of selected text with the included file. The Include pop-up window is shown here:

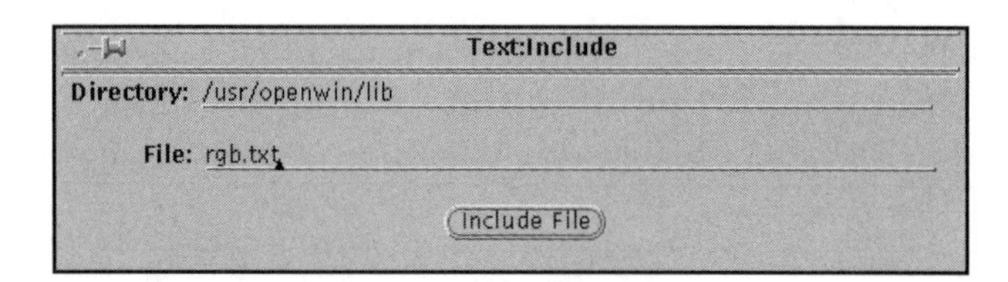

To include a file, enter the name of the directory and file, and press the Include File button.

Empty Document

The Empty Document item from the File menu clears the entire contents of the Text Editor. If the Text Editor contents have been edited, the following warning notice appears, requesting confirmation:

This feature is useful when you want to "start with a clean slate." If you were to save your changes after emptying the document contents, the file would not be deleted, but you would have an empty file.

The View Menu

The View menu lets you perform functions related to the way the file is viewed in the Text Editor's text pane. The View menu is shown here:

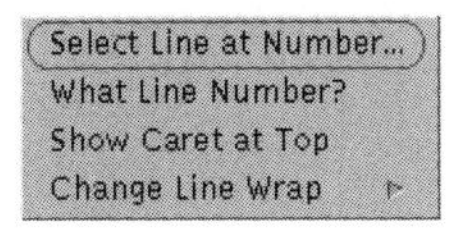

Select Line at Number

The Select Line at Number item on the View menu opens the Line Number pop-up window, which lets you select a specific line number. This feature is particularly useful when you are editing a large file and you need to go to a particular line in the file. If you are a programmer trying to compile a program, and the compiler complains of a syntax error at a given line, you can use the Line Number pop-up window to quickly go to that specific line. The Line Number pop-up window is shown here:

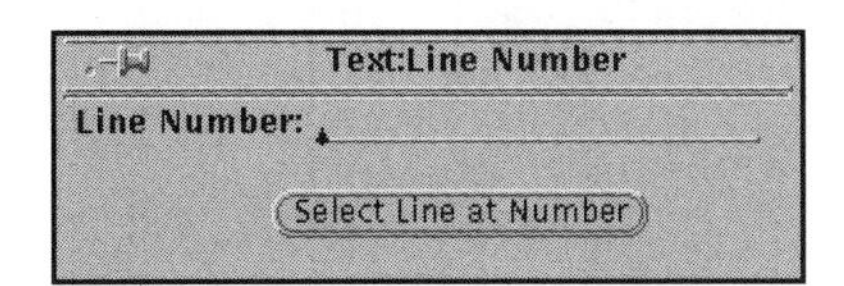

To use this pop-up window, enter the number of the line that you want to go to, and press the Select Line at Number button. The Text Editor highlights that line and automatically scrolls so that the line is displayed in the text pane.

What Line Number?

The What Line Number? item on the View menu lets you identify the line number of the selected text. To use this feature, you must first select some text. The size of the selection does not matter; you can select one character or the entire document. When you select What Line Number?, a notice appears, informing you of the line number of the selected text. If the selection spans multiple lines, the notice provides the line number of the first line of the selection.

Show Caret at Top

The Show Caret at Top item on the View menu lets you reposition the text in the text pane without changing the location of the cursor. When you press Show Caret at Top, the line containing the cursor moves to the third line from the top of the text pane.

Change Line Wrap

The Change Line Wrap item on the View menu displays the Change Line Wrap submenu, which gives you three choices: Wrap at Word, Wrap at Character, and Clip Lines. These choices are shown here:

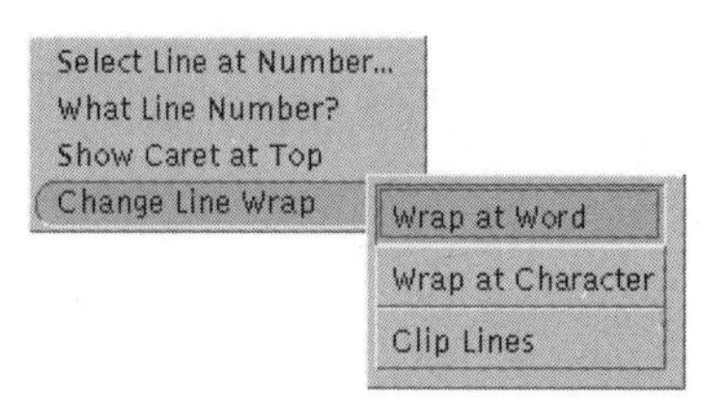

By default, the Text Editor wraps lines at word boundaries. This is the first choice on the Change Line Wrap submenu. Wrapping at word boundaries means that a word is never broken between two lines. If you select Wrap at Character, the lines will wrap at the exact point at which there is no more horizontal space. This could be in the middle of a word or between words.

The last choice, Clip Lines, means that there is no line wrapping. If a line is wider than the horizontal display area provided by the text pane, the line is clipped and no wrapping occurs. A line may continue past the visible right edge of the text pane, and the cursor will not be visible if it is positioned past the right border. The characters past the right border may not be visible, but they still exist.

Your choice of line-wrapping options is mostly a matter of personal preference. There may be times, however, when you will want to choose a particular line-wrapping style. For example, if you are getting ready to print a document that contains lines that wrap, and your printer clips long lines, you may want to choose Clip Lines to get a better idea of how the layout of the document will look on paper. If your printer automatically wraps long lines, it probably wraps at a particular character position, in which case choosing Wrap at Character would more accurately display the hard-copy output. The default wrapping mode wraps at word boundaries, because most documents are easier to read when they don't contain broken words.

The Edit Menu

The Edit menu provides five functions that let you manipulate text: Again, Undo, Copy, Paste, and Cut. These functions are also available through the keys with the same names. The same functions are performed whether you invoke them from the keyboard or from the Edit menu.

Again

The Again item on the Edit menu (or the Again key) repeats the most recent sequence of editing operations, including operations that involve entering characters, deleting characters, or moving the cursor with the keyboard. The editing operations that are considered part of the recent sequence begin with all operations since the last time you moved the cursor with the pointer or chose the Again operation. When you do one of these two operations, a new sequence of operations begins.

You can also invoke the Again operation by pressing Meta-A. (The Meta key is marked by a diamond [✦].)

Undo

The Undo item on the Edit menu lets you undo editing operations. From the Undo submenu you can choose to undo the last edit or all edits, as shown here:

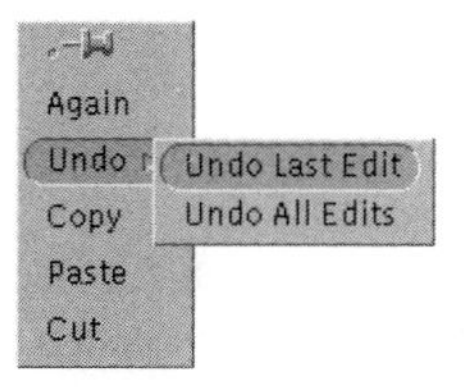

Pressing SELECT on the Undo item activates the default selection from the Undo submenu, which is usually Undo Last Edit. This undoes only the last editing operation. You can choose this item repeatedly to undo each previous editing operation until the file is back to the state it was in the last time you saved it. The Undo key also undoes the last edit operation.

The Undo All Edits item on the Undo submenu removes all editing since the file was loaded into the Text Editor or since the last save. Before all edits are undone, the following notice appears, requesting confirmation:

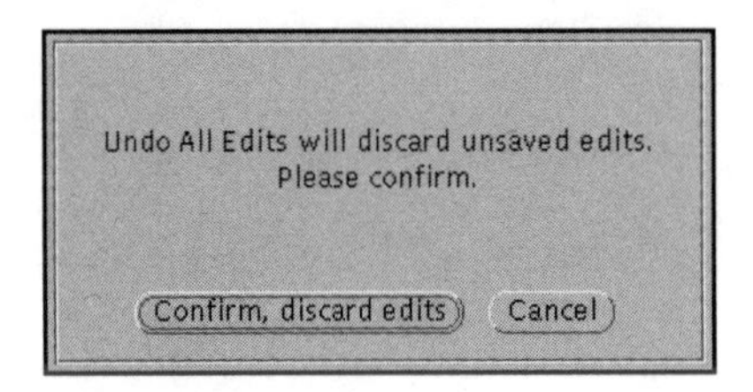

You can also invoke the Undo operation by pressing Meta-U.

Copy

Copying text requires that text be selected. Use the techniques described earlier in this chapter to select any number of characters, words, or lines. With text selected, choose Copy from the Edit menu, or press the Copy key. The selected text is then copied to the clipboard. If the clipboard already contains data, that data is replaced with the newly copied text. You will usually copy text with the intent to paste it somewhere. You can also invoke the copy operation by pressing Meta-C.

Paste

Pasting text requires that the clipboard contain text. When you choose Paste from the Edit menu, or press the Paste key, the contents of the clipboard are inserted at the cursor position. If you perform a paste operation when text is selected, the contents of the clipboard replace the selected text. You can also invoke the Paste operation by pressing Meta-V.

Cut

To cut text from the Text Editor, select the text, and choose Cut from the Edit menu or press the Cut key. The selected text is removed from the text pane and copied to the clipboard. You can cut text to permanently remove it from the text pane or to paste it in some other location. You can also invoke the cut operation by pressing Meta-X.

The Find Menu

The Find menu, shown below, includes items that help you find and replace text, and search for delimiters.

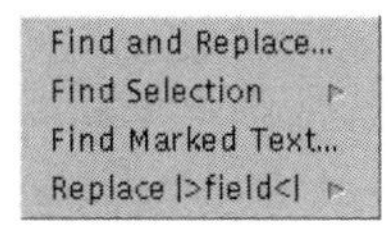

Find and Replace

The Find and Replace item on the Find menu activates the Find and Replace pop-up window, as shown here:

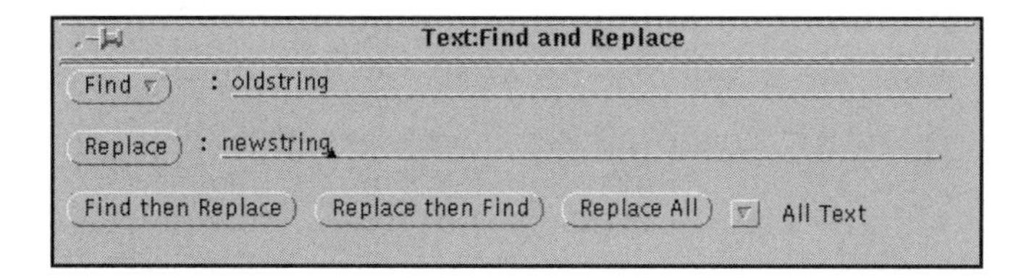

To find text, enter in the top text field the character string you want to search for, and click SELECT on the Find button. The Text Editor then searches forward from the cursor position to find the next occurrence of the string entered in the Find text field. If the string does not exist anywhere in the file, the text pane momentarily flashes and beeps. If the string does exist, it is selected. You can continue searching for the same string by pressing the Find button repeatedly. The search continues to the end of the file and then wraps around to the top of the file to start searching from the beginning of the file. If you plan to repeat a search, you should pin the pop-up window before pressing any buttons; otherwise the pop-up window will automatically pop down.

If you select text before displaying the Find and Replace pop-up window, the selected text is automatically inserted into the Find text field when the pop-up window is displayed. In addition, you can change the current contents of the Find text field by using the selected text. With the Find and Replace pop-up window displayed, select some text from the text pane. Then choose the Find and Replace item from the Find menu again. The selected text replaces the existing text in the Find text field. If you want to search for text that includes a carriage return, you must use this method, because you cannot type a carriage return into a text field on the Find pop-up window.

The Find button is actually a menu button; it displays a menu if you press the MENU mouse button. This menu allows you to change the direction of the search from forward to backward.

Below the Find button and text field are the Replace button and text field, which are used to replace text that has been found. When you press the Replace button, the text in the Replace text field replaces the text found as a result of the find operation. If the Replace text field is empty, the selected text is replaced with the empty string; in other words, that text is deleted.

The three buttons at the bottom of the Find and Replace pop-up window let you combine the find and replace operations.

Find then Replace finds the next occurrence of the find string and then replaces it with the replace string.

Replace then Find assumes that the current find string has been located and is selected. The selected text is replaced with the replace string, and then the next occurrence of the find string is found and highlighted.

Replace All replaces all the find strings with replace strings.

The abbreviated menu button next to the Replace All button allows you to determine the effect of the Replace All button. When you press MENU on the abbreviated menu button, a menu is displayed, showing two choices: All Text and To End. By default, All Text is chosen. This means that Replace All will replace all occurrences of the find string with the replace string. The To End choice will replace with the replace string all occurrences of the find string from the cursor position to the end of the file.

Find Selection

The Find Selection item on the Find menu lets you search for another occurrence of the currently selected text in the text pane. To use this feature you must first select some text. Then choose the Find Selection item from the Find menu, or press the Find key. The next occurrence of the selected text is found and highlighted.

You can reverse the direction of the search by displaying the Find Selection submenu and selecting Backward, or by pressing Shift-Find. If you press the Find key when no text is selected, then the Text Editor searches for the text in the Find text field of the Find and Replace pop-up window.

You can also invoke the Find operation by pressing Meta-F to search forward, or Shift-Meta-F to search backward.

Find Marked Text

The Find Marked Text item on the Find menu displays the Find Marked Text pop-up window, shown here:

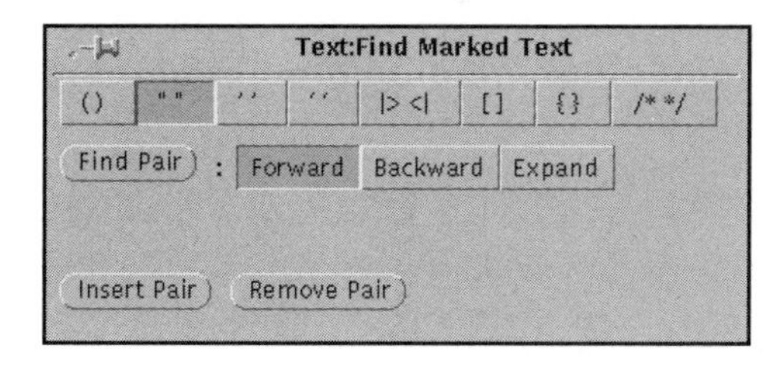

This feature lets you search for commonly used delimiters. These delimiters can be either inserted around text or deleted from text.

The Find Marked Text pop-up window provides eight common delimiter types in an exclusive setting. To search for one of the delimiters, select the delimiter from the exclusive setting and press the Find Pair button. The manner in which the search for the delimiter is conducted depends on the exclusive setting selection to the right of the Find Pair button. The choices are Forward, Backward, and Expand. The Forward and Backward choices determine the direction in which the search takes place.

The Expand choice means that the position of the cursor is expanded in both directions as it searches for a matching set of delimiters. In other words, the cursor must be positioned between the delimiters to find a match. This feature is particularly useful when you have nested pairs of delimiters, such as in a C program. Series of curly braces ({}) usually abound in C programs. You can use the Expand feature to find the innermost set of curly braces, and then press Find Pair again to find the next matching set of curly braces.

When a match is found, the text, including the delimiters, is highlighted, as shown in Figure 5.10.

The Insert Pair and Remove Pair buttons let you insert or remove a pair of delimiters. You will usually select text before using either of these functions, although you can insert a pair of delimiters without having any text selected. To insert a pair of delimiters, select some text and press the Insert Pair button. Before you can remove a pair of delimiters, the selected text must include and be bounded by the delimiters you want to delete. For example, let's say you want to uncomment a line of code in a C program. You first search for C comment delimiters: /* */. When you find the pair that encloses the code that you want to uncomment, you press the Remove Pair button. Only the delimiters are removed, not the text between the delimiters.

Figure 5.10
Marked text found and highlighted

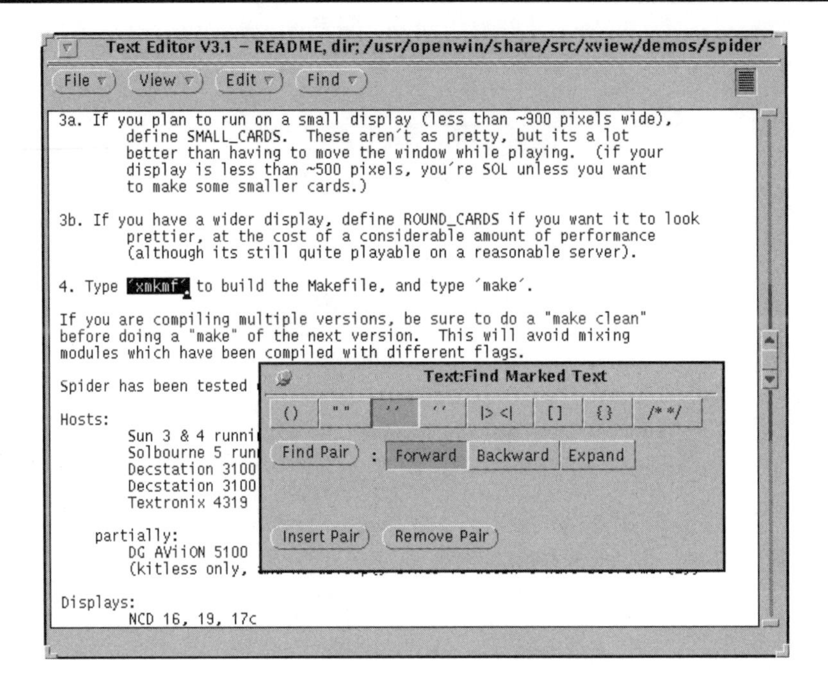

Replace

The Replace |>field<| item on the Find menu is a shortcut method for finding text delimited by the characters |> and <|. The submenu associated with this item lets you select Forward, Backward, or Expand exactly as you did with the Find Marked Text pop-up window.

The Extras Menu

The Extras menu, provided only on the Text Pane pop-up menu (an Extras menu button does not appear in the control area), lets you do some special formatting and inserting or removing of delimiters. Each item on the Extras menu invokes a command on the selected text. Here is the Extras menu:

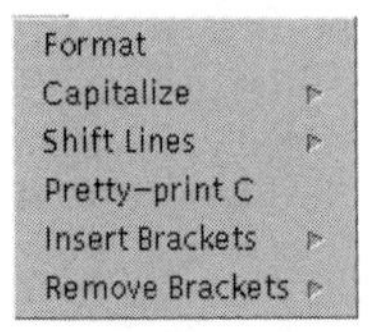

Format

The Format item on the Extras menu lets you format the selected text. All selected lines are reformatted to approximately 72 characters. Short lines are made longer, and long lines are made shorter. This feature is especially useful if you are writing text and the formatting of a paragraph is unbalanced because you have added or deleted text from one or more lines of the paragraph. Rather than reformatting the paragraph by hand (adding the appropriate carriage returns and joining the lines that are too short), you can select the entire paragraph and choose Format from the Extras menu. The paragraph is then reformatted all at once. Figure 5.11 shows a paragraph in the Text Editor before and after it has been formatted.

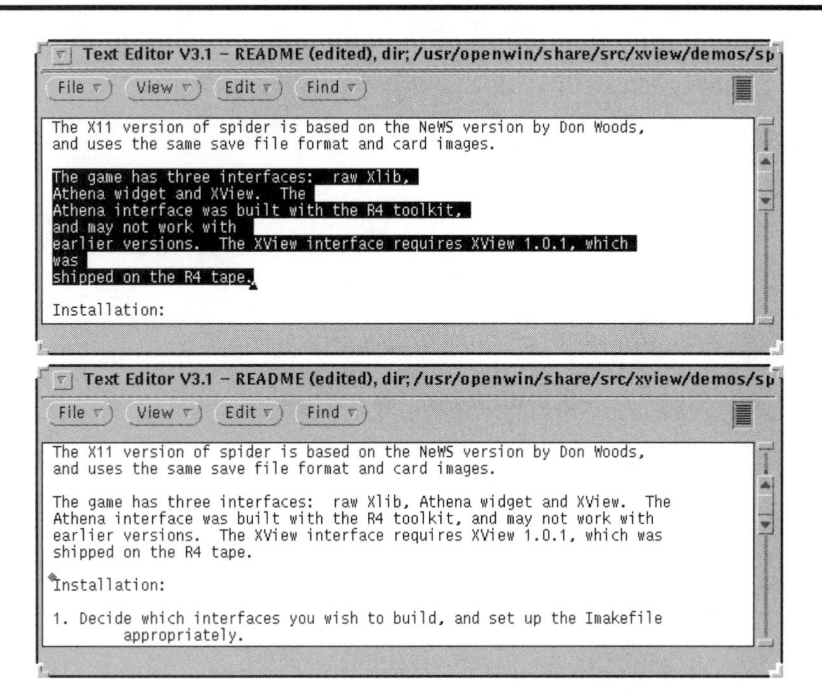

Figure 5.11
A paragraph before (top) and after (bottom) being reformatted

Capitalize

The Capitalize item on the Extras menu lets you change the case of selected text. You can choose to make the selected text all uppercase or all lowercase, or you can change the first character of each word to uppercase. The Capitalize submenu, as shown here, provides the type of capitalization performed:

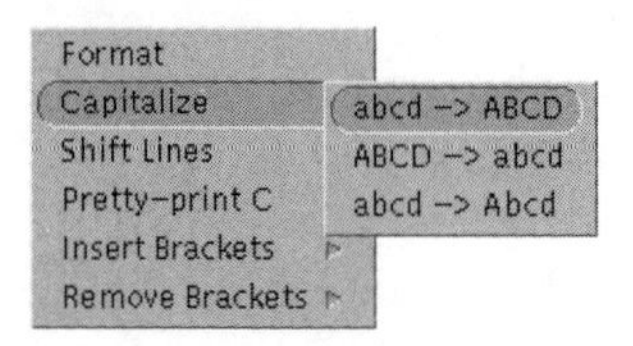

The first item on the Capitalize submenu, labeled abcd -> ABCD, changes all selected characters to uppercase regardless of their current case. This means that characters that are already uppercase will remain uppercase. The second item on the Capitalize submenu, ABCD -> abcd, changes all selected characters to lowercase regardless of their current case. The third item on the Capitalize submenu, abcd -> Abcd, changes the first character of each word to uppercase. The case of any other character in the word is unaffected, however. For example, if a selected word is all uppercase, choosing abcd -> Abcd will not affect that word.

Shift Lines

The Shift Lines item on the Extras menu shifts the selected lines by one tab stop. The Shift Lines submenu lets you select the direction of the shift: left or right.

Pretty-print C

The Pretty-print C item on the Extras menu formats the selected text according to standard C programming conventions.

Insert Brackets

The Insert Brackets item displays a submenu listing four common delimiters that can be inserted at the cursor or around the selected text. The brackets available from the submenu are ( ), [ ], { }, and " ", as shown here:

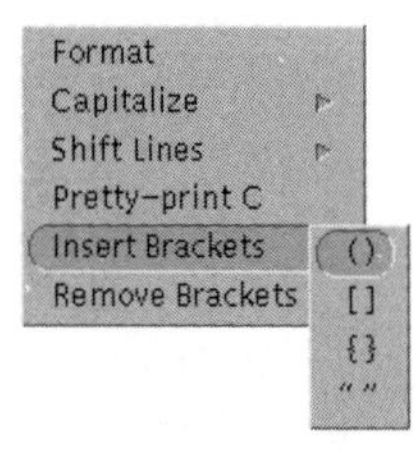

Remove Brackets

The Remove Brackets item also displays a submenu of the same four common delimiters listed in the Insert Brackets item. To remove the brackets from the submenu, you must be sure that the current selection includes the delimiters, and they must be the first and last characters of the selected text.

Other Features of the Text Editor

Thus far in this chapter, you have learned how to manipulate text in the Text Editor by using the Text Editor menus. There are other features available in the Text Editor, including splitting the text pane, using the drag and drop target, and customizing menus. These features are discussed in this section.

Splitting Text Panes in the Text Editor

The Text Editor pane can be split into multiple panes, allowing you to view different parts of the file being edited. This capability is particularly useful if you are editing a big file and you need to refer to a part of the document that would be otherwise out of view. You can have multiple panes, but each pane will contain the same file. You cannot load a different file into a second pane. As you make changes in one pane, you will notice that the changes are reflected in the other pane (if that part of the file is in view). Figure 5.12 shows a Text Editor that has been split into two panes.

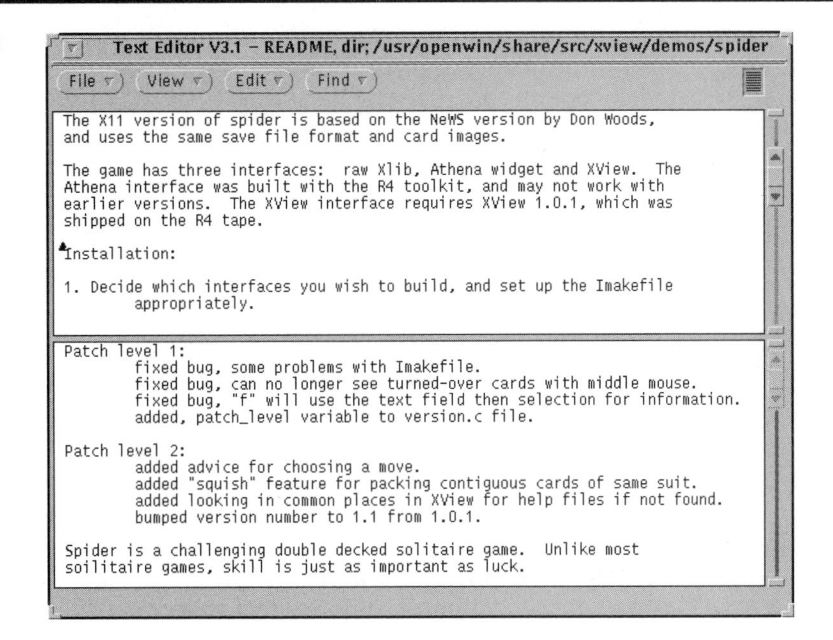

Figure 5.12
A Text Editor split into two panes

To split the text pane, follow these steps:

1. Position the pointer on the top or bottom scrollbar cable anchor. The cable anchors are the small rectangular buttons at both ends of the scrollbar.
2. Press SELECT and drag the pointer to the location where you want the pane to be split.
3. Release SELECT.

Now that the text pane is split, you will notice that each pane has its own scrollbar. You can repeat this process if you want to split the pane again. You can use either of the existing scrollbars.

To join two panes that have been split, follow these steps:

1. Position the pointer on the top scrollbar cable anchor.
2. Press SELECT and drag the pointer all the way to the bottom scrollbar cable anchor.
3. Release SELECT.

You can also split and join panes from the scrollbar pop-up menu. Press MENU with the pointer positioned anywhere along the scrollbar between the two cable anchors, and then select Split View from the pop-up menu to split the text pane. The position of the pointer when you pop up the scrollbar menu determines where the text pane will be split. After you have split the text pane, a new item appears on the scrollbar menu: Join Views. Select this item to join the two split panes.

Drag and Drop Features in the Text Editor

The Text Editor supports the drag and drop function. Entire files can be dragged to or from the Text Editor, or selected text can be dragged from or dropped onto the Text Editor.

The Drag and Drop Target

The Text Editor includes a drag and drop target on the right side of the control area. The drag and drop target has two purposes: it lets you drag the entire contents of the editor to another application, and it lets you load a new file into the Text Editor. When the text pane contains text, a text image appears inside the drag and drop target. If the drag and drop target does not contain a text image, then you cannot perform a drag from the drag and drop target. Figure 5.8 shows a drag and drop target without a text image. Figure 5.12 shows a drag and drop target with a text image.

To drag the contents of the Text Editor, you drag from the Text Editor's drag and drop target. There are several reasons why you might perform a drag and drop. For example, you could drag from the Text Editor and drop in the Print Tool to print the contents of the Text Editor. You could also drop onto the File Manager to create a new file, or drop onto the Mail Tool's Compose window to include the file in a mail message. When you drag from the drag and drop target, you are dragging the current contents of the Text Editor, not the file saved on a disk. This means that all the changes you have made will be included in the dragged file even if you have not yet saved them.

To drag the entire contents of the Text Editor, follow these steps:

1. Position the pointer on the drag and drop target, and press SELECT.
2. Drag the pointer to its destination, and release SELECT.

When you drag the pointer out of the drag and drop target, the pointer changes to the following shape, indicating that a drag and drop operation is in progress:

As you move the pointer, you will see the pointer image change. When the pointer is on a valid drop site, a bull's-eye appears in the pointer image, telling you that you can perform the drop there.

When the drag and drop target is used as the recipient of a drop, the file is loaded into the Text Editor, just as when you load a file by using the Load File pop-up window. The existing contents of the Text Editor are discarded. If changes have been made but not saved, a notice is displayed, as shown in Figure 5.13. You can choose to save the changes before loading the new file, discard the changes before loading the new file, or cancel the drop operation.

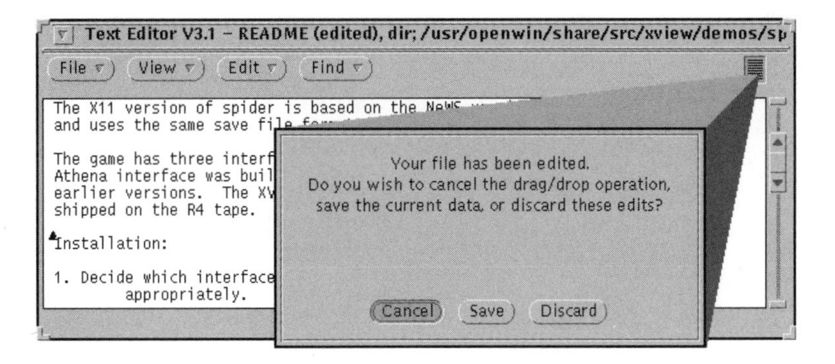

Figure 5.13
Dropping a file onto a modified Text Editor

Drag and Drop Operations from the Text Pane

You can use the text pane directly to perform a drag and drop operation. This capability is useful when you want to drag part of the file, but not all of it, to some other application, or when you want to drop a file or some text onto the text pane to insert it into the current file.

To drag text from the text pane you must first select text. Use the techniques you learned earlier in this chapter to select any amount of text—a few characters or many pages. Here are the steps required for dragging selected text from the Text Editor:

1. Select the text to be copied.
2. Position the pointer on the selected text, and press SELECT.
3. Drag the pointer to its destination, and release SELECT.

You may want to use this technique to print a portion of a file loaded into the Text Editor. For example, if you have a long document and you want to print only one paragraph, you can highlight that paragraph and drag and drop it onto the Print Tool. Only the portion you have selected will be printed.

Depending on the destination, you may find that the highlighted text is deleted from its original location when the drag and drop operation is complete. For example, if you select text from one Text Editor application and drop it onto the text pane of another Text Editor application, the highlighted text will be removed from the source Text Editor. If, however, you drag selected text from a Text Editor and drop it onto the Print Tool drag and drop target, the text will not be deleted from the text pane. Whether or not the highlighted text is deleted depends on the destination application. If you want to ensure that the text will not be deleted (that is, if you want it copied instead of moved), you can hold down the Control key before starting the drag and drop operation. For example, to drag text from one Text Editor to another without deleting the text, follow these steps:

1. Select the text to be copied.
2. Press and hold down the Control key.
3. Position the pointer on the selected text, and press SELECT.
4. Drag the pointer to its destination, and release SELECT.
5. Release the Control key. (Actually, you can release the Control key anytime after you have pressed SELECT. You don't have to wait until you have released SELECT.)

Holding down the Control key will always ensure that the text will not be removed. If you lose text during a drag and drop operation, use the Undo key to restore the lost text.

You can also drop a file or selected text onto the text pane. When you drop data onto the text pane, that data is inserted at the location of the pointer at the time of the drop. The data is inserted into the Text Editor; it does not discard any of the current contents. You can include an entire file by dragging a file icon from the File Manager and dropping it onto the text pane. Or, you can drag one line of selected text from a Command Tool and drop it onto the Text Editor text pane. In either case, the contents of the drag and drop are inserted at the location of the pointer when you release the SELECT button.

Drag and Drop Operations with Icons

You can drop a file onto the Text Editor icon. This process is the same as dropping a file onto the Text Editor's drag and drop target. The file being dropped will be loaded into the Text Editor, which automatically will be deiconified.

You can also drag a file or selected text from the Text Editor and drop it onto an icon. For example, you can drag a file from the Text Editor and drop it onto the Print Tool icon when you want to print the file.

Customizing Your Text Editor

The Text Editor provides several features that make it flexible—even flexible enough that you can customize it. You can modify the Extras menu to add new features according to your liking. You can also bind function keys to specific actions so that some of the features you most often use are easier to access.

Customizing the Extras Menu

The format and functions of the Extras menu are determined by the file /usr/lib/.text_extras_menu. This file determines the label for each item on the Extras menu and the function associated with each item. You can customize the Extras menu by copying this file to your home directory and modifying it. You can use what you have learned in this chapter to edit your copy of the .text_extras_menu file with the Text Editor. Figure 5.14 shows the default .text_extras_menu file when it is loaded in the Text Editor.

The format of the .text_extras_menu file is fairly self-explanatory. Lines that begin with # are comments. Each item enclosed in double quotation marks on the left side is the string displayed on the Extras menu. The corresponding expression on the right is the command that is executed when that item is selected. If the expression on the right is MENU, then the item displays a submenu. The items on the submenu are determined by the indented lines beneath MENU until the item with the END expression is encountered. (This format is the same format you use for creating custom Workspace menus, which you will learn more about in Chapter 10.)

Figure 5.14
The .text_extras_menu file

Text Editor V3.1 – .text_extras_menu, dir; /usr/lib

File ▽ View ▽ Edit ▽ Find ▽

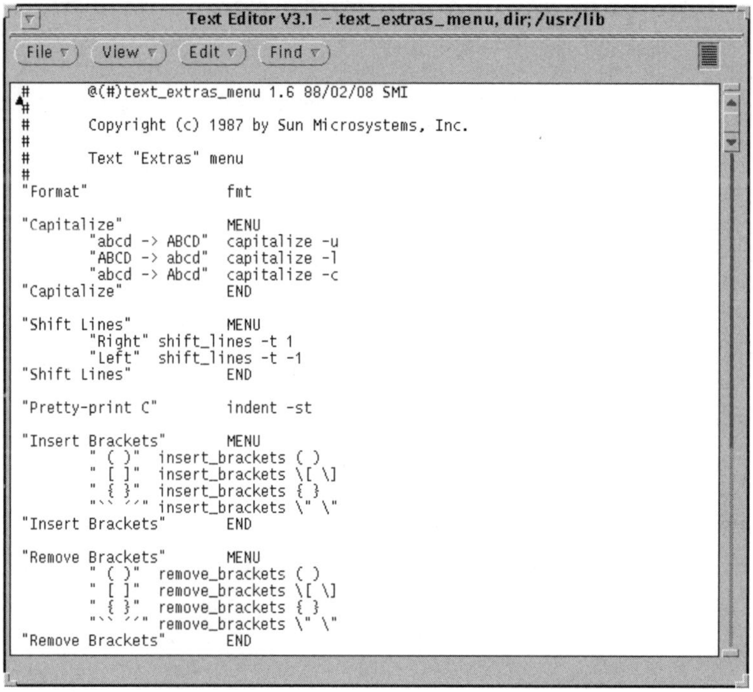

```
#       @(#)text_extras_menu 1.6 88/02/08 SMI
#
#       Copyright (c) 1987 by Sun Microsystems, Inc.
#
#       Text "Extras" menu
#
"Format"                fmt

"Capitalize"            MENU
        "abcd -> ABCD"  capitalize -u
        "ABCD -> abcd"  capitalize -l
        "abcd -> Abcd"  capitalize -c
"Capitalize"            END

"Shift Lines"           MENU
        "Right" shift_lines -t 1
        "Left"  shift_lines -t -1
"Shift Lines"           END

"Pretty-print C"        indent -st

"Insert Brackets"       MENU
        " ( )"  insert_brackets ( )
        " [ ]"  insert_brackets \[ \]
        " { }"  insert_brackets { }
        "`` ''" insert_brackets \" \"
"Insert Brackets"       END

"Remove Brackets"       MENU
        " ( )"  remove_brackets ( )
        " [ ]"  remove_brackets \[ \]
        " { }"  remove_brackets { }
        "`` ''" remove_brackets \" \"
"Remove Brackets"       END
```

To demonstrate how the Extras menu can be customized, let's add three entries to the .text_extras_menu file, as shown in Figure 5.15. This new .text_extras_menu creates a new item on the Extras menu and a new item on both the Insert Brackets and Remove Brackets submenus. The Expand item on the Extras menu will run the expand command on the selected text. The Expand command replaces tabs with the appropriate number of spaces. The two brackets submenus will add or remove the angle brackets (<>). Figure 5.16 shows the new Extras menu. The .text_extras_menu file affects not only the Text Editor's Extras menu but also other DeskSet applications that include an Extras menu, including Command Tool and Mail Tool.

Using Function Keys

You can use the function keys (F1, F2..., R1, R2...) on your keyboard to perform editing operations. The function keys do not have any default actions associated with them. If you want to use the function keys for the Text Editor, you must create the .textswrc file in your home directory. There is a sample .textswrc file in the /usr/lib directory. You can copy this file into your home directory and use it as is, or modify it to your particular needs.

Figure 5.15
A customized .text_extras_menu

Text Editor V3.1 – .text_extras_menu (edited), dir; /export/home/pew

File View Edit Find

```
#       @(#)text_extras_menu 1.6 88/02/08 SMI
#
#       Copyright (c) 1987 by Sun Microsystems, Inc.
#
#       Text "Extras" menu
#
"Format"                fmt

"Expand"                expand

"Capitalize"            MENU
        "abcd -> ABCD"  capitalize -u
        "ABCD -> abcd"  capitalize -l
        "abcd -> Abcd"  capitalize -c
"Capitalize"            END

"Shift Lines"           MENU
        "Right" shift_lines -t 1
        "Left"  shift_lines -t -1
"Shift Lines"           END

"Pretty-print C"        indent -st

"Insert Brackets"       MENU
        " ( )"  insert_brackets ( )
        " [ ]"  insert_brackets \[ \]
        " { }"  insert_brackets { }
        "`` ''" insert_brackets \" \"
        " < > " insert_brackets \< \>
"Insert Brackets"       END

"Remove Brackets"       MENU
        " ( )"  remove_brackets ( )
        " [ ]"  remove_brackets \[ \]
        " { }"  remove_brackets { }
        "`` ''" remove_brackets \" \"
        " < > " remove_brackets \< \>
"Remove Brackets"       END
```

Figure 5.16
The Extras menu with modifications

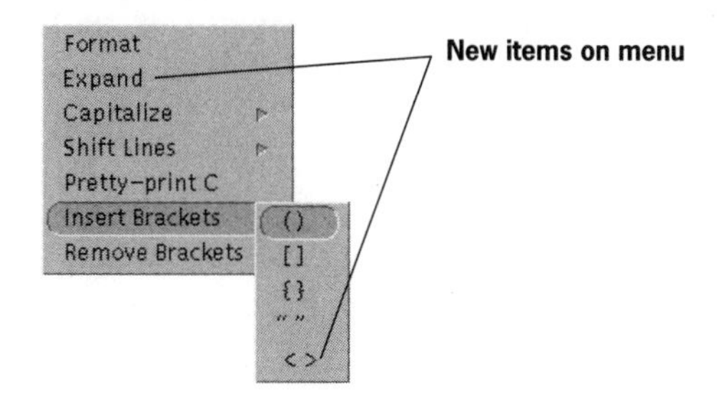

The entries in the .textswrc file have the following format:

```
key name            FILTER
command
```

For example, here is one of the entries in the .textswrc file found in /usr/lib:

```
R4                  FILTER
capitalize
```

When you press the R4 function key, the selected text is capitalized. You can add your own entries to the .textswrc file. If you want to bind the expand command to the F2 function key, you add the following entry:

```
F2                  FILTER
expand
```

If you include a command that does not exist or that cannot be located in your search path, no change is made when the function key is pressed.

If you use the sample .textswrc file in /usr/lib, you may find that some of the function keys don't seem to work. If a function key does not work as expected, try holding down the Meta key while pressing the function key. This may be necessary because some of the function keys are also used for other purposes, such as moving the cursor.

Customization Resources for the Text Editor, Command Tool, and Shell Tool

There are many ways that Text Editor, Command Tool, and Shell Tool can be customized. You can specify such things as margins, line spacing, and tab width. These customization features are enabled when you add an entry to your .Xdefaults file (see Chapter 3).

Table 5.3 lists some of the most common customization features. The table includes the name of the feature, the default value, and a brief description of the feature. To set one of these features, you must add an entry to your .Xdefaults file in the following format:

```
FeatureName: value
```

For example, to set the top margin to 7 lines, the entry would look like this:

```
text.margin.top: 7
```

After you have added entries to your .Xdefaults file, you must load them into the resource database with the xrdb command:

```
dugout% xrdb .Xdefaults
```

This process will not change the behavior of any running Shell Tool, Command Tool, or Text Editor. It will affect only the new invocations of these tools that you start after loading the new .Xdefaults file. Another way to make the new features in your .Xdefaults file take effect is to exit the OpenWindows environment and restart it.

These customization resources also affect Mail Tool's Compose and View windows.

Table 5.3 **Customization Resources**

Feature	Default Value	Description
text.extrasMenuFilename	/usr/lib/.text_extras_menu	The file used for the Extras menu. This file can be set to any absolute pathname.
text.autoIndent	False	When True, begins the next line at the same indentation as the previous line.
text.autoScrollBy	1	The number of lines to scroll when newly entered text has moved insertion point below the view. Valid values range from 0 to 100.
text.undoLimit	50	The number of operations to remember in the undo history log. Valid values range from 50 to 500.
text.confirmOverwrite	True	Specifies whether user confirmation is required to overwrite an existing file when storing the history log.
text.lineBreak	Wrap_word	Determines how text that is too long to fit within the horizontal space provided will be wrapped. Valid values are Clip, Wrap_char, and Wrap_word.
text.margin.bottom	0	The number of lines to allow as the bottom margin.
text.storeChangesFile	True	When True, the name of the current file being edited is changed to the name of the file that is stored.

Table 5.3 Customization Resources (Continued)

Feature	Default Value	Description
text.margin.top	0	The number of lines to allow as the top margin.
text.margin.left	0	The number of pixels to allow as the left margin.
text.margin.right	0	The number of pixels to allow as the right margin.
text.tabWidth	8	The width of the tab characters. Valid values are from 0 to 50.
text.lineSpacing	0	Changes the spacing between lines relative to the size of the font.

Summary

In this chapter you have learned many techniques for entering and manipulating text. These skills apply to both the terminal emulators (the Shell Tool and the Command Tool) and the Text Editor, as well as to other DeskSet applications like the Mail Tool and to many other applications that are not part of the DeskSet. Using the skills you have learned in this chapter for working with text will greatly facilitate your everyday use of the OpenWindows environment.

CHAPTER

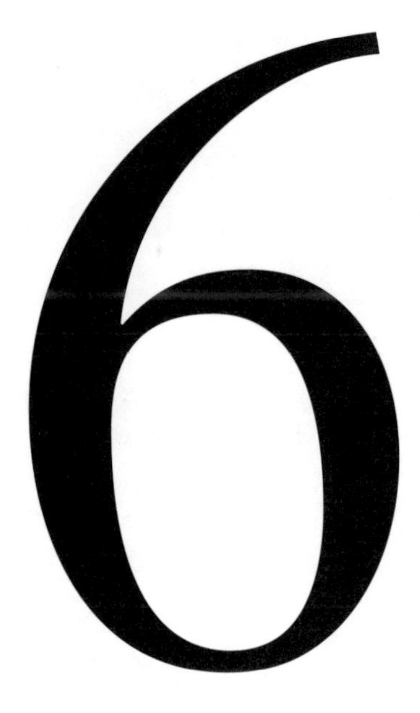

The Mail Tool

Mail Tool Basics

Composing Mail Messages

Receiving Mail Messages

Organizing Mail Messages

Customizing the Mail Tool

OF ALL THE DESKSET PROGRAMS, THE MAIL TOOL IS PROBABLY THE most important. It may also be the one that you will use the most often. The Mail Tool allows you to send and receive electronic mail messages (e-mail) to other users connected to your network. If your system or network is connected to the outside world, you can potentially send e-mail to thousands of users across the country and around the world.

The Mail Tool provides a graphical user interface to the SunOS mail program that is compatible with UNIX mail systems from any UNIX system vendor. Local and regional networks are becoming more and more common, enabling users to easily communicate with colleagues and associates outside their immediate environments. Phone lines also connect hundreds of company and personal UNIX system sites, increasing the already abundant numbers of users with whom you can send and receive mail.

The Mail Tool lets you easily send, receive, and organize mail messages. Messages are usually comprised of text but can also include attached files that may contain voice mail, images, executables, or any other available file type. This feature gives the Mail Tool multimedia capabilities.

In this chapter you will learn how to do the following:

- Compose mail messages
- Include one mail message with another
- Attach a file
- Manipulate attachments
- Include audio attachments
- Use templates
- Receive mail messages
- Reply to mail messages
- Delete mail messages
- Save mail messages
- Use drag and drop with the Mail Tool
- Organize your mail messages
- Customize the Mail Tool

Mail Tool Basics

To start the Mail Tool, choose Mail Tool from the Programs menu, as shown in Figure 6.1.

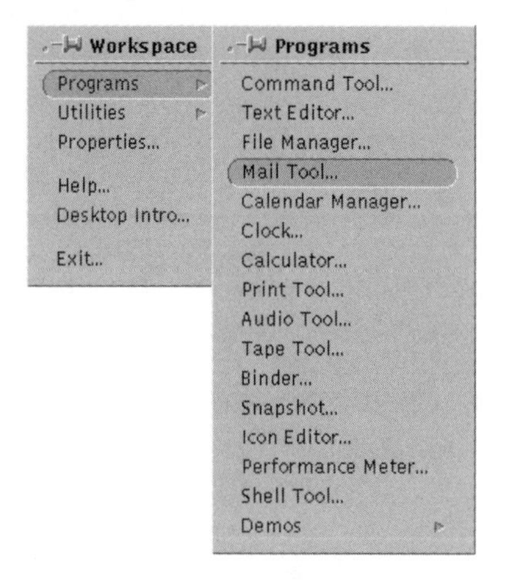

Figure 6.1 Starting the Mail Tool from the Programs menu

You can also start the Mail Tool by entering the mailtool command at the prompt:

```
dugout% mailtool &
```

When the Mail Tool is first invoked, it appears as an icon that looks like an office in-box. When there are no mail messages to be read, the In-Box is empty. When there are new mail messages to be read, the In-Box contains addressed and stamped envelopes. When messages have been read but not discarded, the In-Box contains neatly stacked envelopes. The three Mail Tool icons are shown here:

The Mail Tool includes three basic windows: the Header window, the View Message window, and the Compose Message window. The Header window contains a list of mail messages that you have received but have neither deleted nor moved to another mail file. When you double-click SELECT on one of the messages listed in the Header window, the View Message window appears, showing the contents of the message. Figure 6.2 shows the Header window and the View Message window (displaying message 2).

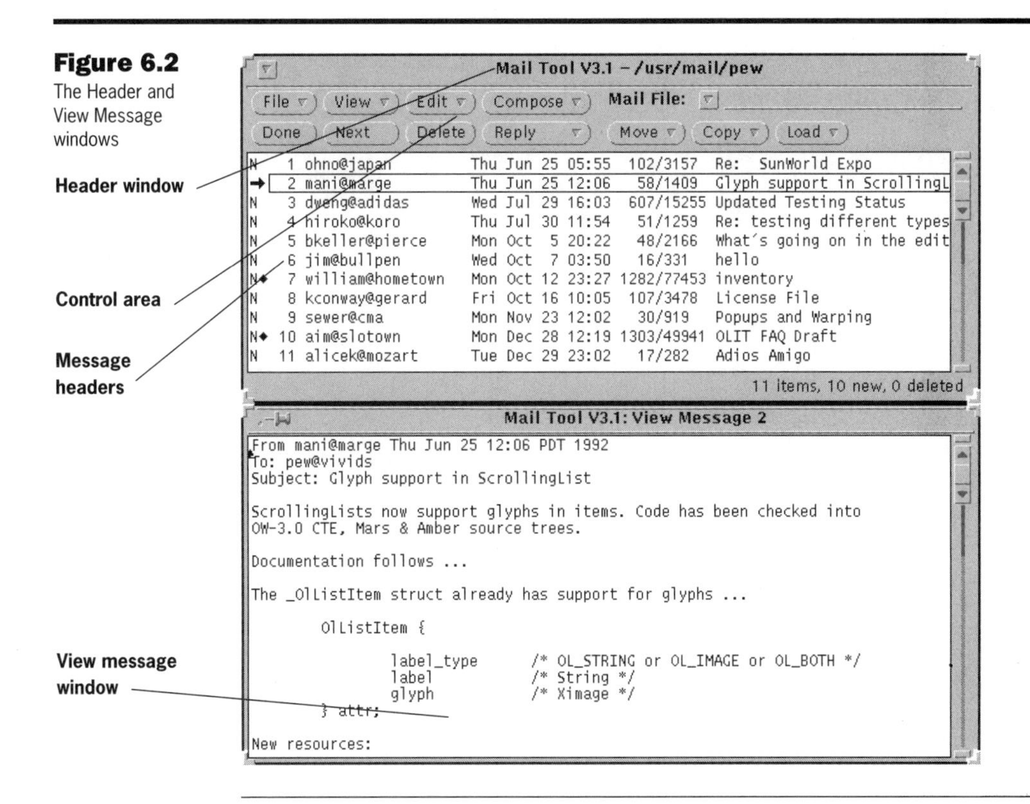

Figure 6.2
The Header and View Message windows

When you want to send a message, either as a reply to a message you have received or as a new message, you use a Compose Message window. Figure 6.3 shows a message being composed in a Compose Message window.

The Compose Message window iconifies independently of the Header and View Message windows. You can start multiple Compose Message windows, and each will iconify separately. The Compose Message window icon looks like this:

The Mail Tool is a sophisticated program that has many options and customizable features. However, the basic sending and receiving of mail messages is really quite simple. You need only a few instructions to get started. Let's start with receiving messages.

Figure 6.3
The Compose Message window

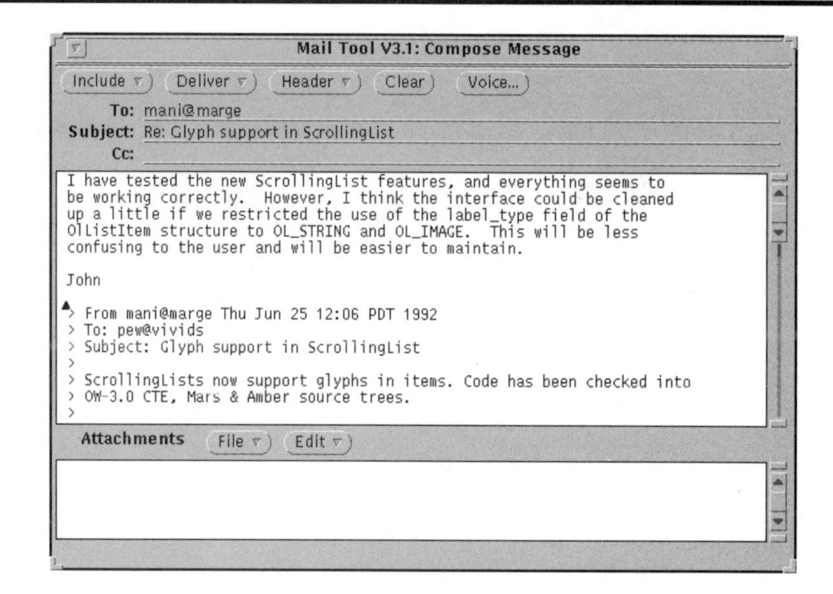

When you receive a new message, you see the Mail Tool icon change and you hear a beep. Deiconify the Mail Tool to display the Header window. The Header window displays header information about each mail message in the In-Box. The first new message is displayed with a rectangular box surrounding it. Position the pointer on the header of the new message, and double-click SELECT. The View Message window appears, showing the contents of the mail message.

After reading the message, you have several choices: you can delete the message, reply to the message, save the message, or leave the message in the In-Box. You use the buttons in the control area at the top of the Header window to make your choice. Press the Delete button if you want to delete the message. Press the Reply button if you want to reply to the message. You can save the message to a mail file by using the Move and Copy buttons. We'll talk more about saving and organizing messages in mail files later in this chapter.

If you do not delete the message, it stays in the In-Box. You view the next message by pressing the Next button. The rectangular box moves forward to the next message in the Header window, and the View Message window is loaded with the contents of the next mail message.

To send mail, you must bring up a Compose Message window. You display a Compose Message window by pressing either the Compose or the Reply button in the Header window. If you press the Compose button, the Compose Message window is displayed with an empty header. You must then fill in the To and Subject fields. If you press the Reply button, the Compose

Message window is displayed with the header already filled in. The To field contains the name of the person from whom you have received mail. The Subject field contains the same subject as the received message, preceded by Re:. When you have finished composing your message, press the Deliver button to send the mail.

There is much more to learn about the Mail Tool, but what you have learned so far in this chapter will enable you to read and send basic mail messages. In the next few sections you will learn more of the details and advanced features about sending and receiving messages.

Composing Mail Messages

To send a mail message, you must display a Compose Message window. You do this by pressing either the Compose or the Reply button on the Header window. Both of these are menu buttons, which means that when you press MENU with the pointer on the button a pop-up menu appears. Here is the Compose pop-up menu:

The first item on the Compose pop-up menu is New. Because it is the default selection, New is automatically selected when you press SELECT on the Compose button. When you choose New, a Compose Message window is displayed with no header information included—that is, the To, Subject, and Cc fields are all blank.

The second item on the Compose menu is Reply. The Reply item includes an arrow, indicating that a submenu will appear when you drag the pointer to the right. That submenu is identical to the menu displayed with the Reply button on the Header window. We'll come back to the Reply options after we finish our discussion of the Compose menu.

The third item on the Compose menu is Forward. You use this feature when you want to forward a mail message to another user. A Compose Message window is displayed with the To field blank and the Subject field filled in with the subject of the message you are forwarding. The text pane area of the Compose Message window is automatically loaded with the mail message that you are forwarding.

The last item on the Compose menu is Vacation. You use the vacation feature to automatically respond to messages you receive when you are on vacation. You will learn about the vacation feature later in this chapter.

The Reply button on the Header window lets you bring up a Compose Message window to reply to a message you have received. Here is the Reply pop-up menu:

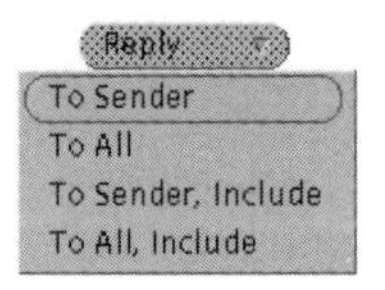

Each of the four items on the Reply menu allows you to reply to the message in a slightly different way. For example, you can use the To Sender item to reply to just the sender of the message, or you can use the To All item to reply to the sender and all the other recipients of the message, including yourself. Of course, if you were the only recipient, then sending the reply to all would be the same as sending the reply to the sender.

You can also use either the To Sender, Include item or the To All, Include item to include the message you are replying to. The receiver of the reply often finds it useful to see the original message so that he or she knows which message you are replying to. You may also want to include the message with your reply whenever you want to make specific comments about parts of the original message.

Using the Mail Tool Compose Message Window

The Mail Tool Compose Message window, shown previously in Figure 6.3, includes a control area, a text pane, and an attachment area. The control area includes several buttons and three text fields. The buttons help you to construct and send your message. The text fields let you specify the recipient of the message, the subject of the message, and the recipient of a copy of the message. The text pane is where you enter the main body of your message. You manipulate this text pane in the same way that you manipulate the Text Editor text pane. The Mail Tool text pane includes the text pane pop-up menu with the same features that were discussed in Chapter 5. The attachment area lets you attach other files to your message. Attachments appear as icons in the attachment area, much like the icons that appear in the File Manager.

Specifying a Recipient and a Subject

Before you send a message, you must specify a recipient in the To field of the Compose Message window. The exact details of how you specify a recipient depends on your network and how you are connected to it. The basic format for specifying a recipient is to enter the recipient's user ID. For example, if you want to send mail to a user whose user ID is *sally*, you would enter **sally** in the To field. You may be required to also include in the To field the name of sally's system. (Check with your system administrator to see if this is required.) You include the system name in the To field by appending an @ to the user ID and then adding the host name. For example, if you wanted to send mail to *sally* on the host name *dugout*, you would specify **sally@dugout** in the To field. If you are sending mail to someone outside your local network, you may have to provide a more complex address. Check with your system administrator for help with addressing complex mail addresses.

You can include more than one recipient in the To field. There is no limit to the number of recipients allowed in the To field. To add recipients, enter all the user IDs, separating each one by either a comma or a space.

The Cc field is used to "carbon copy" the message to other users. It doesn't matter if you include a user ID in the To field or in the Cc field. In either case, the message will be delivered to the specified user. Of course, you usually will have at least one recipient specified in the To field before you will use the Cc field. If you do choose to use the Cc field, you can specify multiple users the same way that you did in the To field: by separating each user ID with a space or a comma. Here is an example of the header area of the Compose Message window with the To, Subject, and Cc fields filled in:

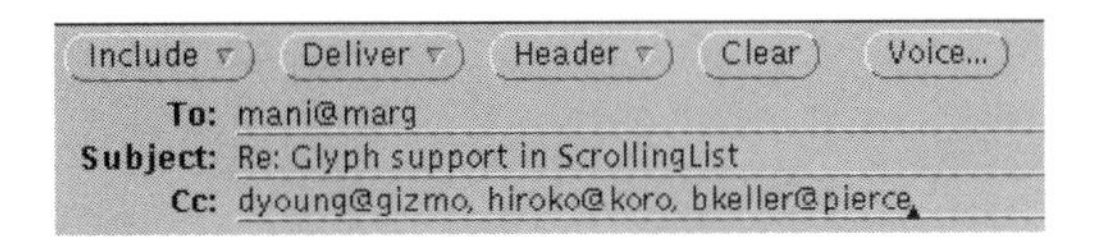

You can also specify a mail file as one of the recipients. We will talk in detail about mail files later in this chapter when we discuss organizing your mail. For now, you can just think of a mail file as a storage place for messages. When you want a copy of a mail message to be added to a mail file, include the name of the file in the To or Cc fields with a plus sign before it. For example, to add the message to the programs file, add **+programs** to the To or Cc fields. The message will be sent to the specified recipients and to the programs mail file. This is like making a photocopy of a letter you write and filing it in your file cabinet for future reference.

The header contains one more field that lets you specify a recipient. An optional text field, labeled Bcc, can be displayed below the Cc text field. Bcc stands for "Blind carbon copy." You can use this feature if you want to send the message to someone but you don't want the other recipients to know that it went to that person. Everyone who receives the message can see the To and Cc fields and therefore know exactly who this message has been delivered to. Using the Bcc field is a way to keep a recipient from being known by the other recipients.

To display the Bcc field in the Compose Message window, you use the Header menu button. When you press MENU with the pointer on the Header button, the Header pop-up menu is displayed, as shown here:

If you select the Add Bcc item from the menu, the Bcc text field is added to the header, as shown here:

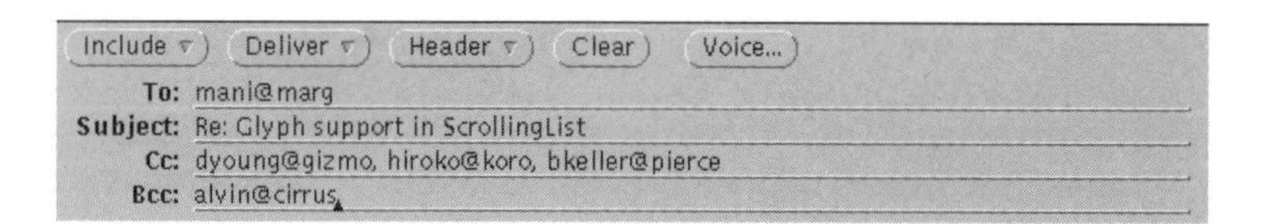

The Header menu also includes an item labeled Aliases. When you select this item, the Aliases Properties window is displayed. (We will talk about the Aliases Properties window in some detail later in this chapter.) You use the Aliases Properties window to reference mail aliases that you have established. Mail aliases are used as a shorthand to represent several recipients and make it easier to send mail to groups of users. It is often convenient to refer to your aliases when you are specifying recipients.

The Subject field of the Compose Message window lets you specify a subject for the mail message. You do not have to specify a subject, but it is usually considered good e-mail etiquette to include one. When the recipients receive the mail message, the subject field is included as part of the message summary displayed in the Header window. This makes it easy for the recipient to quickly ascertain the subject of the message. The Subject field is also the place to specify the importance of the message. You may need immediate action or a quick reply. When I compose such a message, I use the word URGENT in the subject field. This helps bring the message to the attention of the recipient and increases the probability that I will get a quick response.

Composing the Message

The text pane of the Compose Message window is just like the text pane of the Text Editor. It has the same Text Pane pop-up menu with the same features that you learned about in Chapter 5. Before you begin composing a message, make sure that input focus is in the text pane. You do this by clicking SELECT with the pointer over the text pane. You can determine the location of the input focus by locating the black triangular cursor. The cursor will be either in one of the text fields in the header or in the text pane.

You compose a mail message simply by typing into the text pane. You can, of course, use any of the editing features you learned about in Chapter 5 to add text to the text pane. For example, you might want to highlight text in another application, like the Text Editor or a Command Tool, and use copy and paste to copy text into the Compose Message window's text pane. Or, perhaps you are sending mail to your system administrator, asking for help on a command you are having trouble with. You could highlight the text from a Command Tool and copy it into your mail message. Doing this will help the system administrator better understand and solve your problem. You can also include or load files into the text pane by using the File menu of the Text Pane pop-up menu. Recall from Chapter 5 that the File menu has two items you can select to either load or include a file. In either case, a pop-up window is displayed in which you enter the directory and name of the file you want to either include or load.

Another easy way to include files in the text pane is to use drag and drop. You can drag a file from the File Manager and drop it directly onto the text pane. Any existing text will not be deleted, and the file will be inserted into the existing text at the position of the pointer when the drop takes place.

A feature that I often use when composing a mail message is the Format option from the Extras menu. While I'm composing a message, I often go back and rephrase a sentence or delete some text. Doing this can result in lines of uneven lengths. Rather than go through each line to insert the appropriate carriage returns and to join short lines, I highlight all the text that I want reformatted and select Format from the Extras menu. This feature makes all the lines of my selection the correct length and makes the text much more readable.

Besides knowing how to use the available features to compose mail messages, it is also important to know how to compose the text. Here are a few rules of etiquette that are important to keep in mind when composing mail messages:

- *Reread your message before sending it.* It takes just a minute to proofread your message before sending it. It is so easy to make a mistake, such as misspelling or omitting a word. A quick proofread can catch these simple mistakes. The message doesn't have to be perfect, but careless mistakes can frustrate the reader.

- *Use standard line lengths.* By default, the Compose Message window uses a font that can accommodate approximately 80 characters per line. If you resize your Compose Message window to something wider than the default, you can easily enter more than 80 characters when you compose your message. If the recipient uses the default configuration for the View Message window, the format of your message will look jumbled. Long lines will wrap near the end of the line and make the message hard to read. Remember your reader, and keep the line lengths to no more than 80 characters.
- *Avoid emotionally charged exclamations.* When reading your message, the reader cannot hear your tone of voice. A capitalized word or an exclamation mark can be interpreted as an angry tone. Be careful! Some things are communicated better in person or on the phone.
- *Be complete yet brief.* Get the point across, but use words economically. Your reader is much more likely to read and respond to your message if you avoid rambling.
- *Use the narrowest list possible for the recipient list.* I often receive 100 or more mail messages in a single day. Keeping on top of my mail is a time-consuming task. The last thing I want to receive are messages that don't apply to me (sometimes called junk mail). When you reply to mail sent to multiple recipients, don't automatically send the reply to All. Send the reply to only those who need the information.

Common courtesy and common sense go a long way when composing messages.

Including a Message

You use the Include menu button in the Compose Message window header to include a previously written mail message within a message you are composing. The message or messages that you select in the Header window are copied into the text pane of the Compose Message window. You use this feature when you want to forward a message to another user or when you are responding to a message and you want to include a copy of the original message within the response.

The Include menu has four items to choose from:

Bracketed includes the mail message, with delimiters inserted at the beginning and end of the message. The line "----- Begin Included Message -----" is inserted at the beginning of the message. The line "----- End Included Message -----" is inserted at the end of the message.

Indented includes the mail message, with each line preceded by a right-angle bracket (>).

Templates includes a standard template for scheduling with the Calendar Manager. You can also add other customized templates. You will learn how to create customized templates in the section "Customizing the Mail Tool," which appears later in this chapter.

Hide Attachments hides the attachments area of the Compose Message window. When attachments are hidden, this item on the menu becomes "Show Attachments." Attachments are discussed in the next section.

Both the Bracketed and Indented items on the Include menu copy the message into the text pane of the Compose Message window. Each item has its advantages. I use Bracketed when I want to include an entire message as a reference. Figure 6.4 shows an included message with the Bracketed option. I use Indented when I want to include a message and intersperse comments throughout the included message, as in the example shown in Figure 6.5.

Figure 6.4
A Bracketed message

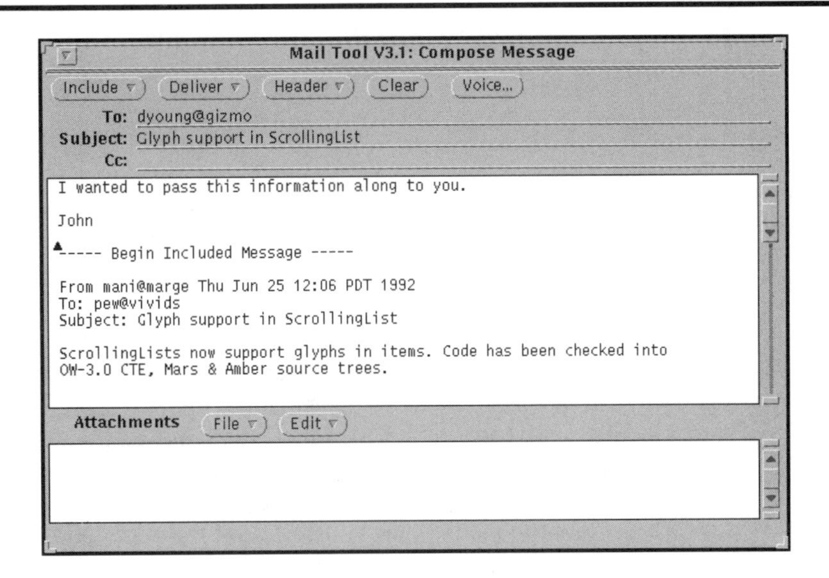

For example, if someone sends me a message with a list of questions to answer, I use Indented. Each line of the included message begins with a right-angle bracket. Each line that I enter does not include the right-angle bracket at the beginning of the line (see Figure 6.5). When the recipient reads the message, it will be easy to identify which lines are the original message and which lines are my reply. The Bracketed message does not provide such a distinction.

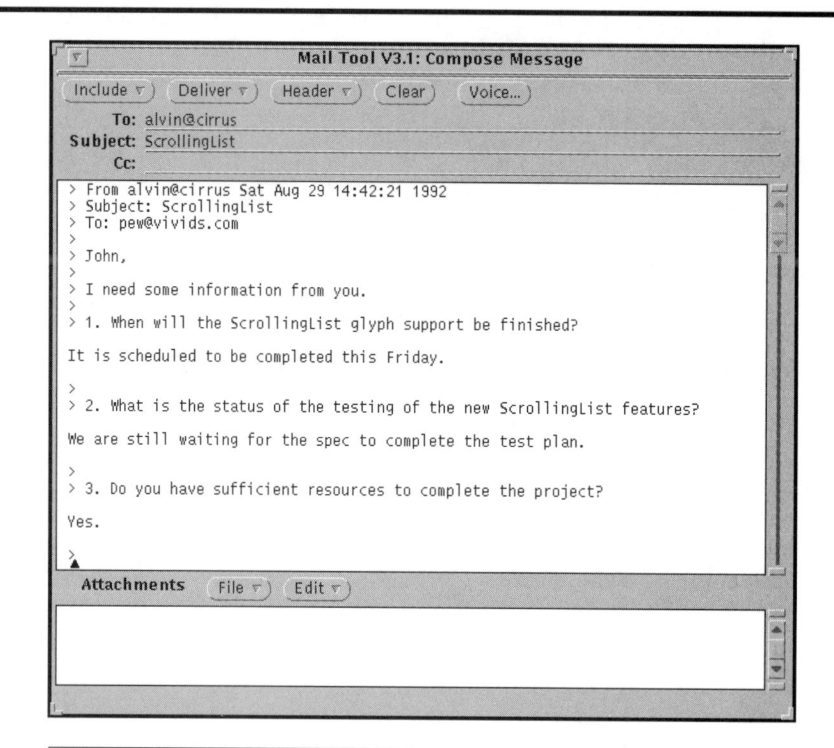

Figure 6.5
An Indented message

Attaching a File

The attachments area of the Compose Message window allows you to attach a file or files to a mail message. The attached files are displayed in the attachments area as icons like those displayed in the File Manager.

It is often better to attach a file rather than include it in the mail message. Attaching a file is like writing a letter and attaching another document to the letter with a paper clip. Your letter is not cluttered with all the details of the attachment, and the reader can simply remove the paper clip and examine the attached document. As an example, you might write a short paragraph that can be used as a cover letter and attach several documents to the cover letter. That is the model you will follow when using the attachments feature. When you are attaching one or more files, you usually write at least a few words of explanation in the text pane (although you are not required to do so). The recipient receives the message, reads it in the text pane, and then opens or saves the attachments.

An important advantage of using the attachments area rather than the text pane is that sometimes you may want a certain file to be included in a mail message that cannot be included in the text pane. The text pane, as its name implies, is for text alone: ASCII text. If you have a file with binary data in it, such as an executable file, you cannot include it in the text pane. You can, however, include it as an attachment. The same is true of files created with SnapShot or Audio Tool: they can be sent as attachments, but they can't be included in the text pane.

Adding an Attachment

You add an attachment by selecting the Add item from the File pop-up menu in the Attachments area of the Compose Message window. The Add Attachment pop-up window is displayed, as shown here:

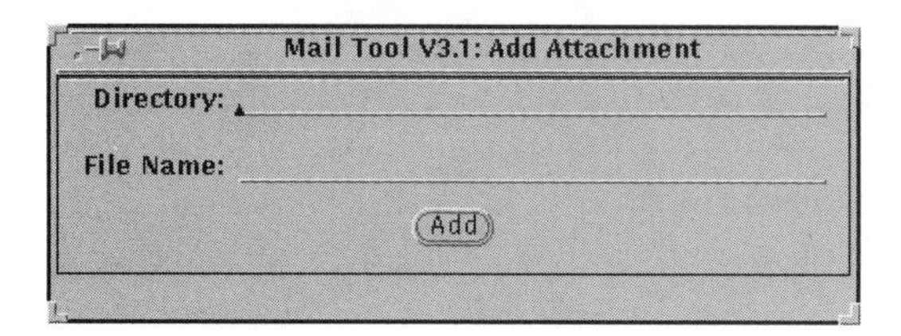

To add an attachment, enter the directory and name of the file in the Add Attachment pop-up window, and press the Add button. You can repeat this procedure to attach multiple files. Each attached file is represented by its own icon. The attachments area can accommodate several icons in its viewable region. If you attach more files than can be displayed in the attachments area, the attachments scrollbar becomes active and lets you scroll the attachments area to see the other icons. Figure 6.6 shows an attachments area that contains several attachments.

You can also add attachments by using drag and drop. For example, you can drag a file from the File Manager and drop it into the Attachments area of the Compose Message window to attach a file. Any of the DeskSet applications that support drag and drop can be used this way. You can drag an image from SnapShot, an audio file from the Audio Tool, or a file you are editing with the Text Editor, and drop it into the Attachments area. You can even highlight text in a text pane (such as a Command Tool or the View Message window of the Mail Tool) and drag just that text to the Attachments area. An icon is then added to the attachments area, representing the text you have just dropped.

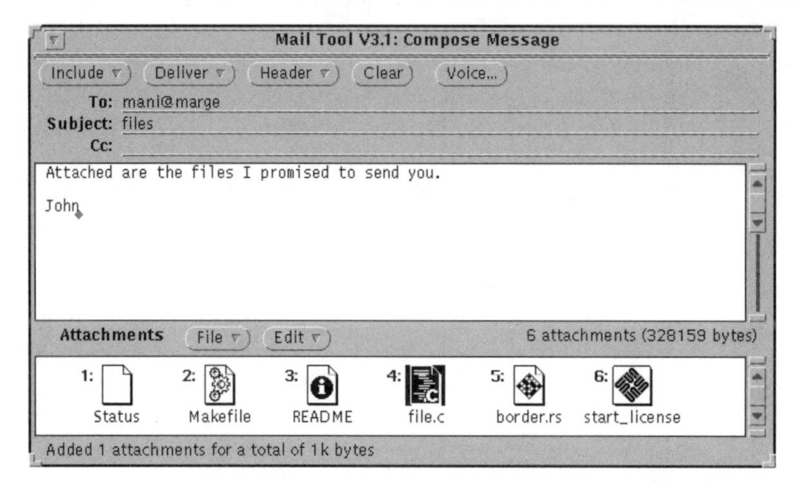

Figure 6.6 Files attached to the Attachments area of a Compose Message window

Working with Attachments

The two menu buttons in the attachments area, File and Edit, let you manipulate the attached files. From the File menu you can choose to add a file, open a file, or copy out a file. We have already discussed adding a file. The Open item lets you open the selected file just as you opened a file from the File Manager (see Chapter 4). The Copy Out item lets you copy the attached file out of the Mail Tool and into the SunOS file system. The time you will most often use this feature is when you are receiving a message.

The Edit menu has four items: Delete, Undelete, Rename, and Select All. The Delete item deletes the file or files selected in the Attachments area. The Undelete item brings back a previously deleted file. The Rename item lets you change the name of an attached file. Select All selects and highlights all the attached files.

When the attachments are very large (a common occurrence), the Mail Tool gives you a warning as you try to deliver the message. You can go ahead and send the message with the attachments, or you can cancel the operation. One option you can consider is to compress the file before you attach it. We talked about the compress program briefly in Chapter 4 when we created a custom command. You can use that custom command at this time to compress the file before attaching it. If you have already attached the file, delete it from the Attachments area, compress the file in the File Manager, and then add the attachment again. You can add the attachment by using either drag and drop from the File Manager or the Add Attachment window. In either case, the compressed file will be attached and will take up much less space. The space consideration may not be important if the message is destined for someone on your local network. If, however, it is headed outside your local environment, especially over phone lines, you may save considerable time and overhead by compressing your attachments first.

Sending Voice Mail

The Mail Tool supports audio mail messages by allowing you to attach an audio file in the attachments area. The user who receives the mail with the audio attachment can listen to the message by double-clicking on the audio attachment.

The Compose Message window includes a Voice button in its header. When you press the Voice button, the Audio Tool is started and appears on your screen. You use the Audio Tool to compose an audio message. When you are satisfied with your audio message, press the Done button in the Audio Tool and the message automatically will be added as an audio attachment to the Compose Message window's attachments area. Figure 6.7 shows the Audio Tool.

Figure 6.7
Audio Tool is started to compose voice mail

In this section we will discuss only the basics of the Audio Tool. Chapter 8 includes a complete discussion of how to use the Audio Tool.

To use the Audio Tool, you must have a microphone connected to your system. If you don't have a microphone, talk to your system administrator about connecting one. (But to listen to an audio message you don't need any extra equipment. Your workstation is equipped with an internal speaker.)

The three buttons at the top of the Audio Tool base window let you file and edit audio files and set the volume. You probably won't need to use these buttons for simple audio creation. The buttons at the bottom are similar to the buttons on a cassette tape recorder. You use the buttons to play, record, rewind, and fast-forward. When you are ready to record your audio message, press the Rec button and begin speaking into your microphone. While you are recording, the Rec button is relabeled Stop. Press the Stop button when you have finished recording. Having the record and stop functions on the same button means that you don't have to search for another button when you are ready to stop recording; your pointer is already over the Stop button. If you want to listen to your message before sending it, press Play. If you are unhappy with what you have recorded, you can select the Clear item from the Edit pop-up menu, which will clear the entire recorded message. Then you can start the process again. In Chapter 8 you will learn other features of the Audio Tool, such as how to edit your message without reentering the entire message.

When you are happy with the audio message, press the Done button. This will automatically add the message as an audio attachment to the Compose Message window and close the Audio Tool. You can press the Voice button again to bring up another Audio Tool. If you know that you want to use the Audio Tool to attach another audio message, you may want to drag the audio file from the Audio Tool and drop it onto the attachments area of the Compose Message window. This process accomplishes the same thing as pressing the Done button, except that the Audio Tool is still displayed.

Using Templates

A *template* is a file that you include in a mail message. Usually, a template file contains text in a format that you are likely to use often in your mail messages, such as a signature line or a calendar appointment. The Mail Tool includes one template for creating calendar appointments. The calendar template is a standard form that can be understood by the Calendar Manager. You can create your own templates for whatever purpose you require. For example, you could define a memo template that you would use to send a memo. This would ensure that your memos all followed the same format, and it would save you the time of typing the standard parts of the memo.

To include a template in your message, display the Include menu on the Compose Message window and choose Templates. If you have not defined any custom templates, Calendar will be the only item displayed on the Templates submenu. When you select an item from the Templates submenu, the template is included in the text pane of the Compose Message window.

Let's look at the calendar template provided with the Mail Tool. The calendar template includes standard marked text that can be easily searched. Use the Find Marked Text pop-up window (see Chapter 5) to search for the fields that you must complete in the calendar template. Fill in the Date, Start, End, and What fields in the calendar template, along with any other message. When you have sent the message, the recipient can drag and drop it onto the Calendar Manager to schedule the appointment. Figure 6.8 shows the calendar template and the Find Marked Text pop-up window.

Another common use of a template is to create a signature. When you send mail, you may want to include your name, e-mail address, and phone number. Rather than type these each time you send a message, you can create a template that contains the information and include it at the end of each mail message.

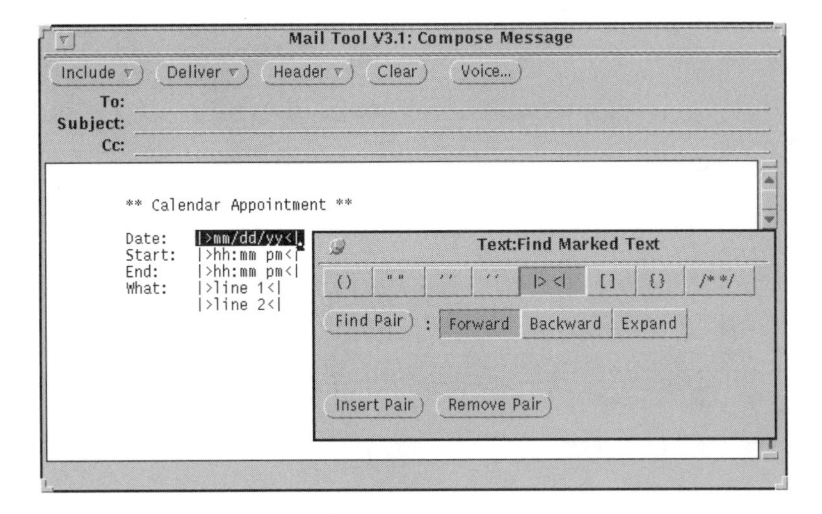

Figure 6.8
The Calendar template

Using the Vacation Notifier

The vacation notifier feature of the Mail Tool lets you automatically send a reply message when you are unable to answer mail for any reason. If you are going on vacation or will be out of town for a few days, you can configure the Mail Tool to respond with a standard format to all the mail you receive. This is a courtesy to the sender. It lets the sender know that you won't be available to reply until you return. The vacation feature is smart enough to keep track of who has received an automatic reply and sends only one reply per week to each user from whom you receive mail. In other words, if you receive several mail messages from one particular user, that user will receive only one automatic reply from the Mail Tool per week.

The Compose menu from the Header window includes a Vacation item that displays the Vacation submenu. The Vacation submenu has two items: Start/Change and Stop. To start the vacation notifier, select Start/Change from the Vacation submenu. The Vacation Setup window is displayed. The text displayed in the Vacation Setup window is the text of the automatic reply that will be sent to each user. The $SUBJECT variable will be replaced with the Subject field of the message being sent. The "Precedence: junk" line indicates that the precedence of the automatic reply is low, and therefore no return messages should be sent if the reply is not successfully delivered. You can modify the contents of the Vacation Setup window to customize your reply message as you see fit. Figure 6.9 shows the Vacation Setup window after it has been customized.

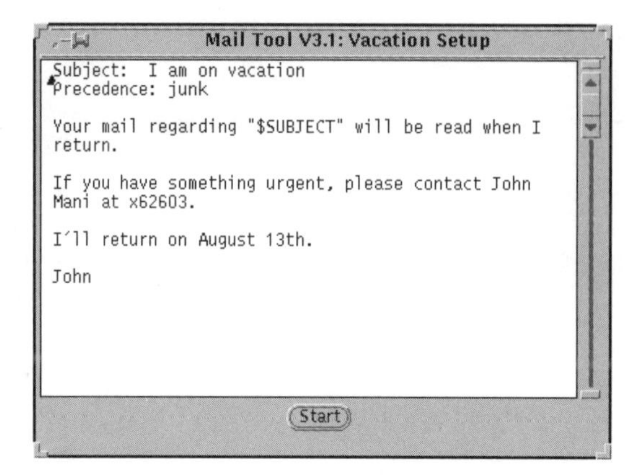

Figure 6.9 The Vacation Setup window

When the vacation notifier is on, the [Vacation] message appears in the header as a reminder. You will still receive messages as long as the vacation notifier is on. When you have returned from vacation, select Stop from the Vacation submenu to turn off the vacation notifier.

Changing Your Mind

In the process of sending a mail message, you may change your mind about the contents of the message or about whether you should send the message at all. If you decide to rewrite your message from scratch, you can clear the entire contents of the Compose Message window, including the header and attachments, by pressing the Clear button in the Compose Message window header.

If you decide not to send the message at all, you can quit the Compose Message window altogether. You quit the Compose Message window the same way you would quit any other window—by selecting Quit from the Window menu. This is the menu provided by the Window Manager that we discussed in Chapter 3. You will receive a warning notice requiring you to confirm that you want to throw away your mail message. If you do quit the Compose Message window, any edits you had in the text pane are stored in the dead.letter file in your home directory. If you decide later that you want to send the message after all, you can recover the contents of the Compose Message window text pane at the time you quit by accessing the dead.letter file. You can load or include the file into the text pane.

Sending the Message

You are ready to send mail when you are satisfied with the message you have composed. You send a message by using the Deliver button in the Compose Message window. The Deliver button is actually a menu button. Each of the four items on the menu delivers the message, but each item treats the Compose Message window differently:

Quit window delivers the message and quits the Compose Message window.

Close window delivers the message, and clears and iconifies the Compose Message window.

Clear message delivers the message and clears the Compose Message window.

Leave message intact delivers the message but leaves the Compose Message window intact. The header, text pane, and attachments area are unaffected.

The Quit window item is the default and is activated if you press SELECT on the Deliver menu button. This is the option that I use most of the time. If I am going to compose another message, I can leave the Compose Message window displayed at the same time. In practice, though, it is very easy to just press the Compose button on the Header window to display a new Compose Message window, and that is what I usually do.

I do occasionally use the "Leave message intact" option if I want to send the same or a similar message to more than one user. Perhaps I have a long message that I need to send to several users but each message must be slightly different. For example, if I was sending confidential information that included a password and some instructions, I might use this feature. The main body of the message would remain the same except for the password, which would be different for each recipient. By leaving the message intact, I can save myself the trouble of reentering the main body for each user. Instead, I can just update the password and send the message again.

You have learned many features in this section that will help you compose mail messages. The technical details are important, but don't underestimate the importance of the contents of the message. Remember the rules of etiquette. Compose messages that are well-formatted, brief, and easy to understand. You will get better results.

Receiving Mail Messages

Every time you receive a mail message, the new message header is displayed in the message headers area of the Header window. You view the contents of a mail message in a separate window: the View Message window. This window is a very simple one. It includes a scrollbar you can use to scroll the contents of the window, but it has no other controls. The Header window, however, has (1) a control area with several buttons; (2) the message headers scrolling list, which displays message headers; and (3) a footer area for displaying warnings and messages.

The controls in the Header window allow you to save, view, delete, reply to, and manipulate incoming mail messages. The message headers area contains a one-line header for each mail message in the In-Box. The header information contained in the scrolling list includes the number of the message, the sender, the date and time received, the size, and the subject. The footer area has two message areas: one on the left and one on the right. The one on the left displays messages about the actions you take. For example, when you delete a message, the left footer area displays "Message deleted." When you drag something from the Mail Tool and drop it onto another application, the left footer area displays "Data transfer in progress." The right footer area displays three statistics: numbers representing the total number of mail messages ("items"), the number of new messages ("new"), and the number of deleted messages ("deleted").

Using Mail Message Headers

The message headers scrolling list contains the header information for each message in the In-Box. Figure 6.10 shows six fields of each message header.

Let's look at each of the six fields in the message header:

The status field, which is optional, contains a symbol and/or a letter to indicate the current status of the message:

- An arrow indicates that the message is currently being displayed.
- An N indicates that the message is new and has not yet been read.
- A U indicates that the message is not new but is unread.
- A blank in the status region indicates that the message has been read.
- A black diamond indicates that the message includes attachments.

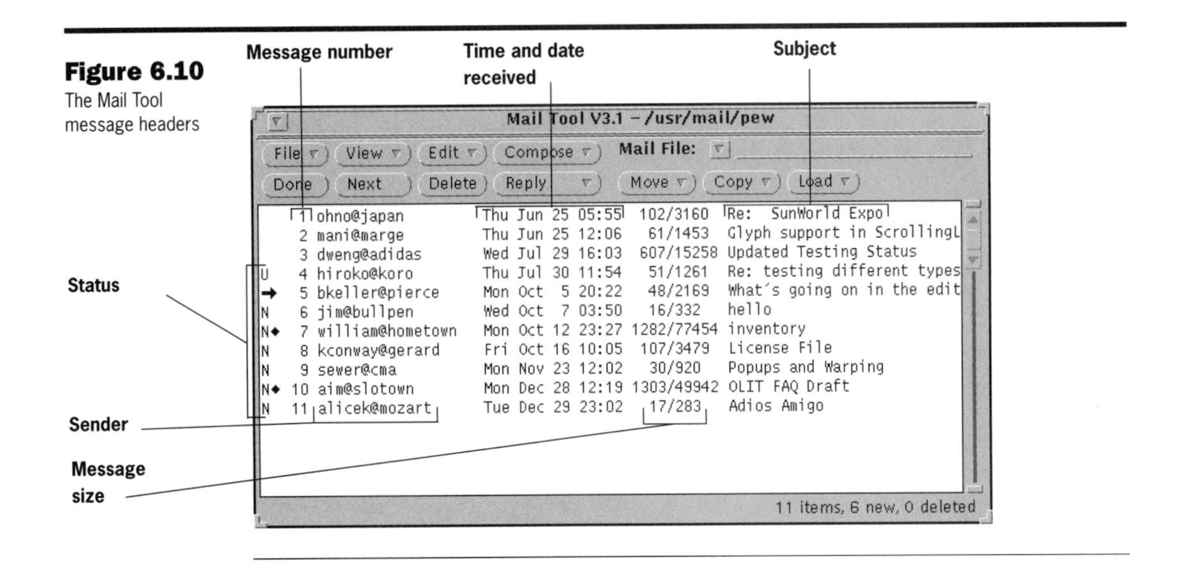

Figure 6.10 The Mail Tool message headers

The message number is a number assigned to the message as it is received. Message numbers are assigned in sequence and are recalculated when mail messages are saved.

The sender field displays the sender's name and host name.

The time and date received field displays the time and date that the message was received.

The message size field has two parts. The first number represents the number of lines in the message. The second number is the number of bytes in the message. Both sizes include the text of the message, the message information contained in the message header, and any attachments.

The subject field displays as much of the subject as can be displayed in the window. If you resize the Header window to make it wider, you will be able to view more of the subject. The subject field is commonly clipped at the right because there is insufficient space to display all of it when you are using the default window size.

Viewing Mail Messages

To display a message, position the pointer over the desired message header and double-click SELECT. The View Message window then displays the message contents. If the View Message window is not currently being displayed when you double-click SELECT, the View Message window pops up. If the

View Message window is already displaying a message, the new message is loaded into the View Message window, replacing the previous contents.

Another way to display the contents of a message in the View Message window is to select the message by clicking SELECT once and then choose Messages from the View menu, as shown here:

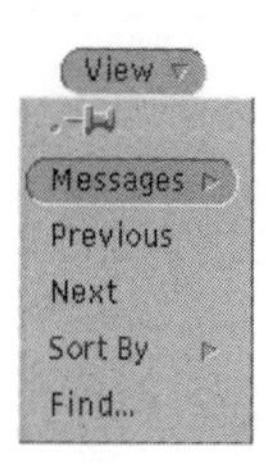

This method allows you to have more than one message selected before you choose View Message. When a message is selected, a rectangular box surrounds the header. You can select additional messages by pressing the ADJUST button over other message headers. When you select View Message, multiple View Message windows are displayed; each message selected is then displayed in its own View Message window.

The View Message window includes a pushpin that, by default, is in the out position. When the pushpin is out, the contents of the View Message window are replaced by the next message that you view. If you pin the View Message window, the contents of the window are not replaced. Instead, when you choose to view another message, an additional View Message window is displayed.

By default, the first few lines of the View Message window indicate who the message is from, to whom it is addressed, and the subject. This is not the complete header information that is stored in the message. To display a full header, display the Messages submenu from the Messages item of the View menu, and select Full Header, as shown here:

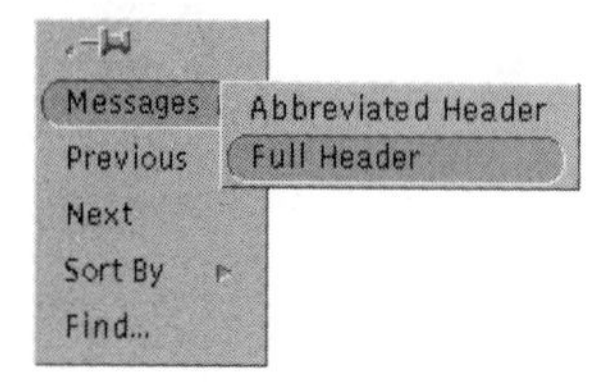

The full header may look very similar to the default abbreviated header, or it may contain many lines of additional information. The way the header looks is determined by the complexity of the path that the message had to take to reach you. Figure 6.11 shows a message with a full header.

Figure 6.11
A message with a full header

```
Mail Tool V3.1: View Message 5
From newbirth.Eng.Sun.COM!sght@netcomsv.netcom.com Sat Jan  2 17:02:23 1993
Return-Path: <newbirth.Eng.Sun.COM!sght@netcomsv.netcom.com>
Received: from netcomsv.netcom.com by noname (4.1/SMI-4.1)
        id AA04558; Sat, 2 Jan 93 17:02:22 PST
Received: from Sun.COM by netcomsv.netcom.com (4.1/SMI-4.1)
        id AA28530; Sat, 2 Jan 93 16:41:25 PST
Received: from Eng.Sun.COM (zigzag-bb.Corp.Sun.COM) by Sun.COM (4.1/SMI-4.1)
        id AA13204; Sat, 2 Jan 93 16:42:50 PST
Received: from newbirth.Eng.Sun.COM by Eng.Sun.COM (4.1/SMI-4.1)
        id AA20440; Sat, 2 Jan 93 16:08:55 PST
Received: by newbirth.Eng.Sun.COM (4.1/SMI-4.1)
        id AA07823; Sat, 2 Jan 93 16:03:26 PST
Date: Sat, 2 Jan 93 16:03:26 PST
From: newbirth.Eng.Sun.COM!sght@netcomsv.netcom.com (Steven GH Tom)
Message-Id: <9301030003.AA07823@newbirth.Eng.Sun.COM>
To: pew@vivids.com
Subject: Re: System access for John Pew
Content-Length: 2558
X-Lines: 70
Status: RO


John,
```

Deleting and Undeleting Mail Messages

After you have read a mail message, you have three options: (1) you can do nothing, and the message will remain in your In-Box; (2) you can delete the message; or (3) you can save the message to a mail file. We'll talk more about saving and organizing mail later in this chapter.

If you have read a message and you do not need a copy of it, you will probably want to delete the message. You delete a message by pressing the Delete button in the Header window control area. All the messages that have been selected are deleted when you press the Delete button. The deletion of a mail message is not permanent until you save your changes (see the next section). You can recover any deleted message, until you save changes, by selecting Undelete from the Edit menu. The Undelete item is a menu button that displays a submenu. This submenu allows you to undelete the last deleted message or choose which messages to undelete from a list. The Undelete submenu is shown here:

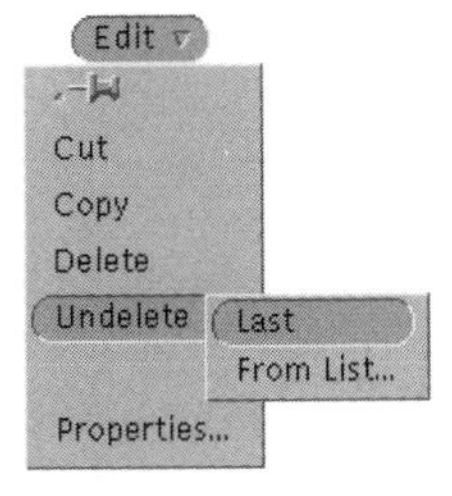

If you choose Undelete Last, the last item deleted is restored to the In-Box and displayed in the Header window. You can continue to undelete the last message until all deleted messages are restored. If you want to undelete a message or messages from a list of all the deleted messages, choose From List, and the Undelete pop-up window will be displayed, as shown here:

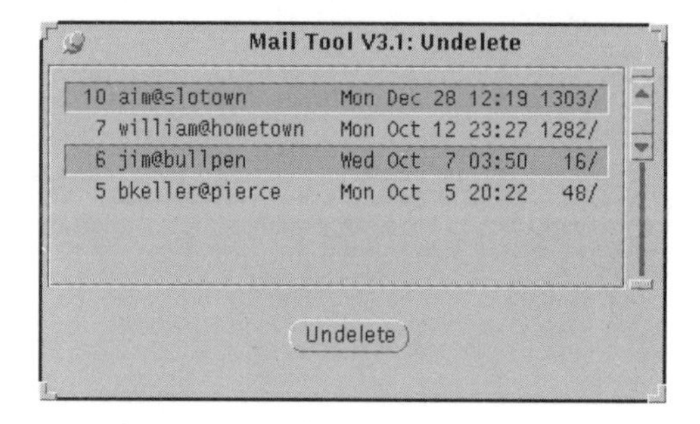

The Undelete window lets you selectively undelete messages. Select the messages that you want to restore, and press the Undelete button. When you save changes in the Mail Tool, all the messages listed in the Undelete window are permanently removed, and you cannot recover them.

Saving Mail Messages

Periodically, you should save the changes you have made while reading your messages. This frees up disk space and renumbers the messages in your In-Box sequentially from 1 to the number of messages in the In-Box. You can save changes by choosing Save Changes from the File menu, shown here:

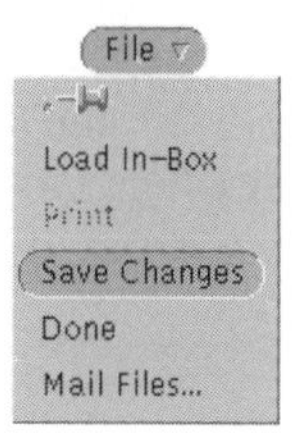

You can also save changes by pressing the Done button. There are actually two Done buttons: one on the File menu and one in the control area of the Header window. Both buttons do exactly the same thing. When you press the Done button, the changes to the Mail Tool are saved, the View Message window is popped down, and the Mail Tool becomes iconified.

Working with Attached Files

When you receive a mail message with an attachment, the status field of the header displays a diamond and the View Message window includes an Attachments area. If a message does not have an attachment, the Attachments area is not displayed. You can operate on the attachments in much the same way that you did with icons displayed in the File Manager. For example, if you double-click SELECT on an attachment, the file will be opened. The action taken when you open an attachment depends on the file type. If the attached file is a regular ASCII file, for example, opening it will invoke the Text Editor program.

You can also open the attached file by selecting it and choosing Open from the Attachments area File menu. The other options available on the File menu are Add and Copy Out. You probably won't use the Add item when you are receiving messages. That feature is usually used when you are composing messages. The Copy Out item, however, is useful when you are reading mail. When you select Copy Out, the Export Attachment pop-up window is displayed. This window contains a field that lets you specify a directory to which the attached file should be written. Once you have specified the directory, you press the Export button. Figure 6.12 shows the File menu and the Export Attachment pop-up window.

Figure 6.12
The Attachments area File menu and Export Attachment window

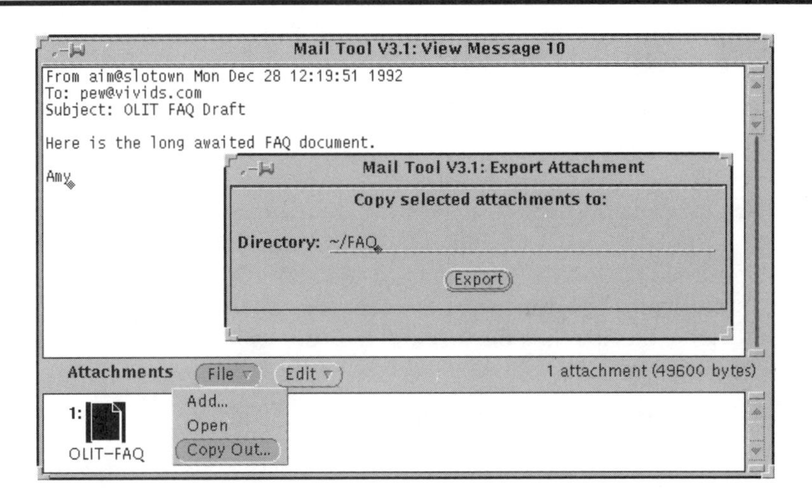

You can also use the drag and drop feature to copy an attached file out of the Mail Tool and into the file system. If you have dropped an attached file onto the File Manager, the file is copied into the current directory that the File Manager has displayed. You can drag and drop attachments to any other DeskSet application just as you have dragged files from the File Manager.

The Edit menu from the Attachments area gives you the flexibility to delete or rename an attachment. You must first select one or more of the attachments. To delete the selected attachments, choose Delete from the Edit menu. To rename an attachment, you must first select one, and only one, attachment. Then choose Rename from the Edit menu to display the Rename Attachment pop-up window. Enter the new name in the Name text field, and then press the Rename button to execute the name change. Figure 6.13 shows the Edit menu and the Rename Attachment pop-up window.

Figure 6.13
The Edit menu and the Rename Attachment window

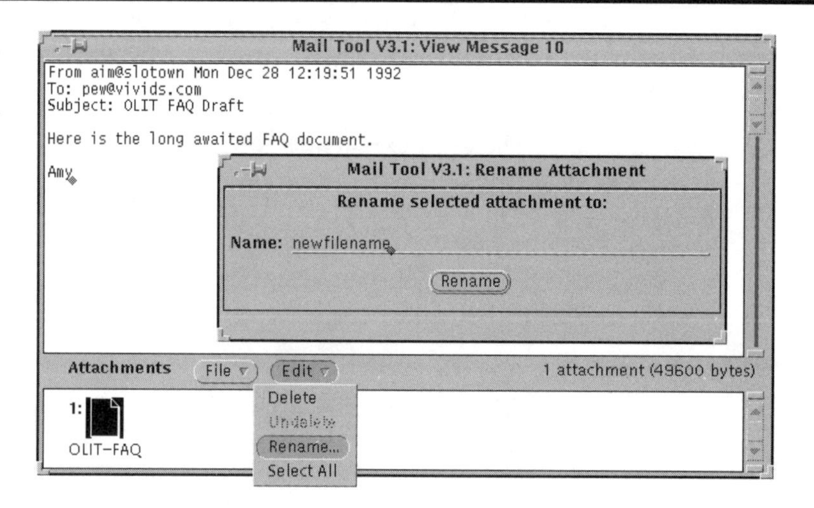

You may need to change the name of an attachment before you copy it out of the Mail Tool and into one of your directories, especially if the attached file has the same name as another file that already exists in the target directory. You don't want to overwrite existing files, so you may want to rename the attached file first and then copy it out to the specified directory.

Finding Mail Messages

You may find that you occasionally need to search for a particular mail message. Perhaps you have been on vacation and you return to find several hundred messages in your In-Box. Or maybe you remember receiving a particular message that you know you didn't delete, but you are having a hard time locating it because you have many messages in your In-Box. To search for messages, you use the Find Messages pop-up window, shown here:

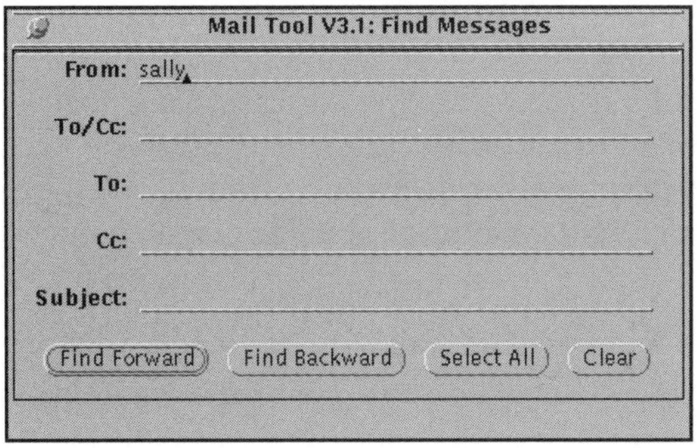

The Find Messages window allows you to specify a field from the header and to search for messages that match the field or fields you specify. For example, if you specify *sally* in the From field, you can search for all messages that you received from sally. After you have filled in the fields you want to search for, press the Find Forward, or Find Backward, or Select All button. The Find Forward and Find Backward buttons find the next message that satisfies all the specified fields. The only difference between the two buttons is the direction of the search. The Select All button selects all the files that match the specified fields. The Clear button clears all the text fields in the Find Messages window.

The entries that you specify in the various fields need not be complete. For example, if you are searching for mail from sally, you can specify a partial name such as *sal* in the From field, and all the messages whose sender matched *sal* would be found—including mail from sally and rosalie. This search method also comes in handy when you can't remember the sender of a particular mail message but you do remember at least one word in the subject. You can specify that word in the Subject field and perform a search based on that word. The matching of characters is case-insensitive.

A match is found only if all the fields specified in the Find Messages window match the corresponding fields in the header of the message. In other words, if you specify more than one field to search for, all the fields specified must match the corresponding header information in order to be considered a matching mail message. The meaning of each of the fields is self-explanatory. Note, however, that an entry in the To/Cc field will match a name in either the To or the Cc field. It doesn't have to be in both—just in one or the other.

Printing Mail Messages

To print a mail message, select one or more messages in the Header window, and choose Print from the File menu.

Each message selected is printed according to the print script defined in the Properties window for Message Windows (accessed through the Edit menu on the Header menu area). We'll discuss this property window later in this chapter when we discuss customizing the Mail Tool.

You can also print mail messages by using drag and drop. To do so, you must have the Print Tool application running on your workspace. Then follow these steps:

1. Select one or more mail messages in the Header window. (They will turn into an icon.)
2. Position the pointer on one of the selected messages, and press SELECT.
3. Drag the pointer to the Print Tool application's drag and drop target (or to the Print Tool icon), and release SELECT.

Each selected message is then printed to the currently chosen printer specified by the Print Tool. Figure 6.14 shows a message being dragged from the Mail Tool and dropped onto the Print Tool's icon.

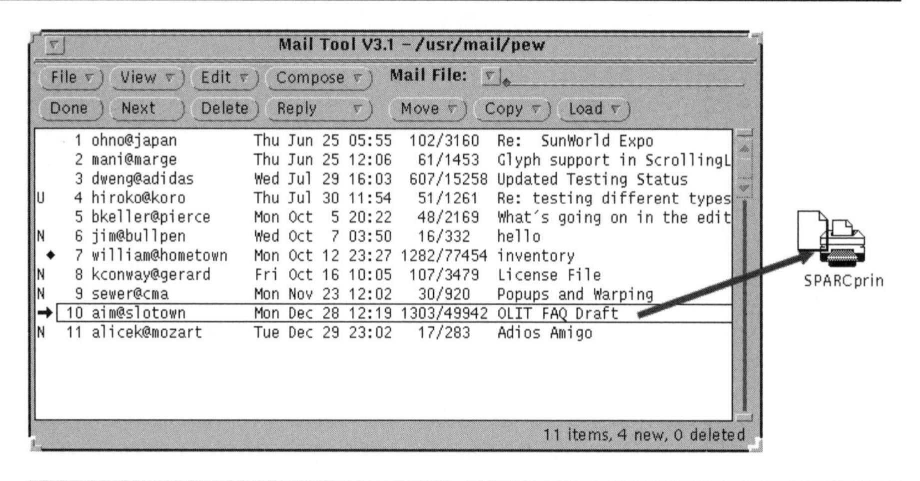

Figure 6.14 Dragging a message from the Mail Tool to the Print Tool

If the message includes attachments, the printed message does not print the contents of any of the attachments but does indicate that there are attachments. If you want to print one or more attachments, drag them to the Print Tool in a separate operation.

Organizing Mail Messages

So far in this chapter, you have learned how to send and receive mail. I've mentioned that when you receive mail you will either delete it or save it. Deleting mail is easy: you just press the Delete button, and the message is deleted. Saving mail, however, requires a little more thought because you have to decide how and where you want to save your messages. In this section, you will learn how to move and copy messages into mail files and how to work with mail files other than your In-Box. You'll also learn how to use the Mail Files pop-up window and some other techniques for organizing your mail messages.

Moving, Copying, and Loading Mail

To understand how mail messages are moved and copied, you need to first understand the concept of a mail file. A mail file is a file that contains one or more mail messages. The mail file that you are probably most familiar with is the In-Box. Each time you receive a new mail message, it is appended to your In-Box mail file. Your In-Box mail file is stored in /usr/mail/<*username*>, where *username* is replaced by your user ID. For example, my In-Box is stored in the file /usr/mail/pew. You can create your own mail files and use them to organize your messages.

The first thing you need to do is to select a mail file directory. By default, your home directory is your mail file directory. However, I recommend that you choose another directory as the location of all your mail files; otherwise your home directory will be littered with files used only for storing mail messages. A conventional place to locate mail files is in a directory named Mail in your home directory. To specify your mail file directory, display the Mail Filing Properties window by following these steps:

1. Select Properties from the Edit pop-up menu.
2. Display the Category menu by pressing MENU on the Category abbreviated menu button.
3. Select Mail Filing from the Category menu.

Figure 6.15 shows the Mail Filing Properties window.

In the Mail File Directory text field, enter **Mail** and then press the Apply button. You do not have to use the name Mail for your directory. If you prefer a different directory name, feel free to use that name. For the purposes of this discussion, however, we will assume that your mail file directory is named Mail.

Now that your mail file directory is set, you can create new mail files. Determining how you will save and organize your messages is a matter of personal preference. You may prefer to save messages in mail files whose names match the names of the senders of those messages. Or, you may want mail files that describe different categories of mail you receive. Choose any method that suits you. If you decide, for example, that you want to save a message to a mail file named *contacts,* you enter **contacts** in the Header window's Mail File text field, and press the Move or Copy button. The Move button moves the selected message to the new mail file. The Copy button copies the selected message to the mail file and leaves the message intact in the In-Box.

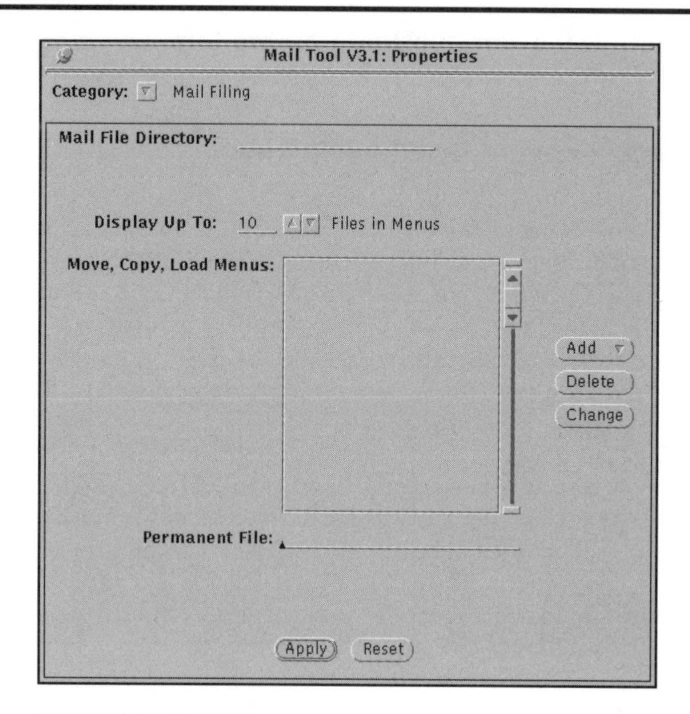

Figure 6.15
The Mail Filing Properties window

You enter the name of a mail file in the Mail File text field by either typing the name of the mail file directly into the text field or by using the abbreviated nemu button next to the Mail File text field. The menu associated with the abbreviated menu button (called the Mail File menu) displays all the mail files you have in your mail file directory. When you select an item from the Mail File menu, the item is inserted into the Mail File text field. This saves you the effort of remembering and typing the name of the mail file.

Each of the three buttons below the Mail File text field displays a pop-up menu that lists the most recently used mail files. Each time you enter and use a mail file in the Mail File text field, it gets added to the menu. The first item on each menu always matches the entry in the Mail File text field. If the Mail file text field is empty, then the first item on the menu is labeled Entry and is made inactive. Since the first item on the menu is the default item, you can specify the mail file in the Mail File text field and then simply press SELECT on the Move or Copy button to move or copy the selected message into the mail file. If the specified mail file does not already exist, it is created, and the selected message becomes the first entry in the mail file. If the mail file does exist, the selected mail message is appended to it. Figure 6.16 shows the Mail File text field and the Move menu.

Figure 6.16
The Mail File text field

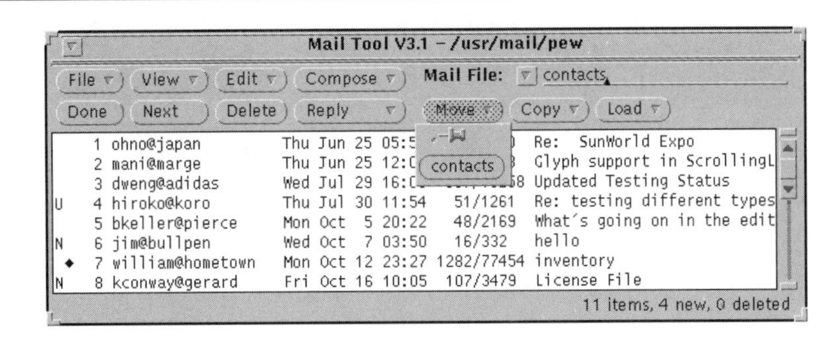

Let's summarize the process of moving or copying a mail message to a mail file. It is really quite simple.

1. Select one or more messages in the Message Headers area of the Header window.
2. Enter the name of a mail file in the Mail File text field.
3. Press SELECT on the Move button or the Copy button to move or copy the selected message or messages to the specified mail file.

Each time you move or copy a message to a mail file, the Mail Tool remembers the mail file and includes it on the menu of each of the three buttons—Move, Copy, and Load. In this way, the Mail Tool saves you the trouble of entering the mail file name in the text field each time you save a message. If, for example, you have already saved a message to the contacts mail file, you can avoid retyping *contacts* in the text field by displaying the menu and selecting the contacts item.

You can also create a subdirectory in your mail file directory. Doing this might be useful if you have several mail files that fit into the same category. To create a mail file within a subdirectory, enter the name of the subdirectory and the mail file, separated by a slash in the Mail File text field. For example, if you want to have a mail file subdirectory named *class* that contains a mail file named *student1,* you enter **class/student1** in the Mail File text field. The class item on the Mail File menu appears with a right arrow, indicating that a submenu is available for that item. The name of each mail file in the class subdirectory is displayed on the submenu, as shown in Figure 6.17.

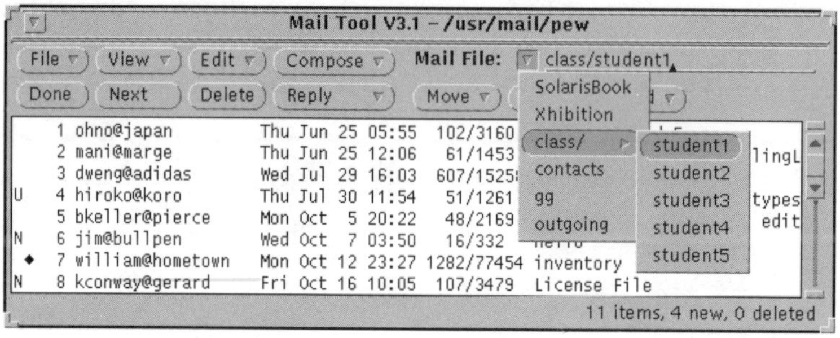

Figure 6.17
The Mail File menu

The Load button lets you load a mail file into the Mail Tool. The messages in the In-Box (which is just another mail file) are usually loaded in the Mail Tool. You can load the messages stored in another mail file by using the Load Button. When you load a mail file, the messages in the file are displayed in the Header window in the same way that messages in the In-Box are normally displayed. Loading a mail file gives you a convenient way to peruse or retrieve saved mail messages. When you want to return the loaded file to your In-Box, select the Load In-Box item on the File menu.

Using the Mail Files window

Another way to manipulate messages and mail files is to use the Mail Files pop-up window. To display the Mail Files pop-up window, select Mail Files from the File menu. Figure 6.18 shows the Mail Files pop-up window.

The Mail Files window lets you perform many of the same operations that you just learned about, such as saving messages, loading mail files, and creating mail files. In addition, you can use the Mail Files window to remove mail files or subdirectories. It also presents the mail file data in a format different from what is available in the Header window.

The scrolling list on the Mail Files window displays the mail files found in the mail file directory. At the top of the scrolling list is a label that displays the current directory. In Figure 6.18 the label displays Mail, which is the mail file directory. When you change directories, the label is updated to identify the current directory. There are two types of entries in the mail file directory: mail files and directories. Mail files are displayed with a mailbox icon, and directories are displayed with a folder icon. For example, in Figure 6.18 the "contacts" item is a mail file and the "class" item is a directory. When you click on an item, the name of the item is entered in the Name text field at the top of the window. When you double-click on a mail file item, the mail file is loaded. When you double-click on a directory, that directory becomes the current directory and its contents are displayed in the scrolling list.

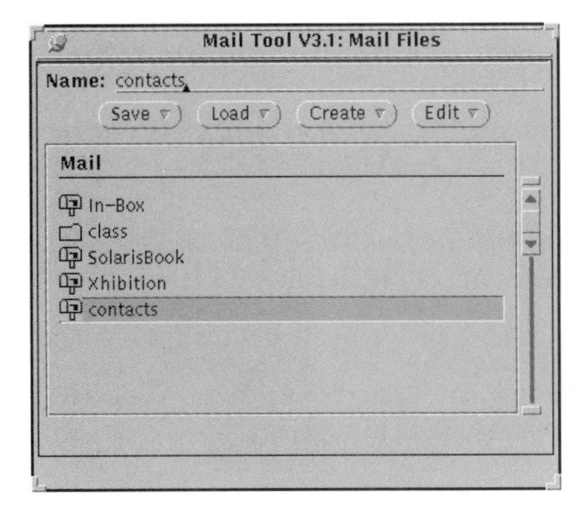

Figure 6.18
The Mail Files pop-up window

Each of the buttons on the Mail Files window operates on the entry in the Name text field. You can enter the contents of the Name text field by either double-clicking on a file in the scrolling list or typing directly into the text field.

The Save menu button lets you move or copy the current selection from the Header window to the specified mail file. The two items on the Save submenu have the following functions:

Move Message into Mail File moves the selected message or messages to the specified mail file. This is the same as the Move button on the Header window.

Copy Message into Mail File copies the selected message or messages to the specified mail file. This is the same as the Copy button on the Header window.

The Load menu button lets you load a mail file into the Header window. The two items on the Load submenu have the following functions:

Mail File loads the mail file specified in the Name text field. This is the same as the Load button on the Header window.

In-Box loads the In-Box. This is the same as the Load In-Box item on the File menu of the Header window.

The Create menu button lets you create a new mail file or directory. The two items on the Create submenu have the following functions:

Mail File creates an empty mail file using the name specified in the Name text field.

Directory creates a directory using the name specified in the Name text field.

The Edit menu button lets you delete, empty, or rename a mail file. The three items on the Edit submenu have the following functions:

Delete deletes the specified mail file. If the specified file is a directory, the directory must be empty before it can be deleted.

Empty empties the specified mail file but does not delete it.

Rename renames the entry selected in the scrolling list. The new name is specified in the Name text field.

Using Drag and Drop to Copy and Load

Another way to copy messages and load mail files is to use the Mail Tool and the File Manager together. Display the File Manager's base window, and change your current directory displayed in the file pane to your mail file directory. Then follow these steps:

1. Select one or more mail messages in the Header window.
2. Position the pointer over one of the selected messages, and press SELECT.
3. Drag the pointer over one of the mail file icons in the File Manager's file pane.
4. Release SELECT.

This procedure copies the selected messages to the mail file that you drop them onto. The result is only a copy, not a move. Of course, you can always delete the messages after you have copied them. Figure 6.19 shows a message being dropped onto a mail file in the File Manager.

You can also use the File Manager with the Mail Tool to load a mail file. Again, you must open the File Manager to the directory that contains the file you want to load. Then follow these steps:

1. Position the pointer over the mail file displayed in the file pane of the File Manager, and press SELECT.
2. Drag the pointer to the message header area of the Header window, and release SELECT.

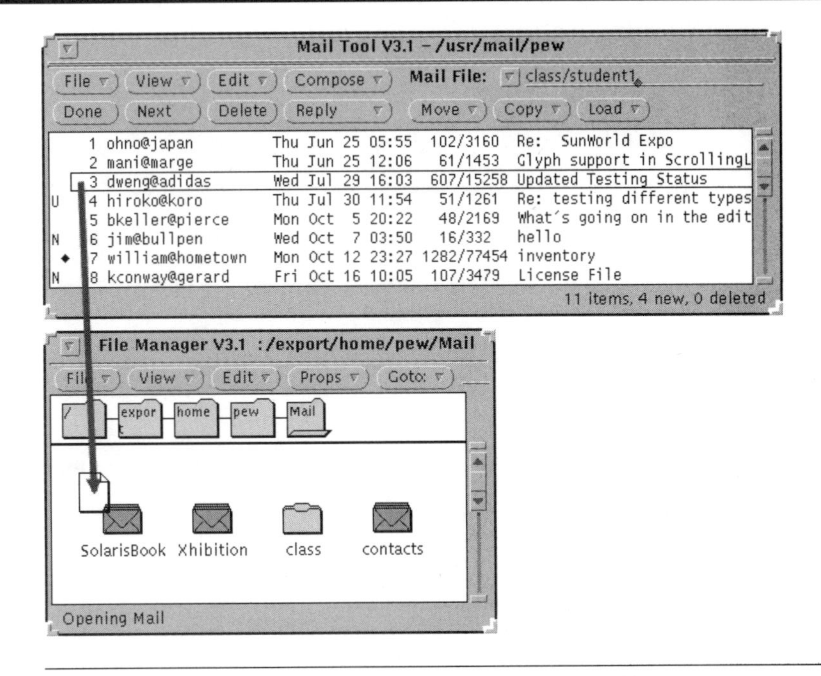

Figure 6.19 Saving a message by using the File Manager and drag and drop

The mail file is now loaded and is displayed in the message header.

Sorting the Contents of a Mail File

Each new mail message that you receive is appended to the In-Box in the order in which it is received. You have the option, however, of rearranging the order of your In-Box or of any mail file. To do so, you use the Sort By submenu. To display the Sort By submenu, you display the View menu and select the Sort By item, as shown here:

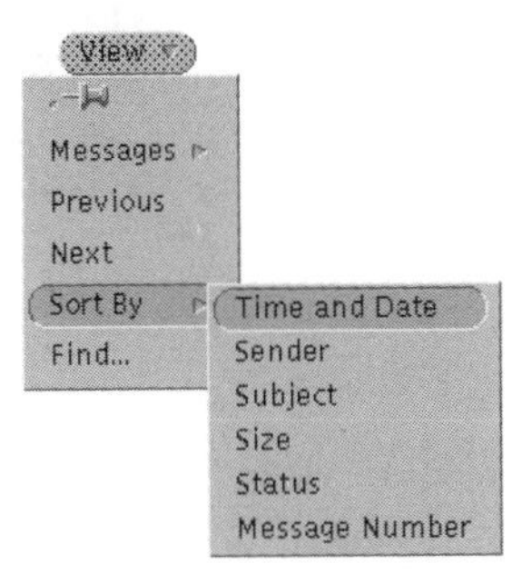

Each item on the Sort By submenu sorts the messages in the current mail file by a different method:

Time and Date sorts the messages according to the time and date received. This is the default ordering.

Sender sorts the messages alphabetically by sender name.

Subject sorts the messages alphabetically by subject field.

Size sorts the messages by size. The smaller files are listed first.

Status sorts the messages by Status field.

Message Number sorts the messages by message number.

When the messages have been sorted, they retain the numbers they had before the sort until you save your changes.

Customizing the Mail Tool

Many customization features are available in the Mail Tool. Throughout most of this chapter, I have described the operation of the Mail Tool based on the default values for these customization options. In this section we will examine the ways you can customize the Mail Tool to your liking.

You customize the Mail Tool through the Properties window. To display the Properties window, select Properties from the Edit menu. Seven categories are available from the Properties window: Header Window, Message Window, Compose Message window, Mail Filing, Template, Alias, and Expert. To select a category, position the pointer over the Category abbreviated menu button, press MENU, and drag the pointer over the desired item in the Category menu. When you release MENU, the corresponding category panel appears.

Whenever you make a change in a property window, you must press the Apply button to effect the change. Most of the properties that you change with the Properties window take effect immediately. There are a few exceptions to this rule because some of the properties affect the way that the Mail Tool is displayed when you invoke it. For these properties to take effect, you must quit Mail Tool and restart it.

The Header Window Properties

The Header Window Properties let you select custom button functions, change message receipt notification, and change the Header window layout. Figure 6.20 shows the Header Window Properties window.

Figure 6.20
The Header Window Properties window

Here is a description of each control on this property window:

Retrieve Every lets you specify the number of seconds between each automatic retrieval and notification of new mail. The default value is 300 seconds, or 5 minutes. If you want to manually check to see if new mail has arrived, you can load the In-Box by selecting the Load In-Box item from the File menu.

Signal With notifies you with beeps and flashes when new mail arrives. This field lets you determine how many, if any, beeps and flashes to provide as notification that new mail has arrived.

Display lets you specify the height and width of the message header region of the Header window. You specify the height in the Headers field and the width in the Characters wide field. A change in either of these fields takes effect the next time you start the Mail Tool.

Delivery lets you determine when and how headers display whenever you receive mail. If you check the Automatically display headers option (which is the default), then the headers of newly received mail messages are automatically displayed. If you check the Show "To: recipient"... option, the Sender field of the message header displays the word *To* followed by the name of the recipient if the mail was sent by you. This option is particularly useful if you load a mail file that contains your outgoing mail messages.

Custom Buttons lets you choose the function of each of the four buttons on the upper-left side of the Header window's control area. The buttons are labeled Done, Next, Delete, and Reply. Each of these controls is available from other Header window menus. In fact, each button appears on the menu associated with the menu button directly above it. For example, Done is found on the File menu, Next is found on the View menu, and so forth. The Custom Buttons choice works together with the Command and Label fields on the property window. Press Done to select the function of the Done button in the Header window, press Next to select the function of the Next button, and so forth.

Command displays the Command menu when you use the abbreviated menu button. The Command menu shows all the available commands that you can use to customize the function of the four buttons specified in the Custom Buttons field. For example, if you prefer that the Done button be used to save changes without iconifying the Mail Tool (as normally occurs with the Done button), select Done from the Custom Buttons field and then select Save from the Command menu. The button will now be labeled "Save," and its function will be to save changes without iconifying the Mail Tool. Figure 6.21 shows the Header Window Properties window with the Command menu displayed.

Label lets you modify the contents of the Label text field to customize your button label. Each choice from the Command menu includes a default label for the button. When you select an item from the Command menu, the default label is entered into the Label text field.

The Message Window Properties

The Message Window Properties let you determine the size of the View Message and Compose Message windows. They also control the function performed by the Print button, and the header fields displayed in the View Message window. Figure 6.22 shows the Message Window Properties window.

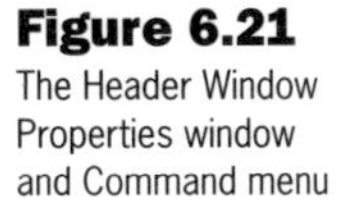

Figure 6.21
The Header Window Properties window and Command menu

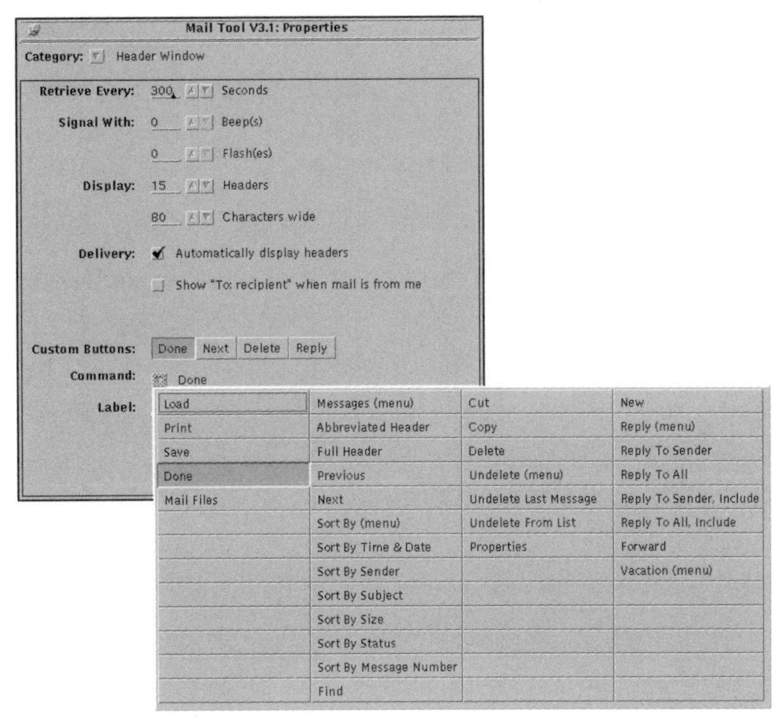

You use the controls in the Message Window Properties window as follows:

Display lets you determine the height of the View Message and Compose Message windows. The number entered in the field determines the number of lines of text displayed.

Print Script is the command that is issued when you press the Print button. If you are connected to a PostScript printer, try using the following print script:

```
mp -l $FILE | lp
```

Your message will be printed in two columns with attractive borders.

Hide lets you hide certain header fields from the View Message window. Every mail message has a header. The number of fields included in the header is potentially large. There are many different fields available that are optional or required by different versions of UNIX mail programs. Each entry in the Hide list identifies a header that should *not* appear when you view the View Message window. The buttons to the right of the list let you add new entries and change or delete existing entries.

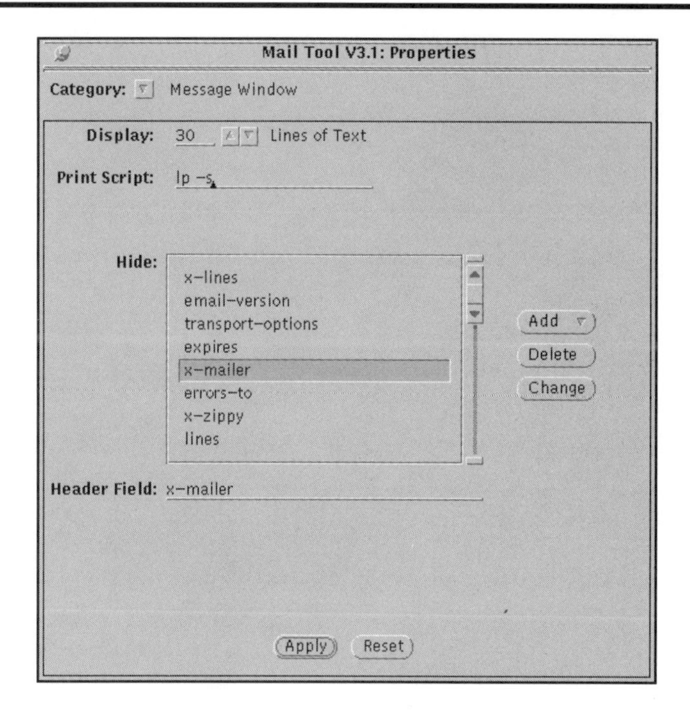

Figure 6.22 The Message Window Properties window

Header Field lets you add or change a header field from the Hide list. To add an entry, enter the new field identifier in the Header Field text field, and press the Add button. To change an existing item, select the item from the list, make the change in the text field, and press the Change button.

The Compose Message Window Properties

The Compose Message window Properties control various features of the Compose Message window, such as the text marker character, the recording of outgoing mail in a mail file, and custom header fields. Figure 6.23 displays the Compose Message window Properties window.

You use the controls in the Compose Message window Properties window as follows:

Included Text Marker lets you specify the characters that appear at the beginning of each line when you include a file in the Compose Message window and specify Indented. The default value is a right-angle bracket followed by a space (>).

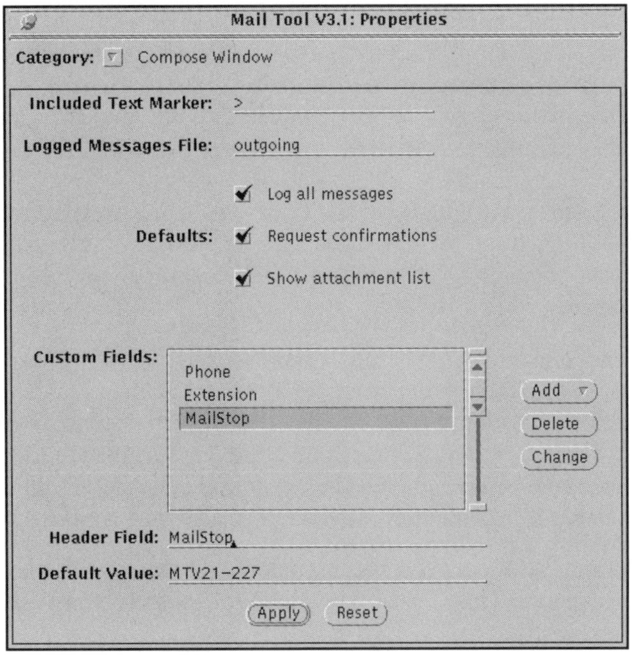

Figure 6.23
The Compose Message window Properties window

Logged Messages File automatically records, in a mail file of your choosing, the messages that you send. By default, this feature is turned off. To turn on this feature, enter the name of the mail file you would like to be used to record messages that you compose. The entry that you specify in the Logged Messages File will be created in the mail file directory. With this option enabled, a check box labeled Log appears in the header of the Compose Message window, as shown in Figure 6.24.

If the Log all messages box is checked, then the Log check box in the Compose Message window will be checked by default. If the Log all messages box is not checked, then the Log check box in the Compose Message window will not be checked by default. In either case, you can check or uncheck the Log check box in the Compose Message window.

Defaults gives you two options. The Request confirmations option lets you determine whether a confirmation is requested before an irreversible action, such as quitting the Compose Message window, is performed. The Show attachment list option lets you determine if the Attachments area of the Compose Message window is displayed initially.

Custom Fields lets you add other fields to the message header. The standard header fields provided by the Compose Message window are To, Subject, Cc, and Bcc. You might want to add a header field that includes your phone number or mail stop. You use the Header Field and Default Values fields to specify the new header fields, and the three buttons to the right of the list to add, delete, or change items in the Custom Fields list.

For each custom field you add there will be a corresponding item on the Header menu of the Compose Message window. This gives you the flexibility of adding or deleting the custom fields when you compose your mail message.

Header Field lets you enter a new custom field or change an existing field. To add a new custom field, enter the name of the field in the Header Field text field and press the Add button. To change an existing field, select the item from the list, change the entry in the Header Field, and press the Change button. The entry in the Header Field will be used as the label for the field in the Compose Message window.

Default Value lets you specify a default value, if you want a custom field to have one. This is optional; you may have a custom header field without a default value.

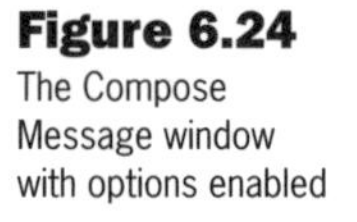

Figure 6.24 The Compose Message window with options enabled

The Mail Filing Properties

The Mail Filing Properties allow you to set the mail file directory and control the permanent entries on the Move, Copy, and Load menus from the Header window. The Mail Filing Properties window is shown in Figure 6.25.

Figure 6.25
The Mail Filing Properties window

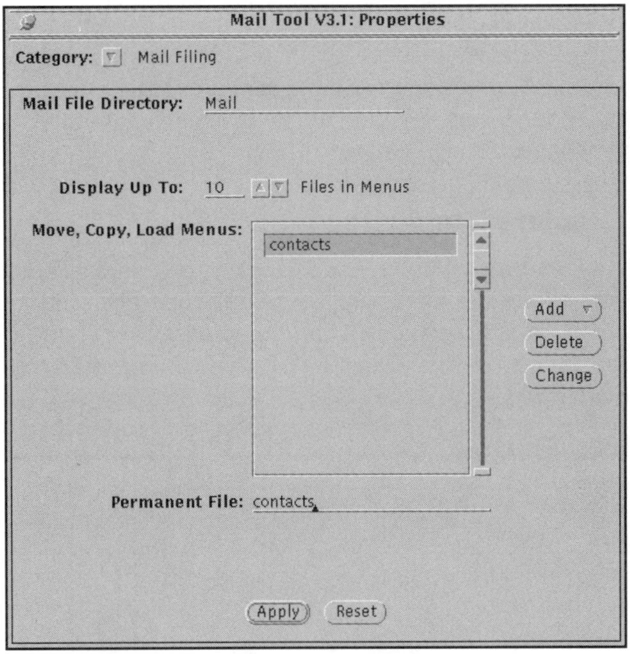

Here is a description of the features available on the Mail Filing Properties window:

Mail File Directory lets you set the location of the mail file directory. This is the default location where mail files are saved.

Display Up To lets you determine the size of the Move, Copy, and Load menus. The default value is 10, which means that only ten items are displayed in each of the three menus.

Move, Copy, Load Menus lets you add permanent entries to the Move, Copy, and Load menus. By default, the Move, Copy, and Load menus each display a list of the most recently used mail files. Each item that you add to the Move, Copy, and Load Menus scrolling list on this property window becomes a permanent item on each of the three menus. Choose as permanent items the mail files that you use frequently.

Permanent File lets you add a new entry to the Move, Copy, Load Menus list. Enter the name of a mail file in the Permanent File text field, and press the Add button to add the mail file to the list. You can change an item on the list by selecting the item, changing it in the text field, and pressing the Change button.

The Template Properties

The Template Properties let you create custom templates that you can use when composing messages. The Template Properties window includes one template by default: calendar. This template lets you create a message that can be understood by the Calendar Manager. Figure 6.26 shows the Template Property window.

Figure 6.26
The Template Properties window

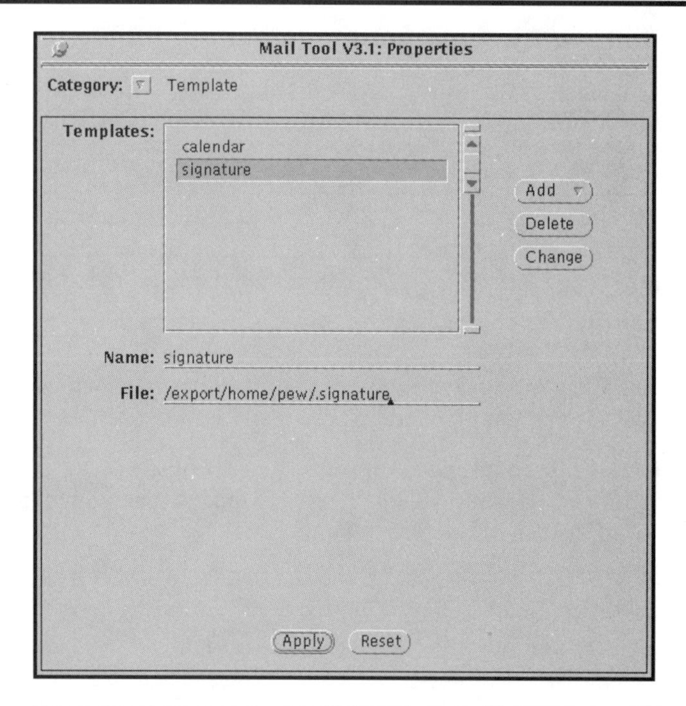

To create a template, you use the controls in the Template Properties window as follows:

Templates lists each template that you have defined. Use the Name and File text fields to enter a new custom template.

Name lets you enter the name of a template. To add a template, enter the name of the template in the Name field and the name of the file containing the template information in the File field, and press Add.

File lets you enter the name of the file that contains the template information.

The Alias Properties

The Alias Properties allow you to create mail aliases. A mail alias is an abbreviation for one or more mail addresses. It is like a distribution list. A mail alias usually represents a list of recipients to whom you would send a common message. These might be the people you work with or a group of people with a common interest. You can also use an alias to specify a single recipient, especially if a user has a complex host address or a user name that is difficult to remember. You can create a mail alias that is easy to remember and then use that alias in the To or Cc field of the Compose Message window. Figure 6.27 shows the Alias Properties window.

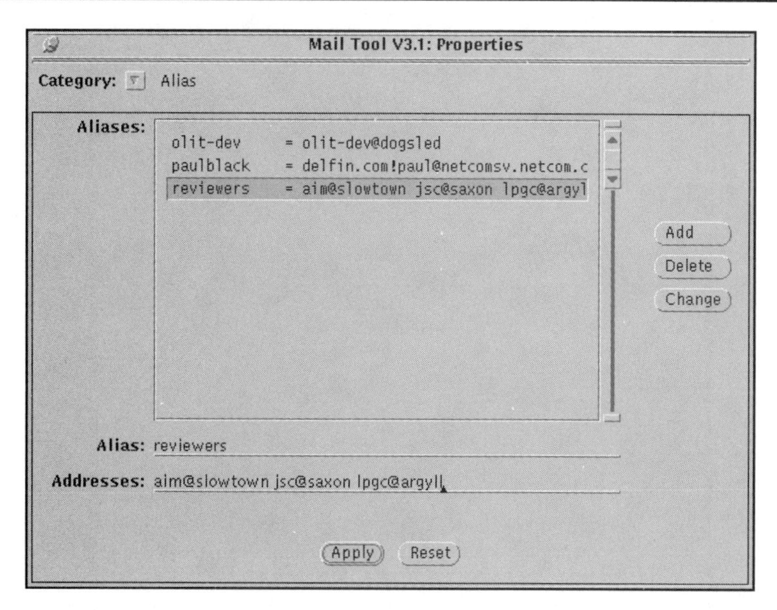

Figure 6.27
The Alias Properties window

To create an alias, use the following controls in the Alias Properties window:

Aliases lists all the aliases you have created. You use the Alias and Addresses fields to create or change an alias. When you select an item from the list, the Alias and Addresses fields display the corresponding alias and addresses.

Alias lets you enter an alias name. To add a new alias, enter the alias name in the Alias text field and the addresses in the Addresses field, and press Add. To change an alias, select the alias from the list, change the Alias or Addresses fields, and press Change.

Addresses lets you enter the addresses for an alias. The addresses are usually users, but you can also include a mail file in the Addresses field. The mail file must be preceded by a plus sign.

The Expert Properties

The Expert Properties let you determine the way mail is addressed when you reply to a message. Figure 6.28 shows the Expert Properties window.

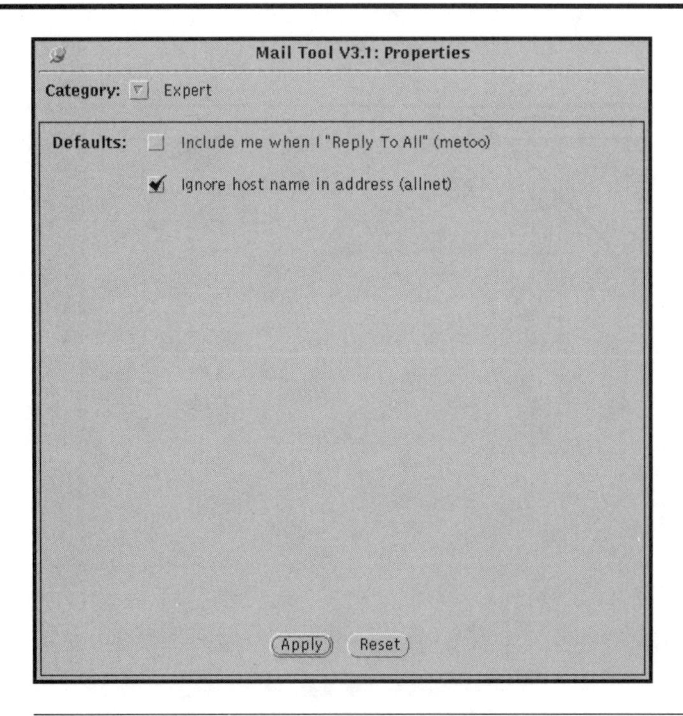

Figure 6.28
The Expert Properties window

The Expert Properties window includes one item, Defaults, which has two check box fields. The first option, labeled metoo, lets you determine whether your user name is included when you reply to a message with the Reply to All option. If this option is checked, you will be included in the To list when you reply to a message with the Reply to All option.

The second option, labeled allnet, has meaning only when the metoo field is not checked. When allnet is checked, your own user name will never be included when you reply to a message with the Reply to All option. If allnet is not checked, your user name will be included only if the host name specified with your user name is different from the system you are replying from.

Summary

The Mail Tool is one of the most important DeskSet utilities, if not *the* most important. Sending and receiving mail is probably one of the tasks that you will do regularly—perhaps several times each day. Electronic mail is the backbone of communications for many companies and organizations. Your mastery of the Mail Tool will contribute to your ability to receive information and communicate with the people around you.

CHAPTER

The Calendar Manager

THE CALENDAR MANAGER LETS YOU SCHEDULE APPOINTMENTS AND create ToDo lists. You can use the Calendar Manager to keep track of your appointments and to remind you of those appointments. By making a single entry, you can schedule an appointment that occurs on a regular basis—once a week, for example. The Calendar Manager then automatically reminds you every week of the scheduled appointment. You can view your appointments in several convenient formats: yearly, monthly, weekly, or daily.

The Calendar Manager also includes a browser facility that enables you to look at the calendars of other users. This feature may help you locate those who are away from their offices, or it may help you to easily schedule appointments at times that are convenient to others. You can even browse the calendars of a group of people simultaneously to find the best time to schedule a meeting with everyone involved.

The Calendar Manager also utilizes Drag and Drop. Appointment notices can be sent as mail messages that are dragged from the Mail Tool and dropped onto the Calendar Manager, which automatically schedules the appointment. The browser facility includes a convenient way to create a mail message in the appropriate format so that other users can drag the mail message and drop it onto their calendars. This capability makes it easy to schedule meetings.

As you start using the Calendar Manager to organize your schedule, you will find it an invaluable tool. You may want to start each day by using the Calendar Manager's printing facility to produce a printout of the appointments and of the ToDo list for the day, and then use the printout for taking notes and updating your future schedule.

In this chapter you will learn how to do the following:

- Use the basic Calendar Manager features
- Display the year, month, week, and day views
- Schedule and edit appointments
- Print Calendar Manager views and lists
- Use the Multi-Browser to schedule meetings for multiple users
- Customize the Calendar Manager
- Use the Calendar Manager from the shell

Calendar Manager Basics

Before getting into all the details, we'll discuss some of the Calendar Manager's highlights in this section. This should be just enough information to get you started in using the Calendar Manager's basic features.

To start the Calendar Manager, choose Calendar Manager from the Programs menu. You can also start the Calendar Manager by entering the cm command at the prompt:

```
dugout% cm &
```

When the Calendar Manager is invoked, it is displayed as an icon. The icon appears as a desktop calendar with the current date displayed, as shown here:

The Calendar Manager also supports an alternative icon that displays a calendar for the current month, as shown here:

November 1993

S	M	T	W	T	F	S
	1	2	3	4	5	6
7	8	9	10	11	12	13
14	15	16	17	18	19	20
21	22	23	24	25	26	27
28	29	30				

If you prefer this icon, you must start the Calendar Manager with the -i 2 command-line options:

```
dugout% cm -i 2 &
```

Double-click on the Calendar Manager icon to display the base window. The Calendar Manager has several display modes. It can display an entire year, a month, a week, or a single day. The default view is the month view, which is shown in Figure 7.1.

Controls

Spanning the top of the Calendar Manager's base window are seven buttons that you use for basic operation. Here is a quick overview of their features:

View lets you change the mode of the base window. You can choose to view your calendar by year, month, week, or day. You can also choose the Find feature to search for an appointment.

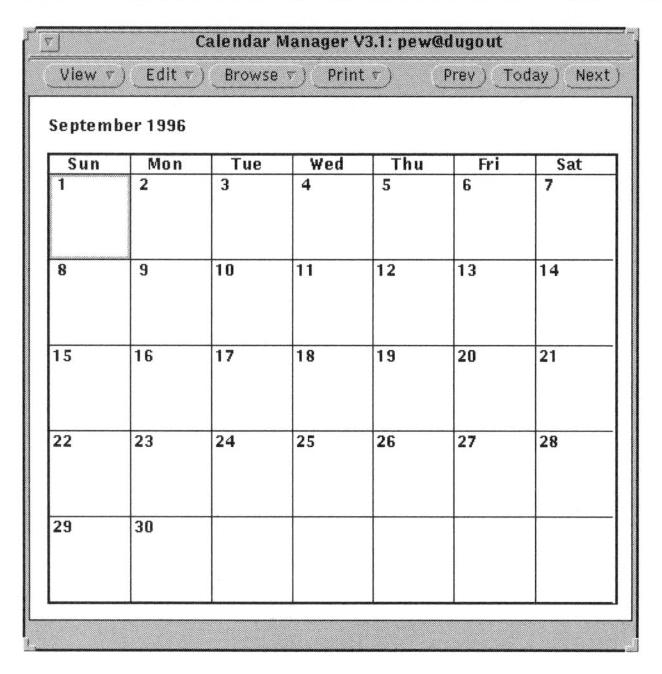

Figure 7.1 The Calendar Manager month view

Edit gives you three choices: Appointment, Time Zone, and Properties. The Appointment choice displays the Calendar Manager Appointment Editor, which you use to create and edit appointments. The Time Zone item lets you choose the appropriate time zone for your geographical region. The Properties item displays the Calendar Manager's Properties window.

Browse lets you look at, or browse, the calendars of other users. You can also choose the Multi-Browser from this menu. The Multi-Browser lets you scan the calendars of several users simultaneously by superimposing the calendars on top of one another in order to determine the best time for a meeting or an event.

Print gives you several options for printing your appointments and ToDo lists. You can choose to print your schedule for a day, a week, a month, or a year.

Prev changes the calendar displayed in the base window. If you are displaying a month view, you can use the Prev button to change the view to the previous month. If you are displaying a day view, the Prev button lets you change the view to the previous day. The same is true for week and year views.

Today changes the calendar displayed on the base window to include and highlight today's date.

Next changes the calendar displayed in the base window. If you are displaying a week view, you can use the Next button to change the view to the next week. If you are displaying a year view, the Next button lets you change the view to the next year. The same is true for day and month views.

Basic Operation

The Calendar Manager's base window has four different views: year, month, week, and day. For this brief introduction of the Calendar Manager's basic features, we will limit our discussion to the month view, which displays an entire month's appointments. Each day displays as many appointments as will fit into the space provided.

The Appointment Editor

To create or edit an appointment, you must use the Calendar Manager's Appointment Editor. To display the Appointment Editor, position the pointer over the day for which you want to schedule an appointment, and double-click SELECT. Figure 7.2 shows the Appointment Editor pop-up window.

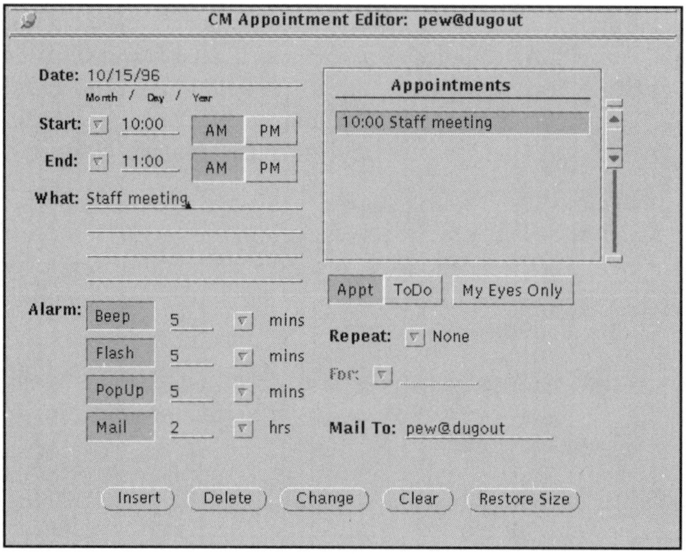

Figure 7.2
The Appointment Editor pop-up window

The Appointment Editor is the heart of the Calendar Manager program. With the Appointment Editor, you schedule and describe appointments and ToDo lists, specify time periods, and determine notification methods.

Here are the steps to follow when you want to schedule an appointment:

1. From the base window, position the pointer over the day for which you want to schedule an appointment, and double-click SELECT.
2. Select a start time and an end time. You can either type the start and end times into the Start and End text fields or use the abbreviated menu buttons to the left of the text fields to select the times in 15 minute increments.
3. Enter a description of the appointment in the What field. You can use one or more of the text fields provided. Only the first line is displayed on the month view of the Calendar Manager's base window.
4. Select alarm options to have the Calendar Manager remind you of your appointment. You can also choose a time interval that indicates the number of minutes, hours, or days before the appointment that the Calendar Manager should provide the alarm.
5. Press the Insert button to schedule the appointment.

When you have scheduled an appointment, the start time and the first line of the What field appear in the Appointments scrolling list. Figure 7.2 shows the Appointment Editor with a staff meeting scheduled.

When you want to change or delete a scheduled appointment, you must first select the appointment from the Appointments scrolling list. When you have done this, all of the corresponding information regarding start and end times, the description, and the alarm settings is displayed. To change the appointment, make the necessary changes to any of the fields on the Appointment Editor and press the Change button at the bottom of the window. To delete the appointment, press the Delete button.

There is much more that you can do with the Appointment Editor pop-up window, but we will save that discussion for later in the chapter.

Appointments and ToDo Lists

The Calendar Manager keeps track of both appointments and ToDo lists. ToDo items are entered the same way that appointments are entered. You use the Appointment Editor but select the ToDo choice under the scrolling list.

Internally, the Calendar Manager keeps track of appointments and ToDo lists separately. This allows you to display or print appointments only or ToDo items only. The Appointment Editor, however, displays all appointments and ToDo items in its scrolling list for the day selected.

Generally, you will schedule an appointment when you need a reminder of the appointment, such as a mail message or a pop-up notice. ToDo lists are best used for keeping track of tasks you want to accomplish when you don't require a reminder. If you choose to add start and end times to a ToDo item, then you will get a reminder as specified in the Alarm section of the Appointment Editor.

You have learned enough now to use the Calendar Manager's basic features. The rest of this chapter is devoted to the details of the Calendar Manager and the Multi-Browser. In the next section we discuss the different views of the Calendar Manager's base window.

Calendar Manager Views

The Calendar Manager provides four views for its base window: year, month, week, and day. As you have already seen, the default view is month. Use the View menu button to select the desired view. When you press MENU with the pointer over the View button, the View menu shown here is displayed:

The first four items on the View menu correspond to the four views available in the Calendar Manager. The last item, Find, displays the Find pop-up window, which you use to locate calendar items. Each of the first four buttons on the View menu has an associated submenu. You can see the Day View submenu in the preceding illustration. From the submenu you can do one of three things: set the Calendar Manager's base window, display a list of appointments, or display a list of ToDo items.

The Appointment and ToDo lists include all of the calendar entries for the specified time period. For example, if you choose the Month ToDo List, then all of the ToDo items for the entire month are included in the list. The list is displayed in a pop-up window with a scrollbar. Figure 7.3 shows the Calendar Manager with the Appt List and ToDo List pop-up windows.

The only difference between the Appt List pop-up window and the ToDo List pop-up window is that the ToDo List includes a checkbox for each item on the list. You can use the checkbox to check off each item as you complete it. This is a convenient way to keep track of "things to do" on a daily, weekly, or monthly basis.

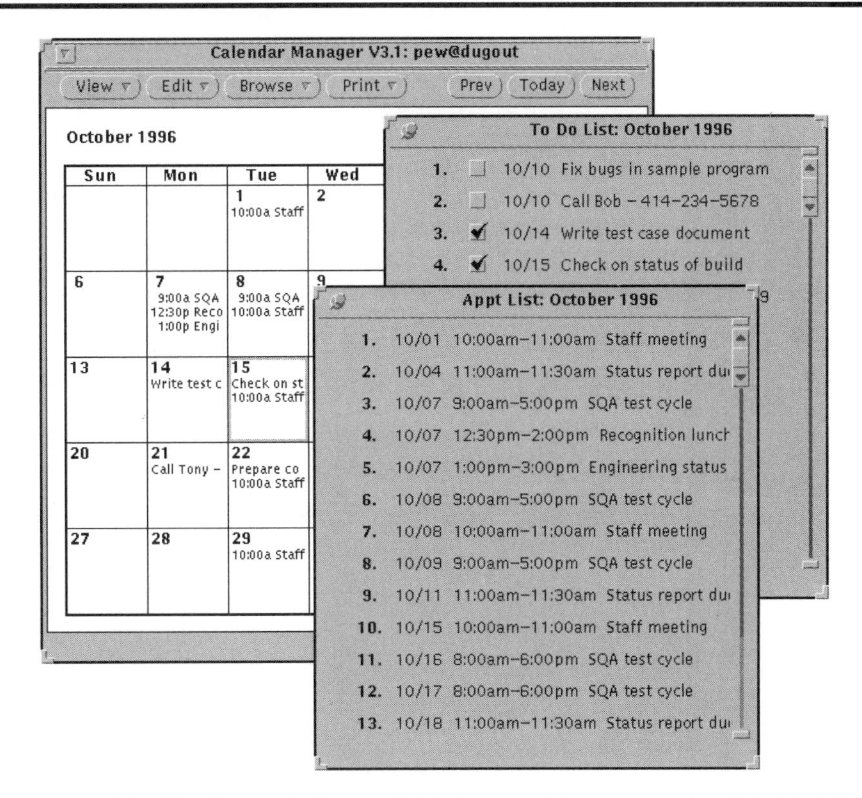

Figure 7.3
The Calendar Manager with Appt List and ToDo List pop-up windows

The Year View

When you select Year from the View menu, any year from 1969 to 1999 can be displayed. Use the year view when you need a year-at-a-glance overview. For example, perhaps you need to know which day of the week a particular day, several months from now, falls on.

You can select a month from the year view by clicking SELECT with the pointer over the desired month. Figure 7.4 shows the year view with October highlighted as the current month. If you now choose Appointments from the Edit menu, the Appointment Editor will display appointments for the first day of the selected month.

The year view is probably not the view you will use every day, but it is very convenient when you need to schedule an appointment well in advance of the date. For example, let's say you are scheduled to speak at a conference that doesn't take place until two years from now. You will find that the quickest way to display the Appointment Editor for the day of the conference is to first display the year view. When you are in the year view, the Next and Prev buttons at the upper right of the base window increment the view by a year at a time. Use the Next button to go to the year of the conference, and double-click SELECT on the month in which the conference takes place to display the month view. With the month view displayed, double-click on the day of the conference to display the Appointment Editor. If you were to start this operation from the month view, you would have to press the Next button a few dozen times to get to the month you were looking for. Using the year view is a much faster technique.

Figure 7.4 The Calendar Manager year view

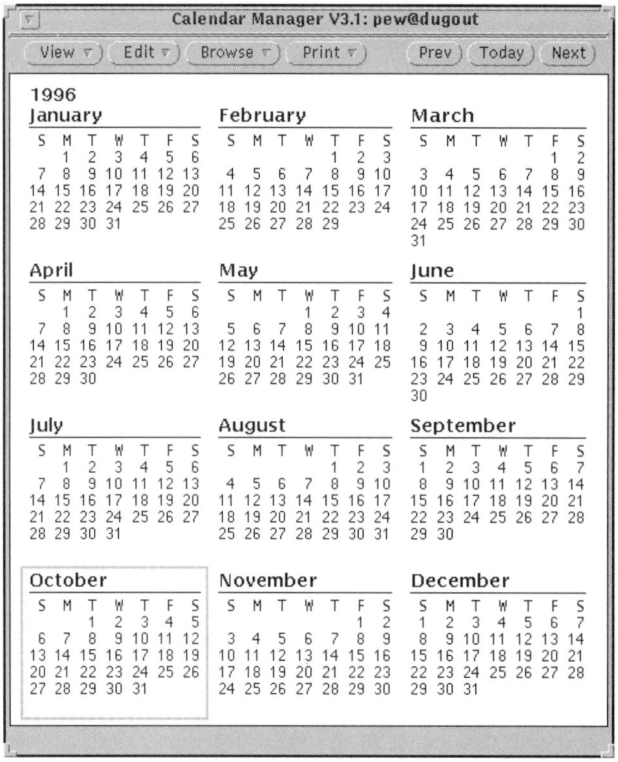

The Month View

The month view is the default Calendar Manager view and is the one you will probably use most of the time. It is much like a monthly calendar that you might hang on your office wall. It gives you a look at the entire month and displays the appointments and ToDo items with their associated start times.

There is limited space available per day in the month view. This means that all of your appointments for a given day may not be displayed because of the lack of vertical space. It also means that the entire description of an appointment or ToDo item may be truncated because of the lack of horizontal space. You can remedy this problem by resizing the Calendar Manager's base window. When you resize the base window, the size of each day grows or shrinks accordingly. Since the characters that are used for displaying your appointments and ToDo items stay the same size, you can display more appointments by increasing the vertical size of the base window. You can also increase the width of the base window to display more of the description of each item shown in each day. Figure 7.5 shows the month view of the Calendar Manager's base window after it has been resized to a larger width (compare with Figure 7.1).

Figure 7.5
The Calendar Manager month view

Calendar Manager V3.1: pew@dugout

View | Edit | Browse | Print | Prev | Today | Next

October 1996

Sun	Mon	Tue	Wed	Thu	Fri	Sat
		1 10:00a Staff mee	2	3	4 11:00a Status rep	5
6	7 9:00a SQA test 12:30p Recogniti 1:00p Engineeri	8 9:00a SQA test 10:00a Staff mee	9 9:00a SQA test	10 Fix bugs in sampl Call Bob - 414-2	11 11:00a Status rep	12
13	14 Write test case d	15 Check on status 10:00a Staff mee	16 8:00a SQA test	17 8:00a SQA test	18 11:00a Status rep	19
20	21 Call Tony - 415-	22 Prepare course o 10:00a Staff mee	23 10:00a Pick up Al	24	25 11:00a Status rep	26
27	28	29 10:00a Staff mee	30	31		

With the month view displayed, you select a day by positioning the pointer over the day and clicking SELECT. The selected day is displayed with a border around it. The color of the border matches your window color (see the discussion of workspace properties in Chapter 3). If the month displayed is the current calendar month, today's date will also be the window color. This helps you easily identify the current day.

You can display the Appointment Editor from the month view by double-clicking SELECT with the pointer over a day. If the Appointment Editor pop-up window is already displayed, selecting a new day from the month view will change the Appointment Editor's appointment date to the day that you selected. In addition, if you double-click SELECT on a day and the Appointment Editor pop-up is already displayed, not only will the appointment date be changed, but the Appointment Editor will be moved to the front of any other windows that may be obscuring it.

The Week View

You can change the view to the week view by positioning the pointer directly over one of the numbers that represent the day of the month, and clicking SELECT. For example, if your calendar is displayed as shown in Figure 7.5, and you position the pointer directly over the 13 and click SELECT, the Calendar Manager changes to the week view, and the week that contains the day you have selected is displayed as shown in Figure 7.6.

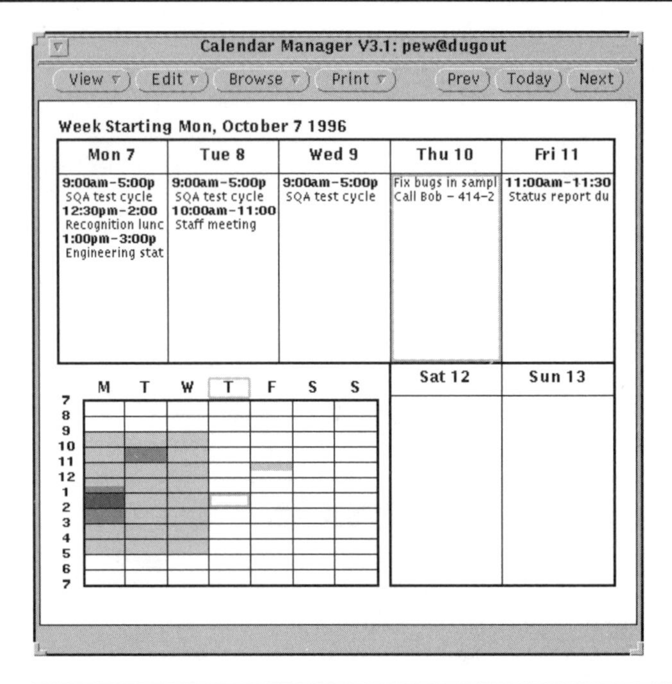

Figure 7.6
The Calendar Manager week view

The week view displays the days for one week, starting on Monday. One advantage of the week view is that it gives you more room to display information about appointments and ToDo items for each day. You also have room to display the start and end times for each appointment. The start and end times are displayed in bold, and the appointment or ToDo items are displayed in the same font used in the month view. Space is still somewhat limited, so only the first line of the description is displayed.

Another important advantage of the week view is that the area in the lower-left corner shows the entire week as hourly blocks of time with scheduled appointments displayed as shaded areas. This helps you quickly determine when you are available to schedule other appointments. If you schedule overlapping appointments, a darker shading appears. In Figure 7.6 you can see that overlapping appointments have been scheduled for Monday between 12:30 and 3:00 and on Tuesday between 10:00 and 11:00. If you schedule three or more appointments that overlap, an even darker shading is displayed. By looking carefully at Figure 7.6, you can see that three or more appointments are scheduled between 1:00 and 2:00 on Monday.

You display the Appointment Editor pop-up window from the week view by double-clicking SELECT with the pointer over any of the day areas or over the weekly block time area in the lower-left corner.

You can select a one-hour block from the weekly block time area by positioning the pointer over the block and clicking SELECT. The block you select is displayed with a border around it. In Figure 7.6, Thursday from 1:00 to 2:00 is selected. If you select a block of time when the Appointment Editor is displayed, the corresponding time in the Start and End fields is selected. This is a convenient way to enter the start and end times for an appointment. It is often faster than any other method for selecting the time of an appointment.

The Day View

If you position the pointer over the date box at the top of one of the day areas and click SELECT, the Calendar Manager displays the day view for the day you have selected. For example, if you position the pointer over the date box labeled Wed 13 and click SELECT, the day view for the 13th is displayed.

The day view shows the appointments scheduled for one day. It does not, however, display any items that do not have times associated with them. On the left side of the day view is a three-month calendar. You can click on any day of any of the three months to display the appointments for that day. Figure 7.7 shows the day view.

The day view contains the complete description of an appointment, not just the first line as in the month and week views. If the entire description is not displayed because of a lack of horizontal space, you can resize the Calendar Manager Window to display more of the information.

Figure 7.7
The Calendar Manager day view

You display the Appointment Editor pop-up window from the day view by double-clicking SELECT with the pointer over any hour of the day. Clicking SELECT anywhere within one of the hour blocks selects that time and updates the Appointment Editor's start and end times if they are displayed.

Finding a Calendar Appointment

The Find item on the View menu displays the Find pop-up window, which you use to search for an appointment or ToDo item. To search for an item, enter some text in the Match Appt text field. You can enter text only to match the description of the appointment or ToDo item; you cannot search for a start or end time or any other fields of an appointment. The Find pop-up window is shown here, with "Meeting" in the Match Appt field:

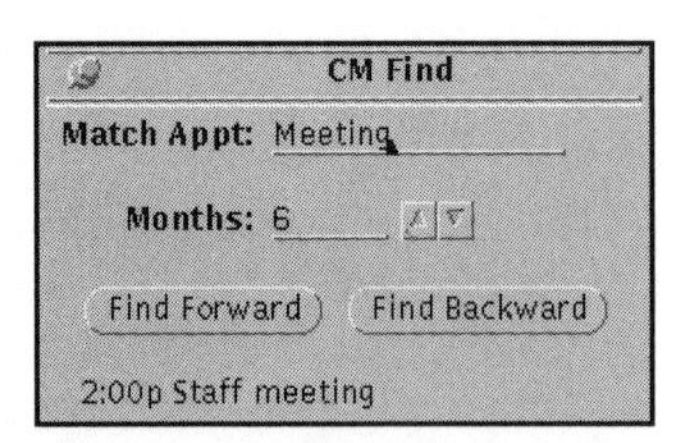

The Months field determines the extent of the search. The default value is 6. You can change the number of months searched from 1 to 100. You can either type the new number or use the increment/decrement buttons to the right of the field to change the value.

The search begins when you click either the Find Forward or the Find Backward button. The search begins from the current day and time selected from the view, in the direction indicated. For example, if you have the day view displayed with the 9:00 to 10:00 a.m. hour block selected and you choose Find Forward from the Find pop-up window, the search begins at 10:00 a.m. on the day displayed in the day view.

When a match is found, the start time and description are displayed in the Find pop-up window's footer, and the view is changed to display the day of the appointment.

The Find feature is especially useful when you know you have an appointment but can't remember the exact date. Rather than searching through weeks or months of calendars, use the Find pop-up window to locate the appointment.

Scheduling Appointments

Earlier in this chapter, you learned some of the basics of scheduling appointments. Now you will learn the details and some different techniques to make scheduling appointments faster and easier.

The Appointment Editor

Every item scheduled by the Calendar Manager has seven parts:

- Date
- Classification
- Start and end times
- Description
- Alarms
- Repeat rate
- Visibility

You set each of these seven parts on the Appointment Editor when you create an appointment. In this section you will learn how to use the Appointment Editor to set each field. Figure 7.8 shows the Appointment Editor displaying information about a staff meeting.

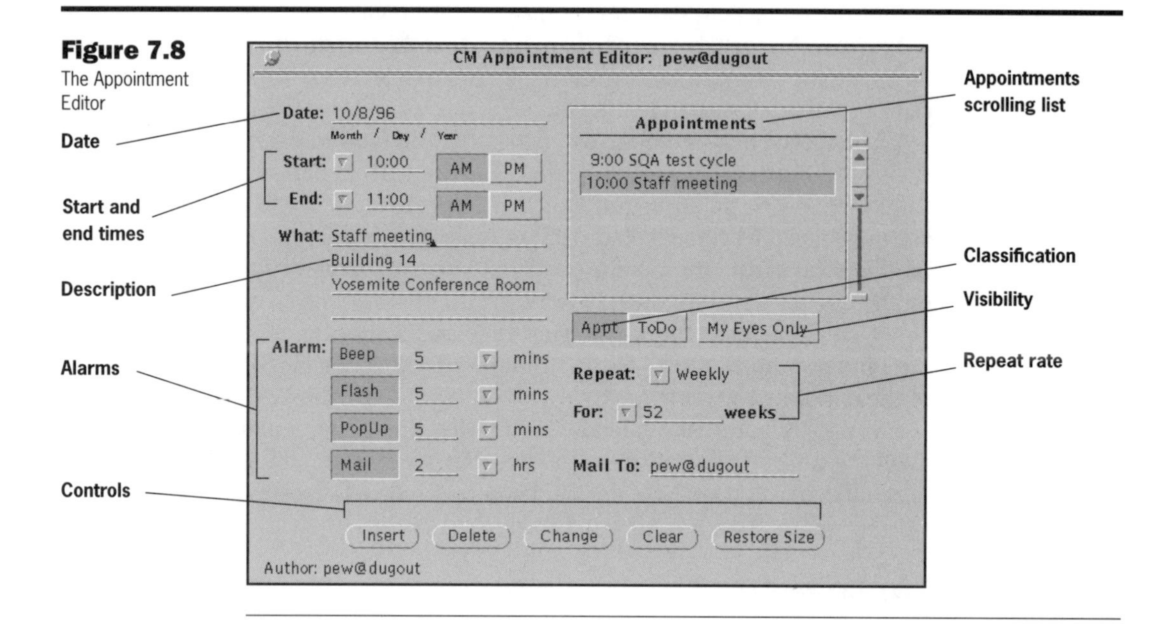

Figure 7.8 The Appointment Editor

Many of the fields that you use for setting appointments have options that you can customize. For example, you can change the available times that are displayed on the Start and End menu. You can also change the default values for each of the alarm settings. These customization features are discussed in the "Customizing the Calendar Manager" section later in this chapter.

Date

The first field is the date of the appointment or ToDo item. This is always a single date, not a range. You use the Date field on the Appointment Editor to set the date. You usually change the Date field by selecting a day from the month or week views.

Classification

There are two types of items scheduled by the Calendar Manager: appointments and ToDo items. You select an appointment or ToDo item by using the Appt/ToDo setting found below the Appointments scrolling list. Every item scheduled by the Calendar Manager must be either an appointment or a ToDo item.

Start and End Times

The start and end times are optional fields for both appointments and ToDo items. Usually, appointments have start and end times. You choose start and end times by filling in the Start and End fields. If you choose not to associate a time with a scheduled item, clear the Start and End fields.

You can choose start and end times in one of several ways. One way is to enter the time in the Start and End text fields from the keyboard. Another way is to use the abbreviated menu buttons to select a time, as shown in Figure 7.9.

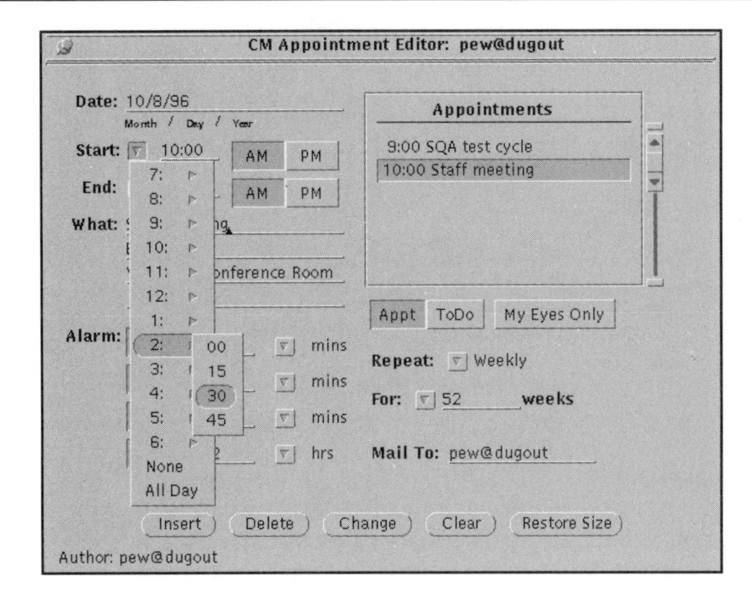

Figure 7.9
Selecting start and end times

Each hour on the menu has an associated submenu from which you can choose a 15-minute interval: 00, 15, 30, or 45. If you need to specify a time other than within a 15-minute interval, you will have to enter the time from the keyboard. When you choose a start time from the menu, the end time is automatically chosen as one hour after the start time. If this is not the correct ending time, enter a new end time. The last two items on the menu, labeled None and All Day, are special options. The None item clears the time field so that no time is associated with the appointment. The All Day item sets the start time to 12:00 a.m. (midnight) and the end time to 11:59 p.m.

Another way to choose start and end times is available when you have the week or day view displayed. You can click SELECT on an hour of the day displayed in the view to set the start and end times on the Appointment Editor. Figure 7.10 shows how to set the date and time to Thursday from 3:00 to 4:00 by clicking SELECT on the week view.

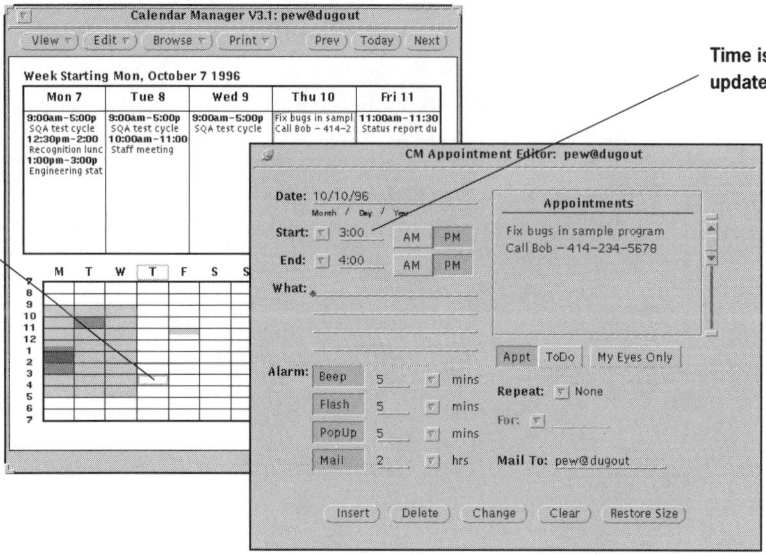

Figure 7.10
Setting the time from the week view

Click SELECT here

Time is updated here

Description

The What text fields on the Appointment Editor allow you to describe the item. You should include a short description on the first line. The text on the first line is displayed on the month, week, and day views. Use the other lines for additional information.

Alarms

If a scheduled item has a time associated with it, then you can receive a reminder by setting one or more alarms. Four types of alarms are available: Beep, Flash, PopUp, and Mail. The Beep and Flash items cause the Calendar Manager to respectively beep and flash when the appointment comes due. If the Calendar Manager is iconified, the icon beeps and flashes. The PopUp alarm causes a pop-up window to be displayed at the appropriate time, showing the time of the appointment and the complete description that you entered into the What field. The Mail alarm lets you send a mail message as a reminder. You use the Mail To field to the right of the Mail alarm choice to designate the intended recipient of the message. By default, this is you, but you can change this designation if you want one or more other users to receive a reminder. For example, if you expect a status report from each person who works for you, you can send a mail reminder to each of them that the status report is due.

To the right of each Alarm setting is a text field that lets you specify a period of time before the scheduled appointment at which you want to be notified. The number in the text field can be interpreted in minutes, hours, or days.

By default, the Beep, Flash, and PopUp alarms are set to minutes and the Mail alarm is set to hours. You can change any of these by using the abbreviated menu button to the right of each text field to display a menu that provides the three choices: minutes, hours, and days.

Repeat Rate

Some appointments occur regularly—a weekly staff meeting, for example. You can choose to specify that an appointment or ToDo item is to repeat at regular intervals, such as daily, weekly, or monthly, and then you would indicate the duration of the appointment. For example, you may want to schedule your seven-day vacation with one appointment entry by specifying a daily repeat duration of seven days.

To specify that an appointment or ToDo item is to repeat, use the Repeat abbreviated menu button to select a frequency. You can choose None (the default), Daily, Weekly, Biweekly, Monthly, or Yearly. When you have chosen a repeat value other than None, the For field becomes active so that you can enter a duration for the repeated appointment. Figure 7.8 shows a weekly appointment scheduled for 52 weeks.

Visibility

An appointment or ToDo item may be public or private. You can choose to have the item available to your eyes only by selecting the My Eyes Only choice found below the Appointments scrolling list. Normally, items in your calendar are viewable to other users to ease the scheduling of appointments for multiple users. If you have a private appointment that you don't want anyone to know about, select the My Eyes Only choice, but be aware that other users who browse your calendar will not know that you are busy at that time.

Appointment Editor Controls

The controls at the bottom of the Appointment Editor allow you to insert and modify appointments and to control the behavior of the Appointment Editor:

Insert inserts a new appointment into the Calendar Manager. Fill in the appropriate fields of the Appointment Editor and press Insert to create a new appointment or ToDo item.

Delete deletes an existing appointment. Choose an appointment from the Appointments scrolling list and press Delete to eliminate an appointment or ToDo item.

Change changes an existing appointment. Choose an appointment from the Appointments scrolling list, make the necessary changes to any of the fields displayed on the Appointment Editor, and press Change to modify an appointment or ToDo item.

Clear clears the fields of the Appointment Editor and supplies the default values for each field.

Restore Size reduces the size of the Appointment Editor. When the Appointment Editor is displayed in the abbreviated size, this button is labeled Full Size and toggles the size of the Appointment Editor back to full size. The Alarm and Repeat fields are not displayed when the Appointment Editor is in the abbreviated size.

Entering a New Appointment

Now let's go through the step-by-step process necessary to schedule an appointment. Suppose you are planning to attend a five-day training course beginning September 30, 1996. The course runs from 9:00 to 5:00 Monday through Friday. Here are the steps you would follow to schedule the course:

1. Change the Calendar Manager's base window view to display the start date of the course (September 30, 1996).
2. Double-click SELECT on September 30 to display the Appointment Editor.
3. Enter the start time of 9:00 a.m. in the Start field and an end time of 5:00 p.m. in the End field.
4. Enter a description of the course in the What field. Use the first line as a general description, and then use the other lines for any additional information such as the location or a reminder of what to bring with you.
5. Select the Alarm options. For this example, turn off Beep and Flash but leave PopUp and Mail turned on. Suppose that it takes 15 minutes to get to the class from your office. You want to come to the office each morning and read your mail before going to class, but you want to allow enough time to get to class without being late, so set the PopUp time to 15 minutes. Leave the Mail time at 2 hours. That will ensure that you receive a mail message each morning reminding you of the class.
6. Since you are creating an appointment, make sure the Appt choice (the default) is selected.
7. Choose whether or not you want the appointment to be seen by others. In this case, there is no need to hide the appointment from anyone, so make sure the My Eyes Only choice is not selected.
8. Select a repeat rate and duration. Display the Repeat menu by pressing MENU with the pointer over the Repeat abbreviated menu button, and select Daily. Then display the For menu by pressing MENU with the

pointer over the For abbreviated menu button, and select 5, which will repeat the appointment for five days.

9. Press the Insert button. The appointment is now scheduled, and the first line of the description appears in the Appointments scrolling list.

Figure 7.11 shows how the Appointment Editor should look after you have filled in all of the fields to schedule the five-day course.

Figure 7.11 Entering a new appointment

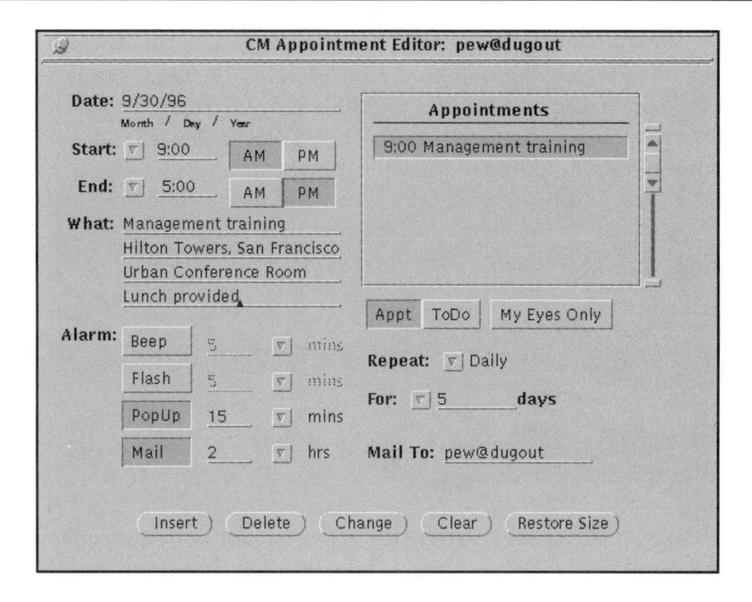

Two hours before the start time of the scheduled appointment you will receive a mail message, and 15 minutes before the start time the following pop-up reminder will be displayed on your screen:

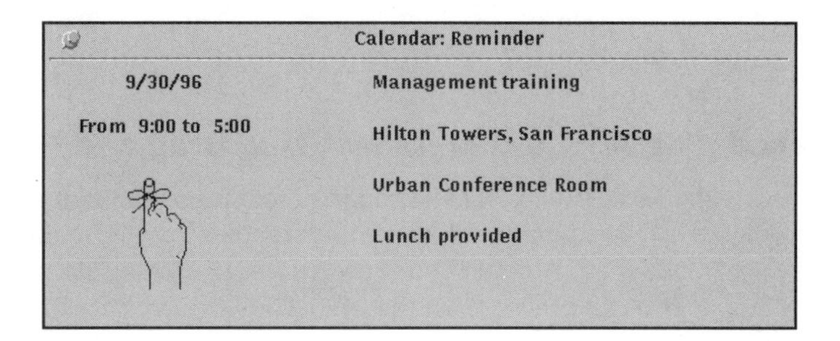

Changing and Deleting Appointments

On occasion you many need to change or delete an appointment or a ToDo item. To change an item, you must first select the item from the Appointments scrolling list by positioning the pointer over the item and clicking SELECT. When a calendar item has been selected, all the information regarding that item is displayed in the Appointment Editor. To make changes to the calendared item, edit the fields on the Appointment Editor and press the Change button. You can change any parameters of a calendared item: the start and end times, the alarm options, the description, or even the visibility.

If you are changing an item that is part of a repeating series, you are given the option of changing just that particular item or all the items in the series. For example, if your five-day class has to move to a new location on Wednesday only, you may want to update the What field for Wednesday's appointment but leave the other four appointments as they are. When you press the Change button, you are presented with the following notice:

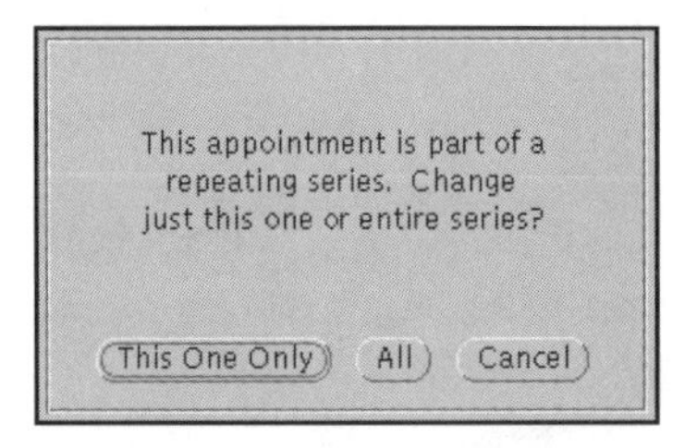

You can choose to alter this appointment only, alter all appointments in the repeating series, or cancel the operation. Press the This One Only button to alter only Wednesday's appointment.

When you want to delete an appointment or a ToDo item, you must first select the appointment from the Appointments scrolling list, just as you would do to change an item. To delete the appointment or the ToDo item, press the Delete button. If the item is part of a repeating series, you will be presented with a notice similar to the one used when you are changing a scheduled item. You can choose to delete just that one item, delete all items in the series, or cancel the operation.

Scheduling Appointments by Using Drag and Drop

By using the Mail Tool, you can send mail messages that contain appointment information. The Calendar Manager understands appointments only when they are in a special format. If you receive a mail message that contains an appointment, you can drag it from the Mail Tool and drop it onto the Calendar Manager. The appointment is then scheduled automatically.

The message you receive will look something like the one shown in Figure 7.12. A calendar appointment includes the date, the start and end times, and a description on one or more lines. The message may also contain other text, but it does not interfere with the scheduling of the appointment.

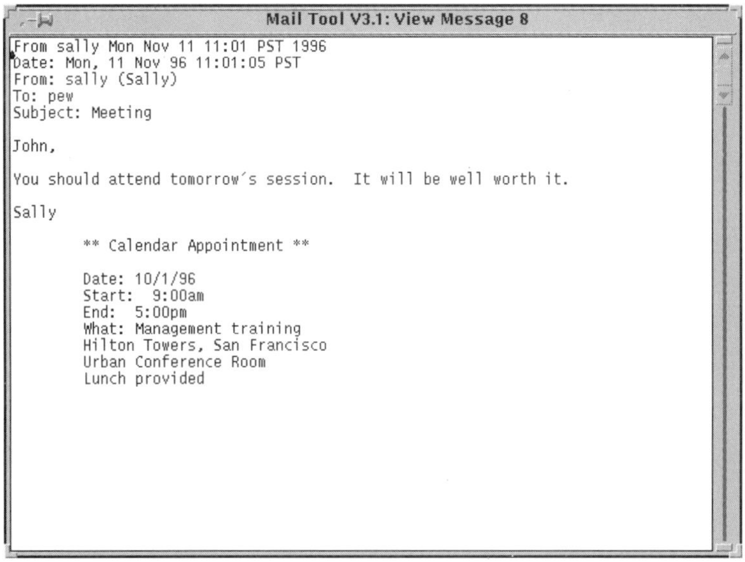

Figure 7.12
An appointment sent through the mail

Mail Tool V3.1: View Message 8

```
From sally Mon Nov 11 11:01 PST 1996
Date: Mon, 11 Nov 96 11:01:05 PST
From: sally (Sally)
To: pew
Subject: Meeting

John,

You should attend tomorrow's session.  It will be well worth it.

Sally

        ** Calendar Appointment **

        Date: 10/1/96
        Start:  9:00am
        End:  5:00pm
        What: Management training
        Hilton Towers, San Francisco
        Urban Conference Room
        Lunch provided
```

A message may also contain more than one appointment. You can use drag and drop in one of two ways to schedule an appointment. The simplest way is to drag the message header from the Mail Tool's base window. Here are the steps to follow:

1. Select the message header from the Mail Tool's base window.
2. Position the pointer over the selected mail message, and press SELECT.
3. Drag the cursor to the Calendar Manager. You can position the pointer over any part of the Calendar Manager's base window or over the Appointment Editor pop-up window.
4. Release SELECT. The appointment is scheduled.

Figure 7.13 shows a message being dragged from the Mail Tool and dropped onto the Calendar Manager. If the message you select contains more than one appointment, this procedure will schedule all of the appointments that the message includes.

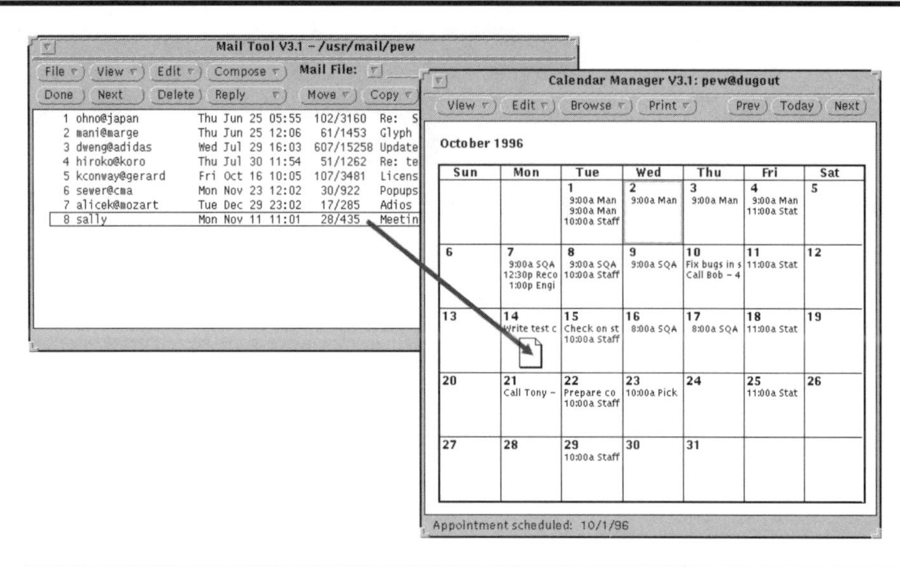

Figure 7.13
Dragging a message containing an appointment from the Mail Tool to the Calendar Manager

Another way to use drag and drop to schedule an appointment is to highlight the appointment in the Mail Tool's Message window and drag the highlighted text to the Calendar Manager. You may prefer this method when multiple appointments are included in a message and you don't want to schedule all of them. You can simply highlight the ones you want to schedule, drag only those appointments, and drop them onto the Calendar Manager. Figure 7.14 shows a message with two appointments, one of which has been highlighted and is being dragged to the Calendar Manager.

You can drop the message anywhere onto the Calendar Manager's base window or the Appointment Editor window. You don't have to drop it onto the correct day, because the message contains the date of the appointment. In fact, you can even drop an appointment message onto the Calendar Manager icon to schedule the appointment.

If you drop a message or text onto the Calendar Manager that is not in the correct format, you will be presented with a notice indicating that the message could not be scheduled. Later in this chapter you will learn how to compose mail messages that include appointments.

Printing

The Calendar Manager supports a printing facility that lets you print any one of the views or a list of appointments or ToDo items. Printing a list of appointments or ToDo items for the day can help you keep track of your schedule while you are away from your computer. In this section you will learn how to print each of the different views and lists that are available. You choose the printer and printer options from the Printer Settings Properties window. You'll learn how to do this in the customization section of this chapter.

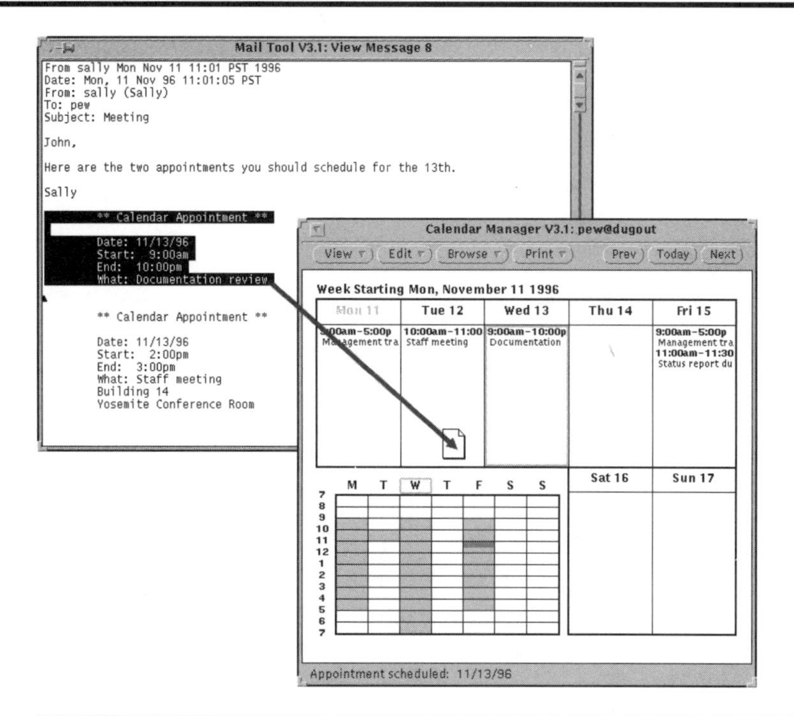

Figure 7.14 Dragging a highlighted appointment from the Mail Tool

Printing Views

The Print button in the Calendar Manager's control area displays a menu from which you can choose your printing options. The items on the menu allow you to choose whether to print a year, month, week, or day view. Each item on the Print menu has a submenu from which you can choose the type of printout. For example, from the Day submenu you can choose to print the day view of the Calendar Manager's base window, or a list of appointments or ToDo items for the day, as shown here:

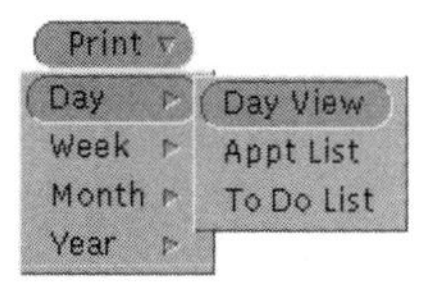

The Day View

To print the day view, select Day View from the Day submenu. The day currently selected is printed in the format shown in Figure 7.15.

Figure 7.15
The day view printout

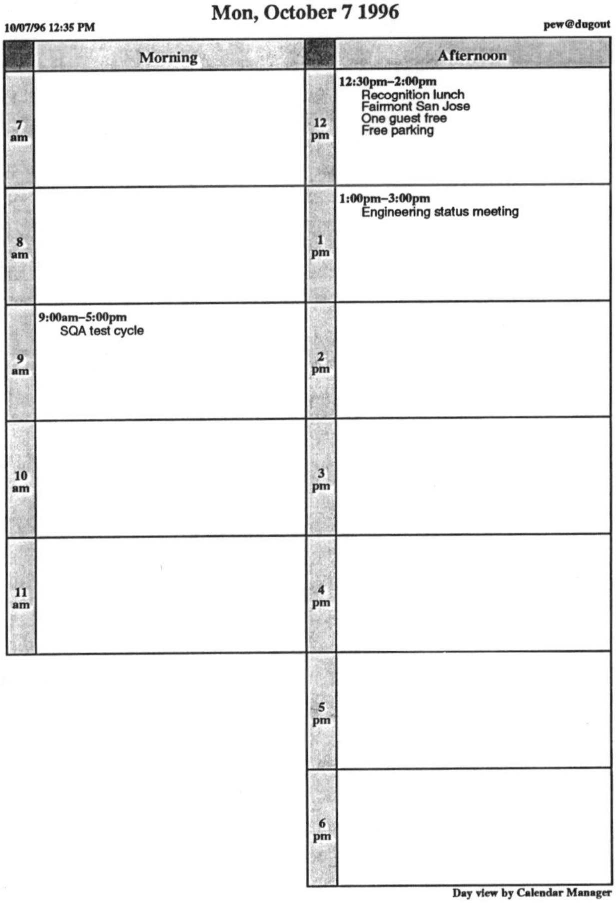

10/07/96 12:35 PM

Mon, October 7 1996

pew@dugout

Morning		Afternoon	
7 am		12 pm	12:30pm–2:00pm Recognition lunch Fairmont San Jose One guest free Free parking
8 am		1 pm	1:00pm–3:00pm Engineering status meeting
9 am	9:00am–5:00pm SQA test cycle	2 pm	
10 am		3 pm	
11 am		4 pm	
		5 pm	
		6 pm	

Day view by Calendar Manager

You can print the calendar for any day by selecting the day before printing it. For example, if the month view is displayed, select a day by clicking SELECT on one of the days. Then choose Day from the Print menu, and that day will be printed.

The Week View

You print the week view by selecting Week View from the Week submenu. The week view printout includes all of the information about each appointment and displays the week as a block with appointment times shaded, as shown in Figure 7.16.

Figure 7.16
The week view printout

Week Starting Mon, October 7 1996

10/07/96 12:59 PM

pew@dugout

Monday 7	Tuesday 8	Wednesday 9	Thursday 10	Friday 11
9:00am–5:00pm SQA test cycle **12:30pm–2:00pm** Recognition lunch Fairmont San Jose One guest free Free parking **1:00pm–3:00pm** Engineering status meeting	**9:00am–5:00pm** SQA test cycle **10:00am–11:00am** Staff meeting Building 14 Yosemite Conference Room	**9:00am–5:00pm** SQA test cycle		**11:00am–11:30am** Status report due

Saturday 12	Sunday 13

M T W T F S S

7 8 9 10 11 12 1 2 3 4 5 6 7

Week view by Calendar Manager

The week view printout prints the week of the day that is currently selected.

The Month View

You print the month view by selecting Month from the Print menu or selecting Month View from the Month submenu. The month view printout appears, as shown in Figure 7.17.

The Year View

Two year view printouts are available: standard and alternate. The Year submenu provides two choices that correspond to the two year view printout types: Yr View (Std) and Yr View (Alt). Figure 7.18 shows the standard year printout, and Figure 7.19 shows the alternate year printout.

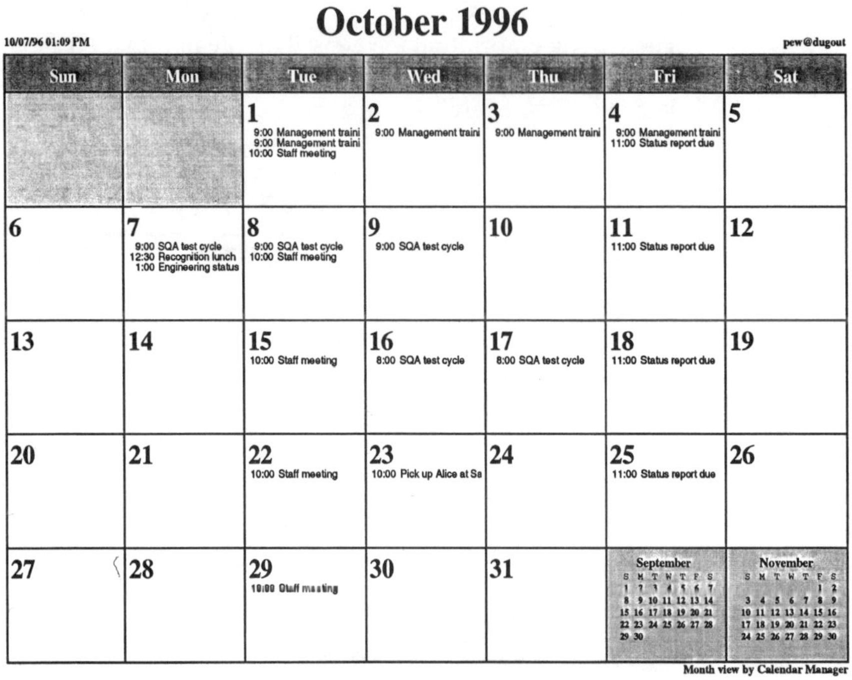

Figure 7.17
The month view printout

October 1996

10/07/96 01:09 PM

pew@dugout

Sun	Mon	Tue	Wed	Thu	Fri	Sat
		1 9:00 Management traini 9:00 Management traini 10:00 Staff meeting	2 9:00 Management traini	3 9:00 Management traini	4 9:00 Management traini 11:00 Status report due	5
6	7 9:00 SQA test cycle 12:30 Recognition lunch 1:00 Engineering status	8 9:00 SQA test cycle 10:00 Staff meeting	9 9:00 SQA test cycle	10	11 11:00 Status report due	12
13	14	15 10:00 Staff meeting	16 8:00 SQA test cycle	17 8:00 SQA test cycle	18 11:00 Status report due	19
20	21	22 10:00 Staff meeting	23 10:00 Pick up Alice at Sa	24	25 11:00 Status report due	26
27	28	29 10:00 Staff meeting	30	31	September S M T W T F S 1 2 3 4 5 6 7 8 9 10 11 12 13 14 15 16 17 18 19 20 21 22 23 24 25 26 27 28 29 30	November S M T W T F S 1 2 3 4 5 6 7 8 9 10 11 12 13 14 15 16 17 18 19 20 21 22 23 24 25 26 27 28 29 30

Month view by Calendar Manager

Printing Appointment and ToDo Lists

In addition to printing the Calendar Manager views, you can also choose to print a list of appointments or ToDo items. Each item on the Print menu has a submenu that includes two items for printing lists: Appt List and ToDo List. When you choose to print a list from the Day submenu, only the items from the selected day are included. If you choose to print a list from the Week, Month, or Year submenus, then the list includes all of the appointments or ToDo items from the week, month, or year of the currently selected day (or month, if you are in year view). As an example, Figure 7.20 displays the appointments for the week of October 7, 1996.

The ToDo list printout is almost identical to the appointment list printout. The only difference is that the ToDo list includes a box in front of each item so that you can check off the item as you complete it. Items that you have already checked on the ToDo list will appear checked on the printout. If you use a daily ToDo list to track your tasks, you can use a weekly or monthly printout as a reference when writing a status report or tracking your progress on a project.

Figure 7.18
The standard year view printout

1996

10/07/96 01:12 PM

pew@dugout

January

S	M	T	W	T	F	S
	1	2	3	4	5	6
7	8	9	10	11	12	13
14	15	16	17	18	19	20
21	22	23	24	25	26	27
28	29	30	31			

February

S	M	T	W	T	F	S
				1	2	3
4	5	6	7	8	9	10
11	12	13	14	15	16	17
18	19	20	21	22	23	24
25	26	27	28	29		

March

S	M	T	W	T	F	S
					1	2
3	4	5	6	7	8	9
10	11	12	13	14	15	16
17	18	19	20	21	22	23
24	25	26	27	28	29	30
31						

April

S	M	T	W	T	F	S
	1	2	3	4	5	6
7	8	9	10	11	12	13
14	15	16	17	18	19	20
21	22	23	24	25	26	27
28	29	30				

May

S	M	T	W	T	F	S
			1	2	3	4
5	6	7	8	9	10	11
12	13	14	15	16	17	18
19	20	21	22	23	24	25
26	27	28	29	30	31	

June

S	M	T	W	T	F	S
						1
2	3	4	5	6	7	8
9	10	11	12	13	14	15
16	17	18	19	20	21	22
23	24	25	26	27	28	29
30						

July

S	M	T	W	T	F	S
	1	2	3	4	5	6
7	8	9	10	11	12	13
14	15	16	17	18	19	20
21	22	23	24	25	26	27
28	29	30	31			

August

S	M	T	W	T	F	S
				1	2	3
4	5	6	7	8	9	10
11	12	13	14	15	16	17
18	19	20	21	22	23	24
25	26	27	28	29	30	31

September

S	M	T	W	T	F	S
1	2	3	4	5	6	7
8	9	10	11	12	13	14
15	16	17	18	19	20	21
22	23	24	25	26	27	28
29	30					

October

S	M	T	W	T	F	S
		1	2	3	4	5
6	7	8	9	10	11	12
13	14	15	16	17	18	19
20	21	22	23	24	25	26
27	28	29	30	31		

November

S	M	T	W	T	F	S
					1	2
3	4	5	6	7	8	9
10	11	12	13	14	15	16
17	18	19	20	21	22	23
24	25	26	27	28	29	30

December

S	M	T	W	T	F	S
1	2	3	4	5	6	7
8	9	10	11	12	13	14
15	16	17	18	19	20	21
22	23	24	25	26	27	28
29	30	31				

Year view by Calendar Manager

The Multi-Browser

The Calendar Manager includes a facility that allows you to access the calendars of other users. This is important for a couple of reasons: (1) you may want to know where to find a certain user at a certain time, and (2) you may need to know another user's schedule so that you can schedule a meeting at a time when that person will be available to attend. The Calendar Manager allows you to load another user's calendar and also includes the Multi-Browser, which lets you browse the calendars of multiple users at one time.

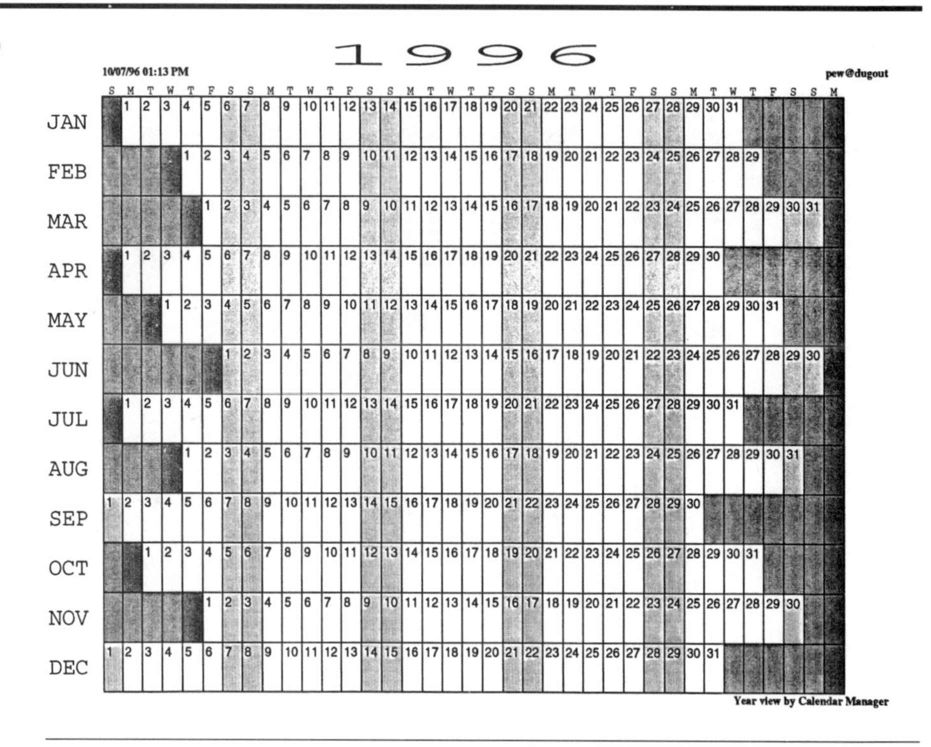

Figure 7.19
The alternate year view printout

The Multi-Browser can be used when you want to simply look at the schedule of other users, or you can (with appropriate permissions) actually schedule an appointment on the calendars of other users. You can also communicate appointments through mail messages—another capability supported by the Multi-Browser. A facility of the Multi-Browser creates a mail message in the proper format from which the recipient can use drag and drop to schedule the appointment.

To start the Multi-Browser, select Multi-Browse from the Browse menu of the Calendar Manager's base window. The Multi-Browser is displayed as shown in Figure 7.21. The Multi-Browser is a separate program, and therefore iconifies independently of the Calendar Manager. The Multi-Browser icon looks like this:

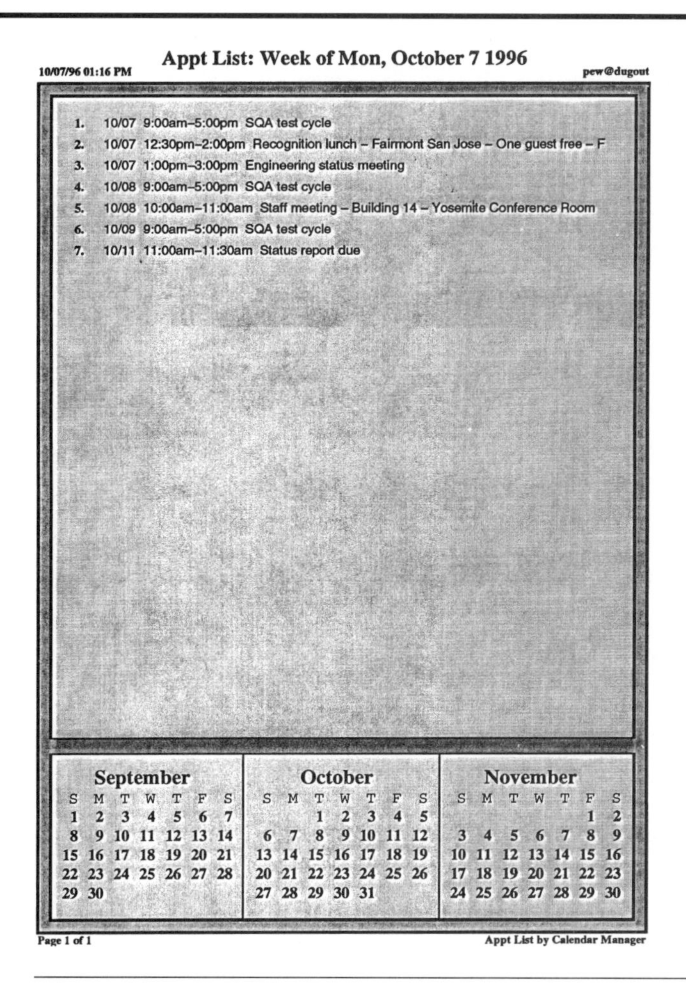

10/07/96 01:16 PM **Appt List: Week of Mon, October 7 1996** pew@dugout

1. 10/07 9:00am–5:00pm SQA test cycle
2. 10/07 12:30pm–2:00pm Recognition lunch – Fairmont San Jose – One guest free – F
3. 10/07 1:00pm–3:00pm Engineering status meeting
4. 10/08 9:00am–5:00pm SQA test cycle
5. 10/08 10:00am–11:00am Staff meeting – Building 14 – Yosemite Conference Room
6. 10/09 9:00am–5:00pm SQA test cycle
7. 10/11 11:00am–11:30am Status report due

September

S	M	T	W	T	F	S
1	2	3	4	5	6	7
8	9	10	11	12	13	14
15	16	17	18	19	20	21
22	23	24	25	26	27	28
29	30					

October

S	M	T	W	T	F	S
		1	2	3	4	5
6	7	8	9	10	11	12
13	14	15	16	17	18	19
20	21	22	23	24	25	26
27	28	29	30	31		

November

S	M	T	W	T	F	S
					1	2
3	4	5	6	7	8	9
10	11	12	13	14	15	16
17	18	19	20	21	22	23
24	25	26	27	28	29	30

Page 1 of 1 Appt List by Calendar Manager

Figure 7.20 The week's appointment list printout

The items on the scrolling list and the menu are user names and host names separated by an @ sign. These are the names of the users whose calendars you can browse. You can add to or delete from this list, as you will learn in the next section.

If you compare the scrolling list on the Multi-Browser and the items on the Browse menu, you will notice that the same names appear on both lists. (The only exception is that the Browse menu includes an additional first item: Multi-Browse.) These two lists always remain identical. Whenever you add or delete a name from the scrolling list, the Browse menu is updated to reflect the change.

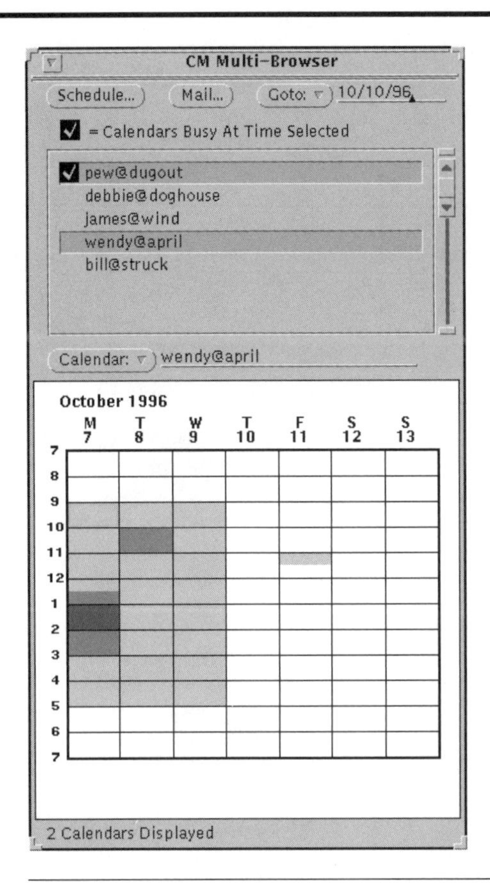

Figure 7.21 The Multi-Browser window

You use the Browse menu to load another user's calendar into the Calendar Manager. This way you can, with the proper permissions, look at the other users' appointments and ToDo lists just as you look at your own. You use the scrolling list on the Multi-Browser to browse another user's calendar or the calendar of several users simultaneously.

Adding and Deleting Users from the Multi-Browser

If you are using the Calendar Manager for the first time, the list of users displayed in the Multi-Browser's scrolling list contains only your user name and host. You can add the name of another user to the list by first entering the name and host, separated by an @ sign, in the text field next to the Calendar menu button. Then either press Return or display the Calendar menu and select Add Calendar. Figure 7.22 shows user debbie at host doghouse being added to the list.

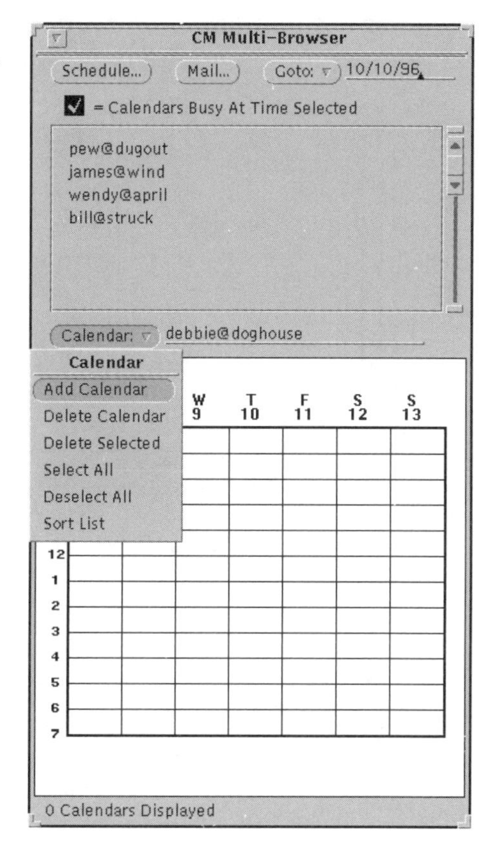

Figure 7.22
Adding a user to the Multi-Browser

After debbie has been added to the list, her name appears on both the Multi-Browser scrolling list and the Browse menu, as shown in Figure 7.23.

The other items on the Calendar menu let you delete names from the list and otherwise manipulate the scrolling list:

Delete Calendar removes from the scrolling list the item displayed in the text field.

Delete Selected removes from the scrolling list the item or items that are selected.

Select All selects all items in the scrolling list.

Deselect All deselects all items in the scrolling list.

Sort List alphabetically sorts the users in the list.

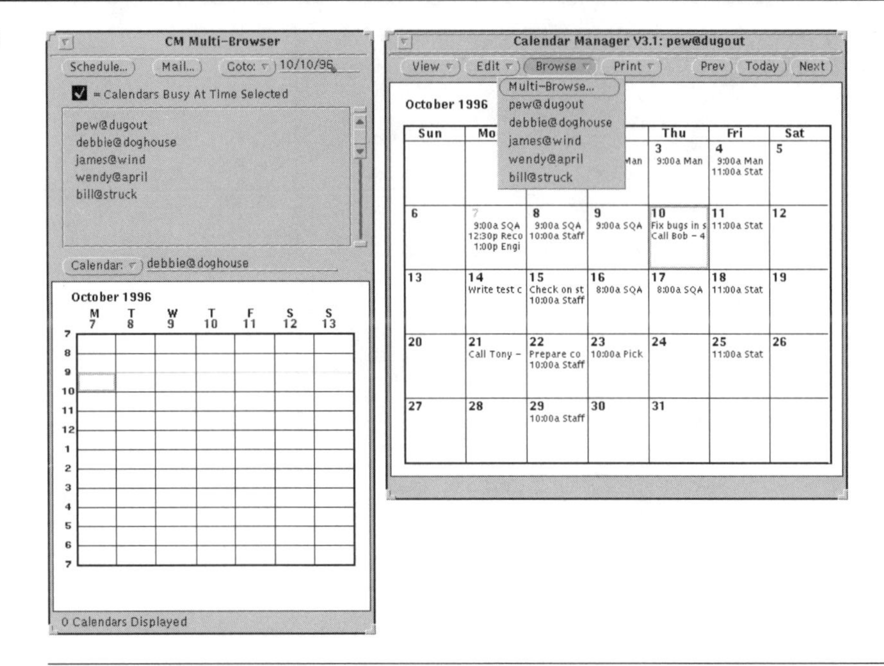

Figure 7.23
The Multi-Browser and Browse menu with a user added

Loading Another User's Calendar

Once you have added a user to your Browse menu, you can load that user's calendar into the Calendar Manager by simply selecting his or her name from the menu. The name and host of the person whose calendar you are looking at is displayed in the header of the Calendar Manager's base window. Figure 7.24 shows the Calendar Manager in the week view after the calendar of wendy@april has been loaded (as indicated in the header).

Each user has the ability to control the permission with which his or her calendar can be accessed by other users. Separate permissions are necessary for browse, insert, and delete. We'll talk about how to set these permissions in the section "Customizing the Calendar Manager," which appears later in this chapter. For now, you should just be aware that these permissions exist. By default, the Calendar Manager allows other users to browse your calendar but not to insert or delete appointments. You can change this capability so that other users can add or delete appointments in your calendar, or you can remove the browse permission. If you load the calendar of a user who has removed browse permission, the times of the appointments will still show, but the description of the appointment will be replaced by the word "Appointment." Figure 7.24 shows a calendar loaded that does not grant browse permission. All the appointment times are included, but no details about the appointments are shown.

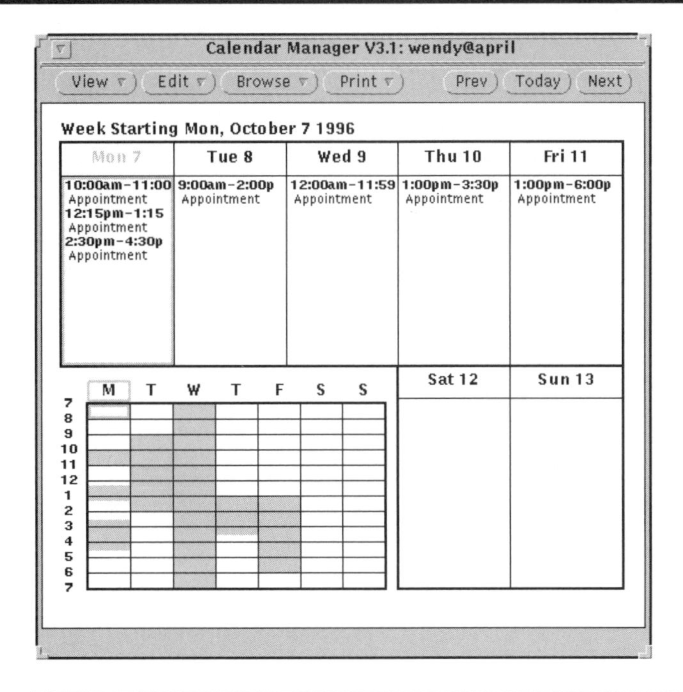

Figure 7.24 Loading another user's calendar

You should also keep in mind that when you load another user's calendar you are seeing only the appointments that were not set to My Eyes Only. When another user creates an appointment or ToDo item and marks it as My Eyes Only, you will not see any indication of it when you browse that user's calendar.

If the calendar you have loaded does grant browse permission, you can see all of the appointments, descriptions, and so forth of that user's calendar, just as if it were your own calendar.

Browsing the Calendars of Multiple Users Simultaneously

One of the advantages of the Multi-Browser is that it lets you look at the calendars of multiple users simultaneously. In the lower half of its window, the Multi-Browser contains a week view of time blocks called the *calendar display.* The calendar display shows you the schedule of the selected user or users. Only a week view is available. Before we go into the details of how to manipulate the Multi-Browser, you need to understand how to select the week that is displayed in the calendar display.

The Goto menu button at the top of the Multi-Browser, shown in Figure 7.25, lets you select the calendar display week. You can either type a date into the text field and press Return, or use the Goto menu to change the week that is displayed.

Figure 7.25
Selecting a week to browse

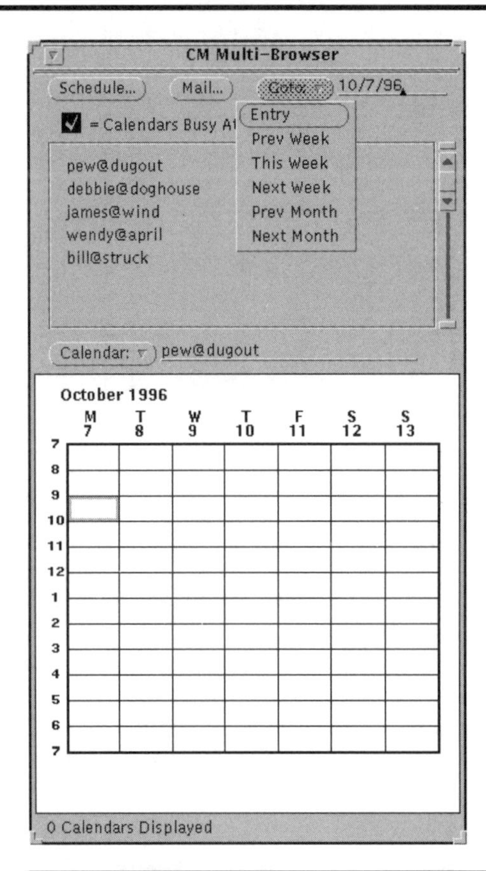

The items on the Goto menu are used as follows:

Entry selects the week displayed in the text field. This is the same as pressing the Return key.

Prev Week moves to the week before the currently selected week.

This Week moves to the week containing today's date.

Next Week moves to the week after the currently selected week.

Prev Month moves to the week one month before the currently selected week.

Next Month moves to the week one month after the currently selected week.

Now that you have the right week selected and you have added users to your list, you are ready to use the calendar display.

To browse the calendar of a user in the list, click SELECT on that user name in the scrolling list. Figure 7.26 shows the Multi-Browser with four users' calendars selected: pew, james, wendy, and bill. Each block of time for the week in the calendar display is either blank or shaded. There are three types of shading: light, medium, and dark. The blocks that are blank represent times in which none of the selected users have appointments scheduled. A lightly shaded block means that one user has a scheduled appointment during that hour, the medium shading indicates that two users have appointments scheduled, and the dark shading indicates that three or more users have an appointment scheduled during that hour.

You'll also notice in Figure 7.26 that users pew, james, and bill have check marks in front of their names. The check marks indicate that they have busy schedules at the time selected. The current time selected is Monday from 9:00 to 10:00 a.m., as shown by the border around that time block. You can change the selected hour by clicking SELECT over a time block. Each time you select a time block, the check marks are updated to indicate which selected users have appointments scheduled during that hour.

If it is your job to schedule a meeting with several people, you can use the Multi-Browser to find a time when all (or most) of the potential participants are not already scheduled. When you have selected all of the users from the scrolling list, look for a block of time that is not shaded. If you were trying to schedule a meeting for users pew, james, wendy, and bill (as shown in Figure 7.26) for the week of October 7, you would see that you have a challenge. The only times available for all the users are early in the morning or late in the afternoon. You could schedule the meeting for 8:00 a.m. or 5:00 p.m. on Tuesday the 8th, but those times may not be good for everyone if they arrive at or leave from work at different times.

If you can't find an open time for all of the participants, you have a couple of choices: you can look for a day in another week, or you can schedule the appointment when *most* of the other people are available. If you choose the latter, you can begin looking for a convenient time for most of the selected users by clicking SELECT on the lightly shaded time blocks. Perhaps there is one key person without whom you cannot hold the meeting. Look for a time slot in which that user does not have a check mark in front of his or her name, and choose that time.

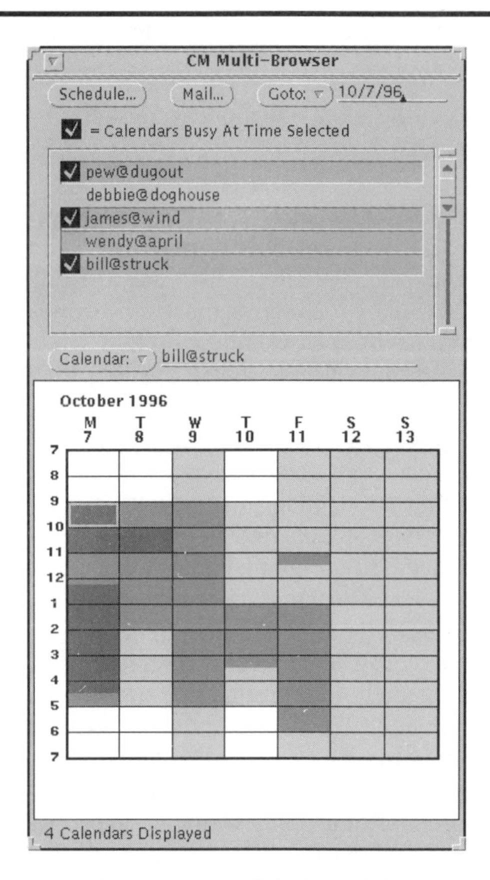

Figure 7.26 The Multi-Browser window with four users selected

Using the Calendar Manager's Browser Editor

The Calendar Manager's Browser Editor is similar to the Appointment Editor. You use it to simultaneously schedule appointments on the calendars of multiple users. You can also use it to gather additional information about a particular user's schedule. To display the Browser Editor, press the Multi-Browser's Schedule button or double-click SELECT on the Multi-Browser's calendar display area. Figure 7.27 shows the Browser Editor.

There are several similarities between the Appointment Editor and the Browser Editor: both include a date, start and end times, a What field, a repeat rate, an Appt/ToDo choice, and an Appointments scrolling list. The Browser Editor does not contain the alarm options or the My Eyes Only choice. It does, however, have an additional scrolling list, which displays the user names selected from the Multi-Browser user list and their corresponding insert access. If a particular user has permitted insert access, that user's name is selected in the Calendars scrolling list. In Figure 7.27 you can see that insert access is available for pew, james, and bill, but not for wendy. This means that you can insert an appointment directly into all of the selected users' calendars except wendy's.

Figure 7.27
The Calendar Manager's Browser Editor

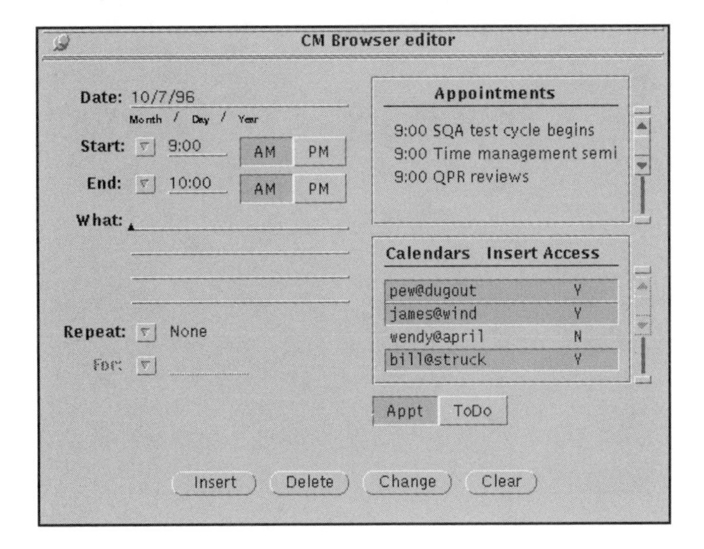

When the Browser Editor is first displayed, the time selected matches the time selected on the Multi-Browser's calendar display. For example, Figure 7.26 shows Monday the 7th from 9:00 to 10:00 a.m. as the selected time period in the calendar display. If you press Schedule with the time period selected as shown in Figure 7.26, the Browser Editor displays the same time period that you have selected from the calendar display, as shown in Figure 7.27. If you click SELECT on another time block in the calendar display, the corresponding time is updated in the Browser Editor.

Getting More Information

The Browser Editor's Appointments scrolling list displays the appointments for each user for the time period indicated. The start time and the description are included in the list. Of course, you don't know which appointment belongs to which user, and this may be important if you are trying to determine who may be able to reschedule an appointment to come to your proposed meeting. If you select one of the appointments from the Appointments scrolling list, the name of the user who has that appointment is displayed in the Calendars scrolling list, as shown in Figure 7.28. As you can see, james is attending an all-day time management seminar in Milpitas for two days. You can click SELECT on the other appointments listed in the Appointments scrolling list to determine who they belong to and to get the details of each appointment, including its start and end times, its duration, and its description.

Figure 7.28
Checking another user's appointment

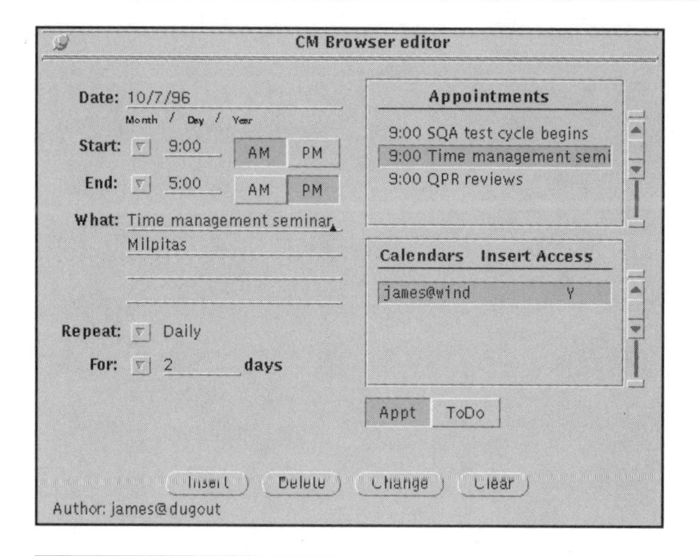

Scheduling a New Appointment

If you have insert access into a user's calendar, you can schedule an appointment directly in that user's calendar from the Browser Editor. Suppose you decide to schedule a meeting for October 10, 1996, from 10:00 to 11:00 a.m. in the Matilda Conference Room. Since you do not have insert access to wendy's calendar, you can schedule the meeting for only the other three people. Here are the steps you would follow to insert the appointment into the calendars of those three users:

1. Display the Multi-Browser if it is not already displayed.
2. Click SELECT on the Multi-Browser's calendar display block that represents the 10:00 a.m. hour block on Thursday, October 10, 1996. This sets the date and the start and end times on the Browser Editor.
3. Display the Browser Editor by pressing the Schedule button.
4. Enter a description of the meeting in the What text fields.
5. Select which users' calendars to insert the appointment into from the Calendars scrolling list. All of the users that you selected in the Multi-Browser's scrolling list of users are included in the Calendars scrolling list. Only the

users that allow insert access are automatically selected in the Calendars scrolling list. If you don't want to insert the appointment into all of their calendars, deselect the names of those who don't need to attend the meeting.

6. Press the Insert button. The appointment is scheduled.

   Figure 7.29 shows the Browser Editor with the new meeting scheduled.

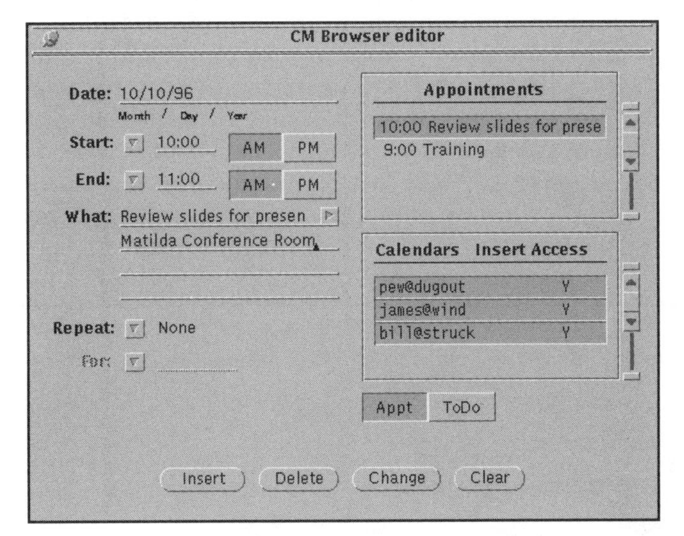

Figure 7.29 Inserting an appointment into the calendars of other users

A word of caution: don't assume that the users know about the appointment just because you inserted it into their calendars. Inserting an appointment into the calendars of other users does not notify them that they have a newly scheduled appointment. They will get their normal default alarms such as mail, a pop-up, and so forth. But this may happen only a few minutes before the scheduled appointment. It is usually considered good etiquette, at the very least, to notify others by mail message that you have scheduled an appointment for them, so that they are not surprised when they are notified that they have a meeting in five minutes.

Sending Mail from the Browser

Many people (including me) do not feel comfortable inserting an appointment or ToDo item directly into someone else's calendar. It's kind of like writing an appointment into someone's hand-held calendar that he or she carries in a briefcase or purse. Most of the time, I don't feel that I have the right (whether or not I have permission) to manipulate someone else's calendar.

There are certainly exceptions to this. You may be responsible for scheduling your manager's calendar, or you may have a close associate who has given you specific permission to insert appointments into his or her calendar. If that is the case, go ahead and use the features of the Calendar Manager and the Multi-Browser as they have been described in this chapter. Otherwise, you may find sending mail a more palatable practice.

I personally always use mail to schedule meetings with multiple users. I do this for two reasons. The first is the reason that I just described: I don't feel comfortable directly manipulating someone else's calendar without permission. The other reason is that I think other people are more likely to remember the meeting if they have had to schedule it themselves by receiving a mail message, reading the message, and then using drag and drop to schedule the meeting.

To create a mail message that includes an appointment notification, use the Mail button in the Multi-Browser window. When you press the Mail button, a Compose Message window is displayed. Figure 7.30 shows the Multi-Browser, the Browser Editor, and the Compose Message window.

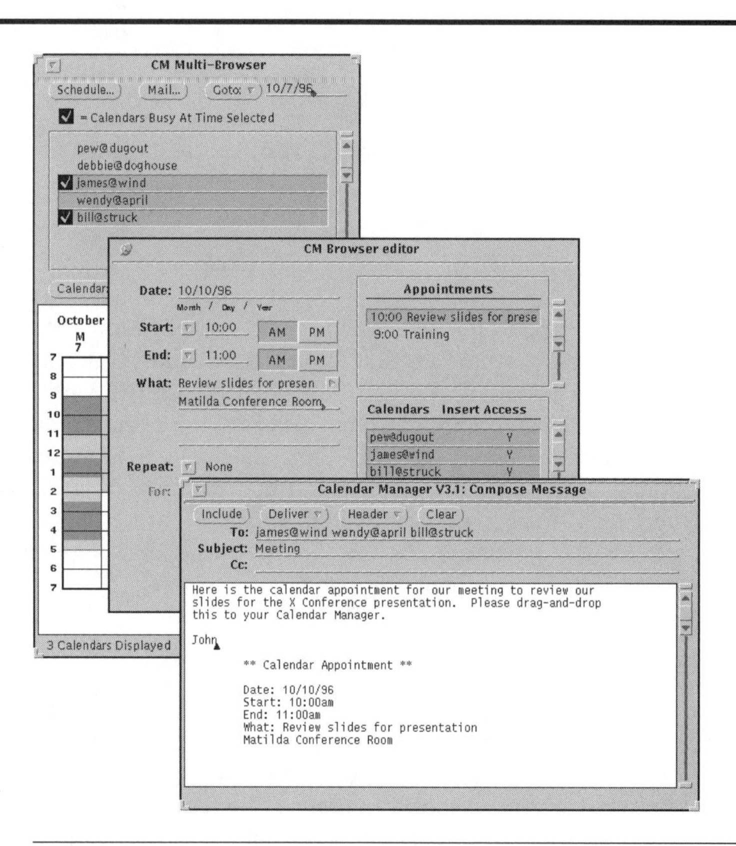

Figure 7.30 Sending a Mail Message from the Multi-Browser

The Calendar Manager Compose Message window is basically the same Compose Message window that is used in the Mail Tool (see Chapter 6). What's special about this Compose Message window is that the message is automatically created in a format that the Calendar Manager understands as an appointment format. The Date, Start, End, and What fields of the Browser Editor are used to fill in the corresponding fields of the appointment notification format that is included in the mail message. Notice that in Figure 7.30 the information included in the mail message matches the information on the Browser Editor. You can also add other text before or after the appointment information, as shown in Figure 7.30.

You will also notice in Figure 7.30 that the To and Subject fields of the Compose Message window are filled in. The Subject field is automatically set to "Meeting," though you can change it to something else if you prefer. The To field is filled in with the names of the users selected in the Multi-Browser's scrolling list. You can see that james, wendy, and bill are included in the list. I deselected myself (pew@dugout) because I already know about the meeting.

When scheduling an appointment for multiple users, a good method is to first schedule the appointment in your own calendar and then use the appointment information you just scheduled to send a mail-message notification to the other people that you expect to attend. Here are the steps to follow:

1. Schedule the appointment in your own calendar.
2. Display the Multi-Browser, and select the users to whom you want to send a message about the meeting.
3. Display the Browser Editor for the date and time of the scheduled appointment.
4. In the Browser Editor's Appointments scrolling list, select the appointment that you just scheduled in step 1. The What field is then filled in automatically, saving you the effort of typing the information again.
5. Press the Mail button on the Multi-Browser. The Compose Message window appears with the appointment information displayed in the format that the Calendar Manager understands.
6. Add a personal message to the mail message, and change any other fields of the message header, such as Subject or Cc. (This is an optional step.)
7. Press the Deliver button to deliver the message.

If you press the Mail button while the Compose Message window is displayed, the appointment information of the mail message is replaced by the current contents of the Browser Editor's Date, Start, End, and What fields. This means that you can alter or change the information on the Browser Editor and update the corresponding data in the mail message by simply pressing the Mail button. If you have added any additional text of your own, pressing the Mail button removes that text.

Another way to use the mail facility of the Calendar Manager is to press the Include button on the Compose Message window to insert a blank appointment format into the message. Then you fill in the fields directly in the Compose window. You may prefer this method if you are sending a message about a meeting that you do not plan to attend and therefore don't want to schedule in your own calendar.

Customizing the Calendar Manager

You can customize several features of the Calendar Manager by using the Properties window. Five categories are available from the Properties window:

- Editor Defaults
- Display Settings
- Access List and Permissions
- Printer Settings
- Date Format

To display the Properties window, choose Properties from the Edit menu or press the Props key on the keyboard. Use the Category abbreviated menu button to display the Category menu, and then select from that menu the category that you want to customize, as shown in Figure 7.31.

Each of the Properties windows has three buttons at the bottom: Apply, Reset, and Defaults. Use the Apply button when you have made changes to the Properties window. The changes you make to any Properties window do not take effect until you press the Apply button. Use the Reset button to change the settings on that particular Properties window to the values you last saved with the Apply button. Use the Defaults button to change the settings on the window to factory defaults. These are the values that the Calendar Manager used before you customized anything.

The Editor Defaults Properties Window

The Editor Defaults Properties window, shown in Figure 7.32, lets you set the default alarm options. By default, all four alarm options are turned off. To set an alarm option, press the button labeled Beep, Flash, PopUp, or Mail, according to your preference. Then update the time fields next to each option. Remember that you are setting the *default values* of the alarm options for the

Appointment Editor. Of course, you can still change the alarm options to whatever you want when you are using the Appointment Editor. This customization window affects only the default values of the alarm options.

The Mail To field lets you specify who will receive a mail notification. By default, mail will be sent to you.

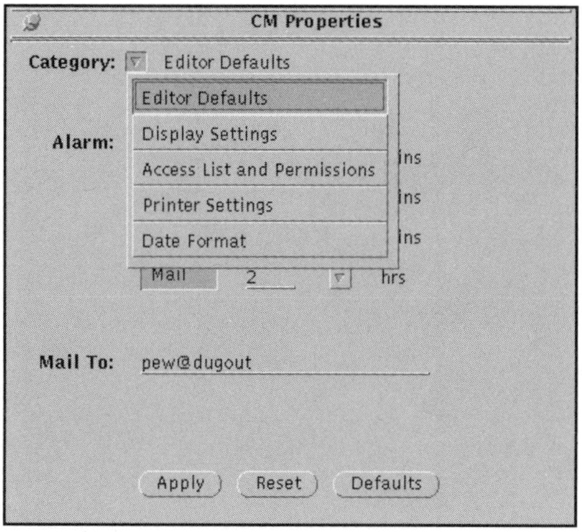

Figure 7.31
Selecting a category from the Properties window

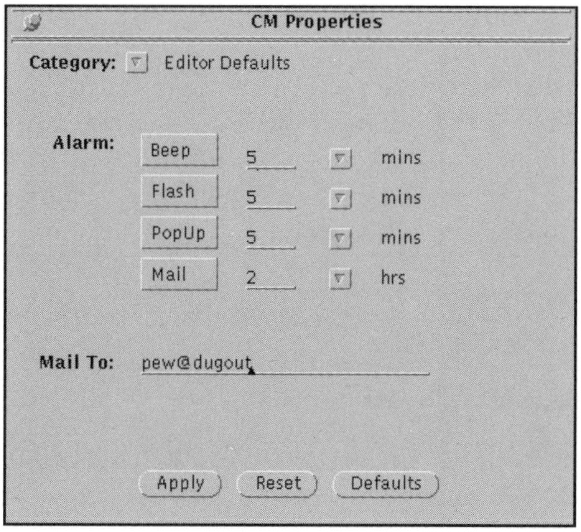

Figure 7.32
The Editor Defaults Properties window

The Display Settings Properties Window

The Display Settings Properties window, shown in Figure 7.33, lets you set the way the Calendar Manager displays boundary times, hour values, and the default view.

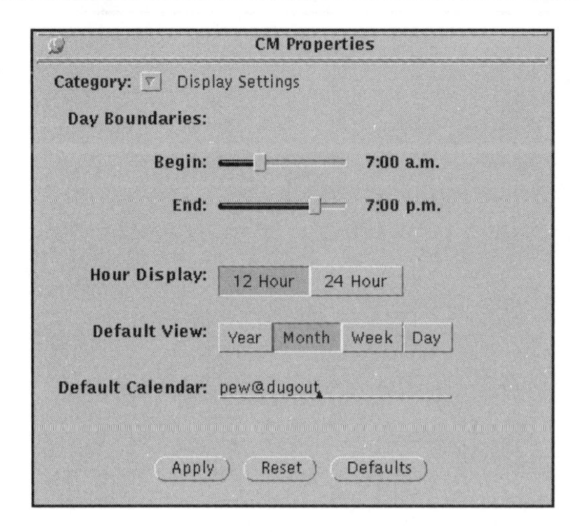

Figure 7.33 The Display Settings Properties window

Let's start with the Day Boundaries settings. Two sliders are used to set the begin and end times for the day. By default, the begin and end times are 7:00 a.m. and 7:00 p.m., respectively. You can adjust either or both of the sliders to change the day boundaries. As you adjust a slider, the corresponding time is displayed to the right of the slider. If, for example, you are scheduling appointments into the evening hours, you probably want to change the end time to a later hour such as 10:00 p.m. Changing the day boundaries affects the Calendar Manager in several places:

- The Calendar Manager day view
- The week chart in the Calendar Manager week view
- The Multi-Browser calendar display
- The Start and End time menus in the Appointment Editor and Browser Editor windows

You use the Hour Display choice to select the way that hours are reported. The default is a 12-hour clock. The other choice is a 24-hour clock. This setting affects the way that hours are displayed anywhere in the Calendar Manager, including the day and week views, printouts, and Start and End time menus.

The Default View choice lets you select which view is displayed when you first invoke the Calendar Manager. The default value is Month.

The Default Calendar text field allows you to select whose calendar is displayed in the Calendar Manager's view. By default, this entry has your name and system in it. You probably won't want to change this unless you need to have another user's calendar loaded by default.

The Access List and Permissions Properties Window

The Access List and Permissions Properties window is used to selectively set permissions for different users. Remember from the section on the Multi-Browser earlier in this chapter that users can turn on or off the permission for other users to browse, insert, and delete appointments and ToDo items in their calendars. This is done by using the Access List and Permissions Properties window, shown in Figure 7.34.

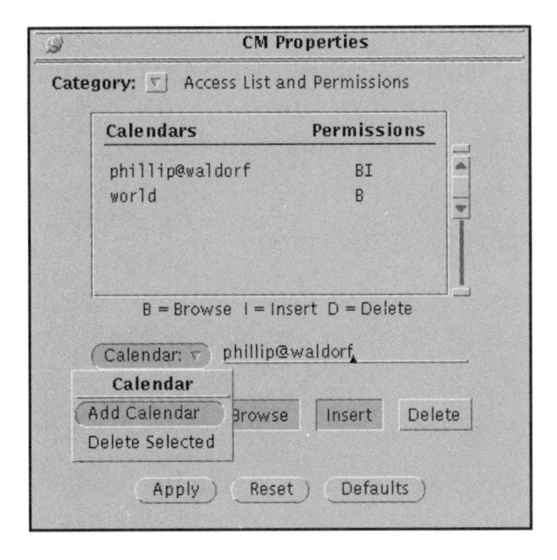

Figure 7.34
The Access List and Permissions Properties window

You can set permissions to browse, insert, and delete for each individual user. There is also a special category called World that applies to all other users. By default, browse permission is allowed for World. This means that other users can look at your calendar, but they may not insert or delete items from your calendar. You may want to keep this policy of allowing all users to browse your calendar, but give insert and delete permissions only to particular users. You can do this by adding a user to the permission list and setting the appropriate permissions for that user.

To add a user to the access and permissions list, follow these steps:

1. In the Calendar field, type the user name and host address of the user you want to add to the list.
2. Select the permissions you want to give to the user from the Permissions nonexclusive choice settings. Figure 7.34 shows the browse and insert permissions being added.
3. Select Add Calendar from the Calendar menu. This selection is also available from the scrolling list pop-up menu.
4. Press the Apply button to record the changes.

When you add a user to the Access list and Permissions, the user's name is included in the scrolling list with the corresponding permissions. Figure 7.34 shows phillip@waldorf added to the list with permissions of BI, representing browse and insert permissions.

If you want to delete the name of a user from the Access list and Permissions, you select that name from the scrolling list. Then select Delete Selected from the Calendar menu, and press Apply.

If you want to change the permissions of a user from the Access list and Permissions, you select the user's name from the scrolling list and change the permissions settings from the Permissions choice. Then select Add Calendar from the Calendar menu, and press Apply.

The Printer Settings Properties Window

The Printer Settings Properties window lets you customize the way printouts are handled. Figure 7.35 shows the Printer Settings Properties window.

Several customizable options are available from the Printer Settings Properties window:

Destination lets you choose whether the output should be printed to a printer or to a file. The default value is printer. If you choose File, the next two fields, Printer and Options, are changed to Directory and File.

Printer lets you specify the printer to which output should be sent.

Options lets you specify command-line options that should be sent to the lp printer command (see Chapter 12).

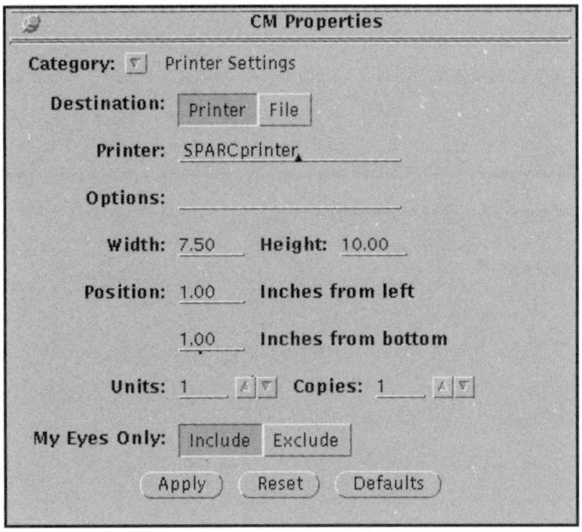

Figure 7.35
The Printer Settings Properties window

Width and **Height** let you change the default width and height values, which are set to 7.5 and 10 respectively. If you change these values, the printout will be scaled proportionally. If you divide both values in half (3.75 and 5.0), you will get a printed calendar that you can carry in a small notebook or shirt pocket.

Position lets you set the distance from the left and bottom edge of the page. The default values are one inch each.

Units lets you specify the number of calendars to be printed. For example, if you are printing the day view, setting Units to 2 will print the calendars of two consecutive days.

Copies lets you specify the number of copies of the calendar to be printed. The default is one.

My Eyes Only lets you choose to include or exclude appointments that you have specified as My Eyes Only.

The Date Format Properties Window

The Date Format Properties window lets you choose the way that the Date field will be used. The Date field is used in three places:

- The Appointment Editor's Date field
- The Goto text field on the Multi-Browser

- The Browser Editor's Date field

By default, the date ordering is month/day/year, with the slash used as a separator. You can choose a different ordering and an alternate separator. Figure 7.36 shows the Date Format Properties window.

Figure 7.36
The Date Format Properties window

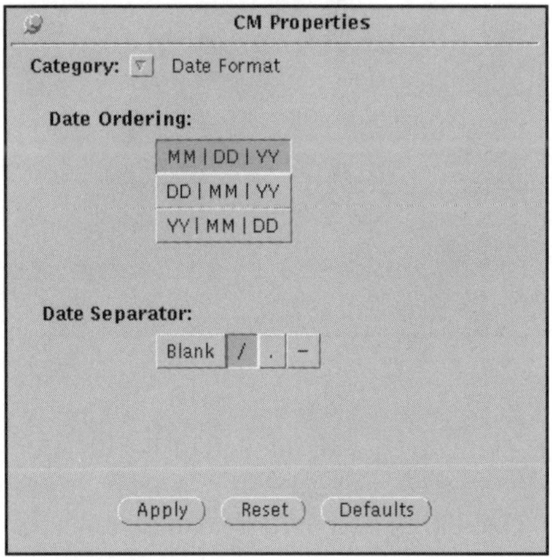

Setting the Time Zone

The Calendar Manager keeps track of the time zone in which you live. If you are browsing the calendar of someone who resides in a different time zone from yours, the Calendar Manager adjusts the time to display the scheduled appointment correctly, For example, if you are in New York and you browse the calendar of someone in California, an appointment that begins at 9:00 a.m. Pacific Standard Time (PST) will display as starting at noon New York time because of the three-hour time difference.

Normally, the time zone in which the Calendar Manager displays appointments is your local time zone. If you want the Calendar Manager to display in another time zone, use the Time Zone item on the Edit menu to display the Time Zone menu.

Each item on the Time Zone menu represents the time zone of a particular country or region of the world. The items that begin with "GMT" represent the time zone in relation to Greenwich Mean Time (GMT). These times are given plus or minus the number of hours before or after GMT. For example, GMT–1 is the time in Sweden, and GMT+8 is the time in California.

If you change your time zone to browse the calendar of someone in a different time zone, don't forget to change it back when you return to your own calendar.

Using the Calendar Manager from the Shell

At some point you will likely need access to your calendar from a remote location. For example, you may be at your home or in a hotel room, using a terminal that is connected to your system by modem, and you need access to the information in your calendar, which is in your system at your office. If you are logging into your system from an ASCII terminal, you have no way of displaying the Calendar Manager DeskSet program. Fortunately, there are three commands that give you a command-line interface to your calendar: cm_lookup, cm_insert, and cm_delete. These three programs are used to browse, insert, and delete appointments, respectively.

Looking up Appointments

The cm_lookup command displays appointments in a calendar. The syntax for this command is as follows:

```
cm_lookup [ -d date ] [ -v view ] [ -c calendar ]
```

The arguments inside the square brackets are optional. With no arguments, cm_lookup displays all appointments and ToDo items for the current day. The -d option lets you specify a date other than today. You can specify a date in the format mm/dd/yy. For example, if you wanted to know the appointments for October 18, 1996, you would enter the following command:

```
dugout% cm_lookup -d 10/18/96
```

The system would respond with something like this:

```
Appointments for Friday October 18, 1996:
          1) 10:00 Staff meeting

          2) 11:30 Lunch with Jim
```

You can also specify a view that describes the period of time that displayed messages represent. The default view is day, meaning that only the appointments scheduled for the day specified (or today by default) are displayed. You can also choose to display a full week's or month's appointments by using the -v options. You select the view by specifying day, week, or month after the -v. When you specify week as the view, the week beginning Sunday of the day specified is displayed. When you specify month as the view, the month that contains the date specified is displayed with all of its appointments. For example, to display all appointments for the current week, enter the following command:

```
dugout% cm_lookup -v week
```

The output would look like this:

```
Appointments for Monday October 11, 1996:
        1) 10:00 Pick up Alice at airport
                 American flight 356

        2)  2:30 Performance review

Appointments for Wednesday October 13, 1996:
        1)  1:00 Meet with Tony
                 Building 21 Room 223

Appointments for Friday October 18, 1996:
        1) 10:00 Staff meeting

        2) 11:30 Lunch with Jim
```

The -c option lets you specify a calendar, other than your own, that you want to access. Using this option is like using the Multi-Browser. For example, you can specify that you want to access the calendar of james@wind by specifying the following command:

```
dugout% cm_lookup -c james@wind
```

You can combine any of the three options to gain access to and display the appointments for any person or day you choose.

Inserting Appointments

The cm_insert command inserts appointments into a calendar. The syntax for the command is as follows:

```
cm_insert [ -c calendar] [ -d date ] [ -s start ] [ -e end ] [ -w what ]
```

To insert an appointment, you use command-line options to specify the date, the start and end times, and the description. You cannot set the alarm options, specify My Eyes Only, or insert a ToDo item. Use the command-line arguments to cm_insert as follows:

–c calendar lets you specify another user's calendar. For example, you can insert an appointment into james's calendar by specifying _c james@wind.

–d date is the date of the appointment. The date is in the format mm/dd/yy. Other keywords are accepted, such as *today*, *tomorrow*, and days of the week like *Tuesday* or *Saturday*.

–s start is the start time for the appointment. The time is in the format hh:mm plus an optional am or pm. If you do not specify am or pm, am is assumed. You can also use a 24-hour clock time.

–e end is the end time for the appointment. The time format is the same as for the start time.

–w what is the description of the appointment. You can use multiple lines for the description by embedding the characters \ and n sequentially into the text.

For example, to schedule a dental appointment for james at 10:00 a.m. on Wednesday, December 4, 1996, you would use the following command:

```
dugout% cm_insert -c james@wind -d 12/04/96 -s 10:00am -w Dentist Appointment
```

Deleting Appointments

The cm_delete command deletes an appointment from a calendar. Its syntax is as follows:

```
cm_delete [ -c calendar ] [ -d date ] [ -v view ]
```

The options to cm_delete are similar to those used with cm_lookup and cm_insert. The –c option allows you to specify another user's calendar to delete from. The –d option lets you specify the date, and the –v option lets you specify the view or time span.

The cm_delete command first prints all of the appointments scheduled for the date specified (today by default). Each appointment for the time period specified is listed with a number. You use the number to specify which appointment you want to delete, and you delete one appointment at a time when prompted. After you have deleted the first appointment, you are prompted to delete another appointment. You may either continue to delete appointments at the prompt or press Return to end the operation. In the following example, the second appointment for james on October 15 is being deleted:

```
dugout% cm_delete -c james@wind -d 10/15/96
Appointments for Tuesday October 15, 1996:
        1)  8:00 Time management seminar
                 Hilton - Milpitas

        2) 11:00 Staff meeting
                 Penitentiary Conference Room

Item to delete (number)? 2
```

```
Appointments for Tuesday October 15, 1996:
        1)  8:00 Time management seminar
                 Hilton - Milpitas

Item to delete (number)? <Return>
```

Summary

In this chapter you have learned how to use the Calendar Manager from its basic features to the details of customization. If you are new to the Calendar Manager, use its basic features first. Schedule your own appointments and ToDo lists, and use the scheduling and printing features regularly. As you gain experience and familiarity with the Calendar Manager facilities, begin to use some of the more powerful features like the Multi-Browser.

You may also have to do a little training of your co-workers if they are not using the Calendar Manager. You can always use the Calendar Manager to schedule your own appointments, but if you are to take advantage of the power that the Multi-Browser gives you, your co-workers must also be scheduling their appointments with the Calendar Manager. You'll find this to be a tool you "just can't live without" once you have begun using and relying on it!

CHAPTER

8

The Daily-Use DeskSet Applications

The Clock
The Print Tool
Snapshot
The Audio Tool
The Performance Meter

YOU'VE NOW LEARNED ABOUT THE MOST IMPORTANT AND COMMONLY used DeskSet applications: the File Manager, the Calendar Manager, the Mail Tool, the Text Editor, the Shell Tool, and the Command Tool. In this chapter you will learn about some other very useful tools that you might use regularly: the Clock, the Print Tool, Snapshot, the Audio Tool, and the Performance Meter. The Clock is a general-purpose clock that provides you with the time of day and lets you set an alarm. The Print Tool gives you an interface to the printer. You can use it to send files to the printer and to check on the status of print jobs. The Snapshot utility lets you capture images from the screen and store them in files. The Audio Tool lets you record and play back audio files. You might use this tool to record an audio message and attach it to a mail message. The Performance Meter gives you information about system services and performance.

In this chapter you will learn how to use the following applications:

- The Clock
- The Print Tool
- Snapshot
- The Audio Tool
- The Performance Meter

The Clock

The Clock program displays the time in analog or digital format. It can be configured to display any time zone around the world. It also has built-in features that let you use the Clock as a stopwatch or as an alarm.

To start the Clock, choose Clock from the Workspace Programs menu. You can also start the Clock by entering the clock command at the prompt:

```
dugout% clock &
```

Here is the Clock's base window:

The Clock has no controls in its base window. All controls for customizing the Clock are available in the Clock Properties window. To display the Clock Properties window, position the pointer on the Clock's base window, and press MENU. The Clock pop-up menu appears. Press the Properties button to display the Clock Properties window, shown in Figure 8.1. You can also display the Clock Properties window by positioning the pointer on the Clock's base window and pressing the Props key.

Figure 8.1
The Clock Properties window

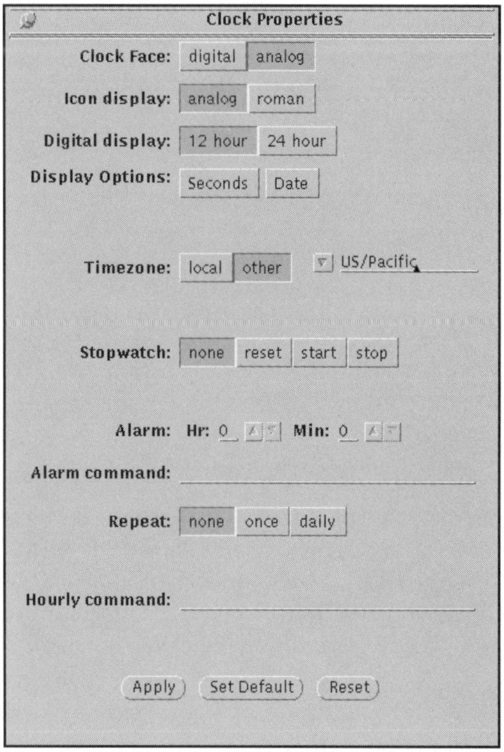

You use the Clock Properties window to customize the Clock. Each time you make changes, you must press the Apply button at the bottom of the window to activate the change. If you want to permanently store the customization options you have chosen, press the Set Default button. The options are stored so that each time you start the Clock the customization options you selected will be set. The Reset button lets you reactivate all the options on the Clock Properties window that were in effect the last time you pressed the Apply button.

Setting the Display Options

The first four fields on the Clock Properties window let you set the way that the Clock is displayed. Some of the settings affect the Clock's base window, some affect the Clock's icon, and some affect both the base window and the icon.

Clock Face

The Clock Face field lets you choose a digital or analog clock face. The default is analog. To change the clock face to digital, select the button labeled digital and press Apply. The digital clock display looks like this:

Only the Clock's base window displays a digital clock face; the icon is unchanged.

You can also use a keyboard accelerator to toggle between the digital and analog clock faces. Position the pointer on the Clock base window and press c to alternate between the two choices. If you have the Clock Properties window displayed when you activate the c keyboard accelerator, you will see the Clock Face setting updated to correspond to the current setting.

You can also provide the -digital command-line option when you invoke the Clock, so that its initial clock face will be digital. For example, to start the Clock with a digital clock face, enter the following command:

```
dugout% clock -digital &
```

Icon display

When you iconify the Clock, the icon displays the current time in either analog or roman format. When the roman icon display option is set, the Clock's icon displays roman numerals for the hours. Here are the two icons:

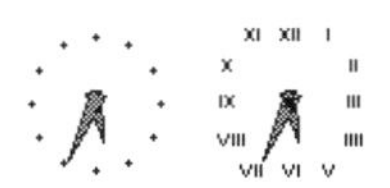

If you have the seconds display option set, the icon also includes a second hand.

The Icon display field lets you choose the way the icon is displayed. The default icon displays hour numbers as dots. The roman choice displays the hour numbers as roman numerals. To change the icon display to roman, select the button labeled roman and press Apply.

You can also use a keyboard accelerator to toggle between the analog and roman icon displays. Position the pointer on the Clock base window and press i to toggle between the two choices. Be aware that all keyboard accelerators are activated only when the Clock's base window is displayed, not when it is iconified.

The -r command-line option lets you set the initial icon display to roman. For example, to start the Clock with a roman icon displayed, enter the following command:

```
dugout% clock -r &
```

Digital Display

The Digital display field lets you choose a 12-hour or 24-hour clock when you are using the digital clock face. If you are using the analog clock face, this option has no effect. The default digital display is 12 hour. The 24-hour choice displays the time in military hours, and the am/pm designation is removed. To change the digital display to 24 hour, select the button labeled 24 hour and press Apply.

You can also use a keyboard accelerator to set the Digital display option. Position the pointer on the Clock base window, and press 1 to choose the 12-hour clock, or press 2 to choose the 24-hour clock.

You can also provide the -24 command-line option when you invoke the Clock, so that its initial digital display will be 24 hour. For example, to start the Clock with a 24-hour digital display, set the clock face to digital and the digital display to 24 hour by entering the following command:

```
dugout% clock -digital -24 &
```

Display Options

The Display Options field lets you choose whether you want the Clock displayed with seconds and/or the date. When the Clock is invoked and the default is in effect, neither the seconds nor the date is displayed. The Seconds choice turns on the second hand for the analog clock face or the number of seconds for the digital display. The Date choice displays the date below the clock face for both the digital and the analog clock faces. Here are a digital and analog Clock with the date and seconds turned on:

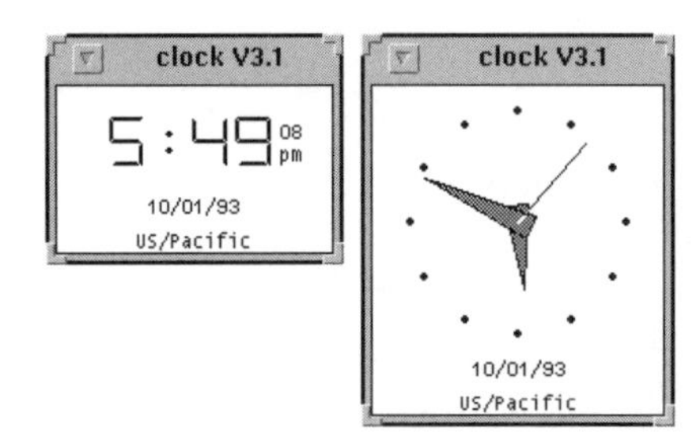

A keyboard accelerator is available for each of these two settings. Again, you must position the pointer on the Clock base window to activate the accelerator, and then press s to toggle the Seconds option or press d to toggle the Date option.

You can also use command-line options to set either of these options. The +seconds option turns on the seconds when you invoke the Clock; the +date option turns on the date. For example, to start the Clock with both seconds and the date displayed, enter the following command:

```
dugout% clock +seconds +date &
```

If the seconds and dates are set as defaults, and you want to start the Clock without them displayed, enter the command

```
dugout% clock -seconds -date &
```

Setting the Time Zone

You can display the time in one of many different time zones. By default, the Clock displays the time according to the time-zone (TZ) environment variable, which is set automatically for you by the operating system. When your system was installed, the appropriate time zone was chosen by whoever set up your system. That time zone is the one that the TZ environment variable is set to by default, and it is the time zone that the Clock will use to display the time.

The Timezone field on the Clock Properties window gives you two choices: local and other. If you choose local, your system's local time is displayed. If you choose other, you must enter a time zone in the text field by either typing directly into the field or using the abbreviated menu button to the left of the field to display and select an available time zone. When other is selected, the corresponding time zone is displayed in the Clock's base window.

Because the TZ environment variable is automatically set in your environment, the Timezone field's other choice is selected and the Timezone text field is set to the value of your TZ environment variable. If you choose the local time-zone option, the Clock will display the local time regardless of the entry in the Timezone text field.

The easiest way to select another time zone is to use the abbreviated menu button to display the Timezone menu. Select one of the times available from the menu, and press the Apply button.

If you want multiple times to appear simultaneously on your workspace, you can run multiple Clocks, each with its own time-zone setting. For example, if you live in the US/Pacific time zone and want to display both your local time and the US/Eastern time zone, you can start two Clock programs and set one of them for the Eastern time zone.

You can toggle between your local time zone and one other time zone by using the t keyboard accelerator. For example, if you live in the US/Pacific time zone, you can set the other time zone to US/Eastern and then toggle between US/Pacific time and US/Eastern time by simply pressing the t keyboard accelerator. Notice that the time zone is not displayed in the Clock's base window when the local time zone is set.

You can set the time zone on the command line by using the -TZ option when you invoke the Clock. Follow the -TZ with the name of the time zone you want displayed. For example, to display the US/Eastern time zone, enter the following:

```
dugout% clock -TZ US/Eastern &
```

Using the Stopwatch

When you need to time a program or keep track of the time it takes to do a certain task, you may want to use the Clock's stopwatch feature. The stopwatch works with either digital or analog clock faces. Use the four choices in the Stopwatch field on the Clock Properties window to control the stopwatch feature. When one of these choices is selected, it takes effect immediately; you don't have to press the Apply button. The normal sequence for using the stopwatch feature is as follows:

1. Press "reset" to set the Clock to 0:00 and display seconds.
2. Press "start" to begin the stopwatch.
3. Press "stop" to stop the stopwatch.
4. Press "none" to return the Clock to the current time.

You can also manipulate the stopwatch feature of the Clock by using keyboard accelerators. Use the Shift-S key to toggle the state of the stopwatch. The first time you press Shift-S the stopwatch is reset. When you press Shift-S again, the stopwatch starts. When you press Shift-S a third time, the stopwatch stops. If you press Shift-S once more, it starts the cycle again by resetting the stopwatch. To return the Clock to normal operation, press the c keyboard accelerator.

Setting an Alarm

The next four fields on the Clock Properties window let you set an alarm. The first three fields work together to set an alarm at a specified time. You use the last field, Hourly command, to specify a command that will be executed every hour.

To set an alarm, you first set the Alarm field to the hour and minute that you want the alarm to signal. To set the alarm time, use the Hr and Min numeric text fields. You can either enter the hour and minute in the two numeric text fields directly from the keyboard or use the increment/decrement buttons to the right of each field.

You use the Alarm command text field to specify the command you want executed when the alarm signals. If you leave the Alarm command field blank, the alarm will consist of a single beep. One of the most popular uses of the alarm command is to specify a command that will deliver an audible message. For example, if your system has a speaker and you have loaded the audio software package (check with your system administrator about this), you can send an audio file to the system's audio device. Use the following alarm command entry:

```
audioplay /usr/demo/SOUND/sounds/doorbell.au
```

When the alarm goes off you will hear the sound of a doorbell.

You select one of the Repeat choices to specify whether the alarm will not signal at all, will signal only once, or will repeat daily at the specified hour. If you set the "none" choice, the alarm command will not execute. If you set the "once" choice, the alarm command will execute once and then will be set to none. If you set the "daily" choice, the alarm command will repeat every day at the specified time.

The last field on the Clock Properties window, the Hourly command field, lets you specify a command that is executed hourly. It is similar to the alarm command except that this command repeats every hour on the hour.

Tables 8.1 and 8.2 list the Clock's accelerators and command-line options.

Table 8.1 Clock Accelerators

Accelerator	Description
1	Sets the 12-hour mode (digital display required)
2	Sets the 24-hour mode (digital display required)
c	Toggles the clock face between analog and digital
d	Toggles the date display on and off
i	Toggles the icon face between analog and roman
s	Toggles the seconds display on and off
S	Sets the stopwatch, and cycles between reset, start, and stop

Table 8.1 Clock Accelerators (Continued)

Accelerator	Description
t	Toggles the time zone between local and one other time zone
q	Quits the Clock

Table 8.2 Clock Command-line Options

Option	Description
-Wn	Starts the Clock with no title line
-TZ [*timezone*]	Starts the Clock with an alternate time zone
-24	Starts the Clock with a 24-hour clock
-alarm setting	Sets how often you want the alarm to go off (none, once, daily)
-alarmtime [*hr:min*]	Sets the time you want the alarm to go off
-alarmcmd [*cmd*]	Sets the command you want to run when the alarm goes off
-digital	Starts the Clock with a digital display
+date	Shows the current date on the Clock face
-date	Turns off current date on the Clock face if it has been set
-hourcmd [*cmd*]	Sets the command you want to be run every hour on the hour
-r	Sets roman numerals on the Clock's icon
+seconds	Shows the number of seconds

The Print Tool

You open a Print Tool by selecting Print Tool from the Workspace Programs Menu. The Print Tool application is the interface to the SunOS printing mechanism. You can use the Print Tool to print files, select a printer, specify the number of copies to print, select a custom filter, and query and manipulate the print queue.

Each time that data is sent to a printer, it enters the print queue. Since a printer can print only one file at a time, the files must be managed in a queue. When one file has finished printing, the next one in the queue is sent to the printer. Each set of data that you send to the print queue is called a *print job*. A print job may consist of a single file, or it may consist of multiple files sent to the printer at one time. Each entry in the print queue is referred to as a print job.

The Print Tool application lets you send print jobs to the print queue with a variety of options. You can also use the Print Tool to examine the print queue and remove any of the jobs that you entered into the queue. To start the Print Tool, choose Print Tool from the Workspace Programs menu. You can also start the Print Tool by entering the printtool command at the prompt:

```
dugout% printtool &
```

Figure 8.2 shows the Print Tool's base window.

Figure 8.2
The Print Tool

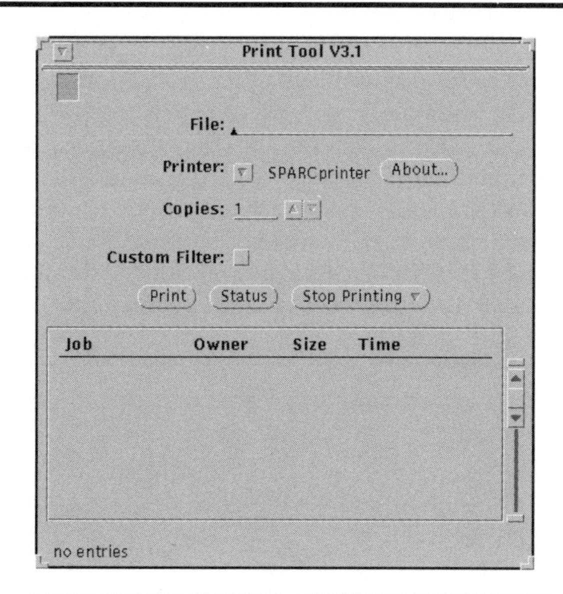

The Print Tool icon looks like this:

The name of the current printer is part of the icon. You can use the Print Tool icon for drag and drop, as you will learn later in this section.

Printing a File

To print a file by using the Print Tool, you enter the name of the file into the File text field and press the Print button. The file that you specify is sent to the queue of the printer that is displayed in the Printer field. You specify in the Copies field the number of copies you want printed. The default is to print one copy, but you can enter another number or use the increment/decrement buttons to the right of the Copies field to change the number of copies to be printed.

When sent to a print queue, a print job cannot be printed until all other print jobs ahead of it in the queue are printed. If no other print jobs are in the queue, that print job is printed immediately.

The Print Tool also supports drag and drop for printing one or more files. The Print Tool's base window includes a drag and drop target in the upper-left corner. You can drag a file from any other application, such as the File Manager, and drop it onto the Print Tool's drag and drop target to print the file or the data associated with the drag and drop operation. You can even select multiple files from the File Manager and drag all of them to the Print Tool in one drag and drop operation. Each file included in the drag and drop operation becomes a separate print job and is included in the print queue of the selected printer. Figure 8.3 shows a file being dragged from the File Manager and dropped onto the Print Tool's drag and drop target.

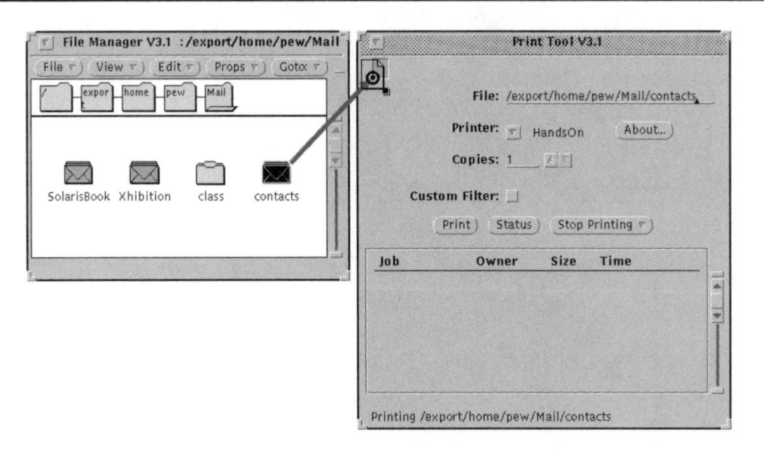

Figure 8.3
Using drag and drop to print a file

You can also perform a drop onto the Print Tool's icon. The file or files dropped onto the Print Tool icon are sent to the print queue of the printer displayed in the icon. This is the same printer that is displayed in the Printer field of the Print Tool's base window. You'll learn in the next section how to set the printer.

One technique you may find useful is to have multiple Print Tool applications running, with each application set to a different printer. You can start two Print Tool applications that are set to separate printers, and then iconify both of them. This saves workspace real estate. When you want to print something, you use drag and drop to the Print Tool icon that is set to the printer you want to use.

This technique can really come in handy when you have two documents that you need to print for a meeting that you're already late for. If you use only one printer, then you must print the two documents in succession, which is more time-consuming than printing them simultaneously. If you can print the documents on separate printers, you save yourself some time. So, you drag and drop the first document onto one icon and then drag and drop the other document onto the other icon. Of course, this technique makes sense only if both print queues are empty at the time that you want to print your documents.

Selecting a Printer

The UNIX printing system allows you to access printers that are connected directly to your system or to other systems on your local network. Your system administrator configures your system with the appropriate information about what printers are available to you.

Each printer available to you on your system is displayed in the Printer menu. You display the Printer menu by positioning the pointer over the Printer abbreviated menu button in the Print Tool's base window and pressing MENU. Figure 8.4 shows the Print Tool with the Printer menu displayed.

To select a printer, display the Printer menu and select one of the printers included on the menu. The selected printer is then displayed in the Print Tool's Printer field. You can learn more about the printer displayed in the Printer field by pressing the About button positioned just to the right of the printer name. When you press the About button, the About the printer window is displayed, giving you information about the printer. Here is an example of an About the printer window:

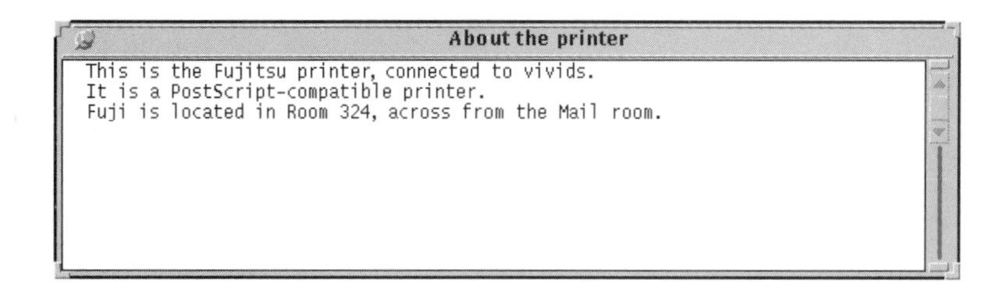

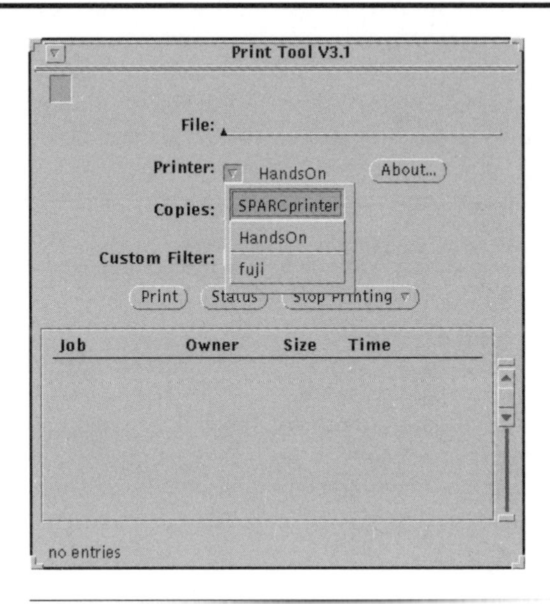

Figure 8.4
Selecting a printer

The information displayed in the About the printer window is determined by the system administrator when the printer is configured. If the system administrator chooses not to enter any information about the printer, the About the printer window will be blank.

Checking the Print Queue

The Print Tool automatically displays the print jobs that are in the print queue for the selected printer. The print jobs are displayed in the scrolling list at the bottom of the base window, as shown in Figure 8.5. The information displayed in the scrolling list includes the job number, the owner, the size of the job in bytes, and the date and time the job was submitted.

The list of print jobs displayed in the scrolling list is updated about every ten seconds. If you want an immediate update of the print queue, press the Status button.

Stopping Print Jobs

You may occasionally want to delete a print job from the print queue. If the print job has not yet begun printing, you can remove it from the print queue, or if it is in the process of being printed, you can terminate the printing.

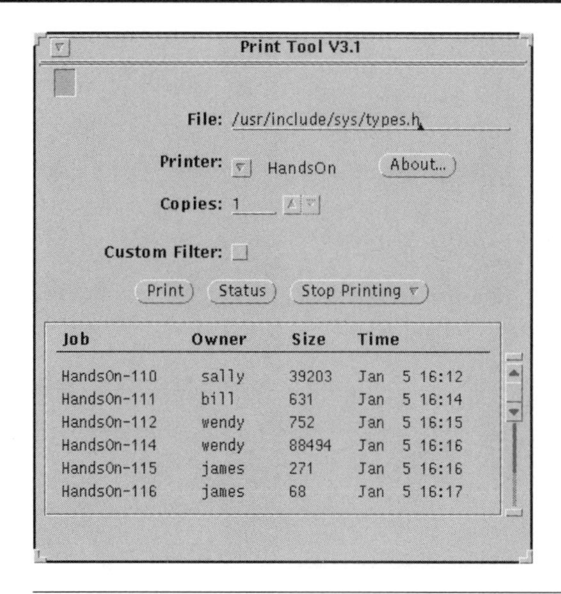

Figure 8.5
The Print Tool with several files in the queue

To be removed from the print queue, the job must be displayed in the scrolling list. You select the jobs that you want to remove, and press the Stop Printing button. To select a job from the scrolling list, position the pointer over the job you want to remove, and press SELECT. Here are the steps for removing a job from the print queue:

1. Select the print job or jobs that you want to remove from the scrolling list.
2. Display the Stop Printing menu by positioning the pointer on the Stop Printing menu button and pressing MENU.
3. Select the Selected Print Job button.

Each job you select is removed from the list. You can remove only the print jobs that are owned by you. Any attempt to remove a print job that you do not own will fail. Figure 8.6 shows three jobs in the HandsOn print queue that have been selected and are about to be removed.

You can also choose to remove all jobs from the print queue by selecting All Print Jobs from the Stop Printing menu. In this case, you do not need to select any jobs from the scrolling list. Of course, only the print jobs that you own will be removed.

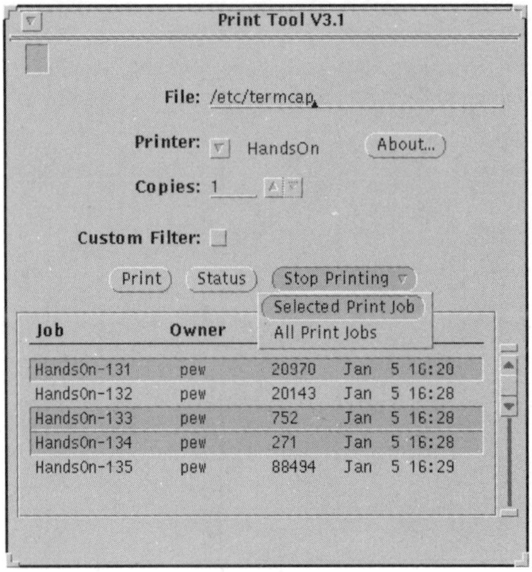

Figure 8.6
Stopping multiple jobs in the print queue

Using Custom Filters

The Custom Filter field lets you specify a filter (a filter is another name for a command) that will run on your print job before the job is printed. To specify a custom filter, check the Custom Filter check box, which displays a text field next to the check box. Enter in the text field the name of the command that you want to act as the filter. For example, if you want your file filtered through the Pretty Printer, you enter

```
mp -l
```

in the text field. This command produces output of two pages per printed sheet in landscape mode.

You can also include the $FILE variable in the custom filter specification. $FILE expands to the name of the file being printed. For example, you could specify

```
mp -o -s $FILE
```

in the Custom Filter text field to filter the file through the Pretty Printer and have the name of the file displayed at the bottom of each page.

Note that the Print Tool ignores custom filters for files that have a print method assigned in Binder properties (see Chapter 9).

Snapshot

The Snapshot program lets you take a snapshot of a window or region of the screen. The snapshot can then be stored as a raster file that contains all the necessary information to reproduce the image. Raster files can be loaded into Snapshot for viewing. This means that you can use Snapshot to generate an image or to view an existing image.

Images created with Snapshot are very useful for several reasons. If you are creating documentation, you may want to include screen images in your document. In fact, most of the images used in this book were captured with the use of Snapshot. You may also want to capture a screen image if you need to communicate information to someone about the visual aspect of an application. For example, you might want to include a screen shot of a program you are having trouble with when you send mail to your system administrator or support person. Raster files can be included as attachments in the Mail Tool, which makes sending images very easy and convenient.

Snapshot supports two file types: raster files and GIF image files. The raster-file format is Snapshot's default format. GIF, which stands for Graphic Interchange Format, is a standard format used on many different computer systems. Files in either format can be loaded into Snapshot for viewing. (When you capture an image and save it to a file, it is always stored in raster-file format.) Snapshot automatically uncompresses compressed images. This means that you can compress an image to save disk space, and Snapshot will still be able to load it.

Snapshot is very easy and intuitive to use. You'll learn how to use all the features of Snapshot in this section, but the basic operation is especially simple. To start Snapshot, choose Snapshot from the Workspace Programs menu. You can also start Snapshot by entering the snapshot command at the prompt:

```
dugout% snapshot &
```

Figure 8.7 shows Snapshot's base window. The Snapshot icon looks like this:

To take a snapshot, you press the Snap button, move the pointer to the window whose image you want to capture, and click SELECT. To view the image you have captured, press the View button. To store the image in a file, press the Save button, which displays a pop-up window. Enter the name of the directory and file in the appropriate fields, and press the Save button on the pop-up window to save the image. Several options are available that you will learn about in the next few subsections, but these basics steps will get you started.

Figure 8.7
The Snapshot base window

Loading, Viewing, and Saving an Image

Before going into all the details of the different ways to capture an image, let's talk about how to load, view, and save files. To load an image into the Snapshot program, you must first display the Load Options pop-up window by pressing the Load button on Snapshot's base window, shown here:

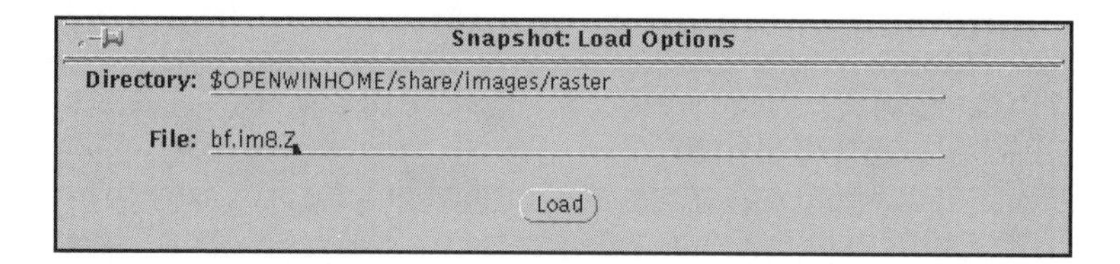

You then enter the directory and file name of the image file that you want to load into Snapshot, and press the Load button.

The directory specified in the preceding illustration, $OPENWINHOME/-share/images/raster, has several images in it. Once you have loaded an image, you can view it by pressing the View button. The image appears in the View pop-up window, shown in Figure 8.8. If the View pop-up window is already displayed, loading a new image file automatically updates the View window with the new image. The View window automatically resizes to accommodate the size of the newly loaded image. To dismiss the View window, unpin it.

You can also load a file into Snapshot by using drag and drop. For example, you can drag a raster or GIF file from the File Manager and drop it onto Snapshot's drag and drop target to load the file. Of course, the file that you drag and drop onto Snapshot must be either a raster or a GIF file. Attempting to drop any other type of file onto Snapshot will fail.

Figure 8.8
The Snapshot View window

You will usually use the Save feature after you have captured a screen image. To save the image, you first display the Save Options pop-up window by pressing the Save button on the base window. The Save Options pop-up window looks just like the Load Options window except that the button is labeled Save rather than Load. To save an image, you enter the name of the directory and file in the Directory and File text fields of the Save Options window, and press the Save button.

You can also save an image by using drag and drop. After you have captured the image, drag the small icon from Snapshot's drag and drop target and drop it onto the File Manager. A raster-image file is created in the File Manager's current directory and is named *raster.* You can also drag and drop to other applications such as the Mail Tool. For example, if you want to include an image in a mail message, you can drag it from Snapshot's drag and drop target and drop it onto the Attachments section of the Mail Tool Compose Message window, as shown in Figure 8.9.

Figure 8.9
Dragging an image from Snapshot to the Mail Tool

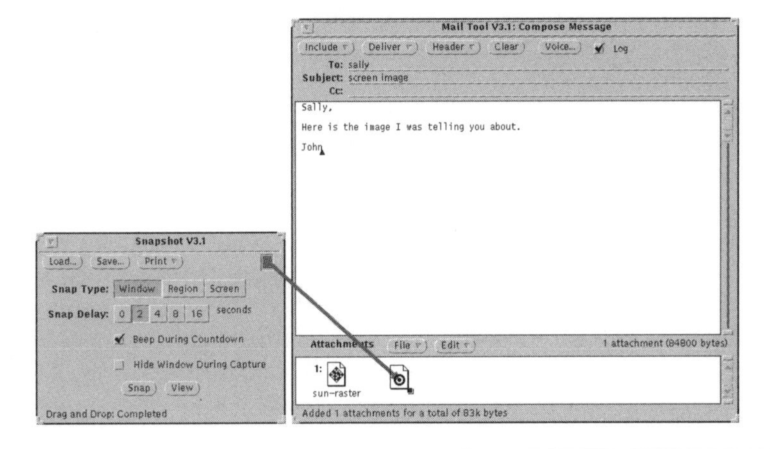

Taking a Snapshot

There are several ways that you can capture an image. The variety of methods is controlled by the options on Snapshot's base window. Be aware, however, that Snapshot can have only a single image loaded at one time. When you take a snapshot, that image is the currently loaded image. If you attempt to take another snapshot without first saving the previous image, you will receive a message that looks like this:

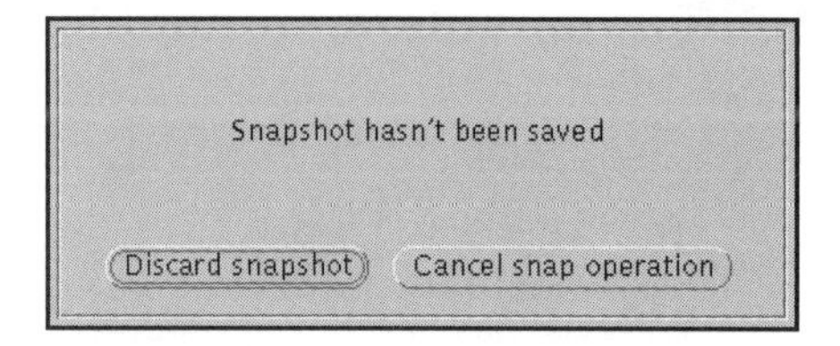

You can choose to discard the previously loaded image or cancel the snap operation.

Snap Type

The Snap Type choice lets you capture an image by window, region, or screen. The simplest way to capture an image is by window. With the Snap Type set to Window, you take a snapshot by pressing the Snap button, moving the pointer to the window you want to capture, and clicking SELECT. The entire window in which the pointer is located is captured. You can cancel a snapshot by clicking ADJUST or MENU after you have pressed the Snap button but before you select the window to capture. Once you have selected the window, you cannot cancel the snapshot.

The Window snap type is the best choice if you want to capture a single window and you want all of the window and only the window. For example, Figure 8.7 shows a screen image that was captured by Snapshot when the Window snap type was set.

The Region choice lets you select a rectangular region to capture. There are no constraints on the size or the contents of the region. You can select the boundaries so that the region contains multiple windows or just a part of one window. When you take a snapshot with the snap type set to Region, you must identify the boundaries of the region before the snapshot is taken. First, you press the Snap button. Then you press SELECT at one corner of the rectangle that you want to capture, drag the pointer to the opposite corner, and release SELECT. An outlined box identifying the region is drawn as you select the region. Once you have selected the region, you click the ADJUST button to take the snapshot. You can cancel the snapshot by clicking the

MENU button, but you must do this before you click ADJUST. Once you have clicked ADJUST, the snapshot is taken; you cannot interrupt it.

The Region snap type is the best choice if you want to capture a part of a window or a region that contains more than one window. For example, Figure 8.9 shows two windows: Snapshot and a Mail Tool Compose window. This screen image was captured by Snapshot when the Region snap type was set.

The last choice available from the Snap Type field is Screen. The Screen choice lets you capture the entire screen. When you press the Snap button, the entire screen is captured without any further selection process. You cannot interrupt a full-screen capture.

Regardless of the snap type, you begin a snap operation by pressing the Snap button. As soon as you press the Snap button, Snapshot's footer is updated with a succinct set of instructions for taking the snapshot. For example, when you have the snap type set to Region, the footer displays the following message:

```
SELECT-Position Rectangle. ADJUST-Snap Image. MENU-Cancel.
```

This message describes the function of each of the three mouse buttons and should help you remember the steps necessary to complete the snapshot.

Snap Delay

The Snap Delay choice lets you specify a delay in seconds between the time that you identify the window or region to capture and the time that the actual capture takes place. This feature is important because you may need to manipulate something on the screen before the image is taken. For example, if you want to take a snapshot of an application that has a button but you want the button to appear pressed in the image, you will need a few seconds after initiating the snapshot to move the pointer to the button and to press the button. Similarly, if you want to include a pop-up menu in your snapshot, you will need to set a delay. Without a delay there would be no way to include the menu, because a pop-up menu (one that is not pinned) cannot stay displayed when you press any other button. So, you must initiate the snapshot with a delay, and then display the pop-up menu in time for the actual capture to take place.

Beep During Countdown

The Beep During Countdown check box is available only when a snap delay other than zero is set. When the check box is checked, Snapshot beeps once per second as it counts down to the time that the image is captured. The beep helps you keep track of how much time remains before the image is captured.

Hide Window During Capture

The Hide Window During Capture check box lets you specify whether the Snapshot base window and all associated pop-ups will disappear while the image is being captured. This feature is particularly useful if you are capturing the entire screen and you do not want to include Snapshot in the image. As soon as the image is captured, Snapshot reappears.

Snapshot Examples

Let's look at a couple of examples of taking snapshots. Regardless of which snap type you specify, it is a good idea to arrange the window, region, or screen the way you want it before you begin the capture. This includes making sure that the entire window or region that you are about to capture is unobscured.

To snap a window, follow these instructions:

1. Select Window from the Snap Type choices.
2. Set the Snap Delay, Beep During Countdown, and Hide Window During Capture options if you want to use them.
3. Click SELECT on the Snap button. The Snap button displays the "busy" (dotted) pattern, and a message is displayed in the footer.
4. Position the pointer on the window you want to capture, and click SELECT. You may want to position the pointer on the header of the window being captured to ensure that the entire window, including the window manager border, is included in the snapshot.
5. If you want to cancel the snapshot, click ADJUST or MENU.

To capture a region, follow these steps:

1. Select Region from the Snap Type choices.
2. Set the Snap Delay, Beep During Countdown, and Hide Window During Capture options if you want to use them.
3. Click SELECT on the Snap button. The Snap button displays the "busy" pattern, and a message is displayed in the footer. The pointer also changes its shape to a southeast-pointing arrow.
4. Position the pointer at one corner of the region you want to capture, and press SELECT.
5. Drag the pointer to the opposite corner of the region you want to capture, and release SELECT. A box outlining the region is drawn as you drag the pointer. You can continue to change the size of the region by pressing SELECT again and adjusting the size of the region.
6. Click ADJUST to capture the image bounded by the region you have specified.

7. If you want to cancel the snapshot, click MENU.

One of the difficulties you may encounter when taking a snapshot is that you don't know the exact size of the object you want to capture, especially if you have to display a window or menu during the countdown. For example, if you are taking a snapshot of an application that has a pop-up menu, you must use a snap delay so that you can display the pop-up menu before the snapshot is taken. The problem is that if the pop-up menu is large it may go outside the boundaries of the base window. If you specify the snap type as Region, you won't know exactly how big to make the region, because the menu is not displayed at the time you specify the region.

There are two ways to solve this problem. One solution is to specify a very large region that you are sure will encompass the entire window and pop-up menu that you want to capture. After you have captured the image, display it in the View window and then take another snapshot—of the image displayed in the View window. The image you have captured includes the pop-up menu, so you can specify the exact region that is just large enough to contain the base window and the pop-up menu without making the image too big. The other way to solve this problem is to capture the entire screen and then use the same technique of recapturing the image from the View window.

Printing a Snapshot

The printing facility provided by Snapshot is quite flexible. It lets you specify orientation, position, and scale. This makes it easy to print any snapshot image regardless of size.

The Print menu button on Snapshot's base window displays the Print menu, as shown here:

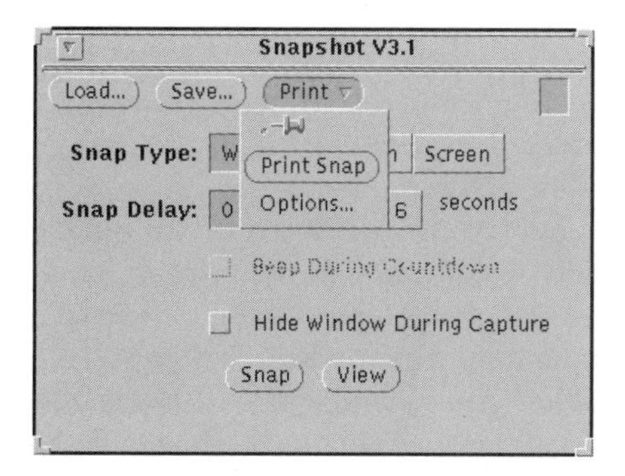

To print the currently loaded image, select the Print Snap item on the Print menu. The snapshot will be printed according to the options set on the Print Options pop-up window. To display the Print Options pop-up window, select the Options item on the Print menu. Figure 8.10 shows the Print Options pop-up window.

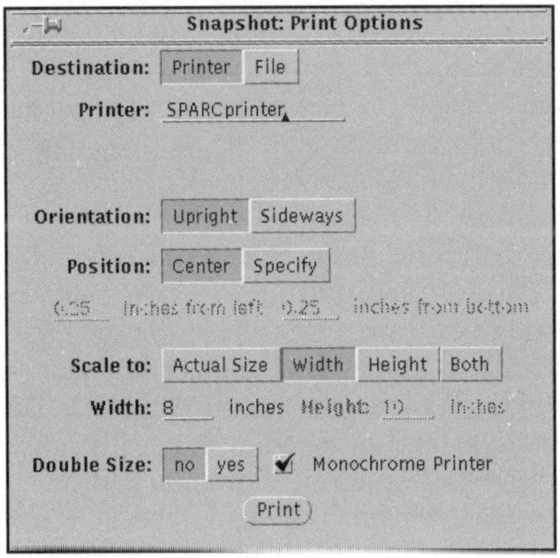

Figure 8.10
Snapshot's Print Options pop-up window

You use the Print Options pop-up window to select the options that control the printout. When you have finished, select the Print button. The Print button on the Print Options pop-up window and the Print Snap item on the Print menu have exactly the same effect.

The first option on the Print Options window is Destination. You can choose either to send the snapshot to a printer or to create a file. The file created when you select File is in PostScript format. It is not the same format as the raster file that is created when you save an image. As soon as you select File, the Printer text field is replaced with two text fields, labeled Directory and File. You must specify the name of the directory and file where you want the PostScript output stored.

If you send the snapshot to a printer, you must specify the name of the printer in the Printer text field, which is directly below the Destination field. The printer that you specify must be one of the printers configured on your system. To see the names of all the printers configured on your system, you display the Printer pop-up menu from the Print Tool application.

The Orientation field lets you specify whether the output will appear upright or sideways. The Upright choice orients the image in portrait mode; the Sideways choice orients the image in landscape mode.

The Position field lets you control the location of the image on the printed page. The default position is Center, which means that the image will be centered on the page. If you select Specify, the "Inches from left" and

"Inches from bottom" text settings, located below the Position field, become activated. Enter the number of inches from the left and bottom of the page into the two text fields to specify the exact location of the printed image.

The "Scale to" field gives you four choices for scaling the image: Actual Size, Width, Height, and Both. The Actual Size choice does just as its name implies: it prints the image in its actual size without scaling.

The Width choice allows you to specify a custom width for the image. The Width field, located below the "Scale to" field, becomes activated when you select Width. Enter the number of inches to which the width should be scaled. When you scale the width, the height of the image is automatically scaled in proportion to the width. This means that the aspect ratio of the width and height will remain the same as the aspect ratio of the original image.

The Height choice works just like the Width choice, except that you specify the height rather than the width. Selecting a height will also keep the aspect ratio of the image proportional to that of the original.

The Both choice allows you to specify both width and height for scaling. This means that you can select any width and height for the output regardless of the original size of the image. Unless you choose dimensions that exactly match the original proportions of the image, the aspect ratio of the printed image will not remain consistent with that of the original image. This can create some strange-looking output.

The Double Size field gives you the option of doubling the size of the image. If you choose yes, the printed output will be twice as big as the original. Remember that the size is doubled in both directions—horizontal and vertical.

The Monochrome Printer check box should be checked if you are using a monochrome printer. This is the default, and it will speed up the printing process when you use a monochrome printer.

Keep in mind that you can use either the Print button on the Print Options window or the Print Snap option on the Print menu to print your image. The options you have chosen will be used regardless of which button you press.

The Audio Tool

The Audio Tool program lets you record, play, and edit audio data. You can record an audio message and then either store it in a file or include it as an attachment in a Mail Tool Compose Message window. You can play an existing audio file and edit it by inserting new audio data or by deleting part of the recording.

To use the Audio Tool, your system must be equipped with a speaker or a jack to which you can connect an externally powered speaker. If you are going to record audio data, you need an audio I/O adapter cable and a microphone. Most SPARCstations (though not all) come with a built-in speaker

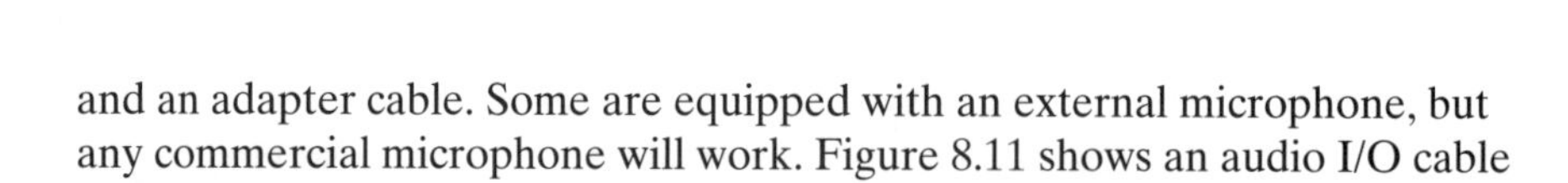

and an adapter cable. Some are equipped with an external microphone, but any commercial microphone will work. Figure 8.11 shows an audio I/O cable and microphone.

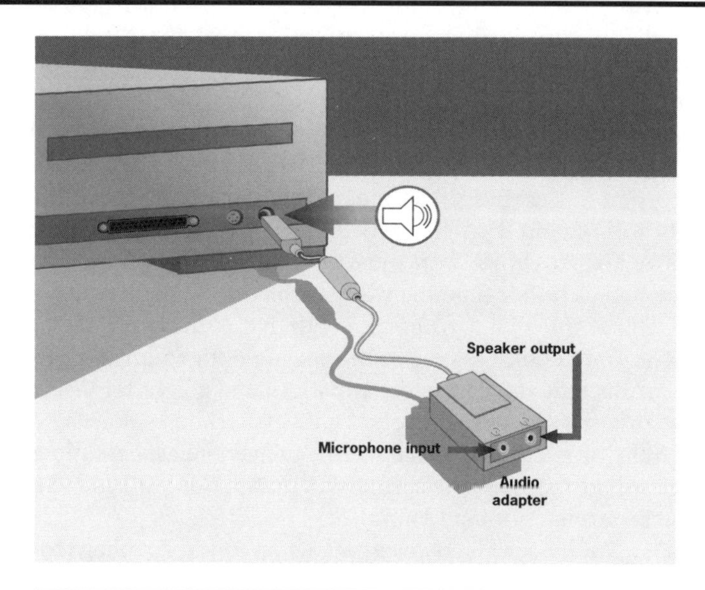

Figure 8.11 The audio I/O adapter cable and microphone

Learning the Audio Tool Basics

You use the Audio Tool much as you use a simple cassette recorder. There are buttons for play, record, forward, and reverse, and you can set the play and record volume. You can save audio data to a file or load an existing audio file into the Audio Tool. In addition, the Audio Tool lets you edit your audio data with a simple cut-and-paste technique.

To start the Audio Tool, choose Audio Tool from the Workspace Programs menu. You can also start the Audio Tool by entering the audiotool command at the prompt:

```
dugout% audiotool &
```

The Audio Tool base window is shown in Figure 8.12.

The Audio Tool icon looks like this:

Figure 8.12 The Audio Tool base window

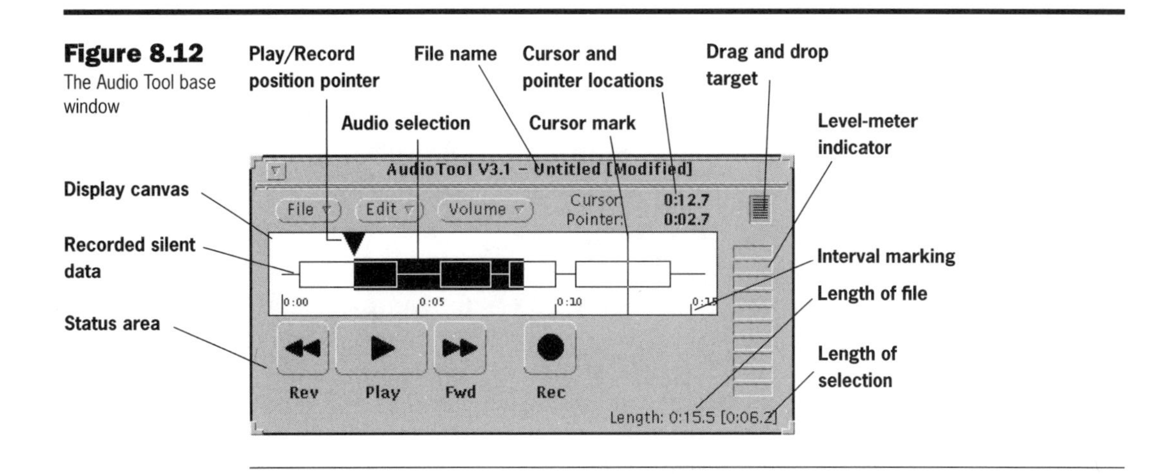

To record audio data, simply press the Rec button and talk into your microphone. When you have finished recording, press the button again (the button has been relabeled Stop). Press the Play button to play the audio data you just recorded. Basic recording and playback require no more sophistication than this.

The Display Canvas

The display canvas region of the Audio Tool's base window gives you a visual representation of the data recorded. Sound data is displayed as a box, and silence is represented as a horizontal line. The display canvas in Figure 8.12 shows four segments of sound data separated by silence. The sound and silence data are somewhat analogous to words of text separated by white space.

The Play/Record position pointer indicates the current position of the audio data. The position pointer moves forward as you play audio data. You can move the position pointer to a particular location by moving the mouse pointer and clicking SELECT. This allows you to start playing from the middle of the sound data.

The vertical line displayed in the display canvas when the mouse pointer is within the canvas is called the *cursor mark*. The numeric values representing the location of the cursor mark and the Play/Record position pointer are displayed above the display canvas. These numbers represent the elapsed time from the current position of the cursor mark or Play/Record position pointer to the beginning of the audio data in minutes, seconds, and tenths of seconds. As the pointer and cursor move, the corresponding locations are updated in the display area.

You can select audio data in much the same way that you select text in the Text Editor or in the Mail Tool Compose Message window. Use the SELECT and ADJUST buttons to highlight a section of audio data. You can use the press-drag-release method with the SELECT button, or you can highlight audio data by clicking SELECT at one location and then clicking ADJUST to delimit the other end of the selection. Click ADJUST again to change the beginning or end of the selection. You can also highlight audio data by using multi-click. If you double-click SELECT in the display canvas with the cursor mark over the sound segment, the entire segment is selected. You can select a silence region the same way: position the cursor mark over a horizontal line in the display canvas, and double-click SELECT to highlight the entire silence region. If you triple-click SELECT, the entire sound data is selected.

Selected data can be copied, cut, or pasted in much the same way as text is handled in the DeskSet applications that support text. You'll learn more about these techniques when we talk about editing audio data later in this section.

The Audio Tool Controls

The Audio Tool's base window contains several controls and display messages about the status of the audio data. The three menu buttons at the top of the window—labeled File, Edit, and Volume—let you control loading and saving audio files, editing audio data, and setting the play and record volume, respectively. The Level meter indicator, located on the right side of the window, displays the current level or intensity of the audio data. The left footer region, also known as the status area, displays a message about the current operation of the Audio Tool. For example, when you are recording, the message "Recording" appears in the status area. The right footer area displays the "Length of file" and "Length of selection" values. The "Length of file" value represents the length of the entire audio data in minutes, seconds, and tenths of seconds. The "Length of selection" value represents the length of the selected audio data.

The four buttons at the bottom of the Audio Tool base window are used for the basic functions of play, record, forward, and reverse. You press the Play button to play the audio data. The audio data begins playing at the location of the position pointer. This is not necessarily the beginning of the data. If any audio data is selected, pressing Play will play the selected data only. The playing will stop when the end of the selected data is reached. As soon as you press the Play button, the label beneath the button changes to Stop. Pressing the button again will stop the playback.

You press the Rec button to record audio data. If there is already audio data displayed in the display canvas, the recorded audio data will be inserted at the position pointer. If any audio data is selected, pressing Rec deletes the selected audio data and inserts the recorded audio data at the position-pointer location. While you are recording, the Rec button is relabeled Stop. Recording continues until you press the Stop button.

The Rev and Fwd buttons allow you to move the location of the position pointer. When you press the Fwd button, the position pointer advances to the beginning of the next sound segment. If you think of the audio data as words (sound) separated by spaces (silence), the Fwd button advances the position pointer to the next word (sound). The Rev button does just the reverse. It moves the position pointer back to the beginning of the current sound segment. If the position pointer is already at the beginning of a sound segment, you press the Rev button to move it to the beginning of the previous sound segment.

You can also use the Fwd and Rev buttons while you are playing audio data. If you click SELECT on either of the two buttons while you are playing audio data, the play continues but the position pointer advances to the beginning of the next or previous sound segment.

If you press and hold SELECT on the Fwd button while playing, the audio data plays at twice the normal speed until you release SELECT. If you press and hold SELECT on the Rev button while playing, the audio data plays backward at twice the normal speed until you release SELECT.

Loading and Saving Audio Files

The Audio Tool can load audio files and store audio data in audio files. To use these features, you first display the File menu by pressing MENU on the File menu button. The File menu is shown here:

The File menu has four items: Load, Save, Save As, and Include File. The Load, Save As, and Include File buttons each display a file selection pop-up window that you use to identify the file you want to load, save, or include. The Save item is active only when a file name is associated with the audio data. When you first start the Audio Tool and begin recording, there is no name associated with the audio data until you use the Save As feature. Once a file name is associated with the audio data, you can simply select the Save item on the File menu to store the audio data to the current name. This capability is useful when you are editing audio data and want to save your changes to the audio file.

Each of the three other functions—Load, Save As, and Include File—use an almost identical pop-up window that includes a file-selection box. Let's start by discussing how to use the file selection box, since it is identical on each of the three pop-up windows. Figure 8.13 shows the Save File pop-up window.

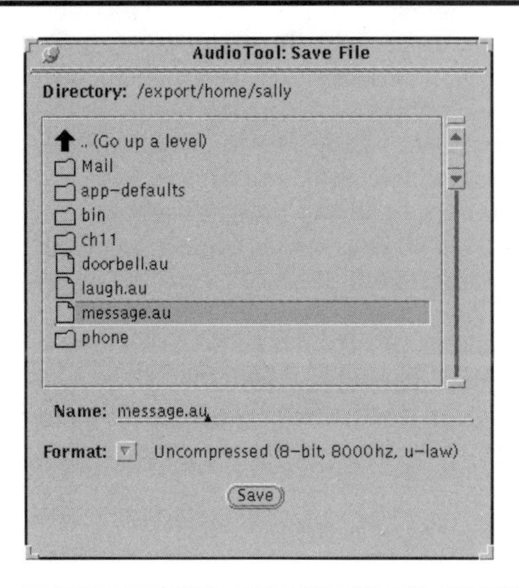

Figure 8.13
The Audio Tool Save File window

You use the file selection box to move around within your directory hierarchy. The current directory is displayed at the top of the window in the Directory field. The current directory shown in Figure 8.13 is /export/home/sally. The scrolling list displays the contents of the current directory. Only directories and audio files are displayed on the list. Other files may exist in the directory, but they are not included on this list unless they are audio files.

The entries on the list that are preceded by a folder glyph represent directories, and the entries preceded by a dog-eared page glyph represent audio files. If you double-click SELECT on a directory item, your current directory changes to that directory. The first entry on every list is an up arrow, representing the parent directory. If you double-click SELECT on that entry, your current directory changes to its parent directory. When you select one of the audio files displayed on the list, the name of the file appears in the Name field at the bottom of the window.

Now let's consider the specifics of the Save File pop-up window. When you want to save an audio file, you use the file-selection box to select a directory where you want the file to be stored. Then you choose a name for the audio file by either entering a name in the Name text field or clicking SELECT on one of the existing audio-file entries on the scrolling list. Of course, you will use an existing entry only if you want to overwrite an existing audio file.

The Save File pop-up window also has a Format field, which you use to determine whether the audio file will be stored in a compressed or uncompressed format. Use the abbreviated menu button to display the Format pop-up menu.

It contains two items: Compressed and Uncompressed. A compressed audio file uses less disk space but may take longer to load than an uncompressed file.

When you have specified a name and have selected a format, press the Save button to store the audio data in an audio file.

The Load File and Include File pop-up windows are nearly identical to the Save File window. The only differences are that the Load File and Include File windows do not have a Format field, and the button at the bottom of the window is relabeled to reflect the function of the window. When you load a file, you are replacing the existing audio data with new audio data from the audio file. When you include a file, you are inserting the data that is in the audio file into the existing audio data. The data is included at the position-pointer location.

You can also save, load, and include files by using drag and drop. The File Manager displays audio files with a unique audio icon, shown here:

You can drag an audio file from the File Manager and drop it onto the Audio Tool's drag and drop target to load the audio file. Any existing audio data in the Audio Tool is then replaced. If you want to drag an audio file from the File Manager and include it in the audio data, drop it onto the display canvas. The audio file is included at the position-pointer location, not at the position where you release SELECT.

You can also save audio data to a file by dragging the glyph from the Audio Tool's drag and drop target and dropping it onto the File Manager. An audio file containing the entire audio data is created in the File Manager's current directory and is named audio.au. If a file named audio.au already exists in that directory, the file is named audio0.au, then audio1.au, and so forth. If you do not want to save the entire audio data, you can select a portion of the audio data from the canvas display, drag it from the Audio Tool, and then drop it onto the File Manager. The audio file you have created will contain only the selected audio data.

Setting the Play and Record Volume

The Audio Tool includes two volume pop-up windows: one for playing an audio file and one for recording. To display either of the two volume pop-up windows, you first display the Volume menu by pressing MENU on the Volume menu button. Then press the Play button to display the Play Volume pop-up window, or press the Record button to display the Record Volume pop-up window.

The Play Volume window includes controls for setting the play volume and the monitor volume, as shown here:

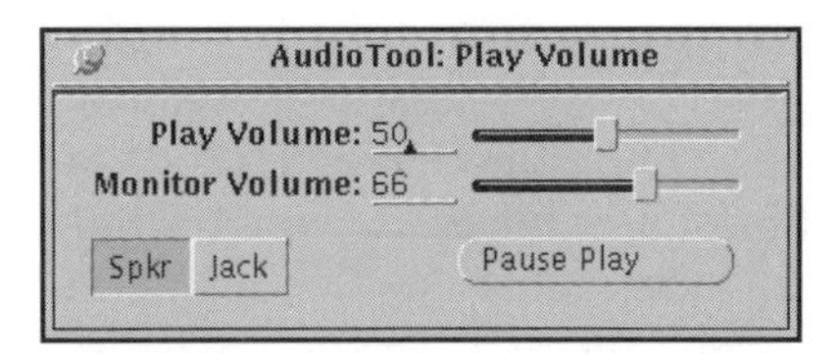

The play volume controls the volume of the audio during playback. The monitor volume is the volume of the microphone input signal. Normally, the monitor volume is set to zero. If the monitor volume is set to a value other than zero, you will be able to hear yourself through the speaker as you talk into the microphone. Even if you are not recording, your voice is carried through the speakers. This feature is more useful if you have another external input source connected to the I/O cable (besides your microphone), such as a CD player.

You adjust the play or monitor volumes by either manipulating the slider or entering a number directly into the text field. Both volumes range from 0 to 100.

In the lower-left corner of the Play Volume window are two exclusive buttons, labeled Spkr and Jack. The Spkr button selects the internal speaker, and the Jack button selects the external jack located on the I/O adapter cable. You might want to plug a set of headphones into the external jack so that you can listen to audio messages privately.

You can press the Pause Play button to pause the playing of audio data. Press it again to resume playing.

The Record Volume pop-up window, shown here, controls the record volume:

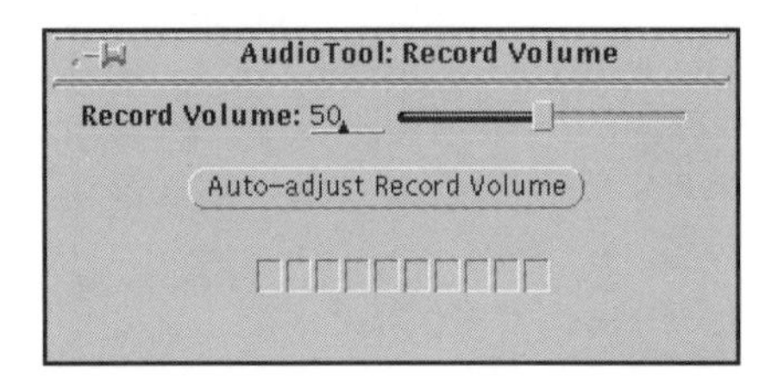

To achieve an optimal recording, you may need to adjust the record level, depending on the sensitivity of your microphone and the loudness of your voice. You can set the record volume by manipulating the Record Volume slider or by directly entering a value in the text field. The preferred way to set the record volume, however, is to use the auto-adjust feature. Press the button labeled

Auto-adjust Record Volume, and then speak into your microphone at a normal level. The Record Volume is automatically adjusted according to the volume of your voice. As you speak you will see the level meter activated and the slider adjusted. When you have finished speaking, press the button again (which has been relabeled Stop). The record volume is now calibrated to your microphone and your voice.

Editing an Audio File

The editing capabilities of the Audio Tool are similar to the text-editing capabilities of the Text Editor. If you think of the audio data as a series of letters that form words (sound) with spaces in between (silence), you will see that editing audio data is analogous to editing text. You can cut, copy, and paste audio data just as you do text. When you cut or copy audio data, it is copied to the clipboard. When you perform a paste operation, you are copying the contents of the clipboard into the audio data. You can even run multiple Audio Tools simultaneously, load each one with a different audio file or record unique audio data in each Audio Tool, and copy and paste audio data from one Audio Tool to the other. You can also copy audio data by using drag and drop. Highlighted audio data can be dragged from one Audio Tool and dropped onto another Audio Tool to copy audio data between applications.

The editing functions are available from the Audio Tool's Edit menu, which is displayed when you press MENU on the Edit menu button. The Edit menu is shown here:

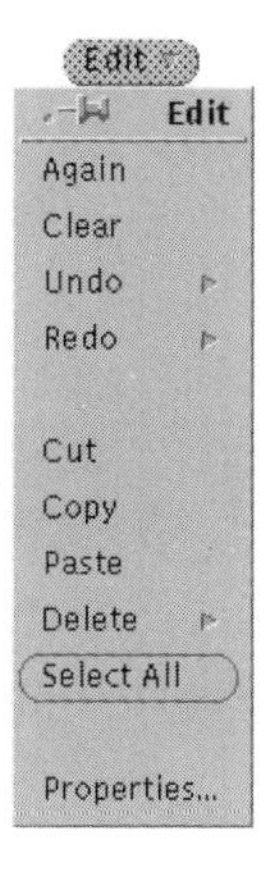

Some of the editing functions available on the Edit menu are also available by means of function keys on the keyboard. For example, the Cut, Copy, Paste,

Again, and Undo keys all perform the same functions as the corresponding items on the Edit menu. Here is a description of each item on the Edit menu:

Again repeats the previous edit command.

Clear removes the entire audio data from the Audio Tool. The display canvas is left blank, and any previously associated file name is eliminated.

Undo supplies a submenu with two items: Last Edit and All Edits. You can choose to undo the last edit only, or all edits.

Redo becomes active only after undo has been used. Redo supplies a submenu with two items that let you redo either the last undo or all undos.

Cut removes selected audio data and moves it to the clipboard.

Copy copies the selected audio data to the clipboard.

Paste copies the audio data stored in the clipboard into the current audio data at the location specified by the position pointer. If any audio data is selected at the time of the paste, the selected data is replaced by the data pasted from the clipboard.

Select All selects the entire audio data. You can also select all by triple-clicking SELECT.

Properties displays the Properties window, which we will discuss in a moment.

Delete displays the Delete submenu. The Delete submenu contain four items for deleting audio data. All of these deletion options remove data without copying it to the clipboard. You can undo a deletion, but you cannot paste the audio data that you have deleted. The Delete submenu is shown here:

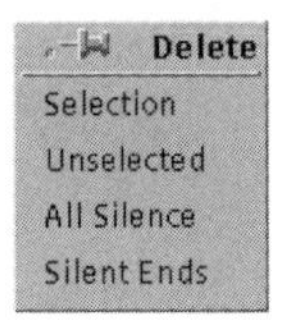

Each of the four items on the Delete submenu deletes audio data, as described here:

Selection deletes the selected audio data. This is the default.

Unselected deletes all unselected data. You can delete unselected audio data only if some audio data is selected.

All Silence deletes all audio data designated as silence by the thin horizontal line in the display canvas.

Silent Ends deletes silent audio data at the beginning and end of the audio data.

Some editing functions are available also on the display canvas pop-up menu. To display this pop-up menu, position the pointer anywhere on the display canvas and press MENU. The menu is shown here:

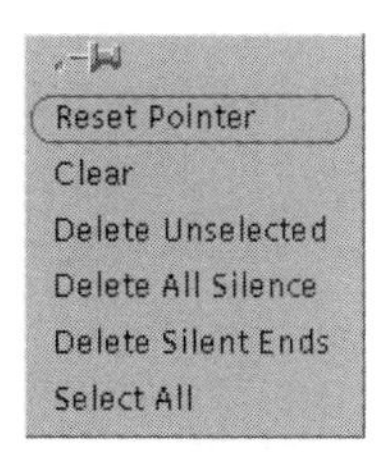

Five of the six items on this pop-up menu are identical to items on the Edit menu or the Delete submenu. The only new item is Reset Pointer, which moves the position pointer to the beginning of the audio data.

Using the Audio Tool Properties

The Audio Tool Properties window, shown in Figure 8.14, consists of various controls for modifying the functions of the Audio Tool.

The controls on the Properties window operate as follows:

Auto Play on Load lets you choose whether the Audio Tool will automatically play a file that is loaded or dragged and dropped onto the Audio Tool's drag and drop target.

Auto Play on Selection lets you choose whether the Audio Tool will automatically play audio data when it is selected.

Confirm before clear lets you choose whether a notification will appear when you clear unsaved data.

Silence Detection lets you turn silence detection on or off. When silence detection is turned off, all audio data appears as a single sound segment.

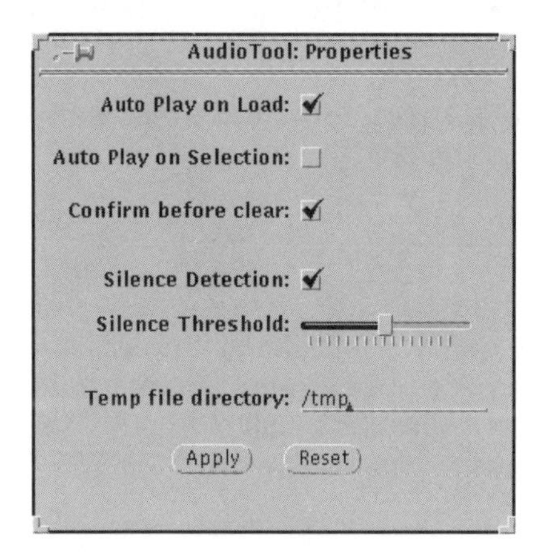

Figure 8.14
The Audio Tool Properties pop-up window

Silence Threshold lets you control the sensitivity to short pauses. It is active only when Silence Detection is activated. Move the slider to the left to increase the sensitivity to short pauses. The number of sound segments will also be increased. Move the slider to the right to decrease the sensitivity to short pauses. The number of sound segments will be decreased.

Temp file directory lets you specify the location for temporary sound files.

Press the Apply button to activate any changes you have made to the Properties window. Press the Reset button if you wish to redo the options on the Properties window.

The Performance Meter

The Performance Meter is a tool for monitoring different aspects of system performance. You can use the Performance Meter to monitor, among other things, CPU usage, disk activity, and network traffic. This information is useful to you when you are trying to determine the reason for a system anomaly. If your computer is not responding to user input, you might glean some information about the problem by using the Performance Meter. You can monitor activity on your own system or on another system on your local network. You also have customization options that allow you to display various performance values simultaneously and in different formats.

The Performance Meter does not have a window header like the other DeskSet applications. To display the Window pop-up menu, position the pointer on the window border and press MENU, or position the pointer anywhere over the application, hold down the Alt key, and press MENU.

To start the Performance Meter, choose Performance Meter from the Workspace Programs menu. You can also start the Performance Meter by entering the perfmeter command at the prompt:

```
dugout% perfmeter &
```

Using the Display Formats

The Performance Meter can display system performance data in two formats: graph and dial. Both formats display the name of the performance option in the lower-left corner and the maximum value of the meter in the lower-right corner, as shown here:

The graph display, which is the default format, acts like a strip chart: it shows you the activity of the performance category over the last few minutes. In other words, it provides some "history" of the performance option you are monitoring. The dial display contains two dial indicators, called the hour hand and the minute hand. The hour hand, which is longer than the minute hand, displays the performance value averaged over the preceding two seconds. The minute hand displays the performance value averaged over the preceding twenty seconds. Both of these time periods can be customized by means of the Properties window, which you will learn about later in this section.

Another difference between the graph and dial displays is the size of the base window. Although the graph and dial windows are about the same size by default, only the graph window can be resized. Resizing the graph window allows you to tailor the amount of "history" you see about the performance activity. Here is the Performance Meter's graph display after being resized:

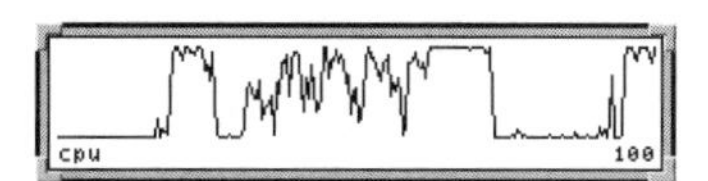

The default size for the Performance Meter is about the same as that of an icon. If you are using the default size, there is little reason to iconify it, since you won't save any workspace. If you do choose to iconify the Performance Meter, it will appear as shown here:

Selecting a Performance Value to Monitor

The Performance Meter has no controls in its base window. You use the Performance Meter pop-up menu to select the performance option that will be displayed in the base window. To display the Performance Meter pop-up menu, position the pointer over the base window and press MENU. The menu is shown here:

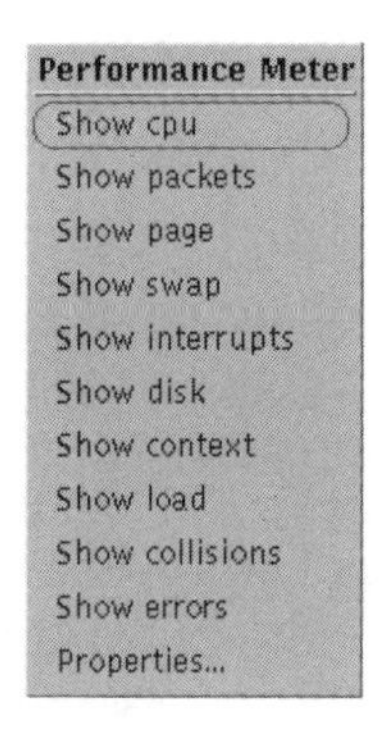

The Performance Meter pop-up menu includes one item for each of the ten performance options. Select an item from the menu, and that performance option will replace the previously displayed option in the base window. If you are monitoring two or more performance options simultaneously, selecting an item from the menu adds that performance option to those already being displayed rather than replacing it. You'll learn how to monitor multiple performance options in a moment.

Here is a brief description of each performance option:

Show cpu monitors the percentage of the CPU being used.

Show packets monitors the number of Ethernet packets received per second.

Show page monitors the paging activity in pages per second.

Show swap monitors the number of processes swapped per second.

Show interrupts monitors the number of device interrupts per second.

Show disk monitors the disk traffic in transfers per second.

Show context monitors the number of context switches per second.

Show load monitors the load average over the last minute. The load average is defined as the number of runnable processes.

Show collisions monitors the number of Ethernet collisions per second.

Show errors monitors the number of Ethernet receiving errors per second.

Customizing the Performance Meter

The controls for customizing the Performance Meter are available on the Performance Meter Properties window. To display the Performance Meter Properties window, position the pointer on the Performance Meter's base window, press MENU, and then select the Properties item.

Another way that you can display the Performance Meter Properties window is by positioning the pointer on the Performance Meter's base window and pressing the Props key. Figure 8.15 shows the Performance Meter Properties window.

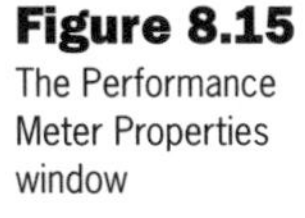

Figure 8.15 The Performance Meter Properties window

You use the Performance Meter Properties window to customize the Performance Meter. Each time you make changes, you must press the Apply button at the bottom of the window to activate the changes. If you want to permanently store the customization options you have chosen, press the Set Default button. The options are stored so that each time you start a new Performance Meter program the customization options you selected will be set. Use the Reset button to set all the options on the Properties window back to the settings that were active the last time the Apply button was pressed.

The Monitor and Direction Options

The Monitor field on the Properties window provides you with ten performance options in a nonexclusive setting. Select each performance option that you want to monitor, and press Apply. The base window expands to accommodate each of the performance options you choose to monitor. The meters are aligned in a single horizontal or vertical row, depending on the Direction choice in the Properties window. Here is the Performance Meter, with ten dial meters displayed horizontally:

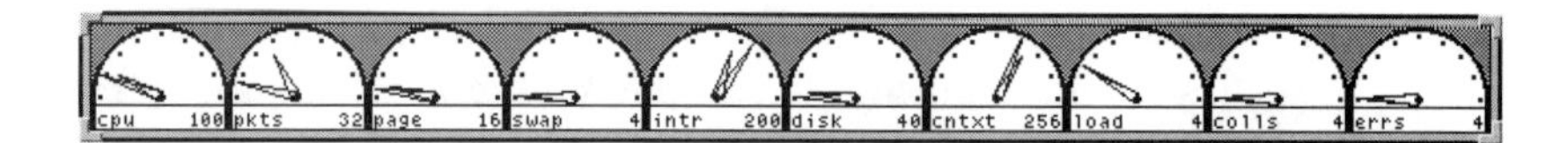

To change the orientation to vertical, select the vertical option from the Direction field. You can also use a keyboard accelerator to change the direction of the layout. Position the pointer on the base window, and press d. Here is the Performance Meter with three vertical graph meters:

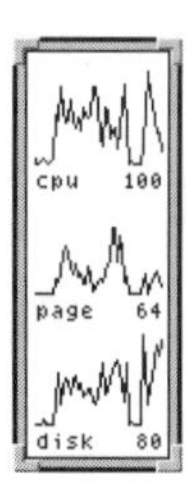

The Display Options

The Display field allows you to choose the type of meter to display: dial or graph. If you choose graph, the Graph type field becomes active. You can then choose either a line graph or a solid graph. The two graph types are illustrated here:

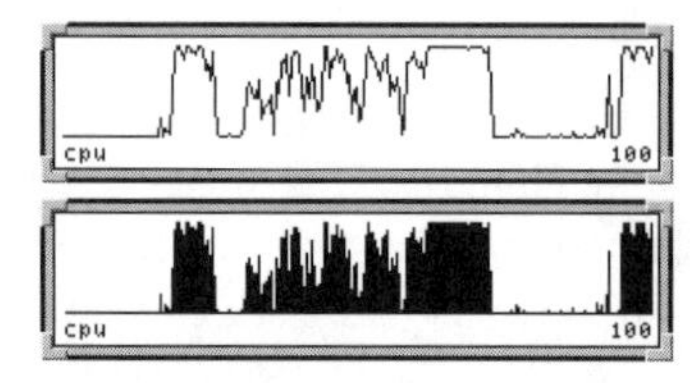

You can also toggle between the graph and the dial meters with the g accelerator, and you can toggle between a line graph and a solid graph by using the s keyboard accelerator.

The Machine Option

The Machine field allows you to specify the machine whose performance you will monitor. The default choice is local, which means that you will monitor the performance of your own machine. If you select remote, you must supply, in the Machine name text field, the name of another machine on your network. If you monitor another machine's performance, the Performance Meter's base window will include the name of the machine at the bottom of the window. You can toggle between monitoring your local machine and monitoring a remote machine by using the t accelerator. In the following illustration, the CPU performance of a remote computer called *wind* is being monitored:

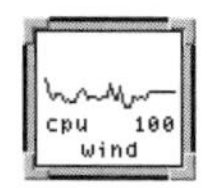

The Time-Interval Options

There are three time-interval options you can customize: Sample time, Hour hand, and Second hand. The Sample time field lets you determine how often the display is updated. The default sample time is 2 seconds, but you can set it to any value greater than zero. The Hour hand and Second hand fields apply only to the dial display. They let you determine the number of seconds over which to average the values displayed by the hour and second hands.

The Log Samples Option

The Performance Meter will log performance values in a file if you check the Log Samples check box. Enter the name of the log file in the Filename field. If you check the Log Samples check box but do not enter a file name, the log file will be created in your home directory and will be called perfmeter.logXXX, where XXX is replaced by a unique identifier.

Table 8.3 lists the Performance Meter's accelerator keys.

Table 8.3 Performance Meter Accelerators

Accelerator	Description
d	Toggles the direction of the meters, horizontal or vertical
g	Toggles the display between graphs and dials

Table 8.3 Performance Meter Accelerators (Continued)

Accelerator	Description
q	Quits the Performance Meter
s	If graphs are being displayed, toggles between line and solid graphs
S	Toggles the saving of samples to file
t	Toggles between monitoring your local machine and monitoring a remote machine

Summary

In this chapter you have learned how to use five DeskSet programs: the Clock, the Print Tool, Snapshot, the Audio Tool, and the Performance Meter. Your understanding of the DeskSet and its capabilities is growing rapidly. In the next chapter you will learn about four other DeskSet applications: the Tape Tool, the Calculator, the Icon Editor, and the Binder.

CHAPTER

More DeskSet Applications

The Tape Tool

The Calculator

The Icon Editor

The Binder

IN THIS CHAPTER YOU WILL LEARN ABOUT FOUR DESKSET UTILITIES THAT you may not need to use everyday but that come in handy when needed: the Tape Tool, the Calculator, the Icon Editor, and the Binder.

The Tape Tool lets you read, write, and list the contents of magnetic tape media and floppy disks. The Calculator program has all the functions of a standard hand-held calculator, including financial, scientific, and logical functions. The Icon Editor and Binder programs are often used together. You create an icon image with the Icon Editor and then bind the icon to a particular file type with the Binder. The File Manager then displays your new icon whenever it displays the file type to which you bound your icon.

In this chapter you will learn how to use the following utilities:

- The Tape Tool
- The Calculator
- The Icon Editor
- The Binder

The Tape Tool

The Tape Tool program lets you manipulate magnetic media such as tapes and floppy disks. You can read, write, and list the contents of tapes and disks with the Tape Tool. The Tape Tool uses the tar (Tape Archive) command for all of its functions. This is a standard UNIX command for reading and writing tapes. Any of the functions available with the Tape Tool can also be entered directly at the prompt with the tar command. The Tape Tool provides a convenient user interface for dealing with tape archives. Files on a tape are displayed in a scrolling list, and you select and deselect files from the list by using the pointer and the mouse.

To start the Tape Tool, choose Tape Tool from the Workspace Programs menu. You can also start the Tape Tool by entering the tapetool command at the prompt:

```
dugout% tapetool &
```

Figure 9.1 shows the Tape Tool base window.

Figure 9.1
The Tape Tool base window

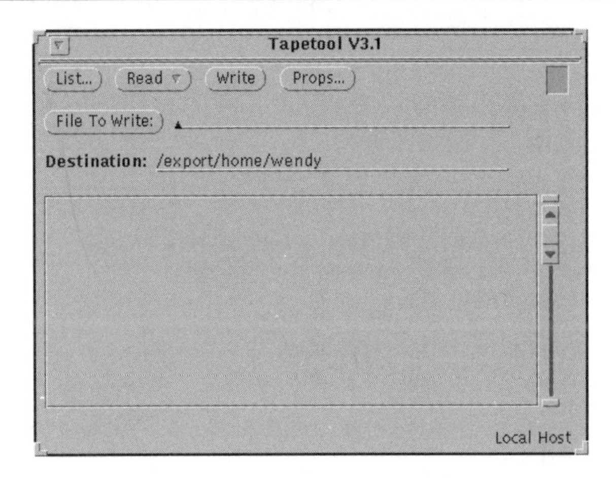

The Tape Tool's icon is displayed in two ways. If you have not selected any files for archiving, the icon displays the tape completely rewound, as shown here:

If you have selected files for archiving, the icon displays the tape partially advanced, as shown here:

Tape Tool Basics

The Tape Tool supports three basic archiving functions: reading, writing, and listing. To write files to tape (archive), you enter the name of a file in the File To Write text field and press Return. You can repeat this process to add other files to the archive list. Each file added to the list is shown in the scrolling list directly below the Destination field. You can also add file names to the archive list by using drag and drop; simply drag the files from the File Manager and drop them onto the Tape Tool's drag and drop target. When you have finished compiling the archive list, press the Write button to archive the files to tape.

To list the files on an existing tape archive, press the List button. The tape archive is read, and the files in the archive are displayed in the scrolling list on the Tape Contents/Files to Read pop-up window.

To read (extract) files from a tape, you first manipulate the list of files in the Tape Contents window. This gives you the ability to read some but not all of the files in an archive. When the list is modified to your satisfaction, use the Read menu button to select one of three read options. This extracts the files from the archive and writes them to the specified destination.

You can resize the Tape Tool's base window or Tape Contents pop-up window to any size. This is particularly useful when you want to enlarge the size of each of the scrolling lists on the two windows. If a file name displayed in a scrolling list is longer than the width of the scrolling list, the file name is truncated. You can increase the size of the window to enlarge the scrolling list so that the entire file name is viewable.

Setting Tape Tool Properties

You will usually want to set Tape Tool Properties before reading or writing an archive. The Tape Tool Properties window is shown in Figure 9.2.

Figure 9.2
The Tape Tool Properties window

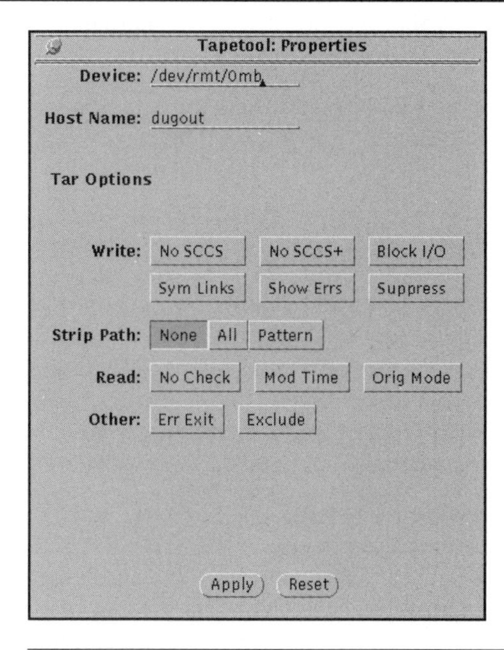

To display the Tape Tool Properties window, press the Props button on the Tape Tool main window.

Here is a brief discussion of each field on the Properties window:

Device lets you specify the hardware device to which read and write operations should be performed. By default, the Device field contains the name of your system tape drive, such as /dev/rmt/0mb. You can enter the name of any device that is appropriate for writing an archive. For example, you can write an archive to the floppy disk drive found on most SPARCstations® by entering /dev/diskette in the Device field. You can also specify the name of a file in the Device field to write to or read from a file rather than a peripheral device. If you have the TAPE environment variable set, the Device field is initially set to the value of this environment variable.

Host Name represents the name of the system on which you want to read and write archive files. By default, this field contains the name of your local system. If you are using a tape drive on a remote system, enter the remote system name in the Host Name field and update the Device field to reflect the name of the device on the remote machine (if it is different from the name of the device on your local machine).

Write affects the way that files are written to an archive. Each of the available options is independent of the others.

No SCCS excludes all directories named SCCS and all files in those directories. SCCS directories are used by programmers for source-code control.

No SCCS+ excludes all SCCS directories plus files with a suffix .o, and files named errs, core, and a.out.

Block I/O lets you specify a blocking factor. When you select Block I/O, the Block Size text field appears below the Other field, as shown in Figure 9.3. The default blocking factor (20) is sufficient for most reads and writes. The only time you would use this feature is when you want to write or read a tape archive from an unbuffered (raw) device in order to increase the speed and efficiency of the write.

Sym Links lets you follow symbolic links (the links that are created in the File Manager when you copy a file as a link). If Sym Links is set, then symbolic-link files are included in the archive as if they were regular files. In other words, the link is followed so that the file that the symbolic link is pointing to is included. The default is to include only the link in the archive, not the file that the link points to.

Show Errs displays error messages if symbolic-link files cannot be resolved. Error messages are displayed only if you have set the Sym Links field to follow symbolic links.

Suppress suppresses information about owner and file modes.

Strip Path allows you to control the way the file names are written to the archive. The None choice indicates that the path should not be stripped. If you drag and drop a file from the File Manager with Strip Path set to None, the entire absolute path name is included. The All choice indicates that the entire path should be stripped from the file name. Files are written to the archive with just their file names; no directory information is included. The Pattern choice lets you customize the way the directory portion of the file name is included in the archive. When you choose Pattern, the Dir Pattern text field appears at the bottom of the Properties window, as shown in Figure 9.3. You use this field to specify the path to be stripped from the file name.

Read lets you choose from three nonexclusive options available when you read an archive.

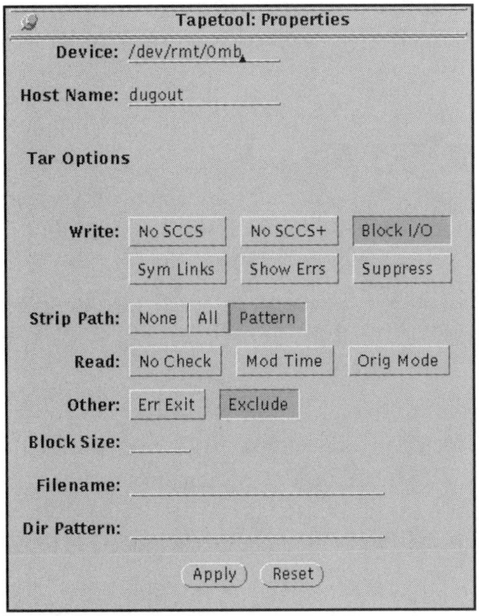

Figure 9.3 The Tape Tool Properties window with optional fields displayed

No Check means that errors during the reading of the archive are ignored.

Mod Time controls the way that the file modification time is set. When you set Mod Time, the modification time of the extracted files is the current system time rather than the modification time stored in the archive.

Orig Mode controls the way that permissions are set. When you set Orig Mode, permission values that were stored in the archive are restored to the extracted files.

Other lets you set two other useful options:

Err Exit lets you control how errors are handled. When you set Err Exit, the read or write operation terminates whenever an error is encountered.

Exclude enables you to exclude a specified file when you read an archive. When you select Exclude, the Filename text field is displayed, as shown in Figure 9.3. Enter in the Filename text field the name of the file that you want to exclude.

After you have made changes to the Properties window, you must click SELECT on the Apply button for the changes to be applied. Use the Reset button to reset all options to the values that were set the last time you selected Apply.

Writing Files to a Tape

Writing files to a tape archive is quite simple. First, set your properties in the Tape Tool Properties window, as described in the preceding section. Then add to the Tape Tool's base window scrolling list the names of all the files or directories that you want to include in the archive. Note that, when you specify a directory, all the files and directories in that directory are included.

You can add file and directory names to the scrolling list in two ways:

- Use the File Manager to drag and drop files onto the Tape Tool drag and drop target. Each file dropped onto the Tape Tool is added to the list. You can select multiple files from the File Manager and drop them all in one operation. Figure 9.4 shows four files (Makefile, README, char.c, and cursor.c) being dragged from the File Manager and dropped onto the Tape Tool.
- Enter the name of a file or directory in the File To Write field and press Return, or click SELECT on the File To Write button. You can add only

one file or directory at a time by using this method. Each name you enter is added to the list of files and directories displayed in the scrolling list. This method is very time-consuming if you are adding many individual files, but if you are adding just one file or one directory, this may be the fastest way to add it to the list.

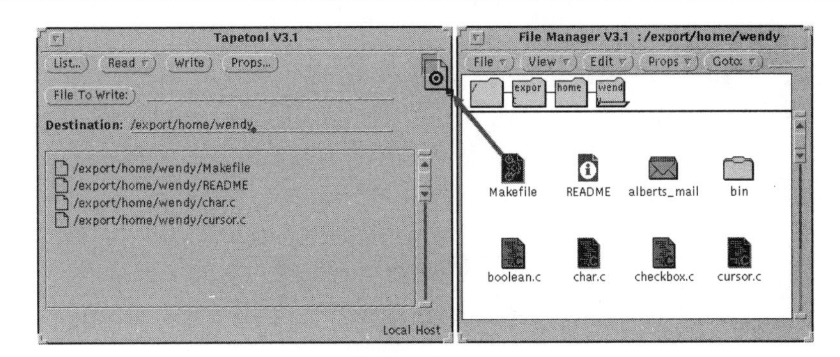

Figure 9.4 Dragging files from the File Manager to the Tape Tool

You can delete any file and directory names from the scrolling list by using the Write Functions pop-up menu. To display this menu, position the pointer on the scrolling list and press MENU. You can use this menu to delete all the names in the list or only the names that you select.

When you are satisfied with the list of files and directories displayed in the scrolling list, click SELECT on the Write button to write the files to tape.

Whenever you are writing an archive to a peripheral device such as a tape or floppy disk, you must make sure that the tape or disk is loaded in the drive and that it is not write-protected. If you are using the floppy drive with a 3½-inch floppy disk, you must format the disk before you can write to it. To format a floppy disk, insert the disk into the disk drive and enter the following command:

```
dugout% fdformat
```

You are prompted to press Return when you are ready to start formatting. When the formatting is complete, you can write files to the disk.

The way that you specify the path name for the files you write to tape is very important. If you are planning to use the tape archive to transfer files to another machine, you probably want to strip the path name so that the file name is not an absolute path name. If you do include an absolute path name for files written to an archive, the files will have exactly the same path when they are extracted from the archive. This means you cannot choose to put the files into another directory on the new system—a limitation that is likely to be inconvenient. If you are writing files to a tape archive that will act as a backup, leaving the complete path name in the file is probably not a problem, because you would be simply restoring the files to their original locations. However, if you are planning to move files between systems, I recommend that you strip all or part of the path name by using the Strip Path field on the Tape Tool Properties window.

Listing Files from a Tape

To display a list of the files in an archive, click SELECT on the List button. The files in the archive are displayed in the scrolling list on the Tape Contents/ Files to Read pop-up window, shown here:

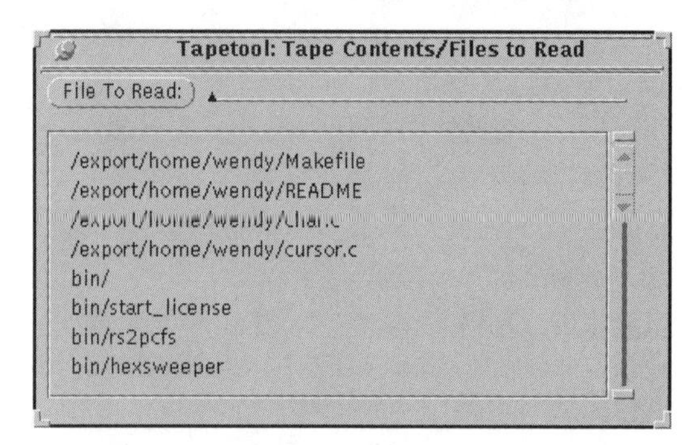

If you are planning to read some, but not all, of the files in the archive, you will need first to edit the list. To edit the list of files in the Tape Contents/Files to Read window, use the Read Functions pop-up menu. To display the Read Functions menu, position the pointer on the scrolling list and press MENU.

The Read Functions menu has three items:

Select All selects every file in the list.

Deselect All deselects every file in the list.

Delete Selected deletes each selected file from the list.

To select a file from the list, position the pointer on the file name and click SELECT. If you click SELECT again on the same file name, it is deselected.

You can also add file names to the list by entering a name in the File To Read text field and then pressing Return or clicking SELECT on the File To Read button. When you are satisfied with the files in the list, you are ready to read them from the archive.

Reading Files from a Tape

To read files from a tape, press the Read menu button on the Tape Tool's base window. This displays the Read pop-up menu, shown here:

For each of these three menu choices, files are extracted from the archive and written to a particular destination. The destination of the files depends on the path name of each file in the archive. If a file in the archive has an absolute path name (an absolute path name begins with a /), then the destination of the file will be the exact path name of the file in the archive. If a file in the archive has a relative path name (a relative path name begins with anything except a /), then the file will be written to the directory specified in the Destination text field. If you are extracting files with relative path names, be sure to enter the appropriate path in the Destination field. In either case, you must have write permission in the specified directories in order to write files to those directories.

Here is a description of each of the three items on the Read menu:

Selected extracts from the archive each file that is selected in the Tape Contents/Files to Read scrolling list. Use this option when you want to extract only a few files from an archive.

Entire List extracts from the archive every file in the Tape Contents/Files to Read scrolling list. Use this option if your archive has many files in it and you want to extract most but not all of the files. Select each file that you do *not* want to read, and delete it from the list by using the Delete Selected item from the Read Functions pop-up menu. When you have deleted all the files that you don't want to read, use the Entire List option to read all the remaining files in the list.

Entire Tape extracts all the files from the archive regardless of the contents of the Tape Contents/Files to Read scrolling list. If you use this option, you do not need to list the archive first, nor do you need to edit the files in the list.

The Calculator

The Calculator program provides all the functions of most common hand-held calculators. The features available with the Calculator include financial, scientific, and logical functions in addition to the standard arithmetic functions that are basic to all calculators.

To start the Calculator, choose Calculator from the Workspace Programs menu. You can also start the Calculator by entering the calctool command at the prompt:

```
dugout% calctool &
```

Figure 9.5 shows the Calculator base window.

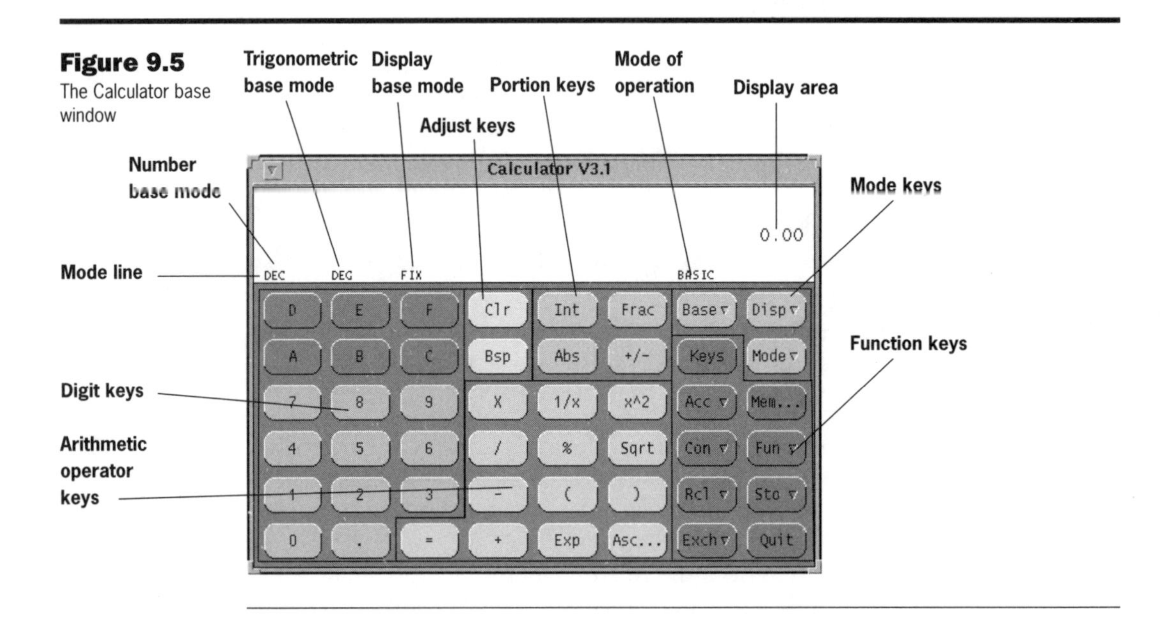

Figure 9.5 The Calculator base window

The Calculator's icon displays a hand-held calculator, as shown here:

Calculator Basics

Before exploring all of the various functions available with the Calculator, let's look at the Calculator's base window to understand some basics. The Calculator has on its base window 48 buttons laid out in six rows and eight columns. At the top of the base window is the display area, where number values are displayed. The bottom of the display area is the mode line, which shows the current modes of operation. The three modes of operation displayed on the left are the Number base, the Trigonometric base, and the Display base. The Calculator's fundamental mode of operation is shown on the right side of the display area. This mode can be BASIC, FINANCIAL, LOGICAL, or SCIENTIFIC. You'll learn more about modes and how to set them later in this chapter.

The Calculator's keys are grouped in several sets of related functions. If you have a color monitor, you can see that the keys are color coded. The keys that belong to the same group are the same color. In the next few sections you will learn how to use each key in the key groups.

If you know how to use a hand-held calculator, you will find using the Calculator very intuitive. Simply click SELECT on the numbers and operators to perform a calculation. Each number you enter is displayed in the Display area, as is the answer at the completion of the problem.

Every button on the Calculator has a corresponding keyboard accelerator. This makes entering numbers in the Calculator particularly easy. For example, if I am doing simple arithmetic, I find it much easier to use the numeric keypad portion of my keyboard for entering numbers than to use the mouse and pointer. The buttons representing digits (0–9, A–F) are activated by using the corresponding digit keys on the keyboard. To determine the keyboard accelerator, press the Keys key. This changes the labels of all the buttons on the Calculator base window to the corresponding keyboard accelerator.

The Calculator Keys

In this section you'll learn about each Calculator key and its corresponding function.

The Digit Keys

The digit keys include the keys labeled 0-9, A–F, and the decimal point. These are the keys for entering numbers on which operations are performed. Not all of these keys are always active. When the numeric base of the Calculator is set to Decimal, digits 0–9 are active. When the numeric base is set to Binary, only digits 0 and 1 are active, and so forth. (You'll learn how to set the numeric base when we talk about Mode Keys.) Inactive keys are dimmed and do not respond to any user input. In Figure 9.5, for example, note that digit keys A–F are inactive.

The Adjust Keys

The Adjust keys group consists of two keys:

- The **Clr** keys clears the number in the display and resets it to zero.
- The **Bsp** (Backspace) key removes the last digit entered.

The Arithmetic Operator Keys

The arithmetic operator keys include some of the most common calculator functions, such as addition, subtraction, multiplication, and division. Here is a description of each:

- The **+** key takes the last number entered and adds it to the next number entered.
- The **-** key takes the last number entered and subtracts from it the next number entered.
- The **X** key takes the last number entered and multiplies it by the next number entered.
- The **/** key takes the last number entered and divides it by the next number entered.
- The **=** key displays the result of the current calculation in the current base.
- The **1/x** key returns the value 1 divided by the currently displayed value.
- The **x^2** key returns the square of the currently displayed value.
- The **%** key takes the last number entered and calculates a percentage by using the next number entered. For example, to calculate 45 percent of 200, you would enter **45 % 200 =**. The answer is 90.
- The **Sqrt** key calculates the square root of the currently displayed value.
- The **(** and **)** keys allow you to group together a set of calculations. For example, to divide 27 by the difference of 12 and 3, you would enter **27 / (12 - 3)**. The answer is 3.
- The **Exp** key starts exponential input. Any numbers typed from now on are the exponent. If you haven't entered a mantissa, the calculator uses a mantissa of 1.0.

- The **Asc** key displays the following window:

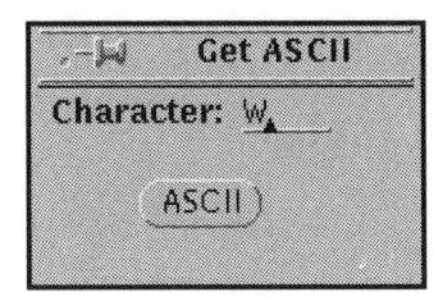

Use this window to determine the ASCII value of a character. Enter the character in the text field, and click SELECT on the ASCII button.

The Portion Keys

You use the Portion keys to control the portion of the displayed value and some other related functions. Here is a description of each key:

- The **Int** key returns the integer portion of the currently displayed value.
- The **Frac** key returns the fractional portion of the currently displayed value.
- The **Abs** key returns the absolute value of the currently displayed value.
- The **+/-** key changes the arithmetic sign of the currently displayed value or of the exponent being entered.

The Mode Keys

The three mode keys control the modes of operation for the Calculator. The current mode for each category is displayed in the mode line of the display area.

The Base Key You use the Base key to set the numeric base of the Calculator to Binary, Octal, Decimal, or Hexadecimal. Position the pointer over the Base key and press MENU to display the Numeric base menu, shown here:

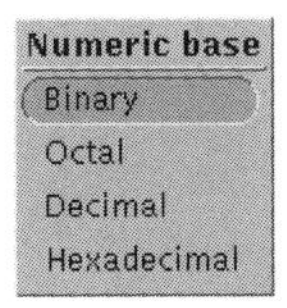

When you change numeric bases, any number displayed in the display area is converted to the new base, and the digit keys that do not apply to that base are deactivated.

The Disp Key You use the Disp key to set the *display type*, or the way that the numbers in the display area are displayed. Press MENU with the pointer over the Disp key to bring up the Display type menu, shown here:

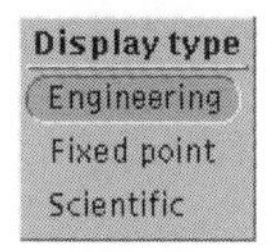

You have three display types to choose from: Engineering, Fixed point, and Scientific. If you use Fixed-point notation and the number is larger than the display allows, the Calculator automatically displays the number in Scientific notation.

The Mode Key The Calculator operates in four fundamental modes: Basic, Financial, Logical, and Scientific. When the Calculator is invoked, it operates in Basic mode. To select another mode, press MENU on the Mode key. The Mode menu appears, as shown here:

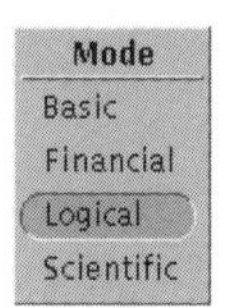

When you choose a mode other than Basic, a pop-up window appears, with additional function keys specific to that mode. When you choose Basic mode, the pop-up window is removed. You'll learn about each of the functions available in the Financial, Logical, and Scientific mode in a moment.

The Function Keys

The Function keys are divided into three categories: memory registers, user-defined functions, and miscellaneous functions. Each key is discussed by category in the following sections.

Memory Registers The Calculator has ten memory registers in which you can store values. You store, retrieve, exchange, and display the contents of the memory registers by using the memory register keys.

- The **Sto** key lets you store a number in a memory register. Position the pointer over the Sto key and press MENU to display the Store pop-up menu. When you select an item on the menu, the number in the display area is stored in the corresponding memory register.

- The **Rcl** key lets you recall a stored memory register. Display the Retrieve pop-up menu by pressing MENU over the Rcl button, and select one of the items on the menu. The contents of the corresponding memory register are displayed in the display area.
- The **Exch** key lets you exchange the contents of a memory register with the number in the display area. Display the Exchange pop-up menu, and select a register from the menu. The value in the display area is exchanged with the value of the chosen register.
- The **Mem** key displays the Memory Registers pop-up window. This window displays the values for each of the ten memory registers.

User-Defined Functions The Calculator lets you define ten constants and ten functions by using the following two keys:

- The **Con** key lets you use a defined constant. Press MENU over the Con key to display the Constants pop-up menu, shown here:

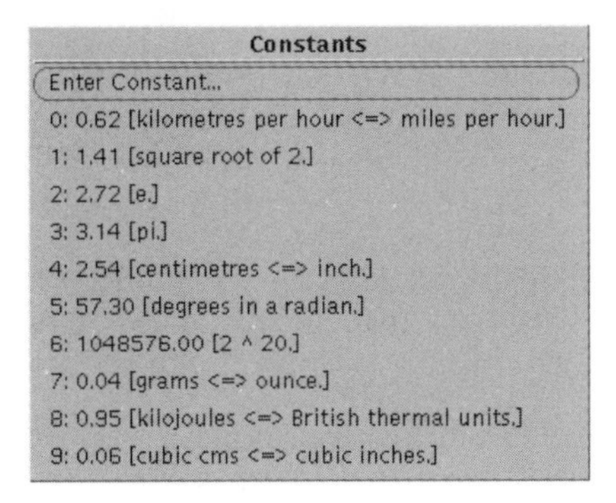

The Constants menu contains ten constants. Select an item from the menu, and the value associated with that item is displayed in the display area.

To create your own constant, select the first item on the menu: Enter Constant. The New Constant pop-up window appears, as shown here:

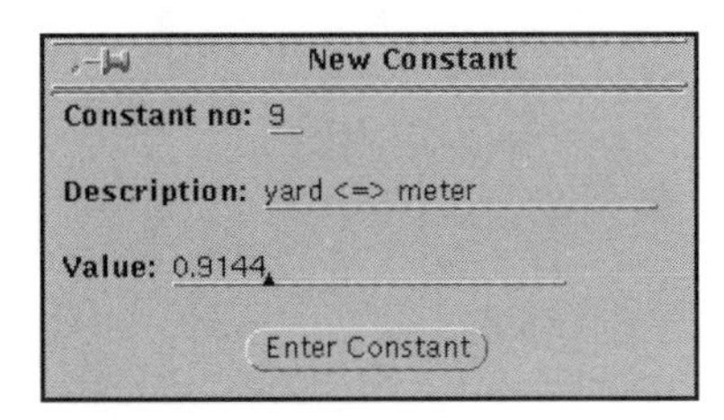

Enter a constant number (a value from 0 to 9), a description, and a value in the corresponding fields of the window, and then press the Enter Constant button to set the new constant.

- The **Fun** key lets you create and use a custom function. There are no predefined functions with the Calculator; you must define your own functions. The first time you display the Functions pop-up menu, the only item on the menu is the Enter Function item. When you choose Enter Function, the New Function pop-up window is displayed. It is identical to the New Constant window except that it is used to create a new function.

  The value field should include a character that represents an arithmetic operation. For example, if you want a function that converts meters to yards, enter **0.9144** * in the value field. When you select this item from the Functions menu, it is the same as if you had entered the number 0.9144, followed by the multiply key. You would then enter a number and press the equals sign to finish the operation.

Miscellaneous Functions Three other keys have miscellaneous functions:

- The **Keys** key toggles the label of the buttons between the standard label and the keyboard-equivalent label. The keyboard-equivalent label represents the key that is the equivalent to the button in the Calculator base window.
- The **Acc** key controls the accuracy of the number displayed in the display area. The default accuracy is two decimal places. You can change the accuracy to a value between 0 and 9.
- The **Quit** key quits the Calculator program.

Financial Functions

The Calculator has nine financial functions that are activated by the keys on the Financial Mode pop-up window, shown here:

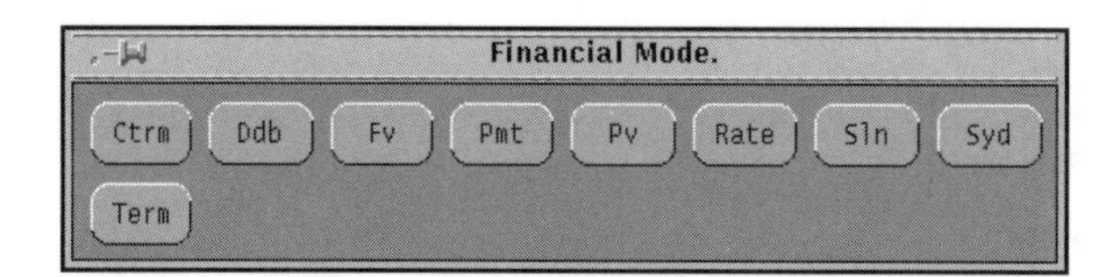

To display this window, select Financial from the Mode pop-up menu.

The financial functions use values stored in the memory registers. For example, to determine the amount of an installment payment, the Calculator needs to know the amount of the loan, the interest rate, and the term of the loan. You must store this information in the appropriate registers before you select the corresponding financial function button.

Each of the following sections describes the information that must reside in each memory register to perform the calculation. An example of each calculation is also included.

Ctrm: Compounding Term

You use Ctrm to compute the number of compounding periods that an investment of present value requires in order to grow to a future value, earning a fixed interest rate per compounding period. For example, to determine how long it will take to double an investment of $8,000 at 9% annual interest compounded monthly, you enter the following values:

Register 0: 0.0075 (periodic interest rate = 9% / 12)

Register 1: 16000 (future value of the investment)

Register 2: 8000 (present value of the investment)

Click SELECT on Ctrm to display the result in the display area (92.77 months).

Ddb: Double-Declining Depreciation

You use Ddb to compute the depreciation allowance on an asset for a specified period of time, using the double-declining balance method. For example, if you paid $8,000 for an office machine that had a useful life of six years and a salvage value of $900 after six years, you would compute the depreciation expense for the fourth year by entering the following values:

Register 0: 8000 (amount paid for asset)

Register 1: 900 (value of asset at end of its life)

Register 2: 6 (useful life of asset)

Register 3: 4 (time period for depreciation allowance)

Click SELECT on Ddb to display the result in the display area (790.12).

Fv: Future Value

You use Fv to determine the future value of an investment. The Calculator computes the future value based on a series of equal payments, earning a periodic interest rate over the number of payment periods in a term. For example, if you deposited $4,000 each year for 20 years into an account paying 8% interest compounded annually, you would compute the value of the account after 20 years by entering the following values:

Register 0: 4000 (periodic payment)

Register 1: 0.08 (periodic interest rate)

Register 2: 20 (number of periods)

Click SELECT on Fv to display the value of the account after 20 years (183047.86).

Pmt: Periodic Payment

You use Pmt to compute the amount of the periodic payment of a loan. Most installment loans are computed like ordinary annuities, in that payments are made at the end of each payment period. For example, if you want to determine the monthly payment for a $120,000 mortgage for 30 years at an annual interest rate of 11.0%, you enter the following values:

Register 0: 120000 (principal)

Register 1: 0.00916 (periodic interest rate is 11% / 12)

Register 2: 360 (term 30 × 12)

Click SELECT on Pmt to calculate your monthly payment (1142.29).

Pv: Present Value

You use Pv to determine the present value of an investment. The Calculator computes the present value, based on a series of equal payments discounted at a periodic interest rate over the number of periods in the term. For example, if you had just won a million dollars in prize money to be awarded in 20 annual payments of $50,000 each, you could determine the value of the award in today's dollars (assuming a 9% rate of interest) by entering the following values:

Register 0: 50000 (period payment)

Register 1: 0.09 (periodic interest rate is 9%)

Register 2: 20 (term)

Click SELECT on Pv to calculate the present value (456427).

Rate: Periodic Interest Rate

You use Rate to compute the periodic interest rate. It returns the periodic interest necessary for a present value to grow to a future value over a specified number of compounding periods. For example, to determine the periodic interest rate of a $20,000 investment that matures in five years with a value of $30,000 and interest that is compounded monthly, you enter the following values:

Register 0: 30000 (future value)

Register 1: 20000 (present value)

Register 2: 60 (term 5 × 12)

Click SELECT on Rate to calculate the periodic interest rate (.00678 per month).

Sln: Straight-line Depreciation

You use Sln to compute the straight-line depreciation of an asset for one period. The straight-line method of depreciation divides the depreciable cost (actual cost minus salvage value) evenly over the useful life of an asset. The useful life is the number of periods, typically years, over which an asset is depreciated. For example, if you paid $8,000 for an office machine that had a useful life of six years and a salvage value of $900 after eight years, you compute yearly depreciation expense by entering the following values:

Register 0: 8000 (cost of the asset)

Register 1: 900 (salvage value of the asset)

Register 2: 6 (useful life of the asset)

Click SELECT on Sln to compute the yearly dollar depreciation allowance (1183).

Syd: Sum-of-the-years'-digits Depreciation

You use Syd to compute the sum-of-the-years'-digits depreciation. This method of depreciation accelerates the rate of depreciation so that more depreciation expense occurs in earlier periods than in later ones. The depreciable cost is the actual cost minus salvage value. The useful life is the number of periods, typically years, over which an asset is depreciated. For example, to compute the fourth year depreciation expense of an $8,000 machine that has a useful life of six years and a salvage value of $900 after eight years, you enter the following values:

Register 0: 8000 (cost of the asset)

Register 1: 900 (salvage value of the asset)

Register 2: 6 (useful life of the asset)

Register 3: 4 (period for which depreciation is computed)

Click SELECT on Syd to compute the depreciation allowance for the fourth year (1014).

Term: Payment Period

You use Term to compute the number of payment periods in a term of an ordinary annuity necessary to accumulate a future value earning a specified periodic interest rate. For example, if you deposit $1,800 into a bank account that earns 11% a year compounded annually, you can determine how long it will take to accumulate $120,000 by entering the following values:

Register 0: 1800 (periodic payment)

Register 1: 120000 (future value)

Register 2: 0.11 (periodic interest rate is 11%)

Click SELECT on Term to determine the number of years it will take to accumulate $120,000 (20).

Logical Functions

The Calculator has nine logical functions that are activated by the keys on the Logical Mode pop-up window, shown here:

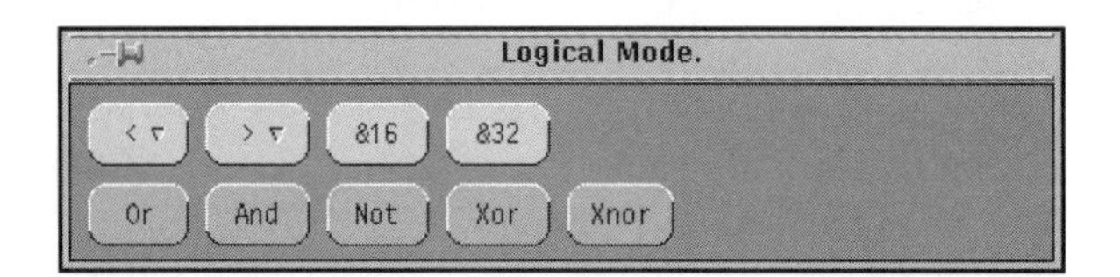

To display the Logical Mode window, select Logical from the Mode pop-up menu.

- The < key lets you perform a left bitwise shift of the displayed value. This key displays a menu from which you choose the number of bits to shift (1 to 15).
- The > key lets you perform a right bitwise shift of the displayed value. This key displays a menu from which you choose the number of bits to shift (1 to 15).
- The **&16** key truncates the current value displayed to a 16-bit integer.
- The **&32** key truncates the current value displayed to a 32-bit integer.
- The **Or** key performs a logical OR operation on the last number and the next number entered, treating both numbers as 32-bit integers.
- The **And** key performs a logical AND operation on the last number and the next number entered, treating both numbers as 32-bit integers.
- The **Not** key performs a logical NOT operation on the values currently displayed in the display area.
- The **Xor** key performs a logical XOR operation on the last number and the next number entered, treating both numbers as 32-bit integers.
- The **Xnor** key performs a logical XNOR operation on the last number and the next number entered, treating both numbers as 32-bit integers.

Scientific Functions

The Calculator has 13 scientific functions that are activated by the keys on the Scientific Mode pop-up window, shown here:

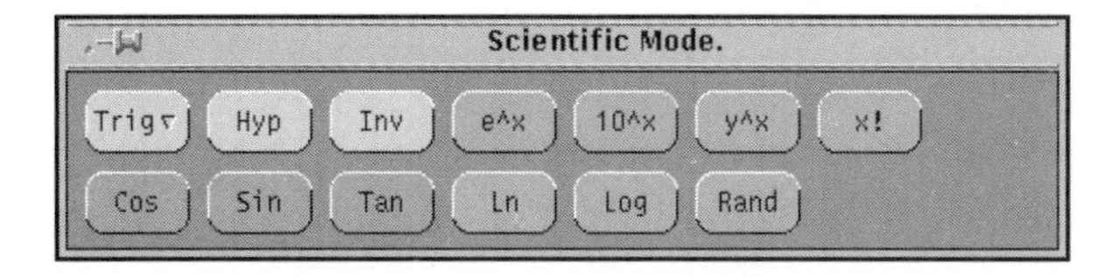

To display the Scientific Mode window, select Scientific from the Mode pop-up menu. The keys are as follows:

- The **Trig** key pops up the Trigonometric type menu from which you can choose the trigonometric base. There are three options: Degrees, Radians, and Gradients. The current trigonometric base is displayed in the mode line of the display area.

- The **Hyp** key toggles the state of the hyperbolic function flag. This flag affects sine, cosine, and tangent functions. When this flag is set, the word HYP appears on the mode line in the display area.
- The **Inv** key toggles the state of the inverse function flag. This flag affects sine, cosine, and tangent functions. When this flag is set, the word INV appears on the mode line in the display area.
- The **e^x** key returns e raised to the power of the currently displayed value.
- The **10^x** key returns 10 raised to the power of the currently displayed value.
- The **y^x** key raises the last number to the power of the next number entered.
- The **x!** kcy returns the factorial of the currently displayed value.
- The **Cos** key returns the cosine of the currently displayed value. It can also return the arc cosine, the hyperbolic cosine, or the inverse hyperbolic cosine if the corresponding hyperbolic and inverse functions are set.
- The **Sin** key returns the sine of the currently displayed value. The Sin key can also return the arc sine, the hyperbolic sine, or the inverse hyperbolic sine if the corresponding hyperbolic and inverse functions are set.
- The **Tan** key returns the tangent of the currently displayed value. It can also return the arc tangent, the hyperbolic tangent, or the inverse hyperbolic tangent if the corresponding hyperbolic and inverse functions are set.
- The **Ln** key returns the natural logarithm of the currently displayed value.
- The **Log** key returns the base 10 logarithm of the currently displayed value.
- The **Rand** key returns a random number between 0.0 and 1.0.

Customizing the Calculator

You can customize the look and layout of the Calculator with the Calculator properties pop-up window. To display the Calculator properties pop-up window, press the Props key or position the pointer anywhere over the Calculator base window and press MENU. The Calculator pop-up menu appears. Then select Properties from the Calculator menu to display the Calculator properties pop-up window, shown here:

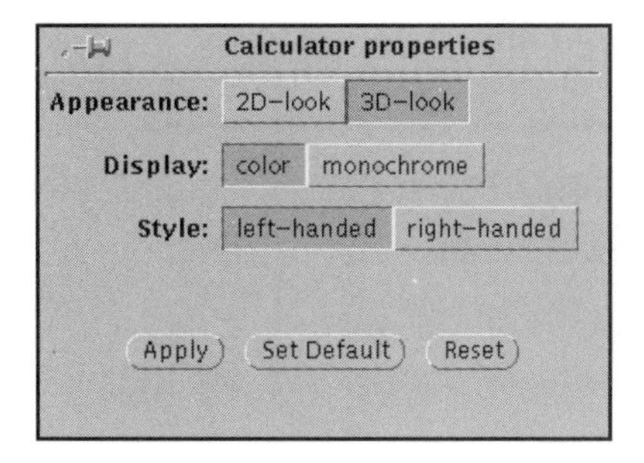

Three settings are available from this window:

Appearance lets you determine if the Calculator buttons appear as two- or three-dimensional objects. The default appearance is two-dimensional. (All of the figures in this section show the Calculator with the three-dimensional appearance.)

Display lets you select a color or monochrome display for the Calculator.

Style lets you select a left-handed or right-handed layout of the buttons on the Calculator. The default left-handed layout displays the number keys on the left. The right-handed layout displays the number keys on the right.

Click SELECT on the Apply button to apply the changes. Click SELECT on Set Default to save the properties as default values that will be used each time you invoke the Calculator.

The Icon Editor

The Icon Editor lets you create and modify icon images. You can use an icon image by binding it to a particular file type so that it is displayed in the File Manager. You use the Binder program (described in the next section) to bind an icon to a file type. Images created by the Icon Editor are also useful to programmers who want to create custom images for use in their applications. To start the Icon Editor, choose Icon Editor from the Programs menu, or enter the iconedit command at the prompt:

```
dugout% iconedit &
```

If you supply the name of an image file on the command line, the Icon Editor will load the Image contained in the specified file, as shown here:

```
dugout% iconedit $OPENWINHOME/include/X11/bitmaps/wide_weave &
```

Figure 9.6 shows the Icon Editor base window.

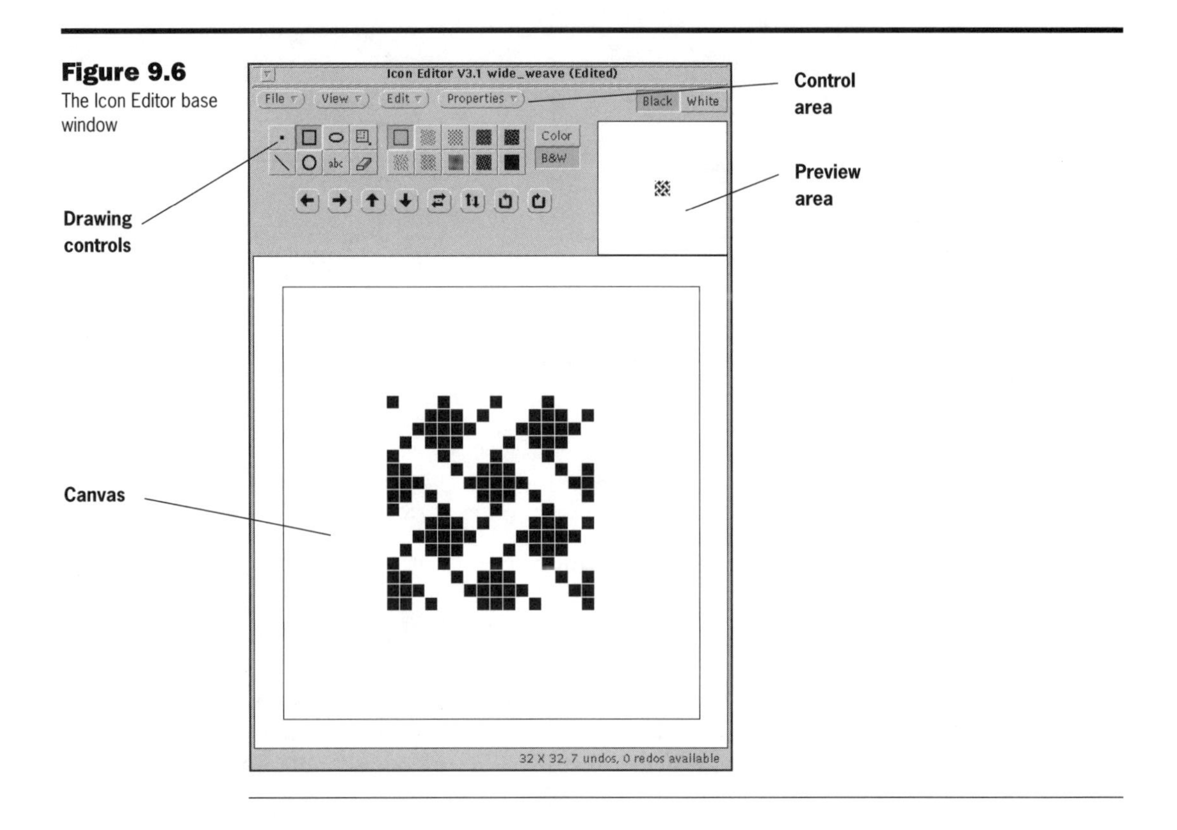

Figure 9.6
The Icon Editor base window

The Icon Editor's icon looks like this:

Icon Editor Basics

The Icon Editor lets you create icons and images that you can use for a variety of purposes. Programmers who write applications with a graphical user interface may want to have user interface components (such as buttons) that display images rather than text labels. Or, a programmer may want to create a custom cursor (a pointer) that will be displayed for that particular application. The Icon Editor is useful for both of these purposes. (In general, the Icon Editor is used to create images, not just icons, so throughout this section we will use the terms *icon* and *image* interchangeably.)

Creating an image with the Icon Editor is easy. You use the mouse and pointer to select dots on the canvas. Each dot on the canvas represents one pixel of the image. As you create an image, the preview area displays the image in its actual size. This is particularly useful when you are creating a new image, because even as you draw it, you can see what the image will actually look like in its true size.

You draw in the canvas area in several ways. You choose controls in the drawing-control area to create circles, rectangles, ellipses, text, and so forth. You can also draw one pixel at a time to create an image. When you create a circle, rectangle, or ellipse, you may choose to fill the area with a pattern, which you choose from the drawing controls. You can also move, rotate, or invert the image—or part of the image—with controls in the drawing-control area. Images can be created in black and white or in color. You choose the colors you want to use by displaying the Color Palette (discussed a little later in this chapter.)

Images vary in size. The Icon Editor lets you select an appropriate size for the image you want to create, and it automatically selects the appropriate size when you load an existing icon. Icons of different sizes are displayed differently in the canvas. Larger icons are displayed in the canvas by using smaller rectangular points so that the entire icon image can fit into the canvas area. The preview area always displays the image in its actual size. For example, Figure 9.7 shows the Icon Editor with a large image loaded. Notice that the size of the points in the canvas area is smaller than the points displayed in Figure 9.6.

You can change the size of the icon by selecting Size from the Properties menu. You can choose from five sizes:

- 16 × 16 pixels (typical cursor size)
- 32 × 32 pixels (the required size for icons displayed in the File Manager)
- 48 × 48 pixels
- 64 × 64 pixels (typical application icon size)
- 128 × 128 pixels

If you change the size of the image when an icon is loaded, the image displayed in the canvas area changes size accordingly. If you choose a size that is smaller than the size of the image, the image is cropped on the right and bottom sides. If you choose a size that is larger than the size of the image, the image is positioned in the upper-left corner of the new canvas size. If you are not happy with the new size you have chosen, you can undo the change by using the undo control discussed later in this chapter.

Figure 9.7
The Icon Editor with a large image loaded

You store an image in a file in one of four formats: XView Icon, X Bitmap, Color X Pixmap, or Monochrome X Pixmap. You select the format when you save the image, or you can set the format from the Format menu. To display the Format menu, choose Format from the Properties menu.

Each of these formats has a particular purpose. If you are creating a color image, the only format available is Color X Pixmap. The other three format types are used for storing monochrome images.

- Use XView Icon when you are creating an icon to be displayed in the File Manager. This is the only format that the File Manager supports, so you must choose this format if you are creating an image that you want to display in the File Manager. Unless you are a programmer, this is probably the only format you will ever need to use.
- Use X Bitmap to create a monochrome bitmap image. This format is a standard format described by the X Window System and is used extensively throughout many X-based applications. All of the files in $OPENWINHOME/include/X11/bitmaps are in X Bitmap format. If

you are writing X-based applications in OLIT, for example, you may want to create images in X Bitmap format to use for your application's icon or other imaging.

- Use Color X Pixmap to store a color image. This stores the image in XPM (X Pixmap) format. The XPM package is a popular library of functions for programmers to store and use color images.
- Use Mono X Pixmap to store a monochrome image in XPM format.

Icon Editor Drawing Controls

Now that you understand some basic concepts about the Icon Editor, let's look at the specifics of the drawing controls. We'll start with the drawing modes.

Drawing Modes

Eight drawing modes are available, as shown here:

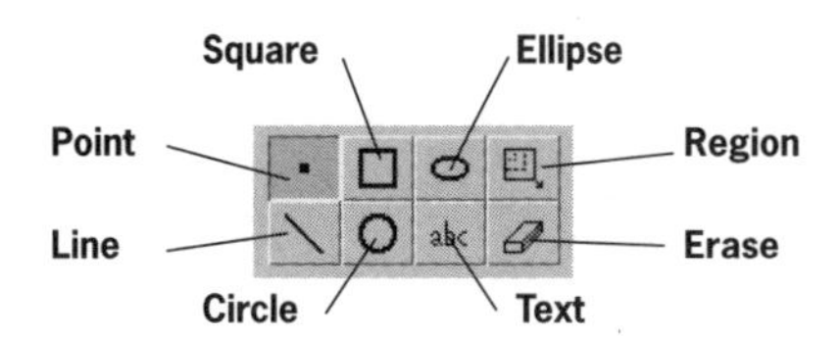

Each one determines the way that points are created, erased, or manipulated in the canvas area. The drawing modes are described here:

Point lets you draw one pixel at a time. To draw a pixel, move the pointer to the desired location and click SELECT. You can also press SELECT and drag the pointer to continuously draw pixels under the pointer until you release SELECT. This is a convenient way to create freehand drawing. To remove a pixel, position the pointer over an existing point and click ADJUST.

Line lets you draw a one-pixel-wide line in any direction. To draw a line, position the pointer at one end of the line and press SELECT. Then drag the pointer to the other end of the line and release SELECT.

Square lets you draw a square or a rectangle. You can also choose to have the area filled with a pattern. When you choose Square, the fill choices become active. When you create a square or a rectangle, it is filled with the pattern chosen from the fill choices. To create a square or a rectangle, position the pointer at one corner of the area and press SELECT. Then drag the pointer to the opposite corner and release SELECT. The square or rectangle is created and filled with the pattern chosen.

Circle lets you draw a circle. You can select a fill pattern when you create a circle, just as you can with the Square mode. To draw a circle, position the pointer at the center of the circle and press SELECT. Then move the pointer in any direction to specify the radius of the circle, and release SELECT.

Ellipse lets you create an ellipse. Ellipses can also be filled objects. To create an ellipse, position the pointer at the center of the ellipse and press SELECT. Then move the pointer in the appropriate direction to create the ellipse of the size and shape you want, and release SELECT.

Text lets you add text to your image. When you choose this option, the Text pop-up window is displayed, allowing you to choose the text, font, weight, style, and size of the characters you want to add. You'll learn all the details of working with text in the next section.

Region lets you specify a rectangular region of the image, which you can then move, flip, rotate, or delete.

Erase lets you erase pixels on the canvas. When you choose this option, the pointer changes to the shape of an eraser. You erase a pixel by positioning the lower-left edge of the pointer over the pixel and clicking SELECT. Or you can press SELECT and then drag the cursor to remove pixels that are beneath the cursor.

Working with Text

When you choose Text from the drawing modes, the Text pop-up window appears, as shown here:

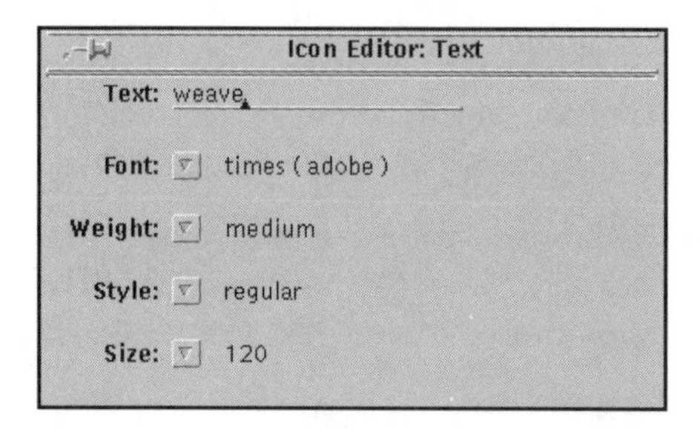

To add text to your image, enter the characters in the Text field. Then choose the font, weight, style, and size of the text from each of the menus provided. To move the text to the image, move the pointer to the desired location in the canvas area and press SELECT. A rectangular box appears, showing you the size of the text. You can move the box to the exact location where you want the text to be displayed while you hold down the SELECT button. When you release SELECT, the text is drawn in the canvas area. Figure 9.8 shows the word *weave* being added to an image.

Figure 9.8
Adding text to your image

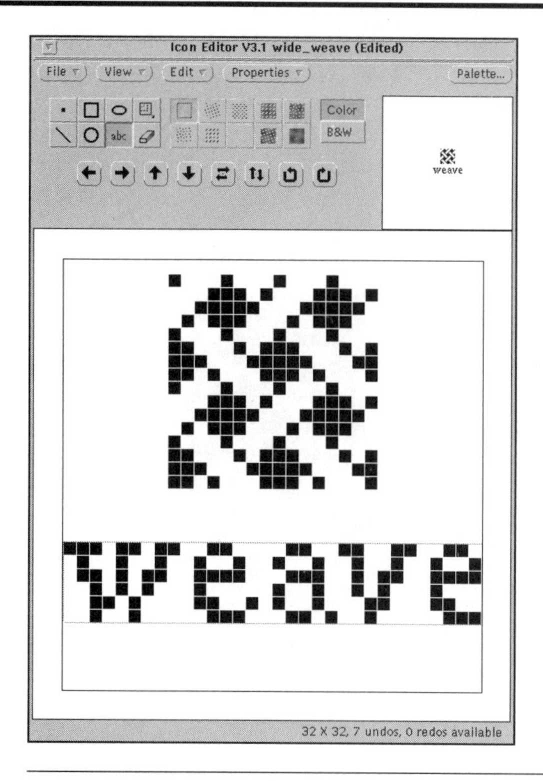

Fill Patterns

When you choose the Square, Circle, or Ellipse drawing mode, the fill pattern choices, shown here, become active:

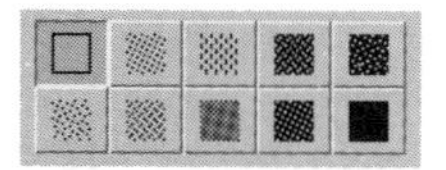

The pattern in the upper-left corner shows an empty square. When you select this pattern, the rectangle, circle, or ellipse is drawn without its interior filled. The pattern in the lower-right corner shows a solid black square. When you select this pattern, the object drawn is filled with solid black (or whatever color is chosen). Each of the other choices fills the object with the pattern displayed in the button image.

Color Controls

You can draw images in black and white or in color. Use the Color control to choose between the two options.

If you choose to draw in black and white, you can draw black pixels or white pixels by choosing the Black or White option located directly above the preview area. Notice that if you choose White the pointer color changes to white.

If you choose to draw in color, the option changes to a button labeled Palette. When you press the Palette button, the Color Chooser pop-up window appears, as shown here:

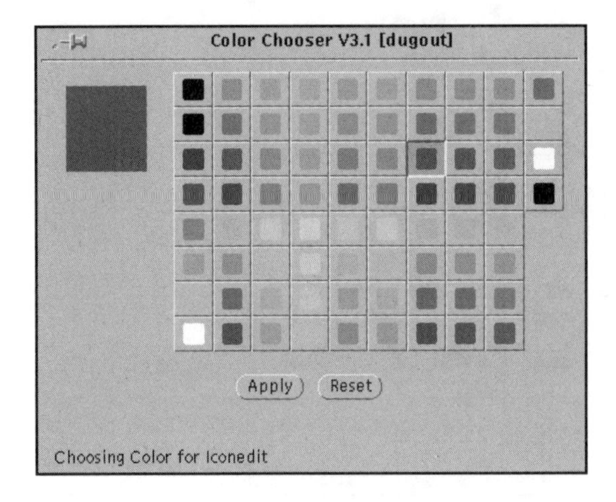

To select a color from the Color Chooser, click SELECT with the pointer over the color you want. The color of the button label you have selected then appears in the color selection area at the upper-left corner of the Color Chooser. Click SELECT on the Apply button to select the color. Notice that, when you position the pointer anywhere over the Icon Editor's base window, the cursor appears in the color selected. You can also apply a color selection by dragging it from the color selection area and dropping it onto the canvas or preview area of the Icon Editor's base window.

If you are creating a color image and then change to black and white, all of the color pixels change to black. A notice appears, asking you to confirm the change before the color information is lost. You can retrieve the color pixels by using the undo function described later in this chapter.

Move Buttons

Eight move buttons are available that let you move, invert, and rotate an image or a region of an image, as shown here:

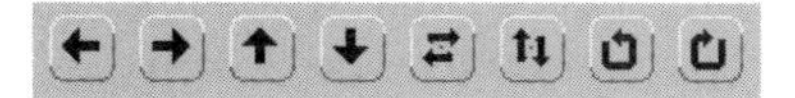

Each move button operates on either the entire image or the region of the image that you have selected. To select a region, press the Region button from the drawing modes, press SELECT with the pointer at one corner of the region, drag the pointer to the opposite corner, and then release SELECT. You will see a flickering box surrounding the region that you specified. Once you have selected a region, any move command that you use applies only to that region. If you do not have a region selected, the move command applies to the entire image.

You use the first four move buttons to move the region or image left, right, up, or down, respectively. The next two buttons invert or flip the image: the button with the horizontal arrows flips the image from left to right, and the button with the vertical arrows flips the image from top to bottom. The last two buttons rotate the region or image 90 degrees counterclockwise and clockwise, respectively.

Loading, Saving, and Printing an Icon File

The File menu button on the Icon Editor's base window provides a pop-up menu that lets you load, save, or print icon files. When you choose Load or Save As from the File menu, the File pop-up window appears, as shown here:

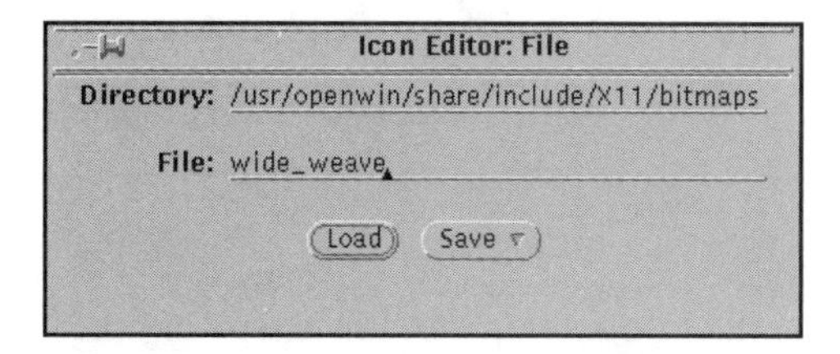

Loading an Image File

To load an image into the Icon Editor, enter the directory and file name into the fields on the File pop-up window and press Load. You may be presented with a notice if you already have an image loaded and you have not yet saved your changes. You can choose to cancel or continue the load operation.

You can also load a file by using drag and drop. For example, you can drag a file containing an icon from the File Manager and drop it onto the Icon

Editor's canvas or preview area to load the image. You can experiment with this feature by changing your File Manager's current directory to $OPEN-WINHOME/include/X11/bitmaps or $OPENWINHOME/include/images and then dragging any of the files in either of these two directories from the File Manager to the Icon Editor. Figure 9.9 shows a bitmap file being dragged from the File Manager and dropped onto the Icon Editor.

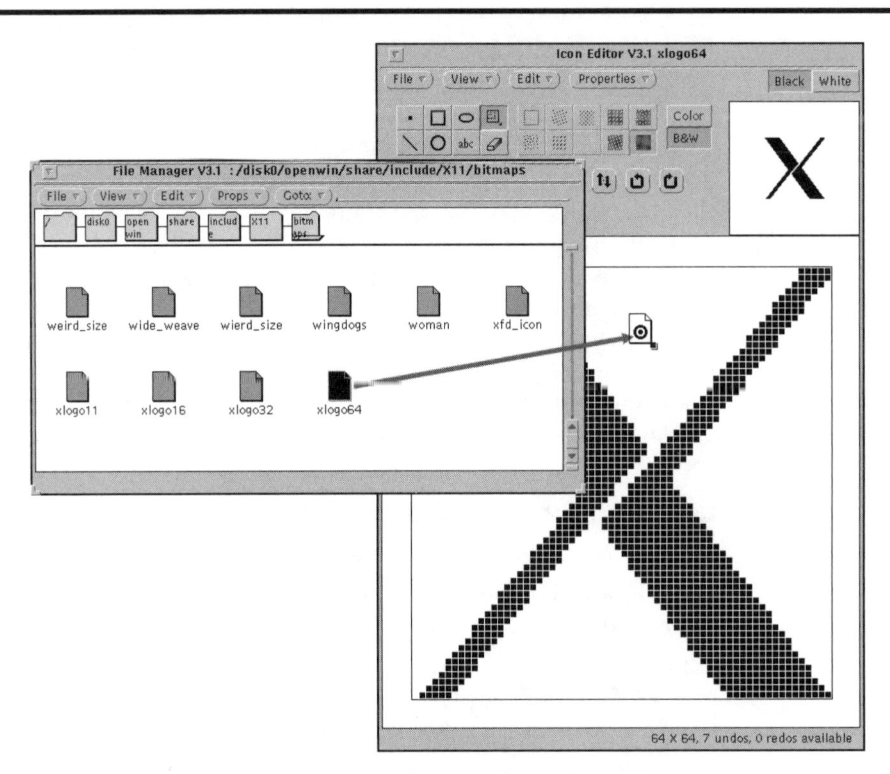

Figure 9.9
Using drag and drop from the File Manager to the Icon Editor

Saving an Image File

To save an image, use the File pop-up window to specify the directory and file name, and press the Save button. If you click SELECT on the Save button, the format of the file is saved to the format that you select from the Properties Format menu. You can explicitly select a format by pressing MENU on the Save button. The Save menu appears, displaying the formats from which you can select.

Printing an Image

To print an icon, select Print from the File menu to display the Print pop-up window shown here:

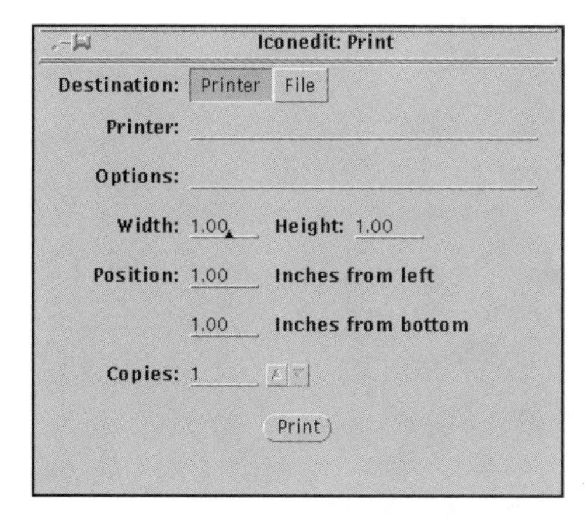

You can choose to send the image to a printer or to a file. If you choose to send the image to a printer, you must specify the printer and then decide whether to set printer options. If you choose to send the image to a file, the Printer and Options fields change to Directory and File fields. You specify the directory and file name of the file in these fields. A PostScript file is produced.

You can also specify the width, height, position, and number of copies of the image to be produced. When you have set the fields on the Print window, press the Print button to print the image or to create the PostScript file of the image.

The View Grid Option

The View menu button on the Icon Editor's base window displays a pop-up menu with a single item: Grid On. If you choose Grid On, the canvas area displays a grid that can be useful when you are trying to align or center all or part of your image. When you turn on the grid, the button on the View menu changes its label to Grid Off. Push the Grid Off button to remove the grid. Figure 9.10 shows the Icon Editor with the grid on.

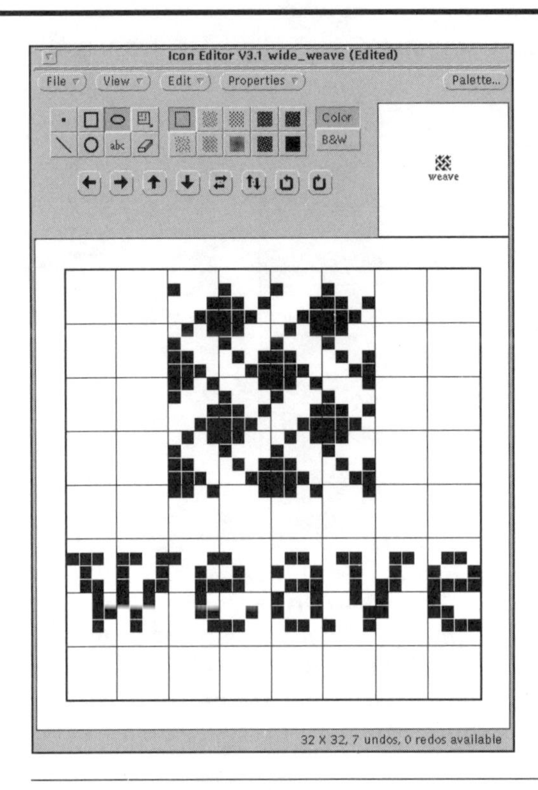

Figure 9.10
Icon Editor with the Grid option on

Editing Commands

The Edit menu button on the Icon Editor's base window displays a pop-up menu with seven items that you can use to edit your icon. You can also display this menu by pressing MENU with the pointer anywhere over the canvas.

Undo undoes the last editing operation. It will undo almost any editing operation, including loading a new file, changing from color to black and white, and performing any of the standard drawing or moving operations. The Icon Editor can undo the latest seven operations. The number of operations that can be undone is displayed in the footer.

Redo redoes an operation undone by the Undo button. The Icon Editor remembers up to seven undo operations so that you can redo those seven operations.

Clear clears the entire canvas or selected region.

Cut cuts the entire image or a region from the image and puts it onto the clipboard. You can retrieve the contents of the clipboard by using the Paste function. You can paste the contents of the clipboard back into the same image at a new location or even into another image being edited in another Icon Editor.

Copy copies the image or region of the image selected to the clipboard without removing it from the image.

Paste copies the contents of the clipboard onto the image. The easiest way to determine the location of the pasted clipboard image is to position the pointer at the upper-left corner of the area where you would like the image placed, and press the Paste key on the keyboard.

Invert changes all the white pixels to black and the black pixels to white within the image or region selected. The Invert item is not available when you are editing a color image.

The Binder

The Binder lets you associate an icon, an open method, and a print method with a file type. You can use the Binder to bind an icon that you created with the Icon Editor to a particular type of file.

The Binder is a user interface to a database called the Classing Engine. The Classing Engine keeps track of file types and the ways they are defined, and associates information with the file type. The Binder program allows you to access and add new entries to the database. Other DeskSet programs use the Classing Engine to determine a variety of information about particular files. For example, the File Manager uses the Classing Engine to determine which icon to display for each file type and which program to invoke when you open a file (the open method) or print a file (the print method).

Some of the features of the Binder are quite advanced for most users, so we will not discuss every detail of the program in this chapter. Instead, we will describe enough of its features so that you can bind an icon of your own creation to a file type that you have specified.

To start the Icon Editor, choose Icon Editor from the Workspace Programs menu, or enter the binder command at the prompt:

```
dugout% binder &
```

Figure 9.11 shows the Binder base window. The Binder's icon looks like this:

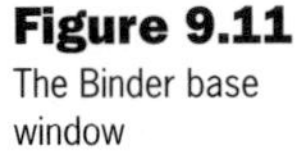

Figure 9.11
The Binder base window

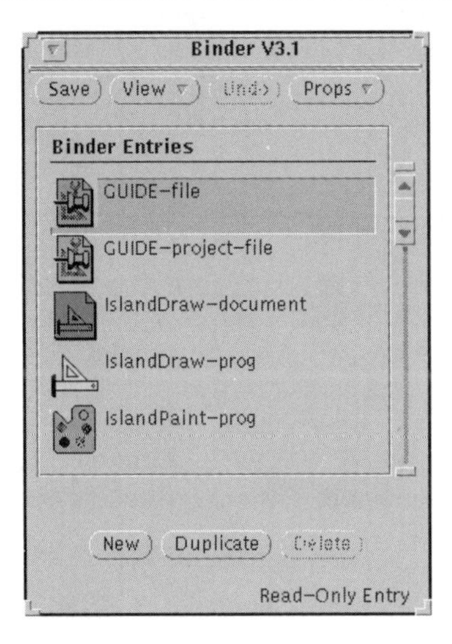

Binder Basics

To understand how the Binder works, it is helpful to display the Properties window and examine the file types that are already defined in the Classing Engine database. To display the Properties window, press the Props button on the Binder base window. In the lower-right corner of the Properties window is a button labeled with a plus sign (+). Press this button to extend the Properties window to its full size, as shown in Figure 9.12.

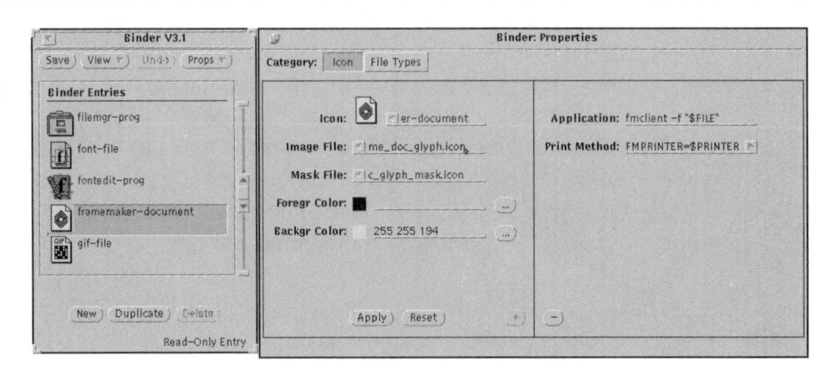

Figure 9.12
The Binder base window and the Icon Properties window

Each file has two sets of properties: icon properties and file-type properties. Figure 9.12 shows the Icon Properties window. Press the File Types button from the Category setting at the top of the Properties window to display the file-type properties. Let's first examine the icon properties.

The scrolling list in the Binder base window displays each icon that the File Manager can possibly display. Click SELECT on one of the items in the scrolling list to display the information regarding that file type in the Icon Properties window. For example, Figure 9.12 shows the FrameMaker-document file type selected in the Binder base window and the corresponding information about the icon, colors, and methods displayed in the Icon Properties window.

Here is a description of each field in the Icon Properties window:

Icon displays the icon image and the name of the file type.

Image File displays the name of the file that contains the icon.

Mask File displays the name of the file that contains the mask image for the icon. You use a mask image to select a nonrectangular area and a background color for the icon.

Foregr Color displays the foreground color for the icon. The color is represented as three numbers that indicate the red, green, and blue content of the color in a range of 0 to 255. The foreground color is set on the black pixels of the icon image.

Backgr Color displays the background color for the icon. The color is represented as three numbers that indicate the red, green, and blue content of the color in a range of 0 to 255. The background color is set on the black pixels of the mask image.

Application displays the program to execute when the file is opened from the File Manager or from a similar application.

Print Method displays the program to execute when the file is printed with the Print Tool or with another application.

The File Types Properties window displays information regarding the criteria that a file must satisfy to belong to a particular file type. Files are identified in two ways: by name and by content. It is possible for one file type to have several ways to identify files that belong to its type. For example, Figure 9.13 shows the gif-file file type selected in the Binder base window and the corresponding information about the way files of this type are identified in the File Types Properties window.

The entry for the gif-file indicates that any files whose name ends with .gif belongs to the gif-file file type. This is an example of identifying a file by its file name. Identifying a file by its contents is the other option for determining a file type.

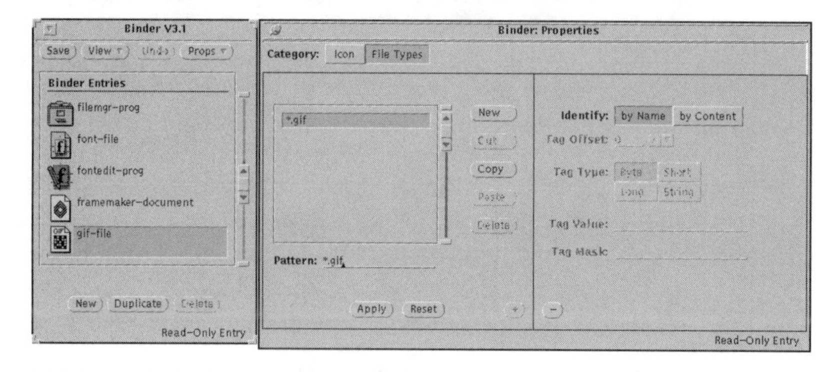

Figure 9.13 The Binder base window and the File Types Properties window

Binding the Memo Icon

To demonstrate how you use the Binder to create your own file icon and associate a particular file type with that icon, we will create a new file type, called *memo-file*. You might send and receive many memos that all have the same naming style or contents, so it would be nice to create a new class of files based on these memos.

First, you will create an icon image by using the Icon Editor. I have created two images: one to be used as the icon image and the other as the icon mask, shown here:

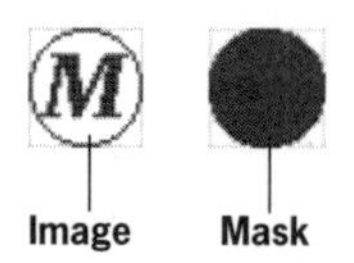

You can use these images or create your own if you like. The purpose of the icon mask is to allow you to create an irregularly shaped icon. The memo icon is circular in shape, so the mask identifies the shape of the icon and allows the nonrectangular shape to be used for the icon image. Once you have created your icon and stored it in a file (see the section on the Icon Editor earlier in the chapter), you are ready to begin adding an entry to the Binder database.

Here are the steps you follow to create the binding:

1. Click SELECT on the New button on the Binder's base window. A new entry, named unnamed_1, is added to the scrolling list, and the Icon Properties window is displayed (if it is not displayed already) with default values in all the fields.

2. Add the name of the new file type to the Icon field. We will call our new file type *memo-file.*
3. Enter in the Image File and Mask File fields the names of the files you created in the Icon Editor. You can choose to leave the Mask File field empty, in which case the icon's background color will extend the full width and height of the icon.
4. Select a foreground and background color. You can either enter the red, green, and blue numbers directly into the text field or press the button (labeled with three dots) to the right of the text field to display the Color Chooser. Select a color from the Color Chooser and press Apply.
5. Enter an application and a print method. Both of these fields are optional. In the Application field, enter the program to invoke when the file is opened from the File Manager. You can include the $FILE symbol to represent the name of the file selected. In the Print Method field, enter the default program to execute when printing the file.

Figure 9.14 shows the Binder base window and the Icon Properties window with all the fields filled in.

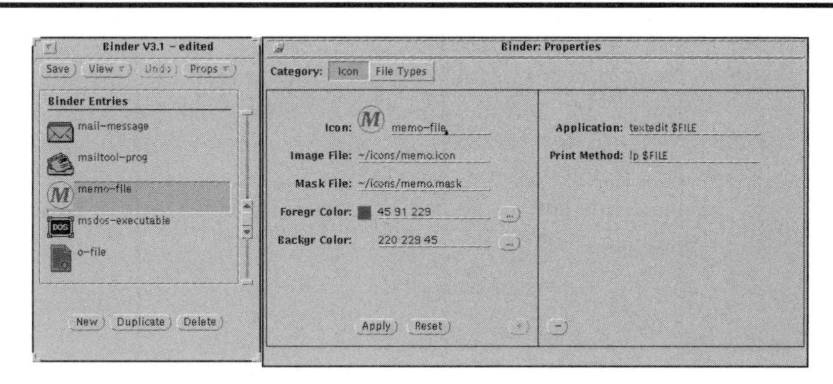

Figure 9.14
Adding a new icon to the Binder

You're not quite finished yet. You now have to select the criteria required for a file to be considered a memo-file. Display the File Types Properties window by selecting File Types from the Category setting. For this example, we will identify a memo-file by name only. Here are the remaining steps necessary to complete the binding:

6. Enter the name or pattern of the file in the Pattern field and press Return. The pattern is added to the scrolling list. For example, we will add two patterns by which the memo-file may be identified: memo* and

*memo. This means that any files whose name begins with memo or ends with memo will be considered a memo-file.

7. Press the Apply button to apply the changes.
8. Press the Save button on the Binder's base window. This stores the information in the Classing Engine database.

   The completed File Types Properties window is displayed in Figure 9.15.

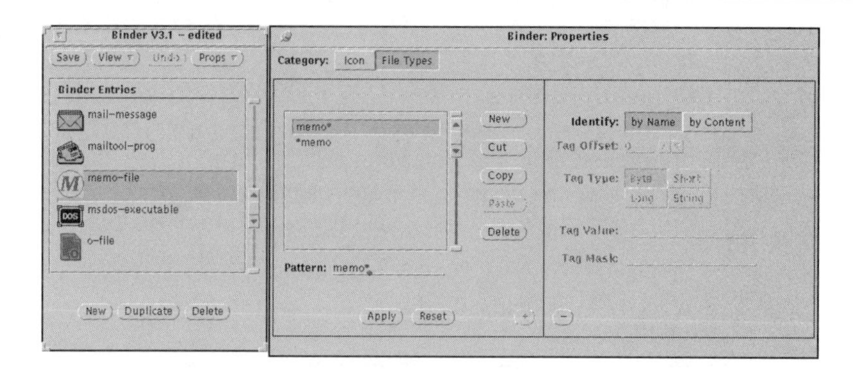

Figure 9.15
Adding a new file type to the Binder

Now that our image is created and bound to the memo-file type, we can display it with the File Manager or with any other application that uses the Classing Engine. Since File Manager reads only the Classing Engine database when it is first invoked, you'll have to restart the File Manager in order to see the new icon you just created. Figure 9.16 shows the File Manager with three memo files displayed.

Summary

In this chapter you have learned about four DeskSet applications: the Tape Tool, the Calculator, the Icon Editor, and the Binder. Although these are probably not the most commonly used applications, they are useful and powerful tools.

You have now learned about all of the DeskSet applications. In the next chapter you will learn some additional techniques for customizing your OpenWindows environment.

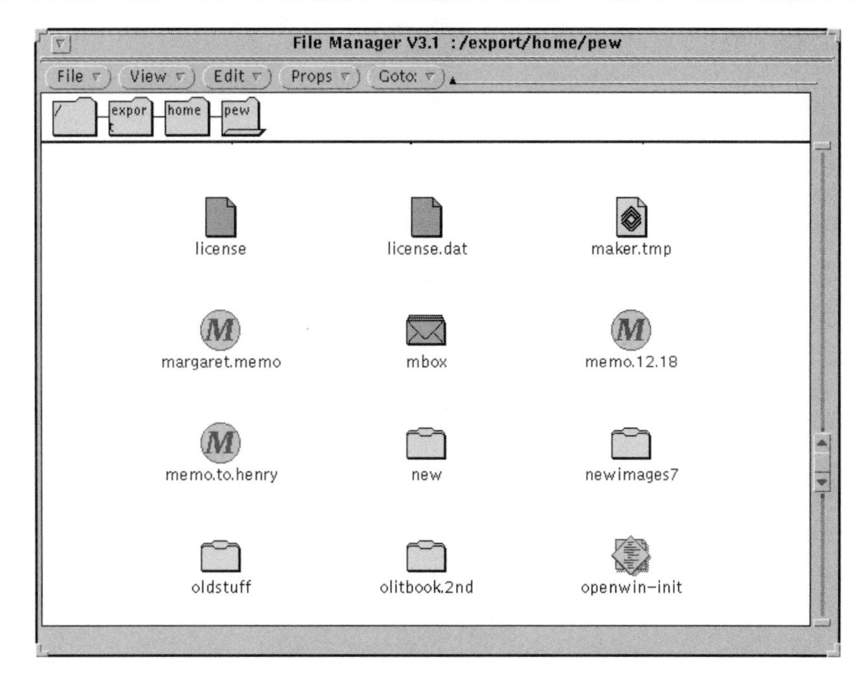

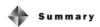

Figure 9.16 The File Manager with the new memo icon displayed

CHAPTER

10

Customizing the OpenWindows Environment

OpenWindows Resources

Common Command-Line Options

Scales and Fonts

The OpenWindows Mouseless Mode

Customizing Menus

Other X Window System Applications

IN CHAPTER 3 YOU LEARNED A LITTLE ABOUT CUSTOMIZING THE OpenWindows environment when we discussed the Workspace Properties pop-up window. You can use the Workspace Properties to choose colors, select icon positions, set the locale, and perform other miscellaneous operations that affect the way the OpenWindows environment looks and feels. Before you proceed with this chapter you may want to review the customization features available from the Workspace Properties pop-up window because these are some of the most common OpenWindows customization features.

In this chapter you will learn how to use the following advanced OpenWindows customization features:

- OpenWindows resources
- Common command-line options
- Scales and fonts
- OpenWindows mouseless mode
- Customizable menus
- Other X Window applications

OpenWindows Resources

The OpenWindows environment has many attributes that you can control by setting the appropriate resource in the .Xdefaults file in your home directory. You have already learned about some of these resources in Chapter 3 when we discussed Workspace properties. Each of the options that you set in the Workspace Properties window adds or modifies an entry in the .Xdefaults file. These options can be modified directly by editing the .Xdefaults file rather than invoking the Workspace Properties window. In addition to the attributes you can set from the Workspace Properties window, there are many other features available. Some of the most useful and common resources are discussed in this section.

Be aware that the .Xdefaults file is usually not read directly by the OpenWindows environment. Rather, the contents of the .Xdefaults file must be loaded in the resource database maintained by the X Window server in order to effect changes. This is done by running the xrdb (X Resource Database) command. The resource database is loaded automatically when you press the Apply button on the Workspace Properties window.

You use the xrdb command to load, list, or merge the resource database. If you edit your .Xdefaults file, you can reload the file by running xrdb with the –load (or –l) command-line options as follows:

```
dugout% xrdb -load .Xdefaults
```

What you may find more convenient is to simply merge a new resource specification with the existing database. Especially if you are just experimenting with a new resource, you may prefer not to bother editing your .Xdefaults file. You can simply add a new entry to the database by using the –merge (or –m) command-line option. Of course, if you use this option, then the resource you merge will not be stored in the .Xdefaults and consequently will not be set the next time OpenWindows is started or the .Xdefaults file is loaded into the X resource database.

To use the –merge options, enter the xrdb –merge command, enter each resource you want to merge into the database, and then enter control-D, as shown here:

```
dugout% xrdb -merge
OpenWindows.AutoRaise: TRUE
OpenWindows.ShowMoveGeometry: TRUE
^D
```

You can also use the xrdb command to print the current contents of the X resource database by using the –query (or –q) option. Here is an example:

```
dugout% xrdb -query
*basicLocale:       C
*displayLang:       C
*inputLang:         C
*numeric:           C
*timeFormat:        C
OpenWindows.AutoInputFocus:                         TRUE
OpenWindows.Beep:                                   always
OpenWindows.DragRightDistance:                      100
OpenWindows.IconLocation:                           bottom
OpenWindows.KeyboardCommands:                       Full
OpenWindows.MultiClickTimeout:                      4
OpenWindows.PopupJumpCursor:                        True
OpenWindows.ScrollbarPlacement:                     right
OpenWindows.SelectDisplaysMenu:                     False
OpenWindows.SetInput:                               select
OpenWindows.WindowColor:                            #cccccc
OpenWindows.WorkspaceColor:                         #40a0c0
Scrollbar.JumpCursor:                               True
```

In many cases you can set a resource on the command line when you execute a program, by providing the –xrm option followed by the resource specification in the exact format as you would provide it in the .Xdefaults file. For example, to run an application and set its window color to green, you enter the following:

```
dugout% application -xrm 'OpenWindows.WindowColor: green'
```

In the next few sections you'll learn about some of the most popular resources settings.

Color Resources

Several resources affect color. To specify the value of a color, you can use the name of a color (color names are defined in $OPENWINHOME/lib/rgb.txt) or a six-digit hexadecimal value such as #40a0c0. The six digits represent the red, green, and blue content of a color. The first two digits after the # represent the red intensity, the next two digits represent the green intensity, and the last two digits represent the blue intensity. The values for each two-digit pair can range from 00 to ff (0 to 255).

WindowColor

The WindowColor resource sets the window color. This resource is set by the Workspace Properties window. The entry in your .Xdefaults file has the following format:

```
OpenWindows.WindowColor: salmon
```

You can also use this resource on the command line to set the color of a particular application by using –xrm as shown here:

```
dugout% printtool -xrm 'OpenWindows.WindowColor: wheat'
```

The default value is #cccccc.

WorkspaceColor

The WorkspaceColor resource sets the color of the workspace (the root window). This resource is set by the Workspace Properties window. The entry in your .Xdefaults file has the following format:

```
OpenWindows.WorkspaceColor: honeydew
```

The default value is #40a0c0.

Background

The Background resource sets the background color of text areas and icons. To set the default background color to lavender, for example, add the following entry to your .Xdefaults:

```
*Background: lavender
```

You can change this resource on a particular application by using the –xrm command-line option, as shown here:

```
dugout% cm -xrm '*Background: SkyBlue'
```

The default value is white.

Foreground

The Foreground resource sets the color of the text of most windows and icon titles. To set the default foreground color to yellow, add the following entry to your .Xdefaults:

```
*Foreground: yellow
```

You might want to combine this resource with the background resource to create a light-on-dark effect, as in this example:

```
dugout% mailtool -xrm '*Background:navy' -xrm '*Foreground: yellow'
```

The default value is black.

BorderColor

The BorderColor resource sets the border color for all windows. For example, to set the border color to green, add the following entry to your .Xdefaults:

```
OpenWindows.BorderColor: green
```

The default value is black.

ReverseVideo

The ReverseVideo resource reverses the foreground and background colors of the application. For example, to run a Shell Tool in reverse video, enter the following command:

```
dugout% shelltool -xrm '*ReverseVideo: TRUE'
```

The default value is FALSE.

Icon Resources

You can control icon behavior and location using the IconFlashCount and IconLocation resources.

IconFlashCount

The IconFlashCount resource sets the number of times the open/close "zoom" lines flash when you iconify or deiconify an application. For example, to set the number of flashes to 20, enter the following entry in your .Xdefaults:

```
OpenWindows.IconFlashCount: 20
```

The default value is 3.

IconLocation

The IconLocation resource determines the general location of icons on the screen. This resource is set by the Workspace Properties window. Valid values for this resource are as follows:

top-lr (or **top**) arranges icons at the top, starting from left to right.

top-rl arranges icons at the top, starting from right to left.

bottom-lr (or **bottom**) arranges icons at the bottom, starting from left to right.

bottom-rl arranges icons at the bottom, starting from right to left.

left-tb (or **left**) arranges icons on the left, from top to bottom.

left-bt arranges icons on the left, from bottom to top.

right-tb (or **right**) arranges icons on the right, from top to bottom.

right-bt arranges icons on the right, from bottom to top.

The default value is bottom.

Stacking Order Resources

The stacking order resources control the stacking of windows on the workspace.

AutoRaise

The AutoRaise resource causes the window that has been given input focus to be automatically raised (brought to the front). If you use the focus-follow-mouse input focus policy (discussed in Chapter 3), this feature lets you simply move the pointer to the desired window, where it is automatically raised to the top. Use this resource with the AutoRaiseDelay resource (see below). To turn this feature on, add the following entry to your .Xdefaults:

```
OpenWindow.AutoRaise: TRUE
```

The default value is FALSE.

AutoRaiseDelay

The AutoRaiseDelay resource specifies the delay, in microseconds, between a window receiving the focus and then being raised above other windows. For example, to set the raise delay to one second, add the following entry to your .Xdefaults:

```
OpenWindows.AutoRaiseDelay: 1000000
```

The default value is 0.

AutoInputFocus

The AutoInputFocus resource sets the policy regarding input focus of newly appearing windows. When this resource is true, newly appearing windows automatically receive input focus. This resource is useful when your input focus policy is set to click-to-focus or when mouseless mode is enabled. To turn on this resource, add the following entry to your .Xdefaults:

```
OpenWindows.AutoInputFocus: TRUE
```

The default value is FALSE.

Window Manager Resources

The Window Manager resources are used to set various features of windows that are controlled by the Window Manager.

DragWindow

The DragWindow resource controls the way a window appears when you move it. If you set DragWindow to true, the entire window and its contents will move, rather than just the outline of the window. To turn on this feature, add the following entry to your .Xdefaults:

```
OpenWindows.DragWindow: TRUE
```

The default value is FALSE.

FlashCount

The FlashCount resource sets the number of times the title bar flashes when the "Owner?" menu item is selected. For example, to set the flash count to 3, add the following entry to your .Xdefaults:

```
OpenWindows.FlashCount: 3
```

The default value is 6.

FlashTime

The FlashTime resource sets the amount of time, in microseconds, that the title bar is flashed when the "Owner?" menu item is activated. For example, to set the flash time to one second, add the following entry to your .Xdefaults:

```
OpenWindows.FlashTime: 1000000
```

The default value is 100000.

MinimalDecor

The MinimalDecor resource sets a minimal amount of Window Manager decorations on a list of applications. Windows that are minimally decorated do not display a window header or window button. Figure 10.1 shows the Print Tool with minimal Window Manager decorations.

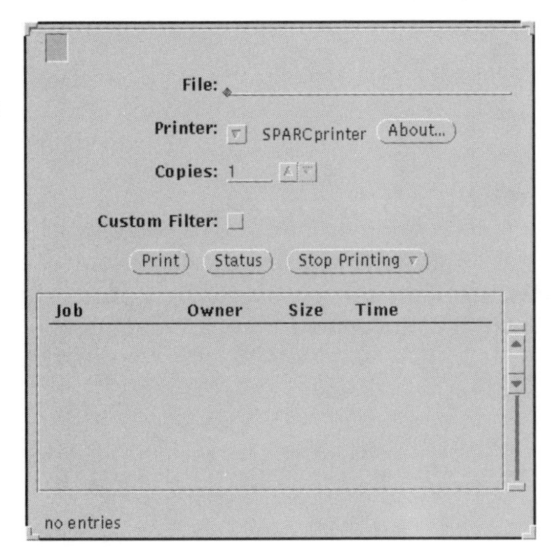

Figure 10.1 The Print Tool with minimal Window Manager decorations

This feature is especially useful if you want to maximize the amount of vertical space available for an application. I sometimes use this feature with the Shell Tool or Command Tool and make the window the maximum vertical size. Eliminating the Window Manager header gives me a few extra viewable lines.

To set the minimal decoration on all applications named shelltool, printtool, and nodecor, add the following entry to your .Xdefaults:

```
OpenWindows.MinimalDecor: shelltool printtool nodecor
```

With this resource set, all Shell Tools and Print Tools and any application named nodecor will have the minimal Window Manager decoration set. You can set the name of an application when you invoke it by using the –name command-line options. By including the name nodecor (a nonexistent application) as one of the minimally decorated applications, you can invoke a program and set its name to nodecor with the –name option so that that instance of the application is drawn with the minimal decor. For example, to start the File Manager with minimal decorations, enter the following command:

```
dugout% filemgr -name nodecor
```

The default value is null.

RubberBandThickness

The RubberBandThickness resource sets the thickness of the "rubber band" line that is drawn when a window is resized or moved. For example, to set the rubber band thickness to 10, add the following entry to your .Xdefaults:

```
OpenWindows.RubberBandThickness: 10
```

The default value is 2.

ShowMoveGeometry

The ShowMoveGeometry resource indicates whether the geometry box will be displayed when windows are being moved. The geometry box displays the current x and y position of a window as it is being moved. The geometry box, shown here, is displayed in the upper-left corner of the root window:

location: 463 , 302

To turn on this feature, add the following entry to your .Xdefaults:

```
OpenWindows.ShowMoveGeometry: TRUE
```

The default value is FALSE.

ShowResizeGeometry

The ShowResizeGeometry resource indicates whether the geometry box will be displayed when windows are being resized. The resize geometry box displays the current width and height of a window as it is being resized. The geometry box is displayed in the upper-left corner of the root window.

To turn on this feature, add the following entry to your .Xdefaults:

```
OpenWindows.ShowResizeGeometry: TRUE
```

The default value is FALSE.

Use3DFrames

The Use3DFrames resource determines the way that window borders are drawn. If you set Use3DFrames to true, the frame borders are given a three-dimensional look. By default, window frames are drawn with a black border (or the color specified by the BorderColor resource). Figure 10.2 shows the Clock displayed twice: once without 3-D frames and once with 3-D frames.

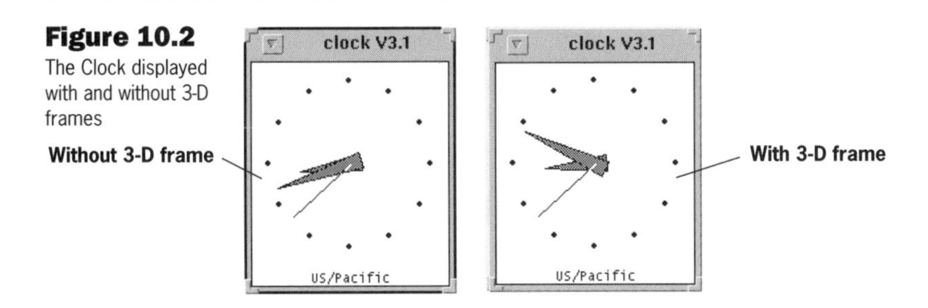

Figure 10.2 The Clock displayed with and without 3-D frames

To use this feature, add the following entry to your .Xdefaults:

```
OpenWindows.Use3DFrames: TRUE
```

The default value is FALSE.

Fonts Resources

Several resources let you set the font that is used to display strings in buttons, icons, and so forth.

ButtonFont

The ButtonFont resource lets you set the font for buttons on Window Manager menus such as the Workspace menu and the Window menu. For example, to set the button font to lucidasans italic, add the following entry to your .Xdefaults:

```
OpenWindows.ButtonFont: lucidasans-italic
```

When you display the Workspace menu, you will see the font set to lucidasans italic, as shown here:

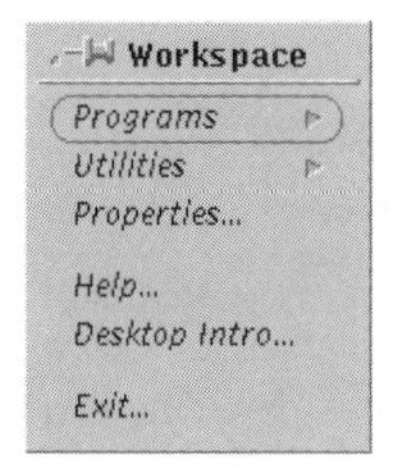

The default value is lucidasans-12.

TitleFont

The TitleFont resource lets you set the font for the title displayed in the window header of each window. The vertical size of the window header is determined by the size of the font used for the title. For example, to set the title font to 32-point helvetica bold, add the following entry to your .Xdefaults:

```
OpenWindows.TitleFont: helvetica-bold-32
```

Figure 10.3 shows how the Tape Tool looks after the title font has been set to helvetica-bold-32.

The default value is lucidasans-bold-12.

IconFont

The IconFont resource lets you set the font used for icon names. For example, to set the icon font to helvetica, add the following resource to your .Xdefaults:

```
OpenWindows.IconFont: helvetica
```

The default value is lucidasans-12.

Miscellaneous Resources

There are many miscellaneous resources you can use to set a variety of characteristics of the OpenWindows environment.

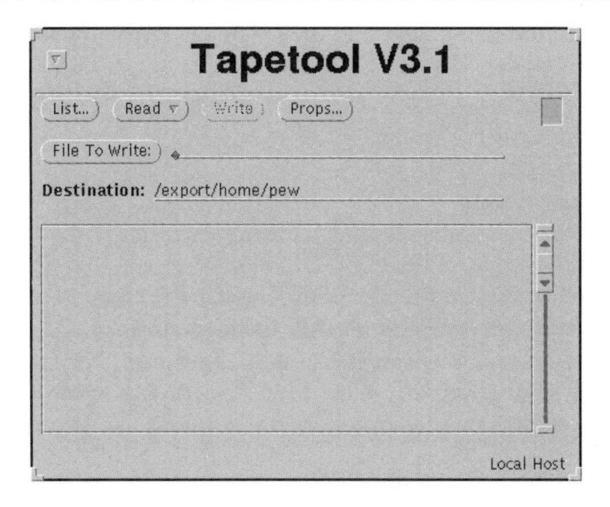

Figure 10.3
The Tape Tool with a large title font

MultiClickTimeout

The MultiClickTimeout resource determines the time, in tenths of seconds, that differentiates a double-click from two single clicks. This resource is set by the Workspace properties. For example, to set the multiclick time to one second, add the following entry to your .Xdefaults:

```
OpenWindows.MultiClickTimeout: 10
```

The default value is 5.

Beep

The Beep resource determines when the Window Manager should beep. The Beep resource can be set to never, notices, or always. The never setting means that the Window Manager should never beep, the notices setting means that the Window Manager should beep only for notices, and the always setting means that the Window Manager should beep whenever appropriate. This resource is set by the Workspace Properties window. For example, to set the Window Manager to never, add the following entry to your .Xdefaults:

```
OpenWindows.Beep: never
```

The default value is always.

DragThreshold

The DragThreshold resource specifies the number of pixels the mouse must move while a mouse button is down in order for the action to be considered a drag. If the mouse moves fewer than this number of pixels while the button is down, the action is considered a click instead of a drag. For example, to set the drag threshold to 2 pixels, add the following entry to your .Xdefaults:

```
OpenWindows.DragThreshold: 2
```

The default value is 5.

KeyboardCommands

The KeyboardCommands resource determines if the Window Manager and applications respond to OPEN LOOK mouseless commands. Valid values for this resource are Full and Basic. With KeyboardCommands set to Full, mouseless operation is turned on. All functions normally handled by the mouse can be entered by using keys on the keyboard. For more information, see the "Open Windows Mouseless Mode" section later in this chapter.

To turn on the mouseless mode, add the following entry to your .Xdefaults:

```
OpenWindows.KeyboardCommands: Full
```

The default value is Basic.

Common Command-Line Options

As you learned in the previous section, there are many resources that affect the look and feel of applications and the entire workspace. Some of these resources can be set directly on applications by using a command-line resource. You have already learned about the –xrm command-line option that you can use with the resources discussed in the previous section. In addition, there are some special command-line options that set attributes of an application at invocation time. Many of these are similar or identical to resources we have already discussed. Table 10.1 lists some of the most common command-line options along with a short description of each.

Table 10.1 Some Common Command-Line Options

Option	Argument	Description
–width (–Ww)	columns	Sets the width to the number of columns specified
–height (–Wh)	lines	Sets the width to the number of lines specified
–size (–Ws)	x y	Sets the width and height to the number of pixels specified by x and y

Table 10.1 Some Common Command-Line Options (Continued)

Option	Argument	Description
–position (–Wp)	x y	Sets the initial x and y position in pixels from upper–left corner of screen
–geometry (–WG)	WxH+x+y	Sets the width and height to W and H and sets the x and y position to x and y
–icon_position (–WP)	x y	Sets the icon position to x and y
–label (–title, –Wl)	string	Displays the string as the window header title
–iconic (–Wi)	N/A	Causes the application to be iconified when invoked
+iconic (+Wi)	N/A	Causes the application to open when invoked
–font (–fn, –Wt)	fontname	Sets the font for the application
–scale (–Wx)	small, medium, large, or extra_large	Sets the scale (size) or the graphical objects and fonts
–foreground_color (–Wf)	red green blue (0–255)	Sets the foreground color to the value specified by red, green, and blue, which must be values between 0 and 255
–foreground (–fg)	colorname	Sets the foreground color to colorname
–background_color (–Wb)	red green blue (0–255)	Sets the background color to the value specified by red, green, and blue, which must be values between 0 and 255
–background (–bg)	colorname	Sets the background color to colorname
–reverse (–rv)	N/A	Reverses the background and foreground colors
–icon_image (–WI)	filename	Sets the icon to the image described in filename
–icon_label (–WL)	string	Sets the icon label to string
–display (–Wr)	server:screen	Displays the program on the server and screen specified by server and screen
–xrm	resource	Sets a resource
–name	appname	Sets the application's name
–help (–WH)	N/A	Prints a list of command–line options

To demonstrate how some of these command-line options are used, let's look at some examples.

To set the size of the Command Tool to 900 pixels wide and 300 pixels long, enter the following:

```
dugout% cmdtool -size 900 300
```

To set the size of a Shell Tool to 600 by 300 pixels and the position to (100,100), enter the following:

```
dugout% shelltool -geometry 600x300+100+100
```

To execute the Calendar Manager and specify that its initial display should be deiconified, enter the following:

```
dugout% cm +iconic
```

To start a Shell Tool with a background of black and a foreground of green, enter the following:

```
dugout% shelltool -bg black -fg green
```

To start the Mail Tool with the scale set to extra large, enter the following.

```
dugout% mailtool -scale extra_large
```

Scales and Fonts

The command-line options and resources that affect scales and fonts deserve a little more attention. Throughout this book you have seen many examples of the DeskSet utilities, but they have always been displayed in their "normal" layout. Setting the scale and font can have a dramatic effect on the look of an application. For example, you may find it difficult to read your mail because of the small font, or you may be frustrated that you cannot fit two 80-column Shell Tools side by side without having them overlap. These are the kinds of problems you can solve by setting the scale and font when you run an application.

You can set the scale to four values: small, medium (the default), large, and extra_large. The scale setting affects two things: the size of the graphical objects such as buttons and scrollbars, and the size of the font. For example, to start the Mail Tool with the scale set to large, enter the following command:

```
dugout% mailtool -scale large
```

Figure 10.4 shows the Mail Tool in large-scale mode.

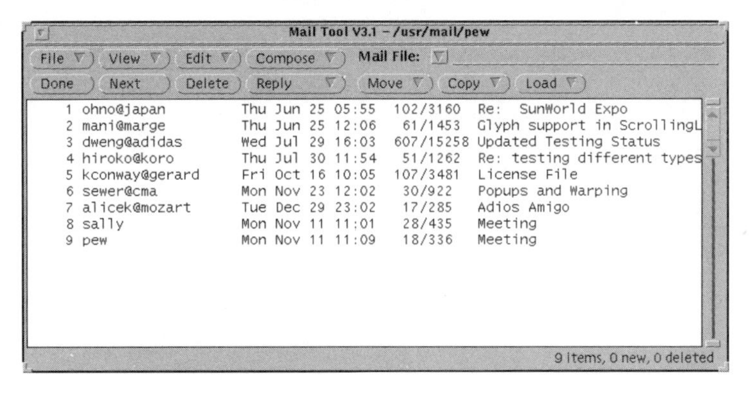

Figure 10.4 The Mail Tool with the scale set to large

I often set the scale of a Command Tool or Shell Tool to small. This enables me to fit two nonoverlapping windows side by side. I often use the following combination of colors and scale when I start a Shell Tool:

```
dugout% shelltool -bg black -fg green -scale small
```

Then I make the Shell Tool full size. If I have set the MinimalDecor resource to shelltool (see the section "Window Manager Resources" earlier in the chapter), then the Shell Tool does not include a window header and I am therefore able to use the full height of my screen for text.

The scale option sets the font to the appropriate size, but you may want to specify a different font. You can do this by using the –font command-line option or one of the font resources. To determine what fonts are available on your system, run the xlsfonts command:

```
dugout% xlsfonts
```

This command produces a long list of fonts (my system lists 714 fonts). Most of the fonts have long, complicated names such as this one:

```
-adobe-courier-bold-o-normal--18-180-75-75-m-110-iso8859-1
```

This format is call the X Logical Font Description format (XLFD). You can use any of the fonts in XLFD format, or you can experiment with some font aliases.

If you look closely at the output to xlsfonts, you will find at the end of the output some fonts with simpler names such as helvetica and lucidasans. These are font-name aliases. You can use these instead of the full XLFD name. Some of the font aliases take an additional point-size designation. For example, lucidasans is listed in the output of xlsfonts, but you can add a point size to it by adding a dash followed by the size. For example, to specify a 24-point lucidasans font, use lucidasans-24. Many of the fonts that are listed with xlsfonts and that have simple names follow this convention.

The OpenWindows Mouseless Mode

The KeyboardCommands resource, discussed earlier in this chapter, is used to turn on mouseless mode. The mouseless mode gives you the ability to operate the OpenWindows environment without the use of a mouse. You may find the mouseless environment easier to use if you set your focus policy to click-to-focus mode, since this mode provides more distinct visual feedback for a window with focus. To change the focus policy, use the Miscellaneous category of the Workspace Properties window and set the Set Input Area field to Click SELECT. As the focus moves to an application, you will see the Window Manager border become highlighted. The input focus within the application is shown by a large triangular caret called the *supercaret*, as illustrated here:

You move the input focus to different components of an application by pressing the Tab key (or Shift-Tab for the reverse order). When the supercaret is over the object you want to select, press the spacebar to activate the object.

There are many key sequences that you can use to maneuver your way around the windowing system. Some of the most important and commonly used mouseless commands are shown in Table 10.2.

Table 10.2 Some Common Mouseless Commands

Name	Key Sequence	Description
Next application	Alt-n	Moves to the next application
Previous application	Alt-Shift-n	Moves to the previous application
Next window	Alt-w	Moves to the next window (pop-up)
Previous window	Alt-Shift-w	Moves to the previous window (pop-up)
Next element	Tab or Ctrl-Tab	Moves the focus to the next element within the application
Previous element	Shift-Tab or Ctrl-Shift-Tab	Moves the focus to the previous element within the application
Workspace menu	Alt-Shift-m	Displays the Workspace menu
Window menu	Alt-m	Displays the window menu for the current window
Select	Spacebar	Selects the element in which the supercaret is displayed

These few commands handle many of the basic operations. You use the arrow keys to move between elements of a similar group. For example, if you move the supercaret around within an application by using the Tab key, you may notice that the supercaret does not move to every element within a common object such as a choice setting. If you want to move the supercaret to other choices within a choice setting, use the arrow keys.

Sometimes you may be in mouseless mode and move the focus to an application but you cannot find the supercaret displayed anywhere. Pressing the Tab key often solves this problem, but if it doesn't, try pressing Ctrl-Tab or Ctrl-Shift-Tab or Ctrl-[. The supercaret will most likely appear.

Table 10.3 lists more of the most common mouseless commands.

Table 10.3 Some Additional Common Commands for OpenWindows Mouseless Mode

Command	Keystroke	Function
Stop	L1 or Escape	Aborts the current action (such as resize)
DefaultAction	Return, Enter, or Meta-Return	Executes the default action for the current menu or notice
Select	Spacebar	Selects the current button
Adjust	Alt-Insert	Toggles the selected state of the current object
Menu	Alt-spacebar	Brings up a menu of the current object
InputFocusHelp	? or Ctrl-?	Brings up Help on the object with input focus
Up	Up Arrow	Moves up one item
Down	Down Arrow	Moves down one item
Left	Left Arrow	Moves left one item
Right	Right Arrow	Moves right one item
JumpUp	Ctrl-Up Arrow	Moves up ten items
JumpDown	Ctrl-Down Arrow	Moves down ten items
JumpLeft	Ctrl-Left Arrow	Moves left ten items
JumpRight	Ctrl-Right Arrow	Moves right ten items
RowStart	Home or R7	Moves to the start of the current row
RowEnd	End or R13	Moves to the end of the current row

Table 10.3 Some Additional Common Commands for OpenWindows Mouseless Mode (Continued)

Command	Keystroke	Function
DataStart	Ctrl-Home	Moves to the start of the data
DataEnd	Ctrl-End	Moves to the end of the data
FirstControl	Ctrl-[	Moves to the first item
LastControl	Ctrl-]	Moves to the last item
Open	Alt-L7	Opens the object with the input focus
Help	Help	Brings up Help on the object under the pointer
TogglePin	Meta-Insert	Toggles the state of the pin of the window with the input focus
Refresh	Alt-F8	Repaints the window with the focus
FullRestore	Alt-F3	Toggles the full-sized/normal-sized state of the window with the focus
Quit	Alt-F9	Quits the window with the input focus
Owner	Alt-F10	Flashes the owner of the pop-up window with the focus
Move	Alt-F6	Moves the window with the focus
Resize	Alt-F7	Resizes the window with the focus

When you display a menu, you can move the input focus to a particular item on that menu by pressing the key that matches the first character of the item label. For example, the Programs menu contains four items that begin with C: Command Tool, Calendar Manager, Clock, and Calculator. You can cycle through each menu item that begins with C by pressing the c key repeatedly. Follow these steps to demonstrate this principle:

1. Press Ctrl-Shift-m to display the Workspace menu. The Programs item is the default.
2. Press the Right Arrow key to display the Programs menu. The Command Tool item is the default.
3. Press c to move the input focus to Calendar Manager.
4. Press c again to move the input focus to Clock, and so forth.

Customizing Menus

The Workspace menu and the associated submenus (Programs, Utilities, and so on) are all customizable. To customize the Workspace menu, you modify the .openwin-menu file. (You used a similar technique when you modified the Extras menu in Chapter 5.)

The format of the .openwin-menu file is very similar to the format of the .text_extras_menu file. Lines that begin with # are comments. The characters enclosed in double quotation marks on the left are the strings displayed on the Workspace menu. The expression on the right is the command executed when the item is selected. The lines with the word MENU include the name of a file that contains the description on the submenu. For example, the item on the Workspace menu labeled Programs displays a menu that is defined in the file $OPENWINHOME/lib/openwin-menu-programs. The default .openwin-menu file is shown here:

```
#
# @(#)openwin-menu      23.13 91/07/10 openwin-menu
#
#       OpenWindows default root menu file - top level menu
#

"Workspace" TITLE

"Programs" MENU         $OPENWINHOME/lib/openwin-menu-programs

"Utilities" MENU        $OPENWINHOME/lib/openwin-menu-utilities

"Properties..."         PROPERTIES

SEPARATOR

"Help..."               exec $OPENWINHOME/bin/helpopen \
                                    handbooks/top.toc.handbook

"Desktop Intro..."      exec $OPENWINHOME/bin/helpopen \
                                    handbooks/desktop.intro.handbook

SEPARATOR

"Exit..."               EXIT
```

The openwin-menu-programs file has the same format as shown in the next listing. Notice that each menu item corresponds to an executable file in $OPENWINHOME/bin except the Demos item, which displays another submenu.

```
#
# @(#)openwin-menu-programs     1.13 92/08/12 openwin-menu-programs
#
```

```
#       OpenWindows default root menu file - Programs submenu
#

"Programs" TITLE PIN

"Command Tool..."       DEFAULT exec $OPENWINHOME/bin/cmdtool
"Text Editor..."                exec $OPENWINHOME/bin/textedit
"File Manager..."               exec $OPENWINHOME/bin/filemgr
"Mail Tool..."                  exec $OPENWINHOME/bin/mailtool
"Calendar Manager..."           exec $OPENWINHOME/bin/cm
"Clock..."                      exec $OPENWINHOME/bin/clock
"Calculator..."                 exec $OPENWINHOME/bin/calctool
"Print Tool..."                 exec $OPENWINHOME/bin/printtool
"Audio Tool..."                 exec $OPENWINHOME/bin/audiotool
"Tape Tool..."                  exec $OPENWINHOME/bin/tapetool
"Binder..."                     exec $OPENWINHOME/bin/binder
"Snapshot..."                   exec $OPENWINHOME/bin/snapshot
"Icon Editor..."                exec $OPENWINHOME/bin/iconedit
"Performance Meter..."          exec $OPENWINHOME/bin/perfmeter
"Shell Tool..."                 exec $OPENWINHOME/bin/shelltool

"Demos" MENU            $OPENWINHOME/lib/openwin-menu-demo
```

To customize the Workspace menu, copy the $OPENWINHOME/lib/-openwin-menu file to your home directory and name it .openwin-menu. If you have a file in your home directory with this name (.openwin-menu), it takes precedence over $OPENWINHOME/lib/openwin-menu. Now that you have your own copy, you can add, delete, or modify entries to your taste.

To demonstrate, let's modify the .openwin-menu file by making the following three changes:

1. Change the Programs menu file to point to a local copy rather than to the one in $OPENWINHOME.
2. Add a new menu item named Mouseless.
3. Add a new menu item named X Applications.

Each of the new menu items has a corresponding menu file. When finished, your .openwin.menu file should look like this:

```
#       OpenWindows root menu file - top level menu
#       Modified 6/19/95
#

"Workspace" TITLE

"Programs" MENU         $HOME/.openwin-menu-programs

"Utilities" MENU        $OPENWINHOME/lib/openwin-menu-utilities
```

```
"Mouseless" MENU        $HOME/.openwin-menu-mouseless

"X Applications" MENU   $HOME/.openwin-menu-xapps

"Properties..."         PROPERTIES

SEPARATOR

"Help..."               exec $OPENWINHOME/bin/helpopen \
                                    handbooks/top.toc.handbook

"Desktop Intro..."      exec $OPENWINHOME/bin/helpopen \
                              handbooks/desktop.intro.handbook

SEPARATOR

"Exit..."               EXIT
```

Now copy the $OPENWINHOME/lib/openwin-menu-programs file to your home directory and name it .openwin-menu-programs. Add one new entry: FrameMaker. It should look like this:

```
#       OpenWindows root menu file - Programs submenu
#       Modified 6/19/95

"Programs" TITLE PIN

"Command Tool..."       DEFAULT exec $OPENWINHOME/bin/cmdtool
"Text Editor..."                exec $OPENWINHOME/bin/textedit
"File Manager..."               exec $OPENWINHOME/bin/filemgr
"Mail Tool..."                  exec $OPENWINHOME/bin/mailtool
"FrameMaker..."                 exec $FMHOME/maker
"Calendar Manager..."           exec $OPENWINHOME/bin/cm
"Clock..."                      exec $OPENWINHOME/bin/clock
"Calculator..."                 exec $OPENWINHOME/bin/calctool
"Print Tool..."                 exec $OPENWINHOME/bin/printtool
"Audio Tool..."                 exec $OPENWINHOME/bin/audiotool
"Tape Tool..."                  exec $OPENWINHOME/bin/tapetool
"Binder..."                     exec $OPENWINHOME/bin/binder
"Snapshot..."                   exec $OPENWINHOME/bin/snapshot
"Icon Editor..."                exec $OPENWINHOME/bin/iconedit
"Performance Meter..."          exec $OPENWINHOME/bin/perfmeter
"Shell Tool..."                 exec $OPENWINHOME/bin/shelltool

"Demos" MENU            $OPENWINHOME/lib/openwin-menu-demo
```

Figure 10.5 shows the new Workspace menu and Programs submenu.

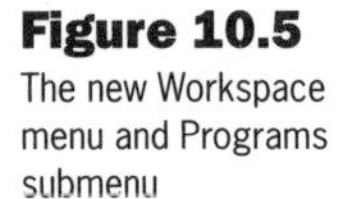

Figure 10.5 The new Workspace menu and Programs submenu

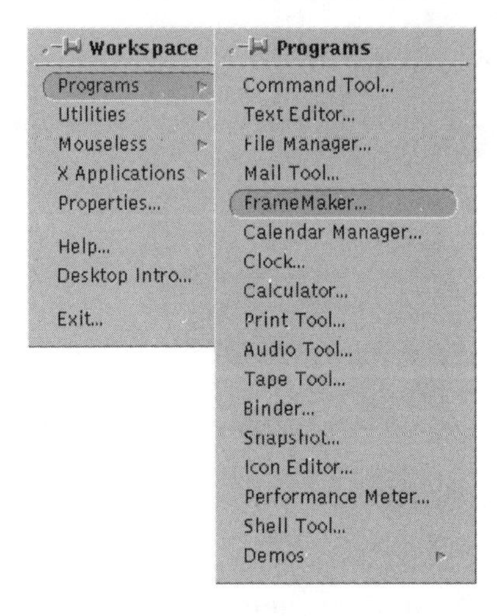

The Mouseless submenu has two items: one to turn on the mouseless feature, and the other to turn it off, as shown here:

```
#        Mouseless submenu
#
"Mouseless" TITLE PIN

"Mouseless ON" DEFAULT exec echo 'OpenWindows.KeyboardCommands:Full'  | xrdb -m
"Mouseless OFF"      exec echo 'OpenWindows.KeyboardCommands:Basic' | xrdb -m
```

Figure 10.6 shows the Workspace menu with the Mouseless submenu.

Figure 10.6 The Workspace menu with the Mouseless submenu

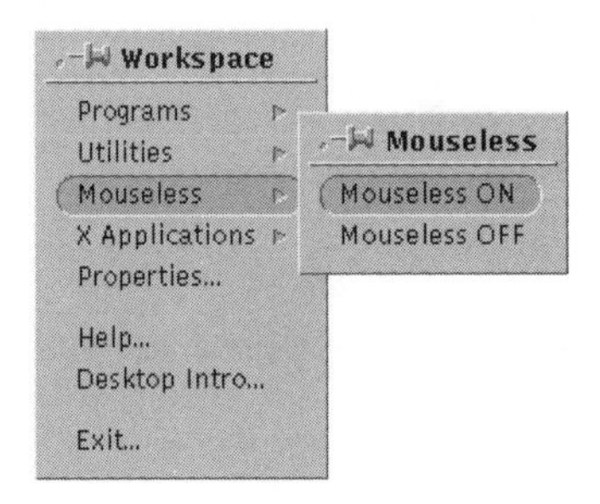

The X Applications submenu has five items: Xcolor, Xlogo, Xmag, Xwininfo, and Oclock. Each of these programs is an X application that is distributed with the X Window System.

```
#       X Applications submenu
#
"X Applications" TITLE PIN

"Xcolor"        DEFAULT exec $OPENWINHOME/bin/xcolor
"Xlogo"                 exec $OPENWINHOME/bin/xlogo
"Xmag"                  exec $OPENWINHOME/bin/xmag
"Xwininfo"              exec $OPENWINHOME/bin/xwininfo
"Oclock"                exec $OPENWINHOME/bin/oclock
```

Figure 10.7 shows the Workspace menu and the X Applications submenu.

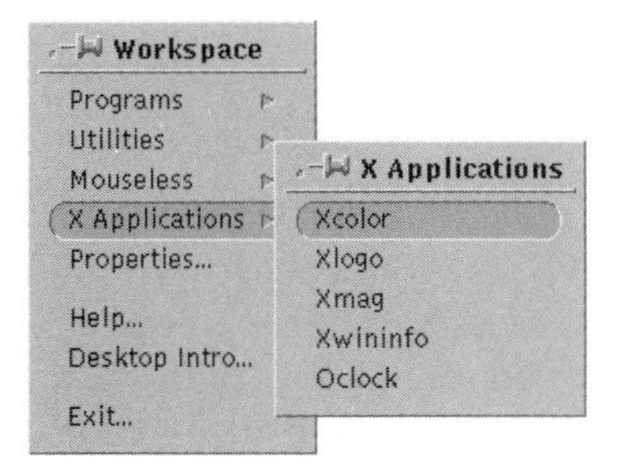

Figure 10.7 The Workspace menu and the X Applications submenu

Other X Window System Applications

The Solaris environment includes many X Window applications. All of the DeskSet programs are included in this category, but there are many others. For example, the five programs included in the X Applications submenu are programs that you may find useful. All of the programs are located in the $OPENWINHOME/bin, which should be in your path. Let's look at a few of the programs in that directory:

xset

The xset program (available from the command line only) sets various user preference options, including keyclicks, autorepeat, mouse acceleration, and screen-saver mode. For example, to set the display to automatically blank the screen after 5 minutes (300 seconds) of idle time, enter the following command:

```
dugout% xset s 300
```

xfontsel

The xfontsel program displays the fonts available to your X server (the same fonts listed by xlsfonts). The fonts are described by using the X Logical Font

Description (XLFD). You can select components of the XLFD and view the corresponding font, as shown in Figure 10.8.

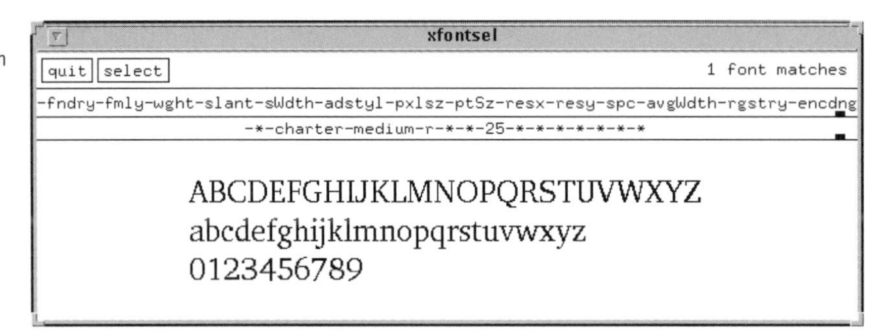

Figure 10.8
The xfontsel program

PageView

The PageView program is an OPEN LOOK application that displays PostScript images. You can load a file by using the File pop-up window, or you can drag and drop a file onto the drag and drop target or the display pane. There are several interesting PostScript images in $OPENWINHOME/share/images/-PostScript. Figure 10.9 shows the butterfly.ps loaded in PageView.

oclock

The oclock program is a circular clock. If you click SELECT on oclock, the Window Manager displays the four resize corners, as shown in Figure 10.10. You can resize the oclock to any circular or elliptical shape.

xwininfo

The xwininfo program (available from the command line only) provides detailed information about a particular window, including its exact location, size, and other features. When you invoke xwininfo, the cursor changes to the crosshair shape and you are prompted to click the mouse in the window that you want information about. Here is an example:

```
dugout% xwininfo

xwininfo ==> Please select the window about which you
         ==> would like information by clicking the
         ==> mouse in that window.

xwininfo ==> Window id: 0xe0000f (cmdtool - /bin/csh)
```

```
==> Absolute upper-left X:  5
==> Absolute upper-left Y:  427
==> Relative upper-left X:  5
==> Relative upper-left Y:  26
==> Width: 595
==> Height: 358
==> Depth: 8
==> Border width: 0
==> Window class: InputOutput
==> Colormap: 0x80076 (installed)
==> Window Bit Gravity State: NorthWestGravity
==> Window Window Gravity State: NorthWestGravity
==> Window Backing Store State: NotUseful
==> Window Save Under State: no
==> Window Map State: IsViewable
==> Window Override Redirect State: no
==> Corners:  +5+427  -552+427  -552-115  +5-115
```

Figure 10.9
The PageView program

Figure 10.10
The oclock program

xhost

The xhost program lets you add and delete hosts to the list of machines that are allowed to make connections to your X server. This is a security feature. For example, to allow host wilbur to connect to and display on your server, enter the following command:

```
dugout% xhost +wilbur
```

To allow any host to connect to and display on your server, enter the following command:

```
dugout% xhost +
```

xterm

The xterm program is a terminal emulator similar to the Shell Tool and Command Tool. You might want to use it if you were going to be working in another X Window environment, such as on a DEC or HP workstation.

There are many other commands in the $OPENWINHOME/bin directory. You can use the man command to get more information about a particular command. For example, to learn more about the xlsfonts command, enter the following command:

```
dugout% man xlsfonts
```

Summary

You have learned some customization features in this chapter that give you a great deal of flexibility in your day-to-day use of the OpenWindows environment. The more you learn about the facilities available in the OpenWindows environment, the more productive you will become.

With this chapter we have completed our coverage of the OpenWindows environment. In the next section of this book you will learn more about how to use SunOS from the command line.

SunOS Fundamentals

More SunOS Fundamentals

Using the vi Editor

The Shell

Using the Network

PART

3

Working from the SunOS Command Line

CHAPTER

11

SunOS Fundamentals

Command-line Basics

File and Directory Basics

File and Directory Operations

Ownership and Permissions

IN CHAPTER 2 YOU WERE INTRODUCED TO SOME BASICS ABOUT ENTERING SunOS (UNIX) commands. You used the ls and passwd commands to list files and to set and change your password. You may find that the vast majority of your time is spent using the DeskSet applications and that your need for using the command line is minor. However, as your experience increases, you will find more and more need for using the command line. You may be away from the office or working from home and not have access to the DeskSet applications. Or, perhaps you need to do some sophisticated processing of data which is not specifically addressed by any of the DeskSet applications. These are times when knowing other commands will be vitally important.

In this chapter, you will learn about

- Using the command line
- File and directory basics
- File and directory operations
- File ownership and permissions

Command-line Basics

When you enter a command at the prompt, you can use several special characters to manipulate the command line and perform special functions. For example, as you enter a command, you will occasionally type the wrong character. To erase the last character that you entered, press the Delete key. If you prefer to use a key other than Delete to erase a character—for example, the Backspace key—you can set the erase character by using the stty command. To change the erase character, use the following command:

```
dugout% stty erase [type new erase key here]
```

You type the actual key that you want to act as the new erase character as the last argument to stty. For example, if you type the Backspace key as the last argument to stty, you may see a Control-H displayed as shown here:

```
dugout% stty erase ^H
```

After entering this command, the Backspace key will actually erase a character rather than input a ^H character. You will probably want to put this command in your .login (or .profile for Korn shell users) so that it is set each time you log in.

Several other characters can help you at the command line. Most of these are control characters, which means you must hold down the key labeled Control when you enter the key. The notation of a character with the ^ in front of it represents a control character. Here is a list of some other commonly used control characters that manipulate the command line:

^U is the "kill" character. It "kills" the entire line of characters you have entered. This character is useful when you want to erase the entire line and start over with a new command.

^C is the interrupt character. Use ^C to interrupt and terminate the running program.

^W is the word-erase character. When you enter ^W, the last word you entered is erased from the input line.

^S is the stop character. Use ^S to temporarily stop the output of a command. This character is useful when the output of a command is scrolling off the screen too quickly for you to read it.

^Q is the start character. ^Q undoes the effect of ^S. Use ^S to stop the output of a command, and use ^Q to restart the output of the command.

^Z is the suspend character. Use ^Z to suspend (but not terminate) the execution of a command. You can leave the program suspended or resume execution in the foreground or background. We'll talk more about foreground and background processing in Chapter 14.

^R is the reprint character. When you enter ^R, the entire command line that you have entered thus far is reprinted on a new line. This character is useful when your command line becomes corrupted or when you are unsure of exactly what you have entered. You can reprint the characters that have been entered, and then continue entering or deleting characters.

You can customize each of these control characters by using the stty command. The controls described here are the default values, but if you prefer to use a different control character to perform one of these operations, use the stty command to change it. For example, you can set ^E to be the kill character by issuing the following command:

```
dugout% stty kill ^E
```

You may want to enter this command in your start-up file (see Chapter 2) so that ^E is set each time you log in or start a new shell. For more information on the stty command, use the man command to read the stty man page.

Using Quotation Marks

When you enter the arguments to a command, you usually separate them with one or more spaces or tabs (called white space). The white space between arguments is ignored by the command. It doesn't matter whether you separate arguments by one space or by 13 tabs; the command ignores the white space. If, however, you want to include the white space as part of the argument, you need to use quotation marks to enclose the entire argument (including the spaces).

To demonstrate this, let's look at the echo command. The echo command echoes each argument it is given and separates the arguments by a single space. For example, the command echo Hello World echoes the two arguments Hello and World, as shown here:

```
dugout% echo Hello World
Hello World
dugout%
```

If you enter the same command but put several spaces between Hello and World on the command line, the output does not display the spaces, as you can see here:

```
dugout% echo Hello          World
Hello World
dugout%
```

That is because the number of spaces or tabs between arguments is ignored by the system. The echo command knows simply that it has been given two arguments: Hello and World. It doesn't know how many spaces are between the two arguments. If you want to display the spaces, you can enclose the two arguments in single or double quotation marks, as in the following example:

```
dugout% echo 'Hello         World'
Hello       World
dugout%
```

All of the characters between a pair of single or double quotation marks are treated as a single argument. So, in the example just given, *echo* interprets the command-line arguments as a single argument consisting of 16 characters, which includes the spaces.

In most cases the choice of single or double quotation marks does not make a difference as long as you use the same type of quotation marks at the beginning and at the end. Quotation marks must always appear in pairs on the command line. If you want a single quotation mark (for example, an apostrophe) to be displayed by the echo command, you can use double quotation marks to enclose the argument, as shown here:

```
dugout% echo "What's your name?"
What's your name?
dugout%
```

One fundamental difference between using single and double quotation marks on the command line is that variables are expanded (replaced with their value) within double quotation marks, but not within single quotation marks. To demonstrate this, notice the output of the following two echo commands:

```
dugout% echo "$OPENWINHOME"
/usr/openwin
dugout% echo '$OPENWINHOME'
$OPENWINHOME
dugout%
```

Notice that in the first case the OPENWINHOME environment variable was expanded to its value; in the second case it was not.

You may find other occasions to use quotation marks. For example, in Chapter 12 you will learn about the grep command, which is used to search for the occurrence of a string of characters in a file. The grep command uses the first argument as the search string and each subsequent argument as the name of a file in which to search for the specified string. If the string of characters that you want to search for includes one or more spaces or tabs, you must enclose that string in quotation marks for the grep command to identify the string. For example, if you want to search for the string "Hello World" in the files geo and saturn, you enter this command:

```
dugout% grep "Hello World" geo saturn
```

If you do not include the quotation marks, the grep command will search for the string "Hello" in the files World, geo, and saturn—which is completely different from what you have in mind.

The man Command

You use the man command (short for *manual*) to display the documentation for a command. This is often more convenient than locating the hard-copy manual. To use the man command, you enter **man**, followed by the name of the command for which you want the manual page (often called just the *man* *page*) displayed. For example, to view the man page for the id command, enter the following:

```
dugout% man id
```

The man page for the id command is then listed in the same window in which you entered the command. The output of the man id command is shown here:

```
id(1M)              Maintenance Commands                id(1M)

NAME
     id - print the user name, user ID, group name, and group ID

SYNOPSIS
     /usr/bin/id [ -a ]

DESCRIPTION
     id displays your user ID, user  name,  group  ID,  and  group
     name.  If  your real ID and your effective IDs do not match,
     both are printed.

OPTIONS
     -a         Reports user name, user ID and all the groups  to
                which the user belongs.

SEE ALSO
     getuid(2)

Sun Microsystems     Last change: 5 Jul 1990                   1
```

As you can see from the description, the id command displays a user's ID and group information.

The man command is especially important when you are using SunOS commands, because the man page may be the only, or at least the primary, source of documentation for the command. When you use the DeskSet applications, you can always get information about the program and its operation by pressing the Help key. You learned about the help mechanism in Chapter 3. SunOS commands that are entered at the command line, however, have no such built-in help facility, so using the man command is important.

The types of man pages available are quite varied. There are man pages on almost every command that you can enter at the command line, including the DeskSet applications. In addition, there are man pages on file formats, library routines, and system calls. Many of these man pages are of interest to programmers only.

Every man page follows a certain format. The man page is divided into several sections. Some of the sections are optional; other sections are found on every man page. Here are some of the most common sections and a brief description of each:

NAME gives the name and a brief description of the command.

SYNOPSIS shows how to execute the command and includes the options and arguments. Optional arguments are displayed enclosed in square brackets. Three dots (...) following an argument means that the argument may be repeated by additional arguments of the same type. The three dots are often used to indicate that multiple files may be included as command-line arguments. For example,

```
grep [ -option ] string filename...
```

means that the grep command can accept an option (not required) as the first argument, followed by a string as the next argument, followed by one or more file names as the next arguments.

DESCRIPTION describes the command. The details of the command and its behavior are contained in this section.

FILES contains a list of files associated with this command.

OPTIONS describes each of the options available with this command.

SEE ALSO includes a list of other related commands or documentation.

DIAGNOSTICS explains error messages that might be displayed when you run the command.

The man command uses the MANPATH environment variable to locate the files that contain the man pages. The MANPATH environment variable is a list of directories through which the man command searches for the man page requested. If the man command does not display the man page for a command that you specify, you may need to find out if your MANPATH environment variable is set correctly. Check with your system administrator for the location of man pages on your system.

Throughout this chapter and the remainder of this book you will learn about many SunOS commands. Each of these commands has a corresponding man page. Since not every command or every detail of each command can possibly be covered in this book, you can turn to the man page for complete information about the command.

File and Directory Basics

In Chapter 4 you learned some basics about files and directories. The File Manager is a graphical user interface that allows you to move, copy, remove, and list files and directories. Each of the facilities available from the File Manager can be accessed directly from the command line. For example, you used the File Manager to copy a file by using the copy and paste feature. You can copy a file on the command line with the cp command.

Since you can manipulate files and directories with the File Manager, you may wonder why you even need to bother learning any other methods such as the cp command. There are several reasons why knowing how to manipulate files and directories outside the File Manager is important. Probably the most important is that there will likely come a time when for some reason you cannot use the File Manager. You may have access to your system but not to the File Manager. Maybe you are at home using your PC and modem to dial into your system at work and you cannot run the DeskSet applications over the phone line. Or perhaps you are visiting a company site at a remote location that provides network access to your system but the only way you can access your home system is through a terminal, not through a workstation running the OpenWindows environment. In such cases you may feel helpless and lost if you don't understand some of the basic commands available for working with files and directories.

Another reason you may want to use the commands discussed in this section is that sometimes it is easier to get your work done by using a Shell Tool or Command Tool than by using File Manager. For example, if your Shell Tool's current directory has the file that you want to copy and the File Manager's current directory is somewhere else, it takes more steps to change the File Manager's current directory, highlight the file, display the menu to copy the file, and then rename the newly copied file to the name you want than it does to simply enter a command such as the following:

```
dugout% cp oldfile newfile
```

However, there are also many examples of how the File Manager can save you time and effort—so knowing both methods is best. Then you can select the fastest way to get your job done.

Hierarchical Directory Structure

As you learned in Chapter 4, files reside in directories that are organized in a hierarchical directory structure. That structure is well illustrated by the File Manager's tree pane, in which each folder represents a directory that can contain files and directories. Figure 11.1 shows the directory hierarchy for sally's home directory.

Figure 11.1
A directory hierarchy

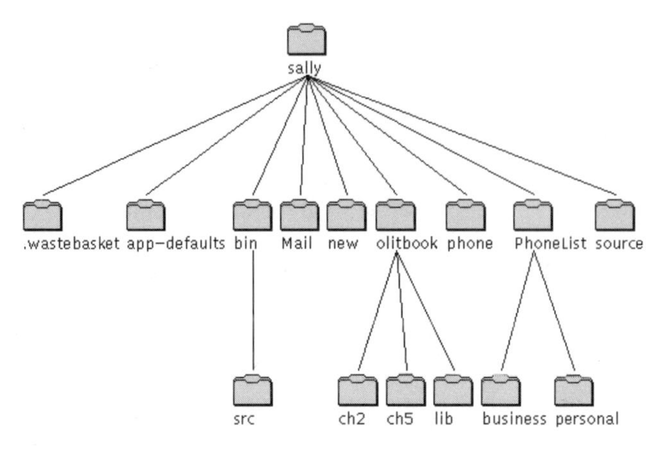

You can reference a file by using an absolute or relative path name. An absolute path name begins at the root (designated by a slash) of the directory hierarchy and names each directory in the path, separating each name by a slash. An example of an absolute path name is /export/home/sally/compressed.Z.

A relative path name specifies a file relative to the current directory. Relative path names do not begin with a slash. The path is relative to the current directory. The way to reference a file depends on your current directory. Using our example of the absolute path name, (/export/home/sally/compressed.Z), if your current directory is /export/home/sally, then the relative path name is simply compressed.Z. If your current directory is /export, then the relative path name is home/sally/compressed.Z.

Maneuvering through the Directory Hierarchy

When you use the File Manager, you always know where you are by looking at the path pane. The path pane displays a folder for each directory, starting at the root directory and traversing down to your current directory. To change your current directory, you can double-click on a folder in the file pane or the path pane, you can open a folder in the file or path pane, or you can choose Up from the File Pane menu.

To locate your current directory from the command line, you use the pwd (present working directory) command. The pwd command takes no arguments and returns the name of the current directory, as in this example:

```
dugout% pwd
/usr/openwin/bin
dugout%
```

To change your directory, use the cd (change directory) command. If you enter the cd command without an argument, your current directory becomes your home directory:

```
dugout% cd
dugout% pwd
/export/home/pew
dugout%
```

Notice from this example that cd does not return any information.

The cd command can also take a single argument that specifies the directory that you want to change to. You can specify either an absolute path name or a relative path name. In either case, cd does not display a message unless you specify a directory that does not exist or a directory to which you are not permitted access. In the following example, the user changes the directory to /export (an absolute pathname) and then changes the directory to home (a relative path name), which is a subdirectory of /export. The user then tries to change to a nonexistent directory: wilbur. The system responds with a message like the one in the following example (the exact message depends on which shell you use). When you try to change to a directory that doesn't exist or to a directory to which you are not permitted access, your current directory remains unchanged.

```
dugout% cd /export
dugout% cd home
dugout% cd wilbur
wilbur: No such file or directory
dugout% pwd
/export/home
dugout%
```

One of the techniques for changing directories that you learned in Chapter 4 is to select Up from the File Pane menu, which changes your current directory to the parent directory. In other words, it moves you up one directory. To indicate a parent directory at the command line use two consecutive dots (..). For example, if your current directory is /export/home, you can move to the parent directory (/home) by specifying two dots as the argument to cd:

```
dugout% pwd
/export/home
dugout% cd ..
dugout% pwd
/export
dugout%
```

You can also combine the .. notation with other directories to specify a relative path name that moves you up and down the directory hierarchy. For example, if your current directory is /export/home/sally/bin, you can change the directory to /export/home/pew with the following command:

```
dugout% pwd
/export/home/sally/bin
dugout% cd ../../pew
dugout% pwd
/export/home/pew
dugout%
```

Listing the Directory Contents

You may recall from Chapter 4 that you had several options for specifying a display mode. By default, the File Manager displayed files as icons. You could also choose to display files by listing them. This produced a list of files with additional information about each file, such as the owner, the permissions, the size, and the date of the last update. This same information is available by using the ls command from the command line.

The ls command gives you many options for customizing its output. You can list just the names of the files in a directory or get complete details such as the owner, permissions, and so forth. Let's start by looking at how the ls command works.

The ls command has numerous options (not all of which we will examine in this book) and can also take one or more file name arguments. Without any options or arguments, the ls command lists the name of each file in the current directory:

```
dugout% ls
Mail            bin             header.h    phone
Makefile        compressed.Z    mailfile    play
README          document.doc    main.c      snapshot.rs
alberts_mail    doorbell.au     memo        sort.c
app-defaults    frame.doc       namelist    start_license
dugout%
```

If you specify file name arguments, ls lists only those files:

```
dugout% ls Makefile memo sort.c
Makefile  memo     sort.c
dugout%
```

You can also use wildcards (sometimes called *metacharacters*) to specify file names. You learned about a few wildcards in Chapter 4, including the asterisk (*), the question mark (?), and the square brackets ([]). As you may recall, the asterisk matches zero or more of any character, the question mark matches any single character, and the square brackets identify a set of characters for which a match is made. For example, you can list all the files that end with .doc by entering the following command:

```
dugout% ls *.doc
document.doc  frame.doc
dugout%
```

Or, you can list all files that end with a dot and a single character by entering the following command:

```
dugout% ls *.?
compressed.Z  header.h      main.c        sort.c
dugout%
```

Or, you can list all files that end with a dot and either a c or an h by entering the following command:

```
dugout% ls *.[ch]
header.h  main.c    sort.c
dugout%
```

Of course, you can provide multiple arguments that each include metacharacters, as in the following command:

```
dugout% ls d* *.?
compressed.Z  doorbell.au   main.c
document.doc  header.h      sort.c
dugout%
```

I should point out that the wildcards are actually expanded (replaced by the corresponding file names) by the shell, not by the ls program. The ls command (and most other commands) does not interpret the wildcards; it doesn't even know that they were entered on the command line by the user. Before the command is executed, the shell expands the wildcards and invokes the command with the expanded file name arguments. We'll talk more about the shell and metacharacters in Chapter 14, but for now be aware that any command that takes files as command-line arguments can use the wildcards we have just described.

You can supply a directory name, rather than a file, as an argument to the ls command to list the contents of that directory:

```
dugout% ls phone
SalesLeads  customers
dugout%
```

You can also use directory names in combination with wildcards to list files within subdirectories. For example, to list all the files that begin with p in each subdirectory of the current directory, enter the following command:

```
dugout% ls */p*
Mail/paul     bin/play      bin/ps2bits
dugout%
```

The first asterisk matches each subdirectory of the current directory. The p* matches any file within these subdirectories that begins with a p.

As mentioned earlier, ls also supports numerous command-line options. These options can be used alone or with file name arguments. If you use an option without a file name argument, ls lists all the files in the current directory according to the options specified. Let's look at just a few of these options.

The –l Option

One of the most common options is –l (long). When you use the –l option, ls provides a long listing of each file, including permissions, number of links, owner, group, size, date, and name:

```
dugout% ls -l
total 150
drwxr-xr-x   2 sally    staff        512 Mar  1 15:33 Mail
-rw-r--r--   1 sally    staff        541 Mar  1 14:04 Makefile
-rw-rw-r--   1 sally    staff         98 Mar  1 14:04 README
-rw-rw-r--   1 sally    staff        315 Sep 25 01:00 alberts_mail
drwxr-xr-x   2 sally    staff        512 Sep 25 01:00 app-defaults
drwxrwxrwx   3 sally    staff        512 Sep 25 01:00 bin
-rw-rw-r--   1 sally    staff         97 Feb 15 09:09 compressed.Z
-rw-rw-r--   1 sally    staff        109 Feb 19 10:59 document.doc
-rw-r--r--   1 sally    staff      17592 Aug  9  1992 doorbell.au
-rw-rw-r--   1 sally    staff        109 Sep 25 00:52 frame.doc
-rw-rw-r--   1 sally    eng           98 Feb 15 09:09 header.h
-rw-rw-r--   1 sally    staff        315 Feb 25 12:33 mailfile
-rw-rw-r--   1 sally    eng           98 Feb 15 09:09 main.c
-rw-rw-r--   1 sally    staff         98 Feb 23 15:02 memo
-rw-rw-r--   1 sally    staff         98 Feb 25 12:33 namelist
drwxrwxr-x   2 sally    staff        512 Sep 25 01:00 phone
lrwxrwxrwx   1 sally    staff          8 Mar  1 16:12 play -> bin/play
-rw-r--r--   1 sally    staff      39203 Aug  8  1992 snapshot.rs
-rw-rw-r--   1 sally    eng           98 Feb 23 15:02 sort.c
```

```
-rwxr-xr-x   1 sally    staff        101 Feb 19 10:59 start_license
dugout%
```

This list may look familiar to you. Remember that in Chapter 4 you learned about using the File Manager to display files by list on the Customize View pop-up window? (Look back to Figure 4.13 to see the File Manager with the display mode set to List.) The format of the ls –l command is identical to that of the File Manager's List display mode.

Let's examine each of the fields on the ls long listing output. The format for the ls output in the long format is shown here:

Permissions	Links	Owner	Group	Size	Date & Time	Name
-rw-rw-r--	1	sally	eng	98	Feb 23 15:02	sort.c

Permissions provide the type of file and the permissions on the file. There are ten characters in the permissions field. The first character indicates the type of file, and the next nine characters indicate the permissions. There are several types of files that ls recognizes. They are not the same types that the File Manager identifies by displaying different icons. Fewer types are available with the ls command. Here is a list of the most common types:

- A regular file
d A directory
l A symbolic link

The other nine permission characters are described in detail later in this chapter.

Links indicate the number of links to the file. Most files have just one link. Directories have two or more links, depending on the number of subdirectories within the directory. The link field indicates the number of hard links to a file, not symbolic links. A hard link is created by using the ln command. (We'll talk more about ln later in this chapter.)

Owner displays the user id of the owner of the file.

Group displays the group ownership of the file.

Size displays the size of the file in bytes.

Date & Time displays the date and time that the file was last modified. This may be the same as the time that the file was created if it has never been modified. If the file's modification time is greater than six months from today's date, the hour and minute part of the time is replaced by the year.

Name contains the name of the file. If the file is a symbolic link, then the name field includes the name of the file that this link is pointing to. For example, the file named play included in the long listing shown earlier is a symbolic link that points to bin/play.

The –a Option

Another common option is –a (all). The –a option lists all the files in the directory. Normally, files that begin with a dot are considered hidden files (sometimes called dot files) and are not listed. Using the –a option lists all the files in the directory, including hidden files, as shown here:

```
dugout% ls -a
.                      .sh_history      frame.doc
..                     .wastebasket     header.h
.Xauthority            Mail             mailfile
.Xdefaults             Makefile         main.c
.desksetdefaults       README           memo
.fmcmd                 alberts_mail     namelist
.mailrc                app-defaults     phone
.mailtool-init         bin              play
.openwin-init          compressed.Z     snapshot.rs
.openwin-init.BAK      document.doc     sort.c
.profile               doorbell.au      start_license
dugout%
```

You can see that this directory has quite a few dot files. Two special files appear in every directory: . and .. (dot and dot-dot). Both of these dot files are directories. The single-dot file represents the current directory; the double-dot file represents the parent directory.

You can combine options to produce a listing that includes the features of each option chosen. For example, you can combine the –l option and the –a option to produce a long listing of all files in the directory by using a single dash (–) followed by both l and a, as shown here:

```
dugout% ls -la
total 190
drwxrwxrwx   7 sally    staff      1024 Mar  1 16:12 .
drwxr-xr-x   8 root     root        512 Dec 30 15:39 ..
-rw-------   1 sally    staff       149 Sep 27 23:05 .Xauthority
-rw-rw-r--   1 sally    staff       492 Sep 27 23:25 .Xdefaults
```

```
-rw-rw-r--   1 sally    staff        957 Sep 25 08:34 .desksetdefaults
-rw-rw-r--   1 sally    staff        375 Sep 25 08:28 .fmcmd
-rw-rw-r--   1 sally    staff       1462 Oct 17 14:35 .mailrc
-rw-rw-r--   1 sally    staff        135 Sep 27 23:25 .mailtool-init
-rwxrwxr-x   1 sally    staff       1088 Sep 27 23:25 .openwin-init
-rwxrwxr-x   1 sally    staff       1088 Sep 27 23:25 .openwin-init.BAK
-rw-r--r--   1 sally    staff        491 Sep 29 19:53 .profile
-rw-------   1 sally    staff       4338 Mar  1 16:17 .sh_history
drwxrwxr-x   2 sally    staff        512 Sep 25 01:27 .wastebasket
drwxr-xr-x   2 sally    staff        512 Mar  1 15:33 Mail
-rw-r--r--   1 sally    staff        541 Mar  1 14:04 Makefile
-rw-rw-r--   1 sally    staff         98 Mar  1 14:04 README
-rw-rw-r--   1 sally    staff        315 Sep 25 01:00 alberts_mail
drwxr-xr-x   2 sally    staff        512 Sep 25 01:00 app-defaults
drwxrwxrwx   3 sally    staff        512 Sep 25 01:00 bin
-rw-rw-r--   1 sally    staff         97 Feb 15 09:09 compressed.Z
-rw-rw-r--   1 sally    staff        109 Feb 19 10:59 document.doc
-rw-r--r--   1 sally    staff      17592 Aug  9  1992 doorbell.au
-rw-rw-r--   1 sally    staff        109 Sep 25 00:52 frame.doc
-rw-rw-r--   1 sally    eng           98 Feb 15 09:09 header.h
-rw-rw-r--   1 sally    staff        315 Feb 25 12:33 mailfile
-rw-rw-r--   1 sally    eng           98 Feb 15 09:09 main.c
-rw-rw-r--   1 sally    staff         98 Feb 23 15:02 memo
-rw-rw-r--   1 sally    staff         98 Feb 25 12:33 namelist
drwxrwxr-x   2 sally    staff        512 Sep 25 01:00 phone
lrwxrwxrwx   1 sally    staff          8 Mar  1 16:12 play -> bin/play
-rw-r--r--   1 sally    staff      39203 Aug  8  1992 snapshot.rs
-rw-rw-r--   1 sally    eng           98 Feb 23 15:02 sort.c
-rwxr-xr-x   1 sally    staff        101 Feb 19 10:59 start_license
dugout%
```

Of course, you can also include one or more file name arguments with the options to list only the files you are interested in. For example, you can produce a long listing of a certain set of files by using the command shown here:

```
dugout% ls -l .X* *.doc */p*
-rw-------   1 sally    staff        149 Sep 27 23:05 .Xauthority
-rw-rw-r--   1 sally    staff        492 Sep 27 23:25 .Xdefaults
-rw-rw-r--   1 sally    staff          0 Mar  1 15:33 Mail/paul
-rwxr-xr-x   1 sally    staff        101 Aug  9  1992 bin/play
-rwxr-xr-x   1 sally    staff        112 Aug  9  1992 bin/ps2bits
-rw-rw-r--   1 sally    staff        109 Feb 19 10:59 document.doc
-rw-rw-r--   1 sally    staff        109 Sep 25 00:52 frame.doc
dugout%
```

The –F Option

The –F option appends the following special characters to the names of files that are directories, executables, or symbolic links:

- / The file is a directory.
- * The file is an executable.
- @ The file is a symbolic link.

Here is an example:

```
dugout% ls -F
Mail/           bin/            header.h        phone/
Makefile        compressed.Z    mailfile        play@
README          document.doc    main.c          snapshot.rs
alberts_mail    doorbell.au     memo            sort.c
app-defaults/   frame.doc       namelist        start_license*
dugout%
```

The –t Option

The –t option sorts the output of the ls command according to the times that the files were last modified. This option is often useful when you want to find the most recently modified or edited files in a directory. You may find it convenient to use the –t option with the –l option so that the date and time fields are displayed:

```
dugout% ls -lt
total 150
lrwxrwxrwx   1 sally    staff          8 Mar  1 16:12 play -> bin/play
drwxr-xr-x   2 sally    staff        512 Mar  1 15:33 Mail
-rw-r--r--   1 sally    staff        541 Mar  1 14:04 Makefile
-rw-rw-r--   1 sally    staff         98 Mar  1 14:04 README
-rw-rw-r--   1 sally    staff         98 Feb 25 12:33 namelist
-rw-rw-r--   1 sally    staff        315 Feb 25 12:33 mailfile
-rw-rw-r--   1 sally    eng           98 Feb 23 15:02 sort.c
-rw-rw-r--   1 sally    staff         98 Feb 23 15:02 memo
-rw-rw-r--   1 sally    staff        109 Feb 19 10:59 document.doc
-rwxr-xr-x   1 sally    staff        101 Feb 19 10:59 start_license
-rw-rw-r--   1 sally    eng           98 Feb 15 09:09 main.c
-rw-rw-r--   1 sally    eng           98 Feb 15 09:09 header.h
-rw-rw-r--   1 sally    staff         97 Feb 15 09:09 compressed.Z
drwxrwxrwx   3 sally    staff        512 Sep 25 01:00 bin
-rw-rw-r--   1 sally    staff        315 Sep 25 01:00 alberts_mail
drwxr-xr-x   2 sally    staff        512 Sep 25 01:00 app-defaults
drwxrwxr-x   2 sally    staff        512 Sep 25 01:00 phone
-rw-rw-r--   1 sally    staff        109 Sep 25 00:52 frame.doc
```

```
-rw-r--r--   1 sally    staff       17592 Aug  9  1992 doorbell.au
-rw-r--r--   1 sally    staff       39203 Aug  8  1992 snapshot.rs
dugout%
```

The –R Option

The –R option recursively lists the directory and each subdirectory. This option might create a very long output, depending on your current location in the directory hierarchy. Here is an example of a shorter listing:

```
dugout% ls -R
Mail            bin             header.h   phone
Makefile        compressed.Z    mailfile   play
README          document.doc    main.c     snapshot.rs
alberts_mail    doorbell.au     memo       sort.c
app-defaults    frame.doc       namelist   start_license

./Mail:
paul

./app-defaults:

./bin:
play        ps2bits     src         xloadimage

./bin/src:

./phone:
SalesLeads  customers
dugout%
```

The –d Option

The –d option lists a directory without displaying the contents of the directory. This option is especially useful when you want to see the long listing for a particular directory itself, not its contents. Here is an example:

```
dugout% ls -ld Mail doorbell.au
drwxr-xr-x   2 sally    staff         512 Mar  1 15:33 Mail
-rw-r--r--   1 sally    staff       17592 Aug  9  1992 doorbell.au
dugout%
```

Other Options

There are many other options for the ls command. Table 11.1 describes some of the other ls options. Refer to the ls man page for a complete description.

Table 11.1 More ls Command Options

Option	Description
–C	Produce multicolumn output with entries sorted down the columns.
–g	List the group but not the owner.
–L	If an argument is a symbolic link, list the file or directory link references rather than the link itself.
–n	The user's ID and group ID are printed as numbers rather than strings.
–o	Same as –l without group.
–r	Reverse the order of sort to get reverse alphabetic or oldest first as appropriate.
–s	List the size of each file in blocks.
–x	Produce multicolumn output with entries sorted across rather than down the columns.
–1	Print one entry per line.

File and Directory Operations

You now know some of the most basic and useful commands for moving around within the directory hierarchy and displaying the contents of directories. In this section you will learn how to display the contents of files, create directories, copy and move files, and remove files and directories.

Looking at File Contents

When you use the File Manager to examine the contents of a file, you open the file by either double-clicking on the file icon or specifying Open from the File menu. Either of these two operations invokes an editor (such as Text Editor or vi) in which the file is edited and loads the selected file. When you are entering commands at the shell prompt, you can use an editor to examine the contents of a file if you wish, or you can use one of several programs available for simply displaying the contents of the file.

The cat Command

The most elementary command for displaying the contents of a file is the cat command. Cat is short for con*cat*enate. The cat command lists the contents of each file provided on the command line. For example, the contents of the README file are displayed as follows:

```
dugout% cat README
This directory is Sally's home directory.
Among other things it contains:

          Mail
          README
          sort.c
dugout%
```

If you supply multiple file name arguments, cat concatenates the files and lists them as shown here:

```
dugout% cat README sort.c
This directory is Sally's home directory.
Among other things it contains:

        Mail
        README
        sort.c
#include <stdio.h>
main()
{
    printf("This program prints the word sort\n");
}
dugout%
```

The cat command has many practical uses. However, when you are displaying a file that has more lines than can be displayed in a single window (or screen), you will often find it more convenient to use the more command, which we will discuss next.

The more Command

The more command is similar to cat except that it lists only one screenful of a file at a time. The cat command displays the entire contents of the file or files specified regardless of the length of the files. If you want to read the contents of a long file, you will find it very difficult to use cat. The more command, however, pauses its output after each screenful of text is displayed, giving you time to examine the contents at your leisure.

The more command pauses each screenful of output and displays --More-- (*xx*%) at the bottom of the window (or screen). The percentage (*xx*%) indicates the amount of the file that has been displayed so far. When you press the spacebar, more displays the next screenful of text and again displays the --More-- prompt. This sequence continues until the file contents are exhausted.

The more command executed in a Shell Tool is shown below. The more prompt indicates that 74 percent of the file has been displayed.

```
dugout% more mailfile
From pew Mon Aug 10 06:23 GMT 1992
Return-Path: <pew>
Received: by dugout. (5.0/SMI-SVR4)
        id AA00552; Mon, 10 Aug 92 06:23:08 GMT
Date: Mon, 10 Aug 92 06:23:08 GMT
From: pew (John Pew)
Message-Id: <9208100623.AA00552@dugout.>
To: pew
--More--(74%)
```

When the more prompt is displayed, you can enter q to quit viewing the file. The remainder of the file will not be displayed, and the prompt will reappear.

If you enter more than one file with the more command, each file is displayed as usual, but the command pauses between files and a special banner appears that delimits the beginning of each file. For example, if you use the more command with README and sort.c, the output looks like this:

```
dugout% more README sort.c
::::::::::::::
README
::::::::::::::
This directory is Sally's home directory.
Among other things it contains:

        Mail
        README
        sort.c
::::::::::::::
sort.c
::::::::::::::
#include <stdio.h>
main()
{
    printf("This program prints the word sort\n");
}
dugout%
```

The more command supports some special options to customize its output. See the more man page for a complete description.

The head Command

The head command lists the first ten lines of the specified file, as in this example:

```
dugout% head /etc/passwd
root:x:0:1:0000-Admin(0000):/:/sbin/sh
daemon:x:1:1:0000-Admin(0000):/:
bin:x:2:2:0000-Admin(0000):/usr/bin:
sys:x:3:3:0000-Admin(0000):/:
adm:x:4:4:0000-Admin(0000):/var/adm:
lp:x:71:8:0000-lp(0000):/usr/spool/lp:
smtp:x:0:0:mail daemon user:/:
uucp:x:5:5:0000-uucp(0000):/usr/lib/uucp:
listen:x:37:4:Network Admin:/usr/net/nls:
nobody:x:60001:60001:uid no body:/:
dugout%
```

You can provide an option that indicates the number of lines to list. For example, if you specify –5 as an option, head lists the first five lines of the file:

```
dugout% head -5 /etc/passwd
root:x:0:1:0000-Admin(0000):/:/sbin/sh
daemon:x:1:1:0000-Admin(0000):/:
bin:x:2:2:0000-Admin(0000):/usr/bin:
sys:x:3:3:0000-Admin(0000):/:
adm:x:4:4:0000-Admin(0000):/var/adm:
dugout%
```

If you specify more than one file, the head command displays a one-line banner for each file:

```
dugout% head -2 README sort.c
==> README <==
This directory is Sally's home directory.
Among other things it contains:

==> sort.c <==
#include <stdio.h>
main()
dugout%
```

The tail Command

The tail command lists the last ten lines of the file. Only one file is accepted on the command line for the tail command:

```
dugout% tail /usr/dict/words
zoology
zoom
Zorn
Zoroaster
Zoroastrian
zounds
z's
zucchini
Zurich
zygote
dugout%
```

You can also provide an option with the tail command to indicate the number of lines to list. For example, if you specify –2 as an option, only the last two lines of the file are listed.

```
dugout% tail -2 /usr/dict/words
Zurich
zygote
dugout%
```

The tail command also has an option for specifying the number of lines from the beginning of the file that it should begin listing. It then lists from that line to the end of the file. This option is invoked by using the plus sign (+) followed by the line number. For example, to list the contents of the file /usr/dict/-words beginning at line 1000 to the end of the file, you enter the following:

```
dugout% tail +1000 /usr/dict/words
Annalen
annals
Annapolis
Anne
anneal
.
.
  <Many lines deleted>
.
.
zounds
z's
```

```
zucchini
Zurich
zygote
dugout%
```

Creating and Removing a Directory

In Chapter 4 you learned how to use the File Manager to create and remove directories. You created a new directory by using the Create Folder item from the File menu and then giving the directory a name. You removed a directory by either moving the folder icon to the Wastebasket or selecting the folder and deleting it (by selecting Delete from the File Pane menu). In this section you will learn how to create and remove directories from the command line.

The mkdir Command

To create a directory from the command line, you use the mkdir command. The mkdir command accepts one or more arguments that specify the names of the directories to create. For example, to create a directory named source, you enter the following:

```
dugout% mkdir source
dugout%
```

If mkdir does not succeed in creating a directory, an error message appears. For example, if you try to create a directory named source when a directory with that name already exists, you will see the following output:

```
dugout% mkdir source
mkdir:  Failed to make directory "source"; File exists
dugout%
```

You can create more than one directory at a time by specifying each directory as an argument to mkdir. You can even create a directory along with subdirectories for that directory by using the same command. For example, you can create a directory named PhoneList and two subdirectories of the PhoneList directory all with the same command, as shown here:

```
dugout% mkdir PhoneList PhoneList/business PhoneList/personal
dugout%
```

The directories are created in order, so you must create the parent directory first. You can use the –p option to create a directory and have nonexistent parent directories automatically created. For example, rather than using the preceding command to create the PhoneList directory and the two subdirectories, you can specify –p and just the two subdirectories to achieve the same results with less typing:

```
dugout% mkdir -p PhoneList/business PhoneList/personal
dugout%
```

The rmdir Command

To remove a directory, you use the rmdir command. The rmdir command removes a directory only if that directory is empty. You must remove all the files and subdirectories within a directory before you can remove the directory itself, as shown here:

```
dugout% rmdir PhoneList/personal PhoneList/business
dugout% rmdir PhoneList
dugout%
```

If the directory is not empty, rmdir displays an error message and takes no action, as shown here:

```
dugout% rmdir PhoneList
rmdir: PhoneList: Directory not empty
dugout%
```

You can also remove directories by using the rm command. We'll talk about the rm command later in this chapter.

Copying, Moving, and Linking Files

You can move and copy files with the File Manager by using the File Pane menu to cut or copy and then paste a file or files, or by using drag and drop. In this section you will learn how to copy, move, and link files from the command line.

The cp Command

The cp command copies one or more files. In its simplest form, cp takes two arguments: the name of the existing file and the name of the new file to create as the copy:

```
dugout% cp existing newfile
dugout%
```

In this example a new file called newfile is created in the current directory. The cp command doesn't return anything unless an error occurs. Common errors include copying a nonexistent file and lacking adequate permission to create the new file.

You can also use cp to copy a file into another directory by specifying an existing directory as the last argument. The cp command copies the file into the specified directory and gives the new file the same name. For example, the command

```
dugout% cp start_license bin
dugout%
```

creates a copy of the start_license file in the bin directory. You can copy multiple files into a directory by listing the files, followed by the directory name as the last argument. For example, you can copy both start_license and Makefile into the bin directory with the following command:

```
dugout% cp start_license Makefile bin
dugout%
```

When you are copying files, you must take care not to overwrite an existing file. The cp command allows you to copy an existing file to a file that already exists. In this case the new file overwrites the existing file, which is then lost; that file cannot be recovered. The cp command does not give you an error message or notification that it has overwritten your other file. You can specify that you want cp to operate in an interactive mode that will provide notification before overwriting a file. To specify the interactive mode, use the –i option. For example, to copy main.c to sort.c in interactive mode, enter the following:

```
dugout% cp -i main.c sort.c
cp: overwrite sort.c? y
dugout%
```

When you use the –i option, the cp command prompts you if a file will be deleted as a result of the operation. You must respond to the prompt with a y to go ahead with the operation, or with an n to cancel it.

You can also use wildcards to copy multiple files to another directory, just as you used wildcards to list multiple files. For example, to copy all files that end with .c or .h to the source directory, enter the following:

```
dugout% cp *.[ch] source
dugout%
```

You can use the cp command to copy entire directory hierarchies by using the –r option, which specifies a recursive copy. For example, to copy the bin directory and all of bin's descendants (files and subdirectories) to bin2, use the following command:

```
dugout% cp -r bin bin2
dugout%
```

The mv Command

To move a file, you use the mv command. The mv command works just like the cp command except that the file is moved rather than copied. The options and arguments are also the same as the cp command.

You can move a file to another directory by specifying the name of the file as the first argument and the name of the destination directory as the second argument. For example, to move the start_license file to the bin directory, you enter the following:

```
dugout% mv start_license bin
dugout%
```

You can move multiple files to a common directory by listing the files, followed by the directory name, as shown here:

```
dugout% mv start_license Makefile bin
dugout%
```

You can turn on the interactive mode for mv so that you will be prompted before any move is performed that would overwrite an existing file. Simply use the –i option, as in this example:

```
dugout% mv -i main.c sort.c
mv: overwrite sort.c? n
dugout%
```

You can also use wildcards with the mv command, as in this example:

```
dugout% mv *.[ch] source
dugout%
```

Note that you can also use the mv command to rename an existing file. Simply specify the existing name as the first argument and the new name as the second argument, as shown here:

```
dugout% mv existing newfile
dugout%
```

There is not, however, a recursive move option available with mv. To rename a directory, just specify the existing directory name as the first argument and the new directory name as the second argument. The following command changes the name of the bin directory to bin2:

```
dugout% mv bin bin2
dugout%
```

Note that if the directory named in the second argument already exists, then the first directory would retain its name and be moved into the second directory.

There is one limitation of moving directories: they cannot be moved across file systems. You haven't learned about file systems thus far in this book (you will in Chapter 16), but you can think of a file system as a separate hardware device. The SunOS directory hierarchy is distributed over one or more disk devices. If you attempt to move a directory hierarchy to another file system, the move will fail. You will have to first copy the directory hierarchy and then remove the original.

The ln Command

You were introduced to the concept of links in Chapter 4. When you copy a file by using the File Pane menu, you have the choice of copying it as a file or as a link. When you choose to copy it as a link, a symbolic link is created. You can perform the same operation on the command line by using the ln command.

There are actually two types of links: hard links and symbolic links. Let's look at these types one at a time.

Hard Links

Recall from the previous discussion of the ls long listing that one of the fields represents the number of links to a file. These are the hard links. A hard link is indistinguishable from the original file. It is like having an additional name and reference given to an existing file. To create a hard link, you use the ln command as you would use the cp command: the first argument is the name of the existing file, and the second argument is the name of the new link, as shown here:

```
dugout% ln memo memo1
dugout%
```

A new file, called memo1, now exists. These two files, memo and memo1, are not only identical but are actually the same file! If you modify the contents of memo, the changes appear also in memo1 because there is really only one file; it is just being referenced by two different names. If you use the ls command to display a long listing, you will see that the permissions, the ownership, the size, and the date and time are identical. The only thing that is different is the name, as shown here:

```
dugout% ls -l memo*
-rw-rw-r--   2 sally    staff          98 Feb 23 15:02 memo
-rw-rw-r--   2 sally    staff          98 Feb 23 15:02 memo1
dugout%
```

Notice also that the link field shows 2 links for both memo and memo1. This means there are two names by which the file contents can be accessed:

memo and memo1. If you create another link to memo (or to memo1), a 3 will be displayed in the links field. If you remove memo or memo1, the links field will be decremented by one, but the file and its contents will still exist, since both memo and memo1 are equal in their "ownership" of the file contents.

You can also link multiple files at once by specifying a directory as the last argument. When you link files into a directory, the links are created in the specified directory with the same file names as the original file names:

```
dugout% ln main.c sort.c source
dugout% ls -l main.c sort.c source
-rw-rw-r--   2 sally    eng          98 Feb 15 09:09 main.c
-rw-rw-r--   2 sally    eng          98 Mar  1 18:05 sort.c

source:
total 4
-rw-rw-r--   2 sally    eng          98 Feb 15 09:09 main.c
-rw-rw-r--   2 sally    eng          98 Mar  1 18:05 sort.c
dugout%
```

Notice that the files main.c and sort.c are now linked in the source directory. You can access either of the two files in the current directory or in the source directory. If, for example, you remove the sort.c file, you can still access the file as source/sort.c.

The limitations of hard links are as follows:

- You cannot link directories.
- You cannot link a file across a file system. (See Chapter 16 for more information on file systems.)

The limitations of hard links make them not as attractive as symbolic links, which we will discuss next.

Symbolic Links

Symbolic links (sometimes called soft links) are similar to hard links, but the differences are distinct. Both links provide a mechanism for accessing a file through a different file name, but a symbolic link contains information only about the file it points to. If that file is removed, it can no longer be accessed through the symbolic link. The symbolic link still exists, but it now points to a nonexistent file. Here are some of the main differences between hard and symbolic links:

- If the file that the symbolic link points to is deleted, the file is truly deleted and can no longer be accessed.
- A symbolic link can point to a nonexistent file.
- A symbolic link can point to a file in another file system.

- A symbolic link can point to a directory.

When you copy a file as a link in the File Manager, you are creating a symbolic link. To create a symbolic link from the command line, you use the ln –s command:

```
dugout% ln -s memo memo1
dugout%
```

As a result of this command, you can access the memo file through memo1, but these two files are not identical as they were when you created a hard link. If you remove memo after creating memo1, the file will be permanently lost. The ls long output shows the differences between the two files:

```
dugout% ls -ls memo*
   2 -rw-rw-r--   1 sally    staff         98 Feb 23 15:02 memo
   2 lrwxrwxrwx   1 sally    staff          4 Mar  2 22:04 memo1 -> memo
dugout%
```

Notice the many differences between the two files: the type of file, the permissions, the size, the date and time, and the name. Symbolic-link files are displayed in a special way by ls. The name of the symbolic-link file is followed by an arrow and the name of the file that it points to.

The most important advantages of symbolic links are that they can point to directories and to files on other file systems. For example, you can use both of these features simultaneously by creating a symbolic link to a directory on another file system. In the following example, a symbolic link is created to the /etc directory:

```
dugout% ln -s /etc etc
dugout% ls -l etc
lrwxrwxrwx   1 sally    staff          4 Mar  2 22:15 etc -> /etc
dugout%
```

If you move into the newly created etc directory, your present directory (etc) will actually be the directory that the symbolic link points to. This is a powerful feature that makes accessing files and directories in distant locations simple.

Removing Files

You use the rm command to remove one or more files or directories. The rm command permanently removes all the files specified on the command line. These files are not moved to the Wastebasket; they are actually deleted, and they cannot be recovered once they are removed (unless you have a backup copy). In this example, two files are being deleted:

```
dugout% rm doorbell.au header.h
dugout%
```

You can use the -i option with the rm command to remove files in interactive mode. When you use the interactive option, you are prompted for a yes or no answer (y/n) for each file specified. This prompt prevents you from accidentally deleting files that you want to keep. Here is an example:

```
dugout% rm -i README compressed.Z
rm: remove  README: (y/n)? n
rm: remove  compressed.Z: (y/n)? y
dugout%
```

You can also use wildcards when removing files. Be very careful, however, because mistyping a remove command when using wildcards can be disastrous. For example, you may want to delete all compressed files in a directory. To do so, you enter the following:

```
dugout% rm *.Z
dugout%
```

If, however, you accidentally insert a space between the asterisk and the dot, you would delete every file in the directory, because * matches all the files in the current directory:

```
dugout% rm * .Z
.Z: No such file or directory
dugout%
```

The shell first expands the * to all the files in the current directory and then invokes rm with the expanded * and .Z. Notice that after rm has removed all the files in the current directory it complains that it cannot find the file named .Z since there is no such file.

You cannot remove a directory with the rm command unless you use the –r option. The –r option recursively removes a directory and all of its contents including subdirectories and their contents. The following command removes the bin directory and all of its contents:

```
dugout% rm -r bin
dugout%
```

Ownership and Permissions

Every file has an owner and a set of permissions. You were introduced to this concept in Chapter 4 when we looked at file properties on the File Properties pop-up window. In this section you will learn more about ownership and permissions and how to set permissions on files from the command line.

Ownership and Permission Basics

The owner of a file is usually the person who created the file, though the owner can be changed (usually by the system administrator). The owner of a file may set or change the permissions of the file. The permissions for a file are separated into categories: user (owner), group, and other (world). Each of these categories has a read, write, and execute permission—making a total of nine permissions. Recall from Chapter 4 that the File Properties pop-up window displays a checkbox for each of the nine permissions. The long listing option of the ls command (–l) also displays the permissions of the file. Let's examine the README file permissions to better understand this concept. The ls command gives the following output:

```
dugout% ls -l README
-rw-rw-r--   1 sally    staff         98 Mar  1 18:10 README
dugout%
```

The first field of the ls –l output provides the permission information. Ten characters are displayed in the permission field. The first character represents the type of file. The next nine characters correspond to the nine permissions, as follows: The first three characters represent the read, write, and execute permissions for the user or owner; the next three characters represent the read, write, and execute permissions for the group; the last three characters represent the read, write, and execute permissions for other (world). Each of the nine characters must be either a dash (–), which means that permission is not given, or one of the letters r, w, or x, which represents read, write, and execute. When the letter is displayed, you know that permission of that type is granted for the file.

For example, a file that has read and write permission for the user (owner), read permission for the group, and read permission for other would have the following permissions field:

```
-rw-r--r--
```

A file that has read and execute permission for user, group, and other would have the following permissions field:

```
-r-xr-xr-x
```

Now let's look at the File Manager's File Properties pop-up window for the README file, shown in Figure 11.2. You can see how the checkboxes correspond directly to the permissions shown by the ls command.

Each permission has a particular meaning that is different for a file and a directory:

- Read permission for a *file* means that the contents of the file can be read. Read permission for a *directory* means that the contents of the directory can be read. A directory that can be read can have its contents listed with the ls command.

Figure 11.2
File Properties for README

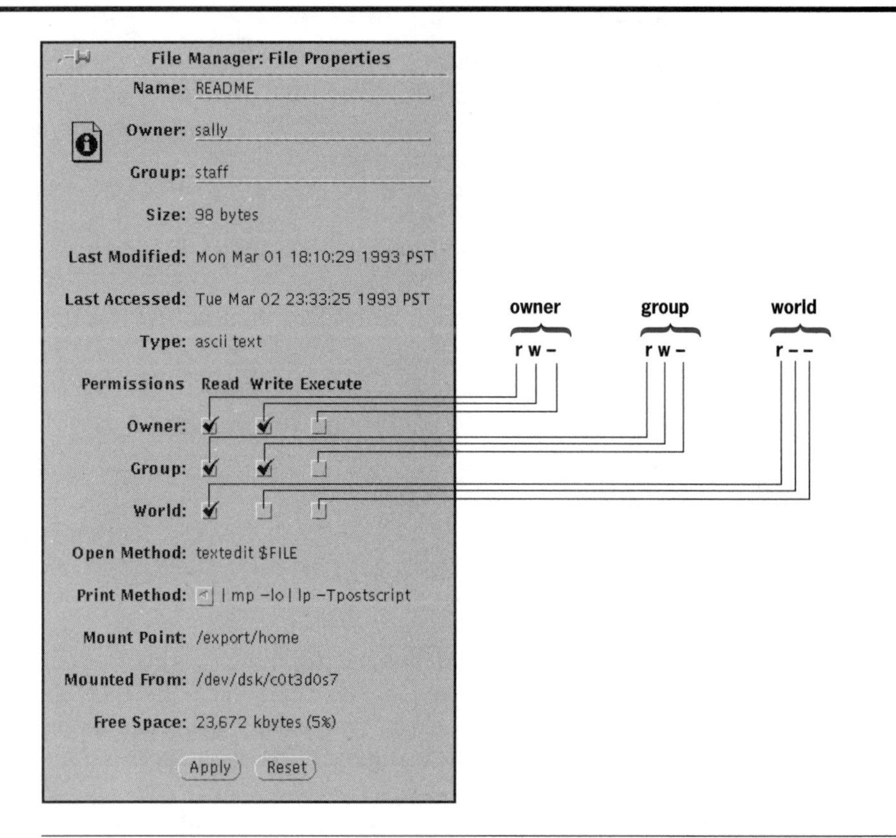

- Write permission for a *file* means that the file can be modified or removed. Write permission for a *directory* means that files can be created in and deleted from the directory.
- Execute permission for a *file* means that the file can be executed as a UNIX command. Execute permission for a *directory* means that you can make that directory your current directory with the cd command.

Changing Permissions

On occasion you may need to change the permissions of one or more files. Perhaps you have a file that contains sensitive information that you do not want anyone else to read. In that case, you can remove all permissions except the ones for user (owner). Or perhaps you have a file that does not have write permission. You can change the permissions to include write permission.

To change the permissions of a file or files, you use the chmod command. The chmod command can be used in two modes: absolute and symbolic. Before you learn exactly how to use the command, you need to know a little more about how to reference permissions.

Let's go back to our discussion of the first field of the ls long listing output. You learned that there are nine permissions, each represented by a character. Another way to reference the particular permissions of a file is by specifying an octal number. To understand this better, let's dissect the permission field of the ls output. If each of the nine permissions is represented as either a 0 or a 1, indicating whether or not the permission is granted, the entire permission field could be displayed as a binary number. For example, the following permissions grant read and write access to user and group, and read access to other:

```
r w -  r w -  r - -          rw-rw-r--
1 1 0  1 1 0  1 0 0
  6      6      4            664
```

The binary number displayed under the permission corresponds to the permissions. The 664 displayed under the binary number (110110100) is the octal equivalent of the binary number. This octal value is used by the chmod command to set permissions.

If you are not familiar with binary and octal numbers, you may find this discussion confusing. Let's consider one other way of looking at this number associated with the permissions. If you assign a numeric value to each of the nine permissions as shown here, you can simply add the numbers to arrive at the same octal permissions value:

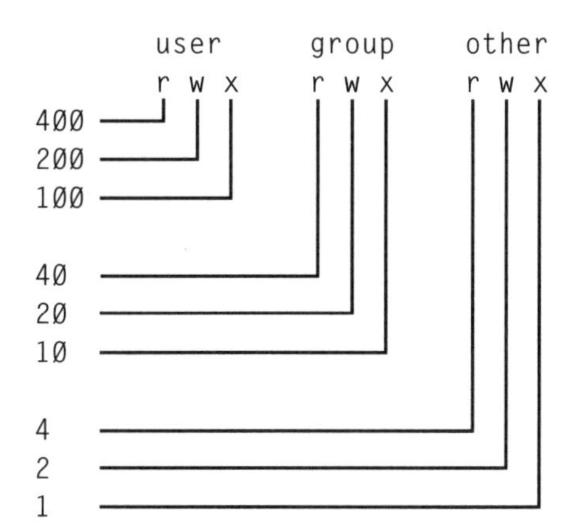

So, using this method, the -rw-rw-r-- permission discussed previously would be evaluated like this:

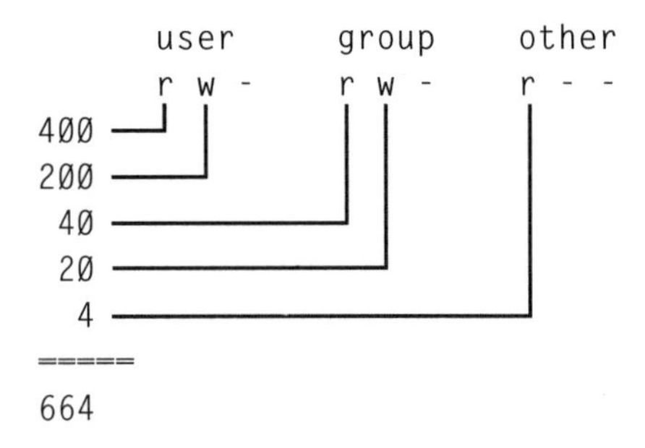

Now that you understand the basic method for determining the octal-equivalent permission mode, examine the following list of commonly used permissions to make sure that you see the correspondence between the permissions and the octal value:

-r--r--r--	444	The file can be read by user, group, and other.
drwxr-xr-x	755	The user can read, write, and execute (change to) this directory. The group and other can read and execute this directory.
-rwxrwxr-x	775	The user and group can read, write, and execute this file. Other can read and execute this file.
-r-xr-xr-x	555	The file can be read and executed by user, group, and other.

You use these octal values to set the absolute permissions of a file or files with the chmod command. For example, to set the permissions of the README file to read-only for user, group, and other, you use the following command:

```
dugout% chmod 444 README
dugout%
```

You can specify multiple files or directories or use wildcards on the chmod command line. Each file specified will be set to the permissions indicated. Of course, you can change permissions only on the files of which you are the owner. The following example changes the permissions of all .c files to read/write for user and read-only for group and other (644):

```
dugout% chmod 644 *.c
dugout%
```

Using octal values to set permissions may seem complicated at first, but it doesn't take long to learn the most commonly used permission values. Several hundred permission values are possible, but in practice fewer than ten are used for most permissions.

The chmod command also allows you to set permissions by using a symbolic mode rather than the octal number. The symbolic mode lets you set a specific permission without affecting the other permissions. To understand this, you need to know the following abbreviations:

u	user (owner) permissions
g	group permissions
o	other (world) permissions
a	all permissions (user, group, and other)
=	assign a permission absolutely
+	add a permission
–	remove a permission
r	read permission
w	write permission
x	execute permission

You combine these characters to specify the permissions that you want to set. The characters are divided into three parts—who, how, and what—as shown here:

who	u g o a
how	= + –
what	r w x

You combine these characters in a certain sequence, as shown here, to specify what permissions you want set for which users:

```
chmod <who><how><what> filename ...
```

The who and what fields can contain multiple characters. Let's look at a simple example that sets write permission for group and other on the file sort.c:

```
dugout% chmod go+w sort.c
dugout%
```

To remove write and execute permission from other on the directory bin, enter the following:

```
dugout% chmod o-wx bin
dugout%
```

The real advantage of using the symbolic mode comes when you want to add or subtract certain permissions on multiple files without setting the same absolute permission on each of those files. For example, if you want to add write permission to group and other on files Mail and doorbell.au, you can use the symbolic mode and not affect the other permissions of the files.

```
dugout% ls -ld Mail doorbell.au
drwxr-xr-x   2 sally    staff        512 Mar  1 15:33 Mail
-rw-r--r--   1 sally    staff      17592 Aug  9  1992 doorbell.au
dugout% chmod go+w Mail doorbell.au
dugout% ls -ld Mail doorbell.au
drwxrwxrwx   2 sally    staff        512 Mar  1 15:33 Mail
-rw-rw-rw-   1 sally    staff      17592 Aug  9  1992 doorbell.au
dugout%
```

Notice that only the write permission was changed for group and other. The Mail directory had execute permission set, and the doorbell.au file did not have execute permission set. The execute permissions were unaffected by this command. It is impossible to perform this task using absolute octal values.

Chmod allows you to combine multiple permission settings in a comma-separated list. For example, to set read permission for all users and to add write and execute permission for the user on files, enter

```
dugout% chmod a=r,u+wx file
dugout%
```

Summary

In this chapter, you've learned a lot about some common SunOS commands—particularly commands that affect files and directories. You have learned how to get more information with the man command and how to manipulate the command line with control characters and quotation marks. You should now feel comfortable doing most of the operations that the File Manager provides at the command line. You can change directories (cd), print the current directory (pwd), list files (ls), use wildcards, examine the contents of files (cat, more, head, and tail), and copy, move, and link files (cp, mv, ln). You have also learned the basics about file ownership and permission and how to change the permissions of a file. You are equipped with the basic tools necessary to be successful when using the SunOS command line.

In Chapter 12 you will continue to increase your knowledge of the command line by learning about some other useful UNIX commands, including the mail and printing systems.

CHAPTER

12

More SunOS Fundamentals

Working with Files

Performing Print Operations

Sending and Receiving Mail from the Command Line

Using Other Utility Commands

IN CHAPTER 11 YOU LEARNED SOME SUNOS FUNDAMENTALS, INCLUDING HOW to copy, move, and delete files and directories. In this chapter you will continue learning about how to work with files, as well as how to use some other general-purpose SunOS commands. You will also learn the command-line interface for two common facilities: printing and mail. As I've mentioned elsewhere in this book, although you will probably use the Print Tool and the Mail Tool most of the time, it is important that you understand how to use the corresponding command-line programs for those times when you do not have direct access to the OpenWindows environment. The topics covered in this chapter include the following:

- Working with files
- Performing print operations
- Sending and receiving mail from the command line
- Using other utility commands

Working with Files

In this section you'll learn about some of the most common commands for manipulating files. You can use these commands to do many things, such as determine the file type, search for a string of characters within the file, sort the contents of the file, and find a file in a directory hierarchy.

Performing Basic Functions

Let's start by talking about three basic commands: file, wc, and diff. You use the file command to determine the type of a file, the wc command to count the words in a file, and the diff command to find the differences between two similar files.

The file Command

The file command displays the file type for the file or files you specify.

```
dugout% file namelist
namelist:       ascii text
dugout%
```

Knowing the type of a file is sometimes very important before you execute a command on that file. For example, you may want to determine the type of a file before you display its contents with the cat or more commands. This is especially important if you are exploring directories and files with which you are not familiar. Rather than just using cat or more directly, it is a good idea to make sure that the file is an ASCII file. If you use cat or more on a binary file, you will have garbage written to your window and you may even have to quit that window. In the following example, the types of all the files in the current directory are displayed when you use the asterisk wild card:

```
dugout% file *
compressed.Z:       data
document.doc:       Frame Maker document
doorbell.au:        audio data: 8-bit u-law, mono, 8000 Hz
namelist:           ascii text
memo:               ELF 32-bit MSB executable SPARC Version 1, dynamically
linked, not stripped
memo.c:             c program text
memo.o:             ELF 32-bit MSB relocatable SPARC Version 1
olitbook:           directory
sort.c:             c program text
sortit.c:           c program text
start_license:      commands text
dugout%
```

As you can see, there are many different file types. The file program uses the file name, the permissions, and the contents of the file to determine its type. By looking at the output of the file command, you can easily determine that you don't want to attempt to use the cat command on the memo or compressed.Z files, since one is an executable and the other is data (which indicates that it contains characters other than ASCII characters).

By default, the file command follows symbolic links. This means that the file type displayed for a symbolic link is the file type of the file to which the link points. You can use the -h option if you do not want to follow symbolic links. For example, if you execute the file command as shown previously, but this time use the -h option, you will see one difference:

```
dugout% file -h *
compressed.Z:     data
document.doc:     Frame Maker document
doorbell.au       audio data: 8-bit u-law, mono, 8000 Hz
namelist:         ascii text
memo:             ELF 32-bit MSB executable SPARC Version 1, dynamically
linked, not stripped
memo.c:           c program text
memo.o:           ELF 32-bit MSB relocatable SPARC Version 1
memo1:            symbolic link to memo
olitbook:         directory
sort.c:           c program text
sortit.c:         symbolic link to sort.c
start_license:    commands text
dugout%
```

Notice that the sortit.c file that was previously listed as c program text is now listed as a symbolic link to sort.c.

The file command is often helpful when you are trying to locate a file whose name you can't recall. Perhaps you created a FrameMaker document in a directory with many other files but you can't remember the name you gave the file. You could use the file command to list the file types of all of the files in the directory and search for FrameMaker document files.

The wc Command

The wc command counts the number of characters, words, and lines in a file.

```
dugout% wc memo.c
     166      529     4573 memo.c
dugout%
```

The output is rather cryptic; it simply prints the number of lines, words, and characters, followed by the file name. If you specify more than one file name on the command line, wc lists the information for each file along with a total. So, if you've been writing some C programs and your boss asks you how many lines of code you have written, you can enter the following command and quickly have the answer:

```
dugout% wc *.c
       8        8       98 main.c
     166      529     4573 memo.c
       5       14       98 sort.c
       5       14       98 sortit.c
     184      565     4867 total
dugout%
```

You can also specify the following three options to customize the output of the wc command:

-l	Count lines only
-w	Count words only
-c	Count characters only

For example, if you want to limit the output to display only the number of lines in a file, use the -l option:

```
dugout% wc -l *.c
       8 main.c
     166 memo.c
       5 sort.c
       5 sortit.c
```

```
     184 total
dugout%
```

You can also combine options. For example, to display only the number of words and characters in the memo.c program, use the following command:

```
dugout% wc -wc memo.c
     529    4573 memo.c
dugout%
```

The diff Command

The diff command displays the line-by-line differences between two text files. It is most useful when the two files being compared are fairly similar. You might use diff if you had made a copy of a file and then made some minor changes to the copy. You could compare the original to the file with the changes. Each line that contains differences, or newly added or deleted lines, is displayed in the output.

To demonstrate how to use diff, let's reuse one of the files we looked at in the previous chapter: README. The README file's contents are shown here:

```
This directory is Sally's home directory.
Among other things it contains:

          Mail
          README
          sort.c
```

Now let's create another file, named README2, that is similar to README but has some slight differences. The README2 file's contents are shown here:

```
This directory is Betty's home directory.
Among other things it contains:

          Mail
          README2
          sort.c
          memo.c
```

The two files are similar but not identical. Let's use the diff command to check the exact differences:

```
dugout% diff README README2
1c1
```

```
< This directory is Sally's home directory.
---
> This directory is Betty's home directory.
5c5
<        README
---
>        README2
6a7
>        memo.c
```

Each line that is different or new is included in the diff output along with some other information. Lines that are identical in both files are not displayed. Each line displayed from either file includes a right- or left-angle bracket at the beginning of the line (> or <). Lines that begin with a left-angle bracket are from the first file listed on the command line. Lines that begin with a right-angle bracket are from the second file listed on the command line. This is easy to remember if you think of the angle brackets as pointers. The left-angle bracket points to the left, reminding you that that line is from the file farthest to the left on the command line. The opposite is true of the right-angle bracket.

The other information in the output describes exactly which lines in the first file would have to be changed to produce the corresponding line in the second file. For example, the line that begins 1c1 indicates that the first line (which includes Sally's home directory) would have to be changed to produce line one from the second file. This information can be used to create scripts that will modify one file to match the contents of the other. In most cases it is enough to be able to just examine the difference from the diff output.

The diff command includes many options for some sophisticated processing. For a complete description see the diff man page.

Searching a File

The grep ("globally find regular expressions and print") command searches a file or files for a string of characters that you specify. You can also use wild cards to specify the search string (also called a *regular expression*). The simplest use of grep requires that you specify a pattern (a string of characters) and the file or files in which to search. The first argument to grep is the pattern; the next arguments (one or more) are the names of the files to search in.

To demonstrate its use, we will use grep on two files named file1 and file2. Each file contains a list of names, as shown here:

file1	**file2**
Patricia Team	Jean Bandforth
Harold Groundhog	John Culver
Bradley McMan	Wendy Clark
Glen Williams	Renee Doornob
John Wilbur	Phillip Jones
Louise Roundtable	Kathleen McMannis
Stephen Philpot	Allister Winthrop
Rebecca Flint	Rebecca Flint
Jim Barclay	Clark Lowrey
John Sunday	Ronald Dilbert
Jeffrey Crossfire	Brian Garth

grep Basics

Let's start with a simple example. To search for John in file1, enter the grep command with the following arguments:

```
dugout% grep John file1
John Wilbur
John Sunday
dugout%
```

Each line of file1 containing the pattern John is displayed. (Note that sometimes the word *grep* is used as a verb. For example, to describe the previous search you might say, "grep for John in file1.")

If you search for a pattern that is not found within the file, no output is given, as in this example:

```
dugout% grep Priscilla file1
dugout%
```

If you want to search for a pattern in multiple files, list each file on the command line. With multiple files listed, grep includes the names of the file in which the line containing the pattern was found. Without this information you would not be able to tell which file contained the pattern you specified.

As you can see from the following example, the name of the file in which the pattern was found precedes each line of output:

```
dugout% grep John file1 file2
file1:John Wilbur
file1:John Sunday
file2:John Culver
dugout%
```

If you want to search for a pattern that includes a space (or tab), you must enclose the pattern in quotation marks. Otherwise, grep will interpret the latter part of the search pattern as a file name, as shown:

```
dugout% grep 'John C' file1 file2
file2:John Culver
dugout%
```

If you do not enclose the pattern in quotation marks, grep tries to search for the pattern John in three files: C, file1, and file2—which, of course, is not your intention.

```
dugout% grep John C file1 file2
grep: can't open C
file1:John Wilbur
file1:John Sunday
file2:John Culver
dugout%
```

grep Options

The grep command supports several options that control the way it searches and the way it displays the search results. In this section, we'll look at five grep options. See the grep man page for details on other options for this command.

Option	Description
-v	Reverse search. All lines that do not match the pattern are displayed.
-i	Ignore case. The pattern is matched regardless of the case of the characters.
-l	File name. The name of the file in which the match was found is displayed rather than the line itself.
-n	Line number. The line number is included with the output.
-w	Word match. The pattern must match an entire word.

Let's look at an example of each of these options to better understand them.

The -v option is useful when you want to find all lines that do not match the pattern you specify. For example, to find all names in file1 that do not include a J, use the following command:

```
dugout% grep -v J file1
Patricia Team
Harold Groundhog
Bradley McMan
Glen Williams
Louise Roundtable
Stephen Philpot
Rebecca Flint
dugout%
```

By default, pattern matching is case sensitive. The -i option indicates that the pattern search should be case insensitive. For example, to search file1 for jeff (regardless of case), use the following command:

```
dugout% grep -i jeff file1
Jeffrey Crossfire
dugout%
```

If you want to know only the name of a file that contains the specified pattern, use the -l option. This option is often useful when you are searching through a large number of files. You might use the asterisk wild card to match all the files in the directory, along with the -l option. Only the files that included the pattern will be displayed, as in the following example:

```
dugout% grep -l Kathleen *
file2
dugout%
```

If you want to know the line number of the line containing the pattern, use the -n option, as in this example:

```
dugout% grep -n John file1 file2
file1:5:John Wilbur
file1:10:John Sunday
file2:2:John Culver
dugout%
```

You can specify that the pattern must match an entire word by using the -w option. For example, to search for Bradley McMan but not Kathleen McMannis, you would specify the -w option with a pattern of McMan, as shown here:

```
dugout% grep -w McMan file1 file2
file1:Bradley McMan
dugout%
```

grep Pattern Matching

There are several special characters that grep recognizes for special pattern matching (character patterns are sometimes called *regular expressions*). These are similar to the wild cards you learned about in the previous chapter. When you use any of these characters in a pattern, it is a good idea to enclose the pattern in single quotation marks. This ensures that the characters are delivered to grep for interpretation rather than being expanded by the shell.

The most common pattern-matching characters are as follows:

Character	Description
^	Searches from the beginning of the line
$	Searches from the end of the line
.	Matches exactly one character
*	Matches zero or more occurrences of the previous character
[ ]	Matches any one of the characters enclosed in the brackets

To search for a pattern that begins a line, use ^. For example, to search for all lines that begin with J, use the following command:

```
dugout% grep '^J' file1 file2
file1:John Wilbur
file1:Jim Barclay
file1:John Sunday
file1:Jeffrey Crossfire
file2:Jean Bandforth
file2:John Culver
dugout%
```

To search for a pattern that ends a line, use $. For example, to search for the pattern Clark at the end of the line, use the following command:

```
dugout% grep 'Clark$' file1 file2
file2:Wendy Clark
dugout%
```

The dot (.) matches exactly one character. (This is similar to the ? character used as a file name wild card.) For example, you could search for a J and an n separated by any two characters, using the following command:

```
dugout% grep 'J..n' file2
Jean Bandforth
John Culver
dugout%
```

The asterisk is used in combination with another character (unlike the asterisk wild card used by the shell). The asterisk matches zero or more occurrences of the preceding character. You can use the dot with the asterisk to match any number of characters. For example, to find all the names of people who have a first name that begins with J and a last name that begins with B, use the following command:

```
dugout% grep 'J.*B' file1 file2
file1:Jim Barclay
file2:Jean Bandforth
dugout%
```

As you can see, both names displayed satisfy the requirement. The .* matched "im " in one case and "ean " in the other.

The square brackets are used to specify one or more characters, any one of which matches one character. For example, to display all names that begin with a B, C, or P, use the following command:

```
dugout% grep '^[BCP]' file1 file2
file1:Patricia Team
file1:Bradley McMan
file2:Phillip Jones
file2:Clark Lowrey
file2:Brian Garth
dugout%
```

Sorting File Contents

The sort command sorts the lines of a file. Sort does not alter the contents of the file specified; it simply reads the file, sorts it, and displays the sorted result. Sorting can be done alphabetically or numerically.

Let's start with a simple example. To sort file1, enter the command, as shown:

```
dugout% sort file1
Bradley McMan
Glen Williams
Harold Groundhog
Jeffrey Crossfire
Jim Barclay
John Sunday
John Wilbur
Louise Roundtable
Patricia Team
Rebecca Flint
Stephen Philpot
dugout%
```

By default, the file is sorted alphabetically. If you have a file containing numbers, you may want to sort it numerically. We'll discuss this feature shortly.

You can provide multiple files for the sort command to sort. All the files are merged first and then sorted:

```
dugout% sort file1 file2
Allister Winthrop
Bradley McMan
Brian Garth
Clark Lowrey
Glen Williams
Harold Groundhog
Jean Bandforth
Jeffrey Crossfire
Jim Barclay
John Culver
John Sunday
John Wilbur
Kathleen McMannis
Louise Roundtable
Patricia Team
Phillip Jones
Rebecca Flint
Rebecca Flint
```

```
Renee Doornob
Ronald Dilbert
Stephen Philpot
Wendy Clark
dugout%
```

It is often preferable to sort from some point other than the beginning of a line. For example, the contents of file1 and file2 are the first and last names of some random people. You may want to sort based on the last name of the person rather than the first name. You can instruct the sort command to skip a number of fields of each line by using the + option followed by a number. Fields are separated by spaces. To skip the first field (the first name), you specify the +1 option, as shown here:

```
dugout% sort +1 file1 file2
Jean Bandforth
Jim Barclay
Wendy Clark
Jeffrey Crossfire
John Culver
Ronald Dilbert
Renee Doornob
Rebecca Flint
Rebecca Flint
Brian Garth
Harold Groundhog
Phillip Jones
Clark Lowrey
Bradley McMan
Kathleen McMannis
Stephen Philpot
Louise Roundtable
John Sunday
Patricia Team
John Wilbur
Glen Williams
Allister Winthrop
dugout%
```

You can use this option to skip any number of fields. If, for example, the file you are sorting has eight fields, you could start the sort on the fourth field by using the +3 option (you are skipping three fields and starting the sort on the fourth).

Sometimes, the files sorted by the sort command have identical lines. When this occurs, both identical lines are included in the output. In the previous two examples, Rebecca Flint's name showed up twice because it was found once in file1 and once in file2. If you use the -u option, sort removes identical adjacent lines, as you can see from this example:

```
dugout% sort -u +1 file1 file2
Jean Bandforth
Jim Barclay
Wendy Clark
Jeffrey Crossfire
John Culver
Ronald Dilbert
Renee Doornob
Rebecca Flint
Brian Garth
Harold Groundhog
Phillip Jones
Clark Lowrey
Bradley McMan
Kathleen McMannis
Stephen Philpot
Louise Roundtable
John Sunday
Patricia Team
John Wilbur
Glen Williams
Allister Winthrop
dugout%
```

Sort is also useful when you are dealing with numeric data. For example, suppose you have a file named filesize that contains the size of the files in your directory, as shown here:

filesize

```
2       README
2       README2
2       document.doc
36      doorbell.au
2       mailfile
2       main.c
18      memo
10      memo.c
```

```
102     memo.o
2       memo1
78      snapshot.rs
2       sort.c
2       sortit.c
6       source
2       start_license
```

By default, the sort command will sort this file alphabetically. To sort the file numerically, use the -n option:

```
dugout% sort -n filesize
2          README
2          README2
2          document.doc
2          mailfile
2          main.c
2          memo1
2          sort.c
2          sortit.c
2          start_license
6          source
10         memo.c
18         memo
36         doorbell.au
78         snapshot.rs
102        memo.o
dugout%
```

If you want to reverse the order of the sort so that the largest files are listed first, use the -r option as well as -n:

```
dugout% sort -nr filesize
102       memo.o
78        snapshot.rs
36        doorbell.au
18        memo
10        memo.c
6         source
2         start_license
2         sortit.c
2         sort.c
2         memo1
2         main.c
2         mailfile
```

```
2         document.doc
2         README2
2         README
dugout%
```

The sort command has many other options for customizing the way that a sort is handled. Refer to the sort man page for complete details.

Finding a File

The find command locates a file in a directory hierarchy. You might want to find all files named *core* or all files that are older than seven days. Find gives you the ability to perform these kinds of searches. When find locates a file (according to your specification), the file name can simply be displayed, or you can specify a command to execute with that file as an argument.

The find command is similar to the find feature that is built into the File Manager (see Chapter 4). Using the Find pop-up window, you can specify a file for which to search (including a wild card). You can also specify an owner, a time stamp, a file type, and a search string. The File Manager uses the information provided on the Find pop-up window to construct a find command, and then executes the command to locate the files specified.

Using the find command from the command line gives you the same capabilities as the Find pop-up window. You actually have more control when using find from the command line because other options are available that cannot be accessed from the Find pop-up window.

The general format of the find command is shown here:

```
find directory... option... action
```

The find command accepts one or more directories from which it begins its search. The directory argument (or arguments) is identical to the field on the Find pop-up, labeled Find files, in and below folder. (Of course, on the Find pop-up you can specify only one directory.) The options available with find correspond to the other fields on the Find pop-up, such as Filename and Owner. For example, to specify the name of a file to find, use the -name option, followed by the file name. To search for a file named core, starting at the current directory, use the following command:

```
dugout% find . -name core -print
./core
./src/core
dugout%
```

In this example, the dot (.) is the directory from which you want to begin the search. There is one option (-name) and one action (-print). The -print action is the most common and the simplest action. It means that when a file is found that matches the options specified, it will be listed (displayed on the screen). If you want to use a wild card in the file name, be sure to enclose it in quotation marks so that it will not be expanded by the shell. The following example finds all files that end with .c, starting at the current directory:

```
dugout% find . -name '*.c' -print
./main.c
./sort.c
./sortit.c
./memo.c
dugout%
```

If you do not specify an option, all files in the hierarchy of the directories specified are included. For example, the following command displays all the files in the directory hierarchy /usr:

```
dugout% find /usr -print
```

The most common find options are as follows:

Option	Description
-name *pattern*	Finds files whose name matches *pattern*
-size *n*	Finds files whose size equals *n* blocks
-mtime *n*	Finds files modified *n* days ago
-mtime +*n*	Finds files modified more than *n* days ago
-mtime -*n*	Finds files modified less than *n* days ago
-type *c*	Finds files of type *c*. Valid values for *c* are as follows: b block device c character device d directory l symbolic link f regular file
-links *n*	Finds files with *n* links
-user *name*	Finds files owned by user *name*
-group *name*	Finds files owned by group *name*

Using these options, you can search for files whose names end with .h, that are owned by sally, and that have been modified in the last four days. You use the following command:

```
dugout% find . -name '*.h' -user sally -mtime -4 -print
```

When multiple options are included, each option must be satisfied for the file to be found. If you want the file to be displayed when one or more of the options are satisfied, separate the options with a -o. The -o indicates an OR operation: either the first option is satisfied or the second option is satisfied. The following command will display all files that end with .h or that are owned by sally:

```
dugout% find . -name '*.h' -o -user sally -print
```

In addition to the -print action, there are two other common actions: -ls and -exec. The -ls action also displays the files found but in a format similar to that of the ls -l command. This action gives you complete information about the file, such as permissions, links, owner, group, size, and so forth.

The -exec action lets you specify a command that should be invoked. For example, you may want to use grep to search for files that contain a particular pattern. To find files that contain the pattern "float," use the following command:

```
dugout% find . -exec grep -l float {} \;
./sort.c
dugout%
```

The grep command is executed on each file in the hierarchy of the directory specified (the current directory in this case) and that satisfies the options specified. The curly braces are a special argument to the find command. They are replaced by each file name. The backslash semicolon is also a special character that find requires to delimit the end of the command following the -exec action.

You can combine options and actions in many ways. Let's look at a few examples. The following command displays all directories beginning at /usr/openwin:

```
dugout% find /usr/openwin -type d -print
```

The next example removes all files named *.o that are more than three days old, starting at the current directory:

```
dugout% find . -type f -name '*.o' -mtime +3 -exec rm -f {} \;
```

The next example finds all files with a .au suffix in the /usr/demo/SOUND directory and current directory, prints each file name, and plays the file with the audioplay command:

```
dugout% find /usr/demo/SOUND . -name '*.au' -print -exec audioplay {} \;
```

Performing Print Operations

In Chapter 8 you learned how to use the Print Tool. The basic operations that the Print Tool provides are printing files, checking the queue, and deleting print jobs from the queue. In this section you will learn how to perform the same operations from the command line by using the lp, lpstat, and cancel commands.

Printing a File

You print a file by using the lp command, which has the following format:

```
lp [options] file ...
```

The simplest usage of lp is to provide a single command-line argument that is the name of the file you want to print, as in this example:

```
dugout% lp file1
request id is SPARCprinter-1191 (1 file(s))
dugout&
```

The lp command displays a one-line response, indicating that one file has been sent to the printer queue, and it gives a request id of SPARCprinter-1191. The request id is made up of the name of the printer to which the file has been spooled, followed by a number representing the printer job. This is the same number that the Print Tool displays in its scrolling list in the Job column (see Figure 8.5). The request id is used when you want to remove a print job from the queue, as you will see shortly.

You are likely to have access to different printers connected to various machines on your network. One of these printers is your system default printer. By default, files are printed to the default printer when you use the lp command. In the preceding example, SPARCprinter was the default printer. To determine what printers are available to you, use the lpstat -v command, as shown in the following example:

```
dugout% lpstat -v
system for SPARCprinter: vivids
device for HandsOn: /dev/lp
system for fuji: vivids
dugout%
```

To determine which printer is the default printer, use the lpstat -d command, as follows:

```
dugout% lpstat -d
system default destination: SPARCprinter
dugout%
```

If you want to print to a printer other than your system default, use the -d option. For example, to print file1 and file2 to fuji, use the following command:

```
dugout% lp -d fuji file1 file2
request id is fuji-1194 (2 file(s))
dugout%
```

You can also specify the number of copies of the file that you want printed by using the -n option. In the following example, six copies of file1 and file2 are being sent to the fuji printer queue:

```
dugout% lp -d fuji -n 6 file1 file2
request id is fuji-1195 (2 file(s))
dugout%
```

Checking the Print Queue

To check the print queue, use the lpstat command. All the print jobs that you have submitted are listed:

```
dugout% lpstat
SPARCprinter-1190     pew      466    Mar 24 22:17
SPARCprinter-1191     pew      161    Mar 25 08:36
SPARCprinter-1192     pew      161    Mar 25 08:37
SPARCprinter-1193     pew      318    Mar 25 08:38
fuji-1194             pew      318    Mar 25 09:38
fuji-1195             pew      318    Mar 25 09:41
dugout%
```

The lpstat output displays the request id, the owner, the size of the print job, and the date and time the print job was submitted. If you want to see all the print jobs in the queue (not just your own), use the lpstat all command:

```
dugout% lpstat all
SPARCprinter-1190     pew      466    Mar 24 22:17
SPARCprinter-1191     pew      161    Mar 25 08:36
SPARCprinter-1192     pew      161    Mar 25 08:37
SPARCprinter-1193     pew      318    Mar 25 08:38
fuji-1194             pew      318    Mar 25 09:38
```

```
fuji-1195                pew        318   Mar 25 Ø9:41
fuji-1196                sally      466   Mar 25 Ø9:44
dugout%
```

You can also restrict the output of lpstat to just the entries for one printer or just a particular user. To display the entries in the fuji printer only, include fuji on the lpstat command line:

```
dugout% lpstat fuji
fuji-1194                pew        318   Mar 25 Ø9:38
fuji-1195                pew        318   Mar 25 Ø9:41
fuji-1196                sally      466   Mar 25 Ø9:44
dugout%
```

To display all the entries for user sally, use only the -u option:

```
dugout% lpstat -u sally
fuji-1196                sally      466   Mar 25 Ø9:44
dugout%
```

Canceling a Print Job

To remove a print job from the queue, use the cancel command, followed by the request id. Of course, you can cancel the job only if it has not yet been printed.

```
dugout% cancel SPARCprinter-119Ø
request "SPARCprinter-119Ø" cancelled
dugout%
```

You can also specify a user name by using the -u option. All print jobs entered by that user are then removed from the queue, as shown here:

```
dugout% cancel -u pew
request "SPARCprinter-1191" cancelled
request "SPARCprinter-1192" cancelled
request "SPARCprinter-1193" cancelled
request "fuji-1194" cancelled
request "fuji-1195" cancelled
dugout%
```

Sending and Receiving Mail from the Command Line

You will probably use the Mail Tool most often to read your mail. It is important, however, to know how to read mail from the command line, because if you are logged in from home or from a remote location, you may not be able to run the Mail Tool. To read mail from the command line, you use the mailx command.

It is important to not have two or more mail programs running simultaneously. If you are currently running the Mail Tool, you should quit that program before using mailx. If you run both, you can corrupt your mail file.

The mailx program is a full-featured mail utility. Nearly every feature available from the Mail Tool is available also from mailx. (Of course, you can't perform a drag and drop or have attachments with mailx.) It would be easy to devote an entire chapter to all the details of mailx, but since Mail Tool is probably going to be your primary mail program, only the basics of mailx are covered here. If you need additional information, see the mailx man page.

Reading Mail

To read your mail, simply enter the mailx command, as shown in this example:

```
dugout% mailx
mailx version 5.0 Tue Nov  3 07:55:52 PST 1992  Type ? for help.
"/var/mail/pew": 7 messages 7 new
>N  1 ohno@japan        Thu Jun 25 05:55  101/3149  Re:  SunWorld Expo
 N  2 mani@marge        Thu Jun 25 12:06   60/1442  Glyph support in Scrol
 N  3 dweng@adidas      Wed Jul 29 16:03  606/15247 Updated Testing Status
 N  4 hiroko@koro       Thu Jul 30 11:54   50/1251  Re: testing different
 N  5 kconway@gerard    Fri Oct 16 10:05  106/3470  License File
 N  6 sewer@cma         Mon Nov 23 12:02   29/911   Popups and Warping
 N  7 alicek@mozart     Tue Dec 29 23:02   16/274   Adios Amigo
?
```

The information on the first two lines includes the version number and creation date of mailx, how to get help, the mail file being read (your in-box), and the number of new messages since the last time you read your mail. This information is followed by the headers of the mail messages. Notice that the format of the headers is nearly identical to that of the headers displayed in the Mail Tool (see Figure 6.2). The last line displays a question mark, which is the mailx prompt.

The first column of each header contains a single character that represents the status of the message. The characters and their corresponding meanings are listed here:

Character	Meaning
N	A new mail message that has not been read
R	A mail message that has been read

Character	Meaning
O	An old message that has been read but is held in the in-box
U	An old message that is unread
S	A saved message
H	A message to be held in the in-box

One of the mail headers has a right-angle bracket (>) at the beginning of the line. This bracket indicates the current message. If you enter p (print) at the prompt and press Return (or just press Return), the current message is displayed, as in the following example:

```
? p
Message  1:
From ohno@japan Thu Jun 25 05:55:24 1992
To: pew@vivids.com
Subject: Re:  SunWorld Expo

John,

Thank you for responding.
    .
    .
    .
<Other lines of the message deleted>
?
```

To redisplay the header, enter h at the mail prompt. Notice that message 1 is marked as read:

```
? h
>R  1 ohno@japan        Thu Jun 25 05:55  101/3149  Re:  SunWorld Expo
 N  2 mani@marge        Thu Jun 25 12:06   60/1442  Glyph support in Scrol
 N  3 dweng@adidas      Wed Jul 29 16:03  606/15247 Updated Testing Status
 N  4 hiroko@koro       Thu Jul 30 11:54   50/1251  Re: testing different
 N  5 kconway@gerard    Fri Oct 16 10:05  106/3470  License File
 N  6 sewer@cma         Mon Nov 23 12:02   29/911   Popups and Warping
 N  7 alicek@mozart     Tue Dec 29 23:02   16/274   Adios Amigo
?
```

To read the next message enter n at the mail prompt. The next mail message is displayed:

```
? n
Message  2:
From mani@marge Thu Jun 25 12:06 PDT 1992
To: pew@vivids
Subject: Glyph support in ScrollingList

ScrollingLists now support glyphs in items. Code has been
checked into OW-3.0 CTE, Mars & Amber source trees.
    .
    .
    .
<Other lines of the message deleted>
?
```

Another way to display a mail message is to enter p, followed by the message number, as shown here:

```
? p 7
Message  7:
From alicek@mozart Tue Dec 29 23:02:08 1992
To: pew@vivids
Subject: Adios Amigo

John,

I just wanted to say goodbye.
Give me a call sometime.

Alice

?
```

When you display a message, the entire text is displayed without pagination. If it is a long message, some or most of it may be scrolled off the screen or window before you can read it. You can avoid this problem by setting the crt variable at the mailx prompt:

```
? set crt
```

Rather than enter this command each time you run mailx, you may want to add it to your .mailrc file in your home directory. The .mailrc file also contains the customization features you set from the Mail Tool Properties window.

With crt set, only one page of the message is displayed at a time. By default, the mailx program uses the pg command to display the message text a page at a time. The pg command is similar to the more command. One page of text is displayed at a time. A colon (:) prompt appears at the end of each page. Press Return to display the next page. If you prefer to use the more command, you can set the PAGER environment variable to more, as shown here. Then mailx will use more instead of pg.

```
dugout% setenv PAGER more
```

After reading a message, you will probably want to either delete it or save it to a file or a mail folder. Another option is to leave the file in your default mail folder (the in-box). To delete a message, enter d at the mail prompt. You can combine the delete and print functions by entering dp to delete the current message and print the next one. If you had just read message 1, entering dp would delete message 1 and print message 2, as shown here:

```
? dp
Message  2:
From mani@marge Thu Jun 25 12:06 PDT 1992
To: pew@vivids
Subject: Glyph support in ScrollingList

ScrollingLists now support glyphs in items. Code has been
checked into OW-3.0 CTE, Mars & Amber source trees.
    .
    .
    .
<Other lines of the message deleted>
?
```

You can also delete selected messages by supplying their message numbers. For example, to delete messages 2, 4, 5, and 6 enter d 2 4-6 at the mail prompt. After you have deleted messages 2, 4, 5, and 6, you can display the headers of the remaining messages by entering **h** at the mail prompt as shown here:

```
? d 2 4-6
? h
 N  1 ohno@japan        Thu Jun 25 05:55  101/3149  Re:  SunWorld Expo
 N  3 dweng@adidas      Wed Jul 29 16:03  606/15247 Updated Testing Status
>N  7 alicek@mozart     Tue Dec 29 23:02   16/274   Adios Amigo
?
```

If you want to save a mail message, enter s at the mail prompt, followed by the name of the file in which you want to store the message. The current mail message is then stored to the specified file.

```
? s sunworld
"sunworld" [New file] 102/3159
?
```

You can also include a message argument when you save a message. This lets you select one or more messages and save them all to a file. For example, to save messages 3 through 5 to a file named keep, enter the following:

```
? s 3-5 keep
"keep" [New file] 762/19968
?
```

You can also save a message to a folder (as you did with the Mail Tool). At the mail prompt, enter s, followed by a plus sign and the name of the folder. The mailx command uses folders exactly the same way as Mail Tool. Mail folders are stored in the mail file directory, specified on the Mail File Properties window from Mail Tool.

```
? s +Xhibition
"/export/home/pew/Mail/Xhibition" [Appended] 101/3149
?
```

You can use one of two commands to exit the mailx program: x or q. The x command exits mailx without saving any of the changes you have made. The q command quits mailx and saves your changes. Messages that you have read and not deleted are automatically removed from your in-box and moved to a file in your home directory, named mbox (sometimes called your mailbox). Files that you have not read remain in your in-box and are marked unread the next time you run mailx. If you have saved a message, it is deleted from your in-box when you quit mailx.

After you have read a message, you may want to keep it in your in-box rather than move it to your mailbox. You can do this with the hold command, as shown here:

```
? hold
? h
 R  1 ohno@japan        Thu Jun 25 05:55  101/3149  Re:  SunWorld Expo
>H  2 mani@marge        Thu Jun 25 12:06   60/1442  Glyph support in Scrol
 N  3 dweng@adidas      Wed Jul 29 16:03  606/15247 Updated Testing Status
 N  4 hiroko@koro       Thu Jul 30 11:54   50/1251  Re: testing different
 N  5 kconway@gerard    Fri Oct 16 10:05  106/3470  License File
 N  6 sewer@cma         Mon Nov 23 12:02   29/911   Popups and Warping
 N  7 alicek@mozart     Tue Dec 29 23:02   16/274   Adios Amigo
? q
```

The header for this message is then marked with an H to indicate that it is being held in the in-box. After you have quit mailx (with q) and have started it again, the message you held is marked with an O, which indicates that it is an "old" message—one that has been read.

To load another mail file or folder into mailx, use the folder command. For example, to load the Xhibition folder, you enter the following command:

```
? folder +Xhibition
Held 7 messages in /var/mail/pew
"+Xhibition": 2 messages 1 unread
?
```

You can get help with mailx commands by entering a question mark at the mail prompt. As you can see from the following listing, there are many mailx commands; we have discussed only a few of them in this section.

```
? ?
                mailx commands

alias,group user ...          declare alias for user names
alternates user               declare alternate names for your login
cd,chdir [directory]          chdir to directory or home if none given
!command                      shell escape
copy [msglist] file           save messages to file without marking as saved
delete [msglist]              delete messages
discard,ignore header         discard header field when printing message
dp,dt [msglist]               delete messages and type next message
echo string                   print the string
edit [msglist]                edit messages
folder,file filename          change mailboxes to filename
folders                       list files in directory of current folder
followup [message]            reply to message and save copy
Followup [msglist]            reply to messages and save copy
from [msglist]                give header lines of messages
header [message]              print page of active message headers
help,?                        print this help message
hold,preserve [msglist]       hold messages in mailbox
inc                           incorporate new messages into current session
list                          list all commands (no explanations)
mail user                     mail to specific user
Mail                          mail to specific user, saving copy
mbox [msglist]                messages will go to mbox when quitting
next [message]                goto and type next message
pipe,| [msglist] shell-cmd    pipe the messages to the shell command
print,type [msglist]          print messages
Print,Type [msglist]          print messages with all headers
quit                          quit, preserving unread messages
reply,respond [message]       reply to the author and recipients of the msg
Reply,Respond [msglist]       reply to authors of the messages
save [msglist] file           save (appending) messages to file
```

```
Save [msglist]               save messages to file named after author
set variable[=value]         set variable to value
size [msglist]               print size of messages
source file                  read commands from file
top [msglist]                print top 5 lines of messages
touch [msglist]              force the messages to be saved when quitting
undelete [msglist]           restore deleted messages
undiscard,unignore header    add header field back to list printed
unread,new [msglist]         mark messages unread
version                      print version
visual [msglist]             edit list with $VISUAL editor
write [msglist] file         write messages without headers
xit,exit                     quit, preserving all messages
z [+/-]                      display next [last] page of 10 headers

[msglist] is optional and specifies messages by number, author, subject or
type.  The default is the current message.
?
```

Composing and Sending Mail

You can send mail either at the shell prompt or from within mailx at the mail prompt. Let's start by looking at the way you enter mail at the shell prompt. To begin, enter the mailx command, followed by the user name or names of the persons to whom you want to send the message. Enter the subject at the prompt, and then enter the body of the message. When you have completed your message, enter a dot (.) at the beginning of the next line and press Return (or press Control-D). Here is an example:

```
dugout% mailx sally
Subject: lunch
Are you available for lunch today?

John
.
EOT
dugout%
```

The dot at the end of the mail message tells mailx to deliver your message; it is not included in the message. The mailx program prints "EOT," which stands for "end of transmission."

You can send exactly the same message from within mailx at the mail prompt. Use the mail command, as shown in this example:

```
? mail sally
Subject: lunch
Are you available for lunch today?
```

```
John
.
EOT
?
```

Notice that in neither case were you prompted for the cc (carbon copy) recipients. Mailx does support cc, but you are not prompted for cc recipients by default. To have mailx prompt you for cc recipients, set the askcc variable:

```
? set askcc
```

You may want to put this variable setting into your .mailrc along with set crt. Once askcc is set, you will be prompted for cc recipients, as shown here:

```
dugout% mailx sally
Subject: lunch
Cc: james
Are you available for lunch today?

John
.
EOT
dugout%
```

The most convenient time to send mail from within mailx is when you are replying to a message you have just received. You can use the r or R command to reply to a message. Either of these commands automatically sets the To and Subject fields of the message for you. When you use the r command, the reply message is sent only to the original sender. When you use the R command, the reply is sent to the original sender and to every user to whom the message was originally sent either from the To line or the Cc line. For example, here is a message sent from dweng to the testers alias:

```
? p
Message  3:
From dweng@adidas Wed Jul 29 16:03:57 1992
To: testers@wind
Subject: Updated Testing Status

Please review the 4/93 OWN RFC.
?
```

If you use the r command, only dweng will receive the reply, as shown here:

```
? r
To: dweng@adidas
```

```
Subject: Re: Updated Testing Status
<Enter message here>
```

If you use the R command, the reply is sent to both dweng and testers, as shown here:

```
? R
To: dweng@adidas, testers@wind
Subject: Re: Updated Testing Status
<Enter message here>
```

While you are entering your message you are under the control of the mailx program. You are not in any editor such as the Text Editor or vi. This means that you need to know some special commands provided by mailx that help you control the way you create your message. Each of these commands begins with a tilde (~) and is entered as you compose your mail message. The tilde must be the first character of the line for the function to operate. If you want to insert a tilde into your mail message as the first character of a line, you use two consecutive tildes.

Let's look at a few of the tilde commands. To display the message entered thus far, enter ~p:

```
dugout% mailx sally
Subject: lunch
Are you available for lunch today?

John
~p
-------
Message contains:
To: sally
Subject: lunch

Are you available for lunch today?

John

.
EOT
dugout%
```

You can use this command before delivering your message, to make sure the message contains exactly what you intended. Or, you might use ~p when you have entered a long message and you want to reread it from the beginning.

If you want to reenter the header information (To, Subject, Cc, Bcc), use the ~h command. In the following example a user is added to the To field and the subject is expanded. You are prompted for each field, as shown here:

```
dugout% mailx sally
Subject: lunch
Are you available for lunch today?
~h
To: sally, james
Cc: <Return>
Bcc: <Return>
Subject: lunch at Milligan's
(continue)
<Enter additional text here>
```

While you are composing a mail message you may want to include a file or another mail message. You can include a file by using the ~r command. You can include a mail message (from the current mail file) with the ~f command. You can use the ~f command only if you are composing a message from within mailx. If you use ~f without an argument, the current message will be included. In the following example the /etc/passwd file and message 5 are being included:

```
? mail sally
Subject: Password File
Here is the password file from my system:
~r /etc/passwd
"/etc/passwd" 17/703
<Enter additional text here>
Here is the license file I received today.
~f 5
Interpolating: 5
(continue)
<Enter additional text here>
```

If you use the ~m command, you can include a mail message in the message you are composing and have each line preceded by a right-angle bracket (>). This is exactly the same thing you did in the Mail Tool when you used the Include Indented function (see Chapter 6). In the following example we'll use ~m to include the current message (the one to which we're replying), and then use ~p to display the entire message (including the included, indented message).

```
? r
To: alicek@mozart
Subject: Re: Adios Amigo
```

```
It's been nice knowing you too!

John
~m
Interpolating: 7
(continue)
~p
-------
Message contains:
To: alicek@mozart
Subject: Re: Adios Amigo

It's been nice knowing you too!

John
> From alicek@mozart Tue Dec 29 23:02:08 1992
> To: pew@dugout
> Subject: Adios Amigo
>
> John,
>
> I just wanted to say goodbye.
> Give me a call sometime.
>
> Alice
(continue)
.
EOT
?
```

Since mailx is not an editor, you have no way of going back to a previous line to correct an error. Once you have pressed Return, you cannot directly edit that line. You can, however, invoke an editor like vi (sorry, but you can't invoke the Text Editor from within mailx). You'll learn all about vi in the next chapter. For now, just be aware that if you want to edit the message that you're composing, you must enter ~v at the beginning of the line. When you exit vi, you are put back into mailx, and all of the changes or additions you made while editing with vi are now included in the mail message. You can then either add more text or deliver the message.

If you decide not to complete a mail message, enter ~q. This quits the composition. You can also enter Control-C twice. After entering the first Control-C, you are presented with a message that one more interrupt (Control-C) is required to kill the message. This prevents you from terminating a mail message if you have entered Control-C accidentally. Here is an example:

```
dugout% mailx sally
Subject: lunch
How about lunch today?
^C
(Interrupt -- one more to kill letter)
^C"/export/home/pew/dead.letter" 2/24
dugout%
```

Using Other Utility Commands

Many other commands are included with SunOS. Let's look at a few that you may find useful.

The bc Command

The bc command is a calculator program. You invoke the bc program and then enter numbers and standard arithmetic operators at the keyboard. To exit bc, enter Control-D. Here is a simple example:

```
dugout% bc
3*8+44
68
68/5
13
^D
dugout%
```

You can do floating-point arithmetic by setting the scale, as shown in the next example. The scale represents the number of decimals points you want bc to provide.

```
dugout% bc
scale=3
58/7
8.285
^D
dugout%
```

The cal Command

The cal command displays a calendar for a specified month or year. With no arguments, cal displays a one-month calendar for the current month:

```
dugout% cal
   October 1996
 S  M Tu  W Th  F  S
       1  2  3  4  5
 6  7  8  9 10 11 12
13 14 15 16 17 18 19
20 21 22 23 24 25 26
27 28 29 30 31

dugout%
```

If you provide a year, cal prints the calendar for the entire year:

```
dugout% cal 1996


                               1996

         Jan                    Feb                    Mar
 S  M Tu  W Th  F  S    S  M Tu  W Th  F  S    S  M Tu  W Th  F  S
    1  2  3  4  5  6                 1  2  3                   1  2
 7  8  9 10 11 12 13    4  5  6  7  8  9 10    3  4  5  6  7  8  9
14 15 16 17 18 19 20   11 12 13 14 15 16 17   10 11 12 13 14 15 16
21 22 23 24 25 26 27   18 19 20 21 22 23 24   17 18 19 20 21 22 23
28 29 30 31            25 26 27 28 29         24 25 26 27 28 29 30
                                              31
         Apr                    May                    Jun
 S  M Tu  W Th  F  S    S  M Tu  W Th  F  S    S  M Tu  W Th  F  S
    1  2  3  4  5  6             1  2  3  4                      1
 7  8  9 10 11 12 13    5  6  7  8  9 10 11    2  3  4  5  6  7  8
14 15 16 17 18 19 20   12 13 14 15 16 17 18    9 10 11 12 13 14 15
21 22 23 24 25 26 27   19 20 21 22 23 24 25   16 17 18 19 20 21 22
28 29 30               26 27 28 29 30 31      23 24 25 26 27 28 29
                                              30
         Jul                    Aug                    Sep
 S  M Tu  W Th  F  S    S  M Tu  W Th  F  S    S  M Tu  W Th  F  S
    1  2  3  4  5  6                 1  2  3    1  2  3  4  5  6  7
 7  8  9 10 11 12 13    4  5  6  7  8  9 10    8  9 10 11 12 13 14
14 15 16 17 18 19 20   11 12 13 14 15 16 17   15 16 17 18 19 20 21
21 22 23 24 25 26 27   18 19 20 21 22 23 24   22 23 24 25 26 27 28
28 29 30 31            25 26 27 28 29 30 31   29 30
```

```
          Oct                        Nov                        Dec
 S  M Tu  W Th  F  S        S  M Tu  W Th  F  S        S  M Tu  W Th  F  S
       1  2  3  4  5                       1  2        1  2  3  4  5  6  7
 6  7  8  9 10 11 12        3  4  5  6  7  8  9        8  9 10 11 12 13 14
13 14 15 16 17 18 19       10 11 12 13 14 15 16       15 16 17 18 19 20 21
20 21 22 23 24 25 26       17 18 19 20 21 22 23       22 23 24 25 26 27 28
27 28 29 30 31             24 25 26 27 28 29 30       29 30 31

dugout%
```

You can print a particular month of any year by specifying that information on the command line:

```
dugout% cal 4 1997
   April 1997
 S  M Tu  W Th  F  S
       1  2  3  4  5
 6  7  8  9 10 11 12
13 14 15 16 17 18 19
20 21 22 23 24 25 26
27 28 29 30

dugout%
```

Be sure to always include the full year. If you specify cal 4 97, you'll get the 4th month of year 97 A.D., not 1997.

The compress Command

You learned about the compress command in Chapter 4. Of course, you can also use it from the command line as well as from the File Manager. The following command compresses file1 and file2:

```
dugout% ls -l file1 file2
-rw-rw-r--   1 pew      staff        703 Mar 25 14:45 file1
-rw-rw-r--   1 pew      staff      88494 Mar 25 14:45 file2
dugout% compress file1 file2
dugout% ls -l
-rw-rw-r--   1 pew      staff        449 Mar 25 14:45 file1.Z
-rw-rw-r--   1 pew      staff      43530 Mar 25 14:45 file2.Z
dugout%
```

As you can see from the ls -l output, there is a considerable savings of disk space when you compress files (in most cases). Compressed files have a

.Z suffix. To uncompress a file, use the uncompress command. You can supply the file name with or without the .Z suffix:

```
dugout% uncompress file1 file2.Z
dugout% ls
file1 file2
dugout%
```

If you include the –v (verbose) option to compress, you are given some additional information about the percentage reduction in the size of the files and the new file name, as shown here:

```
dugout% compress -v file 2 file 2
file1: Compression: 24.03% -- replaced with file1.Z
file2: Compression: 79.71% -- replaced with file2.Z
dugout%
```

You cannot compress already compressed files.

The crontab Command

The crontab command lets you schedule programs to be run at a specified time or at regular intervals. For example, you could schedule an audio file to be played every hour on the hour or have the find command run every night at midnight to remove core files.

To use crontab you must create a file with the information about the command and the time at which it should be executed. Then you run the crontab command with the file as the argument:

```
dugout% crontab crontabfile
dugout%
```

The file provided as the argument to crontab must be in a particular format. Each line of the file contains six fields: the first five fields specify the time, and the last field is the command to execute. Each field is separated by a space or tab. The first five fields are integer patterns that specify the following:

First field: minute (0–59)

Second field: hour (0–23)

Third field: day of the month (1–31)

Fourth field: month of the year (1–12)

Fifth field: day of the week (0–6 with 0 = Sunday)

An asterisk can be used in any of the fields to represent all valid values. For example, the following entry indicates that the doorbell.au file should be played every hour on the hour of every day:

```
Ø * * * * /usr/bin/audioplay doorbell.au
```

If you want this command to be executed every hour between 9:00 a.m. and 5:00 p.m., on Mondays and Wednesdays, you use the following entry:

```
Ø 9-17 * * 1,3 /usr/bin/audioplay doorbell.au
```

Your file can contain as many lines in this format as you like. Here is a sample file that plays the doorbell.au file and executes find every night at midnight:

```
Ø 9-17 * * 1,3 /usr/bin/audioplay doorbell.au
Ø Ø * * *      find / -name core -rm -f {} \;
```

To print the currently loaded crontab file, use the -l option:

```
dugout% crontab -l
          Ø 9-17 * * 1,3 /usr/bin/audioplay doorbell.au
          Ø Ø * * *      find / -name core -rm -f {} \;
dugout%
```

To remove your crontab entry, use the -r option:

```
dugout% crontab -r
dugout%
```

The date Command

The date command displays the current date and time, as shown in this example:

```
dugout% date
Thu Oct 24 15:34:16 PST 1993
dugout%
```

You can also customize the date output by using a series of field descriptors. See the date man page for details.

The du Command

The du command displays the disk usage for the files and directories provided on the command line or for the current directory if no file or directory is specified. Each directory is searched recursively, and the corresponding number of 512-byte blocks that the directory uses is displayed. Here is an example:

```
dugout% du
2          ./app-defaults
6          ./phone
2          ./bin/src
10         ./bin
2          ./Mail
6          ./source
2          ./PhoneList/business
2          ./PhoneList/personal
6          ./PhoneList
2          ./new
2          ./.wastebasket
376        ./olitbook/ch5
2          ./olitbook/ch2
230        ./olitbook/lib
610        ./olitbook
24         ./grep
974        .
dugout%
```

If you provide a directory on the command line, only the disk usage for that directory is displayed, as shown here:

```
dugout% du olitbook
376        olitbook/ch5
2          olitbook/ch2
230        olitbook/lib
610        olitbook
dugout%
```

If you don't want all the details about the sizes of the subdirectories, use the -s option. The -s option displays only the total space used by the directory and all its subdirectories:

```
dugout% du -s olitbook
610        olitbook
dugout%
```

To determine how much space you are using in each of the files and directories in your home directory, use the command shown in this example:

```
dugout% du -s *
2          Mail
```

```
2          Makefile
6          PhoneList
2          README
2          README2
2          alberts_mail
2          app-defaults
10         bin
2          compressed.Z
2          document.doc
36         doorbell.au
2          filesize
2          frame.doc
24         grep
2          header.h
2          mailfile
2          main.c
18         memo
10         memo.c
102        memo.o
2          memo1
2          namelist
2          new
610        olitbook
6          phone
2          play
78         snapshot.rs
2          sort.c
2          sortit.c
6          source
2          start_license
dugout%
```

The information displayed is particularly useful if you are low on disk space and need to do some clean-up. You can quickly determine which files and directories are occupying the most space.

The look Command

The look command is used to "look up" words in the dictionary. The on-line dictionary contains over 25,000 words. It does not include definitions, but it gives you the correct spelling of each word you specify. You use the look command to display all the words in the dictionary that begin with the same characters that you specify as an argument. For example, you can look up words that begin with *hier*, as shown here:

```
dugout% look hier
hierarchal
hierarchic
hierarchy
hieratic
hieroglyphic
Hieronymus
dugout%
```

When you are looking just for a correct spelling, this is usually much faster than picking up a real dictionary.

The tar Command

The tar command is used to create, extract, and read tape archives. These are the same functions that the Tape Tool provides. The tar command gives you a command-line interface for working with tapes and disks. To create an archive, use the c option and specify on the command line each file or directory you want included in the archive. The following example creates an archive that consists of the current directory (specified by .):

```
dugout% tar -c .
dugout%
```

By default, tar writes the archive to a tape in the default tape drive (check with your system administrator to determine your default tape drive). If you want to write the archive to another device or file, use the f option followed by the name of the device or file. For example, to write the same archive to a floppy disk in the floppy disk drive, use the following command:

```
dugout% tar -cf /dev/diskette .
dugout%
```

Or, to write the archive to a file, use the f option and enter the file name rather than the device name. In the following example an archive named tarfile is created that contains the bin and src directories:

```
dugout% tar -cf tarfile bin src
dugout%
```

In each of the examples shown thus far tar is silent. You can ask tar to list each file as it is added to the archive by including the v (verbose) option.

Each file written to the archive is displayed with the corresponding size of the file, as shown here:

```
dugout% tar -cv bin src
a ./ 0 tape blocks
a ./.Xauthority 1 tape blocks
a ./.mailrc 4 tape blocks
a ./.calctoolrc 1 tape blocks
a ./bin/ 0 tape blocks
a ./bin/start_license 1 tape blocks
<More lines of output>
dugout%
```

To read (or list) the contents of an archive, use the t option. This option displays the files included in the archive:

```
dugout% tar -t
./
./.Xauthority
./.mailrc
./.calctoolrc
./bin/
./bin/start_license
<More lines of output>
dugout%
```

The preceding example shows the files in the archive on the default tape drive. You can use the f option to specify another device or file when reading an archive just as you did when creating an archive:

```
dugout% tar -tf /dev/diskette
bin/
bin/xloadimage
bin/cdplayer
bin/cdplayer1
bin/src/
bin/src/mortgage.c
bin/src/payment.c
<More lines of output>
dugout%
```

If you include the v option, you get additional information about each file in the archive, similar to the ls -l output:

```
dugout% tar -tvf /dev/diskette
drwxr-xr-x868/1         0 Mar 15 21:05 1993 bin/
-rwxr-xr-x868/1    139264 May 13 20:15 1991 bin/xloadimage
-rwxr-xr-x868/1     40960 May 23 13:50 1991 bin/cdplayer
-rwxr-xr-x868/1    335872 May 23 13:50 1991 bin/cdplayer1
drwxr-xr-x868/1         0 Dec 10 08:45 1991 bin/src/
-rw-r--r--868/10     5812 Nov 20 22:20 1991 bin/src/mortgage.c
-rw-r--r--868/10     2804 Nov 20 22:22 1991 bin/src/payment.c
<More lines of output>
dugout%
```

To extract files from an archive, use the x option. Files from the archive are written to the current directory. In the following example all the files on the floppy disk are extracted (verbosely) and written to the current directory:

```
dugout% tar -xvf /dev/diskette
x bin/, 0 bytes, 0 tape blocks
x bin/xloadimage, 139264 bytes, 272 tape blocks
x bin/cdplayer, 40960 bytes, 80 tape blocks
x bin/cdplayer1, 335872 bytes, 656 tape blocks
x bin/src/, 0 bytes, 0 tape blocks
x bin/src/mortgage.c, 5812 bytes, 12 tape blocks
x bin/src/payment.c, 2804 bytes, 6 tape blocks
<More lines of output>
dugout%
```

You do not have to extract all the files in an archive. If you specify a file or files on the command line, only those files will be extracted from the archive:

```
dugout% tar -xvf /dev/diskette bin/xloadimage bin/cdplayer
x bin/xloadimage, 139264 bytes, 272 tape blocks
x bin/cdplayer, 40960 bytes, 80 tape blocks
dugout%
```

The spell Command

The spell command uses the same dictionary that the look command uses. The spell command checks the spelling of words in a file. It displays all the words that are not in its dictionary. In the following example, a file named memo is being checked for spelling errors:

```
dugout% spell memo
heirarchy
printtool
dugout%
```

Some words are not in the dictionary because they are misspelled, such as *heirarchy* in the preceding example. Other words may not be in the dictionary but are still correct, such as *printtool.*

Summary

In this chapter you've increased your knowledge of some important commands. You know more about working with files, printing files, sending and receiving mail, and some other utility functions. You are now equipped with some powerful tools. In Chapter 14 you will increase your mastery of SunOS by learning how to use the shell to combine some of the tools with pipes and how to put multiple commands into a shell to create a script program.

Using the vi Editor

vi versus the Text Editor

Getting In and Out of vi

Using Modes

Moving Around within the File

Modifying the File

Using Yank and Put

Searching and Replacing

Reading and Writing Files

Filtering the Buffer

Using Advanced Features

EDITORS PROVIDE AN INTERFACE FOR CREATING AND EDITING FILES. THE first UNIX editor was a line editor called ed. A line editor allows you to edit a file line by line with a command-line–style interface rather than display the file contents on the screen or in a window. The ed editor was the primary editor available on UNIX systems in the early days of UNIX (the early 1970s). Another line editor, developed at the University of California at Berkeley, is called ex. It is quite similar to ed, with some added features. The vi editor (pronounced "vee-eye") was an outgrowth of the ex editor. It is based on ex, so it shares all of ex's commands, but in addition it is a full-screen (full-window) editor, also called a visual editor (hence, the name vi). The vi editor gives you a full-window view of the file you are editing.

In this chapter you will learn about the following:

- Getting in and out of vi
- Using modes
- Moving around within the file
- Modifying the file
- Using yank and put
- Searching and replacing
- Reading and writing other files
- Filtering the buffer
- Using advanced features

vi versus the Text Editor

The vi editor was one of the first (if not the first) UNIX editor to provide visual editing. It became the de facto standard for UNIX editing and is still popular today. Since we have already talked about the Text Editor in Chapter 5, you may be wondering why we are talking about yet another editor. It is true that both the Text Editor and vi are editors that do essentially the same job, but there are a few differences that are important to understand. First, vi can be run when the windowing system is not running. The vi editor was developed originally to run on terminals (before the days of windowing systems like the X Window System). This means that, unlike the Text Editor, you can run vi on your system without running the OpenWindows environment.

Another advantage of vi is that it is found on nearly every version of UNIX from most (if not all) UNIX vendors. So, if you work in an environment in which you do some work on a SunOS system and then use another UNIX system from a different vendor, you will not find the Text Editor available on each system. You will, however, very likely find a version of vi running on any UNIX system.

If you use the Korn shell, you may prefer also using (or at least knowing) vi because the Korn shell supports command-line editing based on vi commands. If you use the Korn shell and know how to edit with vi commands, you will find this a particularly valuable feature. You'll learn about the Korn shell in Chapter 14.

Of course, there are also some important advantages to using the Text Editor. Because the Text Editor uses the standard editing commands found in all DeskSet applications for manipulating text, you'll find more consistency on your desktop by using the Text Editor. The Text Editor also supports the mouse, whereas the vi editor does not.

When you invoke vi (or any other editor), a copy of the file is placed in a *buffer*. The buffer is what you are actually editing when you enter commands or text into the editor. None of the changes, additions, or deletions are made to the actual file until you write the contents of the buffer to the file. You can use this concept to your advantage. For example, if you are editing a file and you make some serious mistakes that ruin your file, you can quit the editing session without writing out the file, and your file remains unchanged. You can also load another file into your buffer without leaving the editor. This means that if you edit one file and then want to edit another one, you do not have to exit the editor and restart it with the new file. You can simply load a new file into the buffer and immediately start editing that file.

Getting In and Out of vi

Throughout this discussion we'll assume you are using vi from a window (either a Shell Tool or a Command Tool), since that is likely to be the most common usage. It is not, however, a requirement, and all the features discussed in this chapter apply to editing with vi either from a window or directly on the terminal screen.

You invoke vi from the shell prompt by entering **vi** followed by the name or names of the files you want to create and/or edit:

```
dugout% vi filename
```

The screen is cleared, and the file (the first file if multiple files are provided) is displayed in the window. If the file is a new one, nothing appears on the screen except a tilde (~) at the beginning of each line. A line that begins with a tilde represents a line that is past the end of the file. Let's begin by invoking vi with a single command-line argument representing a file that does not yet exist:

```
dugout% vi file1
```

Figure 13.1 shows a Command Tool in which vi is running and is editing file1.

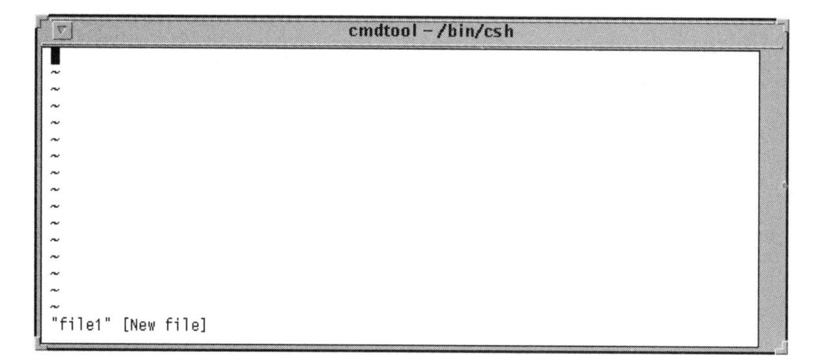

Figure 13.1
Creating a new file with vi in a Command Tool

As you can see from the figure, when you invoke vi with a new file the screen is blank except for the tilde at the beginning of each line and the name of the file being edited on the bottom line of the window. This is called the *status line.* If you invoke vi with an existing file, the contents of the file are displayed in the window, as shown in Figure 13.2. When you edit an existing file, vi displays additional information on the status line of the window: the number of lines and characters in the file.

Figure 13.2
Editing an existing file with vi

```
cmdtool - /bin/csh
Patch level 1:
        fixed bug, some problems with Imakefile.
        fixed bug, can no longer see turned-over cards with middle mouse.
        fixed bug, "f" will use the text field then selection for information.
        added, patch_level variable to version.c file.

Patch level 2:
        added advice for choosing a move.
        added "squish" feature for packing contiguous cards of same suit.
        added looking in common places in XView for help files if not found.
        bumped version number to 1.1 from 1.0.1.

Spider is a challenging double-decked solitaire game.  Unlike in most
solitaire games, skill is just as important as luck.

The X11 version of spider is based on the NeWS version by Don Woods,
"README" 96 lines, 3490 characters
```

If you are new to vi, you may want to use an alternate version of vi that is especially helpful for new users. Instead of using vi, use vedit:

```
dugout% vedit filename
```

Running vedit is the same as running vi, except that vedit has some special features that help new users. For example, when you enter insert mode the right side of the status line displays the message "INSERT MODE." (You'll learn more about modes in the next section.) This will help you as you become familiar with the commands and usage of vi.

Another version of vi is the view command. You use it when you want to examine the contents of a file, but do not want to edit the file:

```
dugout% view filename
```

The view command behaves exactly like vi except that it does not let you save your changes. You can use all the features of vi to search and scroll through the text; you simply cannot save any changes. This is a safety feature to help prevent you from accidentally modifying your file.

The vi editor also has a built-in recovery mechanism. If your system crashes or you lose power while editing with vi, you can recover most of the changes you've made. You'll receive a mail message indicating that vi saved your file, along with instructions on how to restore the file. To restore a lost file, use the -r option:

```
dugout% vi -r filename
```

There are several ways to exit vi. The method you use depends on whether you have made changes to the buffer and, if so, whether you want to save the changes you have made to the buffer. The :q command quits vi, but only if you have not modified the buffer. If you have modified the buffer and want to quit without saving changes, use the :q! command. To save (write) your changes, use the :w command. After you have saved your changes, you can quit with the :q command. You can save a file and quit vi simultaneously with the :wq command. Here is a list of the common commands for quitting vi:

:q Quit vi. You can use this command only if the buffer has not been modified since the last time you saved the file.

:q! Quit vi without saving changes. You can use this command at any time to exit vi, but any changes you have made since the last save will be discarded.

:w Write (save) the buffer to the file. This command copies the buffer to the associated file.

:wq Write and quit vi. This command combines the :w and :q commands.

:x Exit vi. This command checks to see if the file has been modified since the last save. If it has, then the file is saved and vi exits. If the buffer has not been modified, vi exits without writing the file.

ZZ The same as :x.

If you've provided more than one file name on the command line, you can edit multiple files, but only one at a time. The first file on the command line is the one that is initially loaded into the buffer. When you have finished editing that file, you can save your changes and then begin editing the second file with the :n command. This loads the next file into the vi buffer. If you want to discard the edits in the file you are currently editing and load the next file, use the :n! command.

You can edit another file by using the :e command followed by the name of the file you want to edit. This loads the new file into the vi buffer. If the file you are editing has been modified, you must first save the changes. If you want to edit a new file without saving the changes in your buffer, use the :e! command. For example, if you are editing a file and want to load a new file named file2, enter the following command and press Return:

```
:e file2
```

You can return to the previously edited file by entering

```
:e #
```

The pound sign is a special character that represents the file you were previously editing. You can also enter Control-^. This toggles between the two files you are editing.

If you want to load file2 and discard changes you have made to the current file, enter the following command and press Return:

```
:e! file2
```

You can also use the :e! command without a filename argument if you want to reload the current file. This is useful if you've made some modifications to the buffer and are not happy with them. You can reload the file into the buffer (the unchanged file) with this command and start your editing over again.

Here is a summary of the next and edit commands:

:n Edit the next file. Valid only when you have supplied multiple files on the command line.

:n!	Edit the next file. Discard editing modifications in the buffer.
:e *filename*	Edit the file. Load the file into the buffer for editing.
:e! *filename*	Edit the file. Discard editing modifications in the buffer.

Two other fundamental commands of general usefulness are Control-G and Control-L. The Control-G command displays the status line on the bottom line of the window. The status line displays the name of the file, the current line number, and the total number of lines. The Control-L command refreshes the window. If for any reason your window becomes corrupted, you can have vi redraw the window with the Control-L command.

Using Modes

One of the fundamental differences between vi and other visual editors (like the Text Editor) is that vi operates in three different *modes*. It's important to understand each mode in order to understand vi and to know how to take advantage of its features. The three modes are as follows:

Open visual or command mode	Open visual mode is for entering vi commands. The vi editor commands are used to search, move, scroll, and so forth. Commands are not displayed in the window when you enter them. The ZZ command is an example of a command issued in open visual mode. You do not press Return after entering a command in open visual mode.
Insert mode	Insert mode is for entering text. When you are in insert mode, each character you type enters the buffer and is displayed in the window. To begin insert mode you enter a command such as i, a, or o. To exit insert mode press the Escape Key.
Ex command mode	Ex commands are the commands that are compatible with the ex editor. To begin ex command mode enter a colon (:). The cursor moves to the bottom line of the window, where you enter the command and then press Return.

Understanding these modes is essential to using vi. In the Text Editor all you have to do to add characters to the buffer is to begin typing. In vi, however, you can't just start typing text, because you have to first enter insert mode. When you have finished inserting characters, you must press Esc to exit insert mode before you can enter a command in open visual mode or ex command mode.

Many people know little more about vi than how to get in and out of insert mode, how to add or delete a character, and how to move the cursor. You can do a lot of editing with just these simple commands. Most of the remainder of this chapter, however, concentrates on time-saving commands that will help you use vi more effectively. Here is a summary of the basic commands you need for getting started in vi:

i	Enter insert mode.
Esc	Exit insert mode. Return to open visual mode.
x	Delete one character. The character under the cursor is deleted.
Arrow keys	Move the cursor. Each of the four arrow keys (Left, Right, Up, and Down) moves the cursor in the corresponding direction.
:wq	Write the buffer to a file and quit vi.

You can actually get a lot of work done in vi with just these five commands. They allow you to enter characters, delete characters, move the cursor, and write the file to a disk. These are the basic operations that any editor provides. Of course, these five commands describe only the most elementary use of vi. If you have never used vi before, take a few minutes now to play around with what you have learned so far. Invoke vi with the vedit command, and use the commands just described to enter insert mode, enter some characters, exit insert mode, move the cursor around, delete some characters, and write and quit the file. Performing these operations will give you the basic feel of the editor and will help you better understand the features discussed throughout the remainder of this chapter.

Moving Around within the File

The simplest and most intuitive way to move the cursor around in vi is to use the arrow keys. But there are many other ways to move the cursor. The main advantage of these other methods is that you can move the cursor more quickly than you can by holding down an arrow key. You can move the cursor a word at a time, or scroll the window a page at a time, or search for a particular string of characters. Each of these methods increases your efficiency.

Moving the Cursor

You've already learned that you can move the cursor by using the arrow keys. The Left and Right Arrow keys move the cursor one character to the left or right. The Up and Down Arrow keys move the cursor one line up or down. In addition, you can move the cursor with the h, j, k, and l keys. These keys move the cursor left, down, up, and right, respectively. These characters do not represent any mnemonic that helps you remember their function, but you may prefer using them rather than the arrow keys because you can keep your hands in the standard keyboard position rather than move them to the arrow keys.

You can also move the cursor with the +, –, Return, and Spacebar keys. The + and - move the cursor down and up one line, respectively. The Return key moves the cursor down one line and puts the cursor at the beginning of the line (at the first printable character [not a space or tab]). The Spacebar moves the cursor one character to the right.

Since all of the commands discussed in this section are open visual commands, you will not see them displayed in the window when you type them. To reiterate, commands entered in open visual mode are not echoed to the screen and do not require a Return to be entered. They are interpreted by vi as commands. In this case, each of these commands moves the cursor.

Each of these commands can optionally be preceded by a count that tells vi how many lines or characters to move in the direction specified. For example, if you enter 13j, the cursor will move down 13 lines. Or, if you enter 7l, the cursor will move seven characters to the right. Here is a summary of the commands discussed in this section:

← *or* h	Move one character to the left.
↓ *or* j *or* +	Move one line down.
↑ *or* k *or* –	Move one line up.
→ *or* l *or* Spacebar	Move one character to the right.
Return	Move one line down. Position cursor at the first printable character in that line.

Scrolling and Paging

Unlike the Text Editor, vi does not have a built-in scrollbar. In fact, if you use a Command Tool (which has a scrollbar by default), the scrollbar disappears when you invoke vi and reappears when you exit vi. Therefore, you cannot move around in the file by using the scrollbar. You can, however, use several commands to scroll through the contents of the buffer. Here is a summary of the commands you can use for scrolling. Each command is an open visual command, so no characters are displayed or are entered into the buffer when you use that command.

Control-D (^D)	Scroll down one-half page. (The size of the page is determined by the size of the window).
Control-U (^U)	Scroll up one-half page. The cursor advances.
Control-F (^F)	Scroll forward one full page. The cursor advances.
Control-B (^B)	Scroll back one full page. The cursor advances.
Control-E (^E)	Scroll forward one line. The cursor remains at the same line position.
Control-Y (^Y)	Scroll back one line. The cursor remains at the same line position.

Each of these commands can also be preceded by a count, in which case the operation is repeated by the count. For example, if you enter 9^E, you will scroll forward 9 lines, with the cursor remaining at the same line position. If you enter 3^F, you will advance 3 pages in the file.

Moving Word by Word

A *word* is defined in vi as a string of characters separated by a space or a punctuation character. The w (word) command moves the cursor to the next word. This may be the beginning of an actual word, or it may be the next punctuation character. The following line of text is taken from the file shown in Figure 13.2. If you use the w command with this line, the cursor advances to the positions shown here:

```
added, patch_level variable to version.c file.
```

The W (Word) command is similar except that it ignores punctuation. If you use the W command with this line, the cursor advances to the positions shown here:

```
added, patch_level variable to version.c file.
```

The b (back) and B commands move the cursor in the opposite direction of the w and W commands. The b command recognizes punctuation; the B command ignores punctuation.

The e (end) command moves the cursor to the end of a word, recognizing punctuation as word separators. The E command also moves the cursor to the end of a word but ignores punctuation. If you use the E command on the same line shown in the preceding example, the cursor moves as shown here:

```
added, patch_level variable to version.c file.
```

Each of these commands can also be preceded by a count, in which case the cursor moves the specified number of words. For example, if you repeat the command 2W, the cursor moves to the following positions:

```
added, patch_level variable to version.c file.
```

Here is a summary of the commands available for moving word by word:

w	Move forward one word, recognizing punctuation.
W	Move forward one word, ignoring punctuation.
b	Move backward one word, recognizing punctuation.
B	Move backward one word, ignoring punctuation
e	Move to the end of a word, recognizing punctuation.
E	Move to the end of a word, ignoring punctuation.

Using the Search and Goto Commands

To search for a specific string of characters, enter a slash (/) followed by the characters to search for. When you enter a slash, the cursor moves to the bottom of the window. Each character that you enter is displayed at the bottom of the window. When you press Return, the cursor moves forward in the file (from the position of the cursor before you pressed slash) to find the next occurrence of the characters you specified. To repeat the search, enter n (next). To reverse the direction of the search, enter N. If you search for the string "us" in the file shown in Figure 13.2, the cursor moves to the positions indicated:

```
Patch level 1:
        fixed bug, some problems with Imakefile.
        fixed bug, can no longer see turned-over cards with middle mouse.
        fixed bug, "f" will use the text field then selection for information.
        added, patch_level variable to version.c file.

Spider is a challenging double-decked solitaire game.  Unlike in most
solitaire games, skill is just as important as luck.

The X11 version of spider is based on the NeWS version by Don Woods,
and uses the same save file format and card images.
```

You can also search backward through a file by using a question mark (?) rather than a slash. Whether you are searching forward or backward, n repeats the search in the initial direction and N reverses the direction of the search.

You can also use wildcards in your search string. (If you are using vedit, the wildcard feature is turned off.) The wildcards are the same as for the grep command discussed in Chapter 12: dot (.) matches any single character, asterisk (*) matches zero or more occurrences of the previous character, and square brackets ([ ]) denote a set of characters to match (see Chapter 12 for more details). Another special matching-character pair is \< and \>, which match the beginning and ending of a word, respectively. For example, in the previous search we looked for "us." We could limit our search to the characters "us" that begin a word if we specify: "\<us." When we use this search pattern, only two occurrences of "us" are matched, as shown here:

```
Patch level 1:
        fixed bug, some problems with Imakefile.
        fixed bug, can no longer see turned-over cards with middle mouse.
        fixed bug, "f" will use the text field then selection for information.
        added, patch_level variable to version.c file.

Spider is a challenging double decked solitaire game.  Unlike most
soilitaire games, skill is just as important as luck.

The X11 version of spider is based on the NeWS version by Don Woods,
and uses the same save file format and card images.
```

The \> character pair has a similar effect except that the end of a word is matched.

You can move to a specific line in the file by using the G (goto) command. Precede the G with the number of the line that you want to move to. For example, 21G moves the cursor to line 21 and positions the cursor at the first printable character on that line. If you enter the G without a preceding line number, the cursor moves to the last line in the file.

You can move to a specific character in a line by using pipe (|). Precede | with the number representing the character position that you want the cursor moved to. For example, 13| moves the cursor to the 13th character of the current line. If you enter | without a character number, the cursor moves to the first character on the line.

You can also search for a single character within a line by using the f (find) and t (to) commands. Both the f and t commands search for a character in the current line only. You follow the command by the character you want to find. For example, to search for the character x, enter fx. The search goes from the current cursor position to the end of the line. The vi editor finds the next x in the line and positions the cursor on that character. If no x is found between the cursor and the end of the current line, vi beeps. The t command works the same way except that it moves the cursor *up to* the character you search for, or in other words, to the character preceding the search character.

The F and T commands reverse the direction of the cursor: the search is made from the current cursor position to the beginning of the line. The F command moves the cursor onto the search character; the T command moves the cursor up to the search character.

You can repeat a search by using the semicolon (;) and comma (,) commands. The semicolon repeats the search (only on the same line) in the original search direction. The comma repeats the search in the opposite direction.

In the following example, if the cursor is positioned at the first column of the line and you enter the command fe followed by five semicolons, the cursor moves to the positions shown here:

```
added, patch_level variable to version.c file.
```

Here is a summary of the commands described in this section:

/*pattern*<Return>	Search forward in the file for *pattern*.
?*pattern*<Return>	Search backward in the file for *pattern*.
n	Repeat the previous search in the original direction.
N	Repeat the previous search in the opposite direction.
f*X*	Find *X* in the current line. Search from the current cursor position to the end of the line. Position the cursor on the character found.
t*X*	To *X* in the current line. Search from the current cursor position to the end of the line. Position the cursor before the character found.
F*X*	Find *X* in the current line. Search from the current cursor position to the beginning of the line. Position the cursor on the character found.
T*X*	To *X* in the current line. Search from the current cursor position to the beginning of the line. Position the cursor before the character found.
;	Repeat the last find or to command in the original direction of the search.
,	Repeat the last find or to command in the opposite direction of the search.

Positioning the Cursor

You can move the cursor to the top line, the middle line, or the bottom line of the window by using the H (home), M (middle), and L (last) commands, respectively, as shown here. These commands do not change the text displayed in the window—only the position of the cursor.

H	Move the cursor to the top line displayed in the window.
M	Move the cursor to the middle line displayed in the window.
L	Move the cursor to the bottom line displayed in the window.

Marking and Returning

You can mark a particular position in the file by using the m command. Enter m, followed by one of the 26 characters of the alphabet, to mark the position where the cursor is currently located. You can mark 26 different positions in the file—one for each of the 26 characters in the alphabet. Then you can return to the exact position you marked by entering the grave mark (`, sometimes called the back quote) followed by the marked character. For example, if you use the command mq to mark a position, you can return to that position by using the command `q. An alternate method of returning is to use the single quote (') followed by the marked character. This returns the cursor to the beginning of the line that contains the marked position.

This feature is particularly useful when you are editing a large file and you need to move back and forth between two or more sections that are far apart. Rather than scrolling page after page, looking for the exact location you were previously editing, you can mark a position and then easily return to it with the grave or quote command.

The vi editor also automatically keeps track of the last position of the cursor. When you move to a new location, you can return to the previous location by entering grave (`) twice, or to the beginning of the line containing the previous location by entering quote (') twice.

Here is a summary of the commands described in this section:

m*x*	Use the character *x* to mark the position occupied by the cursor.
`*x*	Return to the position marked with the character *x*.
'*x*	Return to the beginning of the line containing the position marked with the character *x*.
``	Return to the previous position.
''	Return to the beginning of the line containing the previous position.

Moving in Other Ways

There are several other ways of moving the cursor position within the file. To understand these movements you need to first understand vi's definitions of *sentence, paragraph,* and *section:*

Sentence	A string of characters that ends with a period, a question mark, or an exclamation point, followed by the end of a line or by two spaces.
Paragraph	One or more adjacent lines. Paragraphs are separated by a blank line (two consecutive new lines).
Section	Text that is delimited by a line beginning with a Control-L or a left curly brace ({).

Here are some ways that you can move around within the file by units of sentence, paragraph, and section, and by some miscellaneous means:

(	Move to the beginning of the sentence.
)	Move to the end of the sentence.
{	Move to the beginning of the paragraph.
}	Move to the end of the paragraph.
[[	Move to the beginning of the section.
]]	Move to the end of the section.
0	Move to the first character in the current line.
^	Move to the first printable character in the current line.
$	Move to the last character in the current line.

Modifying the File

The commands you learned in the previous section are useful for moving the cursor, but they are also useful when you perform editing operations such as deleting, changing, or shifting lines. Many of the commands that move the cursor are considered *targets*. A target is used in conjunction with another command. For example, you learned how to use the slash and a pattern to search for a string of characters. You can combine the pattern search with a command to delete characters in order to delete all the characters between the current cursor position and the string that is found from the pattern search. This is just one example; there are many others. In general, the format of commands to change text is this:

```
[count]command<target>
```

The count field is optional. You will learn about the command field in this section, and you learned about the target field in the previous section, on moving within the file. Not all of the commands follow this exact format. Many do, however, and understanding this basic format will help you to quickly master editing with vi. Let's start by looking at the most elementary editing commands for inserting text.

Inserting Text

The commands that insert text do not strictly follow the command format previously described. These commands are usually used by themselves and simply provide different ways of entering insert mode. You have already learned about the i command, which puts you into insert mode. The other insertion commands also put you into insert mode but in slightly different ways, as described here:

i Begin insert mode. Characters entered are inserted before the current character position.

I Begin insert mode. The cursor moves to the first printable character of the line and begins insertion there.

a Begin insert (append) mode. Characters entered are inserted after the current character position.

A Begin insert (append) mode. The cursor moves to the end of the line and appends characters to the end of the line.

o Begin insert (open) mode. Open a new blank line below the line currently containing the cursor.

O Begin insert (open) mode. Open a new blank line above the line currently containing the cursor.

Regardless of which method you use to enter insert mode, press Esc or Control-[to exit insert mode and return to open visual mode.

Deleting Text

While entering text in insert mode, you can use some special control characters to erase characters you have inserted, as described here:

Backspace or Control-H	Erase last character entered.
Control-W	Erase last word entered.
Control-U	Erase all characters entered on the current line.

In open visual mode, there are two basic commands for deleting characters: x and d. The x command deletes the current character—the one on which the cursor is positioned. The x command does not take a target (as in the general editing-command format), but it can optionally take a count. For example, if you enter 4x, then four characters are deleted: the character under the cursor and the three characters to the right of the cursor. The X command deletes the character before the cursor, and can also take a count.

The d command is the more general-purpose delete command that follows the command format described previously, as shown here:

```
[count]d<target>
```

The count is optional, and the target field represents one of the cursor motions described in the previous section. For example, you can delete one word by entering the command dw. The w is the target and represents a word. Recall from the previous section that the w command moves the cursor forward one word. When used in combination with the d command, dw deletes one word. If you include a count, such as 3dw, then the number of words specified by count are deleted: three in this case.

The target field can be any of the cursor motions you have learned. For example, you can enter the command dL to delete all the lines from the line containing the cursor to the last line in the window. Or, the command d/pattern<Return> deletes all the characters between the current cursor position and the string "pattern."

As you think about all the different ways you can move the cursor, you will begin to understand all the different combinations you can put together to delete as much or as little text as you want, exactly the way you want.

There are two other special delete commands. The dd command deletes exactly one line—the current line. You can precede the dd command with a count to delete multiple lines with one command. The D command deletes all characters from the cursor position to the end of the line.

Each delete command described in this section is summarized here:

x	Delete the character at the cursor position.
X	Delete the character before the cursor position.
d<*target*>	Delete from the current position to *target*.
dd	Delete the current line.
D	Delete to the end of the line.

Here are some other examples of delete commands:

5dd	Delete five lines.
dtW	Delete from the cursor position up to the character W in the current line.
dG	Delete from the current line to the end of the file.
2d}	Delete two paragraphs.
d0	Delete to the beginning of the line.

Replacing Text

There are two commands for replacing characters: r and R. The r command replaces the character under the cursor. Enter r followed by the new character that replaces the existing character under the cursor.

The R command also replaces characters starting at the cursor position but does so by overstriking the characters. When you enter R you are in insert mode, and each character you enter overwrites the existing character at that location. When you have finished replacing characters, you must press Esc to exit insert mode and return to open visual mode. Here is a summary of the replace commands:

r	Replace one character.
R	Replace multiple characters in overstrike style until you press the Esc key.

Changing Text

The basic change command is c. The change command also follows the general command format, as shown here:

```
[count]c<target>
```

The format of this command is identical to the format of the delete command: the count is optional and the target is one of the common move commands. For example, you can change one word by entering the command cw. The w is the target and represents a word. Changing text implies that you are providing new text to replace the old. So when you enter a change command, you are put into insert mode and the end of the change region is identified by a dollar sign ($). In the following example, the cursor is positioned at the v in the word *variable*. If you enter cw to change the word, the cursor remains positioned at the v in variable, and the character at the end of the word, e, is replaced by a dollar sign, as shown here:

```
added, patch_level variabl$ to version.c file.
```

You then enter the new text that should replace the word *variable*. Regardless of the size of the new string you enter, only *variable* is replaced. As you enter new text, it appears to overwrite the old text. If the new text is longer than the word you are replacing, the characters to the right of the word being replaced are "pushed over" so that they are not overwritten.

Of course, you can include a count, such as 3cw, in which case the number of words specified by count (3 in this case) is changed. Or you can use the W command to ignore punctuation. If the cursor is positioned at the v in *variable* in our example, and you enter the command 3cW, the dollar sign appears at the end of the third word forward (ignoring punctuation) as shown here:

```
added, patch_level variable to version.$ file.
```

The s (substitute) command substitutes the character under the cursor with the new characters that you insert. When you enter the s command you enter insert mode and must press Esc to exit insert mode and return to open visual mode. When you enter s, the character under the cursor changes to a dollar sign. If you precede the s command with a count, then count characters are replaced. For example, the command 4s replaces four characters. The dollar sign (indicating the end of the text being substituted) is drawn on the fourth character from the cursor. If the cursor is positioned at the r in the word *variable* and you enter the command 4s, the b is replaced by the dollar sign, as shown here:

```
added, patch_level varia$le to version.c file.
```

There are two other change commands: C and S. The C command changes the characters from the cursor to the end of the line. The S command replaces the entire line. Both commands put you into insert mode.

Here is a summary of the change commands:

c<*target*>	Change from the current position to target.
s	Substitute character.
C	Change from the current position to the end of the line.
S	Substitute the entire line.

Here are some examples of change commands:

3cw	Change three words.
cfq	Change from the cursor position to and including the character q in the current line.
14s	Change 14 characters.
c/*string*<Return>	Change from the current position to the pattern *string*.
c^	Change to the first printable character of the line.

Undoing and Repeating Commands

Anytime you modify the buffer you can always undo the operation. If you insert new text, change text, or delete text, you can enter u (undo) to undo the change. If you enter u again, you redo your change. If you continue to enter u, the change is done and undone repeatedly. A variation of the u command is the U command, which undoes all the changes made to the current line. This could be many individual changes that can all be undone at one time. The U command works only if you have not moved the cursor off the line on which the changes were made. As soon as you move the cursor off the line, you cannot undo all the changes to the line, but only the last change made, and you do that with the u command.

Another convenient feature is the repetition of a command when you enter dot (.). Dot repeats the last editing operation. This can be any operation such as inserting text or deleting a character.

Here is a summary of the undo and repeat commands:

u	Undo the last modification.

U Undo all the changes made to the current line.

. Repeat the last modification.

Shifting Lines

You can shift lines to the right or left with the right- and left-angle bracket commands. To shift the current line one tab to the right, enter two right-angle brackets (>>). (One tab is the default amount of the shift, but this can be customized with the :set shiftwidth variable discussed in the advanced features section later in this chapter.) Enter two left-angle brackets (<<) to shift the line one tab to the left. You can precede the command with a count, in which case count lines are shifted. You can also use a target with these commands (though not in combination with a count). Since the shift command operates on an entire line, only the move commands that would move the cursor to another line make sense in combination with the shift operation. For example, >L shifts to the right all the lines from the current line to the end of the window.

Here is a summary of the shift commands:

>>	Shift one line to the right.
<<	Shift one line to the left.
>(*target*)	Shift all the lines from the current line to the line containing *target* to the right.
<(*target*)	Shift all the lines from the current line to the line containing *target* to the left.

Joining Lines and Changing Case

You can join two lines by using the J command. The line containing the cursor is joined with the next line so that they form one line. If you precede the J command with a count, then count lines are joined starting with the line that contains the cursor. For example, 9J will join the 9 lines that begin at the current line.

You can change the case of a character with the tilde (~). The character under the cursor changes: from upper- to lowercase or vice versa. After the character is changed, the cursor advances to the next character. You can precede the tilde with a count, in which case the count characters' case is changed. If the cursor is over a number or a punctuation mark, no change is made but the cursor is still advanced. In our earlier example, if the cursor is at the beginning of the word *variable* (all lowercase originally) and you enter 5~, the first five characters of *variable* change case, as shown here:

```
added, patch_level VARIAble to version.c file.
```

Here is a summary of the two commands discussed in this section:

J	Join the current line with the next line.
~	Change the case of the character under the cursor.

Using Yank and Put

The vi editor supports a facility called *yank and put* that is very similar to the copy and paste feature that you learned about in Chapter 5. One main difference is that you do not use the mouse and pointer to highlight characters with yank and put the way you did with copy and paste. Rather, you use the keyboard to *yank* text into an internal buffer that vi provides, and then *put* the text into some other location.

We'll start by looking at the yank command, which follows the general command format where y is the command:

```
[count]y<target>
```

To *yank* one line, you enter two y's (yy). When you yank a line or a string of characters, no action takes place other than that of a message appearing on the bottom line of the window (as long as you yank at least the number of lines that the report variable is set to—5 by default). Anytime you yank text, it is copied into an internal vi buffer (we'll call it the *yank buffer*) and no modification is made to your main buffer. For example, 6yy yanks six lines into the yank buffer, and yG yanks all the lines from the current line to the end of the file into the yank buffer. After you have yanked the text, you can position the cursor where you want the yanked text to be inserted and then enter a put command (you'll learn more about put shortly). This is equivalent to a copy and paste operation.

To do a cut and paste operation, you use the standard delete command. Whenever you delete text, that text is automatically put into the yank buffer. You can then insert the deleted text anywhere in the main buffer just as you do when you yank text. For example, dw deletes one word and puts that word into the yank buffer. The command 3dd deletes three lines and puts those three lines into the yank buffer.

To put the contents of the yank buffer into your file, use one of the put commands: p or P. The p command inserts the text *after* the cursor; the P command inserts the text *before* the cursor. If the yanked text is less than an entire line (a word, for example), it is inserted into the current line before or after the cursor (depending on whether you're using p or P). If the yanked text includes at least one full line, that text is inserted into a new line above or below the line containing the cursor (again depending on whether you're using p or P).

In addition to the standard yank buffer, vi has 26 other special buffers called *named buffers*. The named buffers are named by the 26 characters in the alphabet. You can store text into any of these named buffers for later retrieval. For example, you can store one line of text into named buffer a and another line of text into named buffer b. To yank text into a named buffer, you must precede the yank (or delete) command with a double quotation mark and the character representing the named buffer. For example, to yank one line into named buffer x, enter the following:

```
"xyy
```

To retrieve the contents of a named buffer, you precede the put command with a double quotation mark and the character representing the buffer name. For example, to retrieve the contents of buffer x, enter the following:

```
"xp
```

The named buffers are available also when you want to delete lines. Use the delete command exactly as you have learned earlier except first enter the double quotation mark and the name of the buffer. For example, to delete to the end of the file into named buffer t, enter

```
"tdG
```

and retrieve it with

```
"tp
```

When you yank text into a named buffer, any existing text in that named buffer is overwritten. You can append to the text in a named buffer if you use the uppercase form of the letter that represents the named buffer. For example, to append one line to named buffer b, enter the following:

```
"Byy
```

There is no way to examine the contents of a buffer without actually putting the text into the file somewhere. This really isn't a problem, however, because after you have put the contents of a buffer into the file you can easily undo the put operation with the undo command (u).

The yank and put features are particularly useful when you want to copy some text from one file into another. For example, you can edit one file, yank some text into a named buffer, and then put it into another file. After you have yanked text from the first file into a named buffer, use the :e file command (discussed earlier in this chapter) to load the second file into the buffer. Once the new file is loaded, put the contents of the named buffer into it, using the same put command you have already learned. If you want to yank text from one file and put it into another file, you must use a named buffer; the general yank buffer is not maintained across files.

The vi editor maintains another set of buffers that contain the last nine deletions. These buffers are automatically created and maintained by vi. Every time you delete some text it is stored into one of these buffers (we'll call them the *delete buffers*). To retrieve the text in a delete buffer, use the put command preceded by a double quotation mark and the number of the delete buffer. For example, to retrieve the text most recently deleted, enter the following:

```
"1p
```

To retrieve the text deleted five delete operations ago, enter the following:

```
"5p
```

You cycle through each of the delete buffers by using the undo and repeat commands. These commands are useful because you may often find it difficult to remember exactly how many deletions ago you removed some text that you now want to restore. The easiest way to do this is to retrieve the first delete buffer with the "1p command. If this is not the text you want to restore, just undo it with the u command and then repeat the previous operation (the put) with dot (.). When you use dot in combination with putting delete buffers, the delete buffer that is retrieved is automatically incremented. So, when you enter u followed by a period (.), the second delete buffer is retrieved. Then enter u and . again, and the third delete buffer is retrieved, and so on.

Here is a summary of the yank and put commands:

yy	Yank one line into the yank buffer.
y<*target*>	Yank to *target* into the yank buffer.
p	Put the contents of the yank buffer after the cursor.
P	Put the contents of the yank buffer before the cursor.
"*x*y<*target*>	Yank to *target* and put into named buffer *x*.
"*X*y<*target*>	Yank to *target* and append to named buffer *x*.
"*x*p	Put the contents of named buffer *x* after the cursor.

"*x*P	Put the contents of named buffer *x* before the cursor.

Here are a few examples of yank commands:

3yW	Yank three words (ignoring punctuation) into the yank buffer.
"ayG	Yank into named buffer a from the current line to the end of the file.
"v17dd	Delete 17 lines and put them into named buffer v.
"qy/*string*<Return>	Yank into named buffer q from the cursor position to the pattern *string*.

Searching and Replacing

All the commands we have discussed in the previous two sections have been open visual commands. In this section you will learn how to search and replace text in the file by using one of two ex commands: :s and :g.

Let's start with the :s (substitute or search) command. The format of the :s command is this:

```
:[address]s/old/new/[option]
```

All occurrences of *old* are replaced with *new* in the addressed lines. The address field is optional. If the address is not included, the substitution takes place only on the line containing the cursor. You can supply a single line number for an address, or a range of line numbers separated by a comma. For example, to change "caterpillar" to "butterfly" on lines 2 through 27, enter the following:

```
:2,27s/caterpillar/butterfly/
```

You can specify a line number in a variety of ways. You can use the actual line number as shown in the preceding example, or a marked line (such as 'x), or a search string (such as /pattern/). If you use a search string, you must begin and end the pattern with a slash. You can also use dot (.) to represent the current line and $ to represent the last line of the file. The special character % is used to represent the entire file. So, to change all occurrences of caterpillar to butterfly enter:

```
:%s/caterpillar/butterfly/
```

The option field that follows the new replacement string can be a g or c or both. The g represents *global,* which means that the substitution is done globally on each line. By default, only the first occurrence of the old string is replaced by the new string on each line. The g indicates that all occurrences of the old string should be replaced per line.

The c option represents *confirm*. With the confirm option set, vi prompts you before making each substitution. Enter y<Return> to make the change; n<Return> to not make the change.

The :g (global) command executes a command on all the lines that have a particular pattern. The format of the :g command is this:

```
:g/pattern/command
```

The pattern is any standard search string. The command is a command such as d to delete a line. For example, the following command deletes all the lines that contain the string pattern2:

```
:g/pattern2/d
```

Here are some examples of substitute and global commands:

:1,10s/will/won't/g	Change all occurrences of *will* to *won't* in lines 1 through 10.
:.,$s/pattern1/pattern2/	Change all occurrences of pattern1 to pattern2 from the current line to the end of the file. Change only the first occurrence of pattern1 to pattern2 per line.
:4,'cs/string1/string2/gc	Change all occurrences of string1 to string2 from line 4 to the line marked c, and confirm each change.
:g/pattern3/>	Right-shift all the lines containing pattern3.

Reading and Writing Files

In the beginning of this chapter you learned how to invoke vi, write the file, and quit vi. In this section we'll talk more about writing the buffer contents to a file and also about how to read (include) other files into the buffer.

Reading Files

To read a file into the buffer, use the :r command followed by the name of the file to read. For example, to include the file memo in the current file, enter the following:

```
:r memo
```

The file memo is read into the buffer following the line that contains the cursor. You can also specify a line number on which to have the file read if you do not want it read at the current line. For example, the command

```
:5r memo
```

loads the memo file following line 5. If you want to load the file at the beginning of the buffer, use zero for the line number:

```
:0r memo
```

You can load only one file in at a time; the r command accepts only one argument.

Writing files

You have already learned about the basic :w command, which writes the contents of the buffer to the associated file. You can also provide an argument to :w that specifies the name of the file (other than the associated file name) to which the buffer should be written. This is sometimes useful if you want to create a copy of an existing file with some slight modifications. You can invoke vi on the file, make the modifications, and then write the buffer to a new file name. This leaves the original file unchanged. If you want to leave the original file intact, exit vi with :q!.

Sometimes you may need to write a file that is not the file associated with the buffer, but is one that already exists. If you try to use :w with a file-name argument and that file already exists, vi does not write the file but prints a warning message on the status line. To force the write to the existing file (assuming you have the correct permissions), use the :w! command. For example, to write the contents of the buffer to an existing file named memo1, use the following command:

```
:w! memo1
```

If you want to append the contents of the buffer to an existing file, use the :w>> command. Follow the command with the name of the file to append. For example, to append the buffer contents to memo3, enter the following:

```
:w>>memo3
```

When you write a file, you don't have to write the entire contents of the buffer. You can specify a line range before the w and only those lines will be written. For example, to write lines 15 through 27 to a file named memo4, enter the following:

```
:15,27w memo4
```

Or, you can use a line range and append the lines to a file with the following:

```
:15,27w>>memo4
```

Filtering the Buffer

One of the most powerful features available in vi is the ability to filter text from the buffer through a UNIX command and have the output of the command sent back into the buffer. What this means is that you can execute a command on a portion of text in the buffer and have the output of the command replace the original text. For example, you may be editing a list of names and you need to sort them. Instead of having to write and quit the file, run the sort command on the file, create a new file with the sorted output, and then edit that new file, you could simply sort the contents of the buffer from within vi.

Some editors have many features like sorting built into them. The vi editor takes a different approach. Rather than offering built-in features like sorting, vi lets you use any existing command on the text in the buffer. This makes vi much more powerful than editors that have built-in features. The designers of vi (and ex, for that matter) could never have anticipated the needs of every user. But by allowing any regular UNIX command to be executed on the buffer, the needs of the user can be much more easily satisfied.

To execute a command on text in the buffer, use the exclamation (!) command. The format of the exclamation command follows the general command format, as shown here:

```
[count]!<target>
```

By specifying a count and a target, you are specifying the text (perhaps words, lines, or the whole file) that will act as input to the command you specify. When you have entered the [*count*]!<*target*> part of the command, the cursor moves to the bottom line of the window and an exclamation prompt is displayed. You then enter the UNIX command that you want executed on the text you have specified.

To demonstrate this command, let's suppose you are editing a paragraph and you have uneven line lengths that you want to clean up. (This should sound familiar; you do the same thing with the Format item on the Extras menu with the Text Editor.) A UNIX command called fmt does that very operation. To run the fmt command on the paragraph you are working on, follow these steps:

1. Position the cursor at the beginning of the paragraph.
2. Enter **!}** which means that you want to send all the text from the current line to the end of the paragraph (in other words, the entire paragraph) to a UNIX command. The cursor is now displayed on the last line with the exclamation prompt.
3. Enter fmt and press Return.

The entire paragraph is replaced with a new paragraph that has been formatted by fmt.

There are many applications for using this feature. You may want to expand all the tabs in a file by using the expand command. You can sort a file or a portion of a file. You can even run a command like find (which doesn't take a file as input) and insert the output of find into the buffer. With a command like find, you do not need to use any text in the buffer to send to find. You can simply create a blank line and enter !! (which operates only on the current line) and then enter the UNIX command. The output of the command is inserted into the buffer. Try this example yourself: create a blank line in your buffer and enter !!date. The current date provided by the date command is inserted into the buffer on the current line.

Using Advanced Features

The vi editor supports many customization options that you can set with the :set command. To see which options are currently set, enter

```
:set<Return>
```

To see all the options available, enter

```
:set all<Return>
```

In this section I'll briefly describe some of the most common and useful customization options. If you want to set any of these options so that each time you invoke vi they are automatically set, you can do so by setting the EXINIT environment variable. For example, to set the autoindent feature and the wrap margin to 4, you set the EXINIT environment variable to "set autoindent wrapmargin=4." If you are a C shell user, you do this by entering the following command:

```
dugout% setenv EXINIT 'set autoindent wrapmargin=4'
```

If you are using the Korn or Bourne shell, use the following command:

```
$ EXINIT='set autoindent wrapmargin=4'
$ export EXINIT
```

You will probably want to put these commands into the appropriate start-up file such as .cshrc or .profile.

Here are some of the most common and useful options available:

:set autoindent *or* :set ai	Automatically indent the line, based on the indentation of the previous line.
:set list	Show all tabs as ^I rather than as white space.
:set number	Number each line.
:set ignorecase *or* :set ic	Ignore case of characters when doing searches.
:set wrapmargin=*X* *or* :set wm=*X*	Automatically set the right margin to *X* characters. (When the margin is reached, a new line is automatically inserted.)
:set shiftwidth=*X* *or* :set sw=*X*	Set the shift width to *X*. (The shift width is the number of characters that are shifted when you use the shift commands, < and >.)
:map x command	Map a character to multiple commands.
:ab str long_string	Abbreviate a string of characters to a different string of characters. (Useful when you must repeatedly enter a long string.)
:!shell command	Execute a shell command. Don't insert the output into the buffer.

Summary

There are so many commands in vi that it is almost impossible to remember all of them the first time you are introduced to them. Start with the basic commands, and when you are familiar with them, go back and review the material in this chapter and try to put some new concepts into practice. You will likely be surprised at what new features you have not yet tried or mastered. The possibilities are virtually limitless.

CHAPTER 14

The Shell

Job Control

I/O Redirection and Pipes

The History List

Other Useful Shell Features

The Korn Shell

IN CHAPTER 2 YOU WERE INTRODUCED TO THE SHELL, AND IN CHAPTERS 11, 12, and 13 you used the shell to enter commands such as cat, grep, and vi. By now you are probably comfortable with using the shell to execute commands. The shell provides you with an interactive interface to the SunOS operating system and allows you to customize your environment. You can also use the shell to create programs constructed from UNIX commands. In this chapter you will expand your knowledge of the shell and its features.

As you learned in Chapter 2, there is more than one shell. Each shell has a slightly different "flavor." All shells provide basically the same features, but each one has different syntax and options. In this chapter we'll discuss both the C shell and the Korn shell, but we'll emphasize the C shell. In the last part of this chapter there is a short section on the Korn shell and the ways that it differs from the C shell. If you are using the C shell exclusively, you can skip that section. If you are using the Korn shell, you should read the first part of the chapter to learn some standard shell concepts that are shared by both shells, and then also read the Korn shell section. At the end of this chapter is a table that outlines the similarities and differences between the C and Korn shells.

You may also recall from Chapter 2 that a start-up file is executed when you start the shell. The C shell uses the .login and .cshrc files. The Korn shell uses the .profile file. As you learn about features of the shell in this chapter, you may want to put commands in your .cshrc file (or .profile file if you are using the Korn shell) to customize your environment. Setting shell variables and aliases are two of the most common things found in start-up files.

In this chapter you will learn how to do the following:

- Control jobs
- Redirect I/O and pipes
- Use the history mechanism
- Use aliases
- Do command-line editing in the Korn shell

Job Control

When you enter a command at the prompt, you are telling the shell to execute a program (also called a *process*). A process can run in the *foreground* or the *background*. You can stop and restart running jobs without terminating them.

Running a Job in the Foreground

When you enter a command at the prompt and press Return, that command runs in the foreground by default. When you run a foreground process, the shell does not return the prompt until the process has been completed or terminated. To run the find command in the foreground, enter the command at the prompt and press Return, as shown in this example:

```
dugout% find / -name "*.c" -exec grep -l dropTarget {} \;
<Wait for the find command to complete execution before the prompt returns>
dugout%
```

Running a Job in the Background

A background process is started when you enter an ampersand (&) at the end of the command line, before you press Return. This executes the same command but puts it in the background. The prompt is returned to you immediately so that you can enter other commands. Here is an example:

```
dugout% find / -name "*.c" -exec grep -l dropTarget {} \; &
[1] 438
dugout%
```

The advantage of executing a command in the background is especially apparent when that command is one that takes a long time to run. The find command shown in the preceding example can take several minutes to run to completion, depending on the amount of disk space on your system. If you run the command in the foreground, then your shell (the one running in that window) is tied up until find is finished running; you can't enter another command in that window until it is finished. If, however, you execute find in the background, you get the prompt back immediately and you can enter other commands.

Throughout this book you have learned how to execute different DeskSet applications on the command line. In each case, an ampersand was included at the end of the command. This is customary (though not required) because without the ampersand the DeskSet application runs in the foreground. If the application runs in the foreground, the shell does not return the prompt until the application has been terminated. This renders that window unusable for any other purpose until the application is completed. So it makes more sense to run DeskSet applications in the background.

Using the jobs Command

When you execute a command in the background, the shell displays two pieces of information about the command: the job number and the process ID. In the previous example, the job number is one (the number enclosed in square brackets) and the process ID is 438. The *job number* is a number assigned by the shell to keep track of the processes (jobs) that are controlled by that particular shell. Each shell assigns job numbers starting at one and increasing sequentially. The *process ID* is the number assigned to the process by the operating system. Every process running on your system has a unique process ID, regardless of the shell in which it is running. (In most cases, a job and a process are equivalent; however, sometimes one job consists of multiple processes.) These numbers let you change the status of a job. For example, you can terminate a job, stop a job, or move a background job into the foreground.

To get the status of the jobs running in your shell, use the jobs command. This command reports on each job that is running. It displays the job number, the status, and the commands being executed, as shown in this example:

```
dugout% jobs
[1]    Running              find / -name *.c -exec grep -l dropTarget {} ;
dugout%
```

You can get additional information about jobs by using the -l option to the jobs command. It reports the same information, with the addition of the process ID, as shown here:

```
dugout% jobs -l
[1]    438 Running              find / -name *.c -exec grep -l dropTarget
{} ;
dugout%
```

Stopping Jobs

A job can be either running (in the foreground or background) or *stopped*. You might want to stop a vi job, for example, so that you can enter some command and then get right back into vi. It is much faster to stop vi and then restart (continue) it than it is to quit vi and then start a whole new vi process. A stopped job is in a sort of limbo: its execution has been interrupted, and therefore it isn't running, but it can continue running if you want it to do so. If you stop a running job and then restart it, the job picks up at the place it left off. In the preceding example, if you started the find command in the background, you could stop the job by entering the stop command followed by a percent sign and the job number, as shown here:

```
dugout% stop %1
dugout% jobs
[1]  + Stopped (signal)     find / -name *.c -exec grep -l dropTarget {} ;
dugout%
```

You stop a job that is running in the foreground by entering Control-Z (^Z). When you stop a foreground job with Control-Z, the word Stopped is displayed and the prompt is returned. You can use Control-Z with most commands. For example, if you are editing a file with the vi editor, you can use

Control-Z to stop the vi process. If you then execute the jobs command, you will see that your vi process still exists, but has been stopped:

```
dugout% jobs
[1]     Stopped (signal)      find / -name *.c -exec grep -l dropTarget {} ;
[2]   + Stopped               vi .cshrc
dugout%
```

If the job you want to stop is itself a shell, use the suspend command. For example, if you have used the su command to become the super user, a new shell has been started. You can stop the shell process associated with su by using suspend, as shown here:

```
dugout% su
Password: <Enter password here>
# suspend

Stopped (signal)
dugout% jobs
[1]     Stopped (signal)      find / -name *.c -exec grep -l dropTarget {} ;
[2]   - Stopped               vi .cshrc
[3]   + Stopped (signal)      su
dugout%
```

As you can see from the output of jobs, the su command has been stopped by the suspend command. If you attempt to stop a shell process by entering Control-Z, nothing happens; you must use the suspend command.

Changing the Status of a Job

When a job is stopped, you can restart it in the background or foreground by using the bg and fg commands, respectively. Each command is followed by a percent sign and the job number. For example, to restart the stopped find command in the background, enter bg %1 as shown here:

```
dugout% bg %1
[1]     find / -name *.c -exec grep -l dropTarget {} ; &
dugout%
```

If you are editing a file with vi and have stopped it with Control-Z, don't execute vi again; rather, just put the vi job back into the foreground by entering fg %2 (or just %2):

```
dugout% fg %2
<Vi continues running>
```

If you have stopped jobs, you will see when you use the jobs command that one of the jobs has a plus sign in the status line. The plus sign represents the most recently stopped job. If there is more than one stopped job, the second most recently stopped job will include a minus sign in the status line. The following example shows the output of the jobs command identifying four jobs: One is running, and the other three are stopped. The vi /etc/passwd job is the most recently stopped job, and the more /etc/termcap job is the second most recently stopped job.

```
dugout% jobs
[1]    Running          find / -name *.c -exec grep -l dropTarget {} ;
[2]    Stopped          vi .cshrc
[3]  - Stopped          more /etc/termcap
[4]  + Stopped          vi /etc/passwd
dugout%
```

If you enter the bg or fg commands without an argument, the most recently stopped job is the one that is put into the background or foreground. So, if you entered fg with no argument, the vi /etc/passwd process would be put into the foreground. This is convenient when you are editing with vi and want to stop for a moment to enter a command at the prompt. You enter Control-Z to stop vi and then enter your UNIX command at the prompt. When you have finished entering your command and want to get back into vi, you don't have to remember the job number; you just type fg.

Receiving Notification of Completion

When a background job is finished, you receive notification from the shell the next time you enter a Return. If you want immediate notification, use the notify command. For example, if the find process is running in the background and you want immediate notification when it is finished, enter the notify command followed by the job number (including the percent sign):

```
dugout% notify %1
dugout%
```

If you want to be notified for all background jobs when they are finished, set the shell notify variable:

```
dugout% set notify
dugout%
```

Terminating Jobs

When you want to terminate a process running in the foreground, you simply enter Control-C. If you want to terminate a job that is stopped or that is in the background, use the kill command. The kill command takes one or more arguments representing the job numbers or the process IDs of the running process. For example, to terminate the find and more jobs by using job numbers, enter the following:

```
dugout% kill %1 %3
dugout%
```

I/O Redirection and Pipes

Commands such as cat and grep normally write their output to the window (or the screen) in which they are executed. Other commands, such as vi, do not output any text to the screen. The vi editor displays a file in the window and can write to a file, but it does not directly output to the window. When a command does write its output to the window, that output is called the *standard output*. The standard output is the standard or expected output of a command. Output of a command that is not a part of the expected output may also appear in the window. This is called *standard error*, and it includes error or warning messages.

The programmer who wrote the program decided which output would go to standard output and which would go to standard error. Both appear in the window as output of the command; however, there is a difference between the two. The difference is that you have the choice to send standard output only or standard output and standard error to a file or another program. For example, you may want to run the find command and redirect the standard output to a file, but you don't want to see any warning messages that find produced, so you don't redirect standard error. If, however, you are a programmer running the make command you may want to save the standard output and the standard error to a file by redirecting both.

The input that a program expects is called *standard input*. For example, when you use mailx, it is expected that you will input text in the window and that mailx receives and uses that text as the body of the message. That is the standard input for mailx. If you want, you can specify that the standard input be received from a file rather than from the keyboard; this is an example of redirecting standard input.

Redirecting Standard Output

Redirecting standard output is quite simple. On the command line, enter a greater-than sign (>) followed by the name of the file to which you want the standard output written. For example, the output of the find command can be redirected to the file findout with the following command:

```
dugout% find / -print > findout
dugout%
```

Redirection is independent of foreground or background processing. If you are redirecting standard output and want the process to run in the background, put an ampersand at the end of the command as shown here:

```
dugout% find / -print > findout &
[1]   440
dugout%
```

The file findout is created that contains the output of the find command. If a file named findout already existed before you entered this command, it would be overwritten without warning. If you want to avoid overwriting an existing file with redirection, you can set the noclobber variable:

```
dugout% set noclobber
dugout%
```

If this variable is set and a file named findout already existed in the current directory, the shell will not run the command. Instead, it displays a message, as shown here:

```
dugout% find / -print > findout
findout: File exists
dugout%
```

If you have the noclobber variable set, you can force the shell to overwrite an existing file by using an exclamation mark after the greater-than sign:

```
dugout% find / -print >! findout
dugout%
```

Throughout the remainder of this chapter all the examples assume that the noclobber variable is not set.

To append the standard output to an existing file, use two greater-than signs (>>). To demonstrate this, let's look at an example that uses the grep command:

```
dugout% grep Jeff file1 >> phonelist
dugout%
```

This example appends the output of the grep command to the file phonelist. If the phonelist file did not already exist, it would be created.

Redirecting Standard Error

The standard error is reserved for error or warning messages. Many commands rarely output any messages to standard error; others use standard error frequently. The find command, for example, displays a message to standard error every time it attempts to search in a directory for which it does not have permission. If you run the find command demonstrated earlier, you may see output similar to that shown here:

```
dugout% find / -print > findout
find: cannot read dir /lost+found: Permission denied
find: cannot read dir /export/home/lost+found: Permission denied
find: cannot read dir /export/home/sally/.fm: Permission denied
   .
   .
```

```
.
<More output not shown here>
dugout%
```

In this example, the standard output is redirected to the file findout, and the standard error is written to the window. To redirect both the standard output and the standard error to the file findout, use a greater-than sign and an ampersand (>&):

```
dugout% find / -print >& findout
dugout%
```

The ampersand used along with the greater-than sign should not be confused with the ampersand used at the end of a command to put the command into the background. The two are independent, as shown here:

```
dugout% find / -print >& findout &
[1]    441
dugout%
```

You can also append the standard output and standard error to a file by using two greater-than signs and an ampersand (>>&), as shown here:

```
dugout% find / -print >>& findout
dugout%
```

The C shell does not provide a direct way to send the standard output and standard error to different files. However, you can use the following trick to separate the two. Enclose in parentheses the command that redirects standard output, and then redirect the output of that command to standard error, as shown here:

```
dugout% (find / -print > findout) >& finderr
dugout%
```

The standard output is written to the file findout, and the standard error is written to the file finderr. This technique does not work without the parentheses.

Redirecting Standard Input

When a command requires you to input some text, you can redirect that input from a file. To redirect standard input, use the less-than sign (<) followed by the name of the file that the input should be taken from. For example, to use the contents of a file named textfile as the message body of a mail message sent by mailx, use the following command:

```
dugout% mailx sally < textfile
dugout%
```

Normally, when you invoke mailx, you enter the text of the message from the keyboard. By using input redirection, you can construct a message in a file and then use that file as the body of the message. Notice that mailx does not prompt you for the subject or for any other fields when you redirect standard input. If you want to set the subject or cc fields, you can use command-line options provided by mailx (see the mailx man page).

Using Pipes

You've just learned how you can send the output of a command to a file and how you can use a file as the input to a command. You can even combine these techniques to produce a file by redirecting standard output, and then use that file as standard input to a command such as mail. You might do something like this:

```
dugout% find / -print > findout
dugout% mailx sally < findout
dugout%
```

This method works perfectly; you create a file called findout and then use that file as the body of a mail message that you send to sally. However, you can accomplish the same result by sending the standard output of one command (find) directly to the standard input of another command (mailx) with the use of a *pipe*. A pipe (|) sends the standard output of one command to the standard input of the next command. For example, to run the find command and mail the result directly to sally, use the following command:

```
dugout% find / -print | mailx sally
dugout%
```

Or, perhaps you want to send the output of the find command directly to the printer. You enter this command:

```
dugout% find / -print | lp
dugout%
```

The advantages of this method are that you have to enter only one command and you avoid having to create an intermediate file. If you want to pipe both the standard output and the standard error to another program, use |&, as shown here:

```
dugout% find / -print |& mailx sally
dugout%
```

Many commands that normally take a command-line argument representing a file, can also read from standard input. For example, the grep command usually takes one or more file names as command-line arguments through which it searches for character strings. If you do not supply a file name as a command-line argument, grep reads from the standard input. This is useful if you want to first process a file (or files) with a command such as sort, and then send the output to grep. For example, to sort files alpha and beta and then pipe the output to grep, use the following command:

```
dugout% sort alpha beta | grep chapter
chapter1
chapter3
dugout%
```

This example uses grep without a file name argument, so grep reads the standard input and uses it as the "file" through which to search. Many other commands follow this model: If the file name argument is not included, standard input is read. Commands that read from the standard input are sometimes called *filters*. Some of the commands you are familiar with that act as filters are grep, cat, more, sort, and lp.

You can combine more than two commands by using multiple pipes. For example, suppose you want to mail some files to a user named bill, but you first want them sorted and any lines containing "John" removed from the sorted output. You could do this all in one command by entering the following:

```
dugout% sort file1 file2 | grep -v John | mailx bill
dugout%
```

You can also combine pipes and standard output redirection. If you want those same files sorted and "grepped" but want the output stored in a file, enter the following:

```
dugout% sort file1 file2 | grep -v John > sort_john
dugout%
```

On occasion you may want to both store the standard output of a command in a file and pipe it to another command. You can do this with the tee command. The tee command is a filter that sends its output to two places: to the standard output and to the file you specify as an argument. So, if you want to have file1 and file2 sorted and grepped but want a copy of the output put into a file and mailed to bill, you use the following command to do all this in one step:

```
dugout% sort file1 file2 | grep -v John | tee sort_john | mailx bill
dugout%
```

In this case the tee command reads from the standard input (the output of the grep command) and writes the text it received from standard input to the file sort-john, and to standard output, which mailx reads and then mails to bill. If you want to append to the file sort-john, use the -a (append) option to tee, as shown here:

```
dugout% sort file1 file2 | grep -v John | tee -a sort_john | mailx bill
dugout%
```

Chaining Commands

You can execute multiple commands sequentially by *chaining* commands on the command line. You chain commands on a single command line by separating the commands with a semicolon (;). Each command is executed consecutively. For example, to use cd to change to the /tmp directory and then execute the ls command, you enter the following two commands:

```
dugout% cd /tmp; ls
file1 file2 file3
dugout%
```

Or, perhaps you want to print a file, but you would like to specify a delay before printing. You can use the sleep command (which simply pauses for the number of seconds you specify) followed by the lp command to print your file, as shown here:

```
dugout% sleep 60; lp file
request id is SPARCprinter-1234 (1 file(s))
dugout%
```

The History List

The shell maintains a history list of each command you enter at the prompt. The number of commands that the shell remembers depends on the history shell variable (usually set in your .cshrc or .login file). The default is 1. To set the history variable to 20, enter the following command:

```
dugout% set history=20
dugout%
```

With the history variable set to 20, the history list contains the last 20 commands entered. To display the history list, enter the history command, as shown here:

```
dugout% history
    23  set
    24  set history=20
    25  ls /tmp
```

```
    26  cat /etc/passwd
    27  cp .cshrc .cshrc.new
    28  vi .cshrc.new
    29  cmdtool &
    30  jobs
    31  kill %1
    32  vi .cshrc.new
    33  fg
    34  mailx james < .cshrc.new
    35  find / -name "*.c" -exec grep -l dropTarget {} \;
    36  bg
    37  jobs
    38  stop %2
    39  fg %1
    40  ls
    41  rm core
    42  history
dugout%
```

Each item in the history list includes a number (the history number) followed by the command. You can use this list for information only, or you can use it to rerun a command, as you will learn in the next section. You can also supply an argument to history to specify how many previous commands you want to list. For example, to list the five last commands, enter 5 as an argument to the history command, as shown here:

```
dugout% history 5
    39  fg %1
    40  ls
    41  rm core
    42  history
    43  history 5
dugout%
```

Rerunning a Previous Command

You can rerun commands from the history list in several ways. To rerun the previous command, enter two exclamation marks (!!), as shown here:

```
dugout% !!
history 5
    40  ls
    41  rm core
    42  history
```

```
    43  history 5
    44  history 5
dugout%
```

The previous command (history 5, in this case) is displayed and executed. You can execute a particular command from the history list by entering an exclamation mark followed by the history number. For example, to run command 35 again, enter !35, as shown here:

```
dugout% !35
find / -name "*.c" -exec grep -l dropTarget {} \;
<Output of the find command displayed here>
dugout%
```

It's not very likely that you will remember the history numbers of the commands you've entered, so you will probably have to run the history command to find the number of the command you want, and then rerun the command by using this method. Another method you can use to rerun a command is to enter an exclamation mark followed by the first few characters of the command. It's usually easier to remember the first few characters of a command than it is to remember the history number, so you can often do this without having to display the history list. For example, to rerun the cp command, you enter the following:

```
dugout% !cp
cp .cshrc .cshrc.new
dugout%
```

The shell searches through the history list (starting at the most recently entered command), finds the command that begins with the characters you specify (cp in this case), and reruns that command. You do not have to enter the full command name, but only enough characters that the name is not misinterpreted. If you had entered only !c, the shell would have rerun command 29 (cmdtool) because that command also starts with a c and is more recent than cp.

You can also rerun a command by specifying a string of characters that appears anywhere within the command—not just at the beginning—by using !? followed by the string. For example, to rerun the command that includes the string "drop," enter the following:

```
dugout% !?drop
find / -name "*.c" -exec grep -l dropTarget {} \;
<Output of the find command displayed here>
dugout%
```

The find command is rerun because it contains the string "drop."

Another way of executing a previous command is to specify how many other commands you have entered since you entered that command. For example, to enter the fifth most recently entered command, you enter !–5, as shown here:

```
dugout% !-5
history 5
    44  history 5
    45  find / -name "*.c" -exec grep -l dropTarget {} \;
    46  cp .cshrc .cshrc.new
    47  find / -name "*.c" -exec grep -l dropTarget {} \;
    48  history 5
dugout%
```

The shell searches back five commands in its history list and reexecutes that command. This technique is often convenient when you want to reexecute, say, the second most recently entered command. You use !! to reexecute the previous command, and you use !-2 to reexecute the command entered before the previous command.

Modifying a Previous Command

The shell also provides a mechanism that allows you to use a particular argument of a previously entered command. You can use this feature to modify a command, correct a typing error, or reexecute a similar, but not identical, command.

Any of the methods for rerunning a command that we have discussed so far can be followed by new, additional arguments. For example, command 26 in our history list is the cat command. If you want to rerun command 26 but also redirect the output to a file named mypasswd, you enter the following:

```
dugout% !26 > mypasswd
cat /etc/passwd > mypasswd
dugout%
```

This saves you the effort of typing command 26; you simply rerun it and add new command-line arguments. You can do the same thing with any of the techniques that rerun a command. For example, if you want to use vi to edit the .cshrc.new file (command 28) and also edit .Xdefaults, you enter the following:

```
dugout% !vi .Xdefaults
vi .cshrc.new .Xdefaults
<The vi command is run with .cshrc.new
and .Xdefaults as arguments>
```

The shell's history mechanism also allows you to use one or more arguments from a previously entered command that is in the history list. This is a very convenient function that I use frequently. In the preceding example, we ran vi on two files: .cshrc.new and .Xdefaults. After editing those files, you may want to print, copy, or list them. You can reenter the previous command's arguments (.cshrc.new and .Xdefaults, in this case) by using !* as the argument to the next command you enter. For example, if the next command you want to execute is to print the two files that you just edited, you can save yourself the trouble of typing the names of the files again. Instead, enter !* as the argument to the lp command, as shown here:

```
dugout% lp !*
lp .cshrc.new .Xdefaults
request id is SPARCprinter-1232 (2 file(s))
dugout%
```

You can also be more specific about the previous command's arguments. If you want to refer only to the last argument of the previous command, enter !$; to refer to the first argument of the previous command enter !^. To demonstrate this, let's cat the file entered as the first argument of the previous command (lp):

```
dugout% cat !^
cat .cshrc.new
<Output of the cat command here>
dugout%
```

If you have more than two arguments and you want to refer to one of the "middle" arguments, you can use a colon followed by the argument number. For example, if you want to reuse the third argument from the previous command, you use !:3.

Anytime you use special history characters at the prompt, the history list includes the full command—not the history characters (such as !! or !^). Here are the last ten commands we have entered:

```
dugout% history 10
    44  history 5
    45  find / -name "*.c" -exec grep -l dropTarget {} \;
    46  cp .cshrc .cshrc.new
    47  find / -name "*.c" -exec grep -l dropTarget {} \;
    48  history 5
    49  cat /etc/passwd > mypasswd
    50  vi .cshrc.new .Xdefaults
    51  lp .cshrc.new .Xdefaults
    52  cat .cshrc.new
```

```
   53  history 10
dugout%
```

If you want to reuse an argument from a command other than the most recently entered command, you enter the command number after the exclamation mark. For example, to run vi with the last argument from command 49, you enter the following:

```
dugout% vi !49$
vi mypasswd
<The vi command is run with mypasswd as an argument>
```

If you have mistyped a command, you can correct the error without reentering the entire command. Use the caret (^) to delimit the old and new characters from the previous command. For example, let's say you want to copy your .cshrc file to /tmp. You accidentally enter .chsrc (which, of course doesn't exist). The cp command complains that .chsrc doesn't exist. Instead of reentering the entire command, you can use the caret to replace just the characters that you mistyped, as shown here:

```
dugout% cp .chsrc /tmp
cp: cannot access .chsrc
dugout% ^hs^sh^
cp .cshrc /tmp
dugout%
```

When the command you enter is a short one, the time savings may not seem too great. If, however, you have entered a long, complicated command, as in the next example, this technique may save you considerable time.

```
dugout% find / -type f -name '*.[ch]' -exec grep -l dropTarget {} \; >
output
dugout% ^Target^Widget^
find / -type f -name '*.[ch]' -exec grep -l dropWidget {} \; > output
<Output of the find command displayed here>
dugout%
```

Using the caret works only on the most recently entered command. If you want to modify another command, you can use a technique similar to the search-and-replace syntax of the vi editor. To change the word dropTarget in command 35 to WidgetClass, use the s (substitute) command, as shown here:

```
dugout% !35:s/dropTarget/WidgetClass/
find / -name "*.c" -exec grep -l WidgetClass {} \;
<Output of the find command displayed here>
dugout%
```

By default, only one occurrence (the first occurrence) of the string is replaced. If you want to globally replace a string in a previous command, use the gs (globally substitute) command. For example, if you copied three files named memo.c, memo.o, and memo.h to the /tmp directory, you could repeat the command, replacing all occurrences of memo with sort, by using the following command:

```
dugout% cp memo.c memo.o memo.h /tmp
dugout% !!:gs/memo/sort/
cp sort.c sort.o sort.h /tmp
dugout%
```

Table 14.1 summarizes the history commands and characters supported by the C shell.

Table 14.1 The History Commands and Characters Supported by the C Shell

Command	Example	Description
!!	!!	Repeats the previous command.
!*N*	!32	Repeats command number *N* from the history list.
!*pattern*	!cp	Repeats the most recently entered command that begins with the string *pattern*.
!?*pattern*	!?default	Repeats the most recently entered command that includes the string *pattern*.
!-*N*	!-2	Repeats the *N*th most recently entered command.
!*	lp !*	Represents all arguments from the previous command.
!$	vi !$	Represents the last argument from the previous command.
!^	cat !^	Represents the first argument from the previous command.
!:*i*	more !:2	Represents the *i*th argument from the previous command.
!*N**	head !4*	Represents all arguments from the *N*th command.
!*N*$	tail !16$	Represents the last argument from the *N*th command.
!*N*^	vi !22^	Represents the first argument from the *N*th command.
!*N*:*i*	rm !43:3	Represents the *i*th argument from the *N*th command.

Table 14.1 The History Commands and Characters Supported by the C Shell (Continued)

Command	Example	Description
^old^new^	^memo^sort^	Replaces old string with new string in the previous command.
!!:s/old/new/	!!:s/cp/mv/	Substitutes old string with new string in the previous command.
!!:gs/old/new/	!!:gs/memo/sort/	Globally substitutes old string with new string in the previous command.
!*N*:s/old/new/	!27:s/green/red/	Substitutes old string with new string in the *N*th command.
!*N*:gs/old/new/	!35:gs/work/play/	Globally substitutes old string with new string in the *N*th command.

Other Useful Shell Features

We've already covered some of the most important features of the shell in this chapter. Many other features are supported by the shell. In this section, you will be introduced briefly to some of the most popular ones.

Using Built-in Variables

The shell has many built-in variables. Shell variables control features of the shell such as the history list size and the prompt. (Many of the variables in this section are specific to the C shell.) You have already learned about some of them such as the history and notify variables. Others, such as the prompt and filec, are introduced later in this chapter.

You set a variable by using the set command. Some variables, such as filec, do not require an additional argument. You simply set the variable, as shown here:

```
dugout% set filec
dugout%
```

Other variables require a value, such as the history variable. When you set variables that require a value, you use an equals sign followed by the value, as shown here:

```
dugout% set history=100
dugout%
```

You can list the shell's variables by using the set command without an argument, as shown here:

```
dugout% set
argv    ()
cwd     /export/home/pew
filec
history 200
home    /export/home/pew
notify
path    (. /usr/bin /export/home/pew/bin /usr/openwin/bin /usr/ccs/bin)
prompt  dugout%>
savehist        100
shell   /bin/csh
status  0
term    sun-cmd
user    pew
dugout%
```

If you want to use the value of a variable, precede the variable name with a dollar sign ($). For example, you can change directory to your home directory with the following command:

```
dugout% cd $home
dugout%
```

Sometimes you need to isolate a variable name from other characters. You can do this by enclosing the variable name within curly braces, as shown here:

```
dugout% cd ${home}
dugout%
```

For example, let's say you have a variable named "home" whose value is /usr/john. There could possibly be a directory named /usr/john2 that you want to change directly to. If you entered

```
cd $home2
```

the shell would look for a variable named "home2," which doesn't exist and this would fail. You could, however, use the following:

```
cd ${home}2
```

which is the same as

```
cd /usr/john2
```

Table 14.2 briefly describes some of the most commonly used shell variables.

Table 14.2 Some Commonly Used Shell Variables

Variable	Description
cwd	Indicates the current working directory. Usually the same as the return from the pwd command.
filec	Enables file name completion.
history	Indicates the number of lines saved in the history list.
home	Indicates the user's home directory.
ignoreeof	If set, causes the shell to ignore Control-D to logout. You must enter logout instead.
noclobber	Restricts output redirection so that existing files are not overwritten by accident.
noglob	Inhibits the file name substitution.
notify	If set, causes the shell to notify you immediately as jobs are completed.
path	Indicates the list of directories in which to search for commands.
prompt	Indicates the string displayed by the shell as the prompt.
savehist	Indicates the number of lines from the history list that are saved in ~/.history when the user logs out.
shell	Indicates the currently running shell.

Setting the Prompt

The default prompt for the C shell is the host name of the system followed by a percent sign. You have seen the prompt dugout% used throughout this book. Dugout is the host name of my own system. You can change the prompt to any string of characters you desire. For example, to change the prompt to Ready>, enter the following command, which sets the prompt shell variable:

```
dugout% set prompt="Ready> "
Ready>
```

The quotation marks are included so that a single space can be included in the prompt after the right angle bracket (greater-than sign). If you want to customize your prompt, you will probably want to put the set prompt command into your .cshrc or .login file.

You can display the current history number in the prompt by including a \! in the prompt string. For example, to have the prompt display the history number followed by a percent sign, enter the following command:

```
Ready> set prompt="\!% "
19%
```

Each time you enter a command, the prompt displays the new history number, as shown here:

```
19% pwd
/export/home/pew
20% ls -l .cshrc
-rw-r--r--    1 pew      staff        636 Mar 31 23:32 .cshrc
21%
```

Using Aliases

Aliases are a kind of shorthand. By using an alias you can create a custom command with only a few characters. You create an alias for a command that you use frequently, so that you no longer need to type the entire command. An alias also makes it easier for you to execute a complicated command. For example, if you frequently change your current directory to james's home directory, you can create an alias for the command, as shown here:

```
dugout% alias cdj cd ~james
dugout% cdj
dugout% pwd
/export/home/james
dugout%
```

The command cdj is now an alias for cd ~james. When you enter cdj, it is exactly the same as if you were entering cd ~james. The more complicated or frequent the command, the more useful the alias.

You can also pass arguments to an alias. You use \!* to represent all arguments, \!^ to represent the first argument, and \!$ to represent the last argument. For example, if you want an alias that examines the last five lines of a specified file, pipes that text through grep, and mails the output to sally, you use the following command:

```
dugout% alias tgm 'tail -5 \!* | grep VALUE | mailx sally'
dugout% tgm sort.c
dugout%
```

When you execute the tgm alias with sort.c as the argument, the \!* in the alias is replaced by the argument you specify (sort.c).

One of my favorite aliases is the one I use for the cd command. I have aliased cd so that when I enter cd my alias is executed rather than the regular cd command. My cd alias changes my prompt so that it displays the current directory. I use the $cwd shell variable to determine the current directory and set my prompt appropriately. Here is the entry I have in my .cshrc to set the prompt with my cd alias:

```
alias cd 'cd \!*;set prompt="\! ${cwd}> "'
```

This is a fairly complicated alias. It uses command chaining, alias arguments, and shell variables. With this alias set, when I enter cd at the prompt (with or without an argument) the "real" cd command executes to actually change the directory. Then my prompt is set to the history number followed by the new current working directory. Here is an example of how the prompt changes as I change directories:

```
97 /export/home/pew> cd /tmp
98 /tmp> cd ~/bin
99 /export/home/pew/bin> cd /etc/dfs
100 /etc/dfs> cd ~sally
101 /export/home/sally>
```

Using Foreach

The C shell supports a looping mechanism with the foreach command. You use foreach to repeatedly execute a series of commands. The first argument to foreach is a variable name and is followed by a list of items (enclosed in parentheses) that will replace the variable. The following example demonstrates this feature:

```
dugout% foreach no ( 1 2 3 4 5 6 )
? echo looping for number $no
? end
looping for number 1
looping for number 2
looping for number 3
looping for number 4
looping for number 5
looping for number 6
dugout%
```

On the command line you specify the variable (no in this case) and the values that should replace the variable. You are then prompted (with the ? prompt) for the command to run. You can enter as many commands as you like. When you have finished, enter the word "end" at the ? prompt. Foreach then executes each command you entered, replacing the variable ($no) with the values specified. In this example, the echo command is executed six times: once for each of the six arguments enclosed in parentheses.

The foreach command has many useful purposes. For example, suppose you want to send the line containing the user's phone number from a phone list file to each of several users on your system. You can use foreach to simplify the process, as shown here:

```
dugout% foreach user ( sally james wendy wilbur )
? grep $user phonelist | mailx $user
? end
dugout%
```

Expanding an Argument by Using Braces

A technique for expanding arguments is to use curly braces ({ and }) to enclose a comma-separated list of strings. The strings enclosed in the braces are consecutively substituted into the string that contains the braces. For example,

```
A{red,green,blue}B
```

expands to

```
AredB AgreenB AblueB
```

Using this feature will save you some typing. For example, to create three directories, you can enter the following:

```
dugout% mkdir ~/PhoneList/{personal,business,private}
dugout%
```

This would be identical to entering this command:

```
dugout% mkdir ~/PhoneList/personal ~/PhoneList/business ~/PhoneList/private
dugout%
```

The longer the nonbraces portion of the command, the more advantageous it is to use braces. For example, you can use braces to copy several files from a common directory when you can't find a wildcard combination that matches only the files you are interested in. The following command copies three files (escherknot, xlogo64, and stipple) from the /usr/openwin/include/X11/bitmaps directory to the current directory:

```
dugout% cp /usr/openwin/include/X11/bitmaps/{escherknot,xlogo64,stipple} .
dugout%
```

This is still a lot of typing, but look at what you would have to type otherwise:

```
dugout% cp /usr/openwin/include/X11/bitmaps/escherknot
```

```
/usr/openwin/include/X11/bitmaps/xlogo64
/usr/openwin/include/X11/bitmaps/stipple .
dugout%
```

Using Command Substitution

If you enclose a command in back quotation marks (``), it is executed and its output replaces the command on the command line. This is called command substitution and is usually used to supply arguments to another command. For example, if you have a file named list that contains the names of some files, you can cat list and use its output as arguments to another command, such as ls, as shown here:

```
dugout% cat list
memo.c
README
compressed.Z
document.doc
doorbell.au
dugout% ls -l `cat list`
-r--r--r--   1 sally    staff       4573 Mar 24 06:05 memo.c
-rw-rw-r--   1 sally    staff        119 Mar 24 20:02 README
-rw-rw-r--   1 sally    staff         97 Feb 15 17:09 compressed.Z
-rw-rw-r--   1 sally    staff        109 Feb 19 18:59 document.doc
-rw-rw-rw-   1 sally    staff      17592 Aug 10  1992 doorbell.au
dugout%
```

The command

```
ls -l `cat list`
```

is replaced with

```
ls -l memo.c README compressed.Z document.doc doorbell.au
```

Another example of using command substitution is taking the output of the grep -l command and using it as the arguments to vi, as shown here:

```
dugout% vi `grep -l width *.c`
<The vi program executes>
```

This example searches all the files ending in .c for the string "width." By using the -l option to grep, only the names of the files containing a match are listed. That list (the output of grep) is used as the arguments to vi. So, you edit all the .c files containing the string "width."

Other Ways to Change Directories

In addition to the cd command, you can also use the pushd command to change directories. The C shell maintains a list of directories on a *directory stack*. You use the pushd command to take advantage of the directory stack. When you use the pushd command to change directories, the previous directory is pushed onto the directory stack. When you want to return to the previous directory, use the popd command. You can push one or more directories onto the directory stack by using the pushd command repeatedly. The dirs command lists all the directories on the directory stack. The following example shows the use of the pushd, popd, and dirs commands.

```
dugout% cd
dugout% pushd /usr/openwin
/usr/openwin ~
dugout% pushd /tmp
/tmp /usr/openwin ~
dugout% pwd
/tmp
dugout% dirs
/tmp /usr/openwin ~
dugout% popd
/usr/openwin ~
dugout% pwd
/usr/openwin
dugout% dirs
/usr/openwin ~
dugout popd
~
dugout% pwd
/export/home/pew
dugout%
```

Using File Name Completion

The shell's file name completion facility can complete a partially typed file or user name. When you enter an unambiguous partial file name followed by an Escape (Esc), the shell fills in the remaining characters of the matching file name from the current directory. This feature works only if you have set the filec shell variable. For example, if you have a file named license in the current directory, you can enter just the first few characters of the file name, followed by Esc, and the shell completes the name for you. This saves you from typing several characters. The example looks like this:

```
dugout% ls -l lic<Esc>
```

When you enter the Esc, the shell automatically enters the remaining characters of the file name. You can either continue entering more arguments on the command line or press Return. If the characters that you enter do not uniquely identify one file, the shell completes as much of the file name as is matched by all files containing those first few characters, and then beeps. For example, if you have in your directory two files, named license and license.-dat, the shell will not be able to identify which file you intend if you enter only lic<Esc>. In this case, the shell completes the "license" part of the two files and then beeps. You can either enter some more characters at this point in order to provide a unique name, or enter Control-D (^D), which instructs the shell to list all the possible matching files, as shown here:

```
dugout% ls -l lic<Esc>ense<^D>
license license.dat
dugout% ls -l license
```

After you type Control-D the entire command (including the prompt) is re-drawn by the shell. You can now continue entering the command.

Programming with Shell Scripts

You can create your own "programs" by putting commands into a file called a shell script and then executing that file. When you execute the file, each command in the file is executed.

Before you can execute your shell script, the file must be made executable. Use the chmod command (see Chapter 11) to change the permissions so that the file is executable. For example, if you put some commands into a file named summary, you can set the permissions on the file with the following command:

```
dugout% chmod 755 summary
dugout%
```

You can put any command into a shell script. To ensure that the C shell is used when you run your script (as opposed to the Bourne or Korn shell) check to see if the first character of the first line is a pound sign (#). If the first line of the script does not begin with a pound sign, the Bourne shell will be used when you execute the commands in the script. For many scripts, it doesn't matter which shell is used, but if you are using a function that is unique to the C shell (like foreach), you must put the pound sign at the beginning of the file. Note that the pound sign is also used as the comment character. Any line that begins with a pound sign is not executed; it is usually used for a comment (made by the writer of the script).

Here is an example of a simple script that displays the date followed by a long ls listing and the du command to summarize the disk usage of the current directory:

```
#
date
ls -l
du -s *
```

There is much more to writing shell scripts than we have talked about here, but this should get you started.

The Korn Shell

There are probably more similarities between the Korn and C shells than there are differences. For example, starting a process in the background (with the ampersand), redirecting the standard output, and using pipes are identical in the Korn and C shells. Controlling jobs is almost identical too. However, some other concepts are quite different, including redirecting standard error and setting variables and aliases.

One of the most distinctive advantages of the Korn shell is its command-line editing capability. This feature lets you edit previously entered commands. We'll talk about command-line editing later in this section.

In this section we will concentrate on the features that are unique to the Korn shell or that are substantially different from the C shell.

Using the History Mechanism

The Korn shell's history mechanism is conceptually the same as that of the C shell, but the syntax is quite different. The Korn shell history command displays the 16 most recently entered commands, as shown in this example:

```
$ history
350     env
351     history
352     ls -l
353     cd /tmp
354     cp sort.c main.c
355     ls
356     cd -
357     ls -l .profile
358     lp /etc/passwd
```

```
359     cancel SPARCprinter-1236
360     history
361     vi sort.c
362     vi Makefile
363     fg
364     make
365     history
$
```

To rerun the previously entered command, enter r (repeat), as shown here:

```
$ make
$ r
make
$
```

To rerun a particular command from the history list, enter the history number or a string of characters that match the first few characters of the command as shown here:

```
$ r 354
cp sort.c main.c
$ r lp
lp /etc/passwd
request id is SPARCprinter-1237 (1 file(s))
$
```

To rerun a command with changes, specify the old and new character strings, separated by an equals sign after the r. For example, to rerun the lp command but send the /etc/group file to the printer rather than the /etc/passwd file, enter the following:

```
$ r passwd=group lp
lp /etc/group
request id is SPARCprinter-1238 (1 file(s))
$
```

As you can see from these examples, the Korn shell history mechanism provides many of the same features as the C shell history mechanism but with a different syntax.

Editing on the Command Line

One of the most powerful features of the Korn shell is that it enables you to edit commands on the command line. This is a unique feature; it is not shared by the C shell. The Korn shell's editing capability allows you to actually edit the current or previously entered command.

The Korn shell has built-in support for editing the command line with the vi or emacs editor. Since you have already learned about the vi editor, we will only discuss the vi editing option. To enable the editing facility of the Korn shell, you must do one of three things: set the EDITOR variable, set the VISUAL variable, or use the set -o command. To turn on the editing capability of the Korn shell and specify use of the vi editing commands using the set command, enter

```
$ set -o vi
```

Or, you can turn on the editing capability using the VISUAL variable by entering the command:

```
$ VISUAL=vi
```

Or, you can turn on the editing capability using the EDITOR variable by entering the command:

```
$ EDITOR=vi
```

Each of these three commands is equivalent.

To understand the editing capabilities of the Korn shell, imagine that you have resized a Shell Tool so that only one line is displayed. If you executed vi in that Shell Tool, you could edit files that are bigger than one line, but only one line would be displayed at a time. If you think of the command-line editing facility of the Korn shell as a one-line editor with all of the previous commands as part of the file you are editing, many of these concepts will be intuitive.

When you enter a command in the Korn shell, it is like being in insert mode in vi (we're just considering the vi editing case here). By default, you are in insert mode; each key you press enters a character into the buffer (the command line). When you press Return, the command is executed and that command line scrolls out of view (remember, we're thinking of this as a one-line editor). You can press Esc at any time to exit insert mode and go to command mode. As an example, begin entering a command, and before you press Return, press Esc. Now use some of the vi commands you learned in Chapter 13 to move the cursor on that line (don't use the arrow keys, however). Try entering h or b or 0. You will see the cursor move one character to the left (h) or one word to the left (b), or to the beginning of the line (0). At any time, you can enter i (or a) to enter insert mode. This is what command-line editing is all about: You can truly edit the command you are entering!

You can use other vi commands to gain access to previously entered commands. Of course, you must be sure you are in command mode; otherwise these commands will simply be inserted as characters into your command. To enter command mode, press the Esc key. Now try entering k, which moves the cursor up one line in vi. You will see the previous command displayed on the command line. Press k again and you will see the command entered before that one. This all makes sense if you imagine you are editing a file that is being created as you enter commands. The file contents are the commands that you enter. By default, you are at the last line of the file in insert mode.

It's difficult to demonstrate on the printed page exactly what is going on with command-line editing, because the command line is being redisplayed as you enter these commands. Try following the instructions shown here to get a feeling for the command-line editing features that the Korn shell provides. First, make sure you are running the Korn shell and that you have command-line editing enabled by entering the following commands:

```
dugout% ksh
$ set -o vi
$
```

Now follow these instructions exactly:

1. Enter "ls .profile" at the prompt and press Return.
2. Press Esc to enter command mode.
3. Enter k to move up one line in the history list. The previous command (ls .profile) is now displayed on the command line.
4. Enter w to move the cursor forward to the next word. The cursor should now be positioned at the dot in .profile.
5. Enter i to go into insert mode.
6. Enter -l<Space>. These three characters are inserted into the command so that the complete command is now this:

   ```
   ls -l .profile
   ```

7. Press Return. The ls -l .profile command is executed. You can press Return when you are in insert mode or command mode. In either case, the command is executed.

This editing capability is very powerful. You can treat the command line like an editor and use the power and features of the editor to make entering commands quicker and easier. Table 14.3 describes the vi commands that the Korn shell supports for command-line editing.

Table 14.3 vi Commands Supported by the Korn Shell

Command	Description
l	Moves the cursor right one character.
h	Moves the cursor left one character.
k	Moves up (back) to preceding line (command).
j	Moves down (forward) to the next line (command).
G	Goes to the oldest command in the history list.
w	Moves the cursor right one word.
W	Moves the cursor right one word, ignoring punctuation.
e	Moves the cursor to the next end of word.
E	Moves the cursor to the next end of word, ignoring punctuation.
b	Moves the cursor left one word.
B	Moves the cursor left one word, ignoring punctuation.
^	Moves the cursor to the first printable character.
0	Moves the cursor to the beginning of the line.
$	Moves the cursor to the last character of the line.
n|	Moves the cursor to the *n*th character of the line.
f*c*	Moves the cursor to the right to the next *c*.
F*c*	Moves the cursor to the left to the next *c*.
t*c*	Moves the cursor to the right to the character before the next *c*.
Tc	Moves the cursor to the left to the character before the next *c*.
a	Enters insert (append) mode.
A	Enters insert (append) mode at the end of the line.
i	Enters insert mode.
I	Enters insert mode at the beginning of the line.
R	Enters insert mode. Each character that you type replaces the character at the cursor.
c<target>	Changes to the target. (For example, cw changes one word.)

Table 14.3 vi Commands Supported by the Korn Shell (Continued)

Command	Description
C	Changes to the end of the line.
S	Substitutes the entire line.
x	Deletes the character under the cursor.
X	Deletes the character before the cursor.
d<target>	Deletes to the target. (For example, dw deletes one word.)
y<target>	Yanks to target. (For example, ye yanks to the end of the word.)
Y	Yanks from the current cursor position to the end of the line. Notice that this is different from the meaning of Y in vi.
p	Puts the previously yanked or deleted text to the right of the cursor.
P	Puts the previously yanked or deleted text to the left of the cursor.
u	Undoes the last change.
U	Undoes all changes on the current line.
/*pattern*<CR>	Retrieves the most recent command (back) that includes *pattern*.
?*pattern*<CR>	Retrieves the command (forward) that includes *pattern*.
n	Repeats the most recent / or ? search in the same direction as the original.
N	Repeats the most recent / or ? search in the opposite direction from the original.
Control-L	Redraws the entire line.

Other Differences between the Korn and C Shells

There are quite a few subtle differences between the Korn and C shells. The next few sections briefly describe some of the most commonly used features and how they differ within the two shells.

Redirecting Standard Error

Redirecting the standard output is done the same way in the Korn and C shells. Redirecting standard error is different, however. The Korn shell allows you to redirect the standard error by using the 2> followed by the name of the file into which the standard error should be written. For example, to send the find command's standard output to the file "output" and the standard error to the file "error," enter the following:

```
$ find / -name "*.c" -exec grep -l dropTarget {} \; > output 2> error
$
```

If you want both the standard output and the standard error to be redirected to the same file, use 2>&1, as shown here:

```
$ find / -name "*.c" -exec grep -l dropTarget {} \; > output 2>&1
$
```

Reading a Start-up File

If you make changes to your .profile you can reread the file by using the dot (.) command:

```
$ . .profile
$
```

The C shell uses the source command.

Setting the Prompt

To set the prompt in the Korn shell, you must set the PS1 variable. The default value for the PS1 variable is the dollar sign ($). To set the prompt to a string such as "Ready> ", use the following command:

```
$ PS1="Ready> "
Ready>
```

If you want to include the current directory in the path, use the following command:

```
Ready> PS1='$PWD> '
/export/home/pew>
```

Using Aliases

To set an alias, separate the alias and the command with an equals sign, as shown here:

```
$ alias cdj='cd ~james'
$
```

To list all aliases, enter the alias command without any arguments.

Using for Loops

In the Korn shell, you use for rather than foreach to loop through a set of commands. You must also enter do as the first line after the for command, to delimit the beginning of the commands to be executed. End the loop with a line containing done. The following example shows how to use the for command to accomplish the same thing we did with the foreach loop earlier in this chapter:

```
$ for user in sally james wendy wilbur
> do
> grep $user phonelist | mailx $user
> done
$
```

Changing Directories

The Korn shell does not maintain a directory stack, but it automatically remembers the previous directory. You can return to the previous directory at any time with the command cd – :

```
$ pwd
/export/home/pew
$ cd -
/usr/openwin
$ pwd
/usr/openwin
$ cd -
/export/home/pew
$
```

Completing a File Name

The file name completion facility of the Korn shell works only if you have enabled command-line editing as described earlier in this chapter. Using the C shell, you simply enter Esc to complete a file name. To use file name completion within the Korn shell, you must enter Esc (to enter command mode) followed by a backslash (\). If more than one file name matches the entry, use Esc = to list all the files that match. Use Esc * to expand the current partial file name and include all matches on the command line.

A Summary of Korn Shell and C Shell Differences

Table 14.4 lists some of the most common differences between the C and Korn shells.

Table 14.4 Some Common Differences between the C and Korn Shells

C Shell	Korn Shell	Description
hostname%	$	Serves as default prompt.
>& out_err	> out_err 2>&1	Combines standard output and standard error into file out_err.
(...> out) >& err	> out 2> err	Redirects standard output to out, and standard error to err.
`command`	$(command)	Indicates command substitution.
set var=value	var=value	Indicates variable assignment.
setenv var value	var=value export var	Sets environment variable var to value.
source file	. file	Reads commands in file.
end	done	Indicates end of a loop.
foreach	for/do	Loop command.
!!	r	Repeats previous command.
!str	r str	Repeats command that begins with *str*.
!cmd:s/x/y/	r x=y cmd	Edits command and executes.

Summary

The skillful use of the shell can be one of your greatest assets. Knowing the tricks provided by the shell makes the difference between a regular user and a UNIX wizard. Use these features often and you will save yourself considerable time and effort.

CHAPTER

15

Using the Network

The Basics of Networking

Remote Login

Commands for Copying Files between Systems

Commands Executed on a Remote Machine

ONE OF THE NICEST FEATURES OF SUNOS (AND UNIX IN GENERAL) IS HOW seamlessly the network is integrated into the system. You may be using the network right now without even knowing it. If your system is on a network, it is probably connected to the network by a cable that runs out the back of your machine. The network connects each system through some type of cable such as coaxial, fiber optic, or twisted pair. Some networks are even transmitted through the air without the use of a cable. Regardless of the media through which the communication occurs, the network is a link between your system and other systems on the network, and the networking software provides an interface for using other machines on your network.

One common configuration for a low-cost system is called the *diskless* configuration. A diskless workstation does not have its own disk drive and relies completely on the network for access to all files and directories. Another common configuration is called *dataless* configuration, which means that the required files of the core operating system are on the system's local disk but all other files and directories (including users' home directories) are somewhere out on the network. The appeal of this networking environment is that in many cases you (the user) cannot tell that you are even using the network: it just appears that files and directories reside on local disks. You create, read, and access files across the network, but it appears as if they are local to your system.

Not all files from every system on your local network can be accessed as if they are local files. You sometimes have to use specific network commands to log into and access files on other systems. In this chapter you will learn how to do the following:

- Log into a remote system
- Copy files to and from a remote system
- Execute commands on a remote system

The Basics of Networking

Each system has a name by which it is uniquely identified on the network. The name of your system is used when you enter networking commands, and you must always specify the name of the remote machine that you want to interact with. To determine the name of your system, enter the uname -n command, as shown here:

```
dugout% uname -n
dugout
dugout%
```

The name of my own machine is dugout (which is also shown in the prompt). To determine the names of the systems on your network, use the rup command, which stands for "remote up time." The rup command displays several items of information about each system on your local network, including the host name, the system up time, and the load average. The system up time is the number of days, hours, and minutes since the system was last booted. The load average is an average of the number of concurrently running processes over a specified time. The load-average values are displayed as three numbers, representing the number of running processes averaged over 1, 5, and 15 minutes. The rup command is shown in this example:

```
dugout% rup
   localhost    up  2 days,  1:41,    load average: 0.30, 0.43, 0.45
      dugout    up  2 days,  1:41,    load average: 0.30, 0.43, 0.45
      vivids    up  4 days,  7:11,    load average: 0.22, 0.13, 0.00
       storm    up  5 days,  6:05,    load average: 1.52, 0.90, 0.73
        wind    up           9:38,    load average: 0.14, 0.13, 0.05
dugout%
```

If you want to restrict the output of rup to a particular system, you can provide the name of a system (one or more) as an argument to rup, in which case only the information regarding that system will be displayed. In the following example, rup is given two command-line arguments—dugout and wind:

```
dugout% rup dugout wind
      dugout    up  2 days,  1:41,    load average: 0.30, 0.43, 0.45
        wind    up           9:38,    load average: 0.14, 0.13, 0.05
dugout%
```

Rup may not display all the systems on your network to which you have direct access. Some networks are divided into subnets to help decrease the total amount of network traffic. This is a particularly common configuration for large networks, so don't get the mistaken impression that the only systems to which you can communicate over the network are the ones reported by rup. You may want to check with your system administrator for more information about systems available to you on your network. If you work for a company that is connected to a national (or international) network such as the Internet, you may have access to thousands of machines around the world.

In most cases, you will become aware of other systems on your network through co-workers or friends who have files on their systems that you need to access. Usually, they will provide the name of the system on which the data resides, and then you can use that name directly in the networking command.

To determine if a particular system on your network is "up and running," use the ping command. The ping command takes a system name as an argument and determines if that system can be contacted by means of the network. For example, to check to see if system wind is running, enter the following command:

```
dugout% ping wind
wind is alive
dugout%
```

Ping tries to contact the remote system for 20 seconds. If there is no response after that period of time, ping informs you that there was no answer from the specified system:

```
dugout% ping storm
no answer from storm
dugout%
```

You should also be aware that UNIX has a security mechanism that deters users from illegally gaining access to your system and your files. Each system on your network may require different security procedures. You may be able to log into one system without a password, but another system may require you to provide a password. You may find additional obstacles due to similar security procedures.

Remote Login

Logging into a remote machine requires first that you have an account on that machine. If you have an account, use the rlogin (remote login) command to log in. You can use the rlogin command from within a Shell Tool or a Command Tool, or you can use it directly at the shell prompt before you bring up the OpenWindows environment. Specify as a command-line argument the name of the system that you want to log into. To log into a system named wind, enter the following:

```
dugout% rlogin wind
Last login: Thu Apr  1 15:38:01 from dugout
Sun Microsystems Inc.   SunOS 5.1       Generic December 1992
wind%
```

If you are logging into a remote system that has tighter security enabled, you may be prompted for a password as shown in the next example. The password is not echoed to the window or screen when you enter it.

```
dugout% rlogin wind
Password: <Enter password here>
Last login: Thu Apr  1 15:38:01 from dugout
Sun Microsystems Inc.   SunOS 5.1       Generic December 1992
wind%
```

In the preceding two examples, only the name of the system that you wanted to log into is provided. When you supply only the name of the system as an argument, rlogin logs you into the new system by using the same user ID that was used when you were logged into your local system. If you want to log in with another user ID, specify the -l command-line option followed by the user ID. For example, to log into system wind as user robert, enter the following:

```
dugout% rlogin wind -l robert
Password: <Enter password here>
Last login: Thu Apr  1 15:38:01 from dugout
Sun Microsystems Inc.   SunOS 5.1       Generic December 1992
wind%
```

You may need this option if you have accounts on different machines that do not share user IDs. When you log in as another user, you are nearly always prompted for a password.

Once you are logged into the remote machine, you can enter commands just as if you were directly logged into that machine. If you are entering commands at the prompt such as ls or grep, you will see the output of the commands in the window just as if you were executing them locally. However, if you execute a command that displays a window-based program such as one of the DeskSet utilities, you will need to take some additional steps to ensure that the program is displayed on your workstation.

If you log into a remote machine and execute a DeskSet application such as the File Manager, you may be surprised to see that nothing happens. Well, at least nothing appears on *your* screen. What is likely to have happened is that the File Manager program that you invoked on the remote machine now appears on the screen of the remote machine. This may be somewhat alarming to the person using that machine! What you probably want to do is to execute a program on the remote machine but have it displayed on your local screen. To do this, you must use the -display command-line argument when you execute the command. For example, if your local machine's name is dugout and you are remotely logged into wind, and you want to execute the File Manager on wind but have it displayed locally on dugout, you enter the following command:

```
wind% filemgr -display dugout:0.0 &
wind%
```

The display argument indicates that the command should be displayed on the system specified: dugout, in this case. The :0.0 that follows the system name represents the X server process and the screen on which it should be displayed. In most cases, you can simply use :0.0. The only time you would use other numbers is when you have multiple X servers running or you have a configuration that supports multiple screens. Both of these instances are unlikely.

If you are going to execute several applications that you want displayed on your local screen, you may prefer to set the DISPLAY environment variable. If you set the DISPLAY environment variable to dugout:0.0, all programs (window-based programs, that is) will be displayed on dugout. This means you don't have to supply the -display command-line argument for the commands.

There is one other security feature that you may need to be aware of. The X Window System also has a security system built into it. This is in addition to the security that controls remote login, remote copy, and remote execution. You cannot display on a system that has not given permission for you to display. So, if you are logged into wind and you try to display on dugout, you may be denied access, even though dugout is your own system. You will see an error notice like the one in this example:

```
wind% filemgr -display dugout:0.0
Xlib:  connection to "dugout:0.0" refused by server
Xlib:  Internal error during connection authorization check
Error: Cannot open connection to window server: dugout:0.0
wind%
```

What you must do is use the xhost command on the system on which you want to display the program. In this case, you must execute xhost on dugout. As an argument to xhost, supply a plus sign followed by the name of the host representing the system from which you want to display programs. For example, to allow a program running on wind to display locally, use the following command:

```
dugout% xhost +wind
wind being added to access control list
dugout%
```

If you are logging into wind, you can now execute a command on wind and display it locally.

You can completely remove the X Window System security from your own system by using the xhost command with a plus sign on the command line, as shown in the next examples. This means that any system has permission to display on your screen.

```
dugout% xhost +
all hosts being allowed (access control disabled)
dugout%
```

You can also remove permission for a particular system to display on your screen by using xhost with a minus sign followed by the system name. Or, to remove permission for all systems to display on your screen, use only the minus without a system name:

```
dugout% xhost -
all hosts being restricted (access control enabled)
dugout%
```

When you have finished using the remote machine and you want to return to your local system, terminate the remote login session the same way you log out—by entering Control-D or logout:

```
wind% logout
Connection closed.
dugout%
```

Commands for Copying Files between Systems

There are two commands for copying files remotely from one system to another: rcp and ftp. The rcp command is similar to the cp command, but requires that the two systems communicating have appropriate network permission. The ftp command does not require network permission, but does require that you provide a user ID and password before copying files. They are useful commands, so we will discuss both.

Using the rcp Command

The rcp (remote copy) command is very similar to the cp command. You use rcp to copy files from a remote system to your local system, from your local system to a remote system, or even from one remote system to another remote system (though this last combination is rare). Like the cp command, rcp takes the name of an existing file or files and copies it to the file or directory you specify. In addition, you must specify which system you want the file copied to or from. For example, if you have a file named start_license in your current directory on your local machine, and you want to copy that file to a remote machine named wind, you enter the following command:

```
dugout% rcp start_license wind:new_license
dugout%
```

The first argument is the name of the file you want to copy. The second argument is the name of the system and the file name that you want to copy it to. A colon separates the name of the system and the file name. When the file name given is a relative file name, rcp uses your home directory on the specified system as the destination directory. So, a new file named new_license is created in your home directory on wind. An alternate way to use the rcp command is to specify the host name without a file name, as shown here:

```
dugout% rcp start_license wind:
dugout%
```

When only a system name is specified, the file is copied to your home directory on the remote machine and created with the same name as the original file name on your local machine—start_license, in this example. If you want to specify some directory other than your home directory you can provide an absolute path name or a relative path name; however, it must be relative to your home directory on the remote machine. For example, to copy the start_license file to the /tmp directory on wind, enter the following command:

```
dugout% rcp start_license wind:/tmp
dugout%
```

You can also copy multiple files into a common directory on a remote machine by specifying multiple command-line arguments. In the following example, the files start_license and Makefile are copied to the bin directory (that's relative to your home directory) on system forest:

```
dugout% rcp start_license Makefile forest:bin
dugout%
```

The rcp command also supports the -r option (just like cp) to recursively copy a directory and its contents. For example, to copy the bin directory to your home directory on a remote machine tree, enter the following command:

```
dugout% rcp -r bin tree:
dugout%
```

And, of course, you can use wildcards as you have done before. To copy all .c files to your source directory on remote machine leaves, enter this command:

```
dugout% rcp *.c leaves:source
dugout%
```

To copy files in the other direction—from remote machine to local machine—simply reverse the arguments. The first argument must include the host and file names, and the second (or last) argument must be a local file or directory. For example, to copy file sort.c from remote machine wilbur to your current directory, enter the following command:

```
dugout% rcp wilbur:sort.c .
dugout%
```

You can specify multiple files from the remote machine, but each file must include the host name. For example, to copy sort.c and main.c from remote host wilbur to directory source on your local machine, enter the following command:

```
dugout% rcp wilbur:sort.c wilbur:main.c source
dugout%
```

It is possible to use wildcards on the remote machine, but you have to be careful. When you enter a wildcard, such as * or ?, the local shell expands (or replaces) the wildcard with the matching names from your current directory on your local machine. If you tried to match all .c files in your home directory on wilbur by specifying wilbur:*.c, you would not get the desired results, because the * is expanded locally, not remotely. You may not have in your current directory any files that match *.c. To have the wildcard expanded remotely, you must escape (precede) it with a backslash or enclose it in quotation marks. For example, to copy all the .c files from wilbur to your current directory, enter the following command:

```
dugout% rcp wilbur:\*.c .
dugout%
```

or

```
dugout% rcp 'wilbur:*.c' .
dugout%
```

The -r option is also supported for copying files from a remote system to your local system.

If you want to copy a file from one remote machine to another remote machine, include a machine name in both the from and to arguments. For example, to copy file sort.c from wilbur to leaves, enter the following command:

```
dugout% rcp wilbur:sort.c leaves:
dugout%
```

Using the ftp Command

The rcp command is easy to use because it so closely resembles the cp command. However, you can use it only if the remote machine you are interacting with *trusts* you. If a system trusts another system, it grants that system network access without asking for a password. Your system administrator can control which hosts trust each other (at least on your local network). If you want to transfer files between machines that do not trust each other, you must use another facility. You can use the ftp (file transfer protocol) command for this purpose.

When you use ftp, you must supply a user ID and a password to gain access to the remote machine before transferring any files. So, of course, you must have an account on the remote machine before you can use ftp. The process of using ftp is similar to that of remote login: you must enter a user ID and a password before you transfer files. When you log in with ftp, you are not logged in the same way that you are when you use rlogin. You cannot execute any UNIX command as you can when you remote login; you can use only the ftp commands, all of which are specific to transferring files.

To connect to a remote machine with ftp, enter the ftp command followed by the name of the remote machine. You are then prompted for a name and a password, as shown here:

```
dugout% ftp wind
Connected to wind.
220 wind FTP server (UNIX(r) System V Release 4.0) ready.
Name (wind:sally): sally
331 Password required for sally.
Password: <Enter password>
230 User sally logged in.
ftp>
```

When you are prompted for the name, the default name appears within the parentheses after the host name (sally, in this case). You can just enter Return at this prompt if you want to log in as sally, or you can enter the name of the user you want to log in as. When you have successfully entered your user ID and password, you are presented with the ftp prompt: ftp>.

There are several ftp commands that you use to change directory, transfer files, and configure ftp. To see a list of all the available commands, enter help or a question mark at the ftp prompt:

```
ftp> help
Commands may be abbreviated.  Commands are as follows:

!            cr           macdef       proxy        send
$            delete       mdelete      sendport     status
account      debug        mdir         put          struct
append       dir          mget         pwd          sunique
ascii        disconnect   mkdir        quit         tenex
bell         form         mls          quote        trace
binary       get          mode         recv         type
bye          glob         mput         remotehelp   user
case         hash         nmap         rename       verbose
cd           help         ntrans       reset        ?
cdup         lcd          open         rmdir
close        ls           prompt       runique
ftp>
```

To get a brief description of any ftp command, enter help (or question mark) followed by the names of the commands you are interested in. For example, to get information on ascii and mget, enter the following:

```
ftp> help ascii mget
ascii           set ASCII transfer type
mget            get multiple files
ftp>
```

We won't talk about all the ftp commands, but you should become familiar with several that will enable you to successfully transfer files when you use ftp. Table 15.1 describes some of the most important ftp commands.

Table 15.1 Some Important ftp Commands

Command	Description
ascii	Sets transfer type to ASCII. This option should be set when you are transferring ASCII files.
binary	Sets transfer type to binary. This option should be set when you are transferring binary files.
bye	Terminates the ftp session and exits.
cd *<directory>*	Changes directory on the remote machine.
get *<file>*	Copies one file from the remote machine to the local machine.
hash	Toggles printing of # for each block of data transferred. Gives you feedback as file is being transferred. Especially useful for large file transfers.
help [*command*]	Prints ftp help information.
lcd *<directory>*	Changes directory on the local machine.
ls	Lists the contents of the remote directory.
mget	Copies multiple files from the remote machine to the local machine.
mput	Copies multiple files from the local machine to the remote machine.
open *<host>*	Connects to a remote machine.
prompt	Toggles interactive prompting when transferring multiple files with mget and mput.
put *<file>*	Copies one file from the local machine to the remote machine.
pwd	Prints working directory on remote machine.

Table 15.1 Some Important ftp Commands (Continued)

Command	Description
quit	Terminates ftp session and exits.
status	Shows current status of ftp options.

To demonstrate how to transfer files from the remote machine to your local machine, let's suppose you have connected to machine wind by using ftp. At the ftp prompt, you can use the cd, pwd, and ls commands just as you would at the shell. The output to these ftp commands is slightly different from the output produced when you use them with the shell, but they provide basically the same information. The lcd command changes your current directory on your local system, as shown here:

```
ftp> pwd
257 "/export/home/sally" is current directory.
ftp> cd bin
250 CWD command successful.
ftp> lcd bin
Local directory now /home2/sally/bin
ftp> pwd
257 "/export/home/sally/bin" is current directory.
ftp> ls
200 PORT command successful.
150 ASCII data connection for /bin/ls (192.9.200.2,2807) (0 bytes).
hexsweeper
rs2pcfs
start_license
226 ASCII Transfer complete.
36 bytes received in 0.061 seconds (0.57 Kbytes/s)
ftp>
```

To copy the start_license file from the remote machine to your current directory, use the get command:

```
ftp> get start_license
200 PORT command successful.
150 ASCII data connection for start_license (192.9.200.2,2810) (101 bytes).
226 ASCII Transfer complete.
local: start_license remote: start_license
102 bytes received in 0.003 seconds (33 Kbytes/s)
ftp>
```

The get command takes the name of the file on the remote machine and copies it to the local machine, giving it the same name. If you provide a second argument to get, then the file is given that name when it is copied to the local machine.

You can copy multiple files with the mget command. When you use mget, the files always maintain their original names as they are copied to the local machine. The following example shows the files start_license and rs2pcfs being copied with mget. You are prompted for each file to be copied:

```
ftp> mget start_license rs2pcfs
mget start_license? y
200 PORT command successful.
150 ASCII data connection for start_license (192.9.200.2,2814) (101 bytes).
226 ASCII Transfer complete.
local: start_license remote: start_license
102 bytes received in 0.0028 seconds (35 Kbytes/s)
mget rs2pcfs? y
200 PORT command successful.
150 ASCII data connection for rs2pcfs (192.9.200.2,2815) (123 bytes).
226 ASCII Transfer complete.
local: rs2pcfs remote: rs2pcfs
128 bytes received in 0.0022 seconds (58 Kbytes/s)
ftp>
```

You can avoid the prompt for each file if you enter the prompt command at the ftp prompt. Then all the files are copied without any user interaction:

```
ftp> prompt
Interactive mode off.
ftp> mget start_license rs2pcfs
200 PORT command successful.
150 ASCII data connection for start_license (192.9.200.2,2818) (101 bytes).
226 ASCII Transfer complete.
local: start_license remote: start_license
102 bytes received in 0.0023 seconds (43 Kbytes/s)
200 PORT command successful.
150 ASCII data connection for rs2pcfs (192.9.200.2,2819) (123 bytes).
226 ASCII Transfer complete.
local: rs2pcfs remote: rs2pcfs
128 bytes received in 0.0021 seconds (59 Kbytes/s)
ftp>
```

You use the put and mput commands to copy files from your local system to the remote system. The syntax of the put and mput commands is identical to that of the get and mget commands. Here is an example of using the put command to copy a local file named license.dat to a remote machine:

```
ftp> put license.dat
200 PORT command successful.
150 ASCII data connection for license.dat (192.9.200.1,2886).
226 ASCII Transfer complete.
local: license.dat remote: license.dat
```

```
233 bytes sent in 0.036 seconds (6.2 Kbytes/s)
ftp>
```

The ftp command is also used by many systems to provide a type of bulletin-board service. Some systems are set up to allow anonymous users to log in by using ftp to gain access to public files. If your system is connected to a network such as Internet, you may be able to use this feature to access systems around the world. Check with your system administrator to see if your network is connected to any outside networks. You use ftp the same way to connect to the remote machine, but rather than entering your user ID at the Name prompt (since it is unlikely that you have an account there), you enter anonymous. You are then usually requested by ftp to enter your user ID as the password, but that is not required. If this system is configured to handle anonymous ftp, then you can enter anything at the password prompt and you will still gain access. The following example illustrates the use of anonymous ftp:

```
dugout% ftp export.lcs.mit.edu
Connected to sun-barr.EBay.Sun.COM.
220 sun-barr FTP proxy server ready.
Name (export.lcs.mit.edu:pew): anonymous
331 Guest login ok, send ident as password.
Password: <Enter ID here>
230 Guest login ok, access restrictions apply.
ftp>
```

Once you are at the ftp prompt, you can use the same commands you have already learned about in this section to copy files to your local machine.

When you have finished using ftp, enter quit or bye to exit the ftp session:

```
ftp> quit
221 Goodbye.
dugout%
```

Commands Executed on a Remote Machine

Sometimes you may want to execute a command on a remote machine without actually logging into that machine. For example, you may have a file on a remote machine that contains the names and phone numbers of some business associates. Perhaps you want to use the grep command to look for a particular person's phone number in the file. You could remote login to the system and then run grep, but it would probably be faster to simply execute the grep command remotely. If the remote machine is a trusted system, you should be able to use the rsh command to remotely execute a command. The rsh command lets you execute a command on a remote machine without having to rlogin to that machine. To use rsh, provide the name of the remote machine as the first argument, followed by the command as it should be executed on the remote machine. In the following example, grep is being executed on a host named wind, but the output of the grep command is displayed locally:

```
dugout% rsh wind grep Mahler /usr/nameslist
Mahler, Gustav                    (414) 555-1212
dugout%
```

You might want to execute a DeskSet program on a remote machine. We talked about this earlier in this chapter. If the only thing you want to do is execute a single program, it may be easier to simply execute the program rather than first log into the system. For example, to execute the File Manager on system wind and display it on your local system (dugout), enter the following command:

```
dugout% rsh wind filemgr -display dugout:0.0 &
dugout%
```

The rsh command saves you the time and trouble of having to rlogin to a system before executing a command on that system.

Summary

Using the network is easy, and it gives you access to an incredible amount of data. You can log into remote machines, copy files to and from remote machines, and execute commands on remote machines. Skillful use of the network will increase your productivity by giving you quick access to other machines and the data on those machines. In Chapter 16 you'll learn more about the network, including the Network File System (NFS) and the automounter.

System Administration for Users

System Administration with the Administration Tool

PART 4

System Administration

CHAPTER

16

System Administration for Users

System Administration Basics

Monitoring Processes

Starting Up and Shutting Down Your System

File System Administration

Tapes and Floppy Disks

Backups and Restores

Network Services Administration

AFTER GRADUATING FROM COLLEGE IN THE EARLY 1980S, I GOT MY FIRST job as a UNIX system administrator. Back then a desktop workstation was almost unheard of. UNIX ran most frequently on minicomputers that usually resided in a computer room. Each user in various offices had a terminal that was connected to the computer in the computer room. As a system administrator, I worked with a few other administrators maintaining our UNIX systems. We were the only ones authorized to perform any system administration functions. These included such things as creating new accounts, freeing disk space, rebooting the system, doing backups and restores, and killing processes owned by other users.

Things have changed quite a bit over the last ten or so years. Though there are still computer rooms where larger systems (minicomputers, servers, or even mainframes) run UNIX, the desktop environment with a workstation on the user's desk has become increasingly more common. This poses some unique challenges for system administrators. Ten or fifteen years ago, supporting one hundred users may have meant maintaining four or five systems; today it could mean maintaining one hundred systems.

As the trend to move the computer to the desktop has continued, the job of the system administrator has been redefined. As a result, users are often required to perform some simple system administration for their own systems. Many users now know the superuser password for their own systems, which authorizes them to do any of the tasks that the system administrator can do. This can be a blessing or a curse. If you know what you are doing, you can increase your efficiency and save considerable time, because you no longer have to wait for the system administrator to solve your system problems for you. On the flip side, you must also realize that you have the power to destroy your own work! Executing the wrong command can cause disks to become corrupted, network traffic to become congested, and disk space to evaporate. Be careful; with authority comes responsibility.

This book is not intended specifically for system administrators, but because many users may be required to perform some simple system administrator functions, we will discuss some basic administration concepts and commands in this chapter and the next. The job of a system administrator cannot be fully described in these two chapters, so the discussion is limited to the tasks that a regular user is most likely to need and understand. If you have a dedicated system administrator who responds to your every beck and call in a timely manner, you may not need to read this chapter or the next. If, however, you are like most users who have an overworked, extremely busy system administrator, you will want to read these chapters so that you can become your own administrator when handling basic tasks.

In this chapter you will learn about the following:

- Becoming the superuser
- Monitoring processes

- Booting and shutting down the system
- Managing file systems
- Using tapes and floppy disks
- Managing networks

In Chapter 17 you'll learn about some of the other common system administrator functions, including adding new users, configuring printers and print spoolers, and adding new hosts on the network.

System Administration Basics

The job of the system administrator is quite varied. It can involve everything from configuring hardware to managing networks to installing software. In this section we will discuss some of the most basic jobs of a system administrator, including becoming the superuser, learning the locations of some common system directories, and working with processes.

Becoming the Superuser

Nearly every system administration function requires system privileges. System privileges are reserved for the user whose user ID is root (also called the *superuser*). To become the superuser, you must either log in as root or become root by using the su (switch user) command. In either case, you must know the root password if you are to become the superuser. If you don't have the root password for your system, you will not be able to do many of the things described in this chapter.

Using the su command is probably the more common way to become the superuser. The su command takes an argument that specifies the user to whom you want to switch. If you do not supply an argument, then you switch to the superuser, as shown here:

```
dugout% su
Password: <Type root password here>
#
```

A new shell is started by su, and a pound sign (#) is displayed as the default prompt (any prompt can be changed as described in Chapter 14). This prompt helps you remember that you are the superuser. As a general rule of thumb, you should use the root account only when absolutely necessary. Once you have finished issuing privileged commands, go back to being a regular user. You can return to your previous shell by exiting the superuser shell started by su. To do this, use the exit command or enter Control-D.

```
# exit
dugout%
```

Once you have first logged in as root, if you plan to go back and forth between your own user ID and root, you may want to simply suspend the su shell with the suspend command. At a later time, you can put that shell back into the foreground, and you again become the superuser. This saves you the trouble of entering the root password every time you want to execute a privileged command.

```
# suspend

Stopped (signal)
dugout% jobs
[1]  + Stopped (signal)      su
dugout% fg %1
su
#
```

Learning the Locations of Directories

Knowing the locations of system files and directories is often helpful when trying to understand or solve a system problem. In this section, I will briefly describe each system directory and its contents.

The / (root) Directory

The root directory is at the top of the UNIX directory hierarchy. It contains all the other directories described in this section as well as a file called ufsboot. The ufsboot file contains essential information required to boot the system. It should not be altered or removed.

The /tmp Directory

The /tmp directory stores temporary files. The permissions on the /tmp directory allow read, write, and execute for user, group, and other. This means that any user can create, modify, or delete a file in /tmp. When you reboot your system, the files in /tmp are removed. Many different programs use the /tmp directory to write and store temporary files.

The /etc Directory

The /etc directory contains system administration commands and system configuration files. When you become root you will want /etc defined as part of your path so that you can execute commands in that directory. Important configuration files, such as the password file and the system start-up files, are also included in /etc.

The /var Directory

The /var directory contains machine- and user-specific data such as log files, mail and spooling files, accounting files, and a database of installed software packages.

The /dev Directory

The /dev directory contains special files used to access hardware devices. Disk devices are located in /dev/dsk and /dev/rdsk. Tape devices are located in /dev/rmt.

The /bin Directory

The /bin directory is a symbolic link to /usr/bin, which contains most of the commands you execute on a regular basis such as ls, grep, and cat. The /bin directory has historically been the location for many (if not most) of the user commands.

The /sbin Directory

The /sbin directory contains additional executable commands.

The /lib Directory

The /lib directory is a symbolic link to /usr/lib. The files in /usr/lib are primarily libraries that are used by commands at run time and are essential in order to execute nearly every command you enter. Programmers use these libraries when writing programs.

The /opt Directory

The /opt directory contains unbundled or third-party software.

The /kernel Directory

The /kernel directory contains the UNIX kernel (the operating system) and related files.

The /net Directory

The /net directory is used by the automounter (discussed later in this chapter) as the location where file systems from remote machines are automatically mounted.

The /export Directory

The /export directory is the default location for home directories (/export/home). By convention, directories that are to be exported (visible to other systems on the network) are located in /export.

The /proc Directory

The /proc directory contains one file for each running process. The names of the files match the process ID for the corresponding process. These files are created and deleted as processes begin and end. You should not remove or alter files in this directory. They are used by commands like ps to get information about running processes.

The /usr Directory

The /usr directory usually resides on its own file system (see the discussion of file systems later in this chapter). The files in the /usr file system are generally static files, which means they do not change. For example, some of the types of files on the /usr file system are executable commands, libraries, and man pages.

Monitoring Processes

In Chapter 14 you learned about controlling jobs with commands such as jobs, fg, bg, stop, suspend, and kill. Each of these commands takes a job number (preceded by a percent sign) as an argument. The job numbers of processes are maintained by the shell in which the command is executed. You may also remember that there is a process ID for each process. That number is returned when you start a job in the background and is displayed when you use the jobs -l command. Because the job numbers are maintained only by the shell in which the command is executed, you cannot use them to manipulate a particular process from any window or shell other than the one from which it was started. You can, however, use the process ID to manipulate any process. This is sometimes necessary when you need to terminate a process that you cannot access directly by job number or because it is in some way misbehaving.

The ps Command

The ps command gives you status information about running processes. If you use the ps command without an argument, the processes executed in the current window (shell) are displayed, as shown here:

```
dugout% ps
   PID TTY       TIME COMD
   751 pts/0     0:00 csh
   761 pts/0     0:00 ps
dugout%
```

Each command running from this window is displayed with the corresponding process ID (PID), the terminal from which the command was executed (TTY), the accrued CPU time (TIME), and the command name (COMD).

If you want to display process information about all running processes on your system, use the -e option to ps. The fields displayed are the same as when you use ps without arguments, as shown here:

```
dugout% ps -e
   PID TTY      TIME COMD
     0 ?        0:05 sched
     1 ?        0:09 init
     2 ?        0:00 pageout
     3 ?        1:22 fsflush
   374 ?        0:00 syslogd
   312 ?        0:00 lpsched
   386 ?        0:00 sac
   247 ?        0:02 in.route
   255 ?        0:00 keyserv
   259 ?        0:00 kerbd
   252 ?        0:01 rpcbind
   274 ?        0:01 inetd
   277 ?        0:00 statd
   279 ?        0:01 lockd
   289 ?        0:01 automoun
   398 console  0:01 csh
   296 ?        0:00 cron
   725 console  0:00 xinit
   367 ?        0:00 sendmail
   389 ?        0:00 ttymon
   739 console  0:00 sv_xv_se
   322 ?        0:00 lpNet
   733 console  0:00 sh
   720 console  0:00 openwin
   751 pts/0    0:00 csh
   726 console  0:14 xnews
   749 console  0:01 cmdtool
   744 console  0:01 olwm
   740 console  0:00 vkbd
   745 console  0:00 olwmslav
   756 console  0:01 docviewe
   754 console  0:02 filemgr
   475 ?        0:00 rpc.cmsd
   762 pts/0    0:00 ps
dugout%
```

Additional information is available by including the -f (full) option. The full option provides additional fields including the ID of the user who started the process (UID), the process ID (PID), the parent process ID (PPID), the processor utilization for scheduling (C), the time at which the process started (STIME), the terminal from which the command was executed (TTY), the accrued CPU time (TIME), and the complete command name including arguments (COMD). It is not uncommon for process command names to be so long that the entire command name does not fit on one line and therefore wraps to the next line. The following full ps listing includes several such lines:

```
dugout% ps -ef
     UID   PID  PPID  C    STIME TTY      TIME COMD
    root     0     0 80 13:13:13 ?        0:05 sched
    root     1     0 80 13:13:16 ?        0:09 /etc/init -
    root     2     0 20 13:13:16 ?        0:00 pageout
    root     3     0 80 13:13:16 ?        1:22 fsflush
    root   374     1 32 13:15:48 ?        0:00 /usr/sbin/syslogd
    root   312     1 62 13:15:40 ?        0:00 /usr/lib/lpsched
    root   386     1 26 13:15:49 ?        0:00 /usr/lib/saf/sac -t 300
    root   247     1 80 13:15:00 ?        0:02 /usr/sbin/in.routed -q
    root   255     1  2 13:15:03 ?        0:00 /usr/sbin/keyserv
    root   259     1 25 13:15:04 ?        0:00 /usr/sbin/kerbd
    root   252     1 80 13:15:01 ?        0:01 /usr/sbin/rpcbind
    root   274     1 65 13:15:24 ?        0:01 /usr/sbin/inetd -s
    root   277     1 31 13:15:25 ?        0:00 /usr/lib/nfs/statd
    root   279     1 80 13:15:25 ?        0:01 /usr/lib/nfs/lockd
    root   289     1 76 13:15:28 ?        0:01 /usr/lib/nfs/automount
     pew   398     1163 13:17:15 console  0:01 -csh
    root   296     1 80 13:15:34 ?        0:00 /usr/sbin/cron
     pew   725   720 21 16:45:06 console  0:00 /usr/openwin/bin/xinit --
/usr/openwin/bin/xnews :0 -auth /export/home/pew/.xne
    root   367     1 31 13:15:47 ?        0:00 /usr/lib/sendmail -bd -q1h
    root   389   386 45 13:15:54 ?        0:00 /usr/lib/saf/ttymon
     pew   739     1 49 16:45:20 console  0:00 sv_xv_sel_svc
    root   322   312 15 13:15:41 ?        0:00 lpNet
     pew   733   725160 16:45:17 console  0:00 sh /export/home/pew/.xinitrc
     pew   720   398135 16:45:02 console  0:00 /bin/sh /usr/openwin/bin/openwin
     pew   751   749 74 16:45:26 pts/0    0:00 /bin/csh
     pew   726   725 80 16:45:06 console  0:14 /usr/openwin/bin/xnews :0 -auth
/export/home/pew/.xnews.dugout:0
     pew   749     1 80 16:45:25 console  0:01 /usr/openwin/bin/cmdtool -Wp 0 0
-Ws 590 77 -C
     pew   744   733 60 16:45:22 console  0:01 olwm -syncpid 743
     pew   740     1 39 16:45:20 console  0:00 vkbd -nopopup
     pew   745   744 37 16:45:24 console  0:00 olwmslave
     pew   756     1180 16:45:32 console  0:01 /usr/openwin/bin/helpviewer -Wp
620 50 handbooks/desktop.intro.handbook.Z
     pew   754     1 80 16:45:27 console  0:02 /usr/openwin/bin/filemgr -Wp 0
120 -Ws 590 300
    root   475   274 43 13:18:26 ?        0:00 rpc.cmsd
     pew   763   751 31 17:05:53 pts/0    0:00 ps -ef
dugout%
```

If you are looking for one particular process, you may want to pipe the output of ps to grep. For example, suppose that you started the find command in the background in a Command Tool and then quit that Command Tool. You no longer have access to the job number by using the jobs command, but you can get the process ID by using ps piped to grep, as shown here:

```
dugout% ps -ef | grep find
     pew   297     1 80 15:58:06 ?        0:01 find / -print
     pew   328   325  6 16:02:04 pts/3    0:00 grep find
dugout%
```

Notice that two processes are displayed: find and grep. The grep command is the one that you just executed as part of the piped command. The one you are looking for is the first one listed: process 297. You can use the process ID to terminate the process, as you will learn in the next section.

On some occasions you may have a window (a Shell Tool or Command Tool) that does not respond to any user input. You may want to find the process ID of that window so that you can terminate it. You may even have the unfortunate experience of having the entire windowing system "lock up" on you. This rarely occurs, but it is possible. When no window accepts any input and you cannot even display the Workspace menu, there is little you can do except terminate the X window server. You will need to find the process ID of the X server process (called xnews) so that you can terminate it. If you cannot use any of the windows on your screen, you may have to use another system on your network, log into your system remotely, and then run the ps command. If you are looking for the X server process, you run the following command:

```
dugout% ps -ef | grep xnews
     pew   241   240 80 15:35:08 console  0:23 /usr/openwin/bin/xnews :0
-auth /export/home/pew/.xnews.dugout:0
     pew   240   235 17 15:35:08 console  0:00 /usr/openwin/bin/xinit --
/usr/openwin/bin/xnews :0 -auth /export/home/pew/.xne
     pew   338   325  8 16:11:09 pts/3    0:00 grep xnews
dugout%
```

Both processes 240 and 241 in this example are part of the X server process. Terminating either one of them will terminate the X server.

The kill Command

You use the kill command to terminate a process. You learned a little about the kill command in Chapter 14 when we talked about controlling jobs. The kill command takes a job number or a process ID as an argument. For example, to terminate the find command shown in the previous section, you supply the process ID as the argument to kill, as shown here:

```
dugout% kill 297
dugout%
```

After you kill the process, you will probably want to rerun the ps command to verify that the process is no longer running. As you can see here, process 297 no longer appears in the output:

```
dugout% ps -ef | grep find
     pew   338   325  6 16:04:54 pts/3    0:00 grep find
dugout%
```

Sometimes commands are particularly stubborn and do not terminate when you execute the kill command. In these cases you can try using the -9 option to kill. This is sometimes called the *sure kill.*

```
dugout% kill -9 297
dugout%
```

You should try this only after trying kill without the -9 option, because many programs are designed to terminate gracefully when killed. For example, when a program is killed, it may do some clean-up of temporary files or save an edited file. If you use the -9 option, you bypass any possibility for the program to exit gracefully. The program simply dies unceremoniously without the opportunity to do any clean up.

Starting Up and Shutting Down Your System

Starting and stopping your system is occasionally a necessary task. Normally, you will leave your system running continuously. If you need to shut down your system, you should use one of the commands you will learn about in this section; you should never simply turn the power off as you might do with a PC. If you turn off the power to your system without bringing the system down gracefully, you run the risk of damaging or even losing files.

There are many reasons why you might need to turn off your system. For example, there may be a scheduled power outage, or you may be having a new peripheral device added to your system. You should shut down your system in either of these situations. You may also need to restart (reboot) your system if you experience an unusual software problem that you cannot correct otherwise. In this section you will learn how to boot, reboot, and shut down your system.

Using Init States

The SunOS operating system has several distinct software states (run levels) in which it operates. These are called the *init states* and represent different levels at which the system can run. Table 16.1 lists the different init states with a brief description of each.

Table 16.1 System Init States

Init State	Description
0	Power-down state
1, S, s	System administrator state (single-user)
2	Multiuser state (resources not exported)
3	Multiuser state (resources exported)
4	Alternative multiuser state (unused)
5	Software reboot state (unused)
6	Reboot

Init state 3 is the standard multiuser state and is the state in which your machine is usually running. The other states of importance to you are 0, 1, and 6. You use init state 0 when you want to completely stop (halt) your system so that you can turn off the power. Init state 1 (or S or s) is a special state that the system administrator uses to perform certain system administration functions; it is often called the single-user state. Init state 6 is used to reboot (restart) your system. We will concentrate on states 0, 3, and 6 in this section. Init state 1 is important if you are doing some advanced tasks such as installing a new disk. We will not discuss init state 1 in any more detail, but will assume that these kinds of tasks will be performed by your system administrator. The other states are either not used or else are beyond the scope of this discussion.

To determine the current init state, use the who -r command. The who command without arguments reports all the users currently logged into your system. By including the -r option, the who command displays system information, including the run level. The following example shows that the system is running at run level (init state) 3:

```
dugout% who -r
   .         run-level 3  Apr 20 10:21     3      0  S
dugout%
```

To change the init state of your system, you can use one of several privileged commands reserved for the superuser. (Remember that you will have to become root to use any one of these.) The preferred commands are shutdown and init, which are discussed next.

Shutting Down Your System

Before you shut down your system you should, as a courtesy, check to see if any other users are logged into your system and notify them before bringing down your system. To check to see who is logged into your system, use the who command:

```
dugout% who
pew         console       Apr 20 10:43
sally       pts/4         Apr 20 12:05    (bullpen)
dugout%
```

In this example, the output of who displays that I (pew) am logged in and so is sally. Since there is another user on the system, I will use the most *polite* shutdown command: shutdown. When you execute shutdown, a message is sent to each logged-in user, providing a warning that the system is going down and that they should log off now. A grace period of 60 seconds (by default) is provided. Your current directory must be / when you execute shutdown, otherwise an error message is displayed and you must reenter the command. You should exit the OpenWindows environment and enter the shutdown command directly at the console prompt. This is not absolutely required, but it is the cleaner way to shut down the system, because the process associated with the OpenWindows environment already will have been terminated.

By default, shutdown changes the system to init state 1. To specify another state, use the -i option followed by the init state you desire. For example, to shut down your system so that you can turn off the power, use the shutdown -i0 command, as shown here:

```
dugout% su
Password:
# cd /
# shutdown -i0

Shutdown started.    Thu Apr 20 11:00:16 PDT 1995

Broadcast Message from root (console) on dugout Thu Apr 20 11:03:02...
The system will be shut down in 60 seconds.
Please log off now.

Broadcast Message from root (console) on dugout Thu Apr 20 11:04:02...
THE SYSTEM IS BEING SHUT DOWN NOW ! ! !
Log off now or risk your files being damaged.
```

```
Do you want to continue? (y or n):   y
Changing to init state 0 - please wait.
#
INIT: New run level: 0
The system is coming down.  Please wait.
System services are now being stopped.
Print services stopped.
Stopping the syslog service.
Apr 20 11:08:43 1995
 dugout syslogd: going down on signal 15
The system is down.
Halted

Program terminated
Type  help  for more information
ok
```

As soon as you enter the command, a message is sent to every user logged into the system, alerting them to the amount of time before the actual shutdown. When the grace period has expired, another message is sent to all logged-in users, informing them that the system is now going down. We hope that other users will not see this second message because they will have already logged off. After the second message is sent you are prompted as to whether or not you want to continue with the shutdown. If you respond with an n (no), the shutdown does not take place. If you respond with a y (yes), the shutdown continues as shown in the preceding example. When the system is completely down, the ok prompt appears. At this point, it is safe to shut off the power. You should shut off the power to the CPU first and then to the peripherals.

If you want to change the grace period to something other than 60 seconds, use the -g option followed by the number of seconds. For example, if no other users are logged into your system, you might want to eliminate the grace period altogether. You can do this by specifying 0 as the grace period, as shown here:

```
# shutdown -i0 -g0
<Output from shutdown command displayed here>
```

Another way to bring down your system is with the init (or telinit) command. The init command is similar to shutdown, though it is not as polite: it doesn't provide any grace period, warning messages, or opportunity for you to change your mind. If, however, you are the only one logged into your system and you are sure you want to shut down the system, use the init command. The init command takes one argument that specifies the init state to which you want to go. For example, to shut down your system in preparation to turn off the power, enter init 0 as shown here:

```
# init 0
#
<More messages follow>
```

If you use the init command, you do not have to be in the root directory. Remember that you cannot change your mind after issuing the init command.

Under some very rare conditions you may experience a problem with your system such that you cannot enter any commands. This is called a *hung system*. You should try to log in to your system remotely from another machine connected to your network and use the ps command to try to figure out what is going wrong. Sometimes a runaway process can be killed to solve the problem. In the event that you cannot log in remotely and have exhausted all other possibilities, you can abort the operating system by entering Stop-A (the Stop and A keys simultaneously) or L1-A. (If you are on a tty that acts as the console, use the Break key.) This will immediately give you the ok prompt, at which point you can boot your system. You should resort to this method of bringing down your system only when you have exhausted every other possibility, because you greatly increase the risk of corrupting or losing files.

Rebooting Your System

Occasionally, you may need to reboot your system. Installing new software sometimes requires that the system be rebooted, or your system administrator may instruct you to reboot in order to take advantage of system or network configuration modifications. The shutdown and init commands can also be used for rebooting your system. By specifying an init state of 6, you are indicating that you want the system shut down but then immediately started again. Rebooting a system implies that it is currently running. Booting a system implies that it is not currently running (either powered-off or at the ok prompt).

To reboot your system using the shutdown command and a grace period of 30 seconds, use the following command:

```
# cd /
# shutdown -i6 -g30
<Output from shutdown command displayed here>
```

To reboot your system with the init command, log in again and enter init 6. Remember that, when you use init, logged-in users are not notified of the shutdown, nor will you have the opportunity to change your mind as you would with the shutdown command.

```
# init 6
#
<More messages follow>
```

Booting Your System

If you have shut down your system (without rebooting), you will have to boot it to get it back to a working state (init state 3). If you have shut off the power to your system, turning on the power will automatically boot your system. You should power on the peripherals first and then the CPU. If you are at the ok prompt, you must enter **boot** to boot the system. The system then begins the boot procedure as shown in the next example. Your output will probably be slightly different, depending on your exact hardware configuration. When the boot procedure is complete, you are presented with the login prompt.

```
ok boot
SPARCstation 2, Type 4 Keyboard
ROM Rev. 2.4.1, 32 MB memory installed, Serial #4356341.
Ether address 8:0:20:11:38:55, Host ID: 554278f5.

Rebooting with command:
Boot device: /sbus/esp@0,800000/sd@3,0  File and args:
SunOS Release 5.1 Version Generic [UNIX(R) System V Release 4.0]
Copyright (c) 1983-1992, Sun Microsystems, Inc.
configuring network interfaces: le0.
Hostname: dugout
The system is coming up.  Please wait.
checking filesystems
/dev/rdsk/c0t3d0s5: is clean.
/dev/rdsk/c0t0d0s2: is clean
/dev/rdsk/c0t3d0s7: is clean.
/dev/dsk/c0t3d0s7 mounted
/dev/dsk/c0t3d0s5 mounted
/dev/dsk/c0t0d0s2 mounted
starting routing daemon.
starting rpc services: rpcbind keyserv kerbd done.
Setting default interface for multicast: add net 224.0.0.0: gateway dugout
Print services started.
syslog service starting.
The system is ready.

dugout console login:
```

If you have shut down your system to install new hardware peripherals, you should use the boot -r (reconfigure) command to boot your system. The -r option tells boot that it should look for new hardware devices during the boot procedure. If you don't use the -r option, the new hardware you installed is ignored during the boot procedure and you cannot use it.

If you need to interrupt the boot procedure while it is in progress, use the Stop-A or L1-A keys. This is fairly safe to do while booting, though the earlier in the boot procedure the better. When you enter Stop-A, you immediately receive the ok prompt. You might need to do this if you have had to power off your system to install new hardware. When you power on the system, it automatically boots with the boot command. You will have to interrupt the boot procedure (Stop-A) and then enter the boot -r command so that the new hardware is configured into the system.

File System Administration

You have learned elsewhere in this book that UNIX uses a hierarchical directory structure with the root directory (/) at the top of the hierarchy. The directory hierarchy for your system is comprised of multiple *file systems*. A file system is the organizing structure for a group of files and directories. Each file system contains a hierarchy of files and directories. By combining all the file systems on your machine, you come up with the complete directory hierarchy for your system.

Understanding Disks

Disk devices are the primary storage media for files and directories. Some systems do not have any local disks but work exclusively on remote disks across the network. In this section you will learn how disks are organized and named so that you can better understand file systems. For the purposes of this discussion, we will assume that you have at least one local disk attached to your system.

Partitions

Disks are divided into logical sections called *partitions* or *slices*. Each partition of a disk is used for a particular purpose. A partition may contain a file system, or it may be reserved for another purpose such as swap space or raw data. (*Swap space* is a region of a disk that the operating system uses for temporary storage.) If you think of a disk as a pie, a partition would represent one slice of the pie. Some partitions represent multiple pieces, and there is usually one partition that represents the entire pie. Figure 16.1 shows a disk-partitioning scheme represented as a pie, with each partition as a piece of pie.

Most disks can have up to eight partitions. The disk in Figure 16.1 has six partitions defined. Partitions 0, 1, 5, 6, and 7 are distinct, nonoverlapping partitions. Partitions 3 and 4 are undefined, and partition 2 represents the entire disk. It's possible to define other partitions (partition 4, for example) that would define a region on the disk that is the same as two other partitions combined (partitions 1 and 5, for example), though that is not done in this case. The disk in this example has a capacity of 404 megabytes (Mb).

Figure 16.1
Disk partitions

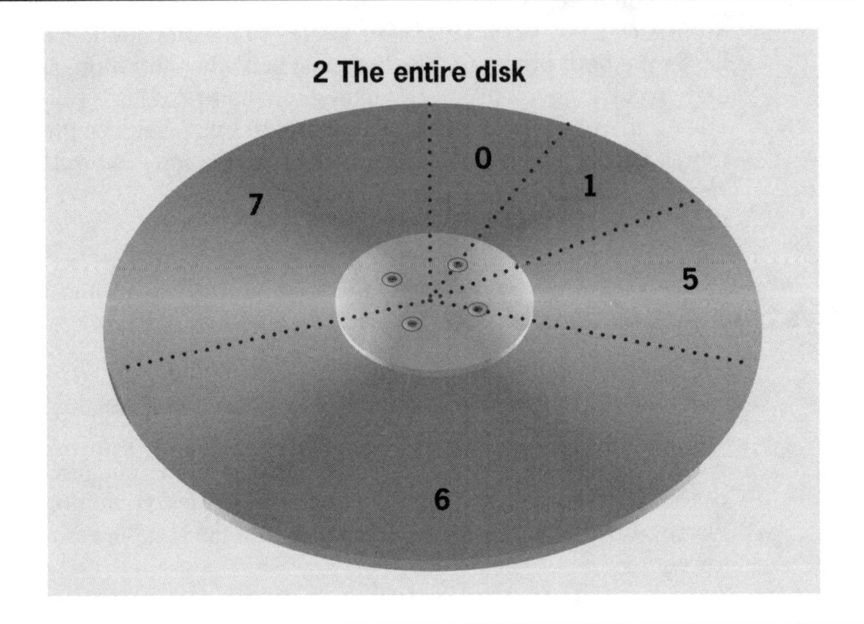

Table 16.2 displays some additional information about each partition of the disk shown in Figure 16.1. We see in the table how several distinct disk partitions are used, each containing a file system or swap space. You could also use just partition 2 and put one big file system (404Mb) on it. If you used partition 2 for a file system, you would not use any of the other partitions (though they still would be defined), because each of them overlaps partition 2. The general rule is that you never use overlapping partitions simultaneously.

Table 16.2 Partition Table

Partition	Type	Size
0	File system	28Mb
1	Swap	64 Mb
2	Unused	404Mb
3	Undefined	N/A
4	Undefined	N/A
5	File system	64Mb

Table 16.2 Partition Table (Continued)

Partition	Type	Size
6	File system	175Mb
7	File system	73Mb

This disk-partitioning scheme gives you the flexibility of using parts of a single disk for different purposes. For example, you may have a collection of files that you want to be read-only. You could have one partition contain a file system that is read-only and the other partitions contain file systems that are read-write. By putting the read-only files on the read-only file system, you are assured that they will not be modified or deleted. The disk partitioning scheme also makes it easier for system administrators to allocate and manage data for various purposes such as backups and restores.

Disk Naming Conventions

Each disk partition has a unique device file by which you access the partition. The device files for disks are found in two places: /dev/dsk and /dev/rdsk. The files in these two directories reference the same devices but with different interfaces. The files in /dev/dsk access the block interface, and the files in /dev/rdsk access the raw interface. (The details of the differences between block and raw interfaces are beyond the scope of this book.) For most cases you will use the block interface files (/dev/dsk).

If you list the files in the /dev/dsk directory, you will see something like this:

```
dugout% ls /dev/dsk
cØtØdØsØ  cØtØdØs4  cØt3dØsØ  cØt3dØs4  cØt6dØsØ  cØt6dØs4
cØtØdØs1  cØtØdØs5  cØt3dØs1  cØt3dØs5  cØt6dØs1  cØt6dØs5
cØtØdØs2  cØtØdØs6  cØt3dØs2  cØt3dØs6  cØt6dØs2  cØt6dØs6
cØtØdØs3  cØtØdØs7  cØt3dØs3  cØt3dØs7  cØt6dØs3  cØt6dØs7
dugout%
```

Each of these files represents one partition on a disk drive. Figure 16.2 shows the device naming convention for disks.

A complete understanding of the device naming convention requires some understanding of the hardware associated with the disk. Here is a brief description of each field:

- The W following the c represents the controller. A *controller* is a piece of hardware that resides in your system and controls one or more disks. If you have only one controller, then W is 0.

Figure 16.2
The naming convention for disks

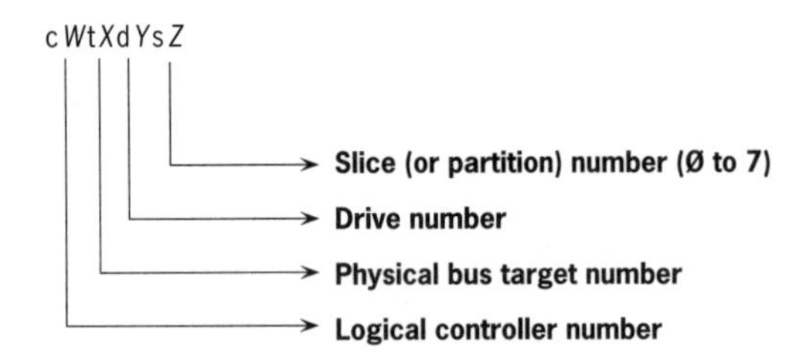

- The X following the t represents the bus target number for the device on that controller. For some controllers, such as SCSI (Small Computer System Interface), the target number should match the target address set by the switch on the back of the unit.
- The Y following the d is the drive number attached to the target. The drive numbers are not necessarily numbered sequentially from zero.
- The Z following the s is the partition (slice) number.

Table 16.3 shows some examples of device names.

Table 16.3 Examples of Device Names

Device Names	Description
/dev/dsk/c0t0d0s0	The first partition (slice) on the first disk at the first target address on the first controller
/dev/dsk/c0t3d0s2	Partition 2 (the entire disk) of the first drive at the fourth target address on the first controller
/dev/dsk/c1t0d1s0	The first partition on the second disk at the first target address on the second controller

Some disks use a slightly different naming convention that does not include a bus target address, as shown in Figure 16.3.

Understanding File Systems

As mentioned at the beginning of this section, a file system is an organization of files and directories. It is like a minidirectory hierarchy with its own root. For example, the /usr directory is usually a separate file system. All the files and directories under /usr are part of the usr file system.

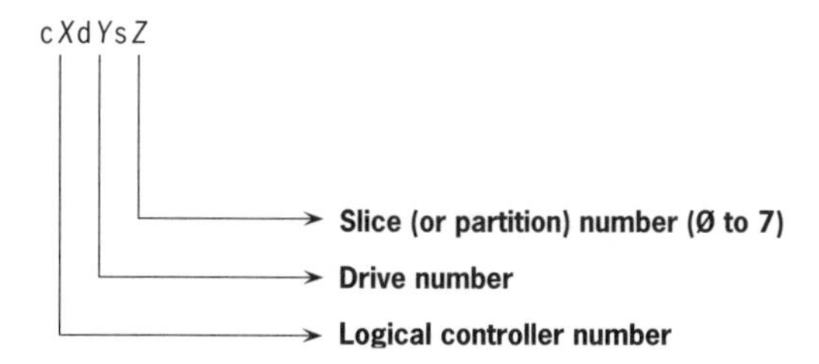

Figure 16.3 Other common disk-naming conventions

To connect file systems into the overall directory hierarchy, a file system must be *mounted*. The root of a mounted file system is associated with an existing directory. For example, the usr file system is mounted on the /usr directory. This may sound a little confusing at first, but think of it as if you were grafting a branch into an existing tree. The tree branch is an existing directory (/usr), and the new branch being grafted in is the file system (the usr file system in this case). A mounted file system then becomes part of the directory hierarchy, and the files and directories in the file system are indistinguishable from other files and directories.

The root file system is a special file system that is always mounted and cannot be unmounted. A file system must be mounted on a directory that resides in the root file system or in a mounted file system. Most file systems are mounted on a directory that resides in the root file system. Remember that each file system is contained within a single partition on a disk. If you have multiple disks with multiple partitions that contain file systems, you mount each of these file systems to create the overall directory hierarchy. Figure 16.4 shows the organization of the four common file systems: root, opt, usr, and export/home.

All the files and directories in the /etc, /var, /dev, /bin, and /lib are located in the root file system. The files and directories in the /usr directory are located in the usr file system, and so on.

The df command

The df (disk free) command reports the amount of free space on each mounted file system. In addition to information about free space, you are also given the file system information, including the partition on which each mounted file system resides. The output of the df -k command is shown here. The -k option reports available space in kilobytes and is the easiest way to examine the df output.

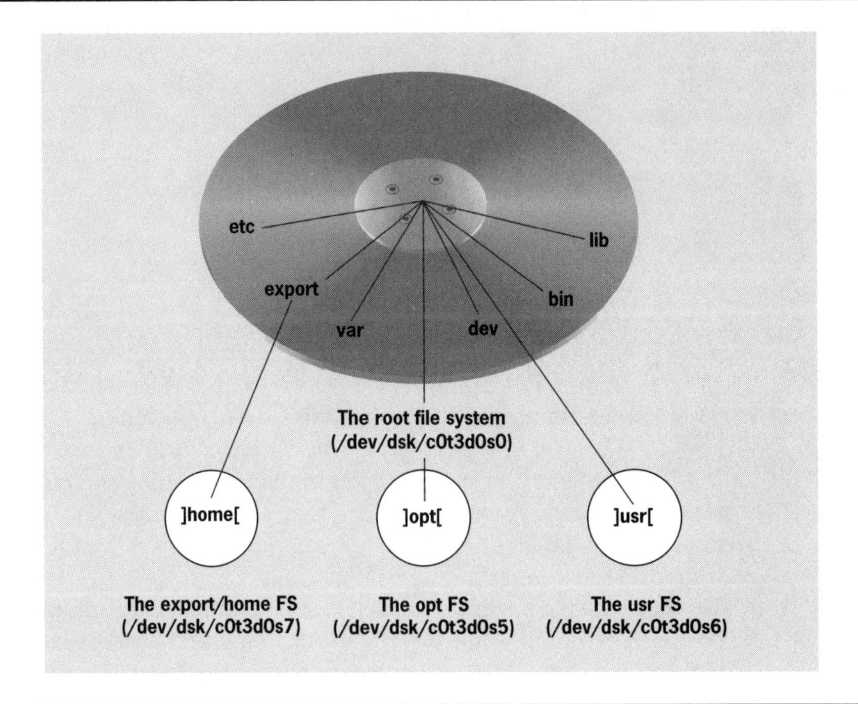

Figure 16.4 File-system (FS) organization

```
dugout% df -k
Filesystem           kbytes    used    avail capacity  Mounted on
/dev/dsk/c0t3d0s0     27023   10295    14028    42%    /
/dev/dsk/c0t3d0s6    168719  105497    46352    69%    /usr
/proc                     0       0        0     0%    /proc
fd                        0       0        0     0%    /dev/fd
swap                  54500     568    53932     1%    /tmp
/dev/dsk/c0t3d0s7     70287   53087    10180    84%    /export/home
/dev/dsk/c0t3d0s5     60559   55933        0   100%    /opt
dugout%
```

The information provided by df is very useful. The first field reports the partition (device) name on which the file system resides. The next four fields display information about the available disk space (in kilobytes) on that file system: the capacity, the space used, the space available, and the percentage used. The last field indicates where the file system is mounted. For example, the second entry is for the usr file system. Its device name is /dev/dsk/c0t3d0s6, it is mounted on /usr, and it is 69 percent full.

Some of the entries in the df output are special file systems (proc, fd, and swap) and do not have an associated device name. In the next section I'll briefly introduce the different file system types.

Understanding File System Types

The standard file system that we have talked about thus far in this chapter is only one of several types available. Some file system types are designed specifically for disks, others for networks, and still others for other special purposes.

Disk-Based File Systems

There are three common disk-based file systems: *ufs, hsfs,* and *pcfs*.

The ufs (UNIX File System) file system is the standard file system that we have been discussing in this chapter. A ufs file system resides usually on a disk, though it can reside also on other media such as a floppy disk or a CD-ROM. (It can reside on tape as well, though this is extremely rare and not very useful.)

The hsfs (High Sierra File System) file system is a read-only file system that is used most commonly for file systems on CD-ROMs.

The pcfs (PC File System) file system is compatible with the DOS-based disk format. A pcfs file system resides usually on a floppy disk. You can read disks made on a personal computer and create files that can be read on a personal computer by using the pcfs file system. You'll learn more about using the pcfs file system later in this chapter.

Other File System Types

Several other common file system types are used for a variety of purposes:

The NFS (Network File System) file system allows a file system from a remote machine to be mounted as if it were a local file system. The NFS file system simplifies network access by allowing you to view and use files from a remote machine as if they were local files.

The tmpfs (Temporary File System) creates a file system in memory. This is the default file system type for the tmp file system (mounted on /tmp). It provides very fast access to the files in this file system. All files in a tmpfs file system are deleted when the system is shut down or rebooted.

The procfs (Process File System) is a special file system that contains a file for each running process.

The Virtual File System Table

Each system has a virtual file system table, /etc/vfstab, that lists the disk partitions and file systems available to the system. The virtual file system table also includes the mount point of the file system and some other options. Here's what a typical /etc/vfstab file looks like:

```
dugout% cat /etc/vfstab
#device          device           mount           FS       fsck     mount    mount
#to mount        to fsck          point           type     pass     at boot  options
/proc            -                /proc           proc     -        no       -
fd               -                /dev/fd         fd       -        no       -
swap             -                /tmp            tmpfs    -        yes      -

/dev/dsk/c0t3d0s0       /dev/rdsk/c0t3d0s0        /        ufs      1        no
-
/dev/dsk/c0t3d0s6       /dev/rdsk/c0t3d0s6        /usr     ufs      2        no
-
/dev/dsk/c0t3d0s7       /dev/rdsk/c0t3d0s7        /export/home      ufs      3
yes    -
/dev/dsk/c0t3d0s5       /dev/rdsk/c0t3d0s5        /opt     ufs      4        yes
-
/dev/dsk/c0t3d0s1       -        -        swap    -        no       -
dugout%
```

Each entry in the virtual file system table includes seven fields, described in Table 16.4.

Table 16.4 Fields in the /etc/vfstab File

Field	Description
device to mount	The device to be mounted. This should always be a blocked device (/dev/dsk).
device to fsck	The device to run file system checks on. This should be the raw device that corresponds to the device to be mounted. (/dev/rdsk).
mount point	The directory on which to mount the file system.
FS type	The type of file system to be mounted.
fsck pass	The fsck pass number, which is used to determine when the file system is checked. A hyphen (-) means don't check.
mount at boot	A yes or no determines whether this file system will be automatically mounted at boot time. (Not related to the automounter software).
mount options	A list of comma-separated options (with no spaces) that are used in mounting the file system. Use a hyphen (-) to show default options. See the mount man page for a list of the available options.

There are at least several occasions when you might use the /etc/vfstab file. You may want to comment out an entry, using a pound sign (#) at the beginning of the line, so that when you boot your system that file system will not be mounted. Or, you may want to change the mount point of a particular file system. You can do this by editing the /etc/vfstab file.

Mounting and Unmounting File Systems

One of the most common things you will do with file systems is to mount and unmount them. The standard file systems such as /usr and /export/home are not likely candidates for mounting and unmounting under normal circumstances. However, you may have a spare partition on a local disk that contains a file system that you use for a special purpose now and then, and you may need to mount and unmount it. To do so, you use the mount and umount commands.

You use the mount command, obviously, to mount a file system. If you are mounting a file system that is already listed in the /etc/vfstab file, you can simply specify the mount point as an argument to mount. You must be root to execute the mount and umount commands.

```
# mount /opt
#
```

To unmount a file system, use the umount command with the mount point as the argument:

```
# umount /opt
#
```

You can unmount a file system only if it is not currently being used. If any user's current directory is anywhere within the file system, or if a file that resides on the file system is being accessed in any way (for example, if it is being edited), you cannot unmount the file system.

If you want to mount a file system that does not have an entry in the /etc/vfstab file, you will have to supply some of the information that would normally appear in the /etc/vfstab file as command-line arguments. Also, the directory on which you are mounting the file system must already exist. For example, to mount the file system that resides on partition /dev/dsk/c0t0d0s4 on /mnt, use the following command:

```
# mount -F ufs /dev/dsk/c0t0d0s4 /mnt
#
```

The -F option specifies the type of file system being mounted. If you do not specify the -F option and the file system type, mount attempts to figure out the correct file-system type (it's usually correct).

If you want to specify an option (such as mounting the file system as read-only), use the -o option followed by the options you want to set. For example, to mount the file system shown in the previous example with the read-only option, use the following command:

```
# mount -F ufs -o ro /dev/dsk/c0t0d0s4 /mnt
#
```

To see which file systems are currently mounted, use the df command (as described previously) or use mount without arguments. The mount command displays the mount point, the device name, the type of mount (read-write, read-only), and the time the file system was mounted. You do not have to be root to use the mount command to display the currently mounted file systems, as shown here:

```
dugout% mount
/ on /dev/dsk/c0t3d0s0 read/write on Tue Apr 18 13:31:23 1995
/usr on /dev/dsk/c0t3d0s6 read/write on Tue Apr 18 13:31:23 1995
/proc on /proc read/write on Tue Apr 18 13:31:23 1995
/dev/fd on fd read/write on Tue Apr 18 13:31:23 1995
/tmp on swap read/write on Tue Apr 18 13:31:28 1995
/export/home on /dev/dsk/c0t3d0s7 setuid on Tue Apr 18 13:31:29 1995
/opt on /dev/dsk/c0t3d0s5 read only on Wed Apr 19 13:17:52 1995
dugout%
```

Tapes and Floppy Disks

Many occasions will require that you use system peripherals such as the tape drive, the floppy-disk drive, and the disk drives. In this section we will look briefly at these two devices to understand how to use and refer to them.

Using Tapes

Tapes are used commonly for making backups, distributing software, and copying files to other systems. If you want to send some files to a user at a remote location that is not connected to your network, you can make a tape and send it to that person. Or, you may have files on a local disk that you want to back up. This requires some knowledge of the tape device.

There are several kinds of tapes: reel-to-reel, 1/4-inch cartridge, and 8mm are the most common. Tape drives also support different densities of data that can be written to them. Every device has a corresponding special file that you use to access that device. Tape devices are located in the /dev/rmt directory. Figure 16.5 shows the standard naming convention for tapes.

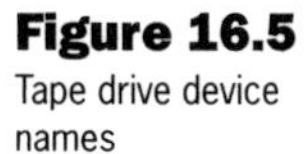

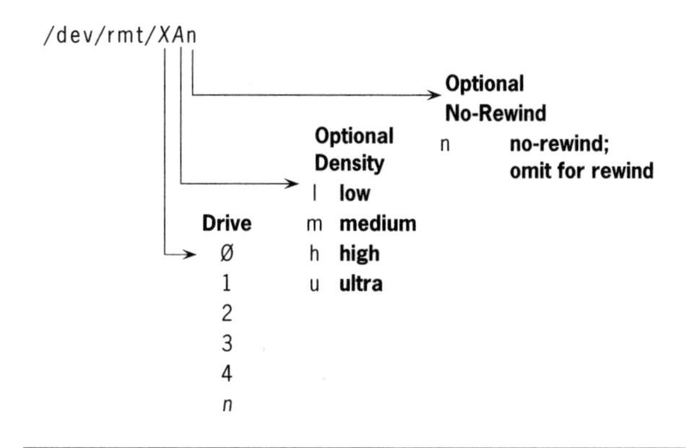

Figure 16.5
Tape drive device names

The first character (X) in the tape drive name specified the drive number. If you have only one tape device on your system, you access that tape drive by using 0 as the drive number. For example, to specify the first drive, use

```
/dev/rmt/Ø
```

If you have a second drive, you access it by using

```
/dev/rmt/1
```

The second character (A) is optional and specifies the density. Every tape device has a default density, so you can leave this character out if you do not need a specific density. If you are planning to create a tape that will be read on a tape drive on another system that supports only a particular density, you may need to use this field in the tape drive specification. For example, to specify the first drive with medium density, use

```
/dev/rmt/Øm
```

The last character (n) is also optional. If n is included in the tape name specification, the tape will not rewind when the tape operation is complete. By default, whenever you use tapes (reading or writing), the tape automatically rewinds when the operation is complete. Using the tape device that includes an n at the end of the tape name specification forces the tape to remain at its current location rather than to rewind. For example, to specify the first tape drive with the default density and the no-rewind option, use

```
/dev/rmt/Øn
```

To specify the low density on the same drive and the no-rewind options, use

```
/dev/rmt/Øln
```

In Chapter 12 you learned about the tar command; it is used frequently to create archives on tape. When using tar, you may need to specify the tape device. For example, to create a tape by using the second tape drive and the no-rewind option, use the following command:

```
dugout% tar cf /dev/rmt/1n .
dugout%
```

When you have created a tape using the no-rewind device, the tape stops at the end of the archive you have created. This archive can be thought of as a *tape file*. A tape can contain more than one tape file. With the tape positioned at the end of the previously created archive, you can write another archive (tape file) to the same tape by using another tar command, such as the following:

```
dugout% tar cf /dev/rmt/1 /export/home/sally
dugout%
```

This time the no-rewind device was not selected, so the tape rewinds when the archive has been written. Now there are two tape files (archives) on the tape.

You can use the mt (manipulate tape) command to position the tape. The mt command lets you rewind a tape or forward it to a particular position. If you have written multiple tape files to a tape, you can then use mt to move the tape position so that you can read or extract the appropriate tape file.

To rewind a tape, use the rew option:

```
dugout% mt rew
dugout%
```

To display the status of the tape, use the status option. This tells you the type of tape drive and also gives you some other arcane information. One useful piece of information given is the file number (file no). The file number indicates at which tape file the tape is currently positioned. In the output shown here, the status option indicates that the file number is 0, which means that the tape is positioned at the beginning.

```
dugout% mt status
Archive QIC-150 tape drive:
   sense key(0x6)= Unit Attention   residual= 0   retries= 0
   file no= 0   block no= 0
dugout%
```

To move the tape position forward, use the fsf (forward space files) option. The fsf option must be used with the no-rewind device; otherwise the tape will advance to the specified position and then automatically rewind, which is of little value. So, use the -f option followed by the name of the no-rewind device, along with the fsf option, as shown here:

```
dugout% mt -f /dev/rmt/0n fsf
dugout%
```

Now the tape is positioned at the beginning of the second tape file. Let's run the mt status command again to see if the file number correctly reflects the position of the tape. We'll use the no-rewind device so that the tape does not rewind after reporting the status:

```
dugout% mt -f /dev/rmt/0n status
Archive QIC-150 tape drive:
   sense key(0x0)= No Additional Sense   residual= 0   retries= 0
   file no= 1   block no= 0
dugout%
```

As you can see from the output, the file number is now reported as 1, indicating that the tape is positioned at the beginning of the second tape file (or tape file 1, counting from 0).

You can supply an additional argument with the fsf option to specify the number of tape files to advance. For example, to advance 3 tape files (from the current position), use the following command:

```
dugout% mt -f /dev/rmt/0n fsf 3
dugout%
```

Of course, this assumes that you have at least that many files on the tape.

The fsf option moves the tape relative to its current position. To move the tape to an absolute position regardless of its current position, use the asf (absolute space files) option followed by the tape file number. For example, to position the tape at the beginning of the fourth tape file (tape file 3, counting from 0), use the following command:

```
dugout% mt -f /dev/rmt/0n asf 3
dugout%
```

To position the tape at the end of any recorded tape files, use the eom (end of media) option. This is useful for appending files onto previously written tapes. The tape is positioned at the end of the last tape file regardless of how many files are on the tape. Of course, you still have to use the no-rewind device. The eom option is shown here:

```
dugout% mt -f /dev/rmt/0n eom
dugout%
```

There are other options to mt, but these few examples should suffice for most cases. See the mt man page for further details.

Using Floppy Disks

Most SPARCstations come equipped with a floppy-disk drive that takes a standard 3½-inch floppy. You can use the floppies in some of the same ways that you use tapes. For example, you can write a tar archive to a floppy. You can also create file systems on floppy disks. By using a special type of file system (pcfs), you can transfer files between a PC running DOS and your SunOS machine.

Disk Basics

Before you can use a floppy, it must be formatted. You were briefly introduced to the fdformat (floppy-disk format) command in Chapter 9. To format a disk, insert a 3½-inch disk into the drive and enter the fdformat command, as shown here:

```
dugout% fdformat
Press return to start formatting floppy.
......................................................................
dugout%
```

You refer to the floppy-disk drive by using the name /dev/diskette or /dev/rdiskette. If you want to create a tar archive on a floppy disk, you enter the tar command, specifying the device as /dev/diskette, as shown here:

```
dugout% tar cvf /dev/diskette file1 file2
a file1 3 tape blocks
a file2 2 tape blocks
dugout%
```

To eject the disk from the floppy-disk drive, enter the eject command:

```
dugout% eject
dugout%
```

Putting File Systems onto Floppy Disks

There are two types of file systems that you can put onto a floppy disk: a ufs file system and a pcfs file system.

Putting a ufs File System onto a Floppy Disk You can put a standard ufs file system onto a floppy disk by formatting it and then using the newfs (new file system) command to create the file system. Once you have created the file system on the disk, you can mount it by using the mount command, which you learned earlier in this chapter. You do not have to be root to format the disk or to make the file system, but you must be root to mount the file system. Making the file system and mounting it on /mnt are shown here:

```
dugout% newfs /dev/diskette
newfs: construct a new file system /dev/rdiskette: (y/n)? y
/dev/rdiskette:  2880 sectors in 80 cylinders of 2 tracks, 18 sectors
         1.5MB in 5 cyl groups (16 c/g, 0.29MB/g, 128 i/g)
super-block backups (for fsck -F ufs -o b=#) at:
 32, 640, 1184, 1792, 2336,
dugout% su
Password: <Enter root password>
# mount -F ufs /dev/diskette /mnt
# df -k
Filesystem            kbytes    used    avail  capacity  Mounted on
/dev/dsk/c0t3d0s0      27023   10307    14016     42%    /
/dev/dsk/c0t3d0s6     168719  105497    46352     69%    /usr
/proc                      0       0        0      0%    /proc
fd                         0       0        0      0%    /dev/fd
swap                   65392      20    65372      0%    /tmp
/dev/dsk/c0t3d0s7      70287   53093    10174     84%    /export/home
/dev/diskette           1263       9     1134      1%    /mnt
#
```

As you can see from the df output, /dev/diskette is now mounted on /mnt. You can treat it just like any other file system. Before you can eject the disk, you must unmount the file system.

Putting a pcfs File System onto a Floppy Disk The other very useful file system type that is commonly used with floppy disks is the pcfs file system. This file system is compatible with DOS floppy disks, which means you can transfer files between SunOS and DOS machines by using the pcfs file system. You can create a floppy on a DOS machine and then read it by mounting it as a pcfs file system. Or, you can create a pcfs file system on a floppy, write files to it, and then transfer those files to a DOS machine by loading the floppy in the DOS floppy-disk drive.

To use a pcfs file system on a floppy-disk drive, you must format the floppy by using the fdformat command, and supply the -d option. This formats the floppy in a way that is consistent with DOS formatting. Alternatively, you can format the floppy on a DOS machine by using the standard DOS FORMAT command. Once the floppy is formatted, you mount the pcfs file system by using the mount command and specifying the pcfs file system type, as shown here:

```
dugout% fdformat -d
Press return to start formatting floppy.
.................................................................
dugout% su
Password: <Enter root password>
# mount -F pcfs /dev/diskette /mnt
#
```

You treat this pcfs file system as you would any other file system. You can copy files to it with the cp command, list files with ls, and examine files with cat or more. The advantage of the pcfs file system is that you can remove the floppy, insert it into a DOS machine, and then access the same files on your SunOS and DOS machines.

You may find it convenient to add an entry to your /etc/vfstab file so that you can easily mount the pcfs file system. First, create a directory on which you want to mount the file system—something like /pcfs. In the /etc/vfstab entry, be sure to specify no in the mount at boot field, as shown here:

```
/dev/diskette   -       /pcfs   pcfs    -       no      -
```

With this entry in your /etc/vfstab file, all you have to do to mount the file system on the floppy is to enter the following mount command:

```
# mount /pcfs
#
```

There are a few things that you should be aware of when dealing with a pcfs file system. Files written to a pcfs file system conform to DOS naming conventions. DOS file names can be up to eight characters, followed by a dot and then three suffix characters. If you attempt to create a file on a pcfs file system that has a longer name than supported, the name will be truncated. For example, if you copy a file named chapter16.text to a pcfs file system, it will be renamed to chapter1.tex on the pcfs file system. There are also some other limitations: a pcfs file cannot begin with a dot (.) or include more than one dot or include a plus sign (+).

DOS and UNIX files also have some slight differences in the way ASCII characters are used. To achieve compatibility, you may need to convert ASCII files from UNIX to DOS format, or vice versa. You can do this with the unix2dos and dos2unix commands. To convert a UNIX ASCII file to DOS format, enter the unix2dos command with two arguments: the name of the existing file and the name of the new files, as shown here:

```
dugout% unix2dos existing new
dugout%
```

To convert a DOS file to UNIX format, use the dos2unix command, specifying the arguments as with the unix2dos command:

```
dugout% dos2unix existing new
dugout%
```

Backups and Restores

Backing up files is an important system administration task. You will usually back up files to some kind of removable media such as tape. Backups are a safeguard against file corruption and accidental deletion. If your system administrator does backups for all the file systems on your machine, you may not need to worry about this task. In many cases, however, you may use some file systems that reside remotely on a server and other file systems that reside locally on your own system's disk. Often, the system administrator backs up files on the server but not the files on a local disk. If this is the case for you, you should take the precaution of backing up your local files.

Backups are done according to file system. If you want to back up only a certain set of files or directories you can simply use tar and make a tape of the data you want to save. If you want to back up all the files on your file systems, you should use the standard backup and restore utilities: ufsdump and ufsrestore.

Backing Up File Systems

To back up a file system (sometimes called *dumping* a file system), you use the ufsdump command. The ufsdump command supports the notion of different *dump levels,* ranging from 0 to 9. The dump level enables you to perform *incremental dumps*. This means you can choose to dump only the files that have been created or modified since a previous dump.

A level-0 dump means that the entire file system is stored. You always need a level-0 dump to act as a base line for any future incremental dumps. When you do a higher-level dump (also called an incremental dump), the ufsdump command dumps only the files that have been created or changed since the highest-level dump that is less than the current level. For example, if you performed a level-0 dump on Tuesday and a level-3 dump on Wednesday, then when you perform a level-5 dump on Thursday, only the files that have been created or changed since the level-3 dump are stored. If, on Friday, you perform a level-2 dump, all the files that have been created or changed since the level-0 dump (regardless of the intervening level-3 and -5 dumps) are stored. This scheme may seem confusing at first, but it provides a very convenient mechanism for doing backups by using the least number of tapes.

For simple backups you probably need to worry only about two dump levels. I do backups of my disk and use only level-0 and level-9 dumps. (Feel free to be more sophisticated if you like.) I perform a level-0 dump on each of my file systems on a regular, but infrequent basis—perhaps once a month (but more frequently when necessary). Then I do a daily backup by using a level-9 dump. Since I don't use any of the other dump levels, the level-9 dump records all the files that have been created or changed since the level-0 dump.

When you run the ufsdump command, be sure that the file system you are dumping is inactive. Your backups can become corrupted if the file system is being actively used. When you perform a level-0 dump, you should first unmount the file system you are dumping. This ensures that there is absolutely no activity on that file system during the dump. This is not an absolute requirement, but it is a good idea.

It is also a good idea to unmount a file system when you are doing an incremental dump, but this is often impractical. I personally don't unmount any file system when I do my daily level-9 dumps, but I perform the dump when there is nothing else happening on my system.

The ufsdump command takes multiple arguments that specify the dump level and the file system to be dumped. For example, to do a level-0 dump of the usr file system, use the following command:

```
# ufsdump 0u /usr
  DUMP: Date of this level-0 dump: Wed Apr 19 15:52:42 1995
  DUMP: Date of last level-0 dump: the epoch
  DUMP: Dumping /dev/rdsk/c0t3d0s6 (/usr) to /dev/rmt/0
  DUMP: mapping (Pass I) [regular files]
  DUMP: mapping (Pass II) [directories]
  DUMP: estimated 225494 blocks (110.10MB)
  DUMP: Writing 32 Kilobyte records
  DUMP: dumping (Pass III) [directories]
  DUMP: dumping (Pass IV) [regular files]
<More output follows>
```

The first argument to ufsdump includes the dump level and other options. In this example we performed a level-0 dump and specified the u (update) option, which indicates that information about the file system being dumped, the dump level, and the time of the dump should be stored in the /etc/dumpdates files. This information is used when incremental dumps are done to determine the time of the previous dumps. The second argument is the file system to dump (/usr).

If you need to store the dump on a tape (or device) other than the default device (/dev/rmt/0), use the f option followed by the name of the device. For example, to perform a level-9 dump on the root file system and store it to the no-rewind device, use the following command:

```
# ufsdump 0uf /dev/rmt/0n /usr
```

If you do not have a tape drive attached to your system, you can specify a tape drive connected to a remote system by preceding the device name by the system name. For example, to dump the usr file system to the first tape drive on system bullpen, use the following command:

```
# ufsdump 0uf bullpen:/dev/rmt/0 /usr
```

It's possible that this will not work because you are trying to access a tape drive on a remote machine as root. SunOS has some built-in security features that normally prevent root access on remote machines. However, you cannot perform the dump as a regular user because you do not have permission to access the file system you are dumping. One possible solution is to specify your user ID with an "at" symbol (@) in front of the remote-machine name—somewhat like a mail address:

```
# ufsdump 0uf pew@bullpen:/dev/rmt/0 /usr
```

This command attempts to access the remote machine (bullpen) as a regular user (pew). But since you are still logged in a root (as shown by the # prompt), you can access the usr file system device. If this still fails due to lack of permission, the remote machine may not consider your system a trusted host (see Chapter 15). In this case, contact your system administrator.

Another important option is c (cartridge tape). If you are using a cartridge or 8 mm tape, use the c option. The ufsdump command knows how to sense the end of the tape when you are using a cartridge tape. This means that you don't have to calculate the size of the tape; ufsdump will simply stop when it gets to the end of the tape. For example, to perform a level-9 dump of the root file system when using a cartridge tape, use the following command:

```
# ufsdump 9uc /
```

If the dump does not fit on a single tape, you are prompted to change tapes. This continues until the dump is complete.

As I described earlier, I do a level-0 dump once a month and then do daily level-9 dumps. I have created a shell script, which I call daily.bu, that contains the commands I use to perform my daily backup. Here are the contents of the file:

```
/usr/bin/mt rew
/usr/sbin/ufsdump 9ucf /dev/rmt/0n / > /export/home/pew/daily.out 2>&1
/usr/sbin/ufsdump 9ucf /dev/rmt/0n /opt >> /export/home/pew/daily.out 2>&1
/usr/sbin/ufsdump 9ucf /dev/rmt/0n /export/home >> /export/home/pew/daily.out 2>&1
/usr/bin/mt rew
```

The first thing that the script does is to rewind the tape by using the mt command. Then it does a level-9 backup of the root file system and writes the output to a file named daily.out in my home directory. Notice that the device being used is the no-rewind device. This means that the tape remains positioned at the end of the dump so that the next command will not overwrite the previous dump. Next, the script does a level-9 backup of the opt file system (also using the no-rewind device) and appends the output to the same daily.out file in my home directory. The same dump command is then used for the /export/home file system. Finally, the tape is rewound, again by using the mt command.

If the three dumps store more data than will fit on a single tape, this method does not succeed. However, each day as the script runs, I check the output file (daily.out) to see if any errors have occurred. If the dumps were too large, then I know I must run a new level-0 dump for at least one of the file systems. I look at the daily.out file to determine which file system took the most space on the tape (the output of ufsdump estimates the amount of tape required for the dump) and then run a level-0 dump on that file system.

To further simplify this daily procedure, I add a crontab entry to automatically run the daily.bu script every morning at 3 a.m. At this time of day there is little activity going on, so getting a clean, uncorrupted dump is likely. Of course, I must be sure that I have a tape loaded in the tape drive or no backup will be made. My crontab entry looks like this:

```
Ø 3 * * *        /export/home/pew/bin/daily.bu
```

Restoring Files from Backup Tapes

To restore files from a backup tape you use the ufsrestore command. This command lets you restore an entire file system or just one or two files. If you need to restore an entire file system, you should probably seek help from your system administrator. If you need to restore just a few files, you should be able to do that yourself.

The first thing you need to understand is which tape you should restore from. To determine which tape has the file or files you need requires that you understand how backups are performed. As you have already learned, backups are done at different levels. This means that if you accidentally delete a file, you may find the backup copy on any one or more of the backup tapes for the file system on which the file resided. If you have created a file since the last backup, then that file is not on any backup tape. So, you can't possibly restore a file that you haven't backed up.

If you have multiple levels of backup tapes stored, you must decide which tape to look on. If you are following the scheme described in the previous section by using level-0 and -9 dumps only, then you know that the file must be on one of those tapes. To determine which dump to look on requires that you know when the file was created or last modified. It's possible that the file is on both tapes if it existed before the level-0 dump was done and has since been modified. Assuming that you want the most recent version of the file, you would, in this case, look on the level-9 dump tape. If the file was created before the level-0 dump and has not been changed since then, it would be on the level-0 tape only. If you are unsure of when the file was created or last modified, you may have to look on both tapes to find the file.

There are several ways that you can use the ufsrestore command. In this section we will concentrate on listing the contents of a dump tape and using the interactive mode of restoring a few files at a time.

To list the files that are on a dump tape, first load the tape. If the dump is part of a multiple-volume dump, load the first tape in the set. Then run the ufsrestore command with the t (table) option. You can optionally specify a device name by using the f option followed by the device name. The following example lists the contents of the dump tape by using the device /dev/rmt/1:

```
dugout% ufsrestore tf /dev/rmt/1
         2       .
         3       ./lost+found
      2688       ./export
      5376       ./export/home
      8064       ./opt
     10752       ./usr
      2689       ./var
      5377       ./var/sadm
      8065       ./var/sadm/install
     10753       ./var/sadm/install/admin
     10909       ./var/sadm/install/admin/default
      2690       ./var/sadm/install/logs
      8066       ./var/sadm/install/.lockfile
      8251       ./var/sadm/install/contents
<More output follows>
```

The preceding method is the quickest way to determine if the file or files you are looking for are on this particular tape. To actually restore files from a backup tape, use the i (interactive) option to ufsrestore. When you use the i option, ufsrestore creates a pseudo shell that contains a simulation of the files and directories on the tape. You are presented with the ufsrestore> prompt, and you can use commands like ls, pwd, and cd to move around within this pseudo shell to locate the files you want to restore. You use the add command followed by the name or names of the files or directories that you want to restore. You can use the add command repeatedly to append to the list of files you want restored. When you have finished adding files, use the extract command to actually extract the files from the tape and write them to the current directory. A directory hierarchy identical to the one on the tape is created in which files are restored. It is a good idea to change to a neutral directory like /tmp before attempting a restore. This avoids overwriting other files with the same name.

To demonstrate the use of the ufsrestore command, let's suppose you have accidentally deleted the /etc/passwd and /etc/group files. You determine that the level-0 dump contains the most recent copies of these files, so you load that tape in the tape drive. (If you have multiple dumps on a single tape, use the mt fsf command, specifying the no-rewind tape device, to advance the tape position to the correct tape file before running ufsrestore.) The following example shows the sequence of commands you would use to restore these two files:

```
dugout% cd /tmp
dugout% ufsrestore i
ufsrestore > ls
.:
 TT_DB/        disk0/       kadb          net/       tmp_mnt/
 bin          *etc/         kernel/       opt/       ufsboot
 cd0/          export/      lib           proc/      usr/
 dev/          home/        lost+found/   sbin/      var/
 devices/      home2/       mnt/          tmp/       vivids/

ufsrestore > cd etc
ufsrestore > ls
./etc:
 clri              ioctl.syscon        passwd            swapadd
 crash             iu.ap               path_to_inst      sysdef
 group             netconfig           remote            wtmpx
<Many other files not listed>

ufsrestore > add passwd
ufsrestore > add group
ufsrestore > ls
./etc:
 clri              ioctl.syscon       *passwd            swapadd
 crash             iu.ap               path_to_inst      sysdef
*group             netconfig           remote            wtmpx
<Many other files not listed>

ufsrestore > extract
You have not read any volumes yet.
Unless you know which volume your file(s) are on you should start
with the last volume and work towards the first.
Specify next volume #: 1
set owner/mode for '.'? [yn] n
ufsrestore > quit
dugout%
```

When you are in the ufsrestore pseudo shell, the root directory (/) is equivalent to the root of the file system you are restoring. If you were restoring files from the usr directory, files that appeared in / would be the files in the /usr directory because /usr is the root of the usr file system.

After you have used the add command to add files to the list of those being restored, the ls output precedes the file name with an asterisk. The asterisk marks that file for extraction. When you enter the extract command, ufsrestore asks you which volume you intend to begin restoring from. If your dump is wholly contained on a single tape, then you can simply enter 1, since there is only one tape in the dump. If you have a multiple-volume dump, you should start with the last tape in the volume and work forward. This speeds the time it takes to locate a file because of the way that the files are written to the backup tapes.

When the extraction is complete, you can quit the ufsrestore program by using the quit command. Every file you have restored is placed in a directory hierarchy matching the original directory hierarchy on the tape. For example, the two files we restored were both from the etc directory. So, an etc directory is created in your current working directory (/tmp), and the passwd and group files are restored in that directory, as shown here:

```
dugout% ls
etc
dugout% cd etc
dugout% pwd
/tmp/etc
dugout% ls
group  passwd
dugout%
```

Finally, you copy the files back into place by using mv or cp, as shown here:

```
dugout% su
Password: <Enter root password>
# mv group passwd /etc
#
```

Network Services Administration

Administrating network services is a large and complex topic that cannot be covered thoroughly in this book. In this section we will discuss some basic concepts regarding the NFS file system and the automounter so that you will understand how they work and how to take advantage of their basic features.

Using the NFS File System

NFS file system is one of the most powerful and useful features of SunOS. Using NFS file system means you can mount a file system from a remote host and use it as if it were a regular file system. When you have mounted a file system with NFS file system, you don't have to use any special network commands such as rcp or rlogin. You just treat the files on the remote file system as if they were local files.

You can mount remote file systems and allow local file systems to be mounted remotely. There are commands to both mount remote file systems and make local file systems available or unavailable to remote systems. You will learn about both in this section.

Mounting Remote File Systems

To mount a remote file system, use the mount command and specify an NFS file system. Then provide the host name and directory to mount. For example, to mount the /export/home directory from system bullpen on /export_bull, enter the following command:

```
# mount -F nfs bullpen:/export/home /export_bull
#
```

The df command also displays remotely mounted file systems. You can see here that bullpen:/export/home is mounted on /export_bull:

```
# df -k
Filesystem            kbytes    used   avail capacity  Mounted on
/dev/dsk/c0t3d0s0      27023   10308   14015    42%    /
/dev/dsk/c0t3d0s6     168719  105497   46352    69%    /usr
/proc                      0       0       0     0%    /proc
fd                         0       0       0     0%    /dev/fd
swap                   61524      20   61504     0%    /tmp
/dev/dsk/c0t3d0s7      70287   53093   10174    84%    /export/home
bullpen:/export/home  189534  160772    9808    94%    /export_bull
#
```

You unmount an NFS mounted file system with the umount command:

```
# umount /export_bull
#
```

If you want a remote file system to always be mounted, you can add an entry to the /etc/vfstab file. Entries in the /etc/vfstab file for NFS file systems are slightly different from ufs file systems. An example of an NFS file system entry is shown here:

```
bullpen:/export/home    -    /export_bull    nfs    -    yes    rw
```

Here is a description of how each field for an NFS file system should be set:

Device to mount includes the remote machine name and the directory on that machine to be mounted, separated by a colon.

device to fsck is always set to a hyphen (-) because you do not run file system checks on remote file systems at boot time.

mount point is the directory on which to mount the remote file system.

FS type is nfs.

fsck pass should be set to a hyphen (-) since no file system checks are done on remote file systems.

mount at boot should be set to yes if you want the file system automatically mounted, or to no if you don't.

mount options is a comma-separated list of options.

In order to successfully mount a remote file system, you must be sure the file system is *shareable*. Whether a file system is shareable is determined by the owner of the system. For example, some users may have file systems on their machines with some particularly sensitive files that they do not want to make available to other users for remote mounting. You can control whether a file system is available for users to mount by using the share command, which you will learn about shortly.

If a remote file system is shareable, you can mount any directory on that file system. You are not limited to mounting only the root of the file system. For example, if sally has her home directory in /export/home on system bullpen, and /export/home is shareable, you can mount just sally's directory by specifying the device to mount as bullpen:/export/home/sally, as shown here:

```
# mount -F nfs bullpen:/export/home/sally /sally
#
```

Making Local File Systems Available for Remote Mounting

You determine whether or not a local file system is available for other users to mount remotely by using the share command. To make your root file system shareable, enter the following command:

```
# share /
#
```

By default, the file system is made shareable with read-write permissions. If you want the file system to be shareable as read-only, use the -o option followed by ro, as shown here:

```
# share -o ro /
#
```

If you use the share command without arguments, it reports all the file systems currently being shared:

```
# share
-               /export/home    rw    "/export/home"
-               /usr    rw    "/usr"
-               /    ro    ""
#
```

You can make a file system unshareable by using the unshare command:

```
# unshare /
#
```

If you want to make a file system permanently shareable, put an entry into the /etc/dfs/dfstab file. The default /etc/dfs/dfstab file provides a sample of how an entry should appear in the file:

```
# cat /etc/dfs/dfstab

#       place share(1M) commands here for automatic execution
#       on entering init state 3.
#
#       share [-F fstype] [ -o options] [-d "<text>"] <pathname> [resource]
#       .e.g,
#       share  -F nfs  -o rw=engineering  -d "home dirs"  /export/home2
#
```

The -d option described in the sample is for a description. So, to share your /usr file system, add an entry such as this to your /etc/dfs/dfstab file:

```
share  -F nfs  -o rw  -d "usr FS"  /usr
```

Every time you boot your system, the usr file system automatically becomes shareable.

To determine which of your local file systems are currently being mounted by remote systems, use the dfmounts command:

```
# dfmounts
RESOURCE      SERVER PATHNAME                        CLIENTS
   -          dugout /export/home                   bullpen
   -          dugout /usr                           wind
#
```

Using the Automounter

The automounter is a sophisticated program that automatically and transparently mounts an NFS file system as needed. When you access a remote directory, the automounter automatically mounts the remote file system for you. It also automatically unmounts a mounted remote file system that has not been accessed for a period of time.

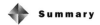

The automounter software is installed by default on Solaris 2.1. All you have to do to use it is to understand how you gain access to remote file systems. By default, the automounter mounts remote file systems on the /net/<hostname> directory. For example, if you want to change directory to sally's home directory on system bullpen (located in /export/home/sally), simply enter the following command:

```
dugout% cd /net/bullpen/export/home/sally
dugout%
```

The /export/home directory on remote system bullpen is automatically mounted on /net/bullpen/export/home.

If you wanted to list sally's .cshrc file, you could simply cat the file, referring to it with the same path name:

```
dugout% cat /net/bullpen/export/home/sally/.cshrc
<.cshrc file contents displayed here>
dugout%
```

The automounter has the same restriction regarding mounting file systems that the mount command has: it can mount only the file systems that are shareable. So, if bullpen:/export/home is not shareable, the automounter cannot mount it.

There are many ways to customize the automounter. One customizable feature is that it can allow remote file systems to be mounted on particular directories. Read the automount man page or check with your system administrator for more details.

Summary

You've learned a number of basic system administration tasks in this chapter. You should now be able to do many of those tasks by yourself, but there are other tasks that require more in-depth coverage than I have provided here. In the next chapter you will add to your knowledge of basic system administration by learning how to add users, configure printers, and perform other administration tasks by using the Administrator Tool.

CHAPTER

17

System Administration with the Administration Tool

Administration Tool Basics

Database Management

Printer Management

Host Management

User Account Management

IN THE PREVIOUS CHAPTER YOU LEARNED HOW TO PERFORM SOME COMMON system administration tasks that help you do your work more efficiently. In this chapter you will learn about some other basic administration tasks; each of these tasks, however, can be performed by using the Administration Tool.

As I mentioned in Chapter 16, these two chapters (16 and 17) are not intended for system administrators, but rather for users who occasionally need to perform some basic system administration tasks. So, our discussion is limited to those areas that you (the user) will most likely need. You probably will still need a system administrator to handle advanced or complex tasks. The Administration Tool is very helpful for a limited number of tasks, but it does not take the place of a system administrator.

In this chapter you will learn how to use the Administration Tool to perform the following tasks:

- Manage databases
- Manage printers
- Manage hosts
- Manage user accounts

Administration Tool Basics

The Administration Tool is really four tools in one. The Administration Tool's base window has four buttons, and each button starts one of the Administration Tool's four tools: the Database Manager, the Printer Manager, the Host Manager, and the User Account Manager. Figure 17.1 shows the Administration Tool's base window.

Each of these tools manipulates an administrative database or table. These tables are maintained by three distinct means: NIS+, NIS, or files in /etc. The NIS+ and NIS tables are network-based tables. The service by which network-based tables are maintained on a network is called a *naming service*. The files in /etc tables are simply files that reside in the /etc directory of your local machine. The files in /etc tables do not use a naming service.

NIS (Network Information Service) was introduced by Sun Microsystems in the mid-1980s. NIS+ is an extension of NIS that provides similar functionality to NIS, with some additional features that make it easier for a system administrator to manage administrative tables.

The advantage to using a naming service (NIS+ or NIS) is that a system administrator has to update only one table rather than one table per machine. For example, in order to log into a machine, you need a user account on that machine. If you work in an environment in which there are dozens or even hundreds of machines, you can imagine the effort that would be required to install a user account for you on every machine in your network. Multiply that by the number of users and the task quickly becomes very large. The concept of a single table that can be accessed by all machines on the network provides a solution to this problem.

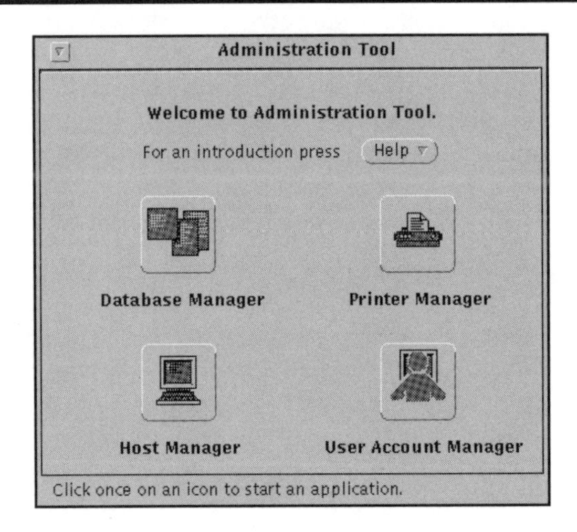

Figure 17.1
The Administration Tool

The advantage of using the files in /etc rather than a naming service is that it may be easier to simply edit a file rather than use a naming service. The disadvantage, however, is that files created in the /etc directory of your local machine cannot be shared across the network. Maintaining tables in files in /etc is especially difficult if you have many systems on your network. For large installations, it is probably not a reasonable solution. For the purposes of our discussion, however, I will explain how to use the Administration Tool by using files in the /etc directory. The methods of adding, modifying, or deleting entries are essentially the same whether you use NIS+, NIS, or files in /etc.

Most of the tasks that the Administration Tool performs are usually reserved for a system administrator and therefore require root access. To run the Administration Tool, you must either be logged in as root or you must belong to a special group: sysadmin. The Administration Tool uses this special group because it needs to access and update tables across the network, and the superuser has limited access privileges on the network (for security reasons). The sysadmin group solves this problem. Any user that belongs to the sysadmin group can run the Administration Tool. If you will be updating tables on remote machines, you will need to belong to the sysadmin group on each machine that requires access. If you run the Administration Tool as root, you will probably not be able to access or update administrative tables on the network (unless you have all the security features turned off). If you will be updating files only on your own machine, then using the Administration Tool as root poses no problem.

The examples in the remainder of this chapter use only the files in the /etc method, so using the Administration Tool as root should be sufficient. If you want to become a member of the sysadmin group, you may need to talk to your system administrator. If you are currently using NIS+ or NIS in your network, you may not be granted membership in the sysadmin group because it may be reserved for the system administrators only. If there are no such restrictions, you will probably still need to ask your system administrator to add you to the group, since you can't use the Administration Tool to add yourself to the group until you are a member. An alternative is to add yourself to the group table in /etc on your local system (/etc/group). Be careful, however, because if you are using NIS+ or NIS, adding a local entry for sysadmin on your machine will override the NIS+ or NIS entry for sysadmin. This could mean that your system administrator no longer has the necessary privileges to run Administration Tool tasks on your system. To be safe, either check with your system administrator about the current configuration and accessibility of the sysadmin group, or use the root account and attempt to update files only on your local machine.

Database Management

The Database Manager lets you add, modify, delete, and view entries in several databases. To start the Database Manager, you press the button labeled Database Manager on the Administration Tool's base window. The Load Database pop-up window is displayed as shown in Figure 17.2.

You choose a database from the Databases scrolling list and a naming service (NIS+, NIS, or /etc files) from the Naming Service choice settings. Then you press the Load button to display the Database Manager that is loaded with the database and that uses the naming service you have specified. Figure 17.3 shows the Database Manager with the Aliases database loaded.

Modifying Supported Databases

The Database Manager supports 14 databases. You will probably not need to modify most of these databases, but here is a brief description of each:

Aliases maintains mail aliases. These mail aliases are similar to the aliases you can create with the Mail Tool or mailx, but they can be accessed by any user.

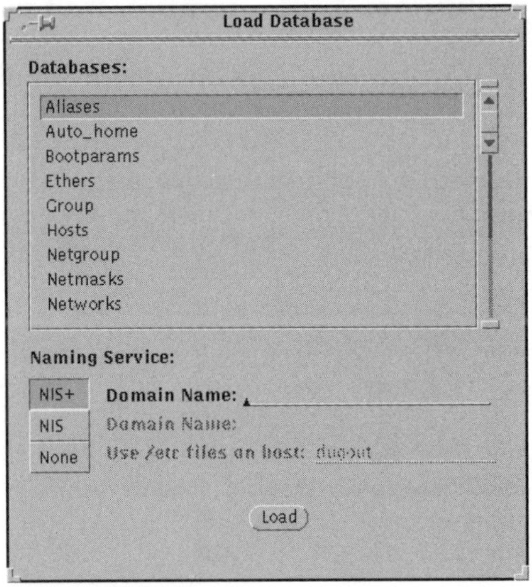

Figure 17.2
The Load Database pop-up window

Figure 17.3
The Database Manager's base window

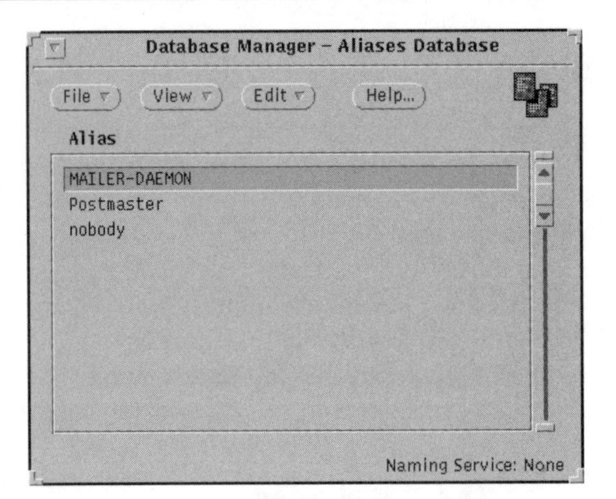

Auto_home defines a path that the automounter uses to mount home directories of particular users.

Bootparams specifies the location (on the network) of file systems for diskless and network clients machines.

Ethers maps host names to the hardware Ethernet addresses.

Group defines the system's groups. Groups are collections of users who share certain files and privileges.

Hosts maps names to Internet Protocal (IP) addresses.

Netgroup classifies network-wide groups of machines and users.

Netmasks database contains network masks used to implement IP standard subnetting.

Networks lists the networks of the Internet. It is created from the official table maintained at the Network Information Control Center (NIC).

Passwd defines user accounts, including user ID password, home directory, and default shell.

Protocols lists the names and numbers of any DARPA (Defense Advanced Research Projects Agency) Internet protocols (for example, ip, tcp, icmp, and ggp) used in your network.

RPC matches rpc program numbers with user-readable names.

Services lists the names of Transmission Control Protocol (TCP) and User Datagram Protocol (UDP) services and their "well-known" protocol numbers. The database is created automatically during OS installation and generally requires no administration.

Timezone sets the installation value for the time-zone environment variable TZ.

Most of these databases are best left to the system administrator to administer. There are a few databases, however, that you may want to administer yourself. The Aliases, Hosts, and Passwd databases are the most likely ones that you will need to modify. Some of the databases are manipulated by other Administration Tool programs. For example, if you use the Host Manager, you will be updating the Bootparams, Ethers, Hosts, and Timezone databases. Using the Host Manager gives you the advantage of updating all the databases you may need when adding a new host to your network. Using the Database Manager to update a single database gives you the advantage of being able to update only the tables that require updating.

The technique to add, modify, or delete an entry from a database is essentially the same regardless of which database you are editing. To show how to use the Database Manager, we will edit the Aliases database, but first let's talk about the general structure and functionality of the Database Manager.

Using the Database Manager Components

The Database Manager has three menu buttons (File, View, and Edit), a Help button, and a scrolling list that displays the entries in the database. The File menu (displayed when you press MENU on the File menu button) has two items that let you load a database from a file into the Database Manager and then write the contents of the database to a file that you specify. The View menu contains several items that let you customize the way that the entries from the database are displayed in the scrolling list. The Edit menu contains three items that allow you to add, modify, or delete an entry from the database.

When you press the Help button, the Help Viewer (see Chapter 3) is invoked and the *Database Manager On-line Handbook* is loaded. This handbook contains some general information about using the Database Manager and some specific information about each database.

Editing the Aliases Database

The Aliases database defines mail aliases that can be accessed by any user. These are similar to the mail aliases that you learned about in Chapter 6 except that those aliases were available only to you. The aliases maintained in the Aliases database are available to users who have access to your naming service on your system. For example, let's say your host name is dugout and you are using files in /etc. If you create a mail alias called reviewers, another user would have access to this mail alias by sending mail to reviewers@dugout.

Adding an Entry

To add an entry to the Aliases database, select Add Entry from the Edit menu. The Add Entry pop-up window is displayed. Enter the name of the alias in the Alias text field, and the address or addresses to which the alias should be expanded in the Expansion text field. Figure 17.4 shows the Add Entry pop-up window with an entry in each of the two fields.

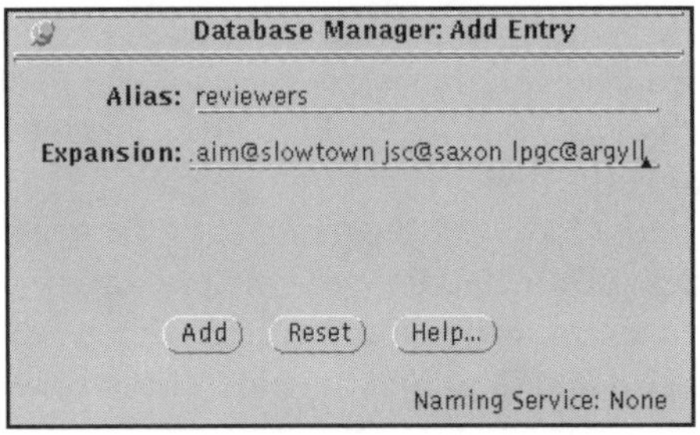

Figure 17.4 The Database Manager: Add Entry pop-up window

Database Manager: Add Entry

Alias: reviewers

Expansion: aim@slowtown jsc@saxon lpgc@argyll

Add Reset Help...

Naming Service: None

After you have entered the alias and expansion data, press the Add button to add the alias to the Aliases database. The alias is added to the scrolling list on the Database Manager's base window.

These two fields (Alias and Expansion) are identical to the Alias and Addresses fields of the Mail Tool's Alias Properties window, shown in Figure 6.27. When you add an alias in the Mail Tool, the alias is available only to you. When you add an alias to the Aliases database, it is available to anyone who has access to your naming service (if you are using NIS+ or NIS) or to your system (if you are using files in /etc).

Modifying an Entry

To modify an existing entry in the Aliases database, first select the item from the scrolling list by clicking SELECT on that item. Then select Modify Entry from the Edit menu to display the Modify Entry pop-up window, shown in Figure 17.5.

Figure 17.5
The Database Manager: Modify Entry pop-up window

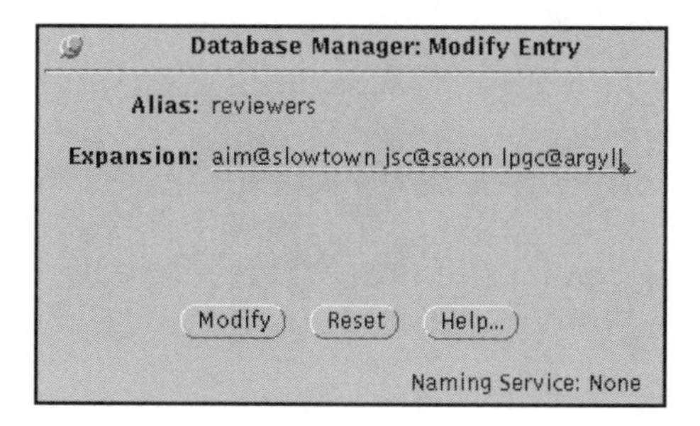

The Modify Entry pop-up window is nearly identical to the Add Entry pop-up window. The only difference is that the only field you can modify is the Expansion field. If you want to change the alias, you must add a new entry with the new alias name. When you have made the changes you want in the Expansion field, press the Modify button to effect the change.

Deleting an Entry

To delete an entry from the Aliases database, first select from the scrolling list the item you want to delete. Then select the Delete Entry item from the Edit menu. You are presented with a notice that asks you if you really want to delete this item. Press the Delete button to delete the alias; press the Cancel button to cancel the deletion.

Editing Other Databases

You use the same basic concepts presented in the previous section to edit any of the databases available from the Database Manager. Of course, each database has a different set of fields, so adding or modifying an entry will be slightly different. For example, if you want to modify an entry in the Passwd database, the Modify Entry pop-up window will look significantly different, as shown in Figure 17.6.

Figure 17.6
The Modify Entry pop-up window for the Passwd database

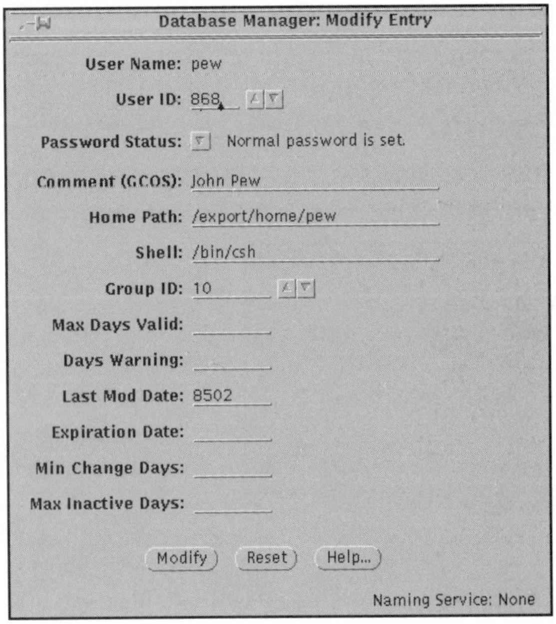

Database Manager: Modify Entry

User Name: pew
User ID: 868
Password Status: Normal password is set.
Comment (GCOS): John Pew
Home Path: /export/home/pew
Shell: /bin/csh
Group ID: 10
Max Days Valid:
Days Warning:
Last Mod Date: 8502
Expiration Date:
Min Change Days:
Max Inactive Days:
Modify Reset Help...
Naming Service: None

The reason the pop-up windows are different is that the fields of an entry in the Passwd database are considerably different from the fields of an entry in the Aliases database. The technique of editing the database, however, is essentially the same.

Printer Management

The Printer Manager lets you configure your system so that it can access a local printer (one attached directly to your system) or a remote printer (one connected to another system to which you have access on the network). To invoke the Printer Manager, press the Printer Manager button on the Administration Tool's base window. Figure 17.7 shows the Printer Manager's base window.

Figure 17.7
The Printer Manager's base window

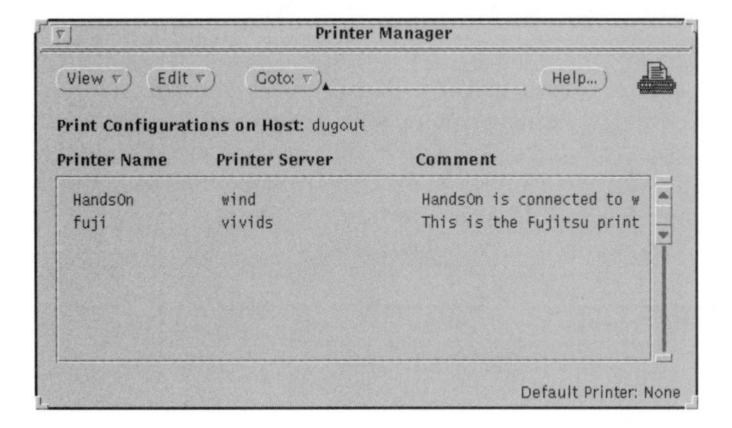

The scrolling list on the Printer Manager's base window displays each of the printers to which you currently have access. The printer name and location and a comment are included. When you add a new printer, it is added to the scrolling list.

To add a printer, you need to know the name of the printer and the system to which it is attached. You can view the printers available on another system by entering the name of the system in the Goto text field and pressing the Goto button (or pressing the Return key). This loads the printer information into the Printer Manager from the system you specify. This works only for systems running Solaris 2.0 or later. If you cannot get information about remote printers by using this method, you may need to check with your system administrator for additional printer information.

The printing system supported by the SunOS system has changed substantially since the introduction of SunOS 5.0 (Solaris 2.0). There are actually two printing mechanisms: BSD and System V. The BSD printing mechanism is supported on SunOS systems that were released before Solaris 2.0. The System V printing mechanism is supported on SunOS systems released since (and including) Solaris 2.0. The System V printing mechanism has the advantage of being compatible with the BSD printing mechanism. This means that if you use the System V printing mechanism you can still have access to printers connected to systems using the BSD printing mechanism. The Printer Manager includes a configuration option that you must specify when you configure the printer as you will see shortly. When you add a printer to your local machine (running Solaris 2.1), it automatically uses the newer System V printing mechanism.

Adding Access to a Remote Printer

Let's start by looking at how you add access to an existing printer that is connected to a remote machine. The Edit menu button on the Printer Manager's base window displays a menu with three items: Add Printer, Modify Printer, and Delete Printer. The Add Printer item is a menu button that displays a submenu with two choices: Add Access to Remote Printer and Add Local Printer. Select Add Access to Remote Printer to display the Access to Remote Printer pop-up window, shown in Figure 17.8.

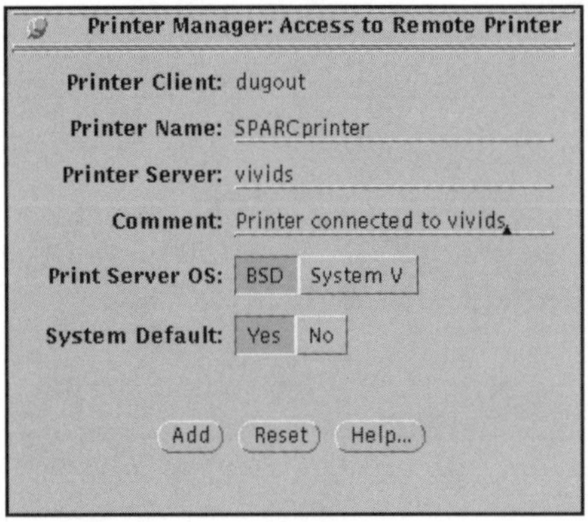

Figure 17.8
The Printer Manager: Access to Remote Printer pop-up window

Printer Manager: Access to Remote Printer
Printer Client: dugout
Printer Name: SPARCprinter
Printer Server: vivids
Comment: Printer connected to vivids
Print Server OS: BSD System V
System Default: Yes No
Add Reset Help...

To add access to a remote printer, simply enter the appropriate information in the fields on this pop-up window and press the Add button. The information that you must provide is described here:

- In the Printer Name field, enter the name of the printer.
- In the Printer Server field, enter the name of the remote system to which the printer (specified in the Printer Name field) is attached.
- In the Comment field, enter a comment about the printer. This is an optional field.
- Select the Printer Server OS choice that matches the operating system of the remote system. If the remote system is running SunOS 5.0 or later, choose System V. If the remote system is running a version of the SunOS system that is earlier than SunOS 5.0, choose BSD.

- Select the System Default choice to determine whether this printer will be the default printer. You can have only one default printer. If you select Yes, this printer becomes the default, replacing the previously configured default printer.

When you press the Add button, you see the printer name, printer server, and comment displayed as a new item in the scrolling list.

Adding a Local Printer

Adding a local printer is similar to adding a remote printer, though you have to supply some additional information regarding the type of printer and how it is connected. When you select Add Local Printer from the Add Printer submenu, the Local Printer pop-up window is displayed, as shown in Figure 17.9.

Figure 17.9
The Printer Manager: Local Printer pop-up window

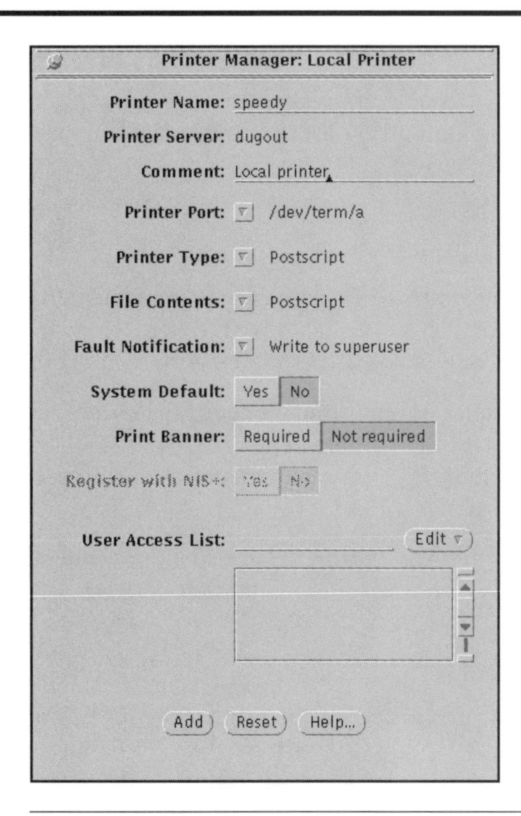

The information that you must provide to add a local printer is described here:

- In the Printer Name field, enter the name of the printer.
- In the Comment field, enter a comment (this is optional). The comment is displayed in the Print Tool's About the printer pop-up window.
- Use the Printer Port abbreviated menu button to display a menu of the ports available on your system. Select the port to which the printer is attached.
- Use the Printer Type abbreviated menu button to display a menu of the printer types. Select the type that matches your printer.
- Use the File Contents abbreviated menu button to display a menu of the types of files that can be printed by this printer.
- Use the Fault Notification abbreviated menu button to display a menu of the actions to take in the event of a printer fault.
- Select the System Default choice to determine whether this printer will be the default printer.
- Select the Print Banner choice to determine whether a banner page is required for each print request.
- Select the Register with NIS+ choice to determine whether the printer will be included in the printer table for the NIS+ naming service. This field is available only if you are using the NIS+ naming service.
- In the User Access List, enter the names of the users to whom you want to restrict the use of this printer. If you leave this field blank, all the users will have access to it. If you specify a list of users, those names are listed in the scrolling list below this field.

When you press the Add button, you see the printer name, printer server, and comment displayed as a new item in the scrolling list.

Modifying a Printer

To modify an existing printer, select the printer from the Printer Manager scrolling list and select Modify Printer from the Edit menu to display the Modify Printer pop-up window, shown in Figure 17.10.

The Modify Printer pop-up window is very similar to the pop-up window that you used to add a printer, with some additional fields. You can change some of the familiar fields you entered when you added the printer, such as the Comment, the Printer Port, the File Contents, the Fault Notification, the

System Default, the Printer Banner, and the User Access List. (The Printer Port, Fault Notification, Printer Banner, and User Access List fields are present only if you are modifying a local printer.) In addition, there are two new fields: Enable Print Queue and Accept Print Jobs. With the Enable Print Queue choice, you can control whether any user will be able to send print jobs to the printer queue. With the Accept Print Jobs choice, you can control whether the printer will print any print jobs in the queue.

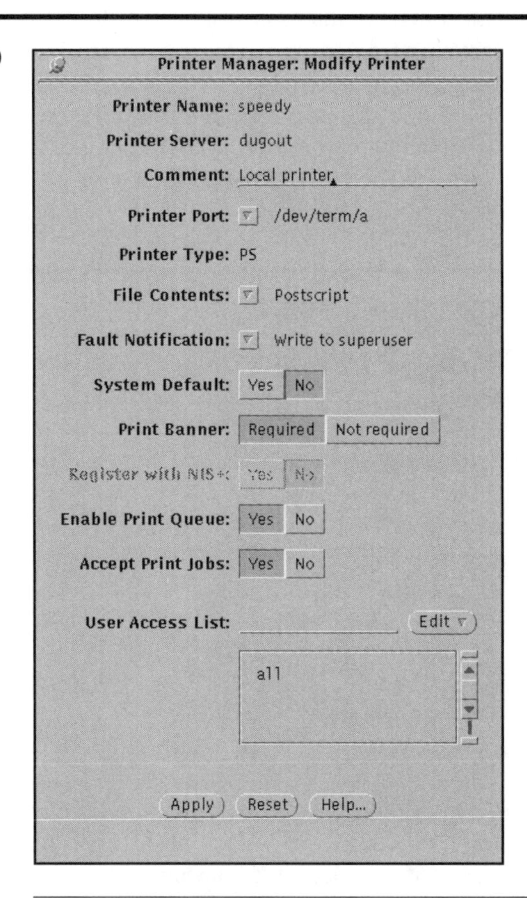

Figure 17.10 The Printer Manager: Modify Printer pop-up window

Deleting a Printer

To delete a printer, select the printer from the scrolling list and select the Delete Printer item from the Edit menu.

Host Management

The Host Manager lets you add, view, and delete hosts on your network. The Host Manager is usually used by the system administrator when adding a new system on the network or modifying the configuration of an existing system on the network. If you want simply to gain access to a machine that is already on the network (and already properly configured), you may find it simpler to update the Hosts database available in the Database Manager. This is simpler and does not require as much detailed information as the Host Manager.

To invoke the Host Manager, press the Host Manager button on the Administration Tool's base window to display the Host Manager: Select Naming Service pop-up window. From this pop-up window, select the naming service and the way you want the hosts displayed (all hosts, one host, or no hosts), and press the Apply button. The Host Manager is then displayed. Figure 17.11 shows the Host Manager's base window.

Figure 17.11 The Host Manager's base window

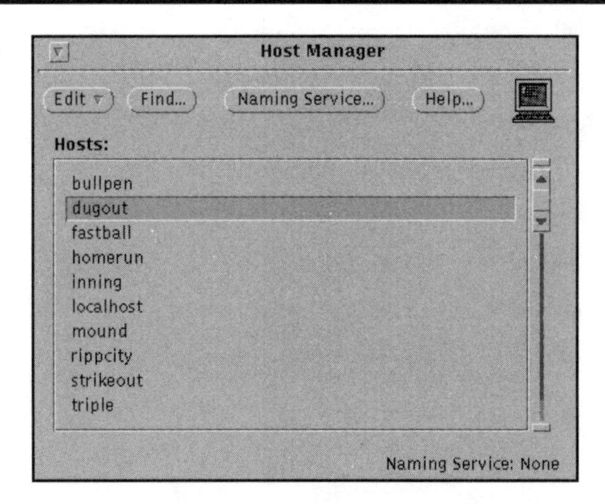

If you choose to display all hosts (the default), then the scrolling list on the Host Manager's base window displays each of the hosts on your network. When you add a new host, it is added to the scrolling list.

Adding a Host

To add a host, select Add host from the Edit menu. The Add Host pop-up window is then displayed, as shown in Figure 17.12.

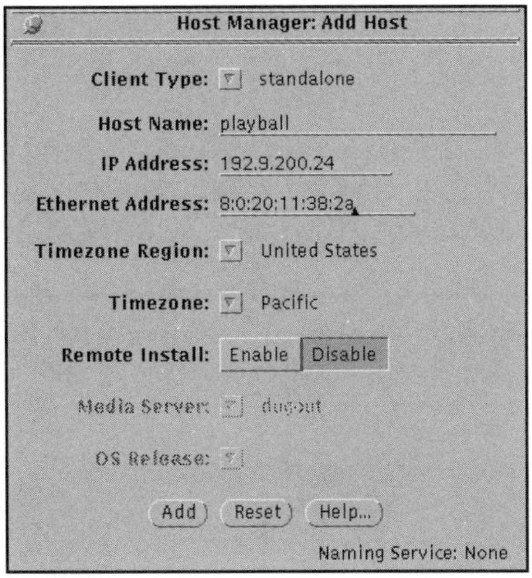

Figure 17.12
The Host Manager: Add Host pop-up window

To add a host, enter the appropriate fields on the Add Host pop-up window and press the Add button. Here is a brief description of each field:

- Use the Client Type abbreviated menu button to select the type of client you are adding: standalone, diskless, or dataless.
- In the Host Name field, enter the name of the host you are adding.
- In the IP Address field, enter the IP (Internet Protocol) address of the host.
- In the Ethernet Address field, enter the Ethernet address of the host.
- Use the Timezone Region abbreviated menu button to select a time-zone region such as United States or Eastern Asia.
- Use the Timezone abbreviated menu button to choose a time zone within the time-zone region you specified in the previous field.
- Select the Remote Install choice to determine whether to allow the machine you're adding to have its operating system software installed from over the network. (This is an advanced feature. You should either disable it or talk to your system administrator.)
- The Media Server field is active only when you enable the remote install. You use this field to specify from which remote machine you will perform remote installations.

- The OS Release field is used to specify the installation that should be performed.

Viewing a Host

To view network information about a host, first select a host from the scrolling list and then select the View Host item from the Edit menu. The View host pop-up window is displayed, as shown in Figure 17.13.

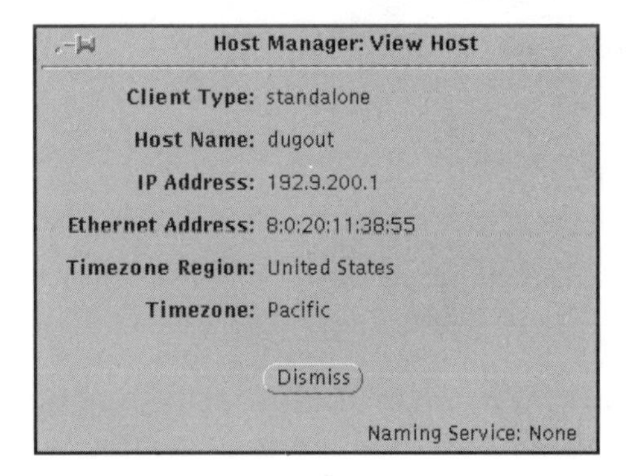

Figure 17.13 The Host Manager: View Host pop-up window

Deleting a Host

To delete a host, select the host from the scrolling list and then select the Delete Host item from the Edit menu.

User Account Management

Adding a new user involves several things, including selecting a user ID, a home directory location, a password, and a default shell. To fully create a user account, you have to update several databases. The databases that are updated when you create a new account (Passwd, Group, Aliases, and Auto_home) can be updated individually when you use the corresponding databases from the Database Manager. The advantage of using the User Account Manager is that it handles all the databases necessary for account creation, modification, or deletion, and also handles other account administration details such as the creation or deletion of the user's home directory.

To invoke the User Account Manager, press the User Account Manager button on the Administration Tool's base window. The User Account Manager: Select Naming Service pop-up window is then displayed. From this pop-up window, select the naming service and the way you want users displayed (all users, some users, or no users), and then press the Apply button to display the User Account Manager. Figure 17.14 shows the User Account Manager's base window.

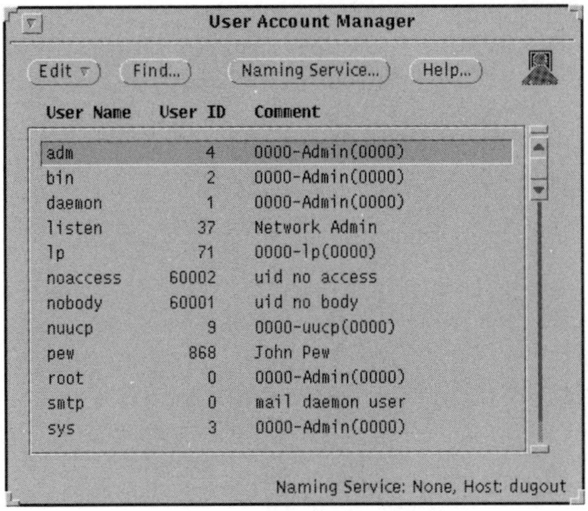

Figure 17.14
The User Account Manager's base window

User Account Manager

Edit | Find... | Naming Service... | Help...

User Name	User ID	Comment
adm	4	0000-Admin(0000)
bin	2	0000-Admin(0000)
daemon	1	0000-Admin(0000)
listen	37	Network Admin
lp	71	0000-lp(0000)
noaccess	60002	uid no access
nobody	60001	uid no body
nuucp	9	0000-uucp(0000)
pew	868	John Pew
root	0	0000-Admin(0000)
smtp	0	mail daemon user
sys	3	0000-Admin(0000)

Naming Service: None, Host: dugout

Adding a User

To add a user, select Add User from the Edit menu. The Add User pop-up window is displayed, as shown in Figure 17.15.

Fill in each of the fields on the Add User window, and press the Add button. Here is a description of each of the fields on the Add User window:

User Identity

- In the User Name field, enter the account name by which this user will be known. A User name may contain the characters A–Z, a–z, and 0–9. The first character must be a letter, and the name must include at least one lowercase letter. The name must be between 2 and 8 characters in length.
- In the User ID field, enter a decimal number between 0 and 60000. User IDs between 0 and 100 are usually reserved for special system accounts. Each user must have a unique user ID.
- In the Primary Group field, enter the user's primary group name or number. This will be the user's default group membership. Only one group may be entered in this field.

Figure 17.15
The User Account Manager: Add User pop-up window

User Account Manager: Add User

USER IDENTITY
User Name: wilma
User ID: 1029
Primary Group: other
Secondary Groups: sysadmin
Comment: Wilma Washington
Login Shell: C /bin/csh

ACCOUNT SECURITY
Password: Cleared until first login
Min Change: 0 days
Max Change: 30 days
Max Inactive: 30 days
Expiration Date: 31 Dec 1995
Warning: 5 days

HOME DIRECTORY
Create Home Dir: Yes if checked
Path: /export/home/wilma
Server: dugout
Skeleton Path:
AutoHome Setup: Yes if checked

Permissions	Read	Write	Execute
Owner:	✓	✓	✓
Group:	✓		✓
World:	✓		✓

MISCELLANEOUS
Mail Server:

Add Reset Help...

- In the Secondary Groups field, enter one or more groups to which the user also belongs in addition to the primary group. This is an optional field.
- In the Comment field, enter a comment about the user. This can be any text, but conventionally is the user's full name and sometimes includes company affiliation. This is an optional field.
- Use the Login Shell abbreviated menu button to select a default login shell for the user. You can select C shell, Bourne shell, Korn shell, or

other. If you choose other, you must supply the complete path name of the shell program in the adjacent text field.

Account Security

- Use the Password abbreviated menu button to select the type of initial password that should be set. The default is to allow the user to set the password when logging in for the first time. You can also choose Normal password, in which case you must supply the password on the Set Password pop-up window.
- In the Min Change field, enter the minimum number of days that must transpire before the user is allowed to change his or her password. This is an optional field.
- In the Max Change field, enter the maximum number of days that a password may remain unchanged. If the user does not change the password within this number of days, the password becomes invalidated and must be reenabled by the system administrator. This is an optional field.
- In the Max Inactive field, enter the number of days that the account may remain unused (no login) before it is automatically locked. This is an optional field.
- In the Expiration Date field, use the three abbreviated menu buttons to specify a day, month, and year on which the account will expire. Select None to specify no expiration.
- In the Warning field, enter the number of days before the password expires that a warning message is displayed to the user. This is an optional field.

Home Directory

- Check the Create Home Dir check box if the user's home directory should be created when the account is added.
- In the Path field, enter the full path to the home directory for this new user account.
- In the Server field, enter the name of the system in which the home directory exists (or will be created).
- In the Skeleton Path, enter the name of the directory that contains the skeleton files (such as .login, .cshrc, or .profile) to be supplied for this account. This path specifies a directory on the system entered in the Server field. This field is active only if you are creating the home directory for the user. This is an optional field.

- Check the AutoHome Setup check box if you want an automount entry for this user's home directory to be set up. This updates the auto_home database.
- Use the Permissions check boxes to specify the permissions for the user's home directory. This field is active only if you are creating the home directory for the user.

Miscellaneous

- In the Mail Server field, enter the name of the system in which this user's mailbox is located. This is an optional field.

Another way you can create an account is to select a user name from the scrolling list on the User Account Manager's base window and then select the Copy User item on the Edit menu. The Copy User pop-up window that is displayed is essentially identical to the Add User pop-up window. The advantage of this technique is that all the fields of the window are filled in with the values from the user whose account you are copying (except the user name and ID). All you have to do is enter the new user name and ID, and modify any other fields that need to be unique (such as Comment and Path). This saves you the time of entering all the fields of the window again.

Modifying a User

To modify an existing account, select from the scrolling list the user you want to modify and then select Modify User from the Edit menu. The Modify User pop-up window is displayed, showing all the same fields as the Add User pop-up window except Create Home Dir and Skeleton Path. This means that you cannot create the home directory of the user from the Modify User pop-up window. All other fields can be modified.

Deleting a User

To delete an existing account, select from the scrolling list the user name you want to delete and then select Delete User from the Edit menu. The Delete User pop-up window is displayed, as shown in Figure 17.16.

When you delete a user, you have the option of simply removing access to the account or additionally removing the user's home directory and its contents and the user's mailbox and its contents. For example, you may want to remove a user's login (because the user has left the company) but retain the files in the user's home directory and mailbox for the benefit of other users. Check the corresponding check box to delete the home directory and mailbox.

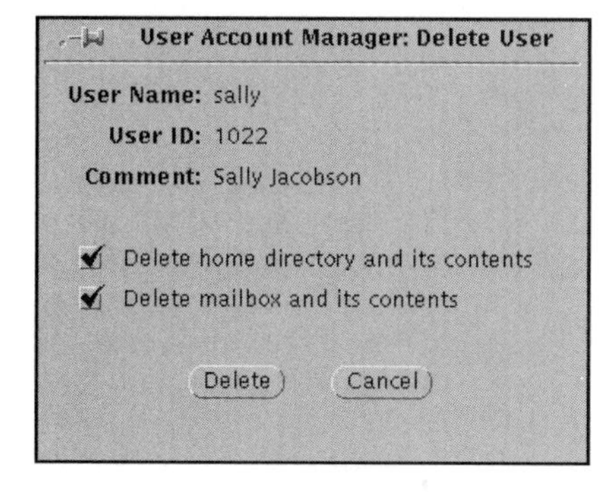

Figure 17.16
The User Account Manager: Delete User pop-up window

Summary

With what you have learned in this chapter and the previous chapter, you should feel fairly confident in your administration abilities. When you do need help, don't be afraid to ask. Then, when your system administrator's skills are required, ask questions about what is being done to solve problems or to configure systems. You probably now have enough of a basic understanding to follow along with what is being done and to learn more as you go.

INDEX

A

B

C

D

E

N

Q

R

T

U

V